Sixth Edition

CORRECTIONS

AN INTRODUCTION

Richard P. Seiter

Vice President, Portfolio Management: Andrew Gilfillan
Vice President, Product Marketing: Brad Parkins
Portfolio Manager: Gary Bauer
Editorial Assistant: Lynda Cramer
Product Marketing Manager: Heather Taylor
Product Marketing Assistant: Liz Bennett
Director, Digital Studio and Content Production: Brian Hyland
Managing Producer, Careers: Cynthia Zonneveld
Content Producer: Holly Shufeldt
Content Producer: Alma Dabral
Manager, Rights Management: Johanna Burke
Operations Specialist: Deidra Headlee

Creative Digital Lead: Mary Siener
Managing Producer, Digital Studio: Autumn Benson
Content Producer, Digital Studio: Maura Snow
Full-Service Management and Composition: Integra Software Services Pvt. Ltd.
Full-Service Project Manager: Philip Alexander
Cover Design: Studio Montage
Cover Art (or Cover Photo): nirut123rf/123RF
Printer/Binder: LSC Communications, Inc.
Cover Printer: LSC Communications, Inc.
Text Font: Sabon LT Pro

Library of Congress Cataloging-in-Publication Data

Names: Seiter, Richard P., author.
Title: Corrections: An Introduction/Richard P. Seiter.
Description: Sixth edition. | Boston, MA : Pearson Education, [2020]
Identifiers: LCCN 2018023143 | ISBN 9780135186190
Subjects: LCSH: Corrections—United States.
Classification: LCC HV9471 .S45 2020 | DDC 364.60973—dc23
LC record available at https://lccn.loc.gov/2018023143

5 2023

Paper Bound: ISBN 10:   0-13-518619-6
ISBN 13: 978-0-13-518619-0
Loose leaf: ISBN 10:   0-13-523547-2
ISBN 13: 978-0-13-523547-8

BRIEF CONTENTS

CONTENTS

PART II Correctional Policy and Operations

Chapter 3 Jails 67

Chapter 4 Probation and Intermediate Sanctions 95

PART III Correctional Clients

Chapter 7 The Clients of Adult Correctional Agencies 205

Chapter 8 The Juvenile Correctional System 234

Chapter 9 Special Offenders 264

PART IV Prison Life

Chapter 10 The Management of Prisons 300

Chapter 14 Treatment and Programs within a Prison 420

PART V Prison Life

Chapter 15 Legal Issues and the Death Penalty 448

Chapter 16 Current and Future Issues in Corrections 481

PREFACE

As an author, I am very excited about this introductory textbook on corrections. Having spent most of my life working in the correctional field, I have had the opportunity to work in many different situations and with many dedicated people. I am pleased to be able to pass on some of the experiences and information gathered over thirty years to students studying corrections and perhaps considering corrections as a career.

As such, the goal of this textbook is to provide students with a practical understanding of today's operations of corrections. The text includes correctional history and theory; however, the text concentrates on what we do in corrections, why we do it, and what challenges face contemporary correctional staff and administrators. The text also presents case studies, information on careers, and real examples of situations to provide students with an understanding of the practical aspects of working in corrections.

New to This Edition

Updated Information

The sixth edition of *Corrections: An Introduction* has been updated to provide faculty and students with state-of-the-art information on the operations of the various elements of corrections and the issues faced by correctional policymakers and practitioners. These updates include the most recent data regarding correctional populations, costs, and new research and findings that impact correctional policy. For example, updates have been made to the following material:

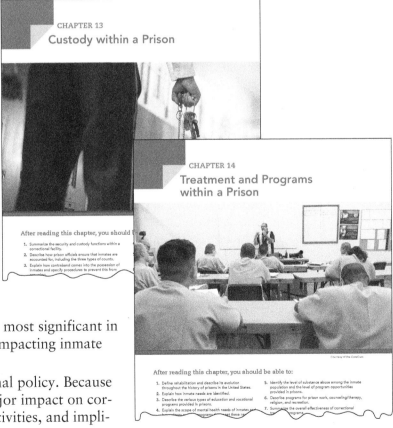

- References to federal court decisions that affect current practices. Although references to court cases have been updated throughout the text, the updates are most significant in Chapter 15 in significant decisions impacting inmate rights and the death penalty.

- The impact of budgets on correctional policy. Because budget issues continue to have a major impact on correctional policy, further updates, activities, and implications have been added.

- Coverage of the challenge of getting and using drugs required in the protocols for administering the death penalty.

- Updated information regarding the continuing problem of jail suicides.

- New information regarding parole effectiveness and inmate reentry.

- Updates on the use of and controversies surrounding supermax prisons and solitary confinement.
- Recent issues and controversies in the operation of private prisons.
- Treatment program effectiveness and their impact on reducing recidivism.

Coverage of Sentencing Policy Reforms

Over the past few years, there have been several reforms of sentencing policy. This edition contains new material that examines state-by-state incarceration rates and addresses these policy decisions. Included as well are the efforts to reduce costs and the resultant impact on correctional budgets.

Expanded Coverage of Current and New Topics

In Chapter 4, there is a new section regarding "reforming probation," and how efforts to improve probation effectiveness and save money serve as a way to reduce violations and sentencing to prison. Chapter 10 includes new issues and information regarding the challenges of recruitment and retention of correctional staff. Chapter 5 includes a new section regarding Federal Prison Industries, a critical work program of the federal prison system. This chapter also describes approaches to prison design by state correctional agencies and trends for state prison populations. Chapter 9 regarding special offenders includes a new section and case study regarding transgender inmates. Chapter 11 has an interesting new case study regarding prison "currency." Chapter 12 includes new information regarding employment of correctional officers, the stress of their work, and recent development regarding union membership. Chapter 14 has new information regarding a pilot program to test the use of Pell Grants for prisoners. Chapter 16 includes updated information on the state of correctional budgets, changes in prison and jail populations, a new interview with a private prison company CEO, as well as important and timely new sections regarding mass incarceration and solitary confinement.

Features of This Text

To give students a realistic and practical understanding of modern corrections, this textbook includes several features and approaches that are designed to heighten the learning process and make it interesting for students. Chapters include realistic experiences and insights into the real world of today's correctional operations. Key features include the following:

Practical Focus

Each chapter includes a brief segment on history and theory, but focuses on the actual operations of prisons, community corrections, and jails. Students are able to experience the challenges that correctional workers face and the practical applications they use to meet these challenges.

A Look Into...

Several chapters include boxed case studies about real issues that have confronted staff members who try to manage today's correctional populations. These examples provide insight into the world of prisons, jails, and community corrections. Some of these describe how certain people look at their jobs or issues facing

---

▶ A Look Into . . .

Prison Reforms through the Twentieth Century

T. Don Hutto is a legend in prison administration and reform from the 1960s through the 1990s. He started as a correctional officer in Texas in 1964, and three years later was the warden of the W Ramsey Unit, one of the largest Texas prisons. At the age of thirty six, he became director of the Arkansas Department of Corrections, just after the incidents around its operation led to the movie Brubaker. Hutto moved to reform both the Ramsey Unit and the Arkansas prison system, ending racial segregation and the use of building tenders (inmates who acted as armed guards over other inmates). He also dealt with reforms needed to move Arkansas from the unconstitutional system it was found to be in *Holt v. Sarver*.

busy redefining our charges as "convicts," "prisoners," "inmates," "offenders," "detainees," "residents," "patients," and even "students."

And, oh yes! We were at various times in the business of "reform," "rehabilitation," "punishment," "incarceration," "treatment," and of course, "reintegration." "Reform" has been a buzzword regarding prisons and corrections for as long as I, and probably any of you, can remember. The New Oxford American Dictionary says that reform means to "make changes in order to improve something." "Reform" is a useful catchword, as, according to someone or some group, just about every societal or cultural institution, needs to be "reformed." Today, the word "change" is more in vogue but "change" means making something different, not necessarily better. The term "change" is neutral and can be either positive or negative. Transform, on the other hand, means to make a thorough or dramatic change, and the radical changes which have taken place in Southern corrections in the last fifty years suggest that "transformed" is the word them, and others are a brief interview with someone working in the field described in the chapter.

Your Career in Corrections

Every chapter includes descriptions of jobs that students may carry out as a specific correctional application. For instance, in a discussion of halfway houses, there is a career box that notes the types of jobs available to staff entering this field, what they do, the requirements of the job, and the possible pay and work conditions they will face.

▶ Your Career in Corrections

Policy Analysts

It may seem odd to start out the "Your Career in Corrections" boxes by describing the job of a policy analyst. Students seldom have heard of this job, and few think about it as a way to begin their career track. However, it is very important to good government that correctional policy be thoughtfully considered with full information regarding cost, effectiveness, and impact. In 2012, American taxpayers contributed over $80 billion to operate our correctional system, while much of what we do is not based on a thorough analysis of cost and impact.[2] This textbook emphasizes the policy choices that must be made as we reform, modify, and update correctional practices, and policy analysts can play a key role in this process.

A policy analyst who works on correctional issues can work for a variety of agencies. Most state (and some large county) correctional departments have a policy and research bureau. Its job is to conduct research and gather

receive grants to conduct correctional research and employ researchers and analysts to examine an issue and write reports as requested by the funding agencies.

There are no reports regarding how many people work in these areas. However, at any one time, easily more than a thousand people are doing the work we have described. Depending on the sophistication of the issue, some will have a doctorate and be experts in research methodology, possibly with some educational emphasis in corrections or criminal justice research. Many others have a master's degree in sociology, criminal justice, business, or public administration and have skills to develop research and policy analysis criteria to be able to provide answers to questions regarding effectiveness or budget impact.

These jobs are not highly visible, yet can have a tremendous impact on the development of good public policy and

---

Case Studies

There are several case studies that provide real situations and approaches that help explain and make clearer some of the policy challenges that confront correctional officials, staff, and offenders. These case studies are both timely and interesting descriptions that further make this book practical for the student and instructors that use it.

▶ You Make the Decision...

Rating the Importance of Correctional Goals

No jurisdiction has to formally rate the importance of the five goals of corrections; however, the following exercise asks students to do just that. It can be done individually, but will be more fun and a better learning exercise in a small group.

Your instructions are to consider each of the five goals of sentencing and create a list of the favorable and unfavorable consequences of focusing on each one. For instance, someone might suggest that focusing on punishment can slowly undermine society's emphasis on fair and just treatment. Or, emphasizing incapacitation may result in positively affecting the crime rate, as incapacitated offenders cannot commit crimes in the community. After creating and discussing the

each goal, go about the difficult task of rating the importance of each goal. There are no guidelines as to what "importance" means, and this should be a very individual decision. Does one person believe that the most important purpose of a criminal sanction is to punish an offender, whereas another believes it should first focus on rehabilitation? Each person should create his or her list, and then the group should discuss the lists and come to a group conclusion about the rating of goals by importance to society. The discussions, debates, and even arguments that result from this exercise should be both fun and a valuable learning opportunity.

You Make the Decision...

At the end of every chapter, this feature presents real situations that someone working in the field may encounter. For instance, in a discussion of probation, students have to struggle with the decision as whether to revoke a probationer for failing to follow all conditions of supervision or not. The chapter regarding parole presents several scenarios for prisoners appearing before the parole board, and students must make a decision whether to recommend parole or not.

A Question of Policy

A valuable learning approach of the book is to focus on the policy implications of different theories and perspectives regarding corrections. All chapters address the practical issues of modern correctional policy development, and some chapters include a box entitled "A Question of Policy." By addressing policy, students receive insight into the critical policy challenges that result from today's practice of corrections. This box presents dilemmas that elected officials and correctional administrators face in creating a policy that is most effective and efficient and that contributes significantly to the accomplishment of correctional goals.

Quality Assurance of Policy

Two activities used to ensure consistent implementation of prison policies are monitoring policy compliance and ACA accreditation. The method most commonly used to monitor policy compliance by staff is an active auditing program to determine the extent to which policy is effectively carried out and contributes to the mission of the prison. Prisons use a variety of auditing procedures to monitor compliance with operational policies. One of these, a **policy audit**, determines whether broad agency policy is in place at the prison. Policy audits match agency-required policy with local prison implementation procedures to ensure that procedures are in place at each prison to address each agency policy. In most states, the central headquarters dictates broad policy with which each prison in the state must comply. An example of a statewide policy regarding keeping contraband from entering the prison is that "all vehicles, carts, and boxes or packages must be thoroughly inspected before being allowed to enter or exit a prison." Each prison is required to develop and implement operational procedures to affect the required statewide policy. In this example, the prison describes how it will inspect the vehicles, carts, and boxes or packages, including where it will be done, who will do it, and what equipment will be necessary. A policy audit is valuable to begin an overall review of security operations, but only identifies whether the required scope of written, authorized, and mandated policies at the prison exists. It does not determine compliance with implementation consistency in practice, or those of procedures.

policy audit
a review to ascertain whether broad agency policy is in place at the prison

An Interview With...

To provide a variety to perspectives from other key players in the correctional system, a feature entitled "An Interview With..." provides personal accounts of correctional administrators, correctional officers, and inmates. These interviews are very valuable, as they add real and practical insights into the issues and operations of corrections.

> ### An Interview With...
>
> **A Jail Administrator**
>
> Herbert L. Bernsen Herb Bensen.
>
> Administrators of large urban jails face many serious challenges in trying to manage their facilities. Herbert L. Bernsen is Director of the St. Louis County Department of Justice Services (DJS), which oversees the St. Louis County Jail. He has worked for DJS since 1972, and served as a probation/parole officer, superintendent of the maximum and medium security correctional institutions, Intake Manager, and Assistant Director. He became Director in 2009. He is a certified Jail Manager by the American Jail Association, and has a national reputation as a knowledgeable and professional jail administrator.
>
> education and work experience that lends itself to the qualities that are needed in this facility. These include dependability, discipline, and the ability to communicate and work with others. Most importantly, individuals must have good skills in communicating with individuals from a variety of backgrounds, and the ability to not only work under supervision, but also independently, being able to think on their feet and make decisions in line with the mission and philosophy we want to achieve.
>
> **Question:** How do you find people with the abilities to perform well in a jail setting?
>
> **Mr. Bernsen:** You have to put the jail out there, in a variety of places where those individuals that are apt to become interested may see or hear about you. You have to do more than just advertise; you have to explain the organization, how it operates professionally, and the critical skills you are looking for. We are looking for more than what the public perceives as a correctional officer, and you emphasize the talent and skill required and the career opportunities that exist. You look at uni-

It is the author's hope that students enjoy this textbook and find it easy to read and study, and that the practical perspectives motivate students to consider a career in corrections. Even if students decide that corrections is not a career opportunity for them, corrections is such an important component in today's criminal justice system that an understanding of how programs operate and how much they cost is important to taxpayers who must support their operation.

Supplements

The sixth edition of *Corrections: An Introduction* is supported by a complete package of instructor and student resources.

Instructor Supplements

Instructor's Manual with Test Bank. Includes content outlines for classroom discussion, teaching suggestions, and answers to selected end-of-chapter questions from the text. This also contains a Word document version of the test bank.

TestGen. This computerized test generation system gives you maximum flexibility in creating and administering tests on paper, electronically, or online. It provides state-of-the-art features for viewing and editing test bank questions, dragging a selected question into a test you are creating, and printing sleek, formatted tests in a variety of layouts. Select test items from test banks included with TestGen for quick test creation, or write your own questions from scratch. TestGen's random generator provides the option to display different text or calculated number values each time questions are used.

PowerPoint Presentations. Our presentations are clear and straightforward. Photos, illustrations, charts, and tables from the book are included in the presentations when applicable. To access supplementary materials online, instructors need to request an instructor access code. Go to **www.pearsonhighered.com/irc**, where you can register for an instructor access code. Within 48 hours after registering, you will receive a confirming e-mail, including an instructor access code. Once you have received your code, go to the site and log on for full instructions on downloading the materials you wish to use.

Alternate Versions

eBooks. This text is also available in multiple eBook formats. These are an exciting new choice for students looking to save money. As an alternative to purchasing the printed textbook, students can purchase an electronic version of the same content. With an eTextbook, students can search the text, make notes online, print out reading assignments that incorporate lecture notes, and bookmark important passages for later review. For more information, visit your favorite online eBook reseller or visit **www.mypearsonstore.com.**

Revel *Corrections: An Introduction,* 6e by Seiter

Designed for How You Want to Teach – and How Your Students Want to Learn

Revel is an interactive learning environment that engages students and helps them prepare for your class. Reimagining their content, our authors integrate media and assessment throughout the narrative so students can read, explore, and practice, all at the same time. Thanks to this dynamic reading experience, students come to class prepared to discuss, apply, and learn about criminal justice — from you and from each other.

Revel seamlessly combines the full content of Pearson's bestselling criminal justice titles with multimedia learning tools. You assign the topics your students cover. Author Explanatory Videos, application exercises, survey questions, interactive CJ data maps, and short quizzes engage students and enhance their understanding of core topics as they progress through the content. Through its engaging learning experience, Revel helps students better understand course material while preparing them to meaningfully participate in class.

Author Explanatory Videos

Short 2-3 minute Author Explanatory Videos, embedded in the narrative, provide students with a verbal explanation of an important topic or concept and illuminate the concept with additional examples.

Point/CounterPoint Videos

Instead of simply reading about criminal justice, students are empowered to think critically about key topics through Point/Counterpoint videos that explore different views on controversial issues such as the effectiveness of the fourth amendment, privacy, search and seizure, Miranda, prisoner rights, death penalty and many other topics.

Source: Federal Bureau of Investigation, *Crime in the United States, 2016*; and U.S. Census Bureau, Small Area Income and Poverty Estimates (SAIPE) Program

New Social Explorer Criminal Justice Data Maps

Social Explorer Maps integrated into the narrative ask students to examine crime and corrections data correlated with socio-economic and other criminal justice data. Maps also show differences in state statutes on major issues such as marijuana legalization, the death penalty, and the distribution of hate organizations across the US.

New Student Survey Questions

Student Survey Questions appear within the narrative asking students to respond to questions about controversial topics and important concepts. Students then see their response versus the responses of all other students who have answered the question in the form of a bar chart. We provide the instructor with a PowerPoint deck with links to each survey and map, making it easy to pull these items up in class for discussion.

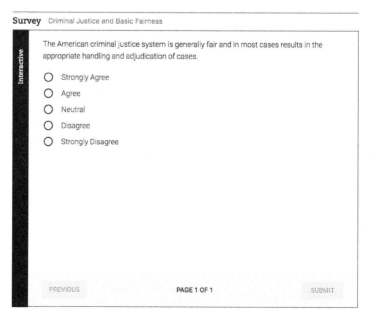

Track Time-On-Task throughout the Course

The Performance Dashboard allows you to see how much time the class or individual students have spent reading a section or doing an assignment, as well as points earned per assignment. This data helps correlate study time with performance and provides a window into where students may be having difficulty with the material.

Learning Management System Integration

Pearson provides Blackboard Learn™, Canvas™, Brightspace by D2L, and Moodle integration, giving institutions, instructors, and students easy access to Revel. Our Revel integration delivers streamlined access to everything your students need for the course in these learning management system (LMS) environments.

The Revel App

The Revel mobile app lets students read, practice, and study—anywhere, anytime, on any device. Content is available both online and offline, and the app syncs work across all registered devices automatically, giving students great flexibility to toggle between phone, tablet, and laptop as they move through their day. The app also lets students set assignment notifications to stay on top of all due dates. Available for download from the App Store or Google Play. Visit **www.pearson-highered.com/revel/** to learn more.

ACKNOWLEDGMENTS

Writing and updating a book is a tremendous undertaking that could not be accomplished without the help of many people. I would first like to thank the many correctional colleagues who assisted me by granting me interviews, providing me advice, and giving me information that was used both for the general book information and to make the book come to life for students through their personal stories and situations. It is not easy to recall some memories of unpleasant situations, but through their candor and openness, readers will get a true understanding of what corrections is really like.

I thank the criminal justice and marketing group at Pearson Education. I also thank the following reviewers selected by Pearson whose feedback guided this edition of the book: Samantha Carlo, Miami Dade College; Jessica Noble, Lewis and Clark Community College; Michael Pittaro, American Military University; Melissa Ricketts, Shippensburg University; Kenneth Salmon, Arizona State University, Jennifer Bradford, Metropolitan State University of Denver; Scott Chenault, University of Central Missouri; Cherly Furdge, North Central Texas College; Carly Hilinski-Rosick, Grand Valley State University; Lorraine Samuels, Huston Tillotson University; John Sieminski, Manchester Community College; William Southern, Jr., Carteret Community College; and Quando Stevenson, Athens State University of Alabama. Their comments and suggestions were the foundation of this revision, are incorporated throughout the sixth edition of *Corrections: An Introduction*, and have made it a more informative and useful book for faculty and students of corrections.

I also thank the correctional agencies that were so helpful in giving me the opportunity to take pictures of their programs and facilities. Of greatest assistance was the Ohio Department of Rehabilitation and Corrections. Several individuals helped arrange the taking of photos and cooperated by providing information. The Missouri Department of Corrections was also helpful in providing material and information. The Federal Bureau of Prisons (BOP) provided several pictures for that agency. And staff members at Facility Support Center and many facilities of the CoreCivic were extremely helpful and cooperative. I also appreciate the assistance of the St. Louis County Justice Center and the St. Louis City Jail for allowing pictures to be taken of their facilities.

Finally, I thank my family and friends who encouraged and supported me throughout the process. My wife, Riffi O'Brien, has been an important part of this book development and progress, and I thank her for her love, support, and encouragement. My son, Matt, has been through this process with me before and continues to provide his common sense advice and humor, and his personal work ethic is a constant motivation to me.

I also prepare and dedicate this edition to the memory of my parents, Paul and Rosemary Seiter, who blessed me with a work ethic and encouraged my continued education and learning.

Thanks to all of you. You made the sixth edition of *Corrections: An Introduction* a reality.

ABOUT THE AUTHOR

Richard P. Seiter is a career correctional professional, having worked in prisons and for correctional agencies for more than thirty years. Following receipt of his PhD in Public Administration from the Ohio State University (OSU), he was a research associate and Assistant Director of the Crime and Delinquency Center at OSU. In 1976, he began a career with the BOP and worked in two federal prisons (the Federal Correctional Institution in Dublin, California, and the U.S. Penitentiary in Leavenworth, Kansas). He was Director of the BOP Staff Training Center in Denver, Colorado, and became the first Chief of the NIC National Academy of Corrections in Boulder, Colorado. He served as warden of two federal prisons (the Federal Prison Camp in Allenwood, Pennsylvania, and the Federal Correctional Institution in Greenville, Illinois). He also served as both Assistant Director for Industries, Education, and Training and Chief Operating Officer of Federal Prison Industries, with sales of over $400 million per year of prison-made products.

Seiter was Director of the Ohio Department of Rehabilitation and Correction for almost six years. In this position, he was responsible for all Ohio prisons, the parole board and parole supervision, and many community correctional programs. He managed an annual budget of $400 million and a staff of 8,000, and he oversaw the construction of more than 10,000 prison beds at a cost of $500 million.

For five years after retiring from the BOP, he was a faculty member at Saint Louis University (SLU). He received tenure and promotion to Full Professor, as well as serving as Director of Criminal Justice. During this time, he wrote two textbooks, published several articles, and expanded the program and course offerings at SLU.

From 2005 until 2011, he was Executive Vice President of Corrections Corporation of America (now CoreCivic), the largest private prison company in the United States. In this position, Seiter oversaw the operation of the sixth largest prison system in the country, with sixty-three prisons, 17,000 staff members, and 75,000 inmates.

CHAPTER 1

The History of Crime and Corrections

Courtesy of Riffi O'Brien

After reading this chapter, you should be able to:

1. Summarize the definition, mission, and role of corrections, and explain the concept of the correctional funnel.

2. Outline the growth of corrections over the past three decades and describe why the scope of correctional budgets, staffing, and clients makes it important for students to study corrections.

3. Contrast the Classical School with the Positive School of criminology.

4. Summarize early responses to crime prior to the development of prisons.

5. Outline the development of the prison in the United States, including the Walnut Street Jail, Pennsylvania System, and the Auburn System.

6. Describe prison development from the Reformatory Era to the Modern Era.

7. Summarize sentencing goals and primary punishment philosophies and the involvement of politics in recent correctional policy.

Introduction

What is corrections, how does it relate to the other components of the criminal justice system, how does it operate, how well does it work, and why should it be studied? This textbook is designed to answer these questions. Although these questions are worded as if "corrections" is a clearly defined and well-bounded activity, this is far from the case. Corrections includes a wide variety of activities, each with a wide variety of emphases and goals; some of the components have direct relationships with other correctional or criminal justice activities, while others operate almost independently. Corrections has been described as a system of fully integrated services and functions, and it has been described as a nonsystem with no coordination or shared mission by any of its components.

Throughout this text, students will learn how government, private, and not-for-profit agencies all contribute to corrections and the correctional process. The text covers history, theories, operations, costs, and effectiveness. It goes beyond providing students a historical perspective, an encyclopedia of terms, and general information regarding corrections. In addition, the text emphasizes practice as well as theory; the challenges to accomplishing the mission of correctional agencies; and the roles of the people who work in, are supervised by, or are affected by the correctional process. The goal of this textbook is to help students understand (1) how various factors throughout the historical development of corrections influenced the basic operating foundations of today, (2) the linkage of theory and practice, (3) how correctional policy is developed and enacted, (4) the manner in which current correctional policy is put into practice by correctional agencies, and (5) the difficulty in carrying out the functions of correctional agencies in a cost-efficient manner.

Defining Corrections

What is meant by "corrections" and why is the term *corrections* used to refer to the legal punishment of criminal offenders? Does the use of the term *corrections* mean that it is the principal function of the management of criminals after sentencing? In this section, we define *corrections*; address these questions; and look at the historical development of terms, titles, and corresponding philosophies as our current practices evolved from the earliest approaches to punishing criminals. Terminology in any discipline usually comes from the role, mission, and expectations of the activities that are described. For our study of corrections, we examine the use of various terminologies over time, how they relate to the mission of corrections, and how corrections fits into the larger activities of the criminal justice system.

What Is Corrections?

Corrections is an interesting term to use to describe the punishment of offenders for the crimes they have committed. However, *corrections* offers a broader perspective on how agencies deal with criminal offenders. Previously, the term **penology** was used instead of corrections. *Penal* is defined as pertaining to or imposing punishment and is derived from the Latin term *peonalis*, meaning "punishment." Penology is simply the study of punishment. Until the 1950s, the functions, components, and actions of carrying out criminal sanctions regularly

penology
the study of the use of punishment for criminal acts

used the term *penal*, and penal institutions (prisons) and penal systems (organizations to carry out punishment) emphasized the principal function of implementing punishment in the handling of criminal offenders after their sentencing.

However, since the founding of the United States and the creation of the prison as a method for punishment in the late eighteenth century, prisons and other correctional agencies have played a broader role. The Walnut Street Jail, established in 1790 as the first prison designed to house sentenced offenders in the United States, had reformation of the offender as its primary objective. Inmates were expected to read the Bible, reflect on their wrongdoing, and do penance for their crimes. Hence, from penance, the term **penitentiary** was established and used for secure facilities used to hold offenders serving a criminal sentence.

As noted, penology is the study of punishment. However, this term generally included a much broader focus than simply punishment and effectively covered the theories, activities, and operations of carrying out the criminal sentence, whether in a prison or in the community. During the 1950s, the nation's penal system evolved such that the rehabilitation of offenders replaced punishment as its primary objective. This philosophical change affected theory and practice, and the term *penology* was replaced by the term **corrections**. For purposes of this textbook, *corrections* is defined as the range of community and institutional sanctions, treatment programs, and services for managing criminal offenders. As such, corrections includes functions such as the supervision and monitoring of offenders in the community, the secure holding of inmates in prisons, the provision of treatment for problems such as drug addiction or mental illness, and residential and other services provided to inmates as a transition from prison to the community.

One of the earliest known bodies of penal codes is the Code of Hammurabi, created during King Hammurabi's reign of Old Babylon, ca. 1780 B.C. The code is best known from this carved stone, now in the Louvre Museum in Paris. Photo by Matthew Seiter.

penitentiary
the term first used to describe secure facilities used to hold offenders serving a criminal sentence; still used today for some older or highly secure prisons

corrections
the range of community and institutional sanctions, treatment programs, and services for managing criminal offenders

In most diagrams of the criminal justice system, corrections is illustrated as the functions for dealing with criminal offenders after a court sentences them. However, the boundaries of corrections have expanded, and corrections now also relates to the detention in jails of offenders charged with crimes, as well as pretrial services such as supervising offenders released on bail. This broader characterization of corrections acknowledges that correctional agencies are often required to deal with offenders who have not yet been found guilty and sentenced to a punishment. This broader definition also makes the establishment of a mission for corrections more difficult and complex.

The Mission of Corrections

A mission is the statement of what an organization is to accomplish. The mission of corrections has traditionally been to implement court-prescribed sentences for criminal violators or to carry out the sentence of the court. Such a mission statement is rather narrow and indicates a lack of control or initiative by correctional agencies as to their functions and how they are to carry them out. However, most contemporary correctional administrators recognize a much broader mission and responsibility. The more complete mission of corrections is to protect society, accomplished through a combination of surveillance and control of offenders, of treatment and rehabilitative services, and of incapacitation during the service of a prison sentence.

In practice, correctional agencies fulfill their mission by assisting courts in the decision to grant bail, by providing the courts with information to guide sentencing, by supervising offenders in the community under court jurisdiction, by imprisoning offenders who receive a sentence of incarceration from the courts, and by overseeing inmates' reentry to the community. Society is protected in the short term as correctional agencies either detain offenders in jail or incarcerate them in prison, thus separating them from society and keeping them from further victimizing citizens in the community. The longer-term protection of society results from correctional agencies providing treatment and services to help offenders become less likely or less motivated to return to a life of crime and more likely to become productive and law-abiding citizens.

Corrections as a Part of the Criminal Justice System

Figure 1.1 is an illustration of the criminal justice system. There are generally thought to be three major components of the criminal justice system: police, courts, and corrections. In the ideal process of criminal justice, the police investigate crimes and arrest suspects, handing over the results of their efforts (investigative information and evidence) to the court system. Prosecutors determine whether a crime has been committed and whether there is probable cause to believe that the suspect has committed the crime. If so, the courts then oversee a determination of guilt for the suspect. If the offender is found guilty, the courts sentence him or her to an appropriate criminal penalty within the state **penal code**, the legislative authorization to provide a specific range of punishment for a specific crime. Once the offender is sentenced, correctional agencies carry out the sentence.

penal code
a legislative authorization to provide a specific range of punishment for a specific crime

However, where the correctional system begins and ends is not as clear as indicated in Figure 1.1. The figure illustrates probation, prison, parole, residential community placement, and revocation of probation and parole, appropriately depicted as part of the "corrections" section of the criminal justice process. However, supervision during bail, detention in jail, diversion programs, and intermediate sanctions are not included in this diagram as part of corrections. Yet these functions are legitimate components of corrections, especially over the past two decades, as corrections (as well as other criminal justice components) has expanded its activities and functions across traditional lines and boundaries. Today, correctional agencies supervise offenders released during the pretrial process; police assist probation officers in supervising community offenders; and courts maintain jurisdiction and supervise offenders even after their release from prison. All of this makes a simple illustration of the criminal justice system and delineation of the major components almost impossible.

Even within the grouping of activities that is referred to as corrections, there are differences among jurisdictions. No one system of corrections exists across the country. There are three governmental levels of correctional systems: federal, state, and thousands of local (county and city) correctional systems. In each state, the role distinctions between what is done at the state versus the local level are different. Some state correctional systems operate all probation activities, whereas in other states counties carry out probation. Some states have a sentencing structure

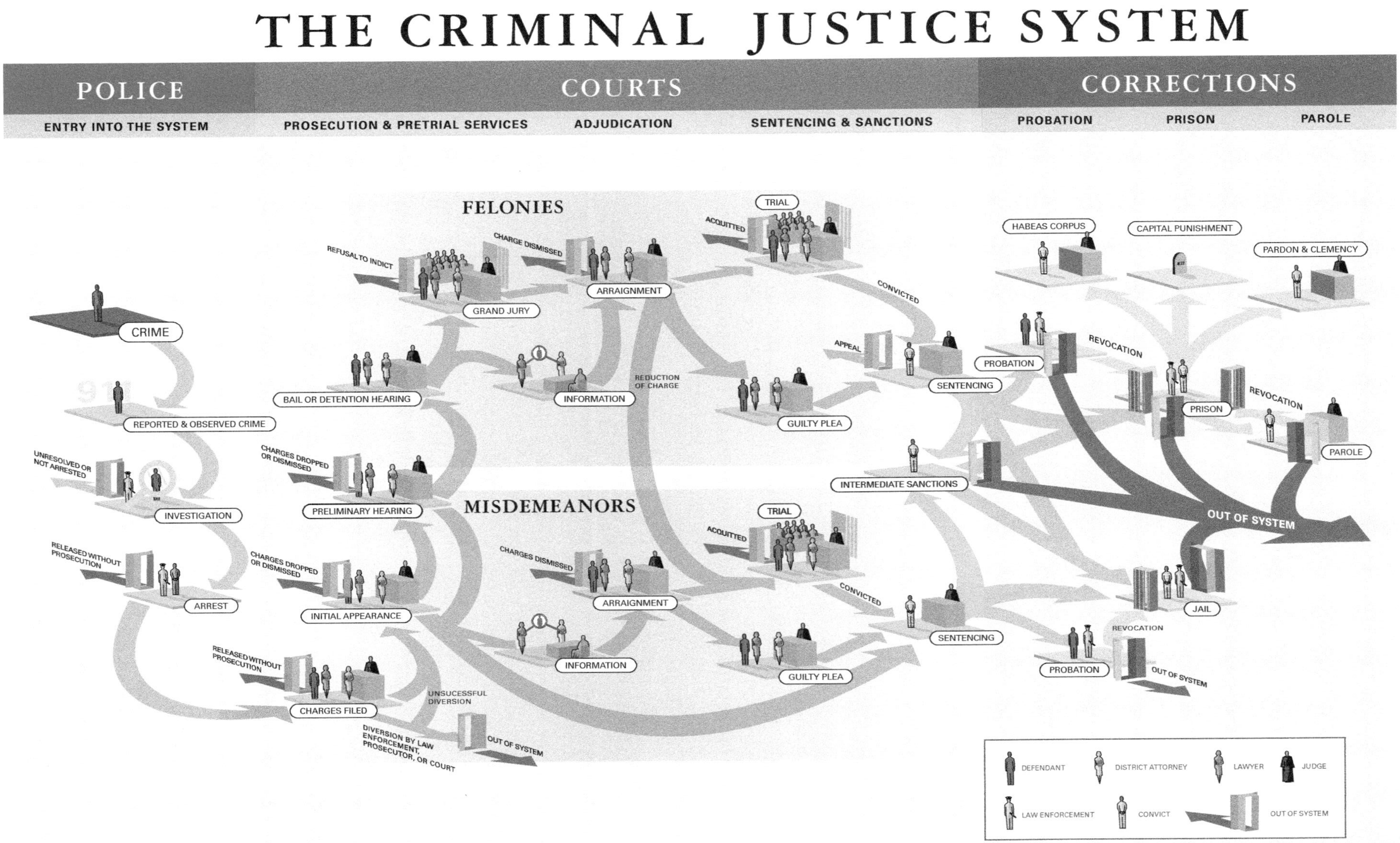

THE CRIMINAL JUSTICE SYSTEM

POLICE	COURTS				CORRECTIONS		
ENTRY INTO THE SYSTEM	PROSECUTION & PRETRIAL SERVICES	ADJUDICATION	SENTENCING & SANCTIONS		PROBATION	PRISON	PAROLE

FELONIES

MISDEMEANORS

CRIME

REPORTED & OBSERVED CRIME

UNRESOLVED OR NOT ARRESTED

INVESTIGATION

RELEASED WITHOUT PROSECUTION

ARREST

CHARGES DROPPED OR DISMISSED

BAIL OR DETENTION HEARING

CHARGES DROPPED OR DISMISSED

PRELIMINARY HEARING

INITIAL APPEARANCE

RELEASED WITHOUT PROSECUTION

CHARGES FILED

DIVERSION BY LAW ENFORCEMENT, PROSECUTOR, OR COURT

UNSUCCESSFUL DIVERSION

OUT OF SYSTEM

REFUSAL TO INDICT

GRAND JURY

CHARGE DISMISSED

ARRAIGNMENT

INFORMATION

REDUCTION OF CHARGE

ACQUITTED

TRIAL

GUILTY PLEA

CHARGES DISMISSED

ARRAIGNMENT

INFORMATION

ACQUITTED

TRIAL

GUILTY PLEA

APPEAL

CONVICTED

SENTENCING

PROBATION

INTERMEDIATE SANCTIONS

CONVICTED

SENTENCING

HABEAS CORPUS

CAPITAL PUNISHMENT

PARDON & CLEMENCY

REVOCATION

PROBATION

REVOCATION

PRISON

OUT OF SYSTEM

JAIL

REVOCATION

PROBATION

OUT OF SYSTEM

PAROLE

DEFENDANT

LAW ENFORCEMENT

DISTRICT ATTORNEY

CONVICT

LAWYER

JUDGE

OUT OF SYSTEM

FIGURE 1.1   The Criminal Justice System

5

that includes release on parole; others do not. And in some states there are state-wide or regionally operated jails, and in others jails are solely within the domain of the city or county.

The Correctional Funnel and Correctional Policy

As stated above, the mission of corrections is to protect society by reducing future crimes. As one of the three major components of the criminal justice system, the pubic considers that corrections, in administering punishment to criminals, prevents future crimes through deterrence and incapacitation, limiting offenders' opportunity to commit further crimes, or reducing their inclination to commit crimes as a result of correctional treatments. The fallacy in this expectation is that the correctional system in reality handles an extremely small percentage of criminals, and an even smaller number is sentenced to prison. The *correctional funnel* (Figure 1.2) is a term used to describe this phenomenon; there is a large numerical difference between the number of crimes reported and the number of offenders convicted and facing a term in prison.

As illustrated in Figure 1.2, of approximately 9.7 million felony crimes known to police in 2010, only 1.7 million individuals (17.7 percent) were arrested, 1.2 million (12.6 percent) were convicted, and about 540,519 (5.6 percent) received a sentence of imprisonment. The remainder of convictions received either or both a short jail term or probation.[1] The public policy issues is that it is often argued that toughening sanctions by lengthening prison sentences will deter offenders, and that keeping them in prison longer will significantly reduce crime. However, the relatively small number of crimes that result in a sentence of imprisonment make it unlikely that even major increases of prison sentences will have a significant impact on crime rates.

The previous few sections included a description of the mission of corrections, a description of the role of corrections within the criminal justice system, and a discussion of the correctional funnel. All of these relate to the outcomes resulting from the development of correctional policy. For discussion purposes in this text, the development of correctional policy is the process that includes considering the mission and role, relevant information, and the best interests of the public (in terms of issues such as safety and cost), and then deciding what broad approaches to take to best meet the goal of protecting society. The correctional funnel is a good example of how, with thoughtful examination, it can be seen that extending sentences significantly may have a deterrent and incapacitative effect on those

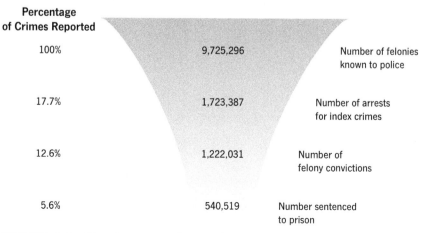

Source: Data adapted from *Sourcebook of Criminal Justice Statistics*, available at http://www.albany.edu/sourcebook (accessed August 6, 2017). Data included in Tables 3.109.2010, 4.7.2010, 5.44.2006, 5.22.2010, 5.47.2006, and 5.25.2008.

FIGURE 1.2 The Correctional Funnel

Your Career in Corrections

Policy Analysts

It may seem odd to start out the "Your Career in Corrections" boxes by describing the job of a policy analyst. Students seldom have heard of this job, and few think about it as a way to begin their career track. However, it is very important to good government that correctional policy be thoughtfully considered with full information regarding cost, effectiveness, and impact. In 2012, American taxpayers contributed over $80 billion to operate our correctional system, while much of what we do is not based on a thorough analysis of cost and impact.[2] This textbook emphasizes the policy choices that must be made as we reform, modify, and update correctional practices, and policy analysts can play a key role in this process.

A policy analyst who works on correctional issues can work for a variety of agencies. Most state (and some large county) correctional departments have a policy and research bureau. Its job is to conduct research and gather statistics that can assist the agency in making policy decisions, provide justification for funding, and assist in creating future strategies and directions for the agency. Legislative bodies always employ policy analysts, and some are assigned to criminal justice or correctional committees. They also conduct research on the effectiveness of correctional programs, usually to aid the legislative body in funding decisions. Some nonprofit agencies employ analysts to examine correctional issues. Groups that are interested in issues such as drug treatment, sentencing, or employment issues for offenders conduct studies to assist in their lobbying efforts to urge that certain policies be implemented. Finally, universities or other research groups often receive grants to conduct correctional research and employ researchers and analysts to examine an issue and write reports as requested by the funding agencies.

There are no reports regarding how many people work in these areas. However, at any one time, easily more than a thousand people are doing the work we have described. Depending on the sophistication of the issue, some will have a doctorate and be experts in research methodology, possibly with some educational emphasis in corrections or criminal justice research. Many others have a master's degree in sociology, criminal justice, business, or public administration and have skills to develop research and policy analysis criteria to be able to provide answers to questions regarding effectiveness or budget impact.

These jobs are not highly visible, yet can have a tremendous impact on the development of good public policy and save taxpayers millions of dollars. A key criterion for someone desiring to work in this field is to be ethically and professionally grounded. Many of the employing agencies noted above may have an "answer" they are looking for to move forward on a policy they would like to see adopted and only want the analyst to give them evidence to use in their arguments in favor of their preferred policy. However, it is critical for analysts to be above justifying a preferred position, without the true data and information to do so. Research and policy analysis should be unbiased and show the true impact of a program or practice. Truly professional analysts will never short-cut their examination or not cite evidence contrary to their agency's desired outcome.

in prison. However, since they represent such a small percentage of the overall population that commits crimes, the direct impact on a reduction of crime rates is questionable.

Throughout this textbook, the "A Question of Policy" boxes encourage discussion of some of the difficult policy issues facing public officials and correctional administrators. Staff members who work in corrections to aid in the policy development process are correctional policy analysts. These positions represent interesting and valuable potential jobs for students majoring in criminal justice and corrections. The "Your Career in Corrections" box presents the role of policy analysts.

Why Study Corrections?

The criminal justice system and corrections are a booming business. The number of clients processed and managed by the criminal justice system is much greater than in the past. The amount of money directed to criminal justice agencies has expanded exponentially. The availability of jobs for those seeking a profession in the criminal justice system has increased significantly. And the interest in corrections by the general public and elected officials has grown tremendously. Today, few citizens of the United States do not have some understanding and knowledge of the criminal justice system, and almost everyone has an opinion on how the system should operate or be changed. Crime and corrections have gone through a metamorphosis from an almost invisible public function to one that seems to be on the minds of almost all members of society.

The number of clients under the supervision of correctional agencies (on probation, in prison or jail, and on parole) has increased significantly over the past three decades. By the end of the twentieth century, more than 6 million offenders were either in prison, in jail, or under supervision in the community. Table 1.1 illustrates the growth from 1980 until 2015, during which there was a 339 percent increase in the number of offenders on probation, a 396 percent increase in the number of offenders in jail, a 478 percent increase in the number of inmates in prison, and a 395 percent increase in the number of offenders on parole.

While this growth has been very dramatic, there has actually been a moderate reduction over the past few years. Most of this reduction was in the number of incarcerated offenders, as states and local jurisdictions have attempted to reduce the overwhelming cost of supervising offenders. It is much less expensive to supervise clients in the community than in prison or jail. Recent estimates are that the average per day cost to incarcerate a prison inmate is over $91,[3] and only $3.42 per day for community supervision.[4]

Yet, corrections is still a significant user of public funds, and therefore continues to be a key focus of elected officials and other criminal justice policy makers. Expenditures for state correctional agencies jumped from $15 billion in 1982 to $58 billion in 2016[5] (Figure 1.3). In fiscal year 1991, state and federal adult correctional agencies' budgets totaled $18.1 billion.[6] But by fiscal year 2011, correctional budgets at federal, state, and local jurisdictions was more than $80 billion.[7]

Over the past two decades, the need has increased for staff to supervise the increasing number of criminal offenders. In 1992, there were 556,500 correctional

TABLE 1.1	Correctional Populations from Selected Years, 1980–2015				
	Probation	Jail	Prison	Parole	Total
1980	1,118,097	183,988	319,598	220,438	1,842,100
1990	2,670,234	405,320	743,382	531,407	4,350,300
2000	3,839,532	621,149	1,316,333	725,527	6,460,000
2005	4,162,495	747,529	1,448,344	784,354	7,051,300
2010	4,055,514	748,728	1,518,104	840,676	7,076,200
2011	3,971,300	735,600	1,505,000	853,900	6,978,500
2012	3,942,800	744,500	1,483,900	851,200	6,937,600
2013	3,912,900	731,200	1,577,000	849,500	6,899,700
2014	3,868,400	744,600	1,562,300	857,700	6,856,900
2015	3,789,800	728,200	1,526,800	870,500	6,741,400

Source: Data from Bureau of Justice Statistics, U.S. Department of Justice, Corrections Facts at a Glance, Selected Years, available at http://www.bjs.gov/index.cfm?ty=pbse&sid=5 (accessed August 8, 2017) and from Danielle Kaeble and Lauren E. Glaze, "Correctional Populations in the United States, 2015," BJS Bulletin (Washington, D.C.: U.S. Department of Justice, 2016, p. 2).

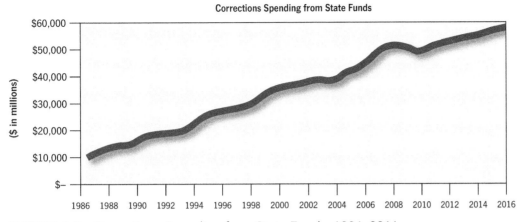

Corrections Spending from State Funds

Source: National Association of State Budget Officers, *State Expenditure Report, 1988–2011,* updated with report of 2014–2016, p. 56, available at https://higher-logicdownload.s3.amazonaws.com/NASBO/9d2d2db1-c943-4f1b-b750-0fca152d64c2/UploadedImages/SER%20Archive/State%20Expenditure%20Report%20(Fiscal%202014-2016)%20-%20S.pdf (accessed August 3, 2017).

FIGURE 1.3 Corrections Spending from State Funds, 1986–2016

employees throughout the United States.[8] The *Bureau of Justice Statistics, Expenditure and Employment Extracts 2012* reports almost a 35 percent increase since that time, as there were 749,418 correctional staff members working at the federal, state, and local levels in the United States in 2012.[9] Many people unfamiliar with corrections believe that only a few types of jobs are held by correctional staff. They understand what correctional officers and wardens do, and perhaps even a probation or parole officer. However, those are only a few of the types of jobs available to those seeking a career in corrections. There are a wide variety of correctional jobs noted below. It is obvious from this list that the variety of correctional jobs is extensive and offers opportunities for employment for students in many fields of study.

Accountant	Industrial specialist
Budget and financial specialist	Personnel/human resource
Caseworker	manager
Chaplain	Probation/parole officer
Computer specialist	Psychologist
Correctional officer	Recreation specialist
Facility maintenance worker	Safety manager
Food service worker	Teacher
Health care professional (physicians,	Training instructor
nurses, dentists, pharmacy staff)	

Corrections continues to be of high interest to citizens and elected officials. Much of this interest results from the misperception that crime is increasing and we as a society must figure out how to make citizens safer. In reality, crime has dropped dramatically over the past three decades. The violent crime rate per 100,000 citizens in 1993 was 747.1 and the property crime rate was 4,740.0, whereas in 2015 the violent crime rate was 372.6 and the property crime rate was 2,487.0. This represents a drop in the violent crime rate of about 50 percent and a drop in the property crime rate of nearly 48 percent from 1993 to 2015.[10] However, crime continues to lead on the news, and as a result, when citizens were asked in polls conducted over the past several years whether there is more crime in the United States now than one year ago, they indicated a belief that crime is increasing (see Table 1.2). In fact, a 2016 Gallup Poll indicated that Americans' concern about crime and violence is the highest in fifteen years.[11]

With the public fear and general concern about crime, public officials will continue to legislate or regulate responses to the perceived crime problem. This results

TABLE 1.2	Attitudes toward the Crime Level in the United States: Selected Years, 1989–2015			
	More (%)	Less (%)	Same (%)	No opinion (%)
2015	70	18	8	
2014	63	21	7	
2013	41	33	21	4
2011	68	17	8	8
2010	66	17	8	9
2009	74	15	6	5
2008	67	15	9	9
2007	71	14	8	6
2006	68	16	8	8
2005	67	21	9	3
2004	53	28	14	5
2003	60	25	11	4
2002	62	21	11	6
2001	41	43	10	6
2000	47	41	7	5
1998	52	5	8	5
1997	64	25	6	5
1996	71	15	8	6
1993	87	4	5	4
1992	89	3	4	4
1990	84	3	7	6
1989	84	5	5	6

Source: The Gallup Organization, *The Gallup Poll* [Online], available at http://www.gallup.com/poll/186308/americans-say-crime-rising.aspx?g_source=position3&g_medium=related&g_campaign=tiles (accessed August 7, 2017). Reprinted With Permission.

Cesare Beccaria
an Italian theorist who in the eighteenth century first suggested linking crime causation to punishments and became known as the founder of the Classical School of criminology

Classical School
the theory linking crime causation to punishment, based on offenders' free will and hedonism

Jeremy Bentham
creator of the hedonistic calculus suggesting that punishments outweigh the pleasure criminals get from committing their crime

in increasing the numbers of police, authorizing more money to be spent by the criminal justice system, and more visibility for criminal justice agencies. As crime and corrections remain on the minds of the public and their elected officials, and there are demands to improve the system and find new ways of operating, those who work in the field will have to create new paradigms to make the system more efficient and enhance the level of support from the citizens whose tax dollars support it. Students studying criminal justice will face this rising interest and increasing expectations as they begin their careers in criminal justice organizations.

Theories of Crime and Punishment

To begin a study of corrections and its historical development, it is important to understand the evolution of theories of crime and its causes. If the purpose of the punishment is to "correct," the punishment must adequately match the reasons why the person committed the crime. There has been considerable thinking and speculation regarding crime and the response to it over the years. For the past fifty years, criminology authors have cited the contribution of the French humanists Montesquieu and Voltaire for encouraging thinking about crime and the then-brutal response to it.[12] This period in the eighteenth century was known as the Age of Enlightenment, and resulted in a move away from feudal ideals, and toward rationalism and equality. However, it was **Cesare Beccaria**, an Italian theorist, who in 1764 first suggested linking crime causation to punishments, as his book *An Essay on Crimes and Punishments* is often credited as the driving force in shaping contemporary thinking about crime and corrections.

Beccaria is known as the founder of the **Classical School** of criminology, the first organized theory of crime causation linked to appropriate punishments. Beccaria suggested that the purpose of punishment is utility, or the prevention of crime. Included in his principles are that crime is an injury to society, that prevention (deterrence of crime) is more important than punishment, that the accused have the right to speedy trials and humane treatment, that there should be no secret accusations or torture, that certainty and swiftness of punishment (more than severity) best deter crime, and that imprisonment should be more widely used as a punishment.

Underlying Beccaria's principles was an emphasis on free will and hedonism. For punishment to deter, individuals must have freedom to choose their actions of committing crime or not. As well, they would judge the impact of the punishment on their own well-being and make a choice regarding the seeking of pleasure and avoidance of pain (hedonism). Building on these principles, **Jeremy Bentham** (1748–1832) created the concept of **hedonistic calculus**, the idea that the main objective of an intelligent man is to achieve the most pleasure and the least pain and that individuals are constantly calculating the pluses and minuses of their potential actions. Bentham therefore theorized that to prevent crime, criminal laws should be organized so that the punishment for any act would outweigh the pleasure that would be derived from the act. Potential offenders would therefore (in line with the Classical School idea of free will) consider the consequences of their actions and be deterred from the commission of crimes.

In reaction to the development of the Classical School emphasizing free will, others began to suggest that not every criminal has complete choice over his or her criminal actions. The **Positive School** was created by **Cesare Lombroso** (1835–1909), with the suggestion that people sometimes commit acts beyond their control. Lombroso, an Italian physician, conducted research into the links between criminality and physical traits. He concluded that criminals had traits that made them throwbacks to earlier stages of evolution: they were not sufficiently developed mentally and had long arms, large amounts of body hair, prominent cheekbones, and large foreheads. This **atavism**, or the existence of features common in the early stages of human evolution, implied that criminals are born, and criminal behavior is *predetermined*.

While several later tests failed to prove Lombroso's theories of atavism, some still support the idea that some factors result in a level of predetermination (not total free will) that influences the chance that someone will commit crimes. Proponents of this approach cite the early works by Dugsdale and by Goddard

hedonistic calculus
the idea that the main objective of an intelligent person is to achieve the most pleasure and the least pain and that individuals are constantly calculating the pluses and minuses of their potential actions

Positive School
the belief that criminals do not have complete choice over their criminal actions and may commit acts that are beyond their control

Cesare Lombroso
the Italian physician who in the nineteenth century founded the Positive School

atavism
the existence of features common in the early stages of human evolution; implied the idea that criminals are born, and criminal behavior is *predetermined*

Cesare Lombroso. Bettmann/Getty Images.

suggesting that there are "criminal families" with a high number of members involved in crime, indicating the possibility of bad genetic influences;[13] the identification by Sheldon of certain body types that are most prone to aggression and violence;[14] or several studies addressing the possibility that chemical imbalances in the body contribute to crime.[15]

Neoclassical School

a compromise between Classical and Positive Schools, while holding offenders accountable for their crimes, allowing for some consideration of mitigating and aggravating circumstances

Another theory developed somewhat as a compromise to the Classical and Positive Schools is the **Neoclassical School** of criminology. Suggested by Gabriel Tarde in 1890, the Neoclassical School recognized there was much ground between total free will and determinism. Tarde argued that no one has complete free will and is uninfluenced by factors such as gender, age, or social and economic environments, yet everyone is still the "author" of his or her own action.[16] The key factors are that, although the Classical School approach to holding offenders accountable makes sense, there should be some consideration of mitigating and aggravating circumstances on account of the criminal activities of any individual. Some authors suggest that the current "get tough" philosophies and transition to determinate sentences are most illustrative of the Neoclassical School in practice today.[17]

Modern theories seem to include a variety of factors that influence people toward criminal behavior. Several theories address the importance of psychological and social factors in determining criminality.[18] Today, however, policy regarding how to punish criminals most often follows the Classical School, emphasizing free will. It is generally believed that offenders must be held accountable and receive just punishments for their crimes. The underlying concept behind this approach is that offenders choose to commit crimes and that punishments must be dire enough to make them consider the result (in both pleasure and pain) of their criminal behavior.

Early Responses to Crime

The types of public responses to crime varied based on the beliefs regarding the causes of crime. The earliest responses to crime were extremely brutal and included torture, beatings, branding, and mutilation. These corporal punishments were often an attempt to relate the punishment as closely as possible to the crime. For instance, liars had their tongues ripped out, thieves had fingers or a hand cut off, and adulterers had a scarlet A branded on their foreheads to reduce their attractiveness and discourage any further adultery. For more serious crimes, offenders were killed in a variety of barbaric methods, such as being hanged, drawn, and quartered, or boiled or burned alive. Besides corporal and capital punishment, removing the offender from the group was commonly used. Banishing someone from the tribe into the wilderness not only resulted in no likelihood of a repeat of the offense, but also often resulted in death, because the person could not survive alone in the wilderness. Another way to remove offenders from society was

transportation

used in England during the seventeenth and eighteenth centuries to remove criminals from society by sending them to British colonies such as America

through **transportation** or deportation. Transportation started in England and was used throughout the seventeenth and eighteenth centuries to send undesirables to the colonies in Australia or America.

The first response to crime in the American colonies was based on the English criminal codes and incorporated the Puritans' linking of crime with sin in developing a rigid and strict system of punishments. Violations of expected community behavior were dealt with severely, using corporal and capital punishment carried out in public to deter both individual offenders and the broader community. Whipping at the town center whipping post or placement in stocks and pillories was common punishment for minor offenses such as drunkenness, slander, or stealing something of minor value. *Pillories* were wooden frames with holes for offenders' hands and head. Offenders had to stand while their hands and head were secured. *Stocks*, similar to pillories, allowed offenders to sit while their hands, head, and feet were all secured in the wooden frame. These punishments were not just for ridicule, as passersby often threw rotten vegetables or even rocks at the offender to aid in the punishment.

Branding was also a popular way to punish offenders; the forehead, face, or hands would be branded, labeling the offender as a certain type of criminal. Adulterers had the letter A carved into their foreheads; thieves had a T carved on their hands; blasphemers were stamped with a B, or perhaps had a hole drilled in their tongues. Torture could also include cutting off a hand or finger of thieves or pickpockets; placing gossips in a *brank*, similar to a birdcage placed over their head with a sharpened shaft with barbs placed in their mouths; or subjecting other minor violators to the *ducking stool*, in which

Historical punishments were both painful and shameful. Stocks and pillories were used both as physical punishment and to ridicule offenders in front of their fellow townspeople, in hopes that they would end their criminal ways. Bettmann/Getty Images.

they were lowered underwater until they almost drowned. More serious offenses resulted in brutal torture, such as stretching and breaking the offender's body on the rack, or in capital punishment by hanging or burning at the stake.

In colonial times, prisons were not yet developed as punishment for crimes. American colonists did use jails, copying the English system of *gaols*, for holding defendants awaiting trial or those already convicted and waiting for their corporal or capital punishment to be carried out. These jails had deplorable conditions, in which poor men, women, and children all lived together in filth, with little food or sanitary conditions. Offenders who could afford it could avoid jail via the *fee system*, an early bail system that enabled the rich to pay a fee and be released. The conditions in both English and colonial jails during the 1600s and 1700s were so deplorable that few doubted the need for reform.

The most famous jail reformer was **John Howard**, who was the sheriff of Bedfordshire, England. Howard himself, while on an English ship, was taken captive by a French privateer and subsequently imprisoned. He was later paroled to England, but never forgot the horrendous conditions resulting in the death of several English prisoners. Once he became sheriff, he was responsible for the operation of the jail and was disturbed over the conditions and the fact that some people were there for weeks because they were unable to pay the fee required for release. He encouraged legislation to do away with the fee system and became a reformer, visiting gaols throughout England to observe conditions. In 1777, he wrote *The State of the Prisons in England and Wales*, which educated the public and Parliament to the problem. As a result, Parliament passed the Penitentiary Act in 1779, providing for "secure and sanitary structures, systematic inspections,

John Howard
the sheriff of Bedfordshire, England, who encouraged reform of English jails in the late 1700s

This replica of a pillory is in St. George, Bermuda. Photo by Richard P. Seiter.

abolition of fees for basic services, and a reformatory regime."[19] Howard coined the term *penitentiary* to emphasize the purpose of offenders doing penance while reflecting on their sins, rather than simply being punished brutally. These ideas not only had an effect on gaols in England, but also influenced the development of prisons in the United States.

The Development of the Prison

In the United States, there were considerable dissatisfaction with the brutality and extensive use of corporal and capital punishment to respond to criminal behavior. One reform-minded individual was William Penn, the governor of Pennsylvania. The Quakers, who settled Pennsylvania, were hardworking and economical people. They realized that the criminal codes were both inhumane and inefficient in that judges often did not follow the criminal codes because they did not want to inflict severe punishments on relatively minor offenders. The Quakers had also been the victims of religious persecution, and freedom to choose their way of life was important to them and the reason they came to America and settled the Pennsylvania colony. Under the leadership of Penn, the Quakers replaced the current criminal code with a new one that included the following:

- The abolition of capital punishment for all crimes other than homicide
- The substitution of imprisonment at hard labor for bloody corporal punishments
- The provision of free food and lodging to inmates
- The replacement of the stocks and pillory with houses of detention.[20]

The Walnut Street Jail

In the late 1700s, Dr. Benjamin Rush (one of the original signers of the Declaration of Independence) became leader of the Philadelphia Society for Alleviating the Miseries of the Public Prisons. He revived the Quaker code, which had been repealed when Penn died in 1718, and the Philadelphia Society established the first prison in the United States in 1790 by converting a wing of the Walnut Street Jail for use in housing sentenced offenders as an alternative to corporal punishment. As in John Howard's concept of the penitentiary, the **Walnut Street Jail** created a regimen of hard work and reflection in order to do penance for criminal offenses.

Walnut Street Jail
the first penitentiary in the United States

Inmates were kept in individual cells and were not allowed to talk to other inmates in order to avoid moral contamination among prisoners. Administrators of the jail did not want prisoners to even know the identity of other inmates and often put masks on inmates as they moved through the prison to avoid identification that would detract from the reform of prisoners in case they met each other after release. Prisoners were given work such as making handicrafts in their cells during the day, and were encouraged to read the Bible and do penance in the evenings. The overall operating theme was one of hard labor, strict discipline, solitary and silent confinement, and religious study.

The Pennsylvania System

When the state of Pennsylvania opened its first two prisons (the Western State Penitentiary in Pittsburgh in 1826 and the Eastern State Penitentiary in Cherry Hill just outside Philadelphia in 1829), the Walnut Street Jail served as the model for their design and operation. The Western Penitentiary was an architectural nightmare, built in an octagon with small, dark cells inside the cellblocks to provide solitary confinement and no labor. It was soon modified in 1833 to provide cells on the outside of the blocks to allow light in through windows and increased cell size to allow for inmate labor within the cell. The mistakes of the Western Penitentiary influenced and improved the design of the Eastern Penitentiary, built with seven cellblocks extending from a hub in the center of the prison walls. Each cellblock was long and narrow, with cells on the outside and a corridor down the middle. The cells had a door through the wall into a small recreation yard, in which prisoners had brief exercise periods by themselves each day.

The basis of these two prisons' operation was the same as the Walnut Street Jail: to emphasize the opportunity for prisoners to reform themselves through hard work while reflecting on their crimes. The **Pennsylvania system** was known as the "separate and silent" system, with silence enforced and inmates not allowed to see or talk with each other. It was believed that this approach would not result in offenders becoming morally contaminated and trained in crime by other prisoners.

Pennsylvania system
the "separate and silent" system of prison operations emphasizing reformation and avoidance of criminal contamination

However, there were several problems with the Pennsylvania system. First, it was almost impossible to keep inmates from seeing and communicating with each other. Second, it was very expensive to operate, as the requirement to keep inmates separate increased the number of staff members needed. Third, there was very limited productivity by inmates, as the requirement to work alone in their cells did not allow for an efficient production of goods for resale as was desired. Fourth, opponents of the operation of the Pennsylvania prisons suggested that the solitude imposed on inmates made many of them mentally ill. As a result of these issues, the prison operations were almost immediately modified. Two inmates were placed in a cell together so one could learn a trade from the other and

This hallway in the Eastern State Penitentiary shows the solid doors that prevented inmates from seeing other inmates as they moved through the hallway. Photo by Richard P. Seiter.

increase the production of goods. As well, the warden of the Eastern Penitentiary, Samuel Wood, used inmates as servants in his home and allowed them to communicate. Therefore, the Pennsylvania system seemed doomed from its beginning and other states that were considering opening prisons as a criminal sanction had to find alternative approaches to overcome the problems. Although there was great interest in the Pennsylvania system, only two states (New Jersey and Rhode Island) fully adopted its "separate and silent" system. Even in those states, the Pennsylvania system was soon abandoned in favor of the improved system that was created in Auburn, New York.

The Auburn System

New York opened a prison in Auburn in 1817 that was originally designed around the Pennsylvania model. Cells were back to back and stacked five tiers high to make it easier to keep inmates separate. However, this design did not allow for the use of individual recreation yards, as did the Eastern Penitentiary. The Auburn prison originally adopted the "separate and silent" system of Pennsylvania, but soon determined that the problems that plagued Pennsylvania were too serious to overcome. In 1823, a modification of the prison began in order to change its unwieldy design and make it more efficient to operate.

The major change was in the Pennsylvania emphasis on keeping inmates separate. Auburn officials determined that they would continue to keep inmates in separate cells at night; however, they would allow them to congregate during the day to work in factories to improve the production of goods, which would be resold to cover some of the prison operational costs. The **Auburn system** became known as the "congregate and silent" system, as officials continued to reduce the spread of criminal ideas by inmates through silence and strict discipline. Barnes and Teeters describe the enforcement of the system through lockstep

Auburn system
the congregate and silent operation of prisons, in which inmates were allowed to work together during the day, but had to stay separate and silent at other times

marching with eyes downcast, hard work and activity while outside cells, and prohibitions of inmates even being face to face.[21]

The operation of Auburn prison was soon copied at Sing Sing prison in New York, and many other prisons in other states followed that approach. There was general consensus that the Auburn system was better than the Pennsylvania system. The prisons were cheaper to build and operate, the congregate style allowed production of goods and more income for the state, and fewer inmates developed mental health problems. This approach was not only adopted by other prisons being built across the country, but the use of imprisonment as a criminal sanction also received international attention, and many countries sent representatives to examine the operation of both the Pennsylvania-style and Auburn-style prisons. Interestingly, although the Pennsylvania style of prisons was seldom favored in the United States, most international visitors found advantages in both, and many preferred the Pennsylvania system because of its effort to avoid contamination among prisoners. During the first half of the nineteenth century, most American prisons practiced the Auburn style of silence, hard labor, separation at night, congregation during the day to maximize production of goods, and strict discipline.

Prisons throughout the Last Two Centuries

During the early 1800s, several large prisons were built and operated on the Auburn model. However, these new prisons were quickly overcrowded, new ones were built, and U.S. prison administrators began to look for ways to improve operations and reduce the growth in the inmate population. Of note were reforms under the leadership of Captain Alexander Maconochie, who in 1840 took over the British penal colony on Norfolk Island, and Sir Walter Crofton, who built on the ideas of Maconochie as head of the Irish penal system. These two men used the concept of indeterminate sentencing, emphasizing preparing offenders for release, giving inmates an opportunity to gradually reduce control and work their way to a less restricted environment, and releasing offenders on a conditional basis when administrators determined that they were prepared to return to the community (the first effort to have conditional release, which led to the development of parole). This operation of the Irish system was seen as more humanitarian, placing

During the Reformatory Era, prisons were often built using gothic style architecture, to remind inmates of their need to reform their ways. Courtesy of Ohio Department of Rehabilitation and Corrections.

Prisons built and operated in the first part of the 1900s were designed to hold large numbers of inmates, in tiers of cells stacked on top of one another. Courtesy of Federal Bureau of Prisons.

Reformatory Era

an environment emphasizing reformation that expanded education and vocational programs and focused offenders' attention on their future

Industrial Prison Era

prison operations with emphasis on having inmates work and produce products that could help to make the prisons self-sustaining

Period of Transition

an era of prison operations in which enforced idleness, lack of professional programs, and excessive size and overcrowding of prisons resulted in an increase in prisoner discontent and prison riots

hands-off doctrine

an avoidance by the U.S. Supreme Court of judicial intervention in the operations of prisons and the judgment of correctional administrators

an emphasis on training and preparation for release, and was believed to do more to return offenders to the community with a greater chance for success.

In 1870, a group of U.S. prison administrators, politicians, and interested citizens met in Cincinnati and formed the National Prison Association, now known as the American Correctional Association. In their discussions, they formally adopted the principles of the Irish system, emphasizing reformation rather than suffering, rewards for good behavior, and the use of indeterminate sentences to release prisoners when they were best prepared to become industrious free citizens.[22] This action and change in approach resulted in corrections entering the **Reformatory Era**, which lasted from 1870 to 1910. Replacing the Auburn emphasis on punishment and reflection on the past, the Reformatory Era provided expanded education and vocational programs aimed at focusing offenders' attention on their future.

As sensible as the Reformatory Era seemed, tremendous growth in the U.S. prison population forced another change after the turn of the century. During the first three decades of the twentieth century, the number of inmates in U.S. prisons grew more than 170 percent.[23] This growth was a significant financial burden for the states, and the new prisons were designed to hold large numbers of inmates in harsh work-oriented environments. This allowed an emphasis on inmates working and producing products that could be sold to help make the prisons economically self-supporting. With their free labor, prisons became very successful as businesses, and prison management emphasized production as much as security and rehabilitation, and the volume of prison-made products sold on the open market increased considerably. Thus the **Industrial Prison Era**, from 1910 to 1935, led to the first major interest in the management of prisons by external parties.

The large volume of prison-made products sold on the open market resulted in challenges from organized labor. As the country entered the Great Depression with the crash on Wall Street in 1929, Congress passed two laws to restrict competition from inmate-made goods with the private sector. The Hawes–Cooper Act in 1929 and the Ashurst–Sumners Act in 1935, amended in 1940, severely limited the sale of prison-made products on the open market. These statutes tolled the death knell for industrial prisons, which suddenly had no marketplace for their goods. Thousands of inmates who had previously been working were idled, and prison administrators were stuck with large prisons designed around work. With nothing for these inmates to do, administrators had to find another way to operate prisons.

From 1935 until 1960, corrections was in the **Period of Transition**, as prison administrators tried to find an answer to their dilemma. During this time, enforced idleness, a lack of professional programs, and the excessive size and overcrowding of prisons resulted in an increase in prisoner discontent and prison riots. Between 1950 and 1966, more than 100 riots and major disturbances occurred in U.S. prisons.[24] Prison managers were constrained in what they could do with the large facilities designed to maximize production they had inherited, and they struggled to find alternative approaches to maintain control of large concentrations of idle prisoners. This era was also greatly affected when the U.S. Supreme Court decided *Cooper v. Pate* (1964) and ended its **hands-off doctrine**, which had restricted judicial intervention in the operations of prisons and the judgment of correctional administrators. By accepting inmate-filed cases alleging

cruel and inhumane punishment under the Fourteenth Amendment to the U.S. Constitution, the Court opened Pandora's box, and federal courts were flooded with requests by inmates to improve the conditions in most prisons.

Things had to change, and resulting reforms included the professionalizing of staff through recruitment and training and implementation of many self-improvement programs to take the place of the industrial work programs. This ushered in the **Rehabilitative Era** (1960–1980), and included the early 1960s adoption of the **medical model** as the dominant theory influencing prison and other correctional practices. Under the medical model, offenders were believed to be "sick," inflicted with problems that caused their criminality; they needed to be diagnosed and treated, and rehabilitative programs would resolve their problems and prepare them for release as "well" into the community, able to be productive and crime-free.

A minor "adjustment" to the medical model was the recognition of the need to strengthen the links between prisons and the community. **Reintegration** was added to the emphasis on rehabilitation. After offenders completed their treatment in prison, they needed transitional care. Reintegration includes the community in the medical model, with recognition that the transition from prisoner to free citizen is difficult. Community correctional programs were expanded, and halfway houses and special parole programs became important elements in the correctional process.

What seemed like the golden age of rehabilitation soon came under attack. In the early 1970s, Robert Martinson and his colleagues completed a review of correctional research to determine "what worked."[25] In the review of more than 200 studies, the researchers concluded that, although there were a few isolated correlations between a treatment program and a reduction in recidivism, no consistent findings indicated that any single treatment program significantly reduced recidivism. Therefore, the Martinson review was commonly known as, concluding, **"nothing works."** For public officials looking for a way to reduce costs and make corrections more punitive, this study provided statistical support and was the death knell for the medical model. Rehabilitative programs lost funding, and parole was eliminated in several states.

Throughout the 1980s, the United States saw an increase in crime, especially violent crimes, and crime and corrections became very important to the public and

Rehabilitative Era
an era of prison management emphasizing the professionalizing of staff through recruitment and training and implementation of many self-improvement programs

medical model
a theory of corrections that offenders were sick, inflicted with problems that caused their criminality, and needed to be diagnosed and treated, and that rehabilitative programs would resolve offenders' problems and prepare them for release into the community able to be productive and crime-free

reintegration
a belief that after offenders complete their treatment in prison they need transitional care, and that the community must be involved in their successful return to society

"nothing works"
a conclusion by Robert Martinson that no correctional treatment program reduces recidivism; it effectively spelled the end to the medical model

During the Retributive Era, some prisons and jails returned to making inmates wear stripes, a tradition that goes back to the 1800s. Although the argument was for security in case of escape, the real reason was to punish inmates in every way legally allowable. Scott Houston/Alamy Stock Photo.

A Look Into . . .

Prison Reforms through the Twentieth Century

Pearson Education.

T. Don Hutto is a legend in prison administration and reform from the 1960s through the 1990s. He started as a correctional officer in Texas in 1964, and three years later was the warden of the Ramsey Unit, one of the largest Texas prisons. At the age of thirty six, he became director of the Arkansas Department of Corrections, just after the incidents around its operation led to the movie Brubaker. Hutto moved to reform both the Ramsey Unit and the Arkansas prison system, ending racial segregation and the use of building tenders (inmates who acted as armed guards over other inmates). He also dealt with reforms needed to move Arkansas from the unconstitutional system it was found to be in *Holt v. Sarver*. The following is a segment of a speech Hutto recently delivered to the North American Wardens and Superintendents Association. Mr. Hutto's comments put into practical perspective the changing beliefs and eras of prison management.

For as long as they have existed, prisons have reflected (although not always accurately) the culture in which they were spawned. Over a period of time, we have coined the term "corrections" to describe the broad process of carrying out the decisions of the courts in a manner which seems to best serve society's interests.

Spanning the generations in our profession, the metamorphosis of terminology has been agonizingly slow, often amusing, and sometimes painful, but the terminology itself has changed far more rapidly than have the actual practices. As too often happens in other endeavors, when we don't know exactly what we ought to be doing or how, we simply change the names. The term "penal," as in "penal system," survived for generations as did its namesake, "penitentiary," which was derived from the word "penitent," based on the vain hope that given enough time and solitude, the offender would somehow see the error of his or her ways (repent, if you will) and be fit to become a law-abiding member of society. In a cultural effort to find an acceptable name for what would preferably be "out of sight and out of mind," we tried "workhouse," "debtors' prison," "prison," "penitentiary," "colony," "camp," "farm," "institution," "center," "facility," and just plain "house." Meanwhile, we were

busy redefining our charges as "convicts," "prisoners," "inmates," "offenders," "detainees," "residents," "patients," and even "students."

And, oh yes! We were at various times in the business of "reform," "rehabilitation," "punishment," "incarceration," "treatment," and of course, "reintegration." "Reform" has been a buzzword regarding prisons and corrections for as long as I, and probably any of you, can remember. The New Oxford American Dictionary says that reform means to "make changes in order to improve something." "Reform" is a useful catchword, as, according to someone or some group, just about every societal or cultural institution, needs to be "reformed." Today, the word "change" is more in vogue but "change" means making something different, not necessarily better. The term "change" is neutral and can be either positive or negative. Transform, on the other hand, means to make a thorough or dramatic change, and the radical changes which have taken place in Southern corrections in the last fifty years suggest that "transformed" is the word that applies, but for convenience sake, I will talk about "positive change."

I mentioned earlier that prisons developed as reflections of the culture in which they existed. Southern prisons certainly fit that pattern. With a few exceptions, the South was an agrarian society, deeply rooted in the plantation and slavery mentality. The large plantation-like prisons which developed in rural areas, particularly in Alabama, Mississippi, Texas, Louisiana, Arkansas and to a lesser extent Oklahoma, Georgia and Virginia, were logical extensions of the prevailing civilization and culture. West Virginia and Kentucky, recognized as border-states during the Civil War, were, in fact more akin to their neighbors, Pennsylvania and Ohio and developed accordingly. The coastal states of North Carolina and South Carolina were influenced heavily by the Piedmont and Appalachian mores and traditions. Florida, with two-thirds of its border being coastline, developed somewhat different traditions. So, when we speak of The South, we are not speaking of one cohesive entity. Nevertheless, it is fair to say that Southern prisons had a tendency to develop along the lines of plantation prisons or roadwork stations known for their "chain" gangs, and these usually widely scattered road station locations were anchored by one or more larger "penitentiaries." Virginia provides an example of a state which developed a combination; road stations, large farms, and a penitentiary.

Up until the nineteen seventies, not much changed.[26]

elected officials. Constant media coverage of violent crime created fear and anger toward the crime issue. Political rhetoric emphasized holding offenders accountable for their acts, and the current **Retributive Era** came into being, emphasizing the need to be tough on criminals while keeping them isolated from law-abiding citizens and making them serve "hard" time. With this model, correctional sanctions are tough, offer few amenities, and emphasize public safety over all else. The Retributive Era is also a return to the Classical School of criminality, in which offenders have free choice to commit their crimes, and a response of lengthening and toughening punishments is believed to deter and prevent crime.

Retributive Era
an era of corrections that emphasizes holding offenders accountable for their acts and being tough on criminals while keeping them isolated from law-abiding citizens and making them serve "hard" time

The Sentencing Goals of Corrections

The sentencing goals of corrections are punishment, deterrence, incapacitation, rehabilitation, and restitution. As one might imagine, it is very difficult to attempt these seemingly conflicting goals at the same time. Can corrections punish at the same time as it rehabilitates? Can prisons incapacitate offenders and at the same time try to get them to repay the victim or society for the damage they have done? Even though correctional officials may admit that these conflicting demands create a management challenge, society continues to expect corrections to pursue all five of these goals.

Punishment

Although different correctional goals have been emphasized in varying degrees over time, the most dominant correctional goal has historically been **punishment**, the infliction of pain or suffering. As a society, we believe that punishment for inappropriate behavior is not only allowable, but also advisable. We use punishment to teach children right from wrong. We believe that punishment helps maintain moral order, with the focus on society rather than on the individual who committed the crime. Criminal offenders are brought to justice by the state, acting for society. Through punishment, society can maintain order and show fairness to those who do not violate the law. Some think of the role of punishment within society as a catharsis, a way for society to feel good about punishing offenders. People need to see that those who demonstrate inappropriate behavior receive their "just deserts," or what is coming to them.

punishment
the correctional goal emphasizing the infliction of pain or suffering

    Punishment for criminal acts is sometimes referred to as **retribution**, which implies the infliction of punishment on those who deserve to be punished. The idea of *lex talionis* (Latin for "law of retribution") is similar to the biblical adage of "an eye for an eye" and indicates that offenders get the punishment they deserve. The idea of punishment and retribution is primarily focused on the past, in that it is in exchange for the commission of a criminal violation. However, punishment is also closely linked to future-oriented correctional goals, such as deterrence or rehabilitation. Punishment is necessary for deterrence, and the presence of punishment encourages rehabilitation. Punishment is reactive in that it focuses on the act or crime, rather than on the offender's particular circumstances or needs. Society believes that it is only fair and just that criminal offenders receive punishment for their crimes.

retribution
infliction of punishment on those who deserve to be punished

    How much and what type of punishment are appropriate in a modern democratic society? It is difficult to determine how much punishment is necessary for the commission of a crime. The U.S. Supreme Court addressed this issue in *Bell v. Wolfish*, when the Court established the "punitive intent standard."[27] The case dealt with conditions and practices at a federal jail for short-term offenders in New York City. Inmates alleged that overcrowded conditions and restrictive security procedures were a violation of the Eighth Amendment, which states that "Excessive bail shall not be required, nor excessive fines imposed, nor cruel and unusual punishment inflicted." The Court ruled that the case should turn only on whether the practices in question violated detainees' right to be free from punishment, using a standard of whether the individual restrictions were punitive or merely regulatory restraints; whether the practice is reasonably related to a legitimate goal other than punishment; and whether it appears to be excessive in relation to the alternative purpose.

The Court also addressed punishment and created the **test of proportionality** in the 1983 case of *Solem v. Helm*, by declaring that

> *a criminal sentence must be proportionate to the crime for which the defendant has been convicted...and be guided by objective criteria, including (i) the gravity of the offense and the harshness of the penalty; (ii) the sentences imposed on other criminals in the same jurisdiction; and (iii) the sentences imposed for commission of the same crime in other jurisdictions...*[28]

test of proportionality
the result of the 1983 case of *Solem v. Helm*; a test used to guide sentencing based on the gravity of the offense and consistency of the severity of punishment

Deterrence

Deterrence is a correctional goal focused on future behavior (or the avoidance of certain actions) by both individuals and society. The expectation is that, as a result of offenders receiving punishment, both they and others will be deterred or discouraged from committing crimes in the future. Jeremy Bentham, in his 1789 concept of hedonistic calculus, argued that if the sanction for committing a crime inflicted a greater amount of pain than the pleasure resulting from the offense, crime would be prevented. When an individual commits a crime and receives a punishment, the punishment is designed to result in **specific deterrence** of that offender from committing further crimes. The idea is that the punishment the offender received created such an unpleasant situation that he or she will not want to experience it again. This certainly seems logical, but requires that offenders receive punishment that is swift, certain, and specifically linked to the criminal act. Unfortunately, justice today often does not end with these results.

Deterrence philosophies are also expected to have an effect on the general society. **General deterrence** presumes that others in society will not commit crimes, because they see that there is a punishment for such acts and that individuals do receive the prescribed punishments. For general deterrence to be effective, the punishment must be visible and the public must believe that if they commit a crime, they will be caught and punished, the punishment will be carried out uniformly, and the benefits of the crime will not outweigh the punishment. This requires logic and rationality. The theory often breaks down, as criminals do not believe they will get caught, think they can get out of trouble with a good lawyer, or do not fear the available punishment enough for it to deter them from the criminal act.

Over the past two decades, legislators have operated under a misconception that if they continue to enhance (increase) penalties for certain crimes, the deterrent effect will expand and commission of these crimes will go down. Public relations campaigns have sought to educate potential criminals regarding the penalties for drug offenses or for using a gun in the commission of a crime. While research has failed to indicate that such penalty modifications have a significant

specific deterrence
the effect of punishment on an individual offender that prevents that person from committing future crimes

general deterrence
the recognition that criminal acts result in punishment, and the effect of that recognition on society that prevents future crimes

deterrent effect, those who favor using prison rather than probation and increasing the length of current prison sentences argue that, even if such enhancements do not have a deterrent effect, they maximize the incapacitative effect.

Incapacitation

Incapacitation is reducing offenders' ability or capacity to commit further crimes. Correctional sanctions restrict offenders' opportunity to continue their criminality and, through this restriction, society is protected from potential criminals. Some suggest that incapacitation is reactive in that it is a punishment for past crimes. Others contend, "sentences based primarily on incapacitation are future oriented,"[29] in that they look at the potential for offenders criminal behavior. Others imply that incapacitation is both reactive and proactive. Carlson and colleagues argue, "Like retribution, incapacitation is reactive, and yet, like deterrence, it attempts to predict and influence future behavior."[30]

incapacitation
reducing offenders' ability or capacity to commit further crimes

Blumstein suggests that there are two ways to define and view the correctional goal of incapacitation. "The most narrow is that incapacitation (through a sentence of imprisonment or death) makes it literally impossible for offenders to commit future crimes. In this view, incapacitation serves to [avert crimes] in the general society by isolation of the identified offenders during periods of incarceration."[31] Thus incapacitation is believed to reduce crime by focusing on the offender who is being incapacitated or imprisoned, while the person is under control of the authorities carrying out the punishment. Incapacitation is based on the belief that most criminals commit several crimes over their lifetimes and therefore, during the time of their criminal sanction, crime is being prevented by their reduced opportunity. However, even a person who is in prison or on death row is capable of committing crimes against victims. In prison, inmates commit crimes of assault against other inmates or prison staff. Offenders in prison still use or deal in drugs. However, society is protected, even while those who work or live in prison are still potential victims of crime.

The second way to consider incapacitation is under a broader definition whereby offenders' opportunities to commit further crimes are lessened by the imposition of the criminal sentence. For instance, house arrest using electronic monitoring to ensure that an offender remains at home at prescribed times reduces the opportunity for criminal activity. Whenever an offender serving a sanction while in the community is under the supervision or monitoring of correctional staff, his or her opportunity to commit crime is reduced.

As noted above, incapacitation is based on a belief that most criminals repeat their criminality. Several studies, beginning with Wolfgang and Sellin's classic work on cohort groups in Philadelphia, have shown that most offenders commit more than one crime, and a small group of offenders commit a large percentage of crimes. A review of this work found the following:

Career criminals, though few in number, account for most crime. Even though chronic repeat offenders (those with five or more arrests by age 18) make up a relatively small proportion of all offenders, they commit a very high proportion of all crimes.... In Wolfgang's Philadelphia study, chronic offenders accounted for 23% of all male offenders in the study, but they had committed 61% of all crimes. Of all crimes by all members of the group studied, chronic offenders committed: 61% of all homicides; 76% of all rapes; 73% of all robberies; and 65% of all aggravated assaults.[32]

selective incapacitation
incarceration of high-risk offenders for preventative reasons based on what they are expected to do, not what they have already done

These findings led to efforts to identify offenders with the greatest potential of committing a high number of crimes and sentence them to long prison terms, an approach referred to as **selective incapacitation**. During the 1980s, the RAND Corporation, recognizing that prison cells were an expensive and therefore scarce resource, created the concept of selective incapacitation. In this work, Greenwood argued that, in order to maximize the incapacitating result (preventing future crimes) of imprisonment, scarce prison and jail space should be reserved for the most dangerous, violent, and repeat offenders.[33] It had earlier been concluded that if selected offenders who commit repetitive crimes were imprisoned and incapacitated for three or even five years, significantly fewer crimes would have been committed.[34] Therefore, a model of selective incapacitation advocates incarcerating, for preventive reasons, high-risk people for what they are expected to do, not for what they have already done.

Selective incapacitation remains hotly debated and has several critics. Gottfredson and Hirschi have challenged the methodological approach and conclusions of the RAND studies.[35] Others have raised the issue of "false positives" and the fairness of incarcerating for long periods of time those who are wrongly expected to commit future crimes. As Allen, Latessa, and Ponder noted, "The evidence is that we would probably incarcerate numerous noneligible (a 'false positive' problem) persons and release to lesser confinement many of those eligible (a 'false negative' problem) persons. Whatever benefits might accrue to this sentencing doctrine have thus far eluded corrections."[36]

Rehabilitation

rehabilitation
a programmed effort to alter the attitudes and behaviors of inmates and improve their likelihood of becoming law-abiding citizens

recidivism
the state of relapse that occurs when offenders complete their criminal punishment and then continue to commit crimes

The next goal of corrections is to rehabilitate offenders, that is, return them to society better able to avoid criminality and less likely to commit further crimes. **Rehabilitation** means returning someone to a prior state. It is assumed that this refers to the life of offenders before they began to commit crimes. However, for most offenders, rehabilitation does not take them back, but to a new and better state, one in which they are self-restrained and not motivated to commit crime. The emphasis of rehabilitation is clearly proactive and focused on preventing future crimes. Correctional officials believe this may be their most important function, protecting society in the long term by reducing **recidivism** (a return to crime). However, it is questionable whether the effectiveness of correctional programs should be judged solely by the recidivism rate. No person or program can force offenders to change their behavior or to make good decisions to avoid crime, especially months after they leave the supervision of correctional officials. The situations and environments facing offenders differ from case to case. Even though recidivism may not be the most appropriate measure of the success of rehabilitation programs, it is likely to remain the one most often examined and used.

Corrections attempts to rehabilitate offenders in many ways. First, correctional programs are aimed at trying to reduce offenders' motivation to commit further crimes. Although there are many reasons why people commit crimes, correctional agencies offer psychological counseling to help offenders understand the factors that trigger certain behaviors, anger management and other programs to help offenders recognize dangerous situations in which they may act wrongfully, and sensitivity training to get offenders to understand the impact of their criminal actions on victims and their families. Second, correctional programs try to build competencies in offenders that may help them avoid problems that heighten their likelihood of committing crime. Such programs are designed to help offenders to increase their educational level, develop a vocational skill, or reduce the use of drugs or alcohol. Finally, correctional programs may simply have a goal of improving offenders' decision-making. Why do offenders choose selling drugs over getting a legitimate job? Why do offenders choose to act out violently rather than avoid confrontation or seek nonviolent resolutions to problems? Or why do offenders steal others' property to try to make an easy buck? Some correctional programs help offenders improve their decision-making skills while considering the values and potential outcomes of their criminal actions.

Although support for rehabilitation has experienced ebbs and flows throughout the history of corrections, public attitudes have consistently favored rehabilitating criminal offenders. A recent public opinion survey indicated that 87 percent of those surveyed favor rehabilitative services for prisoners as opposed to a punishment-only system,[37] and greater than 90 percent of those surveyed rated as "important" that prison inmates receive job training, drug treatment, mental health services, family support, and housing assistance.[38]

Restitution

The first four goals of corrections are acknowledged by almost every author and in almost every textbook. Less mentioned, but currently gaining in popularity, is the goal of **restitution**, or making right by repaying society or victims for the wrongs created by offenders. This is not a new goal in the way it is carried out. Criminal sentences have historically included fines and victim restitution. And it can be argued that the chain gangs of the early twentieth century were public works programs in which inmates had to build roads or clear trails to improve the public good. During more contemporary times, the principle of *restoration* of the damage resulting from crime has increased in importance, and many more criminal sentences include the opportunity for restitution as the sanctions are carried out.

As society took over responsibility for bringing a criminal to justice and removed victims from the process to avoid their seeking revenge, the pendulum swung too far, and the victim became the forgotten participant in the criminal justice process. After police took victims' statements, victims often did not hear anything else official unless they were required to testify at trial. Victims played

restitution
acts by which criminals make right or repay society or their victims for their wrongs

Offenders are regularly required to do some type of community service to help pay back society for their crimes. Courtesy of Ohio Department of Rehabilitation and Correction.

victims' movement
the criminal justice system's recognition that victims should be involved in the process of sentencing criminals

restorative justice
models of sentencing that shift the focus away from punishment of the offender and emphasize involving the victim while holding offenders accountable for the harm they caused and finding opportunities for them to repair the damage

no role in sentencing, few sentences sought to repair the damages they incurred, and they seldom received any progress reports, such as when a criminal would appear before a parole board or was to get out of prison.

Over the past twenty years, a **victims' movement** became popular and the criminal justice system made many adjustments to include victims. Victim assistance programs were created to support victims during the adjudication process and even arranged transportation to the trial if necessary. Sentencing decisions now record and consider victims' statements of their losses. Notifications to victims regarding any change in status in the sentence of a criminal (such as a move from one prison to another) are commonplace. Victims are informed of parole hearings and told how they can provide input if desired. And plans for inmates after release are provided to ensure that the victim sees no conflicts or felt threatened by the proposed release.

All these activities are positive in getting offenders to repay the state or the victim for the damage done by their crimes. However, they still failed to satisfy the needs of most victims, the community, and even the offender. Over the past two decades, an alternative to traditional criminal sentencing, called **restorative justice**, emerged; it more fully implements the overall philosophy of the goal of restitution. Restorative justice models of sentencing shift the focus away from reactive, punishment-oriented sentencing, which has no concern for the victim. These models emphasize involving the victim while holding offenders accountable for the harm they caused and finding opportunities for them to repair the damage. Freeman describes restorative justice as "a process that focuses on the injury resulting from the crime and works to repair the injury by shifting the role of the offender from passive recipient of punishment to active participant in reparation."[39] Meanwhile, public opinion surveys have found that "the process of mediating conflict between crime victims and offenders provides many benefits to the parties involved, the community, and the justice system."[40] As logical as they seem, restorative justice models started with high hope but few have been adopted across the country. However, there is still support for holding offenders responsible for "making right" the harm they have done with their crimes and the importance of involving the victim in the criminal justice process, and restitution is recognized as an important goal of corrections comparable to the other four goals.

The "You Make the Decision" box at the end of the chapter asks you to compare and contrast the five goals of sentencing. Although these goals can all be accomplished in any jurisdiction's penal code and sentencing practices, the exercise makes students think about the relative importance they put on each goal.

Politics and Policy

Why has the U.S. correctional population and especially the prison population raised so dramatically over the past thirty years, and why may its growth now be slowing down? It is important to examine the impact of politics on the formation of correctional policy. Although citizens would like to believe that policy is developed from painstaking research, analysis of costs and benefits, and weighing of many alternatives, unfortunately that is seldom the case. Especially in regard to issues in which there is emotion and strong sentiment, elected officials more often respond by making decisions that will be seen by the public as the "right thing to do" and that will likely win them votes and reelection.

When it comes to the use of incarceration as a sanction for criminal offending, changes in sentencing and incarceration policies had significantly more impact than other changes. Blumstein and Beck examined the growth of imprisonment between 1980 and 1996 and concluded that 88 percent was due to changes in policy, including sentencing to prison rather than probation (51 percent) and lengthening time served by offenders (37 percent). Only 12 percent of the growth was the result of changes in the crime rate or the makeup of criminal offenders.[41] Travis, Western, and Redburn examined both the causes and consequences of this major increase in the prison population from 1980 until 2010. Crime rates began falling for most crimes since the early 1980s. They found the growth in incarceration rate (107 percent) during the 1980s was largely driven by taking discretion away from judges through sentencing guidelines, mandatory minimum sentences, and three-strikes laws which forced more people into prison that might have previously received probation. During the 1990s when the incarceration rate increased by another 55 percent, the major driver was the length of sentence or time served, as state legislatures and the U.S. Congress continually increased prison sentences for almost every crime. There was little growth in the prison incarceration rate from 2000 until 2010.[42]

Why have elected officials moved aggressively toward "tough on crime" policies, even where there is little evidence of their effectiveness and with the knowledge that they are extremely expensive in relation to community alternative sanctions? Perhaps the watershed political event regarding politics and criminal justice policy occurred during the 1988 presidential campaign, when the then vice president George Bush successfully used the public's fear of crime as a campaign tool against his opponent, the then governor of Massachusetts Michael Dukakis. Bush used campaign ads presenting Dukakis as soft on crime for allowing a Massachusetts **furlough** program after Willie Horton, a convicted murderer involved in the furlough program, who committed a heinous rape and murder after absconding from a halfway house in which he had been placed. Even today, you hear candidates for office refer to their efforts to avoid the "Willie Horton" factor of being soft on crime.

furlough
a program in which prison inmates are allowed to leave the prison early to reside in a halfway house and prepare for reentry to the community

As candidates for public office saw the effectiveness of "tough on crime" policies and the dangers of being labeled "soft on crime," campaign promises to keep dangerous offenders in prison longer became the rallying cry for elections across the country, and tougher sentencing laws and funding for prison construction were passed in almost every state. An example is the California three-strikes law, resulting from a similar public campaign to toughen laws after the 1993 murder of twelve-year-old Polly Klaas by Richard Allen Davis, who was on parole after serving only eight years of a sixteen-year sentence for kidnapping. Another example is the nation's war on drugs, in which former president Ronald Reagan pushed through legislation to toughen drug laws, allocate more resources to investigating and prosecuting drug laws, and require mandatory prison terms for federal drug offenders. The dramatic increase in the federal prison population resulted primarily from these policies, to the point that almost two-thirds of the federal prison population were drug offenders.

Unfortunately, once political rhetoric forces correctional policy to move in this direction, it is difficult to change directions and turn back the clock. Increasing costs of correctional budgets usually take money from other public services, such as education, social service programs, and improvement of deteriorating infrastructures. As an example, the National Conference of State Legislatures reported that state spending on higher education experienced the highest reduction in its history during the 1990s, during which state correctional spending had its fastest growth.[43] Addressing this dilemma, Irwin and Austin argue that society must turn away from the excessive use of prisons, which is diverting money from education, child care, mental health, and medical services, all of which have a greater impact on reducing crime than does building more prisons.[44]

An Interview With . . .

An Elected Official, Governor Mike DeWine

Courtesy of Mike DeWine.

Correctional policy has become very visible, and public interest and involvement in the creation of correctional policy are much higher than in the past. Elected officials, therefore, become actively involved in the formulation of correctional policy. One elected official who is very knowledgeable and involved in corrections is Mike DeWine, former U.S. senator, Ohio Attorney General, and now Governor of Ohio. In his more than forty years of public service, Mr. DeWine has worked at all levels of government. He has been a county prosecuting attorney, an Ohio state senator, a four-term U.S. congressman, and Ohio's fifty-ninth lieutenant governor. As lieutenant governor, he oversaw the operations of all of the state criminal justice departments, including the adult corrections and youth services departments. He served as a U.S. senator from 1995 to 2007. He became Ohio Attorney General in 2011, and was elected Governor in November 2018. Governor DeWine was very gracious in sharing his time to be interviewed regarding corrections and public policy.

Question: Governor DeWine, do elected officials care or show much interest in correctional policies?

Governor DeWine: As an elected official who has been closely involved in the criminal justice system throughout my public life, I am very concerned about correctional operations, public opinion, and protection of society. Politicians listen closely to public attitude and opinion regarding corrections and criminal justice. Public opinion is an element in shaping policy, since elected officials have a responsibility to address the concerns of those we serve. Everyone has an opinion, cares about, and wants more information about corrections. Crime is one of the most important issues to the public.

Question: What is most important to the public regarding correctional policy?

Governor DeWine: There are several things. First, the public has an interest in whether prisons have too many amenities and therefore do not really punish or correct offenders. It is clear that the vast majority of the public thinks that prisoners are treated too well. Correctional officials must be proactive and illustrate to the public the many good things going on in prisons that contribute to public safety, benefit the community, and can even improve the chance of offenders returning to society as productive and law-abiding citizens. A good example is the use of community service. In Ohio, we reach out to the communities to identify needs that can be met with prison labor. The state department of corrections provides over a million hours of community service work to local communities per year. The prison staff go to the local community and ask, "What can we do for you? Are there bookcases we can build? Are there teaching tools or kits that you need but cannot afford to have made?" These programs matter, they make a difference, they are good justice, and they are win-win situations for everyone. They keep prisoners occupied and busy, and inmates are able to give something back to the community. This changes the public perception of prisoners sitting in a comfortable place, watching television, eating three meals a day, and living off the taxpayers.

Something else important to the public and elected officials is to have a focus on victims of crime. When I started as a prosecuting attorney, victims of crime were literally the forgotten people in the criminal justice system. It was the State of Ohio versus Defendant. The victim was not even mentioned in the title of the case. We need to involve victims at every step of the criminal justice process. Victims need to be informed and active participants at the sentencing hearing as well as during the parole or release decision process. We also find ways to give something back to victims and require offenders to be accountable for their actions and the pain and loss they have caused. The public expects offenders to give something back to society.

Question: What do elected officials think of rehabilitative correctional programs?

Governor DeWine: Knowing that virtually every offender will be released from prison and living among us, it makes sense to give offenders the tools to make a legitimate living and give them the opportunity to deal with some of the underlying problems that may have contributed to their involvement in crime. The public knows that such programs will not be successful with everyone, but no one supports not doing anything to let inmates improve themselves and prepare for release. It is estimated that up to 80 percent of offenders have a substance abuse problem, and we need to somehow deal with this while they are under correctional supervision.

Question: What would you advise correctional officials regarding understanding and responding to the matters that the public wants regarding correctional operations?

Governor DeWine: First, correctional officials must make an effort to reach out to the public, educate them about how prisons are run, and involve them as much as possible in the correctional process. I do not believe that public opinion and professional correctional judgment are adversarial in regards to correctional policy. I suggest that correctional professionals be more proactive regarding public sentiment when establishing correctional policy. Being consistent with and sensitive to issues that are red flags for the public can go a long way in gaining support from elected officials and their constituencies.[45]

Yet, this has resulted in the implementation of sentencing guidelines, determinate sentencing to replace the use of parole boards, and mandatory sentencing, reducing discretion by judges and correctional professionals, and resulting in an inability to distinguish among offenders by their risk and chance for successful rehabilitation. As Petersilia writes, "One of the most distinguishing characteristics of U.S. crime policy since the 1980s has been the gradual chipping away on individualized decision making and its replacement with one-size-fits-all laws and policies."[46]

One interesting thing in the linkage of politics and correctional policy is that the public is not nearly as strongly in favor of **"tough on crime"** policies as elected officials believe. Public attitudes are becoming less punitive in their belief about the most effective way to handle criminal offenders than in the past. In 1994, only 48 percent of Americans favored addressing the causes of crime and 42 percent preferred the punitive approach. But by 2002, a public opinion poll conducted by Hart and Associates found the public favored addressing the root causes of crime over strict sentencing, by 65 percent to 32 percent. Only 28 percent of Americans surveyed believed that the most effective way to reduce crime is to keep offenders off the street as long as possible. Nearly two-thirds of those surveyed believed that the most effective way to reduce crime is to rehabilitate prisoners by requiring education and job training.[47] And in 2009, a poll by the National Council on Crime and Delinquency found that a strong majority of the U.S. public favored alternatives to incarceration for nonviolent and nonserious offenders.[48]

Americans have also expressed concern with the punitive approach taken by the war on drugs. In the Hart survey, respondents recognized drug abuse as a medical problem, and 63 percent favored handling it primarily through counseling and treatment, whereas only 31 percent believed that it is a serious crime that should be handled mainly by the courts and prison system. Respondents also expressed concern with the overreach of three-strikes laws; 56 percent favored elimination of these policies and other mandatory sentencing laws, and giving judges more discretion to choose the appropriate sentence. In general, only 35 percent supported the direction of the nation's crime approach, and 54 percent believed we are on the wrong track.[49]

In general, the public wants to be protected, and believe that criminals should be held accountable. In the above "An Interview With" box, a good example of how elected officials look at correctional policies and programs is presented through the interview with former U.S. senator and current Ohio Governor Mike DeWine.

"tough on crime"
an attitude that criminals should be severely punished for their wrongdoings, and long prison sentences are the most effective criminal sanction

Chapter Review

Summary

This chapter includes several topics as we begin our study of corrections. Students receive an overview of what corrections is, how it links to the rest of the criminal justice system, and why it is important to study corrections. As the criminal justice system has expanded over the past several decades, the correctional system has grown at the most rapid pace, with elected officials authorizing extensive funds and resources to meet the growing demand for services. As this demand has grown, employment and advancement opportunities have increased, and more students are considering corrections as a career field.

The causes of crime are presented, from the earliest theories based on a range of beliefs that offenders exhibit "free will" to the idea that some offenders are "predetermined" and have no choice in becoming involved in crime. More modern theories, while not discounting any possible cause of crime, emphasize holding offenders accountable and weighing more heavily on the free will concepts than on predetermination. Understanding the theories regarding the causes is critical to determining how to respond to crime. Early approaches included severe corporal punishment, torture, and public humiliation; capital punishment for several crimes; and removing offenders by transporting them out of society. Today we have settled on the use of prisons to punish, deter, incapacitate, and rehabilitate criminals.

The Quakers of Pennsylvania, who opened the Walnut Street Jail in Philadelphia as the first penitentiary for convicted offenders in 1790, are credited with the creation of prisons to house sentenced offenders in the United States. For over 200 years since that time, prisons have undergone many transitions regarding their emphasis on varying correctional goals, from punishment to rehabilitation. Each correctional goal is described in the chapter, and students can realize how correctional practices and various sentences emphasized certain goals over others during various eras of prison and community correctional operations.

The purpose of this chapter is to create a foundation of history and theory so that, as current policies and practices are described, students can link these to theories and goals in order to critically consider the overall effectiveness and public value of correctional policy. In the next several chapters, the operations of the major components of the correctional system are described, beginning with a description of the types of sentences that offenders receive. In Chapter 2, the first stage of correctional operations, including the processes (pretrial diversion, bail, jail, finding of guilt) that lead up to sentencing, is described, as well as various sentencing approaches and options and postsentencing processes for handling the offender and making the actual sentencing decision.

Key Terms

penology

penitentiary

corrections

penal code

Cesare Beccaria

Classical School

Jeremy Bentham

hedonistic calculus

Positive School

Cesare Lombroso

atavism

Neoclassical School

transportation

John Howard

Walnut Street Jail

Pennsylvania system

Auburn system

Reformatory Era

Industrial Prison Era
Period of Transition
hands-off doctrine
Rehabilitative Era
medical model
reintegration
"nothing works"
Retributive Era

punishment
retribution
test of proportionality
specific deterrence
general deterrence
incapacitation
selective incapacitation
rehabilitation

recidivism
restitution
victims' movement
restorative justice
furlough
tough on crime

Review Questions

1. How did the term *corrections* evolve from the earlier use of the term *penology*?
2. What is the mission of corrections?
3. Describe the correctional funnel.
4. What has driven the growth of corrections over the past twenty-five years?
5. What types of jobs are available in corrections?
6. List the principles of the Classical School of criminology.
7. What is Bentham's hedonistic calculus?
8. List the principles of the Positive School of criminology.
9. What reforms were needed that lead to the creation of prisons in the United States?
10. Describe the operation of the Walnut Street Jail.
11. Describe the differences in the Pennsylvania and Auburn systems.
12. How did the Irish system contribute to modern correctional operations in the United States?
13. What legislative acts influenced the changing operations of prisons?
14. How did abandonment of the "hands-off doctrine" affect prison operations?
15. In what ways does corrections attempt to rehabilitate offenders?
16. How does reintegration differ from rehabilitation?
17. Differentiate between specific and general deterrence.
18. What is selective incapacitation?
19. How has the victims' rights movement affected correctional policies and operations?
20. Describe restorative justice.
21. What were the drivers of elected officials' decisions to take discretion away from judges and to also lengthen sentences?

▸ You Make the Decision...

Rating the Importance of Correctional Goals

No jurisdiction has to formally rate the importance of the five goals of corrections; however, the following exercise asks students to do just that. It can be done individually, but will be more fun and a better learning exercise in a small group.

Your instructions are to consider each of the five goals of sentencing and create a list of the favorable and unfavorable consequences of focusing on each one. For instance, someone might suggest that focusing on punishment can slowly undermine society's emphasis on fair and just treatment. Or, emphasizing incapacitation may result in positively affecting the crime rate, as incapacitated offenders cannot commit crimes in the community. After creating and discussing the list for each goal, go about the difficult task of rating the importance of each goal. There are no guidelines as to what "importance" means, and this should be a very individual decision. Does one person believe that the most important purpose of a criminal sanction is to punish an offender, whereas another believes it should first focus on rehabilitation? Each person should create his or her list, and then the group should discuss the lists and come to a group conclusion about the rating of goals by importance to society. The discussions, debates, and even arguments that result from this exercise should be both fun and a valuable learning opportunity.

CHAPTER 2
Sentencing and the Correctional Process

Wavebreak Media Ltd/123RF

After reading this chapter, you should be able to:

1. Summarize the pretrial process and describe the forms of release from jail pending trial.

2. Describe the role of plea bargaining.

3. Summarize the presentence investigation and how the presentence investigation report is used.

4. Compare the different types of sentences and sentencing models.

5. Describe recent efforts to reform sentencing, the drivers for these reforms, and the outcomes of them.

6. Suggest how drug, mental health, and other specialty courts are positive developments in the sentencing of criminal offenders.

Introduction

How does a criminal offender end up in prison or on probation? Once an offender has either pleaded guilty or been found guilty of a crime, a judge must determine the sentence to be received. **Sentencing** is the imposition of a criminal sanction by a judicial authority. Judges do not have total discretion to determine a sentence. Before a judge can prescribe a sentence, the range of allowable sanctions for each crime must be enacted by the legislature and listed in the state or federal penal code. Each year, hundreds of thousands of criminals appear before judges to be sentenced for their crimes. This chapter describes the process, the correctional activities that accompany the process, and the sentencing options and approaches available to judges.

Sentencing descriptions are primarily for **felony** offenses, or those punishable by one year or more of incarceration. **Misdemeanors** are less serious crimes punishable by less than one year of incarceration and have a significantly simpler judicial process. Misdemeanor (lower) courts usually handle all the required judicial steps in one hearing and are often referred to as "assembly-line justice." Offenders charged with a misdemeanor appear in court for their preliminary hearing, usually plead guilty, and receive a sentence of a fine, probation, community service, a short jail term, or a combination of some or all of these. The entire court process may take only a few minutes.

Felony sentencing is much more complicated because the potential sanctions are much more severe. Correctional activities begin even prior to the determination of guilt, as offenders are evaluated for potential release from jail on bail or under some alternative release mechanism. After a finding of guilt, information gathering begins to provide judges with a more complete picture of offenders and the crimes they committed. At sentencing, judges must consider complicated sentencing laws for each individual case and offender. Currently, judges have significantly less discretion in sentencing options than in the past. Mandatory minimum sentences, three-strikes laws, and sentencing guidelines frequently require specific sentences, with little consideration of personal factors regarding offenders, their crimes, and the victims. Various sentencing options and approaches usually available in today's criminal courts are presented next.

sentencing
the imposition of a criminal sanction by a judicial authority

felony
crime that is punishable by a year or more of incarceration

misdemeanors
crimes that are punishable by less than a year of incarceration

Pretrial Correctional Activities

The criminal justice system has three major components: the police, who investigate crimes and arrest suspects; the court system, which includes prosecutors who determine whether to charge suspects with crimes and negotiate plea bargains, and courts that oversee the trial process and sentence guilty offenders; and corrections, which carries out the sentences imposed by the courts. Typically, corrections is considered to begin after the sentencing of criminal offenders. However, over the past thirty years, there have been many innovations and improvements in the way offenders are managed subsequent to booking (the formal identification of a suspect arrested for a crime) and the first appearance (at which charges against suspects are read, suspects are advised of their rights, and they are afforded the opportunity for bail), but before the trial or a guilty plea and sentencing. These innovations include diversion from the criminal justice system, alternatives to traditional bail, and other nontraditional handling of those charged with crimes prior to their sentencing.

These innovations to the pretrial and presentence activities within the criminal justice system have resulted in the blurring of historical process lines and expanded the traditional boundaries of corrections. Today, the diversion of offenders from the criminal justice system into treatment and supervision programs is considered a correctional practice. However, pretrial services activities, including investigating the potential for offenders' release from pretrial detention on bail, release on recognizance, other alternatives to bail, and supervision in the community of those not detained in jail, are also a part of corrections. Some authors describe these activities as part of a chapter on probation. However, these functions are pretrial rather than sentencing as probation and have a great effect on the sentencing process and decision. Therefore, pretrial activities are discussed in conjunction with, and described in terms of how they lead to, the sentencing decision in this chapter.

Diversion from the Criminal Justice System

pretrial diversion
the suspension of criminal process while the offender is provided the chance to participate in treatment programs and avoid further criminal activity

Pretrial diversion provides the opportunity for a criminal offender to be diverted from processing in the criminal justice system by suspending criminal processing while offering offenders the chance to participate in treatment programs and avoid further criminal activity. Diversion occurs without (before) a finding of guilt; therefore, if offenders are successful in the diversion program, the charges against them are dismissed and they will not have a formal criminal record of the offense. Diversion programs are usually used for minor offenders of laws against public intoxication or minor property crimes who have little, if any, prior criminal record and appear to be candidates for some type of treatment in the community.

Pretrial diversion programs are defined as any voluntary option that provides alternative criminal case processing for a defendant charged with a crime and ideally results in a dismissal of the charge(s),[1] and are sometimes referred to as *deferred prosecution* or *probation without adjudication*. Many court systems have bail and diversion staff, separate from the probation staff, which interviews suspects in jail and then recommends to the court whether they should get bail or be released on recognizance or whether they are suitable candidates for diversion. If offenders are charged with a nonviolent crime, have a limited prior criminal record, and possibly have a treatment need, such as for drug or alcohol abuse, the pretrial staff members are likely to recommend that the judge grant the offender the opportunity for diversion. The recommendation will also include certain conditions that must be met over a specified period of time for the offender to successfully complete the diversionary program. Pretrial conditions can be similar to those for probationers (avoiding additional criminality, reporting to the supervising officer as required, maintaining employment, and participating in the identified treatment program). Pretrial services staff members then supervise the diverted offender in the community while making periodic reports to the court.

The following practices define a pretrial diversion program:

- It offers people charged with criminal offenses alternatives to traditional criminal justice or juvenile justice proceedings.
- It permits participation by the accused only on a voluntary basis.
- The accused has access to defense counsel prior to a decision to participate.
- It occurs no sooner than the filing of formal charges and no later than a final adjudication of guilt.

- It develops service plans in conjunction with defendants that address their needs and are structured to assist them in avoiding behavior likely to lead to future arrests.
- It results in dismissal of charges or the equivalent if the divertee successfully completes the diversion process.[2]

One of the earliest diversion programs was Treatment Alternatives to Street Crimes (TASC). TASC started in Philadelphia in the early 1970s to focus on offenders with a drug problem that is believed to be the cause of their criminal involvement. Offenders participated in a drug treatment program and could avoid traditional processing through the criminal justice system. TASC has since broadened its scope beyond drug offenders and is now operational in over 100 communities, and these programs served 17,981 clients in 2013.[3] It sometimes uses names such as Treatment Alternatives for Safe Communities or Treatment Alternatives for Special Clients. TASC and other diversionary drug treatment programs operate under the philosophy that, if offenders become involved in a treatment program for their addiction and successfully deal with their drug problem, their chance of avoiding future criminal activity is improved.

While there is much written, there are no conclusive research to indicate that pretrial diversion programs are more effective than formal criminal processing, even though diverted individuals typically have a lower recidivism rate than those who are not diverted. This is to be expected, as they are less serious offenders, and few evaluations control for the different levels of seriousness when examining such program models.[4] However, diversionary treatment programs have three advantages:

1. They reduce the demands on the court and prosecutors to process the case as a criminal activity. When an offender is diverted from criminal handling, prosecutors save considerable time by not having to prepare the case for trial and not having to assemble evidence to prove the offender guilty beyond a reasonable doubt. Even if the crime is likely to result in a plea bargain instead of a trial, it still reduces the prosecutors' time requirements. In addition, it eliminates several appearances before the court and clogging of the court docket.
2. They cost considerably less than criminal justice processing. Diversion generally moves the offender into community treatment programs (mental health, drug treatment, alcohol treatment) instead of costlier correctional-based programs. The reduction of prosecution and court time previously described also represents considerable cost savings.
3. Offenders avoid the stigma associated with a criminal conviction. For the type of offenders involved in pretrial diversion (nonviolent and usually first-time offenders), this is a significant advantage. It is generally believed that the further offenders penetrate into the correctional process (from probation to imprisonment), the more likely they are to be involved in crime in the future.

For these reasons, pretrial diversion programs are widely supported by criminal justice and court agencies that cannot keep up with their workloads. Today's emphasis on punishment and accountability of offenders has resulted in overcrowded jails and prisons and has overextended the financial resources available to justice agencies. The emphasis of diversionary programs on rehabilitation and reduction of recidivism is considered a bright light in the otherwise dreary environment of the criminal justice system. The National Association of Pretrial Services Agencies Diversion Committee writes,

> *Pretrial diversion is a strong, viable alternative that provides an important service for defendants and the communities in which they live. For defendants, diversion provides an opportunity to make significant changes in their lives and prevent further penetration into the criminal justice system. For communities, the programs assist the courts, prosecutors, and victims in addressing serious problems caused by growing criminal and juvenile justice populations through reducing reliance on traditional case processing and working to stem the "revolving door" syndrome.*[5]

Pretrial Detention in Jail

After arrest, booking, and a reading of their charges, many offenders are detained in jail until their trial or guilty plea. This occurs even though our justice system is based on the belief of "innocent until proved guilty," and there has yet to be a finding of guilt. Offenders are detained for one (or both) of two reasons. First, they are detained if considered a flight risk to ensure that they will appear at all future court proceedings. Second, they are detained if considered a danger to society, in order to protect the public from becoming victims of their future crimes.

There are several alternatives to pretrial detention. It is believed that a variety of bail options (such as pledging money or property) will work for most individuals to reduce the likelihood of flight and ensure their appearance at court processes. These decisions are very objective, based on research identifying several factors that contribute to failure to appear, and the dollar or value of the bond can be increased to a level that the likelihood of failing to appear is minimal.[6] The issue of danger and avoidance of risk to the community is much more difficult to predict. Theoretically, we regularly hold charged-yet-still-innocent offenders in jail for crimes they may possibly commit. This is called **preventive detention**, that is, detaining an accused person in jail to protect the community from crimes he or she is likely to commit if set free pending trial.

preventive detention
detaining an accused person in jail to protect the community from crimes he or she is likely to commit if set free pending trial

Even though the Eighth Amendment specifically provides that "excessive bail shall not be required," there have been recent movements to reduce the risk to the community and weigh in favor of community safety versus freedom for the offender. First, the 1984 Comprehensive Crime Control Act authorized holding allegedly dangerous suspects in jail without bail if a judge finds no conditions that would ensure that the defendant would appear at trial and at the same time ensure the safety of the community. And the U.S. Supreme Court, in the 1987 decision of *United States v.*

The St. Louis County Jail holds more than 800 inmates, most of them on pretrial detention, because they either do not have the funds to make bail or are too high a risk to release to the community pending trial. Photo by Richard P. Seiter.

Salerno, upheld the ability of a magistrate to confine an offender on a presumption that he or she was dangerous.[7] Although some question holding defendants in custody for something they *may* do as a violation of their due process rights, most states have established laws that allow it to occur. Preventive detention can be criticized both in terms of violating one's right to due process and in terms of its effectiveness. Of all defendants released while awaiting trial, only 16 percent are arrested and less than half of those are convicted of a new crime committed during the release period.[8] And there is a strong correlation between denial of bail and a conviction.

If not granted bail, offenders are held in jails, temporary holding facilities that primarily house offenders before trial. In 2013, 62 percent of jail inmates were unconvicted and awaiting court action.[9] Almost every county in the United States has a jail, and many municipalities also operate jails. In the next chapter, operations and issues surrounding contemporary use of jails, jail management, jail crowding, legal liabilities, and offender issues such as suicide prevention, mentally ill offenders, and classification are described.

Release from Pretrial Detention on Bail

Usually within hours after arrest and booking, criminal suspects have a *first appearance* before a judge or magistrate. At this hearing, the charges against them are read, they are advised of their rights, and they are considered for bail or some other method of release from detention. In most cases, release requires the use of **bail**, the pledge of money or property in exchange for a promise to return for further criminal processing. Offenders on bail remain under the jurisdiction and supervision of the courts and have restrictions on travel while they await adjudication, but in most circumstances they have no contact with court personnel other than at formal hearings.

bail
the pledge of money or property in exchange for a promise to return for further criminal processing

The history of pretrial release programs can be traced to medieval England, when those accused of crimes were often detained for months in local jails until the traveling magistrate arrived for trial. These early jails were not designed to hold offenders securely for long periods of time; problems of idleness, sanitation, and disruptive behavior resulted, and many offenders escaped. To avoid these problems, when the offenders were not charged with a serious crime or seen as dangerous, sheriffs began to turn defendants over to willing friends, relatives, or employers. These third parties would offer themselves or money as **surety** (a person who is legally liable for the conduct of another) for the accused person's appearance in court. If the defendant did not appear, the surety could be imprisoned or forced to pay a sum of money to the sheriff. The concept of releasing a defendant before trial with a personal or financial guarantee thereafter developed into today's concept of bail.

surety
a person who is legally liable for the conduct of another; someone who guarantees the accused person's appearance in court

Unfortunately, the practice of bail was often abused and misused from its inception. Therefore, in 1275, specific offenses in England were established as "bailable" and other crimes as "not bailable." Furthermore, the authority to set bail was moved from the sheriff to justices of the peace. To discourage unreasonably high bails, the English Bill of Rights in 1689 stated that excessive bail should not be required, a stipulation later incorporated into the U.S. Constitution, which states in the Eighth Amendment (ratified in 1791) that excessive bail may not be required.

Even with bail amounts not excessive, it is not unusual that offenders' families or friends do not have available funds or property to pledge as bail. To meet the need, the posting of bail bonds became a business enterprise, and bail bonds can be purchased for a fee. *Bail bond agents* are independent

Inmates are placed in a holding cell while booked into jail until a decision is made as to whether they should be granted bail or released on recognizance. Reprinted with permission of CoreCivic.

businesspeople or corporations that usually charge a fee of 5 percent to 10 percent of the bond to provide it as bail. If offenders fail to appear for future criminal proceedings, the bond is forfeited. If they do appear, the full bond is returned to the person or business placing it. However, when using a commercial bond agent, the percentage of the bond given to the agent is not returned to the individual if he or she appears; it is a fee and the cost for the posting of the bond.

There have been many arguments against the use of money to determine who is in or out of jail. A report by the Justice Policy Institute notes how "the ability to pay money bail is neither an indicator of a defendant's guilt nor an indicator of risk in release."[10] There are many problems with this system of bail as a requirement for release. First, the availability of financial resources and the ability to "make bail" are not related to the risk of the offender or the chance of successful criminal processing. Second, the bail process discriminates against the poor. Those unable to afford bail or the bond agent's fee usually end up staying in jail not due to risk, but only because they could not afford bail or even the bond agent's fee. Therefore, the National Association of Counties recommends the use of alternatives to bail for offenders who present a manageable risk.[11] Finally, many find the idea that "freedom can be bought for a price" unfair and antithetical to our system of justice for all. Because of these problems, several alternatives to financial bail developed.

Alternatives to Bail

To respond to the concerns noted previously, several options to traditional bail have been created. For minor offenses such as misdemeanors, summonses are used instead of arrest warrants. A *summons* is a legal order for an individual to appear at a future court proceeding, and requires no bond or property to be promised. For felonies, a variety of bond options have been created, which include the following:

- *Personal recognizance:* The defendant is released upon personal or own recognizance (promise to appear in court) without an appearance bond.
- *Unsecured bond:* The defendant is released on an unsecured appearance bond with a monetary amount that is secured only by the signature of the defendant.
- *Percentage bond:* The defendant is required to execute an appearance bond in a specific amount with the clerk of the court, in cash or other security as directed by the judicial officer.
- *Surety bond:* The defendant is required to execute a bail bond by the deposit of cash or the posting of a bail bond.
- *Collateral:* The defendant is required to execute the bail bond by posting property of a value equal to or greater than the bail set by the judicial officer.
- *Third-party custody:* The court may place the person in the custody of another person or organization.

With the first three options, individuals do not have to place the entire bond amount, but only an unsecured bond or a percentage of the bond required. A survey regarding the use of pretrial detention found that 75 percent offenders were released at arraignment on either bail or personal recognizance, another 7 percent were later released on bail, yet another 4 percent later released on personal recognizance, and only 14 percent were detained until deposition of their cases.[12] There is always much concern about whether release without a monetary pledge is enough of an incentive to insure an offender appears for later hearings or trial. However, a recent study of 1,900 offenders in ten Colorado counties using unsecured bonds found that:

- Unsecured bonds are as effective at achieving public safety as are secured bonds.
- Unsecured bonds are as effective at achieving court appearance as are secured bonds.
- Unsecured bonds free up more jail beds than do secured bonds.[13]

In New York City, there is a push to reduce the use of commercial bond agents and allow defendants to use cash as bail called an "effective cash discount." The theory is that in reality, the percentage the defendant pays to the bond agent is the only money at risk for the offender, and that level provides enough incentive to get them to appear. So the argument is to reduce the bond to that percentage and the defendant then gets the entire cash amount returned when they appear rather than paying it as a fee to the agent.[14]

Pretrial Service Programs

The most frequent mechanism for releasing from jail offenders awaiting trial continues to be **release on recognizance (ROR)**, which is simply the defendants' personal promise to appear. Historically, not many felony offenders were granted this level of trust, and by the middle of the twentieth century, jails were becoming increasingly overcrowded with unsentenced offenders. To improve this situation, the Vera Institute of Justice in New York City created the **Manhattan Bail Project (MBP)** in the 1960s. The purpose of the MBP was to help judges identify individuals who were suitable candidates to be released on their

release on recognizance
release from jail based only on the defendant's promise to appear for further court procedures

Manhattan Bail Project
a program started in the 1960s to assist judges in identifying individuals who were good candidates to be released on their own recognizance without commercial or monetary bond

own recognizance without commercial or monetary bond. The Vera Institute had determined that, even though judges had the authority to release offenders without bail, it was not being used to a great extent.

The staff of the MBP interviewed defendants in jail and contacted their references to verify interview statements. They worked on the assumption that offenders with strong community ties were most likely to appear for trial, and they created criteria to "score" offenders and recommend to judges those who they believed were most suitable for ROR. Because of its positive impact on the detention and bail process, the MBP was replicated by many jurisdictions across the United States. Currently, more than 200 cities have such pretrial release programs to reduce jail crowding. The goal is to decrease the number of offenders detained in jail awaiting trial while providing a more equitable form of release than simple bail.

The popularity of the MBP led to the development of a broader form of ROR program. **Supervised pretrial release (SPTR) programs** were subsequently developed to enable individuals who were considered poor risks for ROR to be released under community supervision prior to trial. While this program started to help unconvicted offenders leave jail and reduce overcrowding, in the 1980s, the SPTR programs began to serve a second purpose. They provided a means to respond to growing public safety concerns by monitoring pretrial releases in the community. In the 1984 Federal Bail Reform Act, the safety of other people was included as a criterion to determine the pretrial release decision. The pretrial services report addresses this factor and weighs community risk as well as appearance at trial. SPTR programs work as follows.

For offenders determined to pose no risk of nonappearance or danger, there is simple ROR. For those who pose some risk, many jurisdictions have created SPTR programs to supervise offenders. The first element is to select who is eligible for jail diversion programs. In a survey of diversion programs, the National Association of Pretrial Service Agencies identified the following criteria used by agencies (the percent is of those agencies surveyed):[15]

supervised pretrial release (SPTR) programs
supervision of offenders released on their own recognizance, similar to supervision while on probation

Prior criminal history	95.7%
Current charge	91.3%
Substance abuse history	39.1%
Mental health history	36.2%
Victim approval	34.8%
Restitution amount imposed	33.3%
Arresting officer approval	30.4%

Under pretrial supervision, offenders must follow certain conditions (no criminal activity, no drug use, and steady employment), must report to a pretrial supervision officer, and can be violated (returned to jail) if they do not follow the conditions.[16] ROR and SPTR programs are considered successful and usually result in only a small percentage of releasees being arrested while on pretrial release status. Although severity of arrest and defendant's criminal history are most important, pretrial detention also influences the likelihood of conviction, in that cases in which a defendant was detained had a conviction rate of 92 percent compared to 50 percent for those released prior to conviction.[17] As well, pretrial detention is associated with the length of prison sentences. A recent study found that pretrial detention or revocation of granted pretrial supervision was associated with increased prison sentences.[18]

Pretrial services are continually growing as more jurisdictions look for safe and effective ways to reduce jail overcrowding, and so there is a growing need for pretrial services staff. The "Your Career in Corrections" box explains the role and responsibilities of these jobs.

Your Career in Corrections

Pretrial Services Officers

Pretrial services officers are officers of the court, serving the court system in most states, most large cities, and thirty-six federal districts. Their job is twofold: investigation and supervision. In most situations, newly arrested offenders are investigated, and recommendations are made to the court regarding their release or detention. The investigation is completed through the creation of a social history regarding the person's life, including family ties, health, mental health status, employment history, financial assets, and other community relationships. The purpose of this history is to determine the strength of the offender's ties to the community, which is critical in the assessment of risk of flight and failure to appear at future court hearings. The social history is created through interviewing the individual, calling family members or other significant parties, doing a credit check, and searching official records. Pretrial services officers also examine the individual's prior criminal history, using computer networks to check prior offenses, gang affiliations, other court histories, and other confinement records. The report usually must be done very quickly, because the hearing to determine bail occurs early in the criminal justice process. In fact, in the federal court system, officers must do the report and make a recommendation within about two hours. The recommendation usually focuses on whether the person should be released or detained. The officer may also address any need for alternatives to detention, such as the use of a halfway house, an inpatient or outpatient drug or mental health treatment center, or electronic monitoring.

If the individual is released, specific conditions are placed on his or her release, and a pretrial services officer supervises the person in a way similar to probation. Many jurisdictions use a "least restrictive" model of supervision, because the individual has a presumption of innocence. This means that supervision conditions are placed according to the individual case, with the fewest conditions possible to ensure that the offender will show up for court and is not a danger to others. Supervision is similar to probation and each case has a separate plan covering the requirements for supervision, including the frequency of contact and other conditions. Almost always, the officer must visit the residence and walk through every room to ensure that the home is an acceptable placement and that there is no evidence of any criminal activity. After this initial home inspection, the supervision begins, and offenders are reminded of court dates and requirements of supervision.

Supervision typically lasts three to six months, until a trial or plea agreement. It can be extended if the conviction is appealed and the person is granted release status. Some individuals are seen daily, whereas others must only make a monthly telephone report. Many contacts are in the field rather than in the office. Officers who do community contacts are usually allowed to carry a weapon, receive special training in personal protection, and wear bulletproof vests for their personal safety. They also make contacts with treatment providers, such as for drug abuse, sex offenders, and mental health. The supervision usually includes urine testing for drug use.

If there is a violation of supervision, the officer reports to the court with a recommendation to either continue supervision as is, change the supervision conditions, or violate and revoke the release status. A detention hearing is held, and the court must show that there are no conditions that can be supervised in the community and still ensure that the person will show up at court. For the hearing, the officer presents a report detailing evidence of the violations and may have to testify.

The Role of Plea Bargaining and Sentencing

"Plea bargaining" is a criminal justice term that has an unsavory perception to many, but it is an essential part of the criminal justice process that is expedient and usually very effective. More than 90 percent of felony cases result in a guilty plea by the defendant instead of a trial to determine guilt or innocence. **Plea bargaining** is an agreement in which the defendant enters a plea of guilty in exchange for a reduced sentence in comparison to the sentence allowable for the charged offense. In practical terms, offenders usually plead guilty to an offense less serious than indicted by the prosecution. For example, instead of first-degree murder, the offender may plead guilty to second-degree murder; instead of armed robbery, he or she may plead guilty to theft. Prosecutors are willing to accept a plea in exchange for a lesser sentence for many reasons. Trials are time consuming and

plea bargaining
an agreement in which the defendant enters a plea of guilty in exchange for a reduced sentence in comparison to the sentence allowable for the charged offense

Do you know where does the term "stand trial" come from? This restored Colonial courtroom in Independence Hall in Philadelphia includes the wrought-iron enclosure where defendants would "stand" during trial before a jury of their peers. Photo by Richard P. Seiter.

costly, and if fewer offenders pleaded guilty, the court resources would be overwhelmed. In addition, even if the prosecution believes it has a sound case against the offender, there is a risk in trying it before a jury, as the jury must be convinced of the offender's guilt "beyond a reasonable doubt." Offenders often plead guilty if they know they are guilty and that the evidence against them is likely overwhelming, and they wish to get a lighter sentence than is possible for the crime they committed.

While there are several arguments as to the negatives of plea bargaining, it is acknowledged that our justice system could not function as it is now organized without it. There are essentially two categories of justifications for its use. The first is an argument that plea bargaining brings about an appropriate result that is likely to reflect the result if a trial was held, yet it has a much lower cost. The second category of justifications is the value of efficiency and resource preservation. Efficiency advocates note the comparative costs of convictions from pleas and convictions from trials, and the prosecutorial and judicial resources saved. Arguments against plea bargaining include the criticism that the outcome does not mirror the likely outcome at a trial, and the process forces pleas of guilt even from those not guilty as innocent persons sometimes accept a plea bargain rather than risk a more serious punishment that could result from a trial.[19] While there continues to be arguments for improving or reforming plea bargaining, it is unlikely to change.

While plea bargaining is primarily a function of the prosecution and the court system, it has many implications for corrections and the sentencing process. Upon a plea of guilty, the court (if accepting the plea agreement) moves immediately to the sentencing process and sentences the offender to the agreed-on sentence. Usually the court, once the plea is negotiated, will ask the probation office to conduct a presentence investigation in order to have more information to ensure that the agreement is within realistic expectations for an offender with this type of background and criminal involvement. Upon sentencing, the offender is then turned over to correctional authorities to carry out the sentence, whether it be probation with certain conditions or a period of imprisonment.

Presentencing Correctional Activities

presentence investigation

a report used during the sentencing process that details the background of a convicted offender, including criminal history, social background, education, employment, mental and physical health, and other significant factors

Following a finding or plea of guilt, criminal courts must determine sentences that will be imposed on criminal offenders. A critical tool used by judges during the sentencing process is the **presentence investigation (PSI)**. The PSI is a report detailing the background of a convicted offender, including criminal history, social background, education, employment, mental and physical health, and other factors valuable to consider in the sentencing process. The PSI often also provides judges the range of sanctions allowable for the crime and recommendations for sentencing based on the risk of the offender and the chance for success if he or she is granted probation and remains in the community.

Most states require a PSI to be completed for felony cases that allow the possibility of probation. When judges have discretion regarding the sentence they will grant offenders, the recommendation within the PSI is followed 80 percent to 90 percent of the time. The PSI is usually prepared by probation officers working for the court. Probation departments usually have a dual responsibility of investigation (preparation of the PSI) and supervision of offenders placed on probation. Some departments have separate groups of probation officers that do only PSIs or only supervision. Others mix officer responsibilities to do some of both these tasks.

Purposes of the PSI

Although the purpose of the PSI is to assist courts in the sentencing decision, it is valuable in many other ways, including the following:

1. *For use in sentencing by the court.* As noted, the information provided by the PSI is critical in the sentencing decision. The PSI provides judges specific factors about the offender that are considered to determine his or her risk to the community and mitigating and aggravating circumstances regarding the offense.
2. *For use in determining supervision needs during probation.* If the offender is granted probation, the information in the PSI is helpful in determining the type of supervision needed and the types of programs that could help the offender succeed in the community. Similarly, if the offender is sentenced to prison with a period of supervision after release, the PSI is valuable in determining postincarceration community supervision needs.
3. *For use by prison officials in classifying offenders and determining program needs.* For offenders given prison sentences, the PSI is very valuable to prison officials in determining the level of prison security (minimum, medium, or maximum) required and the types of programs that should be available to the inmate.
4. *For use by the parole board in making release decisions.* In states that still use indeterminate sentences (described shortly) with release by a parole board, information regarding the current offense, history of crime, and personal background is critical in deciding when an inmate is to be released from prison and put in the community.
5. *For research purposes.* Research studies of the effectiveness of correctional sanctions or programs usually measure outcome as recidivism or return to criminal activity. This outcome variable is much more valuable if it can be correlated with specific factors relative to offenders, such as problems of drug abuse or mental illness, lack of education, or a history of violence.

Throughout the correctional process, officials continually use the PSI to assess the dual needs of offenders for security and supervision and for rehabilitative treatment. Offenders must be placed in a level of supervision (whether in the community or in prison) that is commensurate to their risk of violence or escape. Furthermore, offenders must have the opportunity to participate in programs that can be beneficial in dealing with their problems and treatment needs. Information critical to both of these categories of decisions is collected and included in the PSI.

Collecting Information for the PSI

Shortly after a finding or plea of guilt, the judge sets a date for sentencing of the offender. In addition, the probation office will assign another probation officer to conduct the PSI for presentation to the court to consider for the sentencing decision. The

An important part of the creation of a PSI occurs when the officer visits the family and interviews them regarding the offender. Photo by Richard P. Seiter.

first step in collecting information begins with an interview of the offender. Most states and the federal government provide a worksheet used by probation officers to collect preliminary information during the initial interview. The worksheet includes several questions regarding offenders' criminal history, family situation including marital status and children, physical and mental condition, substance abuse, education and vocational background, and employment record.

Information from the interview is then verified by checking the sources provided by the offender. For instance, all past employers named by offenders are contacted to verify the accuracy of the information. In addition, the investigating officer often interviews other people who can provide additional information or corroborate information provided by the offender. Offenders' spouses or parents are usually interviewed to determine their perspective of the offender and identify other problems not mentioned by the offender. Finally, investigating officers search for official records, such as a copy of the offender's birth certificate, social security card, military records, or verification of high school graduation.

Although the types of information necessary to complete the PSI are generally clear, the detailed information required is not. As noted earlier, correctional officials continually try to balance the goal of risk management with the need for rehabilitation. The investigating officer must keep this balance and the end use of the PSI in mind while collecting information. For example, the officer may note that the offender has a poor employment history and a record of constantly changing jobs. These facts are important, yet are much more valuable if the officer continues to pursue the reasons for the job changes. Did they result from the offender being fired for failure to get along with coworkers, for stealing from employers, or for drug use on the job? Or does the offender simply lack responsibility in finding and maintaining employment? The more detailed the PSI regarding the reasons behind the facts, the more useful the PSI is to correctional officials.

Contents of the PSI

The categories of information noted previously have historically been included in a PSI. However, the approach to writing the PSI has changed significantly. Historically, the PSI was a lengthy narrative of these categories, including many subjective conclusions by the investigating officer. The advantage of this type of report was that it often told a story about the offender, in a way that the reader almost got to know the offender and the types of issues and problems that contributed to his or her involvement in crime. PSIs, with their many subjective statements, were considered the property of the court, and offenders were not allowed to see them. This lack of disclosure was supported in the 1949 case of *Williams v. New York*, in which the U.S. Supreme Court upheld a decision to deny the defense access to the PSI, even though the sentencing judge used evidence in the confidential PSI to give a death penalty over the recommendation of a life sentence by the jury.[20] Since the *Williams* case, many courts have modified their decisions and disclose the PSI, and many state legislatures have passed laws requiring full disclosure of the PSI to the defendants' lawyers.

Face Sheet

- Release status
- Detainers
- Co-defendants
- Related cases

Part A. The Offense

- Charges and convictions
- Plea agreements and stipulations
- Pretrial adjustment
- The offense conduct
- Victim impact statement
- Obstruction of justice
- Acceptance of responsibility
- Offense level computation
- Offense behavior

Part B. Defendant's Criminal History

- Sealed and expunged records § 335.30
  Juvenile adjudications
- Criminal convictions
- Criminal history computation § 335.60
  Other criminal conduct
- Pending charges
- Other arrests (if applicable)

Part C. Offender Characteristics

- Personal and family data
- Physical condition
- Mental and emotional health
- Substance abuse
- Education, vocational, and
  special skills
- Employment
- Financial condition: Ability to play

Part D. Sentencing Options

- Custody
- Impact of the plea agreement
- Supervised release
- Probation
- Fines
- Restitution
- Denial of federal benefits (drugs
  cases only)

**Part E. Sentences Outside of
 the Guideline Range**

- Factors that may warrant departure
- Guided and unguided departures

FIGURE 2.1 Format for Presentence Investigation in U.S. Courts Source: *Guide to Judiciary Policy, Volume 8: Probation and Pretrial Services, Part D: Presentence Investigation Report (Monograph 107)*, Chapter 3 Presentence Report for an Individual Defendant (Washington, D.C.: Administrative Office of U.S. Courts, 2014), pp. 1–3.

With these changes, PSIs have undergone an expected change in the style in which they are written. Many PSIs are now much shorter, factual without opinion, and designed to avoid legal challenges by the defense. In federal courts, the PSI is provided to the defense attorney before sentencing so that any defense objections to facts or statements in the PSI can be noted to the judge. The defense may even point out inaccuracies or provide new information that results in the PSI being changed before it is sent to the judge. Figure 2.1 illustrates the current format suggested for use by federal courts.

Most of the sections in the PSI are fairly clear. However, two important areas that need further explanation are the victim impact statement and the recommendation. As a result of an emphasis of including the victims in the criminal justice process and of emphasizing restitution for the victim as a goal of sentencing, victim impact statements have been added to many states' and to federal PSIs. Victim impact information provides the sentencing judge details regarding both the financial loss and emotional trauma that resulted to the victim of the crime. This information then helps the judge set a required amount of money as a fine or for the offender to pay as victim compensation, when the offender has the potential to pay these costs. Victim statements also sometimes reflect the victims' desire for the type of sentences offenders should receive. Initially, there were questions about the constitutionality and impact of victim statements. However, the U.S. Supreme Court in three decisions ruled such statements did not violate the Eighth Amendment requiring that punishments be proportional to the crime.[21] In addition, there was concern that including statements of the victims' preferences during sentencing would unduly influence judges in their sentencing decision or assignment of monetary payments to the victim. However, studies have indicated that these statements do not overstate victim losses or result in harsher sentencing.[22]

Another key component of the PSI is the recommendation of a sentence by the investigating officer. Because of the recent disclosure of PSIs, some jurisdictions no longer have the officer make a sentencing recommendation in the PSI. However, it is still believed that a recommended sentence is valuable to the sentencing process. First, the recommendation section often identifies the range of sanctions available to the judge. Second, the officer's recommendation is based on fact and offender background and is seen as both professionally developed and without any biases that may have come about during the trial or other court hearings. Third, judges respect these recommendations and follow them in the majority of cases in which recommendations are made. However, with the high level of concurrence by the judge, it can be argued that allowing a probation officer to make a sentencing recommendation gives the officer authority to make a sentence via the judge. Finally, the recommendation is useful during the judicial consideration of the plea bargain agreement. When the defense and prosecution negotiate a specific sentence in exchange for a guilty plea, the judge can compare that sentence to the recommendation by the probation officer to determine whether the agreement is reasonable based on the risk and treatment needs of the offender.

The Sentencing Decision

At this point in the correctional and sentencing process, offenders have either pleaded or been found guilty, a PSI has been provided to the court, and it is time for the sentencing decision. The judge assigned to preside over each criminal case determines the sentence. The range of sentences that can be used by a judge for any criminal case is identified in the state (or federal) penal code, a statute passed by the legislature. In the following sections, various sentencing options, models of sentences, and discretion provided to judges are described.

economic sanction
a requirement that an offender pay a fine or restitution to the victim as a part of his or her sentence

community service
an economic sanction used when offenders do not have funds from which to pay a fine or make restitution; referred to as a "fine on their time," so that indigent offenders do not have to serve prison or jail time merely because they lack the fiscal ability to pay a fine

probation
a prison sentence that is suspended on the condition that the offender follows certain prescribed rules and commits no further crimes

Sentencing Options

Six general categories of sentencing options are authorized in penal codes and therefore are available to judges. They are as follows:

1. **Economic sanctions**: a requirement that an offender pay a fine or restitution to the victim as a part of the sentence, or do **community service** (a requirement that an offender provide personal time to do some public good). In most cases, economic sanctions are a condition of probation; however, in some instances, these are stand-alone sentences without probation.

2. **Probation**: a prison sentence that is suspended on the condition that the offender is supervised in the community, follows certain prescribed rules, and commits no further crimes. If offenders who receive probation meet all the requirements of probation and complete the time they are to be supervised in the community, the suspended sentence is never invoked. Standard conditions of probation include avoiding further crime, maintaining employment, and reporting as required to the probation officer. Additional conditions to have more intensive monitoring or respond to a certain need of the offender (such as substance abuse or mental illness) may be added to standard conditions. Conditions that add monitoring or treatment requirements are sometimes referred to as intermediate sanctions.

3. **Intermediate sanctions**: midrange dispositions that fall between probation and imprisonment. Intermediate sanctions (such as intensive probation supervision or house arrest with electronic monitoring) provide more supervision and monitoring than standard probation, yet are less than a sentence of confinement to a jail or prison. These sanctions are usually added as special conditions of probation.

4. **Short-term confinement**: a sentence in a jail for one year or less. Minor offenders (those who have committed misdemeanors or less serious felonies) may receive a sentence of less than one year. With sentences of this length, offenders are often sentenced to stay in the local community jail, rather than being transferred to a state prison. Often, a period of probation follows the short-term confinement.

5. **Imprisonment**: a sentence in a prison for one year or more to a life sentence. Offenders receiving sentences of more than one year are usually ordered into the custody of the state (or federal) department of corrections for placement in a suitable prison.

6. **Capital punishment**: for the most serious crimes (generally first-degree murder), many states and the federal government provide for the death penalty.

Over the past two decades, there has been an emphasis on creating a broad array of sentencing options to meet the varying needs and requirements of different types of crimes and different types of criminals. Figure 2.2 represents a continuum of the sentencing options as enumerated in many penal codes. This figure illustrates how increasing levels of supervision are provided for more serious criminals.

Even with the "tough on crime" approaches resulting in more prison sentences for longer periods of time for many offenders, the largest proportion of offenders remain on probation or are supervised in the community. As indicated in Table 2.1, the estimated number of people under correctional supervision increased from 1.84 million in 1980 to 6.74 million by 2015. Of these, 3.79 million (56.2 percent) were on probation, 870,500 (12.9 percent) were in jail, 1.527 million (22.6 percent) were in prison, and 728,200 (10.8 percent) were on parole. The trends in this growth are also interesting. As indicated, from 1980 to 1990, the correctional population increased 136 percent and while there was still strong significant growth, the increase was 48 percent from 1990 to 2000. The growth in total correctional population from 2000 to 2007 was 13 percent, but after peaking in 2007, the total population actually declined by 8.1 percent from 2007 to 2015. This reduction coincides with and is influenced by the economic recession and very serious budget challenges facing jurisdictions during this period. This impact and the decisions to adjust sentencing are described in Chapter 16.

An important consideration during sentencing comes in the sequencing of sentences resulting in incarceration. In many criminal cases, offenders are charged with more than one crime or with several counts of the same crime. Penal codes allow the sentences for each crime or count to be aggregated separately. As a result, sentences can be either concurrent or consecutive. **Concurrent sentences**

intermediate sanctions
midrange dispositions that fall between probation and imprisonment

short-term confinement
a sentence in a jail for one year or less

imprisonment
a sentence in a prison of a year or more

capital punishment
punishment for the most serious crimes (generally first-degree murder); most states and the federal government provide for the death penalty

concurrent sentences
sentences that run at the same time

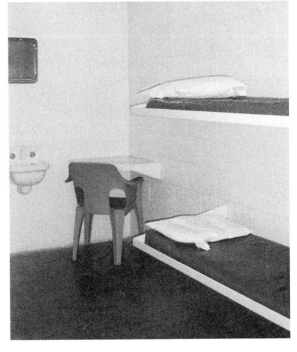

If offenders receive a sentence of short-term confinement, they serve the sentence in a jail and spend much of their time idle in a small cell usually holding two inmates. Photo by Richard P. Seiter.

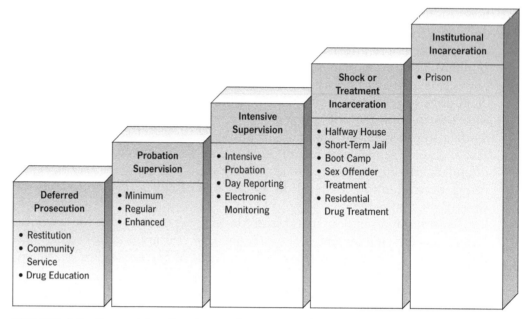

FIGURE 2.2   Supervision Continuum Sentencing Options

are assigned to run at the same time. For example, if an offender is found guilty of three counts of larceny and each count carries a sentence of three years, the total time of the sentences could be nine years. Concurrent sentences would have all three counts begin at the same time, and the offender in the example would then complete the three sentences in three years. However, **consecutive sentences** run

consecutive sentences

sentences that run one after the other

		Community supervision		Incarcerated	
TABLE 2.1	**Estimated Number of Persons Supervised by Adult Correctional Systems, by Correctional Status, 1980, 1990, 2000, and 2005–2015**				
Year	**Total correctional population**	**Probation**	**Parole**	**Jail**	**Prison**
1980	1,842,100	1,118,097	220,438	183,988	319,598
1990	4,350,300	2,670,234	531,407	405,320	743,382
2000	6,460,000	3,839,532	725,527	621,149	1,316,333
2005	7,051,300	4,162,495	784,354	747,529	1,448,344
2006	7,202,100	4,237,023	798,202	765,819	1,492,973
2007	7,337,900	4,293,163	826,097	780,174	1,517,867
2008	7,312,400	4,270,917	828,169	785,533	1,522,834
2009	7,232,800	4,203,967	819,308	767,434	1,524,478
2010	7,076,200	4,055,514	840,676	748,728	1,518,104
2011	6,978,500	3,971,300	853,900	735,600	1,505,000
2012	6,937,600	3,942,800	851,200	744,500	1,483,900
2013	6,899,700	3,912,900	849,500	731,200	1,577,700
2014	6,856,900	3,868,400	857,700	744,600	1,562,300
2015	6,741,900	3,789,800	870,500	728,200	1,526,800

Sources: Data from Bureau of Justice Statistics, *U.S. Department of Justice, Corrections Facts at a Glance, Selected Years,* available at http://www.bjs.gov/index.cfm?ty=pbse&sid=5 (accessed August 8, 2014); and from Danielle Kaeble and Lauren E. Glaze, "Correctional Populations in the United States, 2015," *BJS Bulletin* (Washington, D.C.: U.S. Department of Justice, 2016, p. 2).

one after the other. If sentenced to the three counts in the example to be served consecutively, the offender would have to finish each three-year sentence before beginning the next and would complete the sentences in nine years ($3 + 3 + 3 = 9$ years). The use of concurrent and consecutive sentencing options is usually a consideration during plea bargain negotiations.

Sentencing Models

As noted earlier, nonincarceration sentences include economic sanctions, probation, and intermediate sanctions; incarceration sentences include both short-term and long-term confinement. As described in the next two chapters, short sentences are sometimes linked with an intermediate sanction, so offenders spend part of their sentence in jail or prison and part of their sentence under supervision in the community. Finally, there are sentences of death. For sentences of incarceration, indeterminate and determinate sentences are the two primary models identified in penal codes across the United States, although there are many variations for each of these.

Indeterminate sentences blend the decision by the sentencing judge and a later decision by a release authority to determine the actual time served. At the time of sentencing, judges sentence offenders to indeterminate sentences, with a minimum and maximum amount of time to be served (for example, two to five years or ten to twenty years). After serving the minimum term, offenders are eligible to be released and their cases are reviewed by a parole board (or other labeled commissions that decide release of prisoners). The parole board determines the release date any time between the minimum and maximum sentence. If a parole board never grants parole, the offender serves the maximum sentence and then must be released. The parole decision and postrelease supervision in the community are described in Chapter 6.

As the Reformatory Era of prison operations was initiated in the United States around 1870, many states and prisons began to implement the concepts of rehabilitation and preparing inmates for return to the community. By the beginning of the twentieth century, preparation for release was considered an important part of the prison experience, and correctional systems were organized to provide programs to prepare inmates for the community transition. During the mid-twentieth century, all states used indeterminate sentences with release by parole boards, and by 1977 release on parole reached its peak, as 72 percent of all prisoners were released on parole.[23]

For almost twenty years preceding this high-water mark, the focus of incarceration was rehabilitation, as parole boards reviewed inmates' cases and determined their release dates based on the best judgment of their readiness for successfully returning to the community. Emphasizing rehabilitation made it almost impossible for judges to make a good decision about when offenders should be released at the time of sentencing. Critical to the release decision were efforts by offenders to improve themselves, as demonstrated by their personal status after they had served their minimum sentence. When believed "reformed" and ready to face life in free society, prisoners were released from prison.

As dissatisfaction with parole and indeterminate sentencing increased in the early 1980s, many states moved to implement determinate sentences so there was no opportunity for what was considered early release by a parole board. **Determinate sentences** are sentences of fixed terms. Offenders are eligible for release following the completion of the time to be served (for example, five years). No release authority reviews determinate sentences, as offenders are not subject

indeterminate sentences
sentences that have a minimum and maximum time to serve; a decision by a release authority determines the actual time served within that range

determinate sentences
sentences of fixed terms

to release by parole boards. When offenders complete their sentence terms, they are released. Determinate sentences were almost exclusively used throughout the eighteenth century, and it was believed that sentencing judges were best able to determine the amount of time needed to punish them and deter them from further crimes. Therefore, judges were granted considerable discretion in determining the prescribed sentence. However, as discussed below the 1980s return to determinate sentencing also took much discretion away from judges.

truth in sentencing

requires completion of 85 percent of the sentence before prisoners are eligible for release

A form of determinate sentences that has gained popularity over the past three decades is **truth in sentencing**. In the 1980s, Congress encouraged states to adopt truth-in-sentencing (TIS) statutes and allowed states enacting such laws to qualify for federal funds to aid in prison construction. TIS statutes are determinate sentences, and inmates under TIS statutes must complete at least 85 percent of the sentence before they are eligible for release.[24] By the end of 2000, twenty-nine states and the District of Columbia had adopted TIS statutes.[25] These changes resulted in a significant growth in the prison population; as indicated in Table 2.1, the number of prisoners in state and federal prisons grew from 320,000 in 1980 to 1.5 million in 2015, an almost fivefold increase.

good time

affords inmates the opportunity to reduce their eligibility for release by good behavior in prison

An early reform in determinate sentences was the use of **good time**. The concept of good time was initiated first by Captain Alexander Maconochie, who created a system of marks when he was superintendent of the British penal colony on Norfolk Island in the 1840s. By earning marks, inmates could earn time off their sentence through good behavior and efforts toward personal reform. Good time is now the number of days subtracted from the required time to be served due to good behavior and following prison rules. Good time is used in both determinate and indeterminate sentences and affords inmates the opportunity to reduce the time until their eligibility for release. For example, if an inmate had a two-year sentence, but received ten days good time for each month served, he would effectively be released after eighteen months. For each of the eighteen months, he earned ten days for a total of 180 days, reducing the sentence by six months.

Good time is seen as a critical tool for prison staff to maintain order, because it is a valued reward that can be granted to inmates who behave or not awarded to those who fail to follow the rules of the prison. Most states use good time, yet all vary to some extent on what and how they award it. Many states have made it more difficult to earn good time, and they often must do something in addition to staying out of trouble to earn it. Some states refer to this as "earned time" rather than good time.

As an example, Illinois has three types of good time that inmates can earn.[26] Statutory Sentence Credit refers to the minimum percentage of time an inmate must spend incarcerated, such as 50 percent, 85 percent, or 100 percent of their sentence. This is determined by statute and is based on the offense that was committed. If they behave, inmates are eligible for release at the statutory percentage. However, inmates may lose some of that good time based on their behavior while in custody.

The second category is Supplemental Sentence Credit, and up to 180 days may be granted by the Department of Correction to an eligible inmate based on his or her behavior while incarcerated. Inmates convicted of certain offenses are not eligible for this type of good time credit.

Illinois also allows for Program Sentence Credit to be earned by an inmate for participation in education, drug treatment, or Illinois Correctional Industries programs. However, inmates convicted of violent and other serious crimes are not eligible for the credit, but may participate in programs. Inmates earn one-half day off their sentence for each day of participation in such programs if they successfully complete the programs. For example, if an eligible inmate completes a drug treatment program that is thirty days in duration, he or she may be awarded fifteen days off the sentence.

The reduction in good time—so that offenders do not get out of prison sooner than the public expects and are held accountable for their crimes—seems warranted.

Discretion in Sentencing

In addition to the return to determinate sentencing over the past twenty years, there has also been a move to reduce the amount of discretion granted to sentencing judges and administrative bodies. As noted, early in the history of U.S. sentencing practices, judges were granted considerable discretion in determining the length and severity of criminal sentences. However, reforms to indeterminate sentencing and a "tough on crime" movement also brought about efforts to reduce discretion by judges and parole boards in modifying sentences. There are three forms of sentencing, based on where discretion resides within the system.

The first is the **judicial form of sentencing**, in which judges are granted considerable discretion in sentencing decisions. Under this form, penal codes create broad ranges of allowable sentences for each crime; allow judges to decide whether to grant a sentence of probation or incarceration; and, if sending the offender to prison, define a broad range of the length of time to be served. The second is the **administrative form of sentencing**, which grants discretion primarily to officials of the executive branch of government. This includes prison officials in the award of good time and parole board members in determining when inmates will be released. More recently, the **legislative form of sentencing** has come to dominate sentencing across many states and the federal government. This approach grants most of the discretion to the legislative branch of government; legislative bodies create penal codes with determinate sentences and little (or no) discretion available to judges. Legislative forms of sentencing include truth in sentencing, mandatory minimum sentences, presumptive sentencing, and the use of sentencing guidelines. These sentencing approaches are described below.

judicial form of sentencing
judges have primary discretion in creating the sentence

administrative form of sentencing
administrative bodies (correctional officials and parole/release boards) have primary discretion in granting good time and determining the release time of offenders

legislative form of sentencing
legislative bodies create very structured sentencing codes, and therefore have primary discretion in the length of time served by offenders

▸ You Make the Decision...

Where Should Discretion Reside?

In the above section, you learned that there are three forms of sentencing, based on where discretion resides within the system. These are the judicial form, the administrative form, and the legislative form of sentencing. You have seen the variety of types of sentencing statutes, such as mandatory minimum sentences, three-strikes laws, and sentencing guidelines.

In this "You Make the Decision," you must decide where in the criminal justice system you think discretion should reside. Should judges (who hear the case and know much about the offender) have broad authority to decide a criminal sentence? Should discretion reside with the administrative arm of government (such as correctional agencies) that grant good time or a parole board that decides when to release offenders based on their personal efforts to reform and risk to reoffend? Or should the legislature, who are elected and represent the people of their districts, create sentencing options with little discretion for either judges or administrative officials? First, list the pros and cons for each of these three, and then decide (either yourself or in small groups) where you believe discretion should reside.

Mandatory Minimum Sentences

mandatory minimum sentences

a requirement that for certain crimes or for certain types of offenders, there must be a sentence to prison for at least a minimum term

During the 1980s there was a concern that certain categories of offenders should be sentenced to prison without the opportunity for probation. Since that time, 48 states and the federal government adopted mandatory minimum sentences. **Mandatory minimum sentences** require that for certain crimes (violent crimes, crimes using a gun, distribution of narcotics) or for certain types of offenders (habitual criminals, sexual predators) there must be a sentence to prison for a set minimum term. The sentencing judge may not impose a sentence of probation, assess a fine, or suspend the prison sentence.

As with many criminal justice policy reforms, although the theory behind mandatory minimum sentences makes sense, the practical application results in many unintended consequences. The lack of discretion provided to judges often results in their sentencing offenders to prison that they believe warrant only being supervised in the community. Federal mandatory minimum sentences for drug crimes are particularly telling in this regard. Twenty years ago, 22 percent of the federal prison population were drug offenders, and today drug offenders make up over 46 percent of federal inmates.[27] Many experts are questioning the value of incarcerating large numbers of drug offenders, many with no criminal history, thereby requiring the construction and operation of hundreds of new prisons to hold this population.

Three-Strikes Laws

three-strikes laws

a legislative mandate that judges sentence third-time felons to extremely long or life prison sentences

Another form of mandatory minimum sentence is called **three-strikes laws**, which require judges to sentence third-time felons to extremely long prison sentences (often twenty years, thirty years, or life). These laws were intended to incapacitate habitual and dangerous law violators who commit three felonies so that they could not continue to prey on law-abiding citizens. The initial passage of such a law by the state of Washington in 1993 was intended to target repeat violent offenders. In 1994, California expanded the definition of those who come under the law and allowed some second-felony offenders to be included. At this time, twenty-six states have passed three-strikes laws. As with other mandatory minimum sentences, three-strikes laws are often an overreaction to crime-control efforts.[28]

An often-cited case of overreach of mandatory prison terms was the 1995 sentencing under the California three-strikes law of Jerry Williams. Williams had a record of two prior felony convictions involving violence when he stole a piece of pizza (without a weapon) from four children. The judge, under the mandatory California law, had to sentence Williams to 25 years in prison. The cost to the state for his incarceration for stealing a piece of pizza is estimated to be $500,000. An unintended problem resulting from the California three-strikes law is that offenders with two prior convictions are refusing to plea bargain. For offenders with two prior convictions, any new felony results in their receiving either a 25-year sentence or a life sentence, eliminating the likelihood of a plea and resulting in

Three-strikes laws and other mandatory minimum sentences have resulted in prisons becoming extremely overcrowded. This housing unit with cells around the outside installed beds to handle the overflow of inmates. Photo by Richard P. Seiter.

a demand for a trial. The court systems are being engulfed in trials for relatively simple cases. California prisons now hold approximately 8,500 inmates serving a three-strikes life sentence. Of those, about 3,700 have a third-strike felony that is legally defined as neither violent nor serious.[29]

As a result of the significant increases in prison populations brought about by statutory determinate and mandatory sentences, states began to find they could no longer afford to lock up such a large number of offenders. Since their establishment, there has been much debate about the effectiveness of three-strikes laws and the impact of such laws on crime rates and costs to the correctional system. Since California has one of the oldest of such laws in effect and has used the law more extensively than many other states, it has been the most studied.[30] The most important issue is whether three-strikes laws reduce crime. California's crime rates have decreased since the three-strikes law was adopted. However, the impact of three-strikes laws on this decline is questionable. In one of the most thorough analyses of the California law, Zimring, Kamin, and Hawkins concluded that "declines in crime observed after the effective date of the three-strikes law were not the results of the deterrent impacts of the (three-strikes) statute."[31] For these reasons, California voters in 2012 passed a referendum to limit the negative impact of their three-strikes law by reducing from life to 25 years sentences for violent offenses and allowing inmates serving lengthy three-strike sentences to petition the court for reconsideration.[32]

Presumptive Sentencing

Presumptive sentencing is a predetermined range of a minimum, average, and maximum term for a specific crime. Judges are directed to sentence the "typical" offender committing a crime to the presumptive term. The sentencing judge is then granted limited discretion in determining whether there are *mitigating* circumstances (those that indicate reasons for leniency) that should be considered and used to reduce the sentence to less than the presumptive term, or *aggravating* circumstances (those that indicate that the offender deserves more than the average), resulting in a sentence of more than the presumptive term. Most presumptive sentences include a minimum and maximum sentence, with very limited ranges of discretion. For example, in one presumptive sentencing model, the presumptive sentence is fifty-four months, the minimum sentence is fifty months, and the maximum sentence is fifty-eight months.

presumptive sentencing
a predetermined range of a minimum, average, and maximum term for a specific crime for a "typical" offender, with allowances for mitigating and aggravating circumstances to be considered

Sentencing Guidelines

Sentencing guidelines combine both minimum mandatory and presumptive sentencing approaches. **Sentencing guidelines** are structured sentences, based on measures of offense severity and criminal history, to determine the length of the term of imprisonment. It is a true measure of matching the severity of the offense and offender with the severity of the sentence. Figure 2.3 is the 2017 Minnesota sentencing guideline grid. Minnesota was one of the first states to adopt sentencing guidelines in 1983. The left side of the grid is a list of crime categories in order of increasing severity. Across the top, offenders' criminal histories are scored on factors such as the number of prior offenses, age at first offense, history of violence, or escape from a prison or absconding from community supervision.

sentencing guidelines
structured sentences, based on measures of offense severity and criminal history, to determine the length of the term of imprisonment

States adopt sentencing guidelines for several reasons. First, when it is believed that judges might not be harsh enough on certain criminals and require guidelines to ensure that dangerous criminals are sent to prison. Second, sentencing guidelines provide uniformity, ensuring that offenders who commit similar crimes receive similar sentences. In addition, sentencing guidelines provide planners (using projections of crime rates) a better predictor of the number of inmates in prison

MINNESOTA SENTENCING GUIDELINES GRID

Presumptive sentence lengths are in months. Italicized numbers within the grid denote the discretionary range within which a court may sentence without the sentence being deemed a departure. Offenders with stayed felony sentences may be subject to local confinement.

SEVERITY LEVEL OF CONVICTION OFFENSE (Example offenses listed in italics)		CRIMINAL HISTORY SCORE						
		0	1	2	3	4	5	6 or more
Murder, 2nd Degree (intentional murder; drive-by-shootings)	11	**306** 261–367	**326** 278–391	**346** 295–415	**366** 312–439	**386** 329–463	**406** 346–480[2]	**426** 363–480[2]
Murder, 3rd Degree Murder, 2nd Degree (unintentional murder)	10	**150** 128–180	**165** 141–198	**180** 153–216	**195** 166–234	**210** 179–252	**225** 192–270	**240** 204–288
Assault, 1st Degree	9	**86** 74–103	**98** 84–117	**110** 94–132	**122** 104–146	**134** 114–160	**146** 125–175	**158** 135–189
Agg. Robbery, 1st Degree; Burglary, 1st Degree (w/ Weapon or Assault)	8	**48** 41–57	**58** 50–69	**68** 58–81	**78** 67–93	**88** 75–105	**98** 84–117	**108** 92–129
Felony DWI; Financial Exploitation of a Vulnerable Adult	7	**36**	**42**	**48**	**54** 46–64	**60** 51–72	**66** 57–79	**72** 62–84[2, 3]
Assault, 2nd Degree Burglary, 1st Degree (Occupied Dwelling)	6	**21**	**27**	**33**	**39** 34–46	**45** 39–54	**51** 44–61	**57** 49–68
Residential Burglary; Simple Robbery	5	**18**	**23**	**28**	**33** 29–39	**38** 33–45	**43** 37–51	**48** 41–57
Nonresidential Burglary	4	**12**[1]	**15**	**18**	**21**	**24** 21–28	**27** 23–32	**30** 26–36
Theft Crimes (Over $5,000)	3	**12**[1]	**13**	**15**	**17**	**19** 17–22	**21** 18–25	**23** 20–27
Theft Crimes ($5,000 or less) Check Forgery ($251–$2,500)	2	**12**[1]	**12**[1]	**13**	**15**	**17**	**19**	**21** 18–25
Assault, 4th Degree Fleeing a Peace Officer	1	**12**[1]	**12**[1]	**12**[1]	**13**	**15**	**17**	**19** 17–22

[1] 12[1] =One year and one day

Presumptive commitment to state imprisonment. First-degree murder has a mandatory life sentence and is excluded from the Guidelines under Minn. Stat. § 609.185. See section 2.E, for policies regarding those sentences controlled by law.

Presumptive stayed sentence; at the discretion of the court, up to one year of confinement and other non-jail sanctions can be imposed as conditions of probation. However, certain offenses in the shaded area of the Grid always carry a presumptive commitment to state prison. See sections 2.C and 2.E.

[2] Minn. Stat. § 244.09 requires that the Guidelines provide a range for sentences that are presumptive commitment to state imprisonment of 15% lower and 20% higher than the fixed duration displayed, provided that the minimum sentence is not less than one year and one day and the maximum sentence is not more than the statutory maximum. See section 2.C.1-2.

[3] The stat. max. for Financial Exploitation of Vulnerable Adult is 240 months; the standard range of 20% higher than the fixed duration applies at CHS 6 or more. (The range is 62–86.)

MN Sentencing Guidelines and Commentary, Sentencing Guidelines Grid – Eff. August 1, 2017 |

FIGURE 2.3 Minnesota Sentencing Guideline Grid Source: Minnesota Sentencing Guidelines Commission, *Minnesota Sentencing Guidelines and Commentary* (St. Paul, Minn.: Minnesota Sentencing Guidelines Commission, 2017), available at http://mn.gov/ msgc-stat/documents/2017Guidelines/2017StandardGrid.pdf (accessed August 8, 2017).

or offenders under probation supervision. Most important, sentencing guidelines (by combining factors of offense severity and criminal history) provide a rational approach to determining a sentence.[33]

In some states, judges have very little discretion and cannot vary from the guidelines. In other states, the guidelines are just "guidelines," and judges are not required to follow them. Finally, some jurisdictions allow judges to sentence above or below the sentencing guidelines if the judge includes a written explanation as to the reason for the deviation. At the federal court level, judges had very limited discretion and often complained about this lack of discretion. However, the U.S. Supreme Court in 2005 ruled that federal sentencing guidelines were "advisory" only, giving judges more desired discretion.[34] The impact of sentence guidelines has been regularly reviewed. In a 2011 publication, Stemens and Rengifo analyzed the relationship between sentencing policies and incarceration rates. They recognized that most states have a combination of policies and their study found that when a state used sentencing guidelines combined with determinate sentencing (to reduce the impact of other release decisions such as by a parole board), they resulted in lower incarceration rates.[35]

In states that have moved to sentencing guidelines, there is usually a sentencing commission that first creates the guidelines and then oversees the effectiveness and reviews any needed changes for them. **Sentencing commissions** are expert and nonpolitical groups appointed by government officials, but with the purpose to take politics out of the sentencing decision and to consider the impact of sentences on overall costs and crime policies for the state. North Carolina is an example of a state that decided to take politics out of the sentencing statute. The following "A Look Into" describes how North Carolina made this move and how it continues to monitor the effectiveness of sentences today.

sentencing commissions
expert and nonpolitical groups appointed by government officials, but with the purpose to take politics out of the sentencing decision and to consider the impact of sentences on overall costs and crime policies for the state

A Look Into . . .

Operations of a Sentencing Commission

In the late 1980s, North Carolina (NC) was experiencing large annual increases in the prison population as a result of going from indeterminate to determinate sentences. The state legislature continued to enhance sentences and the state could not keep up with the need for additional capacity by building more prisons. To address the problem, the General Assembly created the North Carolina Sentencing and Policy Advisory Commission in 1990 to make for the modification of sentencing laws and policies. The Commission has twenty-eight members drawn from all three branches of government, from all areas of the criminal justice system, and from the public. The Commission's prior work led to the passage of the Structured Sentencing Act that became effective in 1994. That law established truth in sentencing and prescribed sentencing options for judges based on the severity of the crime and the prior record of the offender.

Arthur F. Beeler, Jr. (Art) is on his third two-year term as a member of the Sentencing and Policy Advisory Commission. He retired from the Federal Bureau of Prisons in January 2009 after a career of more than thirty-three years. Since retiring,

Beeler has been an adjunct instructor at several universities and provided consultation on criminal justice issues as an American Correctional Association auditor and a Certified PREA auditor. He volunteers many hours to the concepts of prisoner reentry and juvenile justice prevention serving as Chair of a Juvenile Justice Prevention Council as well as a local REENTRY council. He has worked with the North Carolina Department of Correction as a consultant and served as a consultant with the Department of State in Afghanistan on issues related to the rule of law in that country. He is currently employed as a Clinical Assistant Professor at North Carolina Central University. He provided the following information about sentencing in North Carolina.

The sentencing guidelines went into effect in 1994, and are now very much a part of the culture in the state, supported by the judges, General Assembly, and all associated with the criminal justice system. The Commission is made up of representatives from across the justice system, including some elected officials and judges. Beeler is a nonpolitical member,

(Continued)

appointed by the lieutenant governor. The work they do is threefold. First, they look at the correctional populations and make recommendations for changes in policy or sentencing. If they believe the prison projections will reach a level that is beyond what is desired, they recommend any changes in sentencing to the General Assembly. Second, they look at recidivism in both the juvenile and adult systems. NC desires sentencing and prevention programs are effective, and they consider the results of both prison sentences and diversionary programs. An example is that each county has a Juvenile Crime Prevention Council that considers the best local diversions for delinquent juveniles. The Commission can recommend modifications of programs if they are not working. And finally, the Commission looks at the results of the Justice Reinvestment Act (JRA), which are described in Chapter 4. In NC, the JRA was put in place about five years ago and has since reduced the prison population from 39,950 to 35,700. The state has been able to repurpose two correctional institutions and turn them into Commitment in Response to Violations (CRV) centers. The CRVs take technical violators and instead of returning them to prison, they are placed in these sites for up to ninety days for heavy programming. In addition, when the General Assembly considers a proposal for new crimes or to modify the severity of a current crime, the Commission considers the appropriateness of it and projects the impact of the proposal on the prison population. They then will report back to the General Assembly with their recommendations.

In addition to the above, the Commission can comment and make recommendations on the policy and effectiveness of other programs. For example, NC created a misdemeanant confinement program whereby offenders convicted of misdemeanors can serve up to three years in a county jail, keeping them locally instead of sending them to a state prison. This program has reduced the state prison population by 1,200 inmates. The Justice Reinvestment Act focused on reducing technical violators returning to prison. As a part of it, the Act gave probation officers more authority to impose sanctions without going to court to ask for a revocation. A sanction often now used is called the "quick dip," whereby probationers with technical violations can be sent to jail for a short stay (one week or less) to get their attention and still give them another chance. It is a taste of what could happen to them if they continue to not meet the terms of their probation. To date, research has indicated these "quick dips" seem to be working.[36]

Reforming Sentencing

The above examples of sentencing approaches put in place by Congress and state legislatures over the past thirty years are the result of discretion moving toward and lying with the legislative branch of government. It is neither wrong nor surprising that discretion has moved to the state legislatures, as that is where sentencing codes are creative and elected officials believe they are the best people to reflect the desires of the citizenry. However, it has led to a major increase in prison population and increased demand for limited budget dollars, and many would argue states have received very little for their dollars spent. There have been many suggestions on how to reform sentencing, yet they often end mired in the politics of changing something as sensitive as criminal sentences.

Sentencing Policies and Incarceration Rates

It is instructive to look at the increase in incarceration rates that resulted from state policies on sentencing. From 1980 to 2015, the rate of imprisonment (defined as the number of offenders in prison per 100,000 population) has risen from 139 to 458.[37] This more than threefold increase represents major policy changes and cost implications for states and the federal government. There are many things that drive rates of incarceration. A study by the Vera Institute of Justice examined ways in which sentencing and correctional policies affected state prison populations over almost thirty years, comparing data for demographic, economic, ideological, and crime-related variables to isolate the impacts of policy changes. Findings suggest that there are many factors that influence incarceration rates. Those policy factors associated with higher growth in state incarceration rates include separate time served for violent offenders, more provisions enhancing sentences for drug offenses, higher statutory minimum sentences for cocaine possession, and more mandatory sentencing laws.

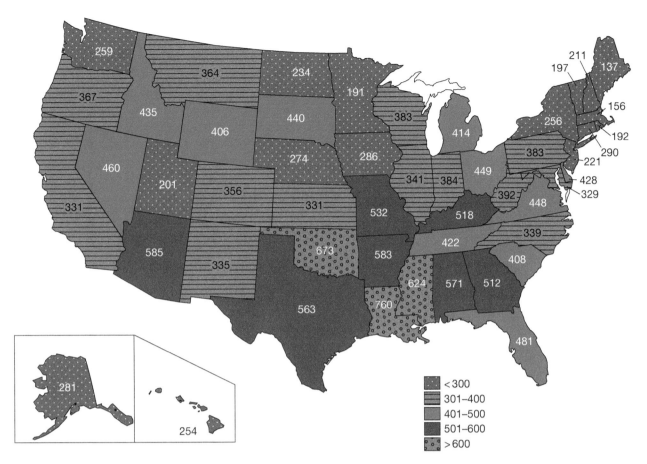

FIGURE 2.4 Map of the United States with Incarceration Rates per State Source: Data from E. Ann Carson, "Prisoners in 2016," *Bureau of Justice Statistics Bulletin* (Washington, D.C.: U.S. Department of Justice, 2018), p. 9.

Other nonpolicy impacts resulting in larger growth in incarceration rates include states with higher property crime rates, states with larger minority populations, states with a higher number of arrests for drug offenses, and states with more law enforcement personnel per capita. Lower rates of incarceration are associated with states with higher income per capita and more generous welfare benefits.[38]

It is interesting to examine incarceration rates by geography of the United States. The five states with the lowest incarceration rates (Maine, 137; Massachusetts, 156; Minnesota, 191; Rhode Island, 192; and Vermont, 197) are in the Northeast and Midwest. The five states with the highest incarceration rates (Louisiana, 760; Oklahoma, 673; Mississippi, 624; Arkansas, 583; Alabama, 571) are in the South. Figure 2.4 is a map of the United States with each state put into a range of colors.

Re-examining Sentencing Policies

Over the past few years, there has been considerable concern with the results in prison incarceration rates and in costs, and there are now movements to reform sentencing and return more discretion to sentencing judges. The impetus for the large growth in prison populations has been the reduction in judicial discretion through the passage of mandatory minimum sentences, sentence enhancements, three-strikes laws, and other requirements to send offenders to prison for relatively long terms. We are now seeing a review and sometimes return to more judicial discretion.

As noted above, a significant legal challenge to mandatory sentencing and the use of sentencing guidelines seems to have begun the move in that direction. In the 2005 U.S. Supreme Court decision of *United States v. Booker*,[39] the Court struck down the requirement by judges to impose a sentence within federal guidelines and instructed judges to impose sentences considering a wider range of factors and to decide sentences based on the "reasonableness" of the case and each specific offender. In essence, the guidelines became just that, guidelines and not requirements. Shortly thereafter, the United States Sentencing Commission issued a report that found that many mandatory minimum sentencing provisions are applied too broadly and are set too high, leading to an increase in prison populations and correctional costs.[40]

In a 2011 report by the National Conference of State Legislatures, a bipartisan work group presented a balanced set of principles for sentencing that provide for justice and protection of the public as fundamental concerns of criminal justice systems. They note that traditional state sentencing approaches have emphasized either incapacitation or rehabilitation, yet contemporary policies need to emphasize reducing recidivism using evidence-based strategies that hold offenders accountable, are sensitive to corrections costs, and reduce crime and victimization. The work group established seven principles they recommend state legislatures consider for sentencing reform:

1. Sentencing and corrections policies should embody fairness, consistency, proportionality, and opportunity.
2. Legislatures should convey a clear and purposeful sentencing and corrections rationale. The criminal code should articulate the purpose of sentencing, and related policies and practices should be logical, understandable, and transparent to stakeholders and the public.
3. A continuum of sentencing and corrections options should be available, with prison space for the most serious offenders and adequate community programs for diversion and supervision of others.
4. Sentencing and corrections policies should be resource-sensitive as they affect cost, correctional populations, and public safety. States should be able to effectively measure costs and benefits.
5. Justice information should be a foundation for effective, data-driven state sentencing and corrections policies.
6. Sentencing and corrections policies should reflect current circumstances and needs.
7. Strategies to reduce crime and victimization should involve prevention, treatment, health, labor, and other state policies; they also should tap federal, academic, and private resources and expertise.[41]

Research results have also put into question the efficacy of mandatory sentencing practices focused on deterrence and incapacitation. One key result was a recent review of recidivism by offenders retroactively released by a change in crack cocaine sentencing statutes. The research compared recidivism by length of sentence for federal drug offenders, and found those released early were no more likely to recidivate than those serving their full term.[42] A 2011 report by the Pew Center suggests that we are not getting much out of our high spending on incarceration. Finding little change in recidivism rates for offenders released from prison in 1999 (45.4 percent) and those released in 2004 (43.3 percent), the report concludes, "The new figures suggest that despite the massive increase in corrections spending, in many states there has been little improvement in the performance of corrections systems."[43]

As a result, between 2007 and 2016, thirty-one states reformed their sentencing practices to control taxpayer costs while improving public safety. These changes primarily emphasized prioritizing prisons for serious and repeat offenders and using savings to expand alternatives to incarceration for low-level offenders.[44] And the Vera Institute for Justice found that over the past decade:

- At least twenty-nine states have taken steps to roll back mandatory minimum sentences.
- At least eighteen states have passed legislation to expand judicial discretion.
- At least thirteen states have passed laws to adjust or limit automatic sentence enhancements (such as committing a crime in the presence of a minor, or while using a handgun, or having a certain number of prior offenses).
- At least seventeen states and the federal government have repealed or revised mandatory minimum sentences downward for certain offenses (mostly for drug offenses).[45]

These reforms by states to re-examine how they impose criminal sentences have in many cases been prompted by the expensive impact that sentencing has on the prison population and the overall cost of corrections. Surveys indicate that voters believe too many people are in prison, we are spending too much on incarceration, and nonviolent offenders can be more effectively managed in less expensive alternatives.[46] California has been the most overcrowded state, but has begun to review its sentencing policies. And the public agrees with the need to change, as the November 2014 elections included California voters passing Proposition 47, a ballot measure to reduce crimes like forgery, fraud, petty theft, and possession of small amounts of drugs from felonies to misdemeanors without a prison sentence.[47] As another example of how states approached these reforms, the following "An Interview With" illustrates how Ohio has twice successfully revised its sentencing code to be more balanced, still considers public safety, and yet saves money by not incarcerating nonserious offenders in prison.

An Interview With . . .

A State Director of Corrections

Gary C. Mohr. Courtesy of the Ohio Department of Rehabilitation and Correction

For several years, Ohio (like most other states) has been challenged with a significant increase in the prison population, straining resources and costing the state millions of dollars each year. By 2010, Ohio's prisons were 33 percent over capacity and the growth was projected to continue over the next several years. For several years, there had been efforts to modify sentences to reduce the population or at least slow the growth. However, the legislature could not agree on an approach that both parties felt comfortable with. But, in 2011, after Governor John Kasich took office and appointed Gary Mohr as the director of corrections, the Ohio legislature finally passed House Bill (HB) 86 to reform sentencing, reduce the prison growth, and save money. The targets were to get the prison population back to the 2008 level and save $46 million.[48] However, after an initial decline in the prison population, the numbers again began to increase. In response, and again with the leadership of Governor Kasich and Director Mohr, the Ohio legislature in 2017 passed further sentencing that could reduce the projected prison population by 3,400. In the updated interview below, Director Gary Mohr of the Ohio Department of Rehabilitation and Correction (DRC) describes the successful passage of these reforms.

(Continued)

Question: Director Mohr, thank you for taking the time to discuss and describe the background and outcome of HB 86. What were the factors that drove the significant increase of the Ohio prison population over the past two decades?

Director Mohr: The prison population in Ohio increased due to three factors. First, our sentencing code lacked viable alternatives to imprisonment. So judges were often left with few options but to send someone to prison. It was passed during the height of the "tough on crime" mentality, and no elected officials ever ran on a platform of reducing the prison population. Second, the prison population was increasing due to increased intake; over 50 percent of these new inmates were serving a sentence of twelve months or less. Finally, our parole rates continued to decline. Although new inmates serve a determinate sentence and are not eligible for parole, there are over 5,000 inmates sentenced under the previous code who are eligible for parole.

Question: I know sentencing reform was tried in the past and failed. What factors were important to its success this time?

Director Mohr: The first was our budget situation. Ohio has been severely hit with the recent economic downturn, and our state budget has been pushed to a breaking point over the past few years. DRC was especially hard hit, with layoffs of more than 1,000 of our staff. In the upcoming 2012/13 biennium budget, DRC was to get another reduction of $190 million less than in the 2010/11 budget. Our biennial budget is approximately $3.2 billion.

The second issue to be considered is that we weren't getting very much for our money. Within the first few weeks of the Kasich administration, it was apparent that we had to reduce prison violence and the key to doing this was to reduce the density of our prisons (in seven prisons, we had triple bunking). This would improve the quality of life for staff and inmates in our prisons and result in less violence. In 2007, DRC had one violent disturbance every twenty-eight days, and by 2010, we had one every 7.6 days.

Question: What were the steps taken and the process to getting the legislation passed?

Director Mohr: The most important was the leadership of the Governor and many key legislative leaders. We also sought the help of the Justice Center at the Council of State Governments. Their credibility and ability to take facts and research and present it in a nonpartisan manner was impressive to many elected officials. I spent much time meeting with legislative leaders to educate them on the problems we had in our prisons and how we needed to reduce violence and improve our programming to reduce recidivism and return to prison. We wanted to rely on the increased use of evidence-based programs that are effective in returning offenders to the community as law-abiding citizens. The legislature passed and Governor Kasich signed HB 86 into law on June 29, 2011.

Question: What has been the outcome of this sentencing reform?

Director Mohr: The biggest piece of the sentencing reform was that there were 12,000 inmates in Ohio prisons that were nonviolent and serving less than one year in prison at an average cost of $26,000 per year. Our community corrections alternatives cost $5,500 per year. Under this bill, first time property and drug offenders are not going to go to prison; local sentencing judges use local correctional sanction funded by the state instead of sentencing them to prison. The reinvestment in local government was the key to support of HB 86. With funds going to local government, they can create viable alternatives to prison. This program does not just take the inmates out of prison, but also provides drug programming and other treatment to help these offenders be successful. As a result of the sentencing reforms, we have seen an immediate impact as the prison population has reduced from approximately 52,000 to less than 50,000. Projections are that from July 2012 to July 2013, we anticipate a further 1,200 inmate decrease in that year period.

A second part of the HB 86 is that once inmates complete 80 percent of their sentence, DRC can petition the sentencing judge to allow them to spend the last part of their sentence in the community. We had some limited but very successful programs in Ohio in which offenders were released on transitional control similar to the new reforms, and they had the lowest recidivism rate of any other program (21 percent). HB 86 expanded the number of inmates eligible, and they are placed in the community in a halfway house or other residential program for two to three months, and then they go into standard community supervision. They are still serving their sentence and classified as an inmate, so if they misbehave, they could be immediately returned to prison.

Question: Director, it has now been over five years since the passage of HB 86. How has it gone, and did it meet expectations?

Director Mohr: I continue to say that we have too many people incarcerated. The highest number of inmates for both males and females is for drug possession, and research indicates that incarceration of nonviolent offenders with a drug addiction actually enhances their criminality. Evidence indicates that the most effective way to manage them is through community-based treatment. In HB 86, first-time, nonviolent offenders were not to be sent to prison; however, many did end up there as probation violators. In 2016, 21 percent of all male and 37 percent of all female inmates were incarcerated after technical violators of probation. So, while we reduced the prison population somewhat soon after passage of HB 86, the population numbers were not dropping to the level we hoped. So, the Ohio legislature just passed HB 89, which will go into effect in September 2017. In this bill, nonviolent offenders (those convicted of a 5th degree felony; the lowest level of severity) are not eligible for prison, even if violated on probation.

We should be able to defer 3,400 Ohioans from prison to the community using these changes. In addition to the change in sentencing, HB 89 will move $58 million during fiscal year (FY) 20018/19 from our prison budget to the counties to fund community supervision and treatment programs. This program is called Targeted Community Alternatives to Prison or T-CAP.

Question: What was the background to pass HB 89?

Director Mohr: In 2016, we initiated this process as a voluntary pilot in eight counties, both to see how it worked and to gain county support when proposed before the legislature. So this pilot was great; very few (none from some counties) 5th degree felons were sent to prison. I really wanted this passed, so we agreed to a reduction in the funded prison population. In FY 2017, our funded budget was 50,017. We dropped this number to 49,104 for FY 2018 and to 47,538 for FY 2019. The savings from this reduction will fund the diversion to the counties, and be overall budget neutral. Even with support from the eight pilot counties, there was opposition from the county commissioners, prosecutors, sheriffs, and county judges. They argued that this was not enough funding and we were taking discretion away from the judges. Therefore, we modified the end result; the first year it is voluntary participation for counties (except it is mandatory for the ten largest counties), and they could still send people to prison, but deduct money they would receive from the diversion fund, and the second year is mandatory.

But we are still worried about our prison count, as we have committed to reduce our funded population. To counter any way around the sentencing intent by counties, we have the authority to cap the length of stay for probation violators who do have a history of violence to 90 days for 5th degree felons and 180 days for 4th degree felons. This should help, as 5th degree probation violators were spending 8.5 months in prison and 4th spending a year in prison in the past. HB 89 takes effect on September 1, 2017, and at this point, have 50 of the 88 counties that have opted in. NOTE: By November 1, 2017, the ODRC prison count was 49,860, the lowest since March 2013.

And another authorization that the legislature gave us was to house nonviolent drug offenders in the community to serve their time. This is called a "treatment transfer." After sentencing to prison, eligible offenders go through a four-week treatment readiness program, and then can be transferred to either a halfway house or electronic monitoring to serve their sentence. Counties are creating great ideas to treat and divert people from prison.

Question: Is there any sentencing reform you are looking at next?

Director Mohr: Yes, and we are hopeful of passage of the Reagan Tokes act, which has just been introduced in both the House and Senate of the Ohio Legislature. I think this could be the most meaning of all our sentencing reforms. I strongly believe that how a person spends their time in prison should count. We in Ohio are a definite sentencing state, and inmates receive very limited good time, so it makes little difference as to when they get out how inmates serve their time. The most horrendous recidivist are those that have behaved poorly in prison, but are still released only because a date on a calendar has passed. Our overall recidivism rate in Ohio is 30 percent, but it is 52 percent form our high security prison in Lucasville. We have to have a sentencing structure to engage those who work their way to high security prison.

Reagan Tokes was a lovely young student at Ohio State University that was raped and murdered by an inmate that fit this description; misbehaving in prison and participating in no programs. There was an interest by members of the legislature to respond with a very punitive sentencing bill. However, Reagan's mother, Lisa Tokes and I talked several times about her daughter and the proposed sentencing, she took an interest, met with legislators, and the original punitive intent of the bill and modified it so that we can provide both incentives and disincentives to inmates. The framework of the legislation is that whatever your sentence is, there is a tail, and inmates can be referred to a parole board who can extend their sentence. As an incentive, if they have a good institutional record and participate in programs, they can be released after either 85 percent or 90 percent of sentence (depending on severity). We will use evidence-based programs to reduce violence and recidivism. But as a disincentive, for 1st and 2nd degree felons, if they do not have good behavior and participate in programs, they appear before the parole board that can extend their stay in prison by up to 50 percent of their original sentence. As example, instead of six-year determinate sentence, the failure to perform well in prison can make it an indeterminate six- to nine-year sentence. I am concerned that some groups will want to keep the disincentives and do away with the incentives. But I will stay strong on it, as will the Tokes. This is also a staff safety issue. When inmates have nothing to lose, they often assault staff. This legislation gives inmates two paths that can reduce recidivism and improve prison safety.[49]

Creative Sentencing Options

One additional and very positive modification in sentencing over the past few years has been the establishment of specialized courts to manage offenders with problems that are believed to be a cause of their criminality. In addition, some alternative courts are established to more efficiently and less costly manage offenders who can benefit from diversion from the criminal justice system. These problem-solving courts include drug courts, mental health courts, and other courts that deal with unique populations such as those driving while intoxicated (DWI), the homeless, veterans, or reentry courts.

Drug Courts

drug courts

an alternative to traditional court models to deal with the underlying drug problem as the basis of the offenders' criminality

The earliest-developed alternative court is the drug court that has now been active for over twenty years.[50] **Drug courts** are an alternative to traditional court models in many ways. First, the overall philosophy is not to punish but to change behavior. Drug courts deal with offenders experiencing a drug problem as the basis of their criminality. Offenders are held accountable and must accept responsibility. Drug courts still oversee the criminal processing, yet all the court players (judges, prosecutors, defense counsel, probation officers, and treatment professionals) acknowledge the need for drug treatment (usually in the community), and therefore the adversarial nature of most criminal court proceedings is replaced with a much more collaborative one. The intent is to quickly and nonbureaucratically get the offender into drug treatment, and early research indicated that the identification of the offender as needing intervention immediately after arrest is believed to improve the offender's motivation for change.[51]

Drug courts are usually a unit within the court system, and drug-addicted offenders are diverted from traditional criminal processing. Courts sentence offenders to treatment programs, recognizing that sanctions that merely increase in punitiveness for repeat offenses do not work for drug addicts. The judge continues to oversee the sentence and holds regular status review hearings with the offender to determine progress and compliance with conditions of the sentence. The National Association of Drug Court Professions has issued standards as suggested best practices for drug court operations.[52]

Drug courts have proved very promising. From 1998 to December 31, 2004, the number of drug courts in operation in the United States grew from 347 to 1,621,[53] and in the most recent overview of the status, it was reported there were over 2,500 drug courts in operation,[54] and were approximately 116,300 participants in drug courts across all states.[55] Drugs courts have continued to be seen as an effective alternative to traditional criminal justice processing. As the opioid epidemic has caused much tragedy and taken an estimated 175 lives per day across the United States, President Donald Trump declared it a "public health emergency." And on November 1, 2017, the President's Commission on Combating Drug Addiction and the Opioid Crisis recommended an expansion of drug courts to all 93 federal judicial districts, in order to provide treatment rather than criminal sanctions to those addicted to opioids.[56]

Preliminary evaluations of drug courts have shown some success in reducing drug use and future criminal activity. An evaluation of one of the first drug courts initiated in Dade County, Florida in 1989 indicates that drug court offenders experienced lower incarceration rates, longer time to rearrest, and less frequent rearrest.[57] A 2000 evaluation found that graduates of drug court programs are less likely to be rearrested than a comparison group of those who do not graduate from the program.[58] A review of recidivism of drug court graduates for 1999 and 2000 found that 16.4 percent were arrested and charged with a serious offense within one year of graduation, and 27.5 percent within two years of graduation.[59] The Government Accounting Office reviewed data for twenty-three drug court programs and in 2005 concluded that lower percentages of drug court participants than those going through traditional criminal justice courts were rearrested or reconvicted and drug court participants had fewer recidivism events.[60] Two other studies utilized meta-analysis and also found positive results. A 2006 experimental design of a Baltimore drug court found sustained effects on recidivism at one and two years after participation.[61] A 2007 study found lower rates of recidivism by drug court participants,[62] and a 2007 study of a larger group of sixty-one drug courts reported an average recidivism reduction of 10 percentage points for adult drug court participants.[63] A 2013 evaluation of drug courts in New York found a positive impact on re-arrest and re-conviction for adult drug court participants.[64] And a 2016 two-year follow-up study found that drug court participants had fewer criminal convictions than an equivalent comparison group.[65]

Mental Health and Other Specialty Courts

In addition to drug courts, courts to deal with the recycling of mentally ill offenders through the criminal justice system have developed over the past decade. As established, mental health courts are not merely drug courts handling people with mental illness. The principal role of mental health courts is to treat mental illness, which unlike drug use, is not a crime. Therefore, the changes included within the purview of mental health courts are very broad, and the operation of mental health courts varies widely. The standard definition of a mental health court is "a specialized court docket for certain defendants with mental illness that substitutes a problem-solving model for traditional criminal court processing."[66] Although only a few existed in 1999, over 300 courts are currently operating.[67] However, it is estimated that these courts handle less than 5 percent of cases dealing with mentally ill offenders.[68]

Even though there is much variation in how they operate, there are some common features of mental health courts. First, they identify individuals who have committed crimes but are mentally ill. The courts screen defendants from any time immediately after arrest to a few weeks later. They look for individuals who are not necessarily criminal in nature, but their mental illness seems to be the key reason they get wrapped up in the criminal justice process. With a priority for community safety, however, most participants are misdemeanor or low-level offenders with no history of serious violence. The courts then attempt to prevent the jailing and detention of these individuals, fearing they will deteriorate even more and end up with greater criminal sanctions as a result of their detention status. The courts use a team approach (judicial officers, treatment providers, prosecutor, defense attorney, and court supervision officer) to identify and recommend candidates for mental health court diversion. The participants must volunteer and agree to participate in treatment. If the individual successfully completes treatment, he or she can avoid a criminal record and continue to seek treatment outside the criminal justice process.

The goals of mental health courts include the following:

- Increase public safety by reducing criminal activity by mentally ill individuals
- Increase treatment to mentally ill individuals
- Improve the quality of life for participants
- More effectively use the resources of communities to treat mentally ill individuals, partly through reducing the repetition of contacts with the criminal justice system.[69]

There are now several studies of the positive effectiveness of mental health courts. Some studies have found that participants in mental health courts had fewer new bookings into jail compared with a similar period prior to their program participation,[70] and other studies found that participants were less likely to have new charges or to be arrested than a comparison group of non-mental-health courts participants.[71] In addition, it has been found that by avoiding expensive inpatient care, overall treatment costs are reduced.[72] These positive outcomes lead one to expect that the number of mental health courts will continue to expand.

Other interesting types of specialty court that have recently been developed are Reentry Courts, Veteran Treatment Courts, and Homeless Courts. Reentry courts were initiated in the last ten years and are part of the growing effort to meet the supervision and services needs of released prisoners returning to the community. With these courts, released prisoners must make regular court appearances, and the court provides case management to provide assistance and supervision after release.[73] The Second Chance Act of 2007 authorized various approaches for improving reentry efforts, to include providing funds for several jurisdictions to pilot the reentry court model.

Many veterans return from their service to our country with mental health and/or substance abuse problems. These individuals often end up the clients of the criminal justice system, and these alternative courts provide treatment and personal accountability to break the cycle of drug abuse and criminal behavior. The courts operate similar to drug courts, as they seek collaboration among the judiciary, community corrections agencies, and drug treatment providers.[74]

As well, in San Diego, they initiated a court for homeless veterans to divert them from the criminal justice process and expedite processing. They also created a tent city to house these homeless vets and provide social services to them.[75] Homeless courts seek to improve the participants' lives in collaboration with multiple partners, and divert participants from traditional criminal processing. A recent review of a Los Angeles County homeless court found that over 90 percent of participants had their warrants or citations dismissed.[76] These examples illustrate how specialty courts can provide a very positive option to traditional criminal processing, and address the basic needs of these populations that can result in criminal behavior.

Chapter Review

Summary

Criminal sentencing is one of the most complicated, yet obviously one of the most critical, components of the criminal justice process. Sentencing attempts to meet several distinct yet often overlapping goals and must take into account a variety of factors, laws, and situations. Some consider sentencing the linchpin of the criminal justice system, in that all the presentence activities are designed to lead up to the sentencing decision, and all postsentence activities are designed to carry out the sentence.

As described in this chapter, the functions of corrections no longer just begin after sentencing. Many critical pretrial functions are now considered a part of the correctional process. Correctional personnel help identify offenders who are good risks for release on recognizance. They may also conduct community supervision of offenders not detained while waiting for their trial dates. Probation officers investigate the background of offenders, conduct a presentence investigation that is extremely valuable for the sentencing decision, and provide information throughout the correctional system to classify and assign offenders to prisons or programs.

Sentencing models and forms have changed significantly over the past several decades. During the nineteenth century, judges had significant discretion in sentencing offenders. During most of the twentieth century, parole boards made decisions regarding offenders' readiness and time of release. Over the past two decades, however, legislatures have taken discretion away from most correctional and court personnel and replaced it with mandatory minimum sentencing, three-strikes laws, truth in sentencing, and sentencing guidelines. Some argue that this provides for uniformity and fairness, but others suggest that this "cookie cutter" form of sentencing, in which all offenders committing similar crimes are treated in a "one size fits all" approach, is not a reform, but a step backward into an overly excessive and inefficient system of justice.

Following this chapter describing sentencing are four chapters that focus on the theoretical approaches, operations, and issues surrounding the various sentencing alternatives. The use of jails and detention facilities is described in Chapter 3, probation and intermediate sentencing options are described in Chapter 4, the rapidly expanding use of prison sentences and the operation of prisons are discussed in Chapter 5, and the release on parole for offenders serving indeterminate sentences and the difficult transition from prison to the community are presented in Chapter 6. By the end of Part 2 of this text, students will have an understanding of the major components that make up the correctional systems of the United States.

As we conclude our study of sentencing, you must decide what type of sentencing model you prefer. In the "You Make the Decision" box at the end of the chapter, you are asked to choose between determinate and indeterminate sentencing for your state.

Key Terms

sentencing

felony

misdemeanor

pretrial diversion

preventive detention

bail

surety

release on recognizance (ROR)

Manhattan Bail Project (MBP)

supervised pretrial release (SPTR)
    programs

plea bargaining

presentence investigation (PSI)

economic sanction

community service

probation

intermediate sanction

short-term confinement

imprisonment

capital punishment

concurrent sentences

consecutive sentences

indeterminate sentences

determinate sentences

truth in sentencing

good time

judicial form of sentencing

administrative form of sentencing

legislative form of sentencing

mandatory minimum sentences

three-strikes laws

presumptive sentencing

sentencing guidelines

sentence commissions

drug courts

Review Questions

1. Differentiate between a felony and misdemeanor.
2. Describe the types of diversion programs currently used.
3. List some of the problems with using bail as a requirement for release from jail pending prosecution.
4. Describe the Manhattan Bail Project and how it has expanded and influenced current detention practices.
5. List the pros and cons of plea bargaining.
6. List the five purposes of the presentence investigation.
7. What are economic sanctions and community service?
8. Differentiate between concurrent and consecutive sentences.
9. Describe how truth-in-sentencing legislation works.
10. Differentiate between judicial, administrative, and legislative forms of sentencing.
11. What are mandatory minimum sentences?
12. List the pros and cons of three-strikes laws.
13. Describe how sentencing guidelines work.
14. Summarize the types of reforms of sentencing and the effect they have had on incarceration across the United States.
15. How do drug courts operate, and what are their advantages?
16. How do mental health courts operate, and what are their advantages?

You Make the Decision...

Determinate or Indeterminate Sentences

As noted, the history of sentencing for criminal offenses has been a combination of determinate and indeterminate sentences. Determinate sentences were used throughout the 1800s, and indeterminate sentences for most of the 1900s. Over the past twenty years, disillusionment with the concept of rehabilitation, the medical model, and parole prompted a "tough-on-crime" philosophy that resulted in an apparent swing back to determinate sentencing and limited discretion with the imposition of mandatory sentencing and truth in sentencing. However, states have more recently become concerned about the increasing costs and prison overcrowding that has resulted from abandoning indeterminate sentences. As a result, some states have reversed themselves and returned to using an indeterminate sentencing structure. It has even been questioned whether the use of determinate sentences reduces public safety. Determinate sentences eliminate the role parole boards play as gatekeepers, keeping inmates who are at high risk of repeating their crimes in prison.

In this "You Make the Decision," you must decide which of these two sentencing models you think is best and want implemented in your home state. List the pros and cons for each sentencing model. Consider the important benefits of each model, and then decide which model you favor. If you are changing from the sentencing model currently used in your state, think of all the potential consequences likely to occur and the possible negative outcomes. You must make a choice: should your state use determinate or indeterminate sentencing?

CHAPTER 3

Jails

John Smierciak/Tribune News Service/MCT/Getty Images.

After reading this chapter, you should be able to:

1. Outline the history of jails.
2. Describe the purpose, function, and operations of today's jails, and the characteristics of jail inmates.
3. Compare the various jail designs and explain the benefits of direct supervision.
4. Discuss the challenges jails face and the efforts being made to address them.

Introduction

Probably no major segment of the criminal justice system is less studied, evaluated, or understood than the nation's jails. Yet no segment of the criminal justice system touches more people's lives. Jails hold only about one-tenth of all offenders under correctional supervision, yet admit and process almost five times as many offenders each year as all other correctional components combined. In the twelve months ending on December 31, 2015, 10.9 million persons were admitted to local jails.[1] Jails are often misunderstood, as the general public regularly confuses prisons and jails. We have all heard someone say something like, "For that crime, I hope the criminal spends years in jail," although jails are not used to hold sentenced offenders for long terms of confinement.

Jails are the watershed of the correctional system. The U.S. jail is the oldest of the correctional components, initiated well before prisons, probation, parole, or halfway houses. And jails have a diverse and difficult mission and role. Almost all offenders pass through a jail as they enter the correctional system. Jails hold a variety of offenders (those who have been arrested, have been detained pending trial, have been sentenced to short terms of confinement for minor crimes, are awaiting transfer to another facility, and are being held administratively for a criminal justice agency). They may hold offenders arrested for public drunkenness or for multiple murders.

Some jail systems are larger than all but a few state prison systems, and some are extremely small (four or five beds). Jails face unique issues, such as dealing with unknown offenders, managing detoxification and medical problems, and serving the court with security and prisoner transportation. Jails can have budgets in the hundreds of millions of dollars per year, or they may have budgets of only a few hundred thousand dollars. Jails may have sophisticated management and professional training of staff, or they may have poor management with patrol deputies with no specialized training assigned to watch prisoners.

This chapter provides an overview of the nation's jail systems, to include their historical development, current operations with the makeup and characteristics of offenders, their organization and physical design, and current issues such as overcrowding, legal issues, dealing with mentally ill offenders, and preventing suicides. Students will find how the diverse makeup of jail clients makes the job of jail staff complex and difficult. Jail inmates may be incarcerated from only a few hours to several months. They hold inmates charged with drunkenness to serial murder, and many offenders are violent and impulsive. These multifaceted challenges of the nation's jails can make other components of the criminal justice system seem simple in their operation and management. By the end of the chapter, students will understand the approaches that jail officials take to deal with these issues and the continuing problems they will face into the next several years.

The History of Jails

gaol
an early English term for a jail

The first jails were created in England. The first **gaol**, as jails were then called, was ordered built by King Henry II in 1166. Originally for use in detaining offenders awaiting trial, as vagrancy became a problem between the fourteenth and eighteenth centuries, the jails were used to house displaced persons, the poor, and sometimes even people with mental illness. These early jails had deplorable conditions of filth, violence, poor food, and little medical care. These conditions came to the attention of John Howard, who was appointed sheriff of Bedfordshire in 1773. While inspecting the local jails, Howard was shocked by the conditions of disease, lack of discipline, and lack of sanitation that he discovered. He visited prisons in other European countries to find models that could be replicated in England and worked with members of the English House of Commons to draft the Penitentiary Act of 1779. This Act created four requirements for English prisons and jails: (1) secure and sanitary structures, (2) systematic inspections, (3) abolition of fees charged to inmates, and (4) a reformatory regime in which inmates were confined in solitary cells but worked in common rooms during the day. The Act also detailed the requirements of diet, uniforms, and hygiene for prisoners. Howard's focus on reform is still remembered today through the work of the John Howard Society, operating primarily in Canada but also in the United States to help offenders and advocate for correctional reform.[2]

Early jails in the U.S. colonies followed the English model and were primarily used to house those awaiting trial. Instead of cells, they often had as many as thirty inmates housed in one large room.[3] As punishment for crimes, offenders were often fined. Those too poor to pay their fines were confined in workhouses until they worked off their debts. The term "workhouse" is still often used across the United States, and while workhouses and jails are sometimes different facilities, the term "jail" is most commonly used. It was not until the end of the eighteenth century that the concept of confinement for punishment and rehabilitation of convicted offenders came to America. The first prison for this purpose was established in 1790 in a wing of the Walnut Street Jail in Philadelphia, and the function of confining sentenced criminals was established in penitentiaries that were built in most states over the next fifty years. Jails continued their role of housing primarily pretrial inmates, and by the end of the nineteenth century, almost every U.S. city had constructed and operated a jail for this purpose.

Current Jail Operations

Role and Functions of Jails

Jails are locally operated correctional facilities that confine people before or after adjudication. Jails serve a variety of functions and hold a variety of categories of offenders, including the following:

jails
locally operated correctional facilities that confine persons before or after adjudication

- Individuals pending arraignment and waiting trial, conviction, or sentencing
- Probation, parole, and bail bond violators and absconders
- Juveniles, pending transfer to juvenile authorities
- People with mental illness, pending their movement to appropriate mental health facilities
- Individuals held for the military, for protective custody, for contempt, and for the courts as witnesses
- Inmates pending transfer to federal, state, or other criminal justice authorities
- Inmates held for federal, state, or other authorities because of crowding of their facilities
- Offenders assigned to community-based programs, such as day reporting, home detention, or electronic monitoring
- Inmates sentenced to short terms (generally less than one year)

This multiple mission makes the operation of contemporary jails very complex and requires systems, staff, and facilities that are flexible enough to meet

Most police departments and even some court buildings have a few cells that are called lockups. These are not full-service jails and can only be used to hold offenders for a few hours. Photo by Richard P. Seiter.

lockup

refers to a small jail with only a few cells and no accommodations for food services, medical care, or recreation

sheriff

the elected official who oversees both policing activities within the county and the operation of the jail

regional jail

a jail that serves more than one county and is overseen by a regional jail commission

these various demands. Although several different terms are now used to describe facilities that carry out these functions (*correctional center, house of correction, detention facility, and even prison*), the roles of these local detention facilities are similar. Jails are full-service facilities that offer security, food service, medical care, and offender programs. Jails are therefore different from **lockups**, which are commonly located in police stations, contain only a few cells, and hold people only for a few hours until they can be transferred to a full-service jail.

The Organization of Jails

The county government almost always operates jails, and almost every county has a jail. In the most recently published census of U.S. jails, there were 3,282 jails in 2006.[4] Since that time, the rated capacity of these jails increased by approximately 50,000 beds, although the number of jails has not increased significantly.[5] In some counties in which there is a large metropolitan area, the county and city may combine the jail function and possibly jointly contribute to the jail budget and management. In rural counties, jail management is the responsibility of the **sheriff**, the elected official who oversees both policing activities within the county and the operation of the jail. In some metropolitan areas, the sheriff only supervises the jail and a county police force takes care of typical law enforcement activities.

Over the past twenty years, a few counties have closed their facilities and combined with other counties. As small counties find it increasingly difficult to afford to meet modern jail standards, a variation of the county-based jail was established. Therefore, many counties form coalitions to jointly fund, build, and operate a **regional jail** that serves all the counties and results in economies of scale that make its operation more financially reasonable. A regional jail commission oversees these regional jails, with each county having one representative to serve on the commission. The commission hires a jail administrator to manage the jail, approves the budget and the proportionate contribution of funds from each county, and approves the general policies and operating practices for the facility. In some cases, the management (and sometimes the construction and ownership) of the regional jail is contracted to the private sector. However, there were only thirty-seven privately operated jails in 2006.[6] The role of the private sector in prison and jail operations is discussed in Chapters 5 and 16.

Jail Populations

As noted in Table 3.1, at midyear 2015, the nation's local jails held 693,300 inmates, a decline from the peak population of 785,500 at midyear 2008. Using the average daily population in Table 3.1, the average population increased

| TABLE 3.1 | Inmates Confined in Local Jails, Average Daily Population, and Incarceration Rates, 2000, and 2005–2015 | | | | | |

	Confined inmates[a]		Average daily population[b]		Jail incarceration rate[c]	
Year	Total	Year-to-year percent change	Total	Year-to-year percent change	Adults and juveniles	Adults only
2000	621,100	2.5%	618,300	1.7%	220	290
2005	747,500	4.7	733,400	3.9	250	330
2006	765,800	2.4	755,300	3.0	260	340
2007	780,200	1.9	773,100	2.4	260	340
2008	785,500	0.7	776,600	0.4	260	340
2009	767,400	−2.3	768,100	−1.1	250	330
2010	748,700	−2.4	748,600	−2.5	240	320
2011	735,600	−1.8	735,600	−1.7	240	310
2012	744,500	1.2	737,400	0.2	240	310
2013	731,200	−1.8	731,400	−0.8	230	300
2014	744,600	1.8	739,000	1.0	230	300
2015	728,200	−2.2			230	
2015	693,300		721,300	−2.4		

[a] Number of inmates held on last weekday in June.

[b] Sum of all inmates in jail each day for a year, divided by the number of days in the year.

[c] Number of inmates confined per 100,000 U.S. residents.

Source: Todd D. Minton and Daniela Golinelli, "Jail Inmates in 2015," *BJS Bulletin* (Washington, D.C.: U.S. Department of Justice, 2016), p. 3.

significantly (25.6 percent) from 2000 to 2008, but then decreased by 7.1 percent from 2008 to 2015. Most of the decline was concentrated in large jails that hold 1,000 inmates or more. And the number of annual admissions during this period has also declined from a high of 13.6 million in 2008 to 10.9 million in 2015.[7]

The use of the nation's jails rose significantly over the past thirty years. The **incarceration rate** is defined as the number of people per 100,000 U.S. residents who are incarcerated in either a jail or a prison. In 1985, the jail incarceration rate was only 114 per 100,000, with an average daily population (ADP) of 265,517.[8] As indicated in Table 3.1, the jail incarceration rate more than doubled between 1985 and 2008, when it peaked at 260 and when 776,600 was the average daily population. Since 2008, there has been a gradual decline, and the 2015 incarceration rate was 230 and the ADP was 721,300.

The makeup of the jail population is very interesting and informative. As indicated in Table 3.2, jails hold primarily male (86 percent) offenders and almost all are adults (99.4 percent). And 62 percent of jail inmates are not yet convicted of a crime. The ethnic and racial makeup of jails also causes concern. While 47.2 percent of jail inmates at midyear 2013 are white, 35.8 percent black, and 14.8 percent Hispanic, the incarceration rates of these groups vary significantly, as the population of the United States in 2013 is estimated to be 77.7 percent white, 13.2 percent black, and 17.1 percent Hispanic.[9] Black and Hispanic offenders are disproportionately represented in jails, which somewhat reflects crime rates among these groups, but also questioning the fairness for granting bail.

incarceration rates
the number of persons per 100,000 who are in jail or prison

TABLE 3.2	Percent of Inmates in Local Jails, by Characteristic, Midyear 2000, 2005, and 2010–2015

| Characteristic | Midyear | | | | | | | Yearend |
	2000	2005	2010	2011	2012	2013	2014[*]	2015
Total	621,100[**]	747,500	748,700	735,600	744,500	731,200	744,600	693,300!
Sex								
Male	550,200[**]	653,000[**]	656,400[**]	642,300	645,900	628,900	635,500	594,200!
Female	71,000[**]	94,600[**]	92,400[**]	93,300[**]	98,600[**]	102,400[**]	109,100	99,100!
Adult	613,500[**]	740,800	741,200	729,700	739,100	726,600	740,400	689,900!
Male	543,100[**]	646,800[**]	649,300[**]	636,900	640,900	624,700	631,600	591,100!
Female	70,400[**]	94,000[**]	91,900[**]	92,800[**]	98,100[**]	101,900[**]	108,800	98,800!
Juvenile[a]	7,600[**]	6,800[**]	7,600[**]	5,900[**]	5,400[**]	4,600	4,200	3,500!
Held as adult[b]	6,100[**]	5,800[**]	5,600[**]	4,600[**]	4,600[**]	3,500	3,700	3,200!
Held as juvenile	1,500[**]	1,000	1,900[**]	1,400	900	1,100	500	300!
Race/Hispanic origin[c]								
White	260,500[**]	331,000[**]	331,600[**]	329,400[**]	341,100	344,900	352,800	335,100!
Black/African American	256,300	290,500[**]	283,200[**]	276,400[**]	274,600	261,500	263,800	243,400!
Hispanic/Latino	94,100[**]	111,900	118,100[**]	113,900	112,700	107,900	110,600	99,000!
American Indian/Alaska Native[d]	5,500[**]	7,600[**]	9,900	9,400	9,300	10,200	10,400	8,600!
Asian/Native Hawaiian/Other Pacific Islander[d]	4,700[**]	5,400[**]	5,100[**]	5,300[**]	5,400	5,100[**]	6,000	5,800!
Two or more races	...	1,000	800	1,200	1,500[**]	1,600[**]	1,000	1,500!
Conviction status[d,e]								
Convicted	271,300	284,400	291,300[**]	289,600[**]	293,100[**]	278,000	277,100	258,800!
Unconvicted	349,800[**]	463,200	457,400	446,000[**]	451,400[**]	453,200	467,500	434,600!

[a] Person age 17 or younger.

[b] Includes juveniles who were tried or awaiting trial as adults.

[c] Data adjusted for nonresponse.

[d] Excludes persons of Hispanic or Latino origin.

[e] Combines American Indians, Alaska Natives and Asians, and Pacific Islanders in an Other Race category.

Source: Todd D. Minton and Zhen Zeng, "Jail Inmates in 2015," *BJS Bulletin* (Washington, D.C.: U.S. Department of Justice, 2016), p. 4.

The U.S. Department of Justice, Bureau of Justice Statistics, does a complete survey of the nation's jails approximately every five years. As a part of this survey, a sample of inmates is interviewed. The survey represents a snapshot examination of inmates in jails on a specific day. The 2013 survey resulted in interviews with more than 936 jails in 874 jurisdictions and created a description of jail inmates. This report was updated one year later in June 2008 and rendered the following information:

- Since midyear 2000, the percentages of men and women in local jails have remained relatively stable.
- The number of women in local jails increased more rapidly than the number of men, and reached 100,940 in 2013, up from 68,100 in 1999.
- Over 51 percent of offenders in local jails were racial or ethnic minorities on December 31, 2013. As estimated, 250,380 were black and 116,630 were Hispanic or Latino.
- At year end 2015, 63 percent of inmates had not been convicted or were awaiting trial, up from 56 percent in 2000.
- At midyear 2013, the jail incarceration rate was 310 inmates per 100,000 U.S. residents, up only slightly from 304 per 100,000 in 1999.[10]

This description does not paint a pretty picture of the jail population. Inmates in jail are a troubled lot and experience many problems (poverty, substance abuse, mental illness) that contribute to their criminal behavior and must be managed by jail staff. Since 2005, more than 60 percent of jail inmates were being held pending court action on their current change, and 68 percent of those held in 2015 were for a felony offense.[11] Yet, it is troubling to note that historically, a high percentage of jail inmates have been charged with or convicted of a nonviolent crime. A recent profile of jail inmates across the United States found that only 25.4 percent of jail inmates were there for violent offenses, while 24.4 percent were incarcerated for property crimes, 24.7 for drug offenses, and 24.9 percent for public-order offenses.[12]

The Increasing Use of Jails

There are several theories that suggest the reasons for the significant increase in the number of jail inmates from the late 1900s to 2008, as well as factors influencing the decline since that time. Several reasons underlie the growth. First, the "tough on crime" mentality of the public affects the percentage of offenders who receive bail or are released on recognizance. Judges do not want to put potentially dangerous offenders back on the streets and are more likely to set higher bail amounts and less likely to grant release without bond requirements. The number of jail inmates who were awaiting trial (not yet convicted of the charged offense) increased from 228,900 in 1993 to 434,600 in 2015.[13]

Second, with extensive overcrowding of state and federal prisons over the past three decades, more jail inmates are being held by jails as they await transfer to prison. At year-end 2015, eighteen states and the federal prison systems were operating above their capacity.[14] In 2000, only 63,140 offenders were held in local jails for state or federal jurisdictions. This figure rose to 81,200 or approximately 11.7 percent of all jail inmates on December 31, 2015.[15] And local jails held another 22,870 offenders (3.3 percent of their population) for the U.S. Immigration and Customs Enforcement ICE) in 2012.[16] Finally, there has been increasing use of a split sentence, or the sentencing of adult felons to a short stay in jail in addition to release to probation. The percentage of felons receiving a jail sentence increased from 25 percent to 28 percent from 1988 to 2006.[17]

Less is known about the reasons for the decline in jail populations over the past two years. However, the serious budget crisis of local governments was most likely the dominant reason and influenced decisions throughout the correctional process. The percent of unconvicted jail inmates decreased slightly, meaning judges are likely considering the cost of incarceration and being more lenient in the use of bail. And with fewer inmates in jails, it is also likely that the judicial process can move them along in a more expeditious manner, and if guilty, sentence them more quickly to the sanction received.

Admissions and Length of Stay

One factor that truly differentiates jails from prisons is the number of admissions and length of stay. The average daily jail population for 2015 was 721,300 offenders, yet jails admitted 10.9 million offenders over that year.[18] This is decidedly different than the number of admissions and releases for prisons, as during 2015, only 608,300 inmates were admitted to state and federal prisons and 641,100 inmates were released.[19]

length of stay
the time served in a jail or prison by any inmate

The average **length of stay** for jails in 2013 was 23 days,[20] much less than the average length of stay within a prison. This average length of stay for jails is misleading, however, as a very large percentage of arrested and jailed offenders make bond and are released within forty-eight hours. Those who do not make bail are likely to spend seventy-five to ninety days in jail awaiting trial, whereas sentenced offenders can serve up to one year in jail. The fact that so many jail inmates are released shortly after arrest creates a logistical nightmare for jail operations in terms of bookings and releases. The sheer volume of these admissions and releases often results in mistakes. Unfortunately, it is not uncommon for jails to be plagued with releasing the wrong person or making errors in identification of offenders. These problems seem to continue, no matter what steps are taken by jails to improve their booking and release processes and their record keeping. And mistaken releases of offenders undermine the public confidence in the ability of jail staff to do a professional job.

The Jail Process and Daily Operations

A number of activities and functions are a part of the daily jail routine. The first major function is admissions and releases. Jails have a central area for booking, admitting, and releasing inmates. Police officers or county sheriff deputies bring arrested offenders to the jail; they are placed in a holding cell that can be for a single or as many as ten to twelve inmates. They are then identified and fingerprinted and their property is inventoried and stored. They receive a brief physical and mental health screening and usually talk to a social worker about the process and how potential release on bail or personal recognizance works. If they are there for a minor offense, they may be quickly released on bond, and are placed in a temporary holding area. In some modern jails emphasizing direct supervision (described later), offenders sit in a relatively unsecured part of the jail booking area until someone comes to the jail to post their bond. If they are arrested for a felony, they will have to wait until their initial appearance before a magistrate (usually within twenty-four hours) to see if they are granted bail. During this time, they

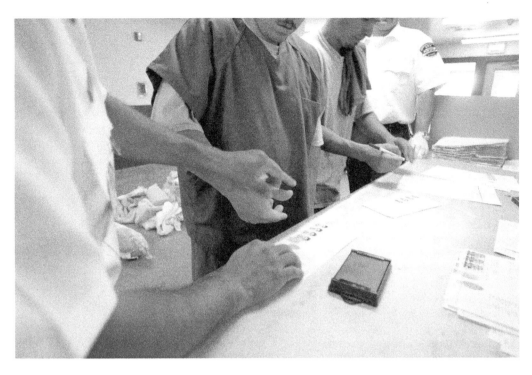

After arrest, offenders are fingerprinted and booked into the jail. Photo Courtesy of CoreCivic.

are placed in a general holding area within the jail, in which they are housed with several other newly arrived offenders.

Offenders not released on bail or personal recognizance are moved to more permanent housing within the jail. They are first placed in a very secure housing unit, often in cells holding only one person, until they can be further interviewed and some preliminary information can be collected regarding their crime and criminal history. This classification process (described below) identifies the dangerousness and risk of the offender and determines whether there are other offenders from whom they should be separated. In addition, any major problems, such as a need for detoxification, potential for suicide, or potential threats by other jail inmates, are identified and considered in the classification and assignment of housing. Once classified, inmates are moved to the housing unit that holds inmates of similar risk of violence or escape.

In their housing unit, inmates begin the normal routine of the jail. Days are filled with boredom, as there is usually little to do. Depending on the jail design, inmates may be let out of their cells and into a common area in which they can talk to other inmates or watch television. Prepared food is delivered to the common area, where inmates eat their meals. If inmates receive visits, they go to the visiting area, which is often adjacent to the housing unit. Visits with family or friends are usually *noncontact*, meaning that inmates and their visitors talk on a telephone or through sound ports with a secure glass in between to prevent the passing of items that are not allowed in the jail. If visited by their attorney, a probation or parole officer, or some other law enforcement official,

Jail inmates have noncontact visiting and have to talk to their visitors through sound ports in the secure glass. Photo by Richard P. Seiter.

Jail inmates can have contact visiting with their attorneys, so they can review and sign papers. Note, however, the handcuffs attached to the wall to prevent inmates from attacking attorneys or trying to escape out the visitors' entrance. Photo by Richard P. Seiter.

inmates usually are provided a small, yet secure area, with direct contact with their visitor, so they can talk in private and sign any necessary papers.

Most jails provide programs such as education, substance abuse counseling, or work, but the programs are very limited and only a few inmates participate. Inmates usually welcome these types of programs and activities, as the boredom of a regular day is extremely difficult for most offenders. Some programs are provided in the common areas of the housing units, but inmates generally move under supervision to another location in the jail for these programs. Inmates who are awaiting trial and not yet sentenced may volunteer, but are not required to work. Work opportunities include cleaning the areas of the jail or assisting in food preparation and service. Even for the few inmates who work, there is normally only enough to do to keep them busy a few hours per day.

Jail Classification

An important aspect of the operation of jails is the classification of inmates. Sophisticated classification systems for jails are a relatively recent phenomenon, having been used extensively only over the past two decades. During the early history of jails, all inmates were mixed together. There was later some segregation of inmates, first by sex, then by age, and finally by crime or risk. In discussing early jail operations, Brennan notes that "Before 1870,...classification was based primarily on type of offense....In the latter part of the nineteenth century,...classification...emphasized offenders' personal pathologies."[21] More recently, **objective classification systems** have superseded early subjective classification processes. Objective systems identify offenders' criminal history and personal characteristics (number of violent offenses, history of violence, age, marital status) that have been found to be statistically linked to dangerousness or escape potential; they result in an actuarial assessment of risk that is used in assigning inmates to a type of housing unit or recommending certain mental health or substance abuse programs. These classification approaches are described in more detail in Chapter 10.

Jail classification systems are plagued with problems not inherent in prison classification systems. First, there is often little information available for jail inmates. Jail social service staff members interview inmates to collect information, primarily relying on self-reported information, as they do not have time to confirm the accuracy of the information. Second, the short stay complicates the process for most inmates, and there is no time for thorough medical or psychological assessments that could aid in the classification process. Finally, Brennan notes that jail classification has "suffered from benign neglect," in that jail administrators have "not accorded classification a central role in management."[22]

objective classification systems

statistical approaches to consider the risk of escape and violence by inmates

However, even as limited as it is, jail classification systems are important for three reasons:

1. They provide a guide for separating violent, predatory inmates from potential inmate victims. One of the most challenging problems for jails is to protect inmates who could be preyed on by dangerous inmates. With little prior information and many housing arrangements in which numerous inmates live together, it is critical to try to separate inmates by risk of assault against one another.
2. They provide a guide for identifying and managing differently inmates with special needs, such as the emotionally disturbed or those at risk of suicide.
3. They provide a guide for identifying inmates with a high risk of escape and housing them in more secure settings than those with a low risk of escape. Such systems allow jails to have a variety of housing assignments, rather than all maximum-security areas that are very expensive to build and operate.

Inmate classification is very important for jail operations, as staff members use the results to make decisions on the housing assignment for inmates, the types of programs they should participate in, the number of staff members assigned to various housing areas, the type of supervision to provide inmates, and whether inmates should be allowed to work or participate in diversion programs. It can be argued that classification is the most important function for effective jail management.

Jail Staffing

One way in which jails and prisons are extremely similar is the importance of professional staff. In all correctional facilities, staff members are more important than any other element in the operations and policies—more important than the facility, the physical security, the services provided, and the programs offered. Poor-quality or poorly performing staff members undermine all these other factors, whereas professional and well-trained staff members can overcome other problems in the jail or its operations.

Jails employed 213,300 full-time staff members at the end of 2015.[23] The largest proportion of jail staff (approximately 79 percent) is correctional officers.[24] Most jail correctional officers are assigned to housing units, but others act as transportation officers and move inmates from the jail to the courthouse to attend hearings. The percentage of correctional officers of the total jail staff

Staff members who work in jails include jail officers, counselors, and transportation officers who move inmates from the jail to the courthouse for hearings. Photo by Richard P. Seiter.

members is higher than in prisons because jails do not offer extensive programs or services, and their primary function is to hold inmates in a secure setting. The next largest categories of staff are clerical and maintenance (12 percent), administrative (6.9 percent), and professional and technicians (5.4 percent).[25]

Jail staff members are always extremely outnumbered by the inmates in any correctional setting. There is no way to "rule" a correctional facility through force; jails must be managed through clear procedures, a consistent routine of operations, and professional staff. It is estimated that the number of inmates per correctional staff member is 3.3.[26] However, this number is misleading, as it calculates ratio for all staff. The ratio of inmates to correctional officers in 2015 was 4.1,[27] and not all correctional officers are at the jail at any single time. Since correctional officers must supervise the jail twenty-four hours per day, seven days per week, only about one-sixth of the total officer workforce is likely to be on duty at any one time. Therefore, on a typical day, there would be one correctional officer for more than twenty-five (4.3 times 6) inmates. Yet correctional officers are assigned throughout the jail, and a typical jail housing unit has approximately seventy-five inmates with one correctional officer. The inmate staff ratio has worsened over the past several years. The 1999 ratio was 2.9 inmates to 1 staff member, and it increased to 3.3 to 1 by 2006.[28] Another change in jail staff has come in the diversity of employees. In 2015, women constituted approximately 35.6 percent (up from 30 percent in 1993) of all jail employees and 30.7 percent (up from 24 percent in 1993) of all jail correctional officers.[29] For a better understanding of the role of jail officers and the opportunities for employment, see the "Your Career in Corrections."

Your Career in Corrections

Jail Officers

As noted in this chapter, there is much less attention, much less research, and much less interest by the public regarding the staffing and operation of county jails than of prisons. Although there are almost three times as many jails as prisons, the nation's jails employ less than half as many staff members as in state and federal prisons. In addition to jail officers, other occupational categories in jails include administrators, clerical and maintenance workers, professional and technical employees, health care, and educational employees. Jails have few inmate programs, but most jails offer limited education, counseling, vocational training, religious programming for inmates.

Jail officers (in some locations called detention or corrections officers) do much of the same work as prison correctional officers. Their primary responsibilities are supervising inmates to maintain order and compliance with rules and performing security procedures such as searching for contraband. However, with most of the staff being officers, and with most inmate programs (visiting, education) and services (food, medical) coming to the inmates in housing units, rather than inmates going to

the program or service, the function of officers often extends into the provision or supervision of these functions. Food service staff members bring meals to the housing area, but the cell block officer supervises the meal service. In addition, visitors come to visiting rooms adjacent to the housing unit, and the housing officer moves the inmates to a noncontact visiting area and maintains some surveillance over the visit.

Similar to prison staff members, jail staff members work in stressful and sometimes dangerous environments. Although not a regular occurrence, staff are assaulted while working in a jail. The total number of assaults compared to the average daily population translated into 17.8 assaults per 1,000 inmates or 48.8 assaults per 1,000 staff members during the twelve-month period.[30] And a 2009 report noted the potential risk of exposure to HIV by officers.[31] Despite this fact, many individuals find work as jail correctional officers challenging and rewarding. Just as in prisons, an officer position is usually the entry-level job, and staff members have the opportunity for advancement and other types of jobs.

Design and Supervision in Jails

Contemporary jails are very different from the earliest jails in the United States. As most can recall from watching old television westerns, every small town had a sheriff's office with a few jail cells to hold those arrested for committing serious crimes or getting drunk in the local saloon. This idea of combining the sheriff's office with the local jail continued into the twentieth century. In many rural counties, the sheriff and his family lived in the second floor of a county-owned house, the main floor was the sheriff's office, and the basement included cells for housing inmates. Most of these jails have now been replaced with more modern facilities. In major metropolitan areas, it is desirable to locate the jail next to the county court building, creating problems for both architectural and security concerns.

Urban leaders do not want a jail to "look like a jail" and ruin the aesthetics of the area in which it is located. Yet jails must be very secure and as escape-proof as possible. Jail designers must take into account requirements for lighting and airflow, for offering inmate programs, and for movement of inmates within the jail and between the jail and the courthouse. Architects take great pride in meeting these sometimes conflicting demands of a jail being secure, yet fitting into the current landscape of the urban environment. The St. Louis city jail, which opened in early 2003, illustrates this effort. A jury of the American Institute of Architects Committee on Architecture for Justice reviewed the design and appearance and stated, "We found this multi-level solution to be sensitive to its urban context and the fabric of the façade while providing good operational solutions."[32]

This sheriff's office from the 1950s was the standard in most county seats, in which the sheriff's family lived upstairs, the administrative office was on the main floor, and the jail was in the basement. Courtesy of the Ohio Department of Rehabilitation and Correction.

The St. Louis City Jail is a good example of modern jail architecture, in which the jail is conveniently located next to the courthouse, yet fits into the urban look of the other buildings. Photo by Richard P. Seiter.

Creating a Secure Setting inside the Jail

Designers of jails must not only make the facility attractive to fit into the city skyline, but also make it functional and secure. Jail functionality begins with the fact that inmates are kept in their housing areas most of the time and are seldom moved to other locations in the jail. Therefore, services (food, laundry, medical), programs (education, counseling), and even visitors must be brought to the inmate housing area. The design of the housing areas has evolved and changed significantly over the past several decades.

Historically, **first-generation jails** housed inmates using a linear design, in which cells are aligned in long, straight rows, with walkways in the front of the cells for jail correctional officers to walk intermittently to observe what is going

first-generation jails
jails using a linear design for housing inmates, in which cells are aligned in long, straight rows, with walkways in the front of the cells for jail correctional officers to walk intermittently to observe what is going on in the cells

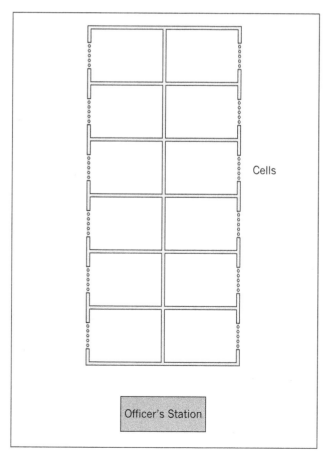

FIGURE 3.1 Linear Design of Jail Housing Units

on in the cells. As illustrated in Figure 3.1, this linear approach did not allow officers to observe and supervise inmates from a single location and resulted in little if any communication between officers and inmates as officers patrolled the corridors and looked into cells. The design of the cells and furnishings was very secure. Cell fronts were open bars (allowing no privacy and increasing the noise level), beds and other furniture were solid metal, and toilets and sinks were often stainless steel and difficult to destroy. There was little space for recreation or programs, and therefore inmates remained in their cells and grew restless and irritated. Food had to be delivered to each cell, taking extensive staff time and making it difficult to maintain quality in food service.

To improve the supervision and resolve some of the program and service issues, jail designers introduced a new style of housing in the 1970s. These **podular designs**, as illustrated in Figure 3.2, have several advantages over linear designs. They usually house smaller numbers of inmates, resulting in

First-generation jails had long rows of cells, and jail personnel saw inmates only as they walked the corridor and looked into cells. Courtesy of the Federal Bureau of Prisons.

a better inmate–staff member ratio. They provide common areas in the center of the unit (called dayrooms) in which inmates can watch television or play table games during the day, thus getting out of their cells and reducing idleness and tension. Podular designs make it easier for officers to view inmate activities in the cells and the dayrooms from one central location.

podular designs
a design of prisoner housing that provides common dayroom areas in the center of the unit to allow inmates to watch television or play table games, thereby getting out of their cells and reducing idleness and tension; podular designs make it easier for officers to view inmate activities in the cells and the dayrooms from one central location

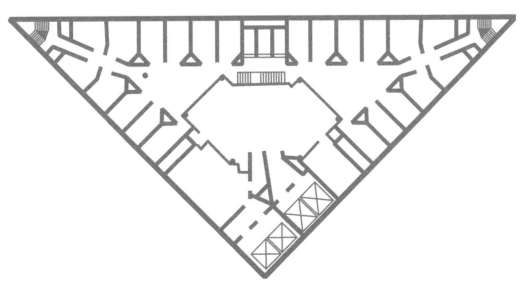

FIGURE 3.2 Podular Design of Jail Inmate Housing Units   Source: National Institute of Corrections, *Direct Supervision Jails Informational Packet* (Washington, D.C.: U.S. Department of Justice, 1993).

Podular jail designs allow for dayrooms in the center, in which officers can easily view inmates allowed out of their cells and into the dayrooms. Photo by Richard P. Seiter.

second-generation jails

jails using podular housing designs and remote supervision; officers are located in a secure control room overlooking the cells and dayroom, with electronic controls to open and close individual cell doors

third-generation jails

jail designs without remote control centers, in which correctional officers are located in the housing unit in direct contact with inmates

The creation of the podular design was an improvement from the linear jails. They resulted in the development of **second-generation jails**, using podular designs with remote supervision. Remote supervision placed officers in a secure control room overlooking the cells and dayroom, with electronic controls to open and close individual cell doors. There was extensive use of secure glass instead of bars to improve visibility. Although second-generation jails had several advantages over first-generation jails, the disadvantage was that with indirect supervision jail staff had limited contact with inmates; thus there was no communication or ability to talk to inmates, find out issues that were developing, and respond to them in a proactive manner.

To improve the problems resulting from the indirect supervision in second-generation jails, jail officials began to design **third-generation jails**, with the remote control center for staff removed and correctional officers placed in the housing unit in direct contact with inmates. This **direct supervision** approach requires staff to continuously supervise and communicate with inmates, thus reducing tension and avoiding the development of conflicts among inmates or between inmates and staff. The design also allows food to be brought to and served in the common area, and there are often laundry facilities in the unit, allowing inmates to take responsibility for these functions rather than staff having to do it for them.

Officials initially feared for staff safety, but direct supervision of jails was found to provide better control, lessen violence, and be safer for staff and inmates. A study of the behavior of inmates across many new direct-supervision jails that replaced old indirect-supervision facilities found a reduction in fifty-one of seventy categories of negative conduct by inmates when the direct-supervision jails

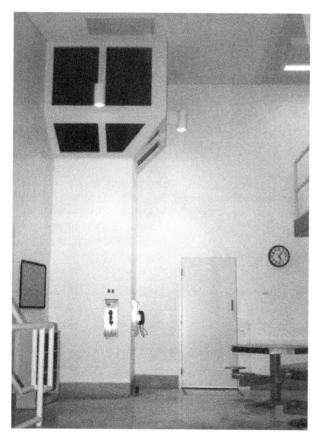

In second-generation jails, officers have no direct contact with inmates, as they oversee activities in the cell house from a remote location, similar to a perimeter tower within the building. Photo by Richard P. Seiter.

In a third-generation jail with direct supervision, officers work in the housing units and interact continuously with inmates. Photo by Riffi O'Brien.

From their remote location in second-generation jails, officers can open and close cell doors electronically simply by pushing a button. Courtesy of CoreCivic.

opened.[33] Since the first podular direct-supervision jail was constructed in 1981 in Contra Costa County, California, more than 100 jails across the country use direct supervision, and most new jails are constructed and managed on this concept.

Issues in Jails

The nation's jails face many significant challenges. With the increased reliance on jails described previously, jails have become increasingly overcrowded, and many new jails have been constructed to accommodate the increasing numbers of inmates. Some jurisdictions have opted to contract with the private, for-profit sector to build and manage a new jail. Jails also receive and hold people with many problems that can require immediate identification and attention. Detained offenders may suffer from mental illness or drug or alcohol addictions or be suicidal. Jail staff must protect inmates from sexual assault. Jails are also increasingly called on to house juvenile offenders who, because of the severity or nature of their crimes, will be processed through the adult court and correctional systems. These issues will be addressed after the following "An Interview With" box.

An Interview With...

A Jail Administrator

Herbert L. Bernsen Courtesy of St. Louis County Department of Justice Services.

Administrators of large urban jails face many serious challenges in trying to manage their facilities. Herbert L. Bernsen is Director of the St. Louis County Department of Justice Services (DJS), which oversees the St. Louis County Jail. He has worked for DJS since 1972, and served as a probation/parole officer, superintendent of the maximum and medium security correctional institutions, Intake Manager, and Assistant Director. He became Director in 2009. He is a certified Jail Manager by the American Jail Association, and has a national reputation as a knowledgeable and professional jail administrator.

Question: What are the major challenges facing you as a jail administrator?

Mr. Bernsen: There are many, but include (1) hiring competent staff and training them in the multiple competencies required of individuals in this field; (2) communicating the philosophy of our agency and the criminal justice field in general in terms of what we are trying to do as far as our mission; and (3) to bring the community into our mission by contacting social service as well as law enforcement agencies, and integrating them into not just how we intake and hold prisoners, but what we do with them to prepare for release.

Question: What are the characteristics essential for staff to work successfully in a large jail?

Mr. Bernsen: It is not necessary that they have prior criminal justice experience, but valuable to have a combination of education and work experience that lends itself to the qualities that are needed in this facility. These include dependability, discipline, and the ability to communicate and work with others. Most importantly, individuals must have good skills in communicating with individuals from a variety of backgrounds, and the ability to not only work under supervision, but also independently, being able to think on their feet and make decisions in line with the mission and philosophy we want to achieve.

Question: How do you find people with the abilities to perform well in a jail setting?

Mr. Bernsen: You have to put the jail out there, in a variety of places where those individuals that are apt to become interested may see or hear about you. You have to do more than just advertise; you have to explain the organization, how it operates professionally, and the critical skills you are looking for. We are looking for more than what the public perceives as a correctional officer, and you emphasize the talent and skill required and the career opportunities that exist. You look at universities, the military, and even use Internet sites so that your message is received by a wide variety of people. Also critical is that your personnel department and administrators that may talk to applicants have a good understanding of what to look for and represent the agency well.

Question: What is the mission of a jail and how do you implement it?

Mr. Bernsen: As a correctional agency, we have a mandate to hold (detain) people that have been assigned to us because of violating a statute or ordinance, and we have to provide a safe, secure, and humane environment for them. Our goal is to provide an environment where staff, inmates, and visitors are free from emotional or physical danger. Inmates must have the opportunity to participate in programs and improve themselves while they are here. This environment should also foster a well-trained staff, capable of direct supervision management. Direct supervision is the philosophy that we use to manage our jail;

we believe it creates a better environment for staff, improves our ability to manage inmates, and increases their chances of successful return to the community.

It is important to get others to understand this mission, and the media can play an important role in this. With a jail setting, negative things can always occur, and the media will want to know why these things happen. Even when mistakes or omissions occur, it is an opportunity to get the message of your mission before the public. You may have a tragic incident such as a suicide, but you can also discuss the type of suicide prevention program you have and the plans you have to improve it. It is important to develop a rapport with the media and invite them to learn about the successful programs within the jail. We need to get agencies to be partners in what we do. An example is the mental health court, in which the community was brought into the facility as a partner with us to get other phases of the community mental health groups to determine how best to handle and provide services to offenders with mental health problems. These can develop into grant opportunities and involvement by other agencies. Today, jails are faced more and more with a higher number of inmates with severe mental illness. Administrators face the dilemma of either providing more space and services to treat people with mental illness within the jail or working to improve community resources to treat people with mental illness and prevent the need to house so many in jail. Another area of significant importance for jails is the need to invest in community reentry programs designed to prevent and reduce recidivism, and partnering with community agencies is critical to implementing successful reentry programs.

Another part of what we can do is to get the courts, judges, and prosecutors involved in what we are trying to do. Any one of these components can block programs from being successful. We have regular meetings to discuss issues of mutual interest. The courts want to be partners with the jail, and

through discussions of issues as mundane as how we transport inmates, doors are opened for further discussions.

Question: Tight budget times always force reducing or ending programs or services you see as valuable. How do you determine what you are going to cut when cuts are needed?

Mr. Bernsen: We look for other funding opportunities, such as grant opportunities that can be found through universities or social service agencies. There may be a source of getting funds to develop a program we would otherwise not be able to afford. Another way is to have contacts to begin doing things in-house you did not realize you could do, such as using intern students, which provides assistance and recruits staff. Social service agencies may decide they should be providing services at the jail, such as our local school board determining they have a responsibility to offer education classes to our population. It is very important that we have an environment that welcomes outside participation, because even though it takes more time and work, the potential payoff is tremendous. As a result of an active use of volunteers, we have more programs and have a calmer institution.

Question: Looking to the future, do you foresee a "new paradigm" for jails?

Mr. Bernsen: I do, because hopefully organizations like the American Jail Association, the National Institute of Corrections, and the American Correctional Association are getting the word out to national and state decision makers that jails are areas that need assistance and are worth investing in. When you look at the number of individuals that come through jails and go out into the community, jails touch many more offenders than prison or community supervision, and many of the individuals they touch have mental, medical, and emotional problems in need of intervention.[34]

Responding to Jail Crowding

The jail incarceration rate has more than doubled, and the population of the nation's jails has almost tripled over the past twenty-five years. Much of the growth has resulted from the increased numbers of minority inmates. As indicated in Figure 3.3, between 1990 and 2015, the number of white and Hispanic jail inmates increased at a faster annual rate than that of black inmates. At the end of 2015, white inmates made up less than one-half (48 percent) of all jail inmates.[35]

Although some jail officials attempted to deal with the increasing number of offenders by increasing the pretrial release and diversion programs, the problem usually resulted in the need to construct new jails or add onto the existing jail to increase capacity. In 1990, local jail capacity was 389,171, and the nation's jails were operating at 104 percent over capacity.[36] During the 1990s, approximately 150 additional jails were built (not including new jails constructed to replace old jails), and the capacity of the nation's jails increased to 677,787 by 2000. Table 3.3 illustrates

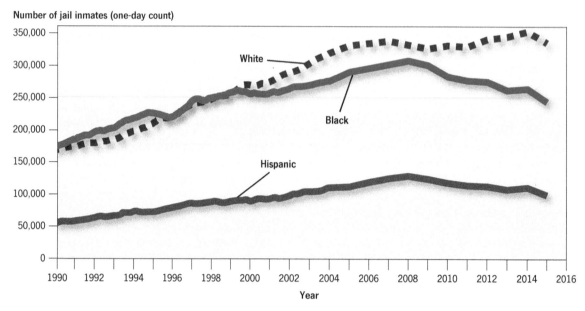

Number of jail inmates (one-day count)

FIGURE 3.3 Jail Population by Race and Ethnicity, 1990–2015   Source: Bureau of Justice Statistics Correctional Surveys, *Correctional Populations in the United States* and *Prison and Jail Inmates at Midyear* (Washington, D.C.: U.S. Department of Justice, various years). Also, Todd D. Minton and Zhen Zeng, "Jail Inmates in 2015," *BJS Bulletin* (Washington, D.C.: U.S. Department of Justice, 2016).

the rated capacity of jails, the amount of capacity that was added each year, and the percentage of the overall capacity of jails that was occupied. From 2000 to 2015, jail capacity was increased by an average of over 20,000 per year, which exceeded the population increase in most of these years. By the end of 2015, jail capacity was 904,900, and the percent occupied was only 79.7 percent of capacity.

Over the past two decades, local governments have done a very good job of managing their jail populations in several ways. First, they have added capacity to more than keep up with the increases in population. Second, they have continued to use bail and other release mechanisms to put low-risk offenders in the community. At the end of 2013, jail officers supervised 46,770 persons in the community, either on electronic monitoring, house arrest, or regular pretrial supervision, and used day reporting centers and work programs to aid in supervision. And a small but decreasing number of inmates are juvenile offenders. In the 1990s, concern over violent juvenile crime and gangs led to several youthful offenders to be detained in jail and then tried as adults (see Chapter 8). By 2000, there were 7,600 juveniles held in local jails, of which 6,100 were to be tried under adult statutes. However, since that time, the number of juveniles waived for handling to the adult court has declined, and by the end of 2015, there were only 3,500 juveniles held in local jails, of which only 3,200 were being held under adult criminal statutes.[37]

Another approach for dealing with jail overcrowding has been to contract out for the detention of jail inmates with a private correctional company. A *private correctional facility* is any correctional facility operated by a nongovernmental agency and usually in a for-profit manner that contract with a governmental entity to provide security, housing, and programs for offenders. According to most reports, the first jail contract with a private company was in 1984, for a 250-bed facility operated by Corrections Corporation of America under contract with Hamilton County, Tennessee. Privatizing the operation of prisons or jails has been very controversial, and arguments surround the issues of benefits and costs, ethics and corruption, quality of service, security and public protection, and liability.[38]

Today, there are dozens of privately operated jails across the country, and privatization of jail construction or management is seen as a viable option for counties

TABLE 3.3	Rated Capacity of Local Jails and Percent of Capacity Occupied, 2000 and 2005–2015

		Percent of capacity occupied based on[b]—		
Year[d]	Rated capacity[c]	Year-to-year percent change in rated capacity[a]	Confined 1-day population[d]	Average daily population[e]
2000	677,800[**]	3.9%[***]	92.0%[**]	91.2%[**]
2005	787,000[**]	4.1[***]	95.0[**]	93.2[**]
2006	795,000[**]	1.0	96.3[**]	95.0[**]
2007	810,500[**]	2.0[***]	96.3[**]	95.4[**]
2008	828,700[**]	2.2[***]	94.8[**]	93.7[**]
2009	849,900[**]	2.6[***]	90.3[**]	90.4[**]
2010	857,900[**]	0.9	87.3[**]	87.3[**]
2011	870,400	1.5	84.5	84.5
2012	877,400	0.8	84.9	84.0
2013	872,900	−0.5	83.8	83.8
2014[*]	890,500	2.0	83.6	83.0
2015[f]	904,900	1.6	76.6!	79.7[**]
Change in rated capacity				
Average annual change, 2000–2015		1.9%		

Note: Data are adjusted for nonresponse and rounded to the nearest 100. See appendix table 6 for standard errors.

! Not compared because the jail population goes through seasonal change, typically with fewer inmates at yearend than at midyear.

[*]Comparison year on rated capacity and percent of capacity occupied.

[**]Difference with comparison year is significant at the 95 percent confidence level.

[***]Year-to-year change is significant at the 95 percent confidence level.

[a]Increase or reduction in the number of beds during the 12 months ending midyear of each year. Number and percentage change for 2000 are calculated using the rated capacity of 652,321 for 1999.

[b]Based on the inmate population divided by the rated capacity.

[c]Maximum number of beds or inmates assigned by a rating official to a facility, excluding separate temporary holding areas.

[d]Data are based on the number of inmates confined on the last weekday in June except for 2015, which was based on December 31, 2015.

[e]Sum of all inmates in jail each day for a year, divided by the number of days in the year.

[f]Data are based on the rated capacity for December 31, 2015.

Source: Todd D. Minton and Zhen Zeng, "Jail Inmates in 2015," *BJS Bulletin* (Washington, D.C.: U.S. Department of Justice, 2016), p. 7.

that need a new jail and do not have the funds available to build one. Between 1993 and 1999, the number of private jails in the United States increased from seventeen to forty-seven, and capacity grew from 3,229 to 16,659.[39] However, by 2006, there were only thirty-seven privately operated jails.[40] This decline is primarily due to the decreasing jail population over the past five years. As the population declines, jurisdictions contracting with private operators can simply cancel the contracts when no longer needed. With the continued decline in the jail population since 2008, it is unlikely there will be an increase in the use of private detention facilities to house jail inmates. The use of private jails and prisons is dealt with in both Chapters 10 and 16.

The Metropolitan Correctional Center in New York City, operated by the U.S. Bureau of Prisons, was the location of one of the major inmate lawsuits regarding jail operations. Courtesy of the Federal Bureau of Prisons.

Bell v. Wolfish

a 1979 U.S. Supreme Court case in which the punitive intent standard was adopted for considering violations of the Eighth Amendment regarding jail operations

Legal Issues for Jails

One of the primary reasons for increased capacity through new jail construction over the past decade has been the increase in the number of successful legal challenges by jail inmates against jails for either overcrowding or other conditions of confinement. Jail inmates file lawsuits over a variety of things: lack of privacy, privileges (or lack thereof), food, brutality by staff, access to their attorneys, or general conditions of overcrowding. Most lawsuits are not successful, but the courts recognize that most jail inmates are not yet convicted, and afford them more privileges than the typical prison inmate.

Jails are expected to provide a constitutionally acceptable environment, which means they must meet all the requirements of health and safety codes, adequately control violence, provide an acceptable level of privacy as allowed by security concerns, and meet basic inmate needs such as medical care and a nutritious diet. When a jail does not meet the expected level and an inmate files a legal action in federal court, the court can impose requirements for action by the jail to remedy the concerns and bring the jail environment up to constitutional standards.

One of the first major cases in which the U.S. Supreme Court addressed jail conditions was the 1979 case of **Bell v. Wolfish**, in which the Court established the "punitive intent standard."[41] The case dealt with conditions and practices at a federal jail in New York City. The jail, although newly constructed, was already overcrowded and "double-bunked," housing two inmates in cells designed for one. The lawsuit by inmates challenged the crowded conditions as well as practices at the jail of not allowing inmates to observe searches of their cells and of requiring them to submit to visual searches of body cavities after visits with family members or friends. The lawsuit alleged violations of the Eighth Amendment of the Constitution, which states, "Excessive bail shall not be required, nor excessive fines imposed, nor cruel and unusual punishment inflicted."

The Supreme Court ruled that the case should turn only on whether the practices in question violated jail inmates' right to be free from punishment (since they were not yet convicted of a crime), using a standard of whether the individual restrictions were punitive or merely regulatory restraints, whether the practices were reasonably related to a legitimate goal other than punishment, and whether the practices appeared excessive in relation to that alternative purpose. This decision is guidance for jails in what is expected by the courts in operating in a safe and secure manner, yet one that does not overly infringe on the rights of yet-to-be-convicted offenders.

Since the *Bell* decision, courts regularly have ruled against the operating conditions at a jail and required jail administrators to make changes or even build a new jail. In a 1999 survey, approximately 15 percent of the reporting jurisdictions reported that they were under a court order or consent decree for crowding or other confinement conditions, and 11 percent were under a court order to limit their population so that it would not be overcrowded.[42] Since then, many new jails have been constructed and procedures have been improved to avoid the likelihood of inmate suits. And with overcrowding going down ever since, there are even fewer successful lawsuits for conditions of confinement in jails today. By 2006, the number reduced and 9 percent of jail jurisdictions had one or more facilities under court order or consent decree.[43] While jail officials have done a good job of proactively managing issues and avoiding legal challenges by inmates, a new challenge they face is in managing legal issues from their own staff. A recent publication of legal issues for jails now illustrates that staff issues (schedules, dress, etc.) are almost as numerous as inmate lawsuits.[44]

Handling Offenders with Mental Illness

Over the last thirty years, the number of criminal offenders with mental illness has been rising. In the 1960s, new anti-psychotropic drugs were created and prescribed for people with mental illness, allowing many mentally ill individuals to remain in the community rather than be placed in mental hospitals. As a result, states closed their hospitals, and the number of mentally ill patients went from a high of 559,000 in 1955 to 69,000 in 1995.[45] When these commu-

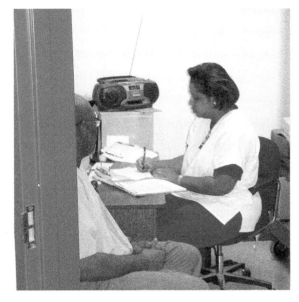

Mental health staff members do assessments of inmates as they enter jails to determine whether they are mentally ill or a serious suicide risk. Photo by Richard P. Seiter.

nity patients stop taking their medication, the symptoms of the mental illness return; many commit crimes and become clients of the criminal justice system. And within twenty years, the National Sheriffs' Association reported that there were 356,268 inmates with severe mental illness in prisons and jails, ten times more than the now approximately 35,000 individuals in psychiatric hospitals.[46] It has been estimated that 16 percent of all jail inmates have a mental illness.[47] And the Bureau of Justice Assistance published that one in four jail inmates self-reported experiences that indicated serious psychological distress (SPD), much higher than one in nineteen of the general U.S. population that meets the threshold for SPD.[48]

Upon arrival in a jail, offenders are usually screened to detect mental illness or the potential for suicide. These assessment instruments are very short, but can accurately indicate a problem that requires immediate attention. The assessment instruments rely on the offenders' honesty and ask them about histories of mental illness, taking of psychotropic medication, and thoughts of suicide. Although most jails (78 percent) do an initial screening, very few offer intensive mental health programs. Of the jails surveyed in 2004 that housed inmates with mental health problems, an estimated 23 percent had received mental health treatment during the year before their arrest, 17 percent had used medication, and about 7 percent had an overnight stay in a hospital as a result of a mental disorder.

There has been considerable discussion and planning for dealing with the high numbers of mentally ill offenders in local jails. A 2017 article advocated local authorities asking themselves six questions to consider when attempting to reduce the number of people with mental illness in jails. These include:

1. Is our leadership committed?
2. Do we conduct timely screening and assessments?
3. Do we have baseline data?
4. Have we conducted a comprehensive process analysis and inventory of services?
5. Have we prioritized policy, practice, and funding improvements?
6. Do we track progress?[49]

Suicide prevention cells have little that inmates can use to harm themselves and are monitored continuously through cameras or personal supervision.

Photo by Richard P. Seiter.

Two other well-documented issues with mentally ill offenders in jails are that they cost much more to house than other prisoners, and their rates of suicide are much higher. Examples of costs include a Florida jail (2007 costs) with a difference of $130 for people with mental illness versus $80 dollars a day for other prisoners. In Washington State, the 2009 cost for seriously mentally ill prisoners was over $100,000 per year compared to approximately $30,000 for other prisoners.[50] Suicide risks are much greater among people with mental illness. A study of suicide attempts in King County (WA) found that 77 percent had a chronic psychiatric problem, and a similar study in California prisons found 73 percent of attempts had a history of mental health treatment.[51] This issue is addressed more fully below.

Preventing Suicides

A serious and challenging issue for jails is the prevention of suicides. Offenders placed in jail (especially those with mental health issues) are a high-risk population for suicides, and there is usually limited information to identify suicide risk inmates when they arrive. Jails do a preliminary screening upon an offender's entry to the jail to determine whether there are immediate concerns about an attempted suicide. In a 2015 report of deaths in correctional facilities, it was identified that of the total number of inmate deaths (967 in 2013) while in jail, 34 percent of them (327) were a result of suicide.[52] From 2000 to 2013, there were 13,728 deaths of jail inmates, and suicide was the leading cause of death in jails in each of these years. However, the mortality rate for suicides per 100,000 jail inmates has remained relatively constant, and was 46 per 100,000 in 2013.[53] Following suicide, other causes of death for inmates in jail included heart disease (23 percent), AIDS related (4 percent), and other illnesses (25 percent).[54] During these fourteen years, there were only 302 deaths by homicides (only 2.1 percent), or only an average of 21 per year.[55]

Jails have three times higher rate of suicide than prisons, partly because offenders entering a jail for the first time face a "shock of confinement" with many uncertainties about their future.[56] Since suicide represents a significant concern for jail administrators, most jails have **suicide prevention programs**. Suicide prevention programs include risk assessment at admission, special staff training, counseling for inmates, and monitoring and special watches of high-risk inmates. An assessment of offenders upon entering jail is critical, as it has been reported that approximately 48 percent of all jail suicides occur during the first week following admission.[57] Inmates who indicate some risk during the assessment are noted and receive specific counseling from mental health professionals regarding their thoughts of suicide. All staff members receive training on the signs of potential suicide among inmates. These include sleeping a lot, depression, staying by oneself, giving away property to other inmates, or confiding their thoughts to family or friends.

If inmates are deemed a high risk of suicide as a result of the assessment or staff observations, they may be specially monitored. Some of the monitoring

suicide prevention programs

jail and prison programs that include early detection of suicide risks, staff education to recognize signs of potential suicide, and procedures for managing inmates who are now suicidal may include **suicide watch** programs, in which inmates are placed in a specially equipped cell without materials that could be used for a suicide attempt (blankets, sheets, belts, shoestrings, places in the cell to hang something from). Some suicide watch cells then have constant supervision by either a camera or a person so that staff can quickly react if the inmate begins any dangerous activity. Others require officers to check on the offender every thirty minutes to ensure his or her safety. Even with all these programs, it is difficult to prevent suicides of inmates truly committed to ending their lives. "A Look Into" describes a best practice approach to preventing suicides in jails.

A very interesting case regarding a jail suicide illustrates the complexities involved even beyond the death of someone under the supervision of jail officials. In 2003, Maury Travis, an alleged serial killer, was arrested and jailed in the St. Louis County Jail for the brutal rape and murder of multiple victims. Because of the nature of the crimes, he was placed on a suicide watch in the jail isolation area with trained inmates assigned to constantly sit outside his cell and watch him to prevent the possibility of a suicide attempt. Several jurisdictions use inmates for suicide watch. It saves staff time and inmates are committed to watching to ensure the suicide risk inmate does not do anything to harm him or herself. If they do, they can immediately contact staff for assistance.

The jail also had a policy that inmates housed in the isolation block would be allowed to come out of their cells and walk on the short range immediately outside their cell for one hour per day. Therefore, the inmate watcher had to move back behind another wall, from which he did not have a direct view of the entire cell. Within thirty minutes after the inmate watcher moved from the cell front, Travis hid in the not-visible corner of his cell, tied his bed sheet around his neck and a ventilation grill in the cell, and hanged himself to death. Besides the fact a life was lost, Travis' death ended the opportunity to question him about several still missing women that fit the description of other Travis victims, and law enforcement personnel were disappointed that they could not question him for information regarding those disappearances. The families of these missing women were kept from finding out what happened to their loved ones. As a result of the suicide, the jail ended their policy of using inmate watchers, and hired several more staff members just to conduct the suicide watch.

suicide watch
management of suicidal inmates who are placed in a specially designed cell and have constant supervision

A Look Into . . .

Preventing Jail Suicides

The risk of suicide is high in jails. Lindsay M. Hayes is a nationally recognized expert on suicides in correctional facilities. He regularly consults and advises correctional agencies around the country on actions to take to prevent suicides. He offers the following background and steps to reduce the likelihood of jail suicides.

The suicide rate in jails is much higher than in prison or in the community. Even though high, the jail and prison rates have come down substantially over the past two decades. The primary reason for the drop is the increase in the awareness of suicide risks and potential ways to reduce the risks have increased. Correctional administrators have become more concerned about it, not accepting that suicides just happen, and have become more proactive in their approach. The current philosophy is more likely to be a question of whether we understand what is going on, how we take a broader look at the picture, see if a suicide was an aberration, or if there is a systemic problem that needs to be addressed. In addition, we are better able to hire and train mental health staff to work in jail facilities and are doing a better job of intake screening and assessing the risk of suicide by new admissions.

Once aware, the important question is how we prevent suicides. The most important thing is to have a written suicide prevention policy. The policy must be comprehensive and include the eight most important prevention activities.

1. *Training of both correctional and mental health staff.*   All staff should receive eight hours of suicide prevention training in their preservice training so that they understand the risk of suicide. Annually, staff should receive a refresher of two hours as a constant reminder that suicide prevention is an important issue to the jail and its management. It also serves as a reminder that every inmate is potentially suicidal.

2. *Intake screening and assessment.*   Specific questions should be asked of every new admission to jail that address the risk of suicide. Are you thinking about committing suicide now? Have you considered it in the past? Have you recently experienced a serious loss? Is there any history of suicide in your family? Do you have a history of mental illness? Arresting or transporting officers should be asked if the inmate mentioned anything or showed any unusual behavior that might be a red flag for suicide.

3. *Communication.*   The first level is between the arresting or transporting officer and the jail staff. The second level is among staff in the jail so that everyone knows if an inmate is likely suicidal and how he or she should be managed. The third level is between the staff and the suicidal inmate, watching and teaching the inmate how to deal with the urge.

4. *Housing.*   Jails must provide a suicide-resistant housing situation for inmates identified as suicidal. It is usually not practical for all jail cells to be suicide resistant, so jailers must identify and create cells that are protrusion free, that is, without things that inmates can use to hang themselves (95 percent of inmates commit suicide by hanging using clothing or sheets attached to a protrusion).

5. *Levels of observation provided to suicidal inmates.*   Most standards recommend at least two levels. The most extreme is constant observation of an inmate who is acutely suicidal, who if not constantly watched will make an effort to commit suicide. The second level of observation is close supervision that results in observation at staggered fifteen-minute intervals (not so routine that inmates can anticipate how frequently the jailer will make the check). This level is appropriate for inmates who are low to medium risk of committing suicide. They may be feeling distraught or suffering from mental illness or depression, or they may have made a suicide attempt in the past.

6. *Intervention in a suicide attempt.*   This is similar to a medical emergency response and includes making sure the responding officer is trained in first aid, has a suicide prevention kit that includes a special knife to cut down a hanging victim, and follows a protocol detailing the role of every staff member when responding to a suicide attempt. There should also be regular mock exercises for staff to practice an emergency situation.

7. *Reporting.*   This is straightforward and includes writing a report by everyone involved in finding a suicide or anyone who had contact with the victim.

8. *Morbidity and mortality review process.*   After any serious suicide attempt (requiring medical attention at the jail clinic or outside hospital), there should be a morbidity or mortality review. Both include a multidisciplinary approach with both mental health and correctional staff involved. They look at the total event and not just how staff members responded to it. They examine a time line of when the inmate arrived at the facility and look for any issues of mental health or medical issues that went undiscovered. This is not an investigation or internal affairs review, but a systemic review to address what happened and what we can learn to reduce the opportunity for suicides in the future. The review may result in a revision of policy, training, revision of screening forms, improvement of emergency response, or physical plan issues.

In the "You Make the Decision" box at the end of the chapter, students consider several factors in a suicide prevention program and decide how they want to structure a prevention policy.

Chapter Review

Summary

Jails today represent one of the most challenging operations in the nation's criminal justice process. Jails not only hold more than 700,000 inmates at any one time, but they also admit more than ten times that number per year, hold a wide variety of categories of offenders, house inmates with several unique problems and needs, and must maintain constitutional standards and protect the rights of offenders charged with, yet not convicted of a crime.

As a result of this multitasked mission, jails are extremely difficult to administer and operate. With the high turnover of offenders, jails sometimes make a mistake by releasing the wrong inmate. With many inmates having mental health, drug abuse, and physical problems, there are regularly cases of suicide, assault, and alleged mistreatment. Located in the center of cities and rural communities, jails get much more public attention than most prisons or other correctional facilities. In many counties, jails are operated by an elected official (the sheriff); sometimes hiring decisions result from political connections or campaign contributions, rather than from the professional or technical skills or knowledge of the applicant.

Through all of these challenges, jails continue to operate almost 900 years after the first jail was opened in medieval England. The jail serves a critical role as an offender intake point to the criminal justice system. Even with major efforts to reform, improve, and reinvent the way jails are operated, few major changes have been made in the basic system of operating jails. And while efforts continue to improve and professionalize the nation's jails, it is not expected that the public's perceptions of how jails run will change.

Jails primarily hold offenders before trial, in addition to some offenders serving short terms of confinement. For more serious inmates who are sentenced to longer periods of incarceration, early U.S. colonists invented the prison. Chapter 5 describes the current status of prisons in the United States, how they operate, the types of jurisdictions that oversee them, and the assignment of inmates to various security levels. After reading Chapter 5, students will have a clear understanding of the differences in the policies and practices between jails and prisons.

Key Terms

gaol	length of stay	direct supervision
jail	objective classification systems	*Bell v. Wolfish*
lockup	first-generation jails	suicide prevention programs
sheriff	podular design	suicide watch
regional jail	second-generation jails	
incarceration rate	third-generation jails	

Review Questions

1. What role did John Howard play in the early development of jails?

2. Name five categories of jail offenders.

3. What are the advantages of a regional jail?

4. List potential reasons for the increase in the jail incarceration rate over the past decade.

5. Compare the average length of stay in a jail to that in a prison.

6. Describe the normal booking process in a jail.

7. Describe the problems associated with the use of classification systems in jails.

8. How are podular jail designs an improvement over linear jail designs?

9. Describe direct supervision.

10. How widely used are private correctional companies to operate jails?

11. Describe the impact of the *Bell v. Wolfish* decision on modern jail operations.

12. Why are there so many mentally ill offenders in jail?

13. What steps do jails take to reduce the likelihood of suicide by inmates?

14. What is a suicide watch?

▌ You Make the Decision...

Preventing Jail Suicides

The story of Maury Travis is troubling for many reasons. First, a life was lost, even though there was significant evidence of his guilt in kidnapping and brutally murdering several women in the St. Louis metropolitan region. Second, with his death, there are still missing women that fit the description of other Travis victims, and law enforcement personnel are disappointed that they could not question him for information regarding those disappearances. And finally, the county jail failed in its responsibility to safely house Travis and prevent him from harming himself during the investigation and pending prosecution for his alleged acts.

It seems that preventing jail suicides would be easy. After all, the inmates are locked in cells. But if someone really wants to commit suicide, it takes only a few seconds, and almost any piece of clothing, sheet, or shoestring can be used to hang oneself. Suicide prevention screenings upon admission are only as good as the information provided by the offender. And, as in the Travis case, even when an inmate is identified as a risk and placed on suicide watch, weaknesses in the procedures can still result in a suicide.

The issues to consider when developing a suicide prevention policy include (1) whom to place on suicide watch, (2) what clothing and bedding are allowed, and (3) whether to use inmate watchers. Keep in mind that it is expensive to place someone on suicide watch, and there are always limited funds for operation. It is easy to decide to place an offender on suicide watch if he or she admits consideration of suicide. But if someone has a minor history or no history yet faces a long sentence or the death penalty, such as Travis, should he or she be on suicide watch? If the person is placed on the watch, do you strip the inmate and not allow any clothing or bedding? This seems harsh, but keep in mind that almost any item can be used as a noose to hang oneself. Finally, many jurisdictions do use inmates trained as suicide watchers. They cost nothing and have proved to be good companions to suicidal inmates. Through their communications, inmates often end their suicidal thoughts quicker than if a correctional officer is watching them. But if something goes wrong, as in the Travis case, it is difficult to justify the use of inmates as watchers to those at the risk of suicide. Consider all these issues and develop your own suicide prevention program.

CHAPTER 4
Probation and Intermediate Sanctions

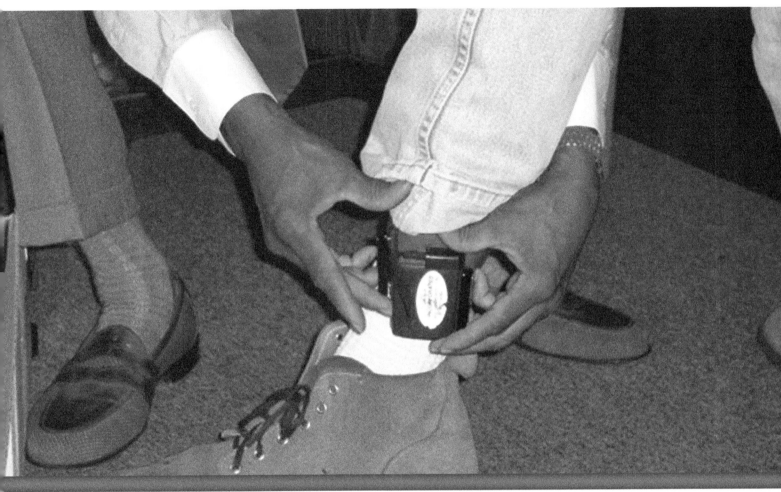

Photo by Richard P. Seiter.

After reading this chapter, you should be able to:

1. Outline the history of probation.
2. Summarize modern probation operations, including conditions of probation and revocation of probation.

3. Outline the results of evaluations regarding the effectiveness of felony probation.
4. Describe the goals of intermediate sanctions and the different types of sanctions.

Introduction

As noted in the sentencing continuum in Chapter 2, probation is the first and least intrusive of the postsentencing options for offenders. Historically, felony offenders were sentenced to either probation or prison. Over the past fifty years, however, the sentencing options available to judges have increased, with the addition of many other sanctions—some that supervise offenders in the community and some that supervise offenders in some type of institutional confinement. In the 1960s, many alternative sanctions to incarceration were developed, and the term **community corrections** was initiated. Community corrections or community-based corrections are criminal sanctions that involve community supervision of offenders, use correctional and program resources available in the community, and require offenders to abide by specified conditions to remain in the community.

Community corrections gained prominence as an adaptation of the Rehabilitative Era of corrections. During this period, offender problems were identified that required treatment to improve and prepare them for a productive and crime-free lifestyle. Most of the treatment was within institutional settings (prisons). However, it was soon recognized that for these treatments to maximize their effectiveness the community must be a part of the provision of treatment. In the restrictive prison environment, offenders could not test their readiness to return to the community or build relationships with community programs that could be continued as they lived in society. Therefore, the Reintegrative Era developed, with the distinct provision that the community be an essential part of the correctional process.

Today, even as retribution has more prominence as a correctional goal, there is still a strong emphasis on community corrections. Yet community corrections has changed from the 1960s and 1970s in that the focus is not on the offender and his or her rehabilitation or reintegration, but on public safety. Additionally, the recent recession and budget crisis for governments have made policy makers realize that we cannot afford the cost of current levels of offenders in prisons. Community corrections has the dual benefit of both holding offenders accountable, and providing safe and cost-effective community alternatives to incarceration.

This chapter describes the history, evolution, and current operations of community sanctions. Probation has been a part of community corrections for more than 150 years. In many ways, probation has changed little from its original philosophies and practices. In many other ways, however, probation has changed significantly, and some suggest there is a "new paradigm" for probation supervision. However, over the past thirty years, dissatisfaction with standard probation as a sanction for criminal offenders, combined with recognition of the need for alternatives to incarceration, has led to an expansion of intermediate sanctions to provide greater supervision than in regular probation, while still monitoring offenders in the community. This chapter therefore presents both a description of probation and the many available community alternatives to incarceration.

community corrections
those criminal sanctions that involve community supervision of offenders, make use of correctional and program resources available in the community, and require offenders to abide by specified conditions to remain in the community

The History of Probation

The earliest history of probation in the United States began in Boston in 1841, when a shoemaker named **John Augustus** posted bail for a man charged with public drunkenness. Augustus had become very interested in the court system and concerned about the dire situation of people charged with crimes who had to spend time in poor jail conditions. While visiting a court hearing, Augustus heard a defendant state that he would drink no more if saved from a sentence

John Augustus
the Boston shoemaker who became the "father" of probation

in the house of correction, and Augustus asked the judge to defer sentencing and release the man into his custody. In doing so, he became the nation's first probation officer (PO).[1] Augustus began to help others in the same way, bailing them out, helping them find work and a residence, and keeping the court appraised of their progress. By the time of his death in 1859, Augustus had bailed out more than 1,800 offenders. His records on the first 1,100 offenders whom he bailed out revealed that only one forfeited bond.[2] Augustus's work had a great impact on how many jurisdictions handled criminal offenders, and he became known as the father of probation. Unfortunately, while he was alive, he received little recognition for his efforts; he died destitute, having used all his funds to help others.

As the successes of Augustus became known, it was recognized that justice could be served without every offender being sentenced to jail or prison. In 1878, Massachusetts passed the first probation statute for juveniles, and probation was officially recognized. Not until 1901, however, did New York pass the first statute authorizing the use of probation for adult felons. Other states quickly followed New York's lead, and by 1938 thirty-seven states, the District of Columbia, and the federal government had passed juvenile and adult probation laws.[3] By 1907, the first directory of POs in the United States listed 795 juvenile and adult POs.

Augustus's acts of supervising offenders slowly crept into the formalization of the role of POs. Augustus himself came up with the term *probation* (based on the Latin term *probatio* meaning "a period of proving oneself"), as well as ideas for requiring offenders to meet conditions of supervision, reporting to the courts, and revoking probation when the conditions were not met.[4] In addition, Augustus's idea of investigating offenders' situations prior to sentencing resulted in the concept of presentence investigations (PSIs) being assigned to POs. Although probation has become much more sophisticated in its operation over the years, most of the original concepts created by Augustus continue to this day.

Modern Probation Operations

Probation is a prison sentence that is suspended on the condition that the offender follow certain prescribed rules and commit no further crimes. Even though probation often suffers from a perception of being "soft on crime," the public and elected officials recognize that not every offender can be sent to prison, and probation is still a sanction regularly used in the United States. In fact, since 1975 the number of offenders under community supervision has risen from less than 1 million to a peak of 4.3 million in 2007, and then declined slightly to 3,789,800 by the end of 2015.[5] However, since that time, the operations of probation have changed significantly. In 1976, a U.S. Comptroller General's Office report criticized probation operations, calling probation a failure due to a lack of adequate resources and recommending a total reevaluation of its operations and practices.[6] As a result, several probation programs, such as intensive probation supervision, house arrest, boot camps, and shock probation, have been created to enhance supervision, increase effectiveness, and increasingly limit offenders' freedom.

Today, probation in the United States is a federal, state, and local activity administered by more than 2,000 separate agencies; there is considerable diversity of operations and no uniform structure. Although probation began as a service to the judiciary and an arm of the court, today, in all but eleven of

probation
a prison sentence that is suspended on the condition that the offender follow certain prescribed rules and commit no further crimes

the states, adult probation is located in the executive branch of government. In more than half of the states, probation operations are centralized in the state department of corrections. This move to the executive branch and toward centralization stems from the need for training, professionalism, and uniformity of standards, which can be better accomplished in larger administrative systems; there can also be better coordination with other correctional services. In approximately eight states and the federal government, probation and parole services are provided by the same state agency, which supervises both probationers and parolees.

Even though prisons and issues focusing on incarceration receive much of the attention and most of the resources, probation operations have a tremendous impact on the correctional systems in the United States. In 2015, the Bureau of Justice Statistics reported a total of 6,741,400 adults under correctional supervision. Of these, 3,789,800 were on probation, 870,500 were on parole, and 2,173,800 were in prison or jail.[7] Even though the "tough on crime" mentality is still strong across the country, probation remains an important component of the correctional process, and the number of people on probation has remained relatively steady for the past several years. And, a recent report to guide elected officials regarding the use of community corrections suggests the following:

> *When officials consider balancing public safety with public spending, community corrections is a public safety asset that is worth the investment. The least expensive alternative to prisons, adult probation and parole supervision and programming is one of the promising methods of controlling crime. Further, when designed with evidence-based practices, adult and juvenile probation, parole, and other community-based programs, can prevent crime, increase offender accountability and competencies, and repair harm to both victims and neighborhoods.[8]*

Organization of Probation

As noted, most probation departments are based in county governments. With thousands of counties, there are many varieties of organizational structures. However, most share many commonalities in their organizational structure, particularly as it comes to supervising probationers in the community. Figure 4.1 illustrates the table of organization for the City and County of San Francisco Adult Probation Department.

The City and County of San Francisco Adult Probation Department is similar to many large city, county, or state probation departments in that it reflects the transition of probation services from standard supervision of all probationers in a similar way to one that has several specialized programs to provide evidence-based supervision practices to match the specific needs and risks of clients. More about some of these specialized supervision and treatment approaches is provided below. San Francisco has four divisions, each of which is described below:

Investigation, Supervision, and Collaborative Courts. This is the division that manages the preparation of PSIs and oversees all standard probation supervision. In addition, as noted in specialty courts in Chapter 2, San Francisco has several specialized courts for clients, such as drug users, DUI offenders, and veterans.

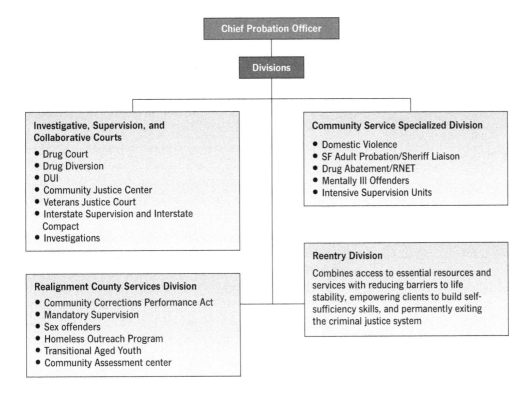

FIGURE 4.1 The City and County of San Francisco Adult Probation Department—Table of Organization Source: Adapted from the City and County of San Francisco Adult Probation Department website, available at http://sfgov.org/adultprobation/ (accessed August 16, 2017).

Community Service Specialized Division. This division is organized to support the services and specialized supervision units, such as offenders with issues of domestic violence, treatment for certain drug offenders, probationers with mental illness, and probationers requiring intensive supervision.

Realignment County Services Division. This division also oversees the programs for some special offenders, such as sex offender, youthful offenders, and the homeless outreach program. As well, it conducts assessments that can lead to supervision and management of probationers resulting in long term change.

Reentry Division. This is a unique division for probation departments, as one usually thinks of reentry from incarceration. But this division takes the same approach: to provide resources and overcome barriers leading to successful exit from the criminal justice program for probationers.

Characteristics of Probationers

One of the unique factors within current probation operations is that there has been a continual decline in the number of offenders on probation in the United States since 2007 when it was a high of 4,293,000. The total number of probation declined every year since then, reaching 3,789,800 at the end of 2015, or by 11.7 percent from 2007 to 2015.[9] This is not a significant concern or major sentencing change, as the total number of offenders under correctional supervision also reached a high of 7,199,600 in 2007 and declined to 6,741,400 or by 8 percent from 2007 to 2015, and the number of people on parole actually increased during that period.[10]

Part of supervision of offenders in the community is through office visits in which probation and parole officers get updates on the activities of their clients.

Photo by Richard P. Seiter.

There is considerable turnover of probation caseloads each year. In 2015, 4.1 million adults moved onto and off probation (almost 2 million individuals entered and just over 2 million exited). The average time served on probation was twenty-three months during 2012. Of probationers exiting supervision in 2015, 62 percent were by successful completion of supervision, 15 percent were incarcerated, 2 percent absconded, and another 13 percent had other unsatisfactory exits.[11]

Probationers are predominantly male (75 percent) and 25 percent are female. Fifty-five percent are white, 30 percent are black, and 13 percent are Hispanic. Fifty-seven percent are under supervision for a felony, 41 percent for a misdemeanor, and 2 percent for other infractions. The largest proportions of probationers are for property (28 percent), drug (25 percent), and public order (15 percent) crimes. Violent offenders are only 20 percent of all probationers, as a violent offense usually results in a prison sentence.[12]

Supervision

probation supervision

the role of a probation or parole officer in monitoring an offender's behavior through office visits; contacts with family, friends, bosses, or treatment providers; and visits to their home or place of work

casework style of supervision

a style of supervising community offenders that places emphasis on assisting the offender with problems, counseling, and working to make sure the offender successfully completes supervision

surveillance style of supervision

a style of supervising community offenders that places emphasis on monitoring and enforcing compliance with the rules of supervision and the detection of violations leading to revocation and return to custody

Once offenders are granted probation, it is the responsibility of POs to supervise them and get them to comply with conditions of their probation. Officers have a dual, and sometimes conflicting, responsibility. The primary purpose of **probation supervision** is to maintain surveillance, enforce conditions of probation, and guide offenders into treatment to protect the public from further crimes. To fulfill this purpose, officers first monitor probationers' activities through a combination of office visits (probationers report to the officer at the probation office), verification of probationers' activities by visiting their homes and contacting their employers or program providers, and monitoring activities such as drug testing of probationers. Second, officers help offenders succeed by determining program or treatment needs and placing probationers in social service programs that address their needs for education, mental health counseling, vocational training, or substance abuse programming.

It has been suggested that officers develop a supervision style that falls into either a casework or a surveillance approach. A **casework style of supervision** emphasizes helping the offender with problems, providing counseling, and ensuring that the offender completes supervision. A **surveillance style of supervision** emphasizes monitoring and enforcing compliance with the rules of supervision and the detection of violations leading to revocation and return to custody. In a survey of probation and parole officers in St. Louis, Missouri, officers were asked what they considered the most important roles for POs and how they spent their time in supervising offenders in the community. Officers responded that the primary role of probation and parole officers is to ensure public safety, to supervise and offer resources to help the client readjust to society, to prevent recidivism, to steer offenders in the right direction, to monitor offenders, and to hold offenders highly accountable for their actions and responsibilities.

Results indicated that officers spend an average of 55.9 percent of their time on casework activities during supervision and 41.4 percent of their time on surveillance activities.[13] These results indicate that officers must do both surveillance (monitoring compliance with conditions) and casework (helping offenders with their problems) in order to enforce conditions of probation and guide offenders to a status that improves their likelihood of success in the community. And a study of federal probation officers also showed a balance between both "social work" and "law enforcement," so that supervision is neither indulgent of antisocial behaviors nor authoritative and heavy-handed.[14] The types of services that most probation and parole agencies provide include referral services, individual counseling, substance abuse counseling, job development, and family counseling.

Probation agencies generally organize caseloads into three types: regular, intensive, and special. **Regular caseloads** are those for standard probationers who may have a significant risk of reoffending or several program needs but do not warrant assignment to one of the other two types of caseloads. **Intensive-supervision caseloads** (described in more detail later in this chapter) are for offenders with too high a risk or a need to be on regular supervision and were created as an alternative to sending these offenders to prison. Intensive-supervision caseloads are significantly less in number, and the required contacts between officers and probationers are significantly higher. Most jurisdictions also use **special caseloads**, whereby an officer's entire caseload is made up of probationers with a specific type of problem, such as substance abuse, mental illness, or a history of violent crimes or sex offenses. Such specialization allows the officer to become knowledgeable and proficient in dealing with this particular problem. Surveys of jurisdictions indicate that 89.5 percent of probationers were on regular caseloads, 15.68 percent were on special caseloads, 4.2 percent were on intensive caseloads, and 0.7 percent were on a caseload using EM.[15]

A good example of a special caseload is for mentally ill offenders. To address these needs, most probation and parole agencies have created special caseloads for managing offenders with mental illness. These caseloads are usually smaller than standard caseloads, averaging between fifty and fifty-five offenders. Most offenders are placed on a special caseload by an order of the court as a condition of their probation. Otherwise, POs may identify an offender as possibly having a mental illness and request his or her placement on a special caseload. A survey found that POs supervising offenders with mental health problems who treated them as special offenders and met with them more often and used mental health community services more than with traditional case management practices were more successful and less punitive in dealing with violations.[16] And for supervision of probationers suffering from severe and chronic psychiatric problems, it is suggested that a dual supervision of both surveillance and therapeutic goals, while cultivating a positive relationship between the officer and probationer is most successful.[17]

The "A Look Into" box is a description of the challenges of managing a special caseload, and how one officer addresses these issues.

There are wide variations in caseload sizes across jurisdictions. *The Corrections Yearbook* reports that the average size of PO caseloads for regular supervision average 127, ranging from 314 cases per officer in Rhode Island to fifteen cases per officer in Pennsylvania.[18] These large caseloads illustrate that although governments recognize the need for probation, they fail to financially support it at a more reasonable level. Large caseload sizes make it very difficult for probation to be an effective sanction in providing services to offenders, monitoring their behavior, and reducing recidivism. And, high caseloads were reported as one of the primary causes of stress among probation and parole officers.[19] The American Probation and Parole Association recommends the caseload approach described in Table 4.1.

Caseload size has been believed to have an impact on recidivism. Historically, most studies failed to show that a smaller caseload size reduces recidivism among

regular caseload
caseload made up of standard probationers, requiring no special program or supervision

intensive-supervision caseload
caseload for offenders with too high a risk or need to be on regular supervision; created as an alternative to sending these offenders to prison

special caseload
caseload is made up of offenders with a particular type of problem, such as substance abuse, mental illness, or a history of sex offenses

A Look Into...

Handling Probationers with Mental Illness

The supervision philosophy of this PO is to build trust with clients, particularly because he is concerned about the client's risk of suicide or violence to others. The officer notes that he would not know these things unless offenders tell him, and they must believe that they can share sensitive information with their PO without fear of immediate violation (return to prison). The officer states that after a few crises with offenders this trust often develops.

Mentally ill probationers report more frequently than standard probationers; weekly contact is not unusual. This frequency of contact often continues even when offenders' behavior is good and they are eligible for less intensive supervision. This is because these probationers may become unstable at any time. Every time the officer sees his probationers, he asks them if they are taking their psychotropic medication, if they are having any thoughts of harming themselves or others, and if they know the date and time of their next psychiatric appointment. He notes that it is very important not just to ask them these questions and accept their answers, but to "pry and push" them. He gave an example of an offender under his supervision that had a history of serious suicide attempts through overdoses of psychotropic drugs. The offender called the PO one day and said his roommate was using drugs, and he was afraid he would get caught up in it. The PO advised him to move as soon as possible, but as they continued to talk, it became clear that something else was bothering him. After some prodding, the probationer finally admitted that he was thinking of harming himself. In fact, he then admitted that he had already begun to take his medicine in a suicide attempt and had called the PO in hopes that the PO would get him to admit what he was doing without his volunteering the information. When asked why someone attempting suicide would not admit it, the PO noted that this is not unusual, as the person planning suicide is often embarrassed and sometimes even concerned about upsetting the PO. Some of his clients become very apologetic about the trouble they cause the PO. In this situation, the PO called emergency medical services (EMS) and continued to talk to the probationer on the phone until the paramedics arrived. He then directed the probationer to go out to meet the EMS workers when they drove up. However, the probationer had kept some pills in his hand, and on the way to

the hospital, he took some more pills. The EMS workers were able to treat and save him, and the probationer is now doing very well, both physically and psychologically.

The PO noted that an important part of his job is to be just one part of the mental health treatment team, with the probationer's psychiatrist, the case manager (who acts as community support to help the person keep track of appointments and monitor medication), the probationer's family (although most mentally ill probationers do not have significant family support), and other treatment providers.

One thing that is very different for a PO who specializes in managing mentally ill offenders is the number of hospital visits. The PO indicated that seven probationers out of his caseload of fifty-three were in a mental institution or a psychiatric wing of a hospital. He noted that he also has to work much more closely with the court and judges to educate them regarding the special circumstances of mentally ill offenders. Sometimes he has to be an advocate for the needs of these offenders and suggest that the court show more tolerance for minor violations of probation. Other times, the PO must act in an unconventional manner and have good relationships with court officials in order to get them to act beyond their normal operations. He gave the example of a female probationer who had stopped taking her psychotropic medication, had just had a baby, and was psychotic and delusional. During an evening telephone conversation with the PO in which he was urging her to go to a hospital for inpatient care, the woman threatened to kill her mother and stated that she did not want to go to the hospital. The PO asked her to hold for a minute, called the probation duty officer, obtained an immediate arrest warrant from the court, and asked the police to arrest the probationer immediately. Within half an hour, the police were at her front door to arrest her.

In closing, the PO indicated that to manage a caseload of mentally ill probationers a person must have a strong desire to do it and must be compassionate and understanding, as these probationers do not respond in the typical manner to threats of a probation violation. If they want to die and are planning to commit suicide, the PO cannot simply demand compliance. He noted that even for most compassionate individuals, this work could lead to a great deal of frustration.

probationers, and some findings actually found higher recidivism as caseload sizes were reduced. This is often explained as officers do not change their supervision style, and those focusing on surveillance are even more likely to find and violate offenders for minor technical violations of conditions. However, a 2011 study reported that when controlling for the type of supervision and approach taken by officers, probation outcomes are more successful when evidence-based

TABLE 4.1	Supervision Caseload Approach	
Case priority	**Hours per month**	**Total caseload**
High	4 hours	30 cases
Medium	2 hours	60 cases
Low	1 hour	120 cases[a]

[a]Based on a 120 work hour per officer per month.

Source: Based on Matthew T. DeMichele, *Probation and Parole's Growing Caseloads and Workload Allocations: Strategies for Managerial Decision Making* (Lexington, KY: May 2007), p. 16.

practices are implemented, meaning that probation agencies use those functions found to be linked to reduced recidivism. Those officers with reduced caseloads that spend their time helping identify treatment needs and working with offenders and treatment agencies to address these problems can effectively reduce recidivism.[20]

Conditions of Probation

The fundamental premise of probation is that offenders must meet certain conditions to successfully complete their probation and avoid having their supervision suspended and being sent to prison. Jurisdictions have **standard conditions of probation** that must be followed by every probationer, and judges usually have the authority to impose **special conditions of probation**. These special conditions are tailored to meet the program needs for an offender, or can be imposed to address an offender's specific risk to the community. During probation, judges may modify conditions as they determine that offenders are performing satisfactorily and no longer need certain conditions or are performing poorly and require added conditions as a part of their supervision.

Standard conditions of probation usually include the following:

1. The probationer shall not leave the judicial district without permission of the PO or the court.
2. The probationer shall report to the PO as directed and shall submit truthful and complete reports.
3. The probationer shall answer truthfully all inquiries by the PO and follow his or her instructions.
4. The probationer shall maintain employment.
5. The probationer shall notify the PO of all changes of address within seventy-two hours.
6. The probationer shall refrain from the excessive use of alcohol and is prohibited from the use of controlled substances.
7. The probationer shall not associate with criminals.
8. The probationer shall not commit any crimes.

Examples of special conditions of probation include requiring drug or alcohol counseling, drug testing, mental health counseling, or vocational training; avoiding a particular person or group; or staying out of bars or poolrooms. Judges may also impose any of the intermediate sanctions described later in this chapter. Judges have considerable discretion in imposing special conditions of probation. If offenders

standard conditions of probation
conditions that must be followed by every probationer

special conditions of probation
conditions of probation tailored to meet the needs for a particular offender; they can be imposed to meet the specific risks or needs of an individual offender

One way to monitor compliance with conditions of no illegal drug use is through random drug testing. Inmates submit urine samples that are sent to a lab for testing. Photo by Richard P. Seiter.

technical violations

violations of conditions of community supervision, without commission of a new crime

new-crime violations

violation of the condition of probation prohibiting the commission of any additional crimes

meet the conditions of their probation, the supervising probation agency may recommend that the sentencing court end the period of probation, terminate supervision, and close the case.

Revocation of Probation

If probationers violate or fail to meet any conditions of their probation, they are subject to having their probation revoked and their original prison sentence imposed. Probationers can have their probation revoked for either **technical violations** (not meeting all the conditions of their supervision) or **new-crime violations** (violating the condition of not committing additional crimes). For minor violations of technical conditions, it is unlikely that probation will be revoked, but for continued violations, serious technical violations, or commission of a new crime, probation most likely will be revoked. One exception resulted from a 1983 U.S. Supreme Court ruling in *Bearden v. Georgia*, in which the Court decided that failure to make restitution payments due to unemployment is not sufficient reason to revoke probation.[21]

For minor technical violations, POs usually have the discretion to determine how they will handle the infraction. They may warn probationers or intensify their own supervision of the case by making more community visits or increasing the reporting requirements. In most jurisdictions, officers cannot impose new conditions without requesting modification by the court. If these actions do not change behaviors or if the violation is serious, POs begin the formal probation revocation process.

The revocation process begins with a report of the violation and a recommendation for action by the supervising PO. The report goes to the sentencing court, and the probationer is given a copy of the alleged violations and directed to appear for a preliminary hearing. The probationer may be arrested and detained in jail until the preliminary hearing. The preliminary hearing is to determine whether there is probable cause to believe that the probationer has committed the violations. If so, a full revocation hearing is scheduled. The probationer may be taken into custody or released on bail or personal recognizance. The probationer may waive the full hearing and plead guilty to the violation at the preliminary hearing, and the judge will decide how to handle the violation at that time. If the case proceeds to a full revocation hearing, the PO bringing the charges and presenting evidence of the violation prepares a full report, and the probationer is given a copy. At the revocation hearing, the officer presents the violation report; the probationer may be represented by legal counsel and have the opportunity to testify and present evidence of his or her innocence of the violations.

In the 1970 case of *United States v. Birnbaum*, the U.S. Supreme Court determined that probation is a privilege and not a right.[22] Once probation is granted, however, the probationer has a liberty interest in avoiding incarceration, and probation cannot be revoked without limited due process requirements. In *Mempa v. Rhay* (1967), probationers were granted the right to legal counsel during the revocation hearing.[23] In 1972, the U.S. Supreme Court decided *Morrissey v. Brewer*, which spelled out the due process rights for parole violations hearings.[24] The next year, the Court decided *Gagnon v. Scarpelli*, which extended the *Morrissey* due process rights to probationers.[25] These include the following rights: (1) to be informed in writing of the alleged violations, (2) to have written notice in advance of the revocation process, (3) to have a preliminary hearing to determine whether there is probable cause, (4) to have a revocation hearing prior to the final decision, (5) to attend the hearings and present witnesses on their behalf, (6) to confront and cross-examine adverse witnesses, and (7) to receive a written decision noting the reasons for the decision.

Gagnon v. Scarpelli
a 1973 U.S. Supreme Court decision that created the due process requirements for revoking probation

If there is a finding of a violation, the court has three options: (1) reprimand and restore to supervision, (2) add conditions and restore to probation, or (3) revoke probation and order imprisonment under the original sentence. Over the past decades, there was an increase in the number of violations of probation and parole, as the "tough on crime" attitude and interest in public safety and avoiding risk encouraged POs to report more violations to the court than previously, and courts violated probationers and sent them to prison at a higher level. In 1978, 82 percent of state prison admissions were new court commitments (rather than probation or parole violations). But the percentage of new court commitments decreased to 57 percent by 2000. After the efforts across the states to reduce the number of probation and parole revocations, new court commitments as a percentage of prison admissions increased back to 70 percent in 2015.[26] Some of these reform efforts are discussed below.

And as indicated in Table 4.2, in 2006, only 58 percent of all probationers successfully completed probation. However, this has increased over the years, and in

TABLE 4.2 Probationers Who Exited Supervision, by Type of Exit, 2006–2015

Type of exit	2006	2008	2009	2010	2011	2012	2013	2014	2015
Total	100%	100%	100%	100%	100%	100%	100%	100%	100%
Completion	58%	63%	65%	65%	66%	68%	66%	64%	62%
Incarceration	18	17	16	16	16	15	15	15	15
Absconder	4	4	3	3	2	3	2	2	2
Discharged to custody, detainer, or warrant	1	1	1	1	1	1	–	–	–
Other unsatisfactory	13	10	10	11	9	9	11	13	13
Transferred to another probation agency	1	1	–	1	1	1	–	–	–
Death	1	1	1	1	1	1	–	–	–
Other	5	4	4	4	4	4	4	4	4
Estimated number	2,230,200	2,320,100	2,327,800	2,261,300	2,189,100	2,089,800	2,131,300	2,129,100	2,043,200

Source: Bureau of Justice Statistics, Annual Probation Survey, 2006–2012, updated from Probation and Parole in the United States, 2015.

2012, 68 percent completed probation. In the "You Make the Decision" box at the end of the chapter, you are asked to consider whether to revoke the probation of an offender who is not complying with all the conditions of his probation.

Issues Regarding Probation

Many issues are discussed when describing the current system of probation operations and determining how the system should be changed or improved. How are offenders supervised in the community, and what is the role of the PO? POs' roles have changed over the past several years, yet there is still little understanding of what they do and how they should do it. Does probation work? Many studies have resulted in serious questions as to whether probation is effective. The true answer depends on what probation is expected to do and what is determined to be successful. And over the past decade, there have been many attempts to reform probation and "reinvest" resources in the most cost-efficient sentencing alternative that still provides public safety. Finally, how do you allocate resources for probation supervision? Most jurisdictions use some method of classifying offenders by risk and need to both create supervision guidelines and expectations and to determine how many offenders a PO will supervise.

Officers going into the field to conduct home visits usually are armed, wear a protective vest, and carry other equipment similar to a police officer. Photo by Richard P. Seiter.

A Changing Style of Supervision

Even while the public recognizes that not every criminal offender can be sent to prison, there continues to be public concern with the effectiveness of probation, spurred by the perception that probations receive minimal supervision, and therefore society is not protected against the repeat crimes by those allowed to remain in the community. However, the manner in which a parolee or probationer is supervised has (until a few years ago) received little attention, even though its importance has always been recognized. In the classic review of prisons and parole, Glaser notes, "The principal functions of parole supervision have been procurement of information on the parolee. . .and facilitating and graduating the transition between imprisonment and complete freedom. . .these functions presumably are oriented to the goals of protecting the public and rehabilitating the offender."[27] Soon thereafter, Alberty analyzed the comparison between styles of parole supervision and violation rates and defined supervision as "the means used to accomplish the goals of protecting society and rehabilitating the offender."[28]

Until the late 1960s, probation and parole supervision focused on the casework style of supervision, or restoring offenders to the community.[29] Under the casework style, officers considered it their responsibility to work with offenders in finding jobs, getting into treatment programs, dealing with problems, and successfully completing supervision. However, from the late 1980s until the early

2000s, there was an increasing reliance on surveillance, or closely monitoring offenders to catch them when they fail to meet all required conditions. This approach emphasizes enforcing compliance with the conditions of supervision, timely detection of violations, and expeditious revocation when violations occur.

An example of the emphasis on public safety is how officers visit offenders' residences or places of employment. These visits lead to concerns about the safety of officers. Therefore, most agencies allow officers to carry a weapon when doing a home visit, and some require them to go with a partner. The safety of officers is a serious and real concern, but there is also a concern that the arming of officers moves supervision even further away from a casework model to more of a policing or surveillance model.

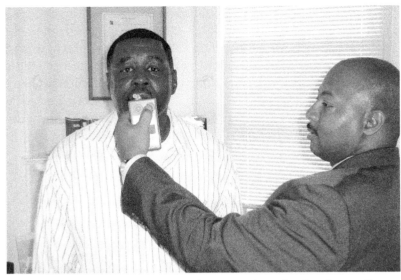

One example of additional conditions and methods of surveillance is the regular use of a Breathalyzer to detect whether an offender supervised in the community has been drinking. Photo by Richard P. Seiter.

This transition from casework to surveillance has occurred for many reasons. First, to emphasize monitoring and public safety, more conditions have been placed on offenders under community supervision. Adams and Roth found that between 1987 and 1996, the percentage of federal offenders with at least one special condition (participation in substance abuse, drug testing, and electronic monitoring) increased from 67 percent to 91 percent,[30] and by 2001, states involved in probation and parole supervision reported conducting 6,403,990 drug tests and revoked 90,796 offenders as a result of a positive test for drug use.[31] Second, there has been very limited tolerance for risk to the community. Instead of focusing on rehabilitation and characteristics of individual offenders, parole and probation agencies now use actuarial methods to classify offenders and manage risk for aggregate populations. These actuarial assessments can result in a psychology of adding surveillance techniques rather than treatment programs to an individual's supervision.

Third, the hiring and training of community supervision officers have changed. Historically, officers had a social work or clinical background and were trained in counseling and rehabilitation of offenders. Today, the majority of entering officers have a college degree with a major of criminal justice, with less than one-third majoring in psychology, sociology, or social work,[32] and training and orientation for officers is increasingly in line with that of law enforcement officers. Finally, community officers and supervisors must be sensitive to public safety, and are cautious when it comes to handling even minor technical violations by community offenders. If that offender later commits a serious crime, the actions of the officer for not acting on the minor violation will be called into question, and in some jurisdictions the officer or agency can be liable to the victim of a subsequent crime. As a result of the focus on surveillance, the number of probation violations rose significantly, and thousands of offenders were sent to prison for technical violations even without commission of a new crime. By 2007, of the 751,593 new admissions to state and federal prisons, 253,856 (33.7 percent) were for technical violations of supervision.[33] This contrasts with 1980, when parole violators constituted only 18 percent of all admissions.[34]

The difficult economic times of the past decade have caused a renewed interest on how we supervise offenders in the community and the result it has on probation and parole revocations. In a pure surveillance style, community officers focus on supervising offenders closely enough to catch them when they fail, but many jurisdictions are revamping their supervision to help offenders be successful and reduce the costly return to prison. An example is in Kansas, which is closing three correctional facilities to save money, and targeting a 20 percent reduction in probationers violated and sent to prison. Kansas has implemented behavior modification as a part of probation supervision. A correctional official noted, "It used to be that it was more about waiting for them [probationers] to mess up and send them back to prison. In this time and this economy, you can't afford to keep doing that. There is a better way to do business."[35]

To save money, Hawaii focused on improving probation, as some judges were sentencing offenders to ten years in prison because they missed appointments with their POs. Judge Steven Alm changed sentencing and probation violators are immediately sent to jail, but only for a few days. As they comply with their probation expectations, they get more freedom and have fewer check-ins with their PO. Modeling the Hawaii approach, Ft. Worth Texas created the Supervision with Immediate Enforcement (SWIFT) court. Offenders supervised by the court have experienced both a reduction in technical probation violations and a reduction of positive drug tests.[36]

A recently advocated supervision approach is the probation or parole officer as a "change agent." This approach is somewhat between the casework and surveillance model. It often begins with the use of a risk-need-responsivity (RNR) model to match the level of service to the offender's level of risk and providing treatment tailored to the needs of the offender.[37] POs focus on what it takes to change the offenders' behavior, and it results in the development of a strategic-therapeutic intervention plan that combines casework and treatment with surveillance and accountability.[38] And Maryland has moved to an evidence-based supervision model that begins with a risk and need assessment to identify treatment and control needs and makes the supervision officer an instrument for facilitating offender change. This Proactive Community Supervision (PCS) model has resulted in fewer rearrests (30 percent for the PCS and 42 percent for traditional models) among offenders. The conclusion is that supervision styles can be transformed and achieve public safety goals by focusing on positive offender change.[39] And this movement to reducing prison populations and saving money by focusing on keeping offenders in the community continues, even while the federal government is advocating a return to tougher sentencing practices. A recent *New York Times* article notes how several conservative states (Louisiana, Texas, and South Carolina as examples) have expanded alternatives to incarceration while U.S. Attorney General Jeff Sessions has "charted the opposite course."[40]

Probation supervision reform has also been influenced by a concept called *broken-windows* probation. This concept mimics the philosophy of community policing, in that all broken windows in a neighborhood are to be promptly repaired, as this small indication of a lack of community concern leads to a larger instability and criminal activity in the community. As such, probation supervision follows the lead of community policing by partnering with citizen groups, churches, and other neighborhood organizations to take joint responsibility for supervising offenders. Emphasizing public safety first, broken-windows probation also allocates resources according to risk and need assessments, locates POs in the probationers' neighborhoods, and uses graduated sanctions, such as house arrest, EM, and mandatory substance abuse treatment.[41] As a result of some of the reforms noted above as well as the Justice Reinvestment initiatives in several states described below, in 2015, there were 608,318 prisoners admitted to state and federal prisons, of whom only 164,626 (27 percent) were for violating their community supervision.[42]

Effectiveness

Studies of regular probation (without some type of enhanced supervision) have demonstrated mixed results in probation's effectiveness in protecting society from future crimes. A 1986 review of 79,000 felons sentenced to probation in thirty-two counties across seventeen states revealed that within three years of sentencing, while still on probation, 43 percent were rearrested for a felony.[43] Yet in the most recent report of probation in the United States, 62 percent of offenders exiting probation during 2015 were successful completions, while 15 percent were incarcerated, and another 15 percent either absconded or had other unsatisfactory exits from supervision.[44] Although these studies question the effectiveness of probation, other studies show some success of probation in reducing recidivism, depending on the seriousness of the offender population, the length of the follow-up, and the type of surveillance provided.

One early review of probation outcomes gives conflicting data. Clear and Braga examined the success of a group of both felony and misdemeanor probationers and found that 80 percent completed their terms without a new arrest.[45] However, Langan and Cunniff examined the same data, but only for felony probationers, and found that 43 percent were rearrested within three years.[46] A review of seventeen evaluations of felony probation found rearrest rates as low as 12 percent and as high as 65 percent.[47] This review concluded that probation without adequate surveillance and treatment is not effective. However, well-managed and adequately funded probation programs do reduce recidivism.

All of the preceding evaluations only cite success rates, with no comparison of alternative sentencing outcomes. In some evaluations, probation success rates are compared to the success of ex-inmates. Probationers' recidivism is consistently lower, but that is expected because offenders who receive probation are a less serious group than those who are sentenced to prison. However, in a study with groups of 511 probationers and 511 parolees matched to have an equal likelihood of recidivism, the results over a two-year follow-up indicated that probationers were more successful; 72 percent of parolees and 63 percent of probationers were rearrested, 53 percent of parolees and 38 percent of probationers had new charges filed, and 47 percent of parolees and 31 percent of probationers were incarcerated in jail or prison.[48] This finding suggests that, although probationers have high rates of recidivism, prison parolees do even worse.

Another study examined outcome by size of caseload and officers' uses of evidence-based practices in the supervision of probationers. This 2011 study reported that probation outcomes are more successful when evidence-based practices are implemented. When officers have reduced caseloads and spend their time helping identify treatment needs and working with offenders and treatment agencies to address these problems, there is a significant reduction in recidivism.[49] A good summary of a variety of approaches to probation and their resultant effectiveness was completed by Skeem and Manchak. In summary, surveillance styles of supervision are largely ineffective; however, a "hybrid" approach somewhere between surveillance and treatment seems most promising in reducing recidivism.[50]

In a study examining arrest rates and offenses of offenders on federal probation and supervised release found fairly positive results, as less than 11 percent were arrested for a serious offense in the first year of supervision, 17 percent were arrested within two years, and almost 23 percent were arrested within three years. And a second study of federal probation and supervised release looked at offenders who successfully completed their supervision. Within one year after supervision, 6 percent were arrested within one year, 12 percent were arrested within two years, and 18 percent were arrested within three years.[51]

Some studies also cite the low cost of probation compared to other sanctions. A recent study by the Vera Institute examined operational and collateral costs of incarceration, and found the average cost per inmate for 2011 was $31,286 per year or $85.72 per day.[52] Costs for regular probation were reported to be an average of only $3.42 per day in 2008.[53] Therefore, particularly during tight budget times, elected officials and correctional administrators continue to support the use of probation, even while looking for ways to increase its effectiveness to protect society and deter crime. Therefore, many jurisdictions are combining probation with one of the below addressed intermediate sanctions to save money while providing safe and effective supervision of offenders in the community.

Overall, while there are many approaches to supervision style and approach that seem effective, a four-decade "look back" fails to show a significant difference in recidivism reduction due to probation versus imprisonment.[54] But, in an effort to focus on reducing recidivism, in order to reduce probationer recidivism, a growing body of knowledge and experience identifies four core practices that most directly improve probation agencies' success. These best practices are as follows:

1. Effectively assess probationers' criminogenic risk and need, as well as their strengths;
2. Employ smart, tailored supervision strategies;
3. Use incentives and graduated sanctions to respond promptly to probationers behaviors; and
4. Implement performance-driven personnel management practices that promote and reward recidivism reduction.[55]

Reforming Probation

All of the above-cited studies illustrate how historically probation has compared in success, against other sanctions, or are cost-efficient. Over the past decade, as prison numbers and costs have climbed, several states have restructured their sentencing and community supervision approaches to "reinvest" in those approaches that are the most cost-effective, while maintaining public safety. The Justice Reinvestment Initiative is a partnership between the U.S. Department of Justice and the Pew Charitable Trusts. Working with the Council of State Governments Justice Center, several states have begun or completed the reinvestment process and in most cases, have both reduced recidivism and reduced projected costs for corrections. A recent report of seven states that participated in such reinvestment shows that in each state, there were reductions in "revocation recidivism" or the return to incarceration from probation or parole due to either arrest and prosecution for a new crime or due to a violation of the technical requirement of their supervision.[56] Reductions of revocation recidivism for these seven states are as follows:

Arizona	29%
Colorado	24%
Georgia	35%
Michigan	43%
North Carolina	42%
South Carolina	46%
Texas	33%

One state that has received much attention for their reforms is North Carolina. From 2000 until 2010, the state prison population had climbed 27 percent to over 40,000, and the budget had increased by 49 percent to $1.3 billion. And the growth was expected to continue and another $500 million would be needed by 2017. So North Carolina used the Justice Reinvestment data-driven approach to identify reforms that could be made, much by transforming their probation supervision approach. In 2009, more than one-half of their prison admissions were because of probation failures; three-quarters of which were for technical violations only. State officials reviewed their supervision practices, finding that everyone was supervised the same, regardless of their risk or need. The state initiated several reforms, to include: (1) adding options for officers other than revocation when probationers missed appointments, curfews, or failed drug tests; (2) trained officers to improve the quality of their interactions with offenders by using evidence based practices that reduce recidivism; and (3) giving officers the authority to immediately place offenders in substance use treatment programs or put them under electronic monitoring without waiting for a judicial hearing. A three-year look at these reforms found that from 2011 to 2014, the state prison population fell by 3,400 inmates, they closed ten prisons, and 175 probation and parole officers were added to guide offenders into treatment with the greatest chance for success.[57]

Another recent example of these reforms took place in Georgia. In 2012, the Georgia legislature enacted HB 1176, to prioritize the use of prison beds for serious and violent offenders, and allow diversion yet accountability while in the community for others. In 2015, they enacted HB 310 to reorganize probation and parole, and in 2016, implemented SB 367 to allow drug-related mandatory sentences to be eligible for community supervision. Through these reforms, Georgia quickly experienced a 6 percent decrease in the prison population, saving the state $264 million in corrections costs and reinvesting $56 million of those savings into recidivism reduction strategies to include accountability (specialty) courts, add evidence-based programming, and enhance reentry. Even with these reforms, the state had the highest use of probation in the country and continued to work to relieve wasted probation money and other resources.[58] Georgia had an extremely high rate of incarceration, and in 2015, two-thirds of the admissions to prison were for violating a condition of probation or parole or committing a new crime while under community supervision. Therefore, in 2017, SB 174 was enacted to reduce lengthy probation terms, improve probation practices, and reduce high probation officer caseloads.

Before SB 174, Georgia had the highest probation rate in the United States, with 6,161 probationers per 100,000 residents, compared to the national average of 1,568 per 100,000 populations. Their felony probation sentences averaged sixty-three months, one of the longest in the United States. Georgia costs for 2014 were $20,509 per incarcerated prisoner per year and $672 per year for each probationer supervised in the community. And in comparing recidivism rates, for nonviolent offenders, 22.9 percent of those sentenced to prison were returned to prison within three years, while a comparison group had 10.3 percent of those on probation returned to prison.[59] Reform efforts included legislative changes to modify some mandatory sentencing practices while giving judges more discretion, and some executive/administrative changes such as implementing automation of pre-sentence assessments, implementing day reporting centers, and realigning budgeting to focus resources on the changes to be made.

One of the initiatives was to move from a reactive to a proactive approach. The reactive approach focused on ensuring probationers were aware of the conditions of probation, checking to ensure they complied with these conditions, performing enforcement functions (drug testing and curfew checking), and measuring outcome by process data (number of appointments made, completion of drug tests). The proactive approach includes assessing probationers for risk and need while focusing officer time on the highest risk/need, developing case plans with performance-based objectives, linking probationers to treatment services, and measuring outcomes by progress made toward case plan objectives. As well, SB 174 created an early termination from supervision policy for certain qualifying offenses, and creating administrative caseloads for those who are qualified and have performed well under supervision. As a result of these changes, projections are that by 2022, 44,104 fewer people will be on probation, 140 probation officers could be reassigned to high-risk caseloads, and $7.3 million in spending will be averted.[60] The reforms in Georgia are a good example and representative of the several changes across the United States. From 2007 to 2015, fourteen states have passed legislation to implement evidence-based practices and twenty states have passed legislation to implement risk and needs assessments.[61]

Probation Classification Systems

A critical issue for successfully supervising offenders in the community is classifying them in terms of risk to the community and need for treatment programs. Classification identifies offender risks and matches appropriate supervision strategies to maximize the resource allocation and focus on public safety. Models of risk assessment were first developed for probation in the mid-1970s and quickly gained support. In 1976, the U.S. Comptroller General tested the predictive power of community risk-prediction models and concluded that "probation prediction models could improve probation systems operations by allocating resources to offenders who most need help.... Model sources appeared to be useful in determining supervision levels and more successfully selected probationers for early release."[62] A National Institute of Corrections report titled *Directions for Community Corrections in the 1990s* noted, "In general, one effective way to increase decision reliability is to make visible the criteria for decisions. For that reason, we advocate the use of statistically based devices to classify offenders according to relative risk."[63]

community classification systems

risk assessments that predict the chance of new crimes being committed; they are used to determine the level of supervision an offender will receive in the community

Community classification systems score offenders based on their offense background and personal characteristics. Figures 4.2 and 4.3 illustrate the Missouri model used to determine levels of community supervision. Probation and parole officers initially complete the Client Analysis Scale-Risk for the offender (Figure 4.2). Each case is scored on the number of prior convictions, employment status, age, present offense, and whether the present offense is a felony. The scores are combined to determine the permanent risk score, which is used to determine the classification of risk and the supervision level.

The highest risk level, *intensive supervision*, applies to offenders posing a significant risk of committing a new offense. They are assigned to smaller caseloads, must report at least once per week to the supervising officer, and are visited two to three times per month at home or at work. Most probationers are placed on *regular supervision*, with larger caseloads and fewer reporting requirements. For offenders who pose little risk to the community, *minimum supervision*, with caseloads as high as 300 offenders, may be satisfactory. These offenders often have contact with their PO only every few months and are basically responsible themselves for following the conditions of their supervision. Some jurisdictions also have *administrative supervision*, under which offenders have no contact with a

STATE OF MISSOURI DEPARTMENT OF CORRECTIONS **CLIENT ANALYSIS SCALE-RISK**		OFFICER CODE
NAME	NUMBER	DATE

PRIOR CONVICTIONS (ADULT-FELONY, MISDEMEANOR, CRIMINAL ORDINANCE INCLUDING SIS)

☐ 1	☐ 2	☐ 3
NONE	1 OR 2 PRIORS	3 OR MORE

EMPLOYMENT/VOCATION

☐ 0	☐ 1	☐ 2
FULL TIME WORK	PART TIME WORK	UNEMPLOYED

AGE (AT ASSIGNMENT)

☐ 0	☐ 1	☐ 2
30 YEARS OR OVER	22 TO 29 YEARS	21 YEARS OR YOUNGER

PRESENT OFFENSE (CHARGE FOR WHICH CONVICTED) (ROBBERY, BURGLARY, STEALING, FORGERY, SEXUAL ASSAULT AS PER RSMo 589.015)

☐ 0	☐ 1
NO	YES

PRESENT OFFENSE A FELONY (OFFICIAL CHARGE)

☐ 0	☐ 1
NO	YES

RISK SCORE

FIGURE 4.2 Missouri Client Analysis Scale-Risk   Source: Provided by the Missouri Department of Corrections (August 29, 2017).

STATE OF MISSOURI
DEPARTMENT OF CORRECTIONS
BOARD OF PROBATION AND PAROLE
SUPERVISION REPORT FORM

OFFICE USE ONLY
☐ INITIAL SCALE
☐ ENTER

OFFICER NAME & NUMBER

DOC NUMBER

NAME	HOME TELEPHONE	CELL PHONE

ADDRESS	CITY	STATE	ZIP CODE

MAILING ADDRESS (if different than above)	CITY	STATE	ZIP CODE

WITH WHOM DO YOU RESIDE? (Include names and relationships)

EMERGENCY CONTACT (Include names, relationship)

EMERGENCY CONTACT ADDRESS	TELEPHONE NUMBER	CELL PHONE NUMBER

NAME OF PRESENT EMPLOYER	EMPLOYER'S PHONE NUMBER

PRESENT EMPLOYER ADDRESS	CITY	STATE	ZIP CODE

NAME OF EMPLOYMENT SUPERVISOR	IS YOUR EMPLOYER AWARE YOU ARE ON PROBATION/PAROLE? ☐ YES ☐ NO	TOTAL INCOME FOR THE PAST 30 DAYS?

DO YOU OWN A VEHICLE? ☐ YES ☐ NO	MODEL	YEAR	LICENSE PLATE NUMBER	VEHICLE COLOR DESCRIPTION

HAVE YOU BEEN ARRESTED IN THE PAST 30 DAYS? ☐ NO ☐ YES - DATE OF ARREST;	ARRESTING POLICE DEPARTMENT	CHARGE(S)

SIGNATURE	ACCEPTED BY	DATE	TIME ☐ A.M. ☐ P.M.

DO NOT WRITE BELOW THIS LINE

_____ **EMPLOYMENT/EDUCATIONAL/VOCATIONAL**
0 = FULL-TIME FOR PAST 3 MONTHS
1 = PART-TIME; SCHOOL; TRAINING; FULL-TIME FOR LESS THAN 3 MONTHS; UNEMPLOYMENT COMPENSATION
2 = UNEMPLOYED; UNDEREMPLOYED (LESS THAN 20 HOURS PER WEEK)
DATE EMPLOYED/UNEMPLOYED _____

_____ **LEGAL (EXCLUDES PRESENT OFFENSE)**
1 = NO ARRESTS IN THE PAST 3 MONTHS
2 = NO CONVICTIONS, 1 ARREST IN THE PAST 3 MONTHS
3 = 2 OR MORE ARRESTS, PENDING CHARGE, OR CONVICTION IN PAST 3 MONTHS
DATE OF ARREST/CONVICTION _____

_____ **TECHNICAL VIOLATIONS**
1 = NO TECHNICAL VR/MANDATORY CITATION IN THE PAST 6 MONTHS
2 = TECHNICAL VR/MANDATORY CITATION IN THE 4–6 MONTHS
3 = TECHNICAL VR/MANDATORY CITATION IN THE PAST 3 MONTHS OR PENDING REVOCATION
DATE OF LAST TECHNICAL VIOLATION/MANDATORY CITATION _____
CONDITIONS CITED _____

_____ **SUBSTANCE ABUSE**
1 = NO DRUG USE/ALCOHOL ABUSE IN THE PAST 6 MONTHS
2 = DRUG USE/ALCOHOL ABUSE IN THE PAST 4–6 MONTHS
3 = DRUG USE/ALCOHOL ABUSE IN THE PAST 3 MONTHS
DATE OF LAST USE/PROBLEM _____

PROBLEM CODES: 1 = NO PROBLEM 2 = IDENTIFIED HISTORY
3 = PROBLEM PAST 4–6 MONTHS 4 = PROBLEM PAST 3 MONTHS

_____ **SOCIAL**
0 = NO PROBLEM
1 = PROBLEM NOT REQUIRING INTERVENTION*
2 = PROBLEM REQUIRING INTERVENTION*
DATE OF LAST OCCURRENCE _____

*A CORRESPONDING SOCIAL CATEGORY MUST BE MARKED

SUBSTANCE ABUSE
_____ ALCOHOL
_____ MARIJUANA/HASHISH
_____ OPIATERS
_____ STIMULANTS COCAINE
_____ DEPRESSANTS
_____ INHALANTS/SOLVENTS
_____ HALLUCINOGENS

SOCIAL
_____ MENTAL PROBLEMS
_____ FAMILY PROBLEMS
_____ FINANCIAL
_____ ASSAULT/AGGRESSIVE
_____ PHYSICAL
_____ REPORTING

_____ # UA_8
_____ # POSITIVE UA_5
_____ # PENDING UA RESULTS

NEED SCORE	RISK SCORE	SUPERVISION LEVEL	☐ DANGEROUS FELON	☐ SEX OFFENDER (NOT ELIGIBLE FOR INTERVENTION LEVEL 1)

NOTES:

MO 931-3698 DI-2009

FIGURE 4.3 Missouri Probation and Parole Monthly Supervision Report Form Source: Provided by the Missouri Department of Corrections (August 29, 2017).

parole or PO. However, they still must meet their conditions and commit no further crimes or their original parole or probation will be revoked. Administrative supervision is used only after low-risk offenders demonstrate a good adjustment to supervision. After the initial classification of risk, each offender is scored on the Monthly Supervision Report (Figure 4.3) to review the status of the supervision and determine the need for changes.

In Missouri, offenders with a risk score of ten or more and a need score of eleven or more are automatically assigned to participate in intensive supervision or another special-supervision caseload. If the review indicates that considerable supervision time has passed without a violation, a lower level of supervision will likely be assigned. Classification processes are extremely valuable to match resources to offenders' risk and needs and help officers make decisions regarding supervision level, revocation, or successful termination of supervision.

A report entitled *Implementing Evidence-Based Policy and Practice in Community Corrections* identifies eight principles that can reduce the risk of community offenders failing their supervision requirements.[64] These include the following:

1. Assess actuarial risk/needs—offenders should be assessed using a valid actuarial instrument as an ongoing process rather than a single event.
2. Enhance intrinsic motivation—offenders are more likely to change behavior if they have an intrinsic motivation, which is influenced by respectful and constructive interactions with officers, treatment providers, and institutional employees.
3. Target interventions—below are listed several effective target treatment of offenders (risk, need, motivation, gender, etc.), as well as treatment characteristics (the intensity and timing as well as the evidence of effectiveness with specific groups).
4. Skill train with directed practice—cognitive and behavioral treatment methods are most effective when delivered by well-trained providers.
5. Increase positive reinforcement—POs should use a high ratio of positive to negative reinforcement as a part of supervision.
6. Engage ongoing support in natural communities—pro-social support is most effective if delivered in the community in which offenders live.
7. Measure relevant processes/practices—it is important to measure progress and outcomes.
8. Provide measurement feedback—the measures of success must be fed back to offenders to hold them accountable and reinforce positive change.

The target interventions fall into five principles:

- The *Risk Principle* is to target and prioritize supervision and treatment resources for higher risk offenders.
- The *Need Principle* emphasizes focusing the resources toward the criminogenic needs that correlate with the likelihood of committing new crimes.
- The *Responsivity Principle* recognizes that not all types of treatments are equally successful with every type of offender population.
- *Dosage* recognizes the first six to nine months of postrelease supervision as the highest risk of reoffending.
- The *Treatment Principle* is to make the treatment plan an integrated component of the full sentence and sanction requirements.

Important for implementing these principles is that they are reflected in the policies, procedures, and day-to-day work of the supervision agency, officers, and treatment providers. The most effective style of supervision is when officers "strike a balance between an enforcement and intervention role; clarify their role with the client; model pro-social behaviors, show empathy without diminishing accountability; and focus interactions on problem solving and addressing criminogenic needs."[65]

A very impressive example of using risk assessment and evidence-based programming is the Tennessee Model of Seamless Supervision put in place in 2017. The T360 (as it is called) is an integrated approach that identifies offender risk and need, creates a treatment and supervision program based on this, and provides a cohesive and continued treatment programs "trilaterally," or across probation, prison, and parole. Tennessee adopted the Status Risk Offender Needs Guide (STRONG-R), which was developed by Washington State University and has proven both reliable and predictable.[66] Seamless supervision also provides a variety of evidence-based programs that community officers can use to provide treatment for offenders and as alternatives to violation and return to prison. Programs include day reporting centers, community resource centers as a "one-stop shop" for high-risk offender needs, substance-abuse peer counseling, and transition centers to aid inmates in preparing for release. These combine with supervision that continues to focus offenders on accountability, discipline, and structure.[67]

Intermediate Sanctions

Defining Intermediate Sanctions

intermediate sanctions
midrange dispositions that fall between probation and imprisonment

Intermediate sanctions are midrange dispositions that fall between probation and imprisonment. Until the past few decades in many U.S. jurisdictions, judges imposing sentences for any but the most trivial of crimes had to choose between what seemed to be "doing something" (imprisonment) and "doing nothing" (probation). However, the problems of prison and jail crowding and the challenge of tight budgets have forced policymakers to develop and more regularly use punishments that fall between these two sanctions. Intermediate sanctions are commonly referred to as *midlevel punishments* and are designed to fill the gap that is widely perceived to exist between probation and prison.

Several factors have been cited in support of intermediate sanctions:

1. Unhappiness with regular probation supervision
2. An increase in the number in prisons and prison overcrowding
3. Tightening of budgets by states and an inability to continue to fund high numbers of offenders sentenced to prison
4. A belief that intermediate sanctions are more effective in providing effective rehabilitative programs
5. A realization that solid ties in the community are critical to the success of offenders and the knowledge that keeping offenders in the community helps them maintain these ties
6. Proportionality of sentencing, in that with a continuum of sanctions the sentence can be crafted to better fit the crime and offender

Since the recession that began in 2008, states began examining the options for use of community sanctions to save money and not undermine public safety.

As noted above, the cost of probation supervision in was $3.42 per day, whereas the average daily cost of imprisoning an offender was $85.72. In comparing the costs of various sentencing options, the Pew Center suggested that U.S. sentencing policies resulted in the discovery that "one unmistakable policy truth has emerged: We cannot build our way to public safety."[68] The current use of intermediate sanctions includes economic sanctions, community service, intensive supervised probation, house arrest, community residential centers, split sentences, shock incarceration (boot camps), and shock probation. Electronic monitoring (EM) often accompanies some of these midrange punishments.

As noted above, the Justice Reinvestment initiatives have often been used to realign resources to look at data-driven and cost-effective alternatives to prison. Another approach often used for such realignment are community corrections acts. A **community corrections act** is passed by a state legislature in order to encourage counties to develop local alternatives to the use of state prisons. As counties reduce the number of prison commitments, the state will reimburse them for a prescribed amount. The county can decide the type of alternatives they create, and judges then sentence suitable offenders to them. The earliest realignment of funds began with the California Probation Subsidy Act in 1965. In 1973, Minnesota passed the first comprehensive community corrections act. Since that time, approximately two-thirds of the states have enacted such legislation.

community corrections acts
acts passed by state legislatures to encourage counties to develop alternatives to prison, reduce the number of people sent to prison from the county, and reimburse the county for costs based on the reduction of prison commitments

Types of Intermediate Sanctions

Economic Sanctions

Economic sanctions use money as the means of carrying out criminal sanctions, such as fines, restitution, or forfeiture of assets. In most cases, economic sanctions are attached as a condition of probation; however, for minor offenses, they may stand alone as punishments for crimes. When people think of economic sanctions, they usually consider small fines for minor offenses. However, fines and forfeiture of assets can be of very large amounts. For instance, during the 1980s, junk bond king Michael Milken defrauded investors of what was estimated to be hundreds of millions of dollars. As a result, in addition to a short prison term, Milken was fined $600 million, although it was believed to be far less than he made from his illegal trading.

Fines are a requirement that offenders pay some dollar amount to the court as punishment for committing the offense. Fines can be a set amount for each type of crime or can be more creative and reflect the individual situation of each offense and offender. Courts usually consider both the seriousness of the offense and the economic gain by the offender to determine the amount of a fine. For instance, fines may be appropriate for white-collar offenders, who have a minimal risk of future criminality and perhaps no need for any rehabilitative programs; the sanction focuses on pure punishment, deterrence, and opportunity to repay the victims or society for the wrong done by the offense.

fines
a requirement that offenders pay some dollar amount to the court as punishment for committing the offense

Although fines are usually paid to the court, a second type of economic sanction is **offender restitution**, which requires offenders to repay society for the harm created by the offense. Restitution can take several forms. One type of offender restitution is **victim compensation**, in which offenders repay their victims directly for their losses and harm caused by the offense. As noted in the discussion of PSIs, federal and many state courts allow victims to submit victimization statements to detail the amount of loss they incurred from the crime. Sentencing judges take this into account when sentencing offenders, and often use the submitted amount for assigning a level of victim compensation. Offenders can also pay

offender restitution
a requirement that offenders repay society for the harm created by the offense

victim compensation
offenders repay their victims directly for their losses and harm caused by the offense

cost of supervision

offenders have to pay for some costs associated with their supervision in the community, such as drug testing or electronic monitoring

asset forfeiture

the authorized seizure by the government of money, negotiable instruments, securities, or other things of value that were obtained through illegal activities

restitution through *community service*. Community service can include cleaning up trash in a public area or counseling teenagers about the negative results of drug use. Community service is included here as an economic sanction, as it is often used when offenders do not have funds from which to pay a fine or make restitution. It is then referred to as a "fine on their time," so that indigent offenders do not have to serve prison or jail time merely because they lack the fiscal ability to pay a fine. Offenders may also be required to pay for their **cost of supervision** by paying to the court the costs affiliated with their supervision, such as drug testing, counseling, or EM, reducing the cost to the taxpayers.

Another extremely effective economic sanction is **asset forfeiture**, the authorized seizure by the government of money, negotiable instruments, securities, or other things of value that were obtained through illegal activities. Created over the past thirty years, asset forfeiture enables courts to punish offenders by taking away assets they accumulated as a result of their criminal activity, ensuring that "crime doesn't pay." Asset forfeiture was first authorized in the RICO (Racketeer Influenced and Corrupt Organization) statute, a part of the federal Organized Crime Control Act of 1970. RICO statutes were created to aid law enforcement in investigating and prosecuting organized crime figures by making it unlawful for anyone involved in a pattern of racketeering to derive any income or proceeds from that activity and allowing the government to seize anything of value that can be shown to have been acquired through the racketeering activity.

Asset forfeiture is also regularly used in the prosecution and punishment of drug offenders. When the federal government expanded its powers and more aggressively targeted the arrest and prosecution of drug offenders during the late 1900s, asset forfeiture became a valuable strategy. As property assets are seized, they are auctioned off and the proceeds are divided among the federal and local law enforcement agencies that participated in the criminal investigation. Local law enforcement agencies use these funds to enhance their own capabilities to target drug crimes, leading to more arrests and prosecution.

Intensive Supervised Probation

intensive supervised probation

supervision of community offenders with higher than average risk, through smaller caseloads and very close monitoring of activities

When regular probation supervision is not considered satisfactory monitoring of offenders who either are high risk or have high treatment needs, yet still do not require incarceration, intensive supervised probation is a viable alternative. **Intensive supervised probation (ISP)** was initiated in Georgia in 1974 to increase the amount of supervision provided to selected felony probationers, and now ISP programs are actively used in every state. The intent of ISP is to identify offenders who need supervision greater than that available through regular probation, yet are not such a risk to the community that they should be in prison.

POs supervising offenders in an ISP program have smaller caseloads, allowing for more frequent contacts with a combination of office reporting by offenders and home and work visits by the officer. The intensity of supervision enhances the goal of incapacitation, since the additional contacts reduce the opportunity for slipping into criminal behavior. Also, ISP is more of a punishment and deterrence because the number of contacts required disrupts the daily lives of offenders. Equally, it can enhance rehabilitation, because officers with smaller caseloads can provide counseling or follow-up on treatment plans for the offenders they supervise.

Early research into the effectiveness of intensive supervision usually did not find a reduction in recidivism, and there have been mixed results in other studies. In a review of fourteen counties in nine states, Petersilia and Turner found that high-risk ISP participants were watched more closely than regular probationers, and while this did not result in more arrests, there were significantly more technical violations, resulting in 27 percent of the ISP participants being returned to prison or jail compared to only 19 percent of regular probationers at the end of one year.[69] However, if the ISP supervision combined drug treatment, community service, and employment programs with surveillance, recidivism rates were 10–20 percent lower than for those who did not participate in such activities. Another analysis of 175 evaluations of ISP programs also found that combining surveillance with treatment resulted in reduced recidivism.[70] More recent research of the use of evidence-based practices was again more positive. A recent review found that those agencies that utilized a more human services philosophy and provided treatment had more promising results.[71] Another study found that smaller caseloads themselves is insufficient to reduce recidivism, yet when combined with evidence-based practices to allocate resources to the highest risk and need offenders, it is likely that recidivism can be reduced.[72] And a meta-analysis of intensive supervision programs combined with treatment-oriented programs found an almost 18 percent reduction in recidivism.[73]

House Arrest

An even greater level of supervision, even while sanctioned offenders remain in the community, results from house arrest. With **house arrest**, offenders are allowed to avoid a prison sentence, yet must be detained or incapacitated in their own homes, while they may remain employed, earn an income, support their families, and pay for their own upkeep and usually the cost of supervision for their house arrest. Offenders under house arrest live at home and must be at home except for times they are to be at work or participating in other activities previously approved by their PO. House arrest has the potential benefits of being economical, imposing severe restrictions on the offender's freedom and opportunity to commit crimes, and allowing for participation in community-based treatment programs.

Although not always necessary, housearrest is commonly used in conjunction with **electronic monitoring (EM)**, or the use of technology to monitor an offender's location. EM requires offenders to wear a tamperproof bracelet around their ankle. The bracelet acts as a receiver for a radio wave sent by a transmitter that is placed in the offender's home. There are two types of systems, active and passive, both of which are monitored from a central location. With active systems, the central location maintains a computerized schedule of when offenders should be in their homes and automatically "alarms" or sends a notice when the signal is not communicated between the transmitter and receiver during those times. This indicates to the monitor or PO that the offender has violated the conditions of his or her house arrest, and someone will be dispatched to check on or arrest the offender. The passive system requires random telephone calls during times the offender should be in the home. When a monitoring telephone call is received, offenders have a certain amount of time to place the receiver against the transmitter, proving that they are in the home as required. These systems are based on

house arrest
offenders live at home and must be at home except for times they are to be at work or participating in other activities approved by their probation officer

electronic monitoring
the use of technology to monitor an offender's location

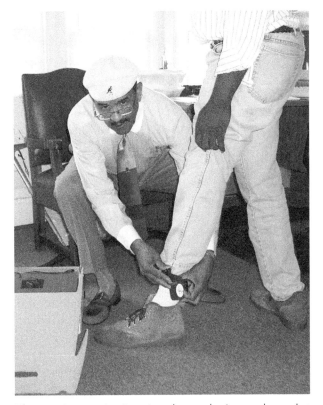

Electronic monitoring involves placing a bracelet around an offender's ankle. The bracelet acts as a receiver and notifies surveillance officers if the offender is not at home at designated times. Photo by Richard P. Seiter.

radio frequency (RF). A more recent technological development is the use of global positioning systems (GPS), which can not only actively monitor if an offender is at home, but identify where the offender is at any time.

EM is not a criminal sanction; it is a method of supervision. The first systems were activated in 1986, more than 40,000 units were in use by 1992, and their use continued to grow.[74] EM is now used in almost every jurisdiction and in many foreign countries as well. The use of EM is also believed to be cost effective, particularly as many states require offenders using the monitors to pay for the cost of supervision. A 2012 report indicated average annual costs across the country for the use of electronic monitoring was only $750.[75]

Generally, house arrest using EM is considered effective. Both quantitative and qualitative positive findings resulted from a major study funded by the U.S. Department of Justice. The 2010 review of almost 3,000 electronic monitored offenders in Florida found that there was a reduction in the risk of failure of about 31 percent compared to offenders placed on other forms of community supervision. And GPS typically had more of an effect on reducing failure with a 6 percent improvement rate in the reduction of supervision failures for offenders placed on GPS supervision relative to offenders placed on RF supervision. Qualitative findings were that administrators and officers supervising EM caseloads had confidence in the systems and their positive outcome. And offenders believed they held them more accountable.[76]

Community Residential Centers

community residential centers

houses in which offenders live in the community that provide supervision, room and board, and some treatment as an alternative to prison

Community residential centers (CRCs) are often referred to as halfway houses, which began as programs to help ex-inmates make the transition between prison and the community. Today, CRCs play a much broader role than simply helping in the postprison transition. As an intermediate sanction, CRCs provide a combination of supervision, structure, accountability, and programming to aid in the community supervision of probationers who require more than standard probation in response to their risk of reoffending and program needs. Thirty years ago, Governor Pierre du Pont of Delaware opened the door to their expanded use when he identified the role of CRCs as an adjunct to traditional community supervision, while providing an increase in supervision leading to enhanced public safety in the management of offenders.[77] CRCs are less expensive than the operation of a prison. In 2011, the average cost for imprisonment was $85.72 per day,[78] even when adjusted for inflation, considerably more than the 2001 average cost of $46.15 per day for a halfway house operated by the department of corrections and the cost of $43.41 for contracted halfway houses.[79] And this cost is further reduced, as most halfway houses or CRCs require residents to pay a portion of the cost of their stay through wages they earn while in the community.

The use of CRCs as an intermediate sanction can occur in two different ways. First, at the time of sentencing, judges can determine that offenders need the services of a residential center and can require probationers to live in a CRC as a condition of their probation. However, CRC placement more commonly occurs later in the period of probation supervision, after probationers are failing under their current supervision requirement. POs may determine that offenders have violated minor conditions of supervision and require more structure and accountability or need a place to live or additional program assistance. The officer then recommends that the court add a CRC requirement as a condition of probation.

The following "An Interview With" illustrates some of the operational issues for halfway houses or CRCs.

CRCs are usually an old boarding house, a YMCA, or some other large residential structure in an urban area. They range in size from thirty to two hundred residents. Resident rooms often hold two people, although some rooms are large enough to accommodate six or eight residents in a dormitory-style environment. The CRCs operate their own kitchen and provide meals to residents. Although CRCs have limited physical security to keep residents from leaving (usually standard residential locks, with cameras throughout the center to assist in supervision), residents are not free to come and go as they please. Residents must stay at the center unless they are approved to go to work or attend an authorized program. If they are complying with center rules, they may receive a weekend pass to visit family or friends.

An Interview With...

A CRC Director

Denise M. Robinson. Denise M. Robertson

Denise M. Robinson is President and CEO of Alvis House, a non-profit community residential center with a mission to serve individuals and families by providing effective programs and services that foster personal responsibility and healthy lifestyles resulting in safer communities for all. Alvis House was established in 1967, and serves over 7,000 clients a year. It has a residential capacity of 500, provides treatment services for many more, has an annual budget of $20 million, and a staff of 400. Programs include:

- Residential reentry programs in Columbus, Chillicothe, Dayton, Lima and Toledo, Ohio.
- Family-focused support programs.
- Supported living programs for individuals with intellectual/developmental disabilities.
- Career-oriented employability skills training.
- Community Reentry Centers in Columbus and Lima that provide employability skills training and GED instruction.
- An Intermediate Care Facility (ICF/IID) and supportive living programs for individuals with intellectual/developmental disabilities.

Ms. Robinson has worked for Alvis House for thirty years, and been in her current position for nine years. She is a highly recognized and award-winning practitioner and advocate of community corrections, as well as for programs and services for individuals with developmental disabilities. She serves on the Board of Governors of the American Correctional Association (ACA), on ACA's Standards Committee, and is a past president of the International Community Corrections Association. She served for eight years as an ACA Commissioner of Accreditation. She has received many honors and awards, but most significantly and recently, was one of two ACA E.R. Cass award winners in 2014, presented annually for distinguished service to the field of corrections. Robinson is only the fourth community corrections practitioner to be a Cass Award recipient since the award was created in 1962. Ms. Robinson holds a Bachelor of Arts degree from The Ohio State University.

Question: What is the specific role of a community residential center as an alternative to incarceration?

Ms. Robinson: Our role is very broad and diverse. In fact, Alvis House calls itself a community residential treatment center (as do many other CRC's nationally), in that we focus very much on treatment as well as residential services. Specifically, we give judges an option to directly sentence offenders to us as an alternative to prison and probation. We have county, state, and federal offenders as clients. With state offenders, Ohio is trying to divert from prison that population usually sentenced to prison for a year or less, and place them for shorter periods in a CRC. We receive offenders who violate their probation or parole supervision. Some state offenders are on a transitional control status, whereby they spend the last part of their prison sentence in a CRC. We also provide pre-trial services to offenders, some as an alternative to jail, and others that need programs and services, and their completion can be considered at sentencing. When these offenders complete programs and show they are stabilized, it often helps them receive a community rather than prison sentence. We also have a work release center, in which county and municipal clients who already have jobs may continue to work and return to the CRC to sleep at each evening.

Question: What type of inmates do you get as a diversion from prison?

(Continued)

Ms. Robinson: They are usually nonviolent offenders, but with significant needs. Research by the University of Cincinnati has indicated that programs are most effective with offenders with medium and high risks of reoffending. They are assessed for risk and criminogenic needs prior to placement. The key needs are substance abuse, peer associations, criminal attitude, and thinking. Eighty percent of our clients have substance abuse treatment needs. So we identify criminogenic needs that can be met in community. Placement in a CRC and remaining in the community allow clients to stay connected with family, get jobs, and take advantage of other community services. And we also have program for women involved in human trafficking.

Question: What types of programs does the halfway house offer?

Ms. Robinson: Alvis House offers a variety of programs to a variety of clients (see the list above). For each client, we develop a treatment plan and offer cognitive behavior treatment in all curriculums we use. Some of the most common and critical are job readiness and job seeking GED instruction, family support and parenting, Life Skills, and personal health and care. We also have a huge commitment to community service. We expect every offender to do something meaningful to give back to the community and make up for what they have taken from others. Through one of our partners, the Harmony Project, we have our clients build playgrounds in neighborhoods harmed by crime. We also serve meals at homeless shelters, go to nursing homes, and do activities with their residents. We support the camps provided by the Central Ohio Diabetes Association. In all, our clients complete approximately 15,000 hours of community service a year.

A new program this year is the Catch Court, a community and criminal justice diversion program for women involved in prostitution and human trafficking, and most have severe substance abuse issues. It is a two-year residential program, whereby they receive all types of services. This court contracts with Alvis House for the residential and some program services. We work with the Southeast Mental Health and Trauma Treatment Center for Women. It is based on the highly acclaimed and successful Magdalene Program of Nashville Tennessee.

Question: Can you describe the process or steps offenders must take to successfully complete the program?

Ms. Robinson: The key is that they must complete all their treatment and case plan goals. These goals are a result of the assessment and determination of needs, and then an individual program to address each need. Federal offenders have a "due out" date, and we have to accomplish their goals by this date. We may have to accelerate what we do for them to complete everything by the out date. State clients do not have a set date of release, as they must complete all goals before they

get out. Some may need only job training, life skills, or cognitive behavior. In addition, they are assessed for eligibility for Medicaid or Social Security, they must get and maintain employment or school, establish financial responsibility, and have an aftercare plan. Some stay for only three months, but others may stay nine to twelve months. I would say that six months is the median period they stay.

Question: What are the three biggest issues and challenges in operating a halfway house for these offenders?

Ms. Robinson: Because we focus on offenders with medium-to high-risk need assessments, they have many programs they must complete. A very big challenge is getting all the treatment hours needed, especially in combination with offenders who work and participate in therapy programs outside of Alvis House. Scheduling is difficult, and we end up providing 12 hours of class a day. This is a challenge for the staff and the clients. But it is worth it. Our recidivism rate for clients who have been out of the program for at least a year is less than 10 percent, well below the national average, so the approach is working.

Drug use and particularly heroin is a serious problem. Heroin use is at epidemic levels. Heroin is relatively cheap at this time, and use has expanded. Other "designer" drugs are also a problem. By designer drugs, I mean those new drugs created in a lab, whereby the use is not indicated in current testing protocols. We, as well as other CRC's throughout the world, are experiencing more overdoses, and we have had deaths in our facilities. While we have good substance abuse programs, some clients are just not ready for change. And they can become a cancer for the facility, and encourage other clients to use.

Question: What is the potential for students to find jobs in a halfway house?

Ms. Robinson: I am so glad we are talking about this, as I believe the potential for careers in our field are amazing. It used to be that people left us to work for state or county government, but now our salaries are pretty commensurate with government and other non-profit organizations. Entry-level jobs as community reentry specialists do not require a college degree. These individuals do monitoring in the residential facilities, and maintain peace and tranquility. They also make calls to client work and programs to verify their participation. Many people start here and work their way up into the degree-required jobs. We also have many student interns; 90 percent of which we end up hiring. Other jobs are for treatment programs and these require a college degree. These positions include social workers, psychologists, nurses, and other licensed clinicians. As I described all the programming we do, these are the staff that provide the treatment. The state and federal agencies with which we contract require both life skills and cognitive programs, so we must have people to do them. So there are job opportunities and careers for all these types of people.[80]

The stay at CRCs is usually only a few months and may be as short as thirty days. There are sometimes emergency placements to provide room and board for probationers who do not have a place to stay, and they stay at the center only until they find another place to live. Other probationers may need supervision or programs that require a longer stay, perhaps up to six months. During this time, many CRCs have stages of privileges, and residents earn the opportunity for more time away from the center as they follow rules and appear successful in their adjustment. In general, CRCs are only for temporary placement when either the need arises for housing or the probationer exhibits less than responsible behavior that requires a period of additional supervision.

Halfway houses are usually large, older homes located in an area close to the central city so that public transportation and other services are readily available. Photo by Richard P. Seiter.

There is no or very minimal physical security at halfway houses. The security relies on offenders taking responsibility for being at the house when they are required to be and staff ensuring that they are accounted for when they come and go from the house. The "Your Career in Corrections" box illustrates some of the roles of halfway house staff in this regard.

Split Sentences

Split sentences are a combination of a short jail sentence and then supervision in the community on probation. The jail sentence can be anywhere from 30 to 180 days. The purpose of a split sentence is to provide a clear combination of punishment and rehabilitation for offenders who have not committed crimes serious enough to require a sentence of imprisonment. However, when offenders' behavior is seen as particularly irresponsible, judges may use a short jail term to get their attention and expose them to the uncomfortable environment of jail to encourage a change of attitude. The jail sentence is simply to add punishment to a sentence of standard probation and, once completed, the offender returns to the community under probation supervision—hence the term *split sentence*, because the sentence is divided between a term in jail and a period of probation.

split sentence
a combination of a short jail sentence and then return to the community on probation

The jail part of a split sentence is sometimes served only on weekends. This lessens the negative impact of serving time in jail, and offenders are able to keep their jobs and maintain ties to family. They must check into the jail on Friday evenings and are released Sunday nights until the total number of days of their sentence has been

A bedroom of a halfway house is of dormitory style, typically shared by three to six residents. Photo by Richard P. Seiter.

Your Career in Corrections

Halfway House or CRC Staff

Most students do not think of working in a halfway house or CRC as they begin a career in corrections, yet there are over 200 community-based correctional facilities (halfway houses) in the United States.[81] So there are many job opportunities in these facilities. Historically, since most of the contracted houses were operated by church-affiliated or other not-for-profit agencies, the program mission of helping offenders was the primary emphasis, salaries were quite low, and staff turnover was high. To a great extent, that is still the case. Yet halfway houses have improved their professionalism in the management of these programs, salaries have improved, and there is improved stability by employees. However, because the houses are small and have few staff members, the lack of promotional opportunities still makes this more likely to be a short-term entry-level job than a career.

Most individuals enter one of two positions when beginning work at a halfway house. The first is a paraprofessional position often called desk monitor. Desk monitors control access into and out of the facility. Most houses have a nonsecure control point at the front door, and residents must sign a logbook when they go in or out. The monitor ensures that residents sign in and are in the house when required. In many ways, it is equivalent to the role of a correctional officer in a prison. If someone leaves when not permitted or fails to return when required, desk monitors notify management and the police and probation or parole officers are likely to be called. When not watching the desk, monitors do room checks to make sure there is no contraband (items not allowed in the possession of residents) or activities such as drinking or drug use. They also search for contraband in rooms or other locations throughout the house. While these positions can be full-time, they are very good part-time positions for students preparing for a corrections career. This experience is very good preparation for work as a police officer, probation or parole officer, or correctional officer.

The second category of halfway house jobs is professional positions, such as counselor, case manager, or substance abuse specialist. Counselors and case managers are assigned a caseload of residents and are responsible for guiding them through their stay by suggesting (or requiring) participation in certain programs, initiating disciplinary action for violation of probation or parole when required, and overseeing the collection of fines or costs for staying at the house. A college degree in criminal justice, social work, psychology, or one of the other social sciences is usually required. These jobs are very interesting and very challenging. The staff members must be directive with residents and hold them accountable for following the rules. They must be knowledgeable of programs and job-finding resources to assist residents. And they must deal with the difficult situation of offenders being restricted in their activities and movements, yet in a nonsecure facility in which they go into the community on almost a daily basis.

Halfway house staff members interact with several categories of criminal justice and social service professionals and get the opportunity to see what they do and network to develop contacts who can help them in future job-finding efforts. The work is challenging and provides a great training opportunity.

---

shock incarceration/ boot camp

alternatives to traditional incarceration that are operated similar to a military boot camp; offenders are required to have short hair, shine their shoes, wear uniforms, do extensive physical exercise, and perform hard physical labor; at times, these are complemented with education or drug programming, but the major components of boot camps are military regimentation, discipline, exercise, and hard work

met. Split sentences have become more common over the past twenty years, as the "tough on crime" mentality has emphasized punishment as well as rehabilitation for even minor offenders. Data from the Bureau of Justice Statistics show that of offenders entering probation, approximately one-fourth have a split sentence of incarceration plus probation.[82]

Shock Incarceration or Boot Camps

An interesting correctional sanction that developed during the late 1900s is **shock incarceration or boot camp**. The first boot camps were initiated in Georgia in 1983 and Oklahoma in 1984. Quickly gaining in popularity, boot camps were implemented in many other states over the next ten years. This development is interesting in regard to the accomplishment of correctional goals, as boot camps were created with the purpose of holding offenders accountable for their crimes with a harsh punishment and deterrent effect. Correctional boot camps are operated similarly to a military boot camp; offenders are required to have short hair, shine their shoes, wear uniforms, do extensive physical exercise, and perform hard physical labor. At times, these activities are complemented with education or drug programming, but the major components of boot camps remain military regimentation, discipline, exercise, and hard work. Boot camps appeal to both liberals and conservatives because they focus on being tough on crime and tough on the offender, but are also a community alternative to traditional imprisonment. If offenders complete boot camp, they receive a shorter sentence than if they had received a traditional prison sentence. Boot camps are usually reserved for young, first-time prisoners who are deemed likely to benefit from structure and discipline while gaining self-control with the rigorous daily routine.

Graduation from the boot camp illustrates the regimentation and discipline gained by participants over their stay. AB Forces News Collection/Alamy Stock Photo.

While early evaluations in some states have indicated that offenders who complete boot camp programs leave with more positive attitudes, boot camps were later criticized as expensive and not effective. Boot camps are expensive because they are usually small in number of offenders and require a high staff to inmates ratio. They are especially expensive compared to minimum-security prisons, where most of the boot camp offenders would otherwise be incarcerated. Several findings have been very critical of the impact of boot camps on reducing recidivism.[83] A review by the U.S. General Accounting Office (GAO) reported that boot camps only marginally reduce recidivism, and the differences between boot camp and non-boot camp offenders diminish over time.[84] Although the GAO study found an improvement in attitudes, it determined the impact on recidivism to be at best negligible. As a result of the negative findings, several states closed their boot camp operations. A few states still operate them for various reasons. For example, Pennsylvania reviewed the history of their boot camp, and determined that while there is no evidence of reducing recidivism, they found the boot camp saves money and did not compromise public safety.[85]

Shock Probation

A final intermediate sanction is **shock probation**, a short period of imprisonment to "shock" the offender, with a return to the community within a few weeks to continue supervision on probation. The concept originated in Ohio when 1965 legislation authorized the sentencing judge to reconsider a sentence of imprisonment within 90–130 days after incarceration of the offender. If the offender meets the criteria (a nonviolent offense with no offense history) and the judge believes that the punitive and deterrent value of the sentence has already been met, the sentence can be modified and the offender released to regular probation. Shock probation is based on a specific deterrence model, with a belief that the shock of the sentence and admission to prison shows offenders the punishment they will receive if they continue to commit crimes. The theory is that, as a result of placement in prison for a short period of time, offenders-granted shock probation will be deterred from commission of further crimes.

In an evaluation of the effectiveness of shock probation, this theory proved to be true, as Vito concluded,

1. The shock experience should not be limited to first-time offenders; eligibility should properly include those with prior records, as deemed eligible by the judge.

shock probation
a short period of imprisonment to "shock" the offender, with a return to the community within a few weeks to continue supervision on probation

2. The length of incarceration necessary to secure the deterrent effect could be much shorter, probably thirty days or less.

3. Reincarceration rates have never exceeded 26 percent and, in Ohio, have been as low as 10 percent. The level of these rates clearly indicates that the program has potential for reintegration.

4. Shock probation has considerable potential to reduce institutional overcrowding characteristics of contemporary corrections.[86]

Shock probation is generally believed to be a low-cost and effective intermediate sanction for less serious felons, and many states have implemented shock probation as a part of their sentencing structure.

The Effectiveness of Intermediate Sanctions

The use of intermediate sanctions has increased significantly over the past two decades, and with recent budget crises in many jurisdictions, it will continue to play a more important role in the next decade. However, there are still a fairly limited number of research studies from which to evaluate the effectiveness of these programs against their desired outcomes. The following list suggests some reasons for the limited number of studies of effectiveness and the lack of use of these evaluations for correctional policymaking:

1. Political, ethical, and programmatic reasons may not permit random assignment of clients to either the treatment or control group.

2. Treatment or program effects "bleed over" to the control group, or the intended treatment is inappropriately or unevenly applied.

3. It is rare to have only one treatment in operation at a time, thus contaminating the impact of the measure of outcome.

4. Varying measures of success and failure make it difficult to generalize across studies and program results.[87]

In the preceding descriptions of the intermediate sanctions, some outcome studies were identified, with mixed conclusions as to their overall effectiveness. To fully evaluate their success, intermediate sanctions should be analyzed against their desired goals. Examples of such analyses follow:

Goal 1: Intermediate sanctions should be used to divert offenders from prison. Most experts would agree that one goal of intermediate sanctions is to manage more offenders in the community who would (without intermediate sanctions) have to be sentenced to prison. However, it is generally concluded that intermediate sanctions are not always used with high-risk probationers, and therefore add to the supervision of probationers who would not have been sent to prison even if the intermediate sanction did not exist. This phenomenon is called **net widening**, the overlapping of criminal sanctions and added supervision for community-placed offenders, rather than diversion of offenders from prison.

Goal 2: Intermediate sanctions should reduce the cost of corrections. Common sense would seem to indicate that it would be less expensive to maintain offenders in the community rather than sentence them to prison. However, most offenders who are assigned to intermediate sanctions would, if sentenced to prison, be assigned to minimum-security prisons and sentenced to short terms of confinement. If offenders are maintained in the community

net widening
the overlapping of criminal sanctions and added supervision for community-placed offenders, rather than diversion of offenders from prison

and net widening occurs, the overall cost of supervision could end up being more than if they are sent to a minimum-security prison. For instance, placement in a boot camp or CRC can cost more per day than placement in a minimum-security prison.

> *Goal 3: Intermediate sanctions should reduce the level of recidivism for offenders.* The studies noted earlier provide mixed indications of the effectiveness of intermediate sanctions in reducing recidivism. However, the most consistent conclusion is that recidivism is not significantly affected by mere community surveillance unless it is combined with participation in treatment programs. Petersilia, in reviewing studies of intermediate sanctions, concluded, "The empirical evidence regarding intermediate sanctions is decisive: without a rehabilitation component, reductions in recidivism are elusive."[88] When these two components are combined in a quality fashion, intermediate sanctions have proved effective in reducing recidivism.

Over the past fifteen years, there has been more emphasis on identifying programs that show evidence of success in reducing recidivism and funding those for intermediate sanctions. At the forefront of this movement was Oregon, which in 2003 mandated that all treatment programs receiving state funds are to be evidence based. And soon thereafter, almost 54 percent of Oregon's addiction treatment budget of $94 million funds programs that are evidence based. Before the 2003 legislative mandate, only 25–30 percent of programs were evidence based.[89] After Oregon made this move, almost every state now has followed suit and focuses attention and funding on evidence-based programs. Another example of the transition to evidence-based programming are the recommendations of the Charles Colson Task Force on Federal Corrections, established by a 2014 Congressional mandate. Their recommendations included using data and evidence-based programming both within federal prisons, as well as postrelease supervision.[90]

Chapter Review

Summary

This chapter has described the first set of sentencing sanctions in the correctional process: probation and intermediate sanctions. The least intrusive and least intensive sentencing option is probation. Probation has the advantages of maintaining offenders in the community so that family and employment ties are maintained, of being less costly than imprisonment, and of focusing on offender rehabilitation to a greater extent than does imprisonment. For many minor offenders who have a low risk of reoffending and little or no history of violence, probation is a viable sanction.

For offenders who have a greater risk of reoffending or treatment needs that cannot be met through regular probation but who are not such a risk to the community that they need imprisoned, intermediate sanctions can provide additional supervision and program opportunities. When they are used for offenders who (without their availability) would be sent to prison, intermediate sanctions have all the benefits of probation and are generally less expensive than imprisonment. Intermediate sanctions add proportionality to the sentencing process, in that they provide a wide range of alternative supervision and treatment options and can be more appropriately matched to the crime committed and to the offenders' risks and needs. Research has also determined that if surveillance is combined with treatment, intermediate sanctions can effectively reduce recidivism.

Probation and intermediate sanctions represent community-based alternatives to institutional-based sentences. The next chapter continues the discussion of modern correctional operations by moving further into the continuum of correctional sanctions and describing the theories and operational approaches of U.S. prisons. We will then complete our overview of correctional operations by describing the postprison programs of supervision and reentry to the community. At the end of Part II of this textbook, students will have a thorough understanding of the major correctional components used today, and we can move into a more detailed examination of correctional perspectives, issues, and challenges.

Key Terms

community corrections	technical violations	intensive supervised probation (ISP)
John Augustus	new-crime violations	house arrest
probation	*Gagnon v. Scarpelli*	electronic monitoring
probation supervision	community classification systems	community residential centers (CRCs)
casework style of supervision	intermediate sanctions	split sentences
surveillance style of supervision	fines	shock incarceration
regular caseloads	community corrections acts	boot camp
intensive-supervision caseloads	offender restitution	shock probation
special caseloads	victim compensation	net widening
standard conditions of probation	cost of supervision	
special conditions of probation	asset forfeiture	

Review Questions

1. What contributions to modern probation did John Augustus make that continue today?

2. Approximately how many people were on probation in the United States in 2015?

3. What are the primary emphases of probation supervision?

4. Differentiate between the casework and surveillance styles of probation supervision.

5. What is the difference between standard and special conditions of probation?

6. List five standard conditions of probation.

7. Name three types of probation caseloads.

8. What are the two types of probation violations?

9. What were the important findings in the *Gagnon v. Scarpelli* decision regarding revocation of probation?

10. Describe the philosophy of the broken-windows approach to the operation of probation.

11. How do community classification systems work, and what is their impact on probation supervision?

12. What is an economic sanction?

13. Differentiate between offender restitution and victim compensation programs.

14. What is asset forfeiture and why can it be called an economic sanction?

15. Describe the results of evaluations regarding intensive supervised probation.

16. How is electronic monitoring used to enforce the requirements of house arrest?

17. Differentiate passive and active electronic monitoring systems.

18. What are the two ways that community residential centers are used as intermediate sanctions?

19. What is a split sentence?

20. Describe the operation of a boot camp.

21. How long does an offender usually stay in prison under shock probation?

22. How can net widening reduce the effectiveness of an intermediate-sanctions program?

You Make the Decision...

Should I Revoke Him

One of the most difficult challenges for a probation officer (PO) is deciding whether to initiate a revocation process for a probationer. To some, it may seem very clear-cut. If probationers violate the conditions of their supervision, their probation should be revoked. Most probation agency policies require that violations be brought to the attention of the court for action to either revoke or modify probation conditions. Yet courts do not want to see every technical violation of a probationer, and officers have considerable discretion in how to handle most minor infractions. For instance, a probationer may be required to report several times per month to the officer and is usually very responsible in doing so. If the offender misses one appointment, agencies do not want officers reporting it as a violation to the court. However, all criminal activities should be reported.

The officer must decide whether to initiate a revocation process for several situations that fall between these two obvious extremes. It is easy for officers to take a hard line and report almost any violation. They can never be criticized if the offender later commits a serious crime. However, research findings indicate that recidivism is not reduced by only surveillance techniques of probation, but by a combination of casework and surveillance and by the officer's getting offenders to take responsibility for their crimes and the behaviors that lead to criminal acts. The best officers use this discretion wisely and counsel offenders or issue agreements to modify supervision conditions as intermediate actions. Many probation agencies now give officers limited authority to add requirements to be better able to hold the offender accountable, such as drug testing, additional reporting to the officer, or even (in a few situations) residence in a halfway house or electronic monitoring. The following scenario is for students to consider and then decide how to handle the case.

You are the PO for John Smith. Smith is a 32-year-old offender with a history of serious drug use, three misdemeanor theft offenses, and one prior felony conviction for breaking and entering. The current offense is auto theft and possession of cocaine. He received a sentence of two years of probation with standard conditions and a requirement to participate in drug abuse counseling and random drug testing. Smith did rather well the first eight months of supervision, but his behavior then began to deteriorate. In month nine, he missed two of his four appointments with you, with excuses that his car broke down and that there was a family emergency. He also lost his job and has yet to find another. His sister called and told you that Smith was again using drugs. You had him come in immediately for a random drug test, which proved negative.

In month ten, he missed two of his drug counseling sessions, claiming that he was not using drugs and the sessions were a waste of time. He said he would rather spend his time trying to find a job. In month eleven, he tested positive for cocaine use. You had not notified the court before this time, but had counseled Smith repeatedly and told him that continued failure to meet the conditions of his probation could result in revocation and a prison sentence. You believe that Smith is not a dangerous person, as he does not have a violent history. You also believe that if he could stay in the community and conquer his drug use, he could stay out of trouble. Yet he has not been honest with you and seems to not respond to your more intensive counseling (and threats). You now must report the violations to the court and recommend how to deal with Smith. You can recommend continuation of probation with current conditions, added conditions as an intermediate sanction, or revocation and implementation of Smith's eighteen-month prison sentence. What do you recommend, and why?

CHAPTER 5
Prison Systems

Courtesy of CoreCivic.

After reading this chapter, you should be able to:

1. Summarize the characteristics and status of prisons in the United States, including the changing demographic trends in the inmate population.

2. Summarize the organization of the federal and state prison systems.

3. List the other public correctional systems.

4. Suggest the reasons for the development of private prisons, and speculate regarding their role in the future.

Introduction

We now turn our study of corrections to **prisons**, institutions designed to house convicted, adult felons serving a sentence of one year or more. Prisons are a relatively new phenomenon in criminal justice and corrections. As described in Chapter 1, the early sanctions for convicted offenders were primarily corporal and capital punishment, mixed with public humiliation. It was not until the end of the eighteenth century that the Quakers of Pennsylvania decided that a more humane and efficient way to punish and reform criminals was needed, and the penitentiary was first established in Philadelphia.

prisons
institutions designed to house convicted, adult felons, serving a sentence of one year or more

Over the next 200 years, prisons evolved with a variety of theoretical foundations influencing policies and practice. Over the past thirty years, a toughening public attitude toward crime and criminals has helped prisons emerge as the sanction believed to most effectively meet the correctional goals of punishment, deterrence, and incapacitation. Unfortunately and inaccurately, the public had come to believe that probation and intermediate sanctions do not successfully meet their concern for public safety, and increasingly more offenders are sentenced to prisons, many for extremely long periods of time. Fortunately, these attitudes are beginning to soften, primarily as a result of budgetary shortages at state and local levels.

This change in philosophy and practice has resulted in an unprecedented level of prison construction, a burgeoning industry of prison operations, and a significant percentage of federal and state budgets going toward construction and operation of prisons. In 1980, almost 200 years after prisons were first used as a criminal sanction, there were only 316,000 sentenced prisoners under state or federal jurisdiction. In just over thirty years, from 1980 to 2016, the number of prisoners increased by almost 500 percent, to over 1.5 million inmates. This chapter describes recent trends in the makeup of the prison population in the United States, the construction of prisons to keep up with the increase in inmate numbers, the types of prison systems in the United States, and the way in which prisons are organized by security levels to manage the different levels of offender risk.

Current Status of Prisons in the United States

There has been tremendous growth in the role of prisons in the United States as well as swings in philosophy over the past several years. As an example of the changing philosophy regarding the operation of prisons, the 1967 report by the President's Commission on Law Enforcement and Administration of Justice, Corrections Section, recommended the following:

1. Long sentences are self-defeating in regard to rehabilitation.
2. Most offenders do not need to be incarcerated and could function in the community under supervision.
3. Most inmates derive maximum benefit from their incarceration during the first two years.
4. Community-based corrections are less expensive than and at least as effective as incarceration.
5. Corrections must encompass all aspects of rehabilitative service, including mental health, employment services, education, and social services.

6. Because of their dangerousness, some offenders will require extensive incarceration in secure institutions.

7. Most inmates do not have a mental illness but suffer from a variety of educational, medical, maturational, economic, and interpersonal handicaps that are seldom reduced or resolved in prison.

8. Inmates must be given the opportunity and capability to earn a living wage to compensate their victims and support their families.

9. The pay for inmates is too low. The rates of pay should be at least the minimum wage for similar labor.

10. The private sector should be used to provide training and work programs that are realistic to develop employable workers at the end of their sentence.[1]

As is obvious, public opinion and the purpose of prisons in the criminal justice system have changed significantly since this report was written. In 1967, state and federal prisons held less than 300,000 inmates.[2] The medical model, with an emphasis on rehabilitating offenders, was the prevailing philosophy. Shichor noted that rehabilitation was strongly emphasized as the goal of prisons until the 1970s, when this emphasis began to diminish as the United States experienced large increases in crime rates, resulting in rising numbers of prison commitments.[3] Before that time, however, prisons were reserved for the most violent and dangerous offenders, and property offenders were usually granted probation and supervision in the community. Also, prisons held a generally homogeneous group of offenders, with very similar histories of criminality, sentences, age, and treatment needs.

Today, the role and prevailing philosophies of prison operations have changed significantly. The "tough on crime" mentality of the public and elected officials has forced prisons to become a catchall for all types of offenders, as punishment became favored over rehabilitation. Property offenders are now as likely to be imprisoned as violent offenders. Drug offenders, even those with no prior

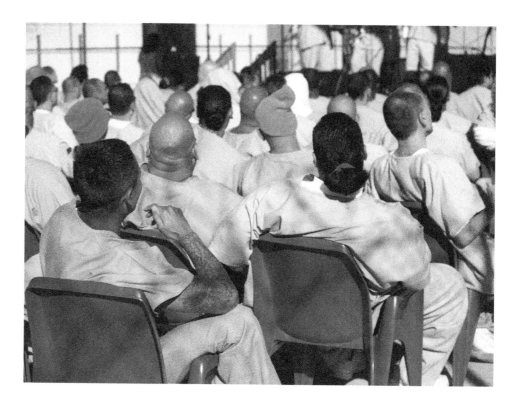

Inmates are now very diverse in terms of age, race, gender, and ethnicity.
Courtesy of CoreCivic.

involvement in crime, often receive mandatory prison sentences of five to ten years. The prison population is much more heterogeneous in terms of prior criminal history, sentence, age, and treatment needs. Even though the past few years have seen a modest decline, by the end of 2016, the number of prisoners under the jurisdiction of federal or state adult correctional authorities was still 1,505,397.[4]

The Role and Mission of Prisons

The primary function of prisons is to hold convicted felons, usually serving a sentence of one year or more, whereas convicted felons serving shorter sentences usually serve their time in local jails. Inmates consider jail sentences very "hard time," since jails do not have the full range of education, vocational training, work, recreational, or other treatment programs that are available in prisons. Therefore, jail inmates spend most of their time just sitting in their cells, watching television, or playing cards with other inmates. Since prisons are designed to hold inmates for longer terms, they need to provide a full range of programs, both for rehabilitative purposes and to keep inmates productively busy.

Many people perceive that prison inmates just sit in cells. This could not be further from the truth. For both management and legal reasons, prison administrators develop activities to keep inmates out of their cells and busy as much of the day as possible. During the period of transition of prisons described in Chapter 1, prison administrators discovered how difficult it was to operate prisons without the ability to let inmates out of their cells and keep them busy. When Congress passed laws in the 1930s restricting the sale of inmate-made goods in the open market, prisons engaged in production with full-scale factory operations had to find another way to manage growing number of inmates (many prisons during that time housed 3,000–4,000 inmates). Fearful of violence and tension erupting from the forced idleness, prison administrators tightened security and kept inmates locked in their cells for much of the day. This resulted in even more tension and, after a series of prison riots, officials were forced to find better methods to operate modern prisons.

Prison administrators now understand the problems that can result if inmates are confined to housing units for long periods of time. Although not specifically stating that inmates had to be out of cells and involved in work and program activities for any particular number of hours, the federal courts have also encouraged this type of operation through their decisions regarding prison operations. In *Rhodes v. Chapman* (1981), the U.S. Supreme Court decided that overcrowded conditions resulting from two inmates housed in cells designed for one person at the Southern Ohio Correctional Facility (SOCF) was not a violation of the Eighth Amendment right of protection from cruel and unusual punishment.[5] Very important in the decision was the Court's consideration of the "totality of conditions" at SOCF, finding that inmates were out of their cells for much of the day, and no other problems, such as poor medical care or food service, resulted from the crowded conditions. If prison officials attempted to keep inmates locked in their cells without adequate programs and work activities, the Court would likely reconsider the *Rhodes* decision.

The federal courts have allowed inmates to be locked in cells for all but five hours per week in the case of *Bruscino v. Carlson*.[6] However, this case did not involve the operations of a traditional prison. *Bruscino* is based on a lockdown of a U.S. penitentiary (USP) in Marion, Illinois, and the elimination of inmate programs outside cells resulting from continued violent acts by inmates that culminated in the murder of two correctional officers in the same day. The Court

Rhodes v. Chapman
a 1981 U.S. Supreme Court decision that overcrowded conditions resulting in two inmates housed in cells designed for one person was not a violation of the Eighth Amendment right of protection from cruel and unusual punishment

considered the fact that inmates were placed in USP–Marion because they were unmanageable and had violated rules at other prisons. There was a process for reviewing their assignment to and their removal from USP–Marion. A federal judge, in denying a motion by inmates to stop the lockdown, stated, "The Court is of the firm conviction that this litigation was conceived by a small group of hard-core inmates who are bent on the disruption of the prison system in general and of USP–Marion in particular."[7] However, it is unlikely that the federal courts would accept this type of lockdown for a standard prison not designated for the most violent and dangerous inmates.

Currently, prison officials keep inmates locked in cells (or confined to their housing areas in dormitory-style facilities) for only about eight hours per day, generally from 11:00 P.M. to 7:00 A.M. During the day, inmates work or participate in educational or vocational programs. In the evening (from dinner until lockdown time), inmates participate in recreational activities or other treatment programs, such as substance abuse programs, religious activities, or counseling. The key to a successfully operated prison is to keep inmates productively occupied and under the supervision of staff for the sixteen hours per day that inmates are not confined to their housing units.

mission

a statement of an organization's major function and what it is to accomplish, or its basic purposes, to include general outcomes that it is committed to achieving

A **mission** is a statement of what an organization is to accomplish, or a "statement of its basic purposes, often in terms of broad outcomes that it is committed to achieving or the major function it carries out."[8] In many cases, the mission is the statement of why an agency exists. For most state prison systems, the mission is legislatively created. State legislatures, in creating the agencies that operate prisons, often include the purpose or function of the agency in the authorizing legislation. A common mission statement for a prison is "to supervise criminal offenders during the period of their sentence, protect the public, and offer programs that assist in the rehabilitation of criminals." When not created by the legislature, agencies will generate their own mission statement. The mission statement for the Federal Bureau of Prisons (BOP) appears on its website:

> *It is the mission of the Federal Bureau of Prisons to protect society by confining offenders in the controlled environments of prisons and community-based facilities that are safe, humane, cost-efficient, and appropriately secure, and that provide work and other self-improvement opportunities to assist offenders in becoming law-abiding citizens.*[9]

As is clear from both the example of a legislatively created mission and the BOP mission, most prisons have a dual-purpose mission statement. First, prisons are to be safe and secure, protecting inmates and staff from harm while they live and work in the prison environment and protecting the public from further criminality by not allowing inmates to escape and further prey on society. Second, prisons provide programs that assist in the management of prisons by keeping inmates busy but, more important, prepare offenders for release and the transition to the community. By concentrating on the rehabilitation of offenders in addition to simple incapacitation, prisons further protect society by improving the chance of inmates' successful return to society and reduction of the long-term likelihood of further criminal activity.

Creating a safe and secure prison environment, and one that encourages inmates to participate in meaningful treatment programs, is a difficult balance. This balancing act usually falls on the shoulders of the warden, who must set the tone and ensure that both security and treatment get the appropriate level of attention. Not many students go through college studying to be a warden. Yet the warden's job is one of the most challenging and interesting in the public management arena. The "Your Career in Corrections" box illustrates some of these challenges.

Growth of the Prison Population

Currently, it is generally believed that confinement facilities are the most effective sanction to protect the public, punish criminals, and deter them from committing further crimes after release. Over the past few decades, we have continued to increase the number of offenders sentenced to correctional institutions, and by the end of 2016, there were 1,505,397 offenders incarcerated in state and federal prisons.[10] Whenever criminal justice policymakers have a concern about the risk of placing offenders in the community, they shift to a policy of increased use of confinement. Although this option undoubtedly maximizes community safety, in many cases it does so marginally and comes at a great expense to taxpayers.

Your Career in Corrections

Wardens

The author of this textbook is a career correctional administrator and was warden of two federal prisons. He thoroughly enjoyed these jobs and often described a warden's job as similar to that of a city manager, in that wardens are responsible for many service functions (food service, health care, sanitation and maintenance, policing, construction, human resources, and budget management), as well as the correctional aspects of security, inmate programs, and legal issues.

Today, there are approximately 2,000 state and federal prisons, each having a warden as the chief executive of the prison. While these CEOs manage budgets of multiple millions and supervise hundreds of staff members, they are not paid at a level similar to a chief executive in the private sector; yet pay can range from $60,000 to $150,000 depending on the jurisdiction and the size and complexity of the prison. Wardens usually begin working for their agency at an entry level, and move up the chain of command, and are very experienced when taking the position of warden. In most states, there is no minimum educational level, although most wardens have a college degree. There is also no specific requirement for education or experience, as wardens can begin their correctional careers in almost any discipline, including security, counseling, or any other area of corrections.

College students do not usually plan a career toward the job of warden. In fact, most college students do not plan to go to work in a prison. Many who end up in institutional corrections often plan to be a social worker or counselor and later find opportunities to work in prisons both exciting and challenging. Warden is a job that takes many years of training and experience. As noted previously, the average correctional job experience for wardens was more than fifteen years. No matter how much education, how much experience in management,

or how much willingness to work a person has, nothing is more important to prepare someone to be a warden than working in a prison at a variety of levels. Most decisions that come to a warden's desk are not simple, and there are no easy or obvious solutions. Many have multiple problems and risks, and the difficulty lies in selecting a solution that has the least likelihood of dire consequences. There are always so many varying impacts from what a warden does (if it helps security, it may hurt treatment; if it is something positive for inmates, it may be problematic for staff; if it has great potential for a positive outcome, it may not be affordable within the budget) that each decision must be thoughtfully considered as to how it affects different groups or other prison functions.

Perhaps the most important skill required of a warden is the management and leadership of people. Corrections is a people business, and everything must be accomplished through the staff members that work in a prison. The most effective wardens are those who can lead and motivate staff through involving and engaging them in the overall management of a prison. In a challenging and sometimes dangerous job of prison employees, the staff members must believe in the warden and feel they are consulted and their input is important in the decisions of managing the facility and the inmates. Surveys have indicated that prison wardens have much greater job satisfaction than all but a few other professions. There is never a boring day, and each day brings something different. It takes skills in every different area of management (budget, human resources, security and treatment, and facility maintenance). But most important, being a warden is a very people-oriented job. Wardens get things done by dealing with people—staff and inmates—and must enjoy and be good at getting others to implement and follow what has been decided.

It is interesting that from the invention of the prison in 1790 until about 1980 (almost 200 years) the state and federal prison population rose from zero to only about 300,000. In less than four more decades, the prison population grew by 500 percent, to over 1.5 million. This growth illustrates a remarkable shift in the policies that had previously influenced the use of prisons as a criminal sanction throughout our history. Why the tremendous increase? Several factors have predisposed the increase.

First, since the 1980s, the public has become more fearful of crime, less tolerant of criminals, and more demanding of tougher sentencing laws. This was understandable during the 1980s, when crime rates (particularly for violent crime) were increasing. According to Gallup polls, in 1989, 84 percent of citizens polled felt there was more crime in the United States than the year before. Since that time, crime rates have been declining and have gone down in almost every category of felonies every year since 1993. Yet, in a Gallup poll conducted in October 2016, 45 percent of citizens still believed that there was more crime now than the year before, 33 percent believed there was less, and 20 percent believed it was the same as a year ago.[11] As a result of this belief and the resulting fear of crime, the public demands that criminals be sentenced for longer periods of time and wants punishment and offender accountability to be the primary focuses of such sentences.

In response, elected officials significantly lengthened sentences. With every high-visibility, heinous crime, elected officials respond by proposing an increase in criminal sanctions for that crime or type of criminal. As a result, the average length of incarceration has increased significantly since 1990. The average length of stay for inmates released during 1990 was 23.7 months.[12] For the 413,400 inmates released during 2012, the average time served was 17 months, yet for those released after committing a violent offense, the average time served was 28 months.[13]

Unfortunately, many elected officials do not have confidence in alternatives to incarceration, and are afraid if they do not seem "tough" enough, voters will not support them. Therefore, these officials continue to emphasize the use of incarceration, rather than alternative sanctions or preventive approaches. Crime has become a partisan political issue, and both Republicans and Democrats try to show they are tough on crime by using "sound bites" that fit into thirty-second commercials, rather than thoughtfully debating the substance and effectiveness of crime policy alternatives. Tonry, in analyzing reasons for the increase in incarceration rates in the United States, suggests that the partisan political approach to crime policy results in "widespread adoption of broadly defined three-strikes laws, mandatory minimum-sentence laws, sexual psychopath laws, and the federal sentencing guidelines.... [These laws] are too rigid and often result in unjustly harsh penalties...."[14]

Sentencing practices have also changed. During the mid-1900s, all states used indeterminate sentences, and release on parole peaked in 1977, as 72 percent of all prisoners were released on parole.[15] But with the demise of the medical model, the "tough on crime" attitude of the public and elected officials, and the belief that rehabilitation did not work, fifteen states and the federal government moved to the use of determinate sentences, and only 28 percent of offenders were released on parole in 1997.[16] By the end of 1999, forty-one states had adopted truth-in-sentencing (TIS) statutes, requiring inmates to serve 85 percent of a determinate sentence before release.[17] These sentencing changes have resulted in an unprecedented level of the prison population.

This toughening of philosophical approaches has influenced not only sentencing decisions, but also supervision in the community. For most of the 1990s, community supervision (probation and parole) underwent a transition from help-ing and counseling offenders to risk management and surveillance. This resulted in the allocation of resources for increased monitoring, rather than for counsel-ing and rehabilitative programs for offenders on probation and parole. In this **new penology** perspective, Rhine writes, "The traditional corrections objectives of rehabilitation and the reduction of offender recidivism give way to the rational and efficient deployment of control strategies for managing (and confining) high-risk criminal populations."[18]

As a result, there were more strident parole and probation monitoring with less tolerance for risk of crime by offenders, and increasing numbers of offenders are sent to prison as community supervision violators. The state prison popula-tion peaked at 1,405,622 in 2009, and of the 674,836 state prison admissions in that year, 237,449 (35 percent) were from parole violations.[19] Even more alarm-ing is that, for states reporting reasons for which individuals were incarcerated in 2010, 117,968 of 187,702 (63 percent) probationers were revoked under their new sentence without a new conviction and 127,918 of 177,252 (72 percent) parolees incarcerated were for a revocation and not a new sentence.[20] Courts and parole boards do not want to risk keeping uncertain offenders in the community. If minor violators later commit a serious crime, those deciding to allow them to continue in the community face criticism or even legal action. This risk-free ap-proach has a tremendous impact on prison populations and the commitment of taxpayer dollars to the prison systems of the United States.

In addition, since the 1980s, society has operated on the premise that il-licit drug use and trafficking create a serious danger to our society and way of life, and we have declared a **war on drugs**. Soon after this declaration, the U.S. Department of Justice took the position that "there is extensive evidence of the strong relationship between drug use and crime,"[21] noting that drug users report more involvement in crime, people with criminal records are more likely than those without criminal records to report being drug users, and crime rises as drug use increases. And by the turn of the century, the office of National Drug Control Policy's Operations budget was spending $10 billion a year for inter-diction or investigations.[22] With the continued increase in the dollars directed toward law enforcement efforts to find and arrest drug dealers and users, the increased federalization of drug crimes, and the enactment of federal criminal statutes requiring either five- or ten-year mandatory sentences for drug offend-ers, almost one-half of the BOP inmates are currently serving sentences for drug crimes.[23] These statutory and policy or operational changes have resulted not only in an increase in the total number of prisoners, but also in a continuous and dramatic rise in the incarceration rate of the United States. In 1980, the United States incarcerated 139 individuals per 100,000 population. This rate increased to 506 per 100,000 population in 2008, before declining to 450 people per 100,000 population in 2016, which was the lowest rate of imprisonment since 1997.[24]

Yet it is interesting to examine the outcome of all the additional inmates in-carcerated and dollars spent to add prison capacity. It has been more than twenty years since the passage by Congress of the Violent Crime and Law Enforcement Act of 1994, and studies are analyzing the impact of the increased use of incar-ceration. The Pew Center for the States reported that over the past two decades, the nation's imprisonment rate has climbed 24 percent and crime has declined 40 percent.[25] Some could suggest that is the benefit of the increased use of incar-ceration. However, deeper analysis illustrates that there are other factors associ-ated with this decrease in crime. The Pew report indicates that the five states with

new penology
an emphasis on the rational and efficient deployment of control strategies for managing and confining high-risk criminal populations

war on drugs
a Reagan initiative to reduce the availability and dependence on illicit drugs through interdiction, criminal sanctions, and treatment

Over the past two decades, billions of dollars have been spent to construct new prisons to keep up with the increase in the number of inmates. Courtesy of Federal Bureau of Prisons.

the largest decreases in crime (45 percent) also all had reductions in their rates of imprisonment. The state with the highest reduction in crime from 1994 to 2012 (New York at 54 percent) also reduced their prison population by 24 percent during the same period.

Meeting Growth Demands

To respond to the major increase in prison population over the past three decades, most jurisdictions have expanded capacity by building new prisons or by contracting with the private sector. As the inmate population increased, state legislatures and the U.S. Congress responded with financial support to construct hundreds of thousands of new prison beds. From 1993 to 2000, there were 288 new prisons constructed and opened,[26] and from June 30, 2000, to December 30, 2005, 153 new state and federal prisons and 151 new private prisons were constructed and opened.[27] As well, by the end of 2016, 128,323 state and federal offenders were held in prisons owned and operated by private facilities, and another 83,679 inmates were being held in local jails.[28] Yet in 2016, there were still fourteen states and the federal prison system that housed more inmates than they had capacity.[29] When building new prisons, there are many options for designs, and the way a prison is built will influence the style of management for years to come.

Federal and State Prison Systems

Most people think that only the federal and state governments operate prisons for adult offenders, but there are actually several other correctional systems and agencies in the United States. These include private companies that contract to house offenders for government jurisdictions, immigration facilities that hold noncitizens subject to deportation to their home country, military prisons that house violators of the military justice system, and U.S. territories and commonwealths that often operate their own prison systems. However, by far the largest numbers of prisoners are housed in state and federal prisons. The most recent census of correctional facilities indicated that at the end of 2005, there were 1,821 state and federal prisons in the United States, with a capacity of housing (without overcrowding) 1,430,208 prisoners.[30] However, the Bureau of Justice Statistics reported that state and federal prisons confined 1,505,397 inmates at the end of 2016, with fourteen states operating above their highest capacity and the federal prison system was operating at 114 percent of capacity.[31]

Historically, there has been a significant difference between federal and state prison systems. Each holds offenders convicted under the jurisdiction's specific criminal statutes. State penal codes usually include the standard **street crimes**, or those defined by the FBI as index crimes, including murder, robbery, rape, aggravated assault, burglary, larceny or theft, and motor vehicle theft. In the past, federal crimes included fraud and other white-collar offenses, movement of criminal activity across state or national boundaries, and crimes specific to the federal government, such as postal fraud or treason. However, over the past few decades, Congress has continually **federalized** crimes such as bank robbery, kidnapping, murder of public officials, drug distribution, and certain crimes using a weapon. As a result, there is now less distinction between the types of inmates in state and federal prisons than in the past. The sections below describe the current status and operation of both the federal and state prison systems.

street crimes
traditional reference to crimes with little sophistication required, such as murder, robbery, burglary, assault, and theft

federalized
the making of a crime a federal rather than a state offense; results when the U.S. Congress decides that it desires federal law enforcement and prosecution of certain offenses

The Federal Prison System

Until the late 1800s, offenders convicted of federal crimes were housed in state prisons if their sentence was for more than one year and in local jails if they were to serve less than one year. After the establishment of the U.S. Department of Justice in 1870, an official of the department was charged with the responsibility for the "care and custody" of all federal prisoners. However, as state prisons became more overcrowded, the states became reluctant to house federal offenders and pressured the Department of Justice to create facilities to maintain federal inmates.

As a result, Congress passed the **Three Penitentiary Act** on March 3, 1891, authorizing the construction of three penitentiaries to house federal offenders.[32] The Act included the construction and operation of federal prisons in Leavenworth, Kansas (construction beginning in 1896),[33] McNeil Island, Washington (constructed from 1892 to 1895), and Atlanta, Georgia (construction completed in 1899). These three prisons served the needs of the federal government and housed almost all federal inmates for several decades. As these facilities became more crowded, however, the Department of Justice sought the authority to construct additional prisons. As a result, Congress in 1925 authorized the construction of a reformatory for male prisoners between ages seventeen and thirty at Chillicothe, Ohio, and a federal prison for women was opened in Alderson, West Virginia, in 1927.

Three Penitentiary Act
the 1891 act of Congress that authorized the construction of the first three federal prisons

Establishment of the Federal Bureau of Prisons

By the end of the 1920s, officials in the Department of Justice determined that a separate agency within the department was needed to oversee the operation of the growing number of prisons. The Congressional Special Committee on Federal Penal and Reformatory Institutions agreed and recommended the establishment of a central agency to administer federal prisons. In 1930, Congress passed an

The U.S. Penitentiary in Leavenworth, Kansas, was one of the first three federal prisons authorized and built under the Three Penitentiary Act of 1891. Courtesy of the Federal Bureau of Prisons.

Federal Bureau of Prisons

an agency within the U.S. Department of Justice charged with housing and managing federal law offenders

Sanford Bates

the first director of the Federal Bureau of Prisons

Act to establish the **Federal Bureau of Prisons (BOP)** for the "management and regulation of all federal correctional and penal institutions,"[34] while providing more progressive and humane care for federal inmates, to professionalize the prison service, and to ensure consistent and centralized administration of the 11 federal prisons in operation at that time. President Herbert Hoover signed the Act into law on May 14, 1930, and **Sanford Bates** was appointed the first director of the BOP. Bates had been chief of the Massachusetts prison system, and his appointment began a trend (that continues today) of the director of the BOP being an experienced correctional administrator, rather than a political appointment. Since its origination, the BOP has had only nine directors:

Sanford Bates	1930–1937
James V. Bennett	1937–1964
Myrl E. Alexander	1964–1970
Norman A. Carlson	1970–1987
J. Michael Quinlan	1987–1992
Kathleen Hawk Sawyer	1992–2003
Harley G. Lappin	2003–2011
Charles E. Samuels, Jr.	2011–2016
Mark S. Inch	2017–present[35]

Growth of the Bureau of Prisons

It is interesting to examine the growth of the BOP over its history. Since federal offenders are those who commit crimes that Congress has placed under federal jurisdiction, growth comes primarily as a result of such Acts of Congress. The growth of the federal prison population, from the establishment of the BOP to current times, resulted from passage of criminal statutes extending the authority of the federal government to prosecute new crimes that were difficult for local law enforcement agencies to handle. Early examples of these Acts include the following:

- The *White Slave Act* in 1910 (interstate commerce of prostitution)
- The *Harrison Narcotic Act* in 1914 (taxing and records must be kept on controlled substances)
- The *Volstead Act* in 1918 (prohibition of the sale and consumption of alcohol)
- The *Dyer Act* of 1919 (interstate transportation of stolen vehicles)

By the end of the year the BOP was established (1930), there were fourteen federal prisons housing just over 13,000 inmates. By 1940, the bureau had grown to twenty-four institutions with 24,360 inmates. This total population did not change significantly between 1940 and 1980. However, the bureau decided that large institutions (averaging more than 1,000 inmates) were difficult to manage, and several new prisons were opened to reduce the average prison size. By 1980, there were forty-four federal prisons, just over 24,500 inmates, and approximately 10,000 employees.

The U.S. Bureau of Prisons has been fortunate to have had only nine directors since its creation in 1930. The first three Bureau directors are shown here. Courtesy of the Federal Bureau of Prisons.

During the 1980s, the bureau experienced the beginning of a tremendous population growth, the result of the **Sentencing Reform Act of 1984**, which abolished parole, established determinate sentencing, and reduced the amount of good time available to federal offenders. Other acts of Congress in 1986, 1988, and 1990 created mandatory minimum sentences for various crimes. At the end of the 1980s, the federal government acted again, declaring the war on drugs and passing several new laws to prosecute drug offenders under federal statutes. These included federalizing drug possession and distribution (the federal role had previously been limited to the prosecution of importers of illegal drugs), imposing mandatory minimum sentences of five and ten years for any offenders distributing illegal drugs, and lengthening other drug crime sentences. About the same time, federal government efforts to crack down on illegal immigration resulted in placement of more illegal aliens in federal prisons. As a result, the federal prison population again more than doubled, reaching approximately 136,000 at the end of 1999.[36] During the late 1990s, Congress ordered the District of Columbia to close its prison system, and the Bureau of Prisons was directed to house District of Columbia felons. This transfer was completed in 2001, and on December 31, 2001, the federal prison system held 6,930 District of Columbia inmates.[37]

During the early 2000s, some state prison systems actually reduced their prison populations. However, with the federalization of many offenses and increased BOP responsibility for housing District of Columbia and immigration offenders, the federal prison population has grown every year from 2000 to 2013, when it peaked at 219,298.[38] For the ten-year period from 2003 to 2013, the BOP grew at an average of 2.2 percent while the state prison population increased only by 0.5 percent.[39] During 2014, however, the BOP had its first population reduction in over two decades, and ended the year with 214,149 prisoners. This has been the result of the Congress following the lead of some state prison systems and modifying sentences to reduce prison terms for low-risk and nonviolent

Sentencing Reform Act of 1984
the act of Congress that abolished parole, established determinate sentencing, and reduced the amount of good time available to federal offenders

TABLE 5.1	U.S. Bureau of Prisons Population on January 4, 2018

Type of facility	Number of inmates
BOP-operated prisons	155,057
Long-term privately managed facilities	18,068
Community correctional centers	10,368
Total	183,493

Note: Community correctional centers include offenders in halfway houses, home confinement, and jails.

Source: Data from Federal Bureau of Prisons, available at http://www.bop.gov (accessed January 10, 2018).

offenders. This trend continued, and after several reforms of sentencing since that time, on January 4, 2018, the BOP population had declined to 183,493.[40]

Table 5.1 breaks this population into categories in terms of the type of facilities in which they are held.

The Bureau of Prisons Today

The federal prison system is a nationwide system of prisons and detention facilities for the incarceration of inmates sentenced for federal crimes and for the detention of individuals awaiting trial or sentencing in federal court. In January 2018, the BOP consisted of 109 secure prisons, and employed 38,133 staff.[41] Institutions are classified as one of five different **security levels** (minimum, low, medium, high, and administrative), with each level holding inmates with similar risks of violence and escape. The various security levels of prisons are distinguished by features such as towers and other perimeter security barriers (fences or walls) with detection devices, the type of housing for prisoners (cells or dormitory), and the staff member-to-inmate ratio.

Minimum-security institutions (federal prison camps) have dormitory housing, a relatively low staff member-to-inmate ratio, and limited or no perimeter fencing. Low-security prisons (federal correctional institutions) have double-fenced perimeters, mostly dormitory housing, strong work and program components, and a staff member-to-inmate ratio higher than in minimum-security facilities. Medium-security prisons (also called federal correctional institutions) have double fences with electronic detection systems, mostly cells for housing, and an even higher staff member-to-inmate ratio than in low-security prisons.

High-security institutions (U.S. penitentiaries) have highly secure perimeters (featuring walls or reinforced fences), cell housing, high staff member-to-inmate ratios, and close control of inmate movement within the prison. The fifth category of federal prisons, administrative facilities, comprises institutions with special missions, such as detention of pretrial offenders, treatment of inmates with serious or chronic medical problems, or containment of extremely dangerous, violent, or escape-prone inmates. The BOP also houses prisoners under the jurisdiction of the U.S. Marshals Service and therefore must build and operate detention facilities (jails) to house these inmates in several cities across the country. The Administrative Maximum (ADX) U.S. Penitentiary in Florence, Colorado, is an example of a BOP administrative facility; it is a "supermax" prison designed to hold federal inmates who have proved unmanageable by being violent or attempting escape at other secure prisons. The BOP has many institutions that are a part of a Federal Correctional Complex

security levels

levels such as minimum, low, medium, high, or maximum are distinct by such features as the presence of towers and other perimeter security barriers (fences or walls) with detection devices, the type of housing for prisoners (cells or dormitory), and the staff-to-inmate ratio

(FCC). At FCCs, institutions with different missions and security levels are located in close proximity to one another, and increase efficiency through shared services. As noted in Table 5.1, the BOP makes extensive use of community correctional centers (halfway houses or residential reentry centers), placing many inmates in these facilities thirty days to six months prior to their release from prison to help them adjust to life in the community. Some of these offenders are then placed in home confinement at the end of their halfway house terms. These placements not only aid in prison–community transition, but also reduce cost and prison population. In 2015, the Bureau released over 60,000 inmates, and approximately 75 percent were released through a community correctional center. Figure 5.1 illustrates the location of current BOP-operated facilities.

Dormitory housing, in which beds are lined up next to one another and inmates are not locked into cells, is used for minimum-security prisons. Photo by Richard P. Seiter.

As noted previously, the BOP has had a stable leadership over its more than eighty-year history. An interview with Harley G. Lappin, the seventh director of the Bureau of Prisons, is presented below.

An Interview With...

A Former Director of the Federal Bureau of Prisons

Harley G. Lappin. Courtesy of Harley G. Lappin

In 2003, Harley G. Lappin became the seventh director of the BOP. He is a career public administrator, who began his career with the BOP in 1985 as a case manager at a prison in Texarkana, Texas. Since that time, he has worked in four other prisons, serving as camp administrator, associate warden, and warden of two facilities. He was promoted to regional director in July 2001 and sworn in as director on April 4, 2003. He retired from that position in 2011, served as the chief corrections officer for Corrections Corporation of America (now CoreCivic) until 2018, and then retired from that position.

Question: What makes the BOP a successful correctional organization?

Director Lappin: It is really a combination of several important factors. The first and most significant one is our employees; our staff are our single most important resource. They facilitate the accomplishment of our mission and the outcomes we strive for every day. In that regard, quality training, on-the-job development, and an experienced cadre of employees who assist new employees in understanding the culture and expectations are critical to our success. The fact that our experienced staff have a commitment to our new employees certainly contributes to the success of this agency.

A second is leadership. Last week at our national wardens' training we had a panel of past directors who discussed leadership and the importance of selecting leaders at every level of the organization. It was fascinating to hear how each of the former directors understood the critical role leadership plays in continuing the success of the BOP. It was quite clear that one of the most important decisions we make as leaders is selecting future leaders like wardens, associate wardens, and other senior and middle-level managers who will lead the agency into the future.

And finally, I would have to say the availability and consistent application of policy and oversight. The BOP is a policy-driven agency. While we encourage staff to be innovative, we

(Continued)

recognize that we have many tried and true methods that have been developed through years of experience that are consistently carried out at all BOP facilities through our written policy and procedures.

Question: How has the BOP been successful in creating a culture of professionalism?

Director Lappin: Again, leadership and experienced employees who continue this spirit of professionalism are critical. We establish high standards in terms of how our prisons look and are managed, as well as how employees approach their jobs and their personal and professional responsibilities. Another important consideration is our emphasis on communication among employees and between staff and inmates. We constantly reinforce the importance of communication and how it is essential to proactive and effective prison management.

Question: What were some of the key challenges facing the BOP when you were director?

Director Lappin: The key to our continued success was the recruitment and development of good people for our workforce. Predictions are that the work-force of the future will vary in skill level and there will more than likely be a smaller pool of candidates than in years past. Our challenge is to recruit and retain staff with skill levels consistent with our needs or deploy a training program that enhances the skill level of the candidate pool to meet our needs. For example, for us to be successful we must have staff that communicate effectively and are problem solvers. With greater competition for this group, we must ensure that if we hire less skilled people, we provide them with training opportunities to acquire the level of skill necessary in these areas to succeed as correctional professionals.

A second challenge was the continued expansion of the federal prison system. We saw that even while the prison population of some states was declining, some of that decline is due to the federalization of crimes and lead to continued growth for the BOP. In addition, the post-9-11 focus on terrorism and the immigration/border initiatives will result in an increase in the federal inmate population.

Question: What advice would you give to college students thinking about a career in corrections or a career with the Bureau?

Director Lappin: I would encourage them to consider public service of any kind. Serving your country in this manner is not only personally rewarding, but also critically important to the future of our country. Specifically, corrections provides a wealth of opportunities and experiences that may not be found in many other occupations. I encourage our high school and college students to prepare themselves for entrance into the work-force of the future. It is critically important they be effective, skilled communicators. I suggest they take advantage of every opportunity to improve writing and public speaking skills, whether they intend to work in the public or private sector.

Federal Prison Industries

One of the most unique and successful program in U.S. corrections is Federal Prison Industries (FPI), which operates under the trade name of UNICOR. FPI is a wholly owned corporation of the U.S. government and it was created to serve and is administratively housed in the Bureau of Prisons. As noted in Chapter 1, the Industrial Prison Era (from approximately 1910 to 1935) essentially ended as Congress passed the Hawes-Cooper Act in 1929 and the Ashurst-Sumners Act in 1935, drastically restricting the sale of prison-made goods on the open market and idling thousands of inmates who were working in both state and federal prison industry programs. The current use of prison industry programs is presented in Chapter 14.

As a result of this idleness in prisons, there were several prison riots and disturbances throughout the United States. The leadership of the BOP (Director Sanford Bates and Assistant Director James V. Bennett) set out to create a work program that could work around the concern for prison goods being sold on the open market, and still have the positive impact by keeping inmates productively occupied. They worked with the Department of Justice to craft legislation, whereas the industry products would be sold exclusively to the federal government, and a board of five directors representing outside interests would balance the work program's correctional needs while minimizing private industry impact.[42] There was initial

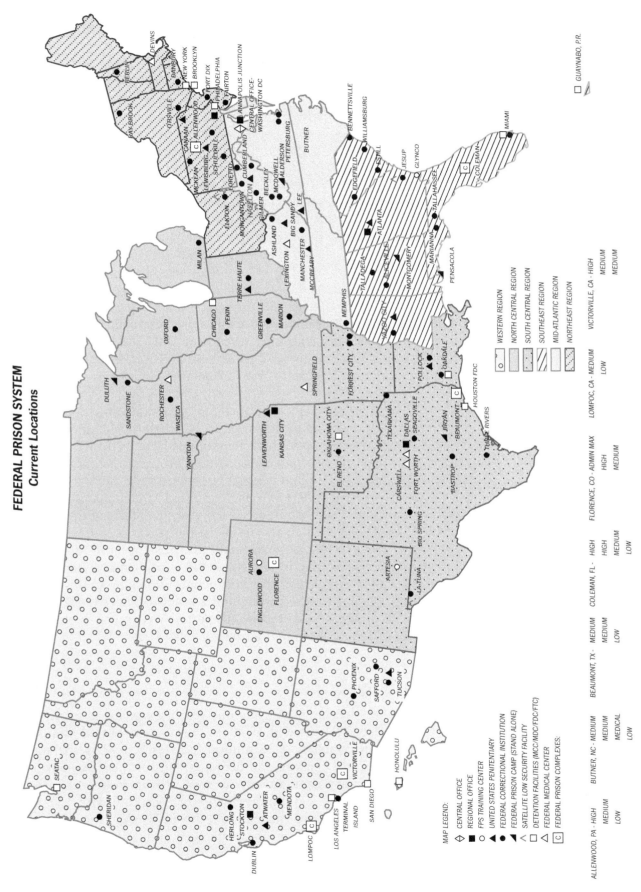

FIGURE 5.1 Federal Prison System: Current Locations   Source: Bureau of Prisons website, available at www.bop.gov (accessed August 27, 2017).

opposition from labor groups; however, President Franklin D. Roosevelt took a personal interest in working to overcome the opposition, and signed the law establishing FPI on June 23, 1934, and on January 1, 1935, FPI officially began operations under Executive Order 6917.

Initial products and industrial operations were limited, and included a textile mill, a shoe factory, and a broom and brush operation. FPI soon added production of mattresses, clothing, wood and metal furniture, a brick plant, and laundry operations. As the Bureau of Prisons grew, FPI continued to grow to meet its mission to "protect society and reduce crime by preparing inmates for successful reentry through job training."[43] The goal is to employ a significant number of inmates, both to reduce idleness and provide them training and work experience essential for success after release. By the 1990s, FPI had over 100 factories producing 150 different products, and had grown to employ over 20,000 inmates with annual sales of over $400 million.[44] Over the next two decades, the private sector became much more aggressive in their opposition to FPI, and lobbied Congress to restrict their sales. These efforts were successful to a point, and with Congressional action and partnership with the private sector, FPI reduced their sales and impact. However, by the end of fiscal year (FY) 2016, they still operated 63 factories and three farms, while employing 10,896 inmates in their six business segments: Agribusiness, Clothing and Textiles, Electronics, Office Furniture, Recycling, and Services. And for FY 2016, FPI had sales and other revenue of $605,252,000 and earnings of $4.057 million. Of these revenues, 72 percent is purchased from U.S. vendors for materials and supplies, 23 percent is for staff salaries, and 5 percent is for inmate salaries.[45]

FPI promotes that they are a correctional program, and not a business. However, if they are a program, they need to be self-sufficient and not use taxpayer dollars for their operation. There are multiple benefits from FPI. First is the self-funding provision of a valuable correctional program. Estimates are that it would cost well over $100 million per year to provide space and pay staff to provide an alternate program (if there was one) for over 10,000 inmates. Second, even inmate wages go to a valuable purpose. Each year, inmates pay over $1 million of their earnings to meet their financial obligations, such as court-ordered fines, child support, or crime restitution. And finally and perhaps most importantly, FPI has been shown to be effective in reducing recidivism. Inmates who participate in prison industries or completed other vocational training programs were found to be 24 percent less likely to recidivate and 14 percent more likely to be gainfully employed up to twelve years following release.[46] As argued by the Bureau of Prisons, FPI is a prison program that works.

State Prison Systems

Most adult prisoners serving more than one year are housed in facilities operated by the fifty states. At the end of 2016, the states operated almost 1,250 prisons holding approximately 1.32 million inmates.[47] Just as the states are very different in terms of the size and demographics of their populations, the state prison systems vary dramatically as well. Prison populations in 2016 ranged from Texas with 163,703 inmates to North Dakota with 1,791,[48] and in 2005, the number of prisons ranged from five in Washington, D.C., to 132 in Texas.[49] The state prison systems have changed dramatically in the past fifty years, both in terms of organization (moving from a decentralized to a centralized system of management) and in terms of the number of prisons and inmates supervised.

⬛ You Make the Decision...

Support Prison Industries?

The above section describes the history and growth of Federal Prison Industries. As noted, over the past two decades, there has been a strident debate regarding prison industries; inmates manufacture products that are sold to states or (with limited allowances) on the open market. The open market option under the PIE program is described in more detail in Chapter 14. But the argument is the same even when prison industries sell only to government agencies. FPI sells primarily to the federal government, and most state prison industries sell their products to the state or local governments. Trade associations and labor unions argue that any prisoner-made products compete with products manufactured in the private sector and since prisoners are paid minimal (if any) wages, that puts private companies at a disadvantage, and prisoners therefore take the jobs of law-abiding citizens.

The argument by correctional agencies is that: (1) prison industries is a training program that reduces recidivism, (2) while inmates are paid minimal amounts, the cost of operating in a prison is much greater than operating in the community and therefore the total costs are similar, and (3) that prison industries buy their materials and supplies locally, and many of the products they manufacture are actually imported and they bring back jobs to the United States rather than cost us jobs.

Students should examine many factors and then come to their own conclusion as to which position (that of the correctional agency or that of the private sector) they support. First, analyze and find those arguments you agree with. Then, either in a group or individually, make a decision as to which position you support. You can't be in the middle; support either prison industries or the private sector.

Since the first prison was created in Pennsylvania in 1790, there had been very slow growth with the state prison population, reaching 294,918 in 1980.[50] In the next ten years, the population climbed to 678,446, an increase of 130 percent.[51] Another decade of growth, and the state prison population reached 1,245,845 by 2000, another increase of 84 percent.[52] Things then began to slow down, and after growth of only 13 percent from 2000 to 2009,[53] the state prison population actually declined by 6.5 percent from 2009 to 2016.[54] The growth from 1980 until 2009 was driven by the major changes in sentencing, to include the replacement of indeterminate sentences and parole with determinate sentences, mandatory minimum sentences, three-strikes laws, and tough sentencing guidelines. State legislatures took discretion away from both judges and administrative officials (limiting good time and parole), and continually changed not only who went to prison, but also lengthened the time served for most offenses. Since 2009, the challenge of fiscal needs of the large number of prisons, inmates, and staff resulted in several sentencing reforms. Yet, each state adopts its own penal code, specifying what acts are considered felonies, what range of sentences is available for each category of crime, and what type of sentencing structure it will have. As noted in earlier chapters, this results in considerable differences in the incarceration rates and therefore in the prison populations among states. Figure 5.2 illustrates the growth and then decline in the number of state prisoners over the past several decades.

The Organization of State Prison Systems

Over the past decades, state correctional agencies have gone through a slow but deliberate transformation. The early eras of state prison operations were similar to the pre-1930s for the federal prison system, with no central control of prisons and legislatures allocating budgets and personnel directly to each individual prison. State prison wardens were often said to have their own individual

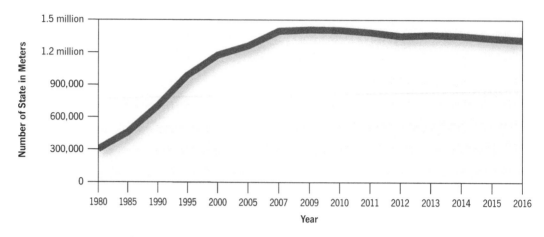

FIGURE 5.2   Trends in the State Prison Population over the Past 35 Years

"fiefdoms," with complete control over the hiring and firing of staff and the management and discipline of inmates.

Even as late as the first half of the twentieth century, many wardens of state prisons were appointed by governors, with no cabinet-level agency to oversee prison operations. However, as prison systems became larger, as their missions became more complex resulting from the increasing intervention of courts defining expected constitutional standards, and as prisons became more visible and accountable to the public, many states formed cabinet-level departments specifically to oversee the state prisons. Riveland writes, "Thirty-two states are organized with separate Departments of Corrections reporting to the Executive; 11 as separate departments reporting to boards or commissions; 5 under a Department of Public Safety umbrella, and 1 under a social services umbrella. Twenty-four of the separate departments have been so organized since 1979."[55] These state correctional agencies have become very large and very complex. Of the fifty state adult correctional systems, nine are also responsible for juvenile corrections, twenty-seven have some probation responsibility, thirty-three supervise parole functions, and twenty-nine manage community corrections programs.[56]

The most common organizational model (twenty-four states) has the director, commissioner, or secretary of corrections as a cabinet-level officer, appointed by and reporting directly to the governor. In eleven other state correctional agencies, the corrections chief reports to a board or commission. The purpose behind this type of organizational model is to have some separation between politics and correctional policy.

The members of the corrections boards or commissions are appointed by the governor and usually must be made up of individuals from different political parties (often a like number of Republicans and Democrats) and serve overlapping terms. Therefore, governors are not able to immediately replace the board or commission with their own appointees, having to wait until terms end to replace members. The boards and commissions are relatively stable as a result, maintaining consistency of policy and leadership in the correctional agency. Figure 5.3 illustrates three models of reporting by correctional agencies. In the first, the corrections director reports directly to a governor. In the second, the director reports to a board or commission. The third is the federal model, in which the BOP director is appointed by and reports to the attorney general of the United States. An interesting trend in the appointment of correctional directors is described in the "A Case Study" box.

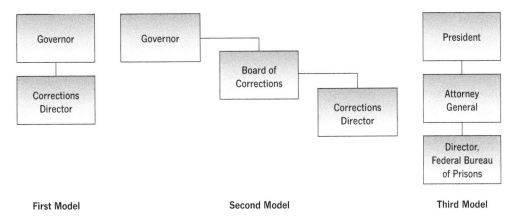

First Model   Second Model   Third Model

FIGURE 5.3 Three Models of Correctional Agency Relationship to the Chief Executive

A Case Study

Appointing Correctional Directors

A very important issue is how directors of state and federal prison systems are appointed. As noted previously, there are three types of organizational structures for departments of corrections: reporting to a governor, a state board of corrections, or the U.S. attorney general. The most relevant factor is the stability of the director in the position, how often there is a change of leadership, and the continuity of leadership that results. As noted in the discussion of the BOP, the agency has had only nine directors since 1930. In Ohio, I was one of only eight state directors since 1970. However, many states have governors that serve only one four-year term, and with each turnover of governors, there is a new director of corrections. Such rapid turnover usually results in a lack of continuity of programs, operations, and leadership that reduces the quality of the overall operation of the correctional agency.

There are three scenarios in which directors of corrections are appointed. The first is the career correctional professional, in which the politics of the governor or the attorney general have little impact on the selection of the corrections chief. With the federal prison system, there has never been a "political" change of directors, even though there have been dozens of attorneys general and changes in political parties throughout the seven decades of the BOP. A few states are similar in that the corrections director survives changes in governors and political parties, as the professionalism and competence of the leader are considered more important than being of the same political party or the person that the governor wants in the position. This, in most people's opinions, is the best situation, allowing for competent leadership and a long-term shaping of the department's culture and organization to best accomplish its mission. As well, staff members see the agency as a career and strive to work to the top of the agency, without fear that promotion will at some point lead to dismissal.

The second scenario is that in which a professional correctional person is appointed as director of a state correctional agency, but the leadership turns over with every new governor. Most states unfortunately fall into this category, although a few state directors prove themselves so accomplished at their jobs that the governor decides to keep that person rather than replace him or her with someone new just for the sake of change. I have several close associates and friends who have been directors of state correctional agencies in several states, moving on as they are replaced in one state, but with the knowledge and reputation to get a job in another state almost immediately (as governors are elected at the same time in many states). Even with professional leadership, this lack of continuity is usually a negative in the ability for the agency to reach its maximum potential.

The third scenario is, in most professional correctional administrators' minds, the worst. As correctional agencies become more of a political concern to elected officials, they sometimes decide not to appoint a correctional professional, but instead to appoint someone with a strong political background. This occurs when governors believe there is more danger to their reelection from making political than correctional management mistakes. These governors sometimes look to the state legislature to select someone who they know supports their criminal justice policies, or sometimes select a sheriff who may have some correctional background in running a jail but has also stood for election for the office of sheriff. One of the worst examples of this scenario occurred in a state in which the governor had originally appointed a professional correctional administrator who was extremely well respected throughout the country. However, after some disagreement between the governor and director regarding some issues of correctional policy (such as whether to have a chain gang), the director was fired. The governor appointed a funeral director as head of corrections, whose only experience was as a member of the state legislature.

Inmates in State Prison Systems

At the end of 2016, the makeup of state prison inmates was predominantly male (93 percent); the racial breakdown was 34 percent white, 35 percent black, 20 percent Hispanic, and 11 percent other minority; 53 percent were violent offenders.[57] Table 5.2 illustrates the percentage of sentenced state inmates by type of crime in 1990, 2000, and 2016. The Bureau of Justice Statistics reports that in 2016, in addition to the 55 percent of offenders serving sentences for violent offenses, 18 percent were serving sentences for property offenses, 15 percent for drug offenses, and 12 percent for public-order offenses. Of the violent offenses, murder accounted for 13.7 percent, manslaughter 1.3 percent, robbery 13.2 percent, rape 12.5 percent, and assault offenses 10.5 percent of all offenses.[58]

The largest growth of state prison inmates at the end of 2015 was among violent offenders. This is very different from the growth by offense category (predominantly drug offenses) within federal prisons. As many drug crimes were federalized, the federal prison population grew, resulting in almost one-half of all federal prison inmates serving sentences for drug offenses. In 1980, in both state and federal prisons, drug offenders made up less than 10 percent of the nation's prisoners and violent offenders, almost 60 percent. By 1993, the number of drug offenders had risen to 26 percent of the total, and the number of violent offenders had dropped to 45 percent of the total.[59] By 1995, there were 52,782 drug offenders in federal prisons, and by July 2017, 81,049 (46.3 percent) federal prisoners were drug offenders.[60] Therefore, the growth of violent offenders in state prisons comes about from two phenomena. First, violent offenders are receiving much longer sentences than in the past and therefore, as more are admitted to prison without others being released, the overall number increases. Second, the percentage of the total inmates who are serving sentences for violent offenses increases as many drug offenders are diverted to federal prisons.

A phenomenon over the past several years among state prison systems is the decline in the growth of inmates. After almost two decades of dramatic increases, the growth has begun to slow and the level of overcrowding in state prisons has decreased. Table 5.3 illustrates the growth in the number of state inmates over the past fifteen years. State prison populations grew by 12.9 percent between 2000 and 2009, but declined by 6.5 percent between 2009 and 2016. There was a small increase in 2013, but only by 6,293 (0.4 percent) inmates, as twenty-eight states experienced an increase in their populations.

There is debate over what issues have most influenced the decline in the number of state prison inmates over the past few years, and several possible reasons

TABLE 5.2	Percentage of Sentenced State Inmates by Type of Crime, 1990, 2000, and 2016		
Type of crime	**1990**	**2000**	**2016**
Violent	46%	49%	55%
Property	25	20	18
Drug	22	21	15
Public order/other	7	10	12

Sources: Data from Heather C. West and William J. Sabol, *Prisoners in 2007* (Washington, D.C.: U.S. Department of Justice, Bureau of Justice Statistics, December 2008), p. 27; and E. Ann Carson, *Prisoners in 2016* (Washington, D.C.: U.S. Department of Justice, 2018), p. 18.

TABLE 5.3	Persons Held in State Prisons, December 31, 2000, 2005–2016
Year	**State**
2000	1,245,845
2005	1,338,292
2006	1,375,628
2007	1,397,217
2008	1,407,002
2009	1,407,369
2010	1,404,032
2011	1,382,606
2012	1,352,582
2013	1,358,875
2014	1,351,752
2015	1,330,148
2016	1,316,205
Average annual change,	1.4%
2000–2009	+1.4%
2009–2016	−6.5%

Sources: Data from E. Ann Carson, "Prisoners in 2016," *BJS Bulletin* (Washington, D.C.: U.S. Department of Justice, 2018); and Heather C. West, William J Sabol, and Sarah J. Greenman, "Prisoners in 2009," *BJS Bulletin* (Washington, DC: U.S. Department of Justice, 2010).

exist for the drop. The first possibility is that demographics have changed; fewer Americans are in the high-crime age group and have enough criminal history to be sent to prison. Second, crime rates have been dropping. In addition, more crimes are being prosecuted at the federal level, and offenders who would have otherwise been in state prisons are now in federal prisons. But the most often cited reason for the reduction in prison populations is the impact of tightened budgets, as states looked for ways to reduce costs by reducing the number of offenders in prison. This issue is presented in more detail in Chapter 16.

Classification within State Prison Systems

State prison systems use security-level classifications similar to the federal prison system. One major difference, however, is that many states have central reception centers at which all inmates are initially placed until they are classified. Upon their arrival at the reception center, state inmates receive a **security classification** to determine to which prison they will be assigned. The purpose of a security classification is to match offenders to institutions that have the physical security and staff resources to prevent escapes and control their behavior. However, also important for the assignment to a prison is the need for specific programs for the inmate. Both security and program need determinations are the result of several factors. Inmates go through psychological, educational, or vocational testing, and their past records are reviewed. The presentence investigation (PSI) provides much of the information regarding criminal history, family and social history, education and vocational achievement, and employment history.

security classification
to match offenders to institutions that have the physical security and staff resources to prevent escapes and control their behavior

Objective classification systems, or actuarial methods to score past criminal behavior and program needs and predict offenders' risk of violence and escape, are used in most states to determine security classification. Points are assigned based on offenders' history, and the point totals indicate the level of security (minimum, medium, maximum) that is required for each inmate. In addition to security classification, inmates' program needs and home are also considered in the decision of prison assignment. Most states have many similar-security-level prisons (for instance, Michigan has twenty-five medium-security prisons), and inmates are assigned both geographically (as close to home as possible) and to meet specific program needs (some prisons may have specialized mental health or substance abuse programs).

The states use somewhat different terminologies for security classifications. In 2005, slightly more than a third of inmates were classified as maximum security, two-fifths as medium security, and one-fifth as minimum security.[61] The following illustrates the number of prisons by security level at the end of 2005:

Maximum security	372
Medium security	480
Minimum security	969

The number of facilities by security classifications has shifted a little from 2000 to 2005, as the number of maximum-security prisons has increased by 12 percent, the number of medium-security facilities has declined by 8 percent, and the number of minimum-security facilities has increased by 19 percent. Objective classification systems put much weight on the length of time to be served before release. Part of the reason for the growth of maximum-security facilities is that as sentences lengthen, the security level of an inmate with the same criminal history and background may be increased, only because he or she is serving a longer sentence. Minimum-security numbers have increased as many more offenders who used to get probation for such crimes as drunk driving or low-level drug sales are now serving short prison terms.

The security levels of state prisons are similar to those of federal prisons. Minimum-security institutions often have dormitory housing or sometimes dorm rooms like colleges with four to ten inmates sharing a room, with a low staff-to-inmate ratio, and without a secure perimeter. There will either be a single fence or sometimes no fence, as the purpose is not to physically keep inmates from escaping; their short sentences are usually enough to keep them from taking that risk. Inmate movement is very free flowing; inmates move without supervision from their housing area to assignments, the cafeteria, or recreation. Medium-security prisons have double-fence perimeters with electronic detection systems, mostly cells for housing, and a higher staff member-to-inmate ratio than in minimum-security prisons. Inmates still move somewhat freely, but under constant supervision, and they are outside their cells during much of the work or program day.

Maximum-security prisons have highly secure perimeters with walls or reinforced fences and often armed control towers. There is cell housing and a high staff-to-inmates ratio, and inmate movement is very structured and often escorted by staff. Inmates still work and are in programs, but usually in smaller numbers of inmates at any time. Another security level sometimes utilized are "supermax" prisons. The development and use of these for very violent offenders are described in Chapter 9, and the controversies and reforms of these facilities are discussed in Chapter 16. In supermax prison, inmates spend almost all their time in their cells, as the mission is to control behavior and limit violence. When inmates leave their cells, they are often in handcuffs and under multiple-staff supervision.

After classification at the reception center, inmates are transferred to the prison at which they begin serving their sentence. At their assigned prison, inmates go through an orientation regarding rules and regulations, policies and procedures, and processes such as adding people to their visiting or telephone list. Inmates then go through another classification process to determine what type of prison job they will have and what type of programs they will be assigned. This classification and assignment process uses the results of the education, vocational and mental health tests, and assessments that were completed in the reception center. These are discussed with inmates, who state their preference for work and program assignments. In most states, all inmates must have a job unless they receive a full-time program assignment. Most programs (education and substance abuse) are voluntary, although in some states and under certain sentences, education (up to the level of basic literacy) and substance abuse programs may be mandatory. Table 5.4 illustrates the types of assignments inmates receive in prisons. After assignment, inmates begin the daily routine that they will carry out throughout their sentence. These routines and inmate activities are described in Chapters 12 and 13.

Prisons are classified by the physical security features, primarily focused on preventing escapes. Courtesy of CoreCivic.

The Design of State Prisons

The importance of the architectural design of prisons cannot be overstated. Although some minor modifications may be possible, the type or design of housing units, the location of the buildings within the secure perimeter, and even the perimeter itself mandate certain operational and staffing patterns. Prison architecture has evolved slowly over the past 150 years, with few major changes since the first prisons were built in the United States in the early 1800s.

TABLE 5.4	Inmate Prison Assignments	
Assignment	**Number of inmates**	**Percent of total**[a]
Prison industry	78,881	7.8
Prison farm	34,180	3.6
Other work	550,583	47.0
Full-time education or vocational	129,049	13.9
Part-time education or vocational[b]	129,683	14.5

[a]The total will not be 100 percent because some inmates are unassigned and some states have other assignments not included in these categories.

[b]Part-time includes release preparation, adult continuing education, parenting, and fitness and wellness programs.

Source: Data from Camille Graham Camp and George M. Camp, *The 2002 Corrections Yearbook: Adult Systems* (Middletown, Conn.: Criminal Justice Institute, 2003), p. 82.

In the early days of prison design, housing units had either inside or outside cells, which were "linear" in that the cells were arranged side-by-side in one long row. With inside cell design, the cells back up to one another, with a corridor for staff movement around the cells, and between the cell fronts and the cellblock walls. With **outside cells**, the staff corridor is between the rows of cells, which face each other and are abutted to the wall. With outside cell arrangements, each cell usually has its own window, and there is only one barrier between the inmate and breaking out of the cellblock. The **inside cells** are considered more secure, because inmates attempting escape would have to both get out of their cells and get through the cell block walls. In either cell configuration, the linear design required staff to be directly in front of a cell to see inside.

As prison architects laid out the prison footprint, they placed cellhouses in one of two formats. The first is a radial design, with cells and corridors extending like a wheel from a central control point. The first prison constructed specifically as a prison, the Eastern State Penitentiary in Philadelphia, Pennsylvania, was laid out in a radial design. Most prisons built in the nineteenth and twentieth centuries used the telephone-pole design, where the housing units were like the extensions from the top of a telephone pole, off a long and wide central corridor. The problem with this design is that all inmate movement had to occur at one time through the central corridor, making it hard for staff to see and to supervise. Figure 5.4 illustrates inside cell, outside cell, and radial and telephone pole designs.

The most significant change in prison design occurred since the 1970s, as correctional architects began to use a campus-style design. Campus-style prisons were initiated by the federal BOP and were first used at the federal correctional institutions in Morgantown, West Virginia; Pleasanton (now called Dublin), California; and Miami, Florida. Campus designs are now commonly used in state as well as federal prisons. In campus designs, the buildings are separated and spread out within the secure perimeter. It is believed that forcing inmates to move from one building to another, and walking outside instead of within a corridor have a positive effect on the environment of the prison. Also, with the decentralized location of the buildings, there is less inmate congestion as they move through the prison, reducing the likelihood of tension. As the benefits of the campus style of prisons became better known, this model was adopted by several states.

As the campus design was used more regularly, a further refinement came into being. As illustrated in Figure 5.5, the campus design was modified to take advantage of potential cost savings. Instead of each area of the prison being a separate building, some buildings are put together to use common walls and a common roof. An example of this style of architecture is the Federal Correctional Institution (FCI) in Greenville, Illinois. At FCI Greenville, one large programs and operations building includes space for maintenance, food/inmate services,

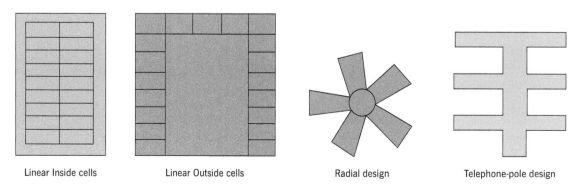

| Linear Inside cells | Linear Outside cells | Radial design | Telephone-pole design |

FIGURE 5.4   Early Styles of Prison Designs

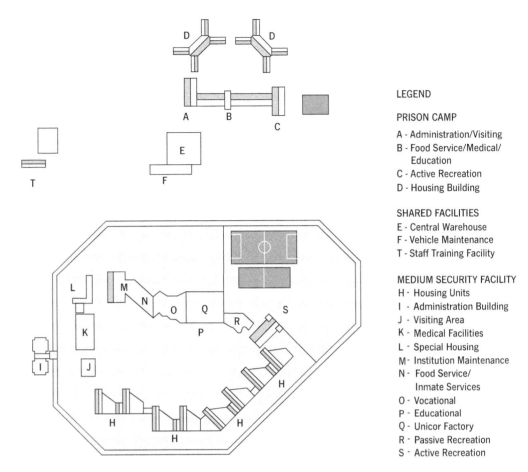

LEGEND

PRISON CAMP

A - Administration/Visiting
B - Food Service/Medical/
    Education
C - Active Recreation
D - Housing Building

SHARED FACILITIES

E - Central Warehouse
F - Vehicle Maintenance
T - Staff Training Facility

MEDIUM SECURITY FACILITY

H - Housing Units
I - Administration Building
J - Visiting Area
K - Medical Facilities
L - Special Housing
M- Institution Maintenance
N - Food Service/
    Inmate Services
O - Vocational
P - Educational
Q - Unicor Factory
R - Passive Recreation
S - Active Recreation

FIGURE 5.5 The Design of FCI Greenville Source: Federal Bureau of Prisons, *Greenville Federal Correctional Institution* (Washington, D.C.: U.S. Department of Justice, no date), p. 3.

vocational training, education, Unicor (industries), and passive recreation. As the "footprint" of FCI Greenville illustrates, the prison is still a campus style, even with these several activities sharing a common roof and walls.

Another development in prison design that is often used in campus designs is podular designs which are considered to have several advantages over linear designs. They provide common areas in the center of the unit (called dayrooms), in which inmates can watch television or play table games during the day, thus getting out of their cells and reducing idleness and tension. Podular designs also make it easier for officers to view inmate activity in the cells as well as the dayroom from one central location. And podular designs easily lend themselves to the use of direct supervision of inmates. Podular housing units often use a "triangle" design, and two triangles can be connected by central staff offices and record storage areas, creating a "bow tie," as illustrated in the housing building in Figure 5.6.

As noted in Chapter 3, direct supervision puts staff in direct contact with inmates, as inmate cells are situated around the outside of the building, with staff offices, showers, and quiet recreation rooms interspersed among the cells. During the day, in minimum and medium security prisons, cell doors are often kept unlocked, and inmates may move from their cells into the open, central day room space. Correctional officers move freely with inmates in the day room and can easily see into cells. And other staff offices are located among the cell locations and make staff easily accessible to inmates. Direct supervision is used in most states, as it has been found to be effective in both reducing serious incidents and lowering correctional costs.[62]

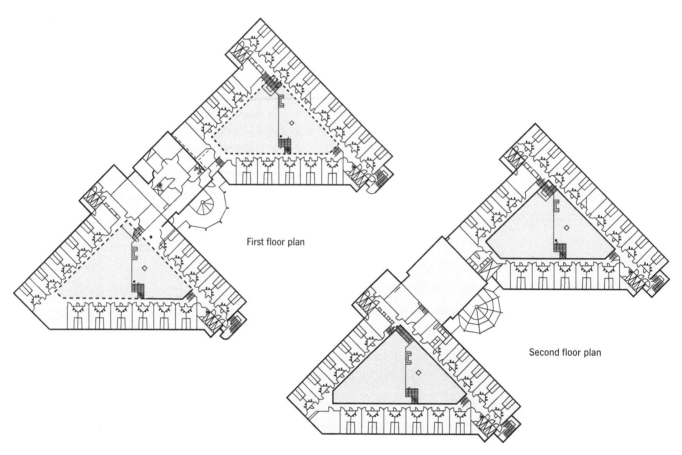

FIGURE 5.6   Popular Design of Prison Housing Units   Source: Federal Bureau of Prisons, *Greenville Federal Correctional Institution* (Washington, D.C.: U.S. Department of Justice, no date), p. 8.

Other Public Correctional Systems

State and federal prisons by far hold most of the adult prisoners housed in correctional facilities in the United States. However, there are also almost 34,000 individuals detained in immigration facilities, approximately 1,400 inmates in military facilities, and 10,000 in U.S. territories and commonwealths. First, the U.S. **Immigration and Customs Enforcement (ICE)** is responsible for housing illegal aliens pending a hearing or deportation back to their home country. Individuals are usually detained in three ways: first, if caught while attempting to illegally enter the United States; second, if they are arrested for commission of a crime and then held because they are in the United States without permission; and if there are raids by ICE officials of housing or workplaces and the officials find individuals who are in the country illegally. Whenever an illegal alien is detained, they are subject to potential deportation.

The number of ICE detainees has been increasing over the past few years (see Table 5.5) as enforcement efforts to catch and detain individuals attempting to enter the United States illegally increased. This number has remained relatively consistent through the end of 2015. In the last few years of the Obama administration, ICE placed increased emphasis and focus on the removal of convicted felons and other public safety threats over noncriminals. This resulted in a reduction

Immigration and Customs Enforcement (ICE)
the agency of the U.S. government responsible for housing illegal aliens pending a hearing or deportation back to their home country

TABLE 5.5	Number of Detainees Held by the U.S. Immigration and Customs Enforcement (ICE), December 31, 1995, 2002, 2006, and 2011			
	2011	**2006**	**2002**	**1995**
Total	33,384	27,368	21,065	8,177

Sources: Data from Paige M. Harrison and Allen J. Beck, "Prisoners in 2002," *Bureau of Justice Statistics Bulletin,* July 2000 (revised August 27, 2003), p. 8; and Heather C. West and William J. Sabol, "Prisoners in 2007," *Bureau of Justice Statistics Bulletin* (Washington, D.C.: U.S. Department of Justice, December 2008), p. 26, and ICE website at www.ice/gov/about/offices/enforcement-removal-operations (accessed February 17, 2012).

in the total number of removals and returns (from approximately 370,000 in 2013 to just over 230,000 in 2015). However, this did not have a great impact on the number of detainees, as most of those were arrested for a criminal act beyond illegal immigration.

ICE operates some facilities itself, and ICE facilities detain only about a third of its total detainees. The remainder is housed by the BOP or other federal facilities, under contract to private facilities, or under intergovernmental agreements in state prisons or local jails. At the end of 2015, ICE either operated or contracted with 111 facilities to house illegal alien detainees.[63] During 2015, ICE arrested, removed, or returned 235,413 illegal immigrants. Of this total, 165,935 were apprehended while, or shortly after, attempting to illegally enter the United States. The remaining 69,478 were apprehended in the interior of the United States and the vast majority were convicted criminals who fell within ICE's civil immigration enforcement priorities.[64] However, many more noncitizens are convicted of crimes and serve their sentences in state or federal prisons, and, upon completion of the sentence, are turned over for ICE for removal hearings. At the end of 2015, there were 65,107 in 49 states (not including California) and the federal prison system. This does not include the number of detainees noted above in ICE-operated or -contracted facilities.[65]

Another type of correctional organization, the U.S. military services, also operates prisons or **brigs** to house offenders convicted of violating the military justice codes. Table 5.6 illustrates that the military branches held 1,338 detainees in 2016, with 78 percent serving sentences of one year or more.[66] This number has declined by over 40 percent since reaching 2,420 in 2000. Table 5.7 indicates the offenses for which these offenders are sentenced in military prisons.

The final category of public correctional institutions is that of territorial prisons. The five U.S. territories and commonwealths operate correctional facilities that serve as jails and prisons for these jurisdictions. Each has a court and correctional system similar to those of a state, and these correctional populations seem to be following the same trends as states, in that they grew during the first decade of the twenty-first century, but now the growth is slowing or even declining. As indicated in Table 5.8, these five authorities held a total of 12,266 offenders in custody, of which 88 percent were in Puerto Rico.[67] The total in custody has declined almost 24 percent from 16,130 in 2000 to 112,266 in 2016. The largest proportion of the territorial population (78 percent) are serving a sentence of one year or more.

brig
a military term meaning a correctional facility

TABLE 5.6	Prisoners Under Military Jurisdiction by Branch of Service, Year-Ends 2015 and 2016					
	Total population[a]			Sentenced population[b]		
Jurisdiction	2015	2016	Percent change 2015–2016	2015	2016	Percent change 2015–2016
Total number of prisoners	1,398	1,338	−4.3%	1,092	1,084	−0.7%
Military branch of service						
Air Force	250	236	−5.6%	187	192	2.7%
Army	668	646	−3.3	589	577	−2.0
Marine Corps	255	245	−3.9	157	153	−2.5
Navy	202	191	−5.4	141	145	2.8
Coast Guard	23	20	−13.0	18	17	−5.6
In custody of—						
Air Force	33	27	−18.2%	2	5	:
Army	802	781	−2.6	736	713	−3.1%
Marine Corps	80	109	36.3	13	27	107.7
Navy	483	421	−12.8	341	339	−0.6

: Not calculated.

[a]Includes all prisoners under military jurisdiction, regardless of conviction status or sentence length.

[b]Includes prisoners sentenced to more than 1 year under military jurisdiction.

Source: E. Ann Carson, "Prisoners in 2016," *BJS Bulletin* (Washington, D.C.: U.S. Department of Justice, 2018), p. 23.

Private Correctional Institutions

Although the use of private facilities to house prisoners is a relatively recent phenomenon, the private sector has been involved in the administration of various correctional aspects almost since the origination of penal codes. During the 1960s, the use of halfway houses as a transition from prison to the community grew rapidly. Most of the halfway houses were privately operated, although most were owned by faith-based or not-for-profit charitable organizations such as the Salvation Army. By the 1980s, almost every state had contracts with privately operated halfway houses to provide residential services, supervision, and transitional programs for inmates leaving prison and returning to the community.[68] Also, many states with very small juvenile offender populations have often found it cost-effective to contract with privately operated facilities, rather than to open state-run juvenile facilities. In 1984, it was reported that 65 percent of all juvenile facilities were private, housing approximately 32,000 offenders.[69]

Although these uses of the private sector in corrections did not cause controversy, contracting to house adult prisoners in private for-profit prisons raised serious ethical and practical questions, resulting in a slow beginning to the use and role of private prisons. A **private prison** is any secure correctional facility, operated by an organization other than a governmental agency and usually in a for-profit manner that contracts with the government to provide security, housing, and programs for adult offenders. In a private prison, staff members are

private prison
any secure correctional facility, operated by other than a governmental agency and usually in a for-profit manner, which contracts with a governmental entity, to provide security, housing, and programs for adult offenders

TABLE 5.7	Prisoners Under Military Jurisdiction with Sentence of Any Length by Most Serious Offense, Year-End 2016				
Most serious offense	Total[a]	Air Force	Army	Marine Corps	Navy
Total	100%	100%	100%	100%	100%
Violent offenses	42.9%	41.8%	44.7%	41.7%	39.6%
Nonviolent offenses	57.1%	58.25%	55.3%	58.3%	60.4%
Total	100%	100%	100%	100%	100%
Sexual	65.5%	70.5%	66.4%	55.7%	64.5%
Violent	27.9	31.8	26.4	29.2	26.0
Nonviolent[b]	37.5	38.6	39.9	26.6	38.5
Other violent	15.0%	10.0%	18.2%	12.5%	13.6%
Murder[c]	6.4	5.0	8.0	5.2	4.1
Manslaughter	0.5	0.5	0.3	0.0	1.8
Robbery	0.5	0.0	0.8	0.5	0.0
Aggravated/simple assault	6.8	4.1	8.0	6.3	7.1
Other	0.8	0.5	1.1	0.5	0.6
Property	4.2%	2.3%	4.2%	6.3%	4.7%
Burglary	0.6	0.5	0.3	1.6	0.6
Larceny-theft	0.0	0.9	2.2	4.2	3.0
Motor vehicle theft	0.0	0.0	0.0	0.0	0.0
Fraud	0.7	0.9	0.9	0.0	0.6
Other	0.6	0.0	0.8	0.5	0.6
Drug[d]	6.4%	11.8%	2.7%	9.4%	10.1%
Public order	0.3%	0.5%	0.3%	0.0%	0.6%
Military	5.2%	3.6%	2.5%	15.1%	5.3%
Other/unspecified	3.5%	1.4%	5.7%	1.0%	1.2%
Total number of prisoners	1,236	220	636	192	169

Note: Counts are based on prisoners sentenced to any length of time under military correctional authority. Excludes pretrial detainees. Coast Guard offense distribution not shown due to too few cases.

[a]Includes prisoners who served in the Coast Guard (not shown separately).

[b]Includes sexual harassment, indecent exposure and other acts, prostitution, stalking, and other nonviolent sexual misconduct.

[c]Includes nonnegligent manslaughter.

[d]Includes possession, use, trafficking, and other drug crimes.

Source: E. Ann Carson, "Prisoners in 2016" *BJS Bulletin* (Washington, D.C.: U.S. Department of Justice, 2018), p.23.

not public employees, but are employees of the company that owns and operates the prison. Such prisons can be administered without cumbersome governmental purchasing and personnel policies, although they are still held to the same constitutional standard for treatment of inmates as a public prison.

The first private contract to house adult offenders was in 1984, for a small, 250-bed facility operated by Corrections Corporation of America under contract with Hamilton County, Tennessee. Soon thereafter, additional contracts with the private sector to house illegal aliens (contracted with the INS) and youthful offenders (with the BOP) were established. The growth over the next few decades in

TABLE 5.8	Prisoners in Custody of Correctional Authorities in the U.S. Territories and Commonwealths, December 31, 2016					
	Jurisdiction population			**Capacity**		
Jurisdiction	**Total[a]**	**Sentenced to more than 1 year[a]**	**Total custody population**	**Rated**	**Operational**	**Design**
Total	10,613	9,560	12,266			
American Samoa[b]	/	/	189	/	/	/
Guam[c]	752	358	738	443	...	443
Commonwealth of the Northern Mariana Islands	262	169	262	559	272	559
Commonwealth of Puerto Rico	8,930	8,655	10,500	14,511	14,632	14,632
U.S. Virgin Islands[d]	669	378	577	468	355	550

Note: Jurisdiction refers to the legal authority of state or federal correctional officials over a prisoner, regardless of where the prisoner is held. Custody refers to the physical location where the prisoner is held.

...Not available. Specific type of capacity is not measured by territory.

/Not reported.

[a]Excludes counts for American Samoa.

[b]American Samoa has not submitted NPS data since 2011. Custody data were located in the 2015 American Samoa Statistical Yearbook (http://doc.as.gov/wp-content/uploads/2011/06/2015-Statistical-Yearbook.pdf) and represent the number of persons in custody as of December 2015.

[c]Guam did not submit 2016 NPS data. Population data represent populations on January 1, 2017, and were located in a Guam Department of Corrections report (http://doc.guam.gov/wp-doc-content/uploads/2016/09/Guam-DOC-Population-Report-for-January-01-2017.pdf). Capacity data are from 2014, the last time Guam submitted NPS data.

[d]U.S. Virgin Islands did not submit NPS data from 2014 to 2016 and had inconsistent 2013 data. Data are from 2012.

Source: E. Ann Carson, "Prisoners in 2016," *BJS Bulletin* (Washington, D.C.: U.S. Department of Justice, 2018), p. 24.

the privatization of correctional facilities was spurred by the increasing number of inmates and the rapid need to build new prisons, the budgetary challenges required to fund these new prisons, and the Reagan-era support of using the private sector to help downsize the scope of government. Welch notes,

> At that time, the prevailing political and economic philosophy encouraged government officials to turn to the private sector to administer public services, such as sanitation, health care, security, fire protection, and education. As a result of the introduction of free-market principles into the administration of public services, ... the privatization of corrections appeared to be a new and novel approach to some old problems (i.e., overcrowding and mounting costs).[70]

By 1990, Logan reported that private prisons held just over 9,000 adult inmates,[71] but by December 31, 2016, there were 128,323 state and federal prisoners held in private prisons, accounting for 8.5 percent of all prisoners.[72] Table 5.9 illustrates the numbers and percentage of all state and federal inmates held in private prisons. The use of private prisons grew rapidly in the 1990s, jumping almost ten times. This growth continued to its high point of 137,200 in 2012, but has since declined. A more detailed discussion of the use of private prisons, trends and policy issues impacting their use, and the pros and cons of private prisons is covered in Chapter 16.

TABLE 5.9	Number of Prisoners Held in Private Facilities, December 31, 2000–2015

	Number of Prisoners			
Year	Total	Federal	State	Percent of all prisoners
2000	90,542	15,524	75,018	6.5
2001	91,053	19,251	72,702	6.5
2002	93,912	20,274	73,638	6.5
2003	95,707	21,865	73,842	6.5
2004	98,628	24,768	73,860	6.6
2005	107,940	27,046	80,894	7.1
2006	113,697	27,726	85,971	7.2
2007	123,942	31,310	92,632	7.8
2008	129,482	33,162	96,320	8.0
2009	129,333	34,087	95,246	8.0
2010	128,195	33,830	94,365	8.0
2011	130,992	38,546	92,426	8.2
2012	137,200	40,446	96,774	8.7
2013	133,044	41,159	91,885	8.4
2014	131,273	40,017	91,706	8.4
2015	126,272	34,934	91,338	8.3
2016	128,323	34,159	94,164	8.5

Sources: Data derived from Paul Guerino, Paige M. Harrison, and William J. Sabor, "Prisoners in 2010," E. Ann Carson and Daniela Golinelli, "Prisoners in 2012," and E. Ann Carson, Prisoners in 2016," *BJS Bulletins* (Washington, D.C.: U.S. Department of Justice, 2011, 2013, and 2018).

Private Correctional Companies

The use of private prisons has continued to expand, and on January 30, 2005, there were 107 privately operated secure prisons contracting to hold adult criminal offenders.[73] Several companies contract with government agencies to house adult offenders, but only three have a significant market share. Two of these are publicly traded private prison companies, with their size and approximate revenues listed in Table 5.10. These companies include **CoreCivic**, **The GEO Group, Inc.**, and **Management Training Corporation**. There are at least four other private prison companies with significant contracts and revenues to hold federal, state, or county inmates.

Although still controversial, the operation of private prisons is now an accepted practice, and more than one-half of the states, the Federal Bureau of Prison, ICE, and the District of Columbia all use private facilities. The issues concerning the use of private prisons are more fully addressed in Chapter 16. However, it is expected that private correctional operations will continue to remain strong due to a number of factors. Although the growth in the number of state and federal prisoners has slowed over the past five years, there is still expected to be modest increases in the number of prison inmates in some states. Due to tight state and federal budgets since the 2008 recession, very few jurisdictions have constructed new prisons, and do not have the capacity to return inmates currently in private facilities to their own public prisons.

CoreCivic
Formerly Corrections Corporation of America, CoreCivic is the largest in revenue of the private prison corporations, and opened the first private, for-profit correctional facility in 1984 in Tennessee

The GEO Group, Inc
a private correctional company headquartered in Florida that operates correctional facilities in the United States and several foreign countries

Management Training Corporation
a private correctional company headquartered in Utah that started as a job training company, and now operates several correctional facilities in the United States

TABLE 5.10	Major Private Correctional Companies	
Company	**Number of secure facilities**	**Revenues for 2016**
CoreCivic	55	$1.850 billion
The GEO Group, Inc.	67	$1.373 billion
Management Training Corporation	27	Undisclosed

Note: CoreCivic was formerly Corrections Corporation of America. They list 90 total facilities on their website, 55 secure facilities, and 36 reentry centers or halfway houses. Revenue includes all facilities. GEO has 67 secure facilities as well as several other community centers and several facilities out of the United States. The GEO revenue is only their U.S. corrections and detention division.

Sources: Each company's website accessed September 3, 2017. Data derived from the 2016 annual reports of CoreCivic website, www.cca.com; The GEO Group, Inc., website, www.geogroup.com; and Management Training Corporation (MTC) website, http://www.mtctrains.com. MTC is a privately held company and does not have to disclose revenues or earnings.

This private prison owned by the CoreCivic is one of many private prisons now operated throughout the United States. Courtesy of CoreCivic.

A Question of Policy

The increase in the number of inmates in the past two decades and the resultant cost to construct new prisons to keep up with this growth lead to an important question of policy. In the "You Make the Decision" box at the end of this chapter, students are to consider the policy of construction and cost implications of this option to respond to the constant expansion of the prison population and the increasing resources necessary to operate new prisons.

Chapter Review

Summary

Although prisons have been an important component in the criminal justice system since shortly after the creation of the U.S. Constitution and the formation of our current system of justice, they have changed in scope and role only minimally during their first 200 years of operation. However, over the past two decades, there have been major changes in their role, mission, and scope; the attributes of inmates; and the length of time that inmates serve. This chapter has described these trends and discussed our nation's current approach of constructing new prisons to avoid severe overcrowding of correctional facilities. This policy decision, however, has been at great cost to the taxpayers; direct expenditures to correctional agencies are now greater than $80 billion per year.

This chapter has also presented the different correctional agencies that operate prisons, including states, the BOP, ICE, the military, territories and commonwealths, and private correctional companies. Major changes in policies and populations within the public agencies were described, specifically how changes in federal laws regarding crimes affect the federal and state prison systems. Also, the controversial issues surrounding for-profit private companies operating correctional institutions were described.

Much of the challenge in operating prisons under today's approach of construction of new facilities to keep up with the increasing number of inmates has to do with finding the budgetary resources to continue to operate correctional agencies. In the final two chapters of this textbook, this challenge and the future approaches and alternatives to our current overreliance on prisons are addressed. It is critical to examine and consider alternative methods of managing offenders and to search for preventive approaches to offenders becoming involved in crime. We must also consider diversion from the criminal justice system for minor, first-time offenders and juveniles and using alternatives to incarceration that do not seriously endanger public safety as reasonable sanctions for minor property and drug offenses. Our society cannot continue to fund the growth of imprisonment to the detriment of other important government functions.

The next chapter examines what happens to inmates as they get out of prison. The declining use of parole and indeterminate sentences and the changing issues that confront prisoners as they leave prison and return to the community are reviewed. The past two decades have witnessed not only a change in the prison population, but also a change in the makeup of those being released. These changes require a renewed examination of how we prepare inmates for release and the ability of the community to readily accept them upon their return.

Key Terms

prisons	Three Penitentiary Act	Immigration and Customs
Rhodes v. Chapman	Federal Bureau of Prisons (BOP)	Enforcement (ICE)
mission	Sanford Bates	brig
new penology	Sentencing Reform Act of 1984	private prison
war on drugs	security levels	CoreCivic
street crimes	security classification	The GEO Group, Inc.
federalize		Management Training Corporation

Review Questions

1. How did *Rhodes v. Chapman* change the operations of prisons?

2. What is the general mission of most correctional agencies?

3. How many inmates are there in U.S. correctional facilities?

4. Describe recent trends in terms of the inmate population, commission of violent crimes, and length of sentence.

5. Describe the increase in the number of prisons over the past decade.

6. What three prisons were included in the Three Penitentiary Act of 1891?

7. What was the result of the Sentencing Reform Act of 1984, and what impact did it have on the Bureau of Prisons?

8. What factors influenced the continued significant growth of the Bureau of Prisons into the 2000s?

9. Describe the physical security factors that go with prison security levels (minimum, medium, maximum).

10. Why do some inmates go to state and others federal prisons?

11. What factors have influenced a recent decline in the number of prison inmates in some states?

12. What state prison security level has the highest percentage of inmates?

13. What is the role of the U.S. Immigration and Customs Enforcement?

14. When and where was the first private prison opened under contract to house adult offenders?

15. Describe the most controversial issues in the use of for-profit private companies to house inmates.

You Make the Decision...

Is Incarceration Worth the Cost?

The question to consider is whether the changes in laws resulting in an increase in the number of inmates, construction of new prisons, renovation of existing facilities, and spending tens of billions of dollars to house prisoners are good public policy. As noted previously, the absolute number of violent and dangerous offenders in prison has not increased significantly. The largest portion of the growth has come from the incarceration of drug offenders. Whether our nation can withstand another decade of a policy to try to build our way out of prison crowding is a question that must be addressed in a thoughtful and pragmatic manner by corrections and elected officials.

The dramatic differences in the incarceration rates among various states require the review of perhaps the most important policy issue regarding corrections in the United States: Does the increase in the use of incarceration reduce the risk to citizens of being victimized and, if so, is that reduction of risk worth the additional cost of such incarceration? This is an important issue for students of corrections to confront. Look at the states with the highest incarceration rates (Louisiana,

Oklahoma, Alabama, Arkansas, Mississippi, and Arizona). Compare these states with those having the lowest incarceration rates (Maine, Rhode Island, Massachusetts, Minnesota, North Dakota, and New Hampshire). Do trends in crime rates provide any parallels to increases in rates of incarceration?

Students should examine many factors and then come to their own conclusion as to whether the increased use of incarceration is worth the cost. Factors that should be considered include the trends in crime rates (particularly violent crime), the cost of building and operating new prisons, the available alternatives to incarceration, the mission and goals of corrections, and the effectiveness of both imprisonment and community correctional programs. Students should weigh the cost of incarceration against the impact it has on crime, while considering the need for these tight funds for other uses. Unfortunately, this policy deliberation does not occur in the public policy debate among legislative bodies or most elected officials. It is a critical public policy dilemma that deserves a thorough debate.

CHAPTER 6

Parole and Prisoner Reentry

Lawrence Bartlett/AFP/Getty Images

After reading this chapter, you should be able to:

1. Outline the history of parole, and specify the role played by Maconochie and Crofton.

2. Explain the significance of the Elmira Reformatory and the medical model in the history of parole in the United States.

3. Compare and contrast the ways inmates can be released from prison, and explain the use of parole guidelines to determine parole readiness.

4. Identify how the number of offenders on parole supervision has changed over the past three decades.

5. Explain the conditions of parole supervision, and how classification is used to determine offender risk.

6. Describe the process of parole revocation and list the due process rights for offenders during this process.

7. Describe the reentry process, the issues inmates face when reentering the community, and what can be done to address them.

Introduction

Throughout the history of the United States, prisons have held criminal offenders sentenced to their authority under many different sentencing structures. During the 1800s, prisoners served set amounts of time in crowded prisons, with little emphasis on rehabilitation or preparation for release. During the first half of the twentieth century, criminals continued to be confined in prisons under determinate sentences; however, there was a developing emphasis on work and some rehabilitative programs. By the middle of the twentieth century, prison sentences began to be for indeterminate terms, prisons accentuated rehabilitation programs, and parole board experts decided when prisoners would be released based on their readiness for returning to the community. This move to the use of parole was a major change in philosophy, as well as sentence structure, and affected not only prison operations, but also the type of supervision that offenders received after release. This approach continued until the last two decades of the twentieth century.

Over the past twenty years, traditional parole with release by a parole board and indeterminate sentences have been abandoned in many states, and there has been a return to set, determinate sentences. Offenders are often limited in the amount of good time they can earn during their sentences, as truth-in-sentencing laws requiring the completion of 85 percent of the sentence before prisoners are released have been enacted and implemented in many states. This emphasis on holding offenders accountable through tough sentencing laws results in a focus on punishment, incapacitation, and deterrence. Prison rehabilitation programs are often reduced in importance, both to save money and to avoid making prisons too soft a punishment for crime. Many offenders are now released without the review of a parole board to determine readiness or consider the soundness of their release plans. However, most states still use a conditional and supervised release of offenders, even when their determinate sentence ends.

These changes make the status of prisoner reentry to the community very different from that of only a few decades ago. The number of releasees is greater, the majority is not released through parole, and the prisoners serve longer sentences. They are also less prepared to return to their communities, and their communities are less able to accommodate them. A large number of releasees are subsequently returned to prison, many for violating the technical conditions of their parole or release supervision rather than for the commission of a new crime.

This chapter reviews the development of parole in the United States and how it is administered for those states in which it is still in use. The release decision, supervision on parole, the violation process when offenders fail to meet their parole conditions, and the overall effectiveness of parole and indeterminate sentences are discussed. The challenge of reentry to the community is also described, and the types of challenges faced by returning prisoners are illustrated. Knowing that reentry is difficult and many offenders fail, there has been an increasing effort and resources directed toward improving the reentry process. There is also a review of the types of programs that help prisoners reenter the community and examples of the types of programs that are used to both supervise and aid offenders as they leave prison and return to the community.

The History of Parole

The term *parole* is from the French word *parol*, meaning "word of honor." It was first used in the 1700s as a means of releasing prisoners of war upon their promise not to resume arms in the current conflict. This evolved to the modern meaning of

parole as a conditional release of inmates by a parole board prior to the expiration of their sentence. It is often thought that parole had no history in U.S. prisons until the mid-1900s, but a much earlier use of conditional release influenced the development of parole as currently used. In colonial America, there was a shortage of labor, leading to the transportation of children and pardoned criminals from England to the American colonies to provide a ready workforce. As the pardoned criminals returned to England after serving their indentured time, specific conditions for their freedom had to be created. Even with the end of the transportation of children and convicts to the United States after the Revolutionary War, the idea of a period of punishment and work followed by a requirement to meet conditions of freedom was established.

Maconochie and the Mark System

The more formal use of conditional release from prison most likely had its roots in 1840, when **Alexander Maconochie** became superintendent of the British penal colony on Norfolk Island, about 1,000 miles off the coast of Australia. Maconochie had been captured by the French while serving as a British naval officer and was sensitive to the brutal way prisoners were often treated. Upon his appointment as superintendent, he decided to initiate a revolutionary philosophy of reforming the prisoner by instilling self-discipline with an emphasis on "punish for the past, and train for the future."

Since the amount of time necessary to instill self-discipline could not be estimated in advance, Maconochie advocated open-ended (indeterminate) sentences and a **mark system**. Instead of sentences for a specific amount of time, Maconochie required offenders to earn a specific number of marks based on the severity of the crime, and they would be released once they earned the required level of marks through work and good behavior. His system consisted of four stages on the way to release, each providing more personal liberty to the prisoner.[1] The *penal stage* emphasized punishment and included solitary confinement and a diet of bread and water. The *associated stage* allowed inmates to associate and begin to earn marks through work, program participation, and good behavior. Poor behavior resulted in an increase in the number of marks required for release. The third stage was the *social stage*, in which inmates were grouped and held jointly responsible for the conduct of each other, as a way to begin the process of living responsibly in society. The final stage was a **ticket of leave**, in which prisoners earning the required level of marks received a conditional pardon and were released to the community.

Norfolk Island had deplorable conditions prior to the arrival of Maconochie. Hughes described conditions as so bad that "convicts would choose two men by drawing straws: one to die, the other to kill him ... the killer and witnesses would have to be sent to Sydney for trial ... a boon to the prisoners, who yearned for the meager relief of getting away from the ocean of hell."[2] The mark system worked well on Norfolk Island and brought tranquility to what had been a violent prison with regular riots. Unfortunately, his English overseers saw Maconochie's approach as "coddling" criminals, and he was relieved of his duty in 1844. After his return to England, Maconochie continued to write and encourage prison reform. In a review of some of Maconochie's writings, Morris noted that Maconochie desired to maintain a sanitary prison with adequate diet and decent treatment for prisoners. In his view, "punishment, allowing for and facilitating redemption, dignifies society, makes prison service a constructive occupation, and enhances public safety. By contrast, vengeance-based punishment, posing as effective deterrence, demeans society, makes torturers of prison guards, and lessens public safety."[3] Word of Maconochie's approach and system became widely known even after his dismissal and influenced others, particularly Sir Walter Crofton.

parole
the conditional release of inmates by a parole board prior to the expiration of their sentence

Alexander Maconochie
the superintendent of the British penal colony on Norfolk Island from 1841 to 1844, who created a system of marks for good behavior that could lead to a graduated release from prison

mark system
credits against a sentence that allowed for inmates to be released once they earned the required level of marks through work and good behavior

ticket of leave
a form of release used by Maconochie; on earning the required level of marks, prisoners received a conditional pardon and were released to the community

Walter Crofton and the Irish System

Sir Walter Crofton

the director of Irish prison system in 1854, who began to implement many of the ideas of Maconochie's work

Even though Maconochie was dismissed as superintendent of Norfolk Island, some of his ideas were later accepted, and the Penal Servitude Act, enacted by the British Parliament in 1853, enabled prisoners to be released on a ticket of leave and supervised by the police. In 1854, **Sir Walter Crofton** was appointed director of the Irish prison system and began to implement many of the ideas of Maconochie's work. He created the following four-stage system of graduated release from prison and return to the community:[4]

1. *Solitary confinement* of approximately nine months. Much like Maconochie's first stage, it included an emphasis on punishment, little interaction with other prisoners, silence, chapel, and work.
2. *Special prison* in which the offender worked with other inmates and earned marks to gain privileges and move further toward release. Inmates also had to complete three conduct classes, taking up to twelve months.
3. *Open institution*, a transitional stage to society, with training on the freedoms and requirements of release and continued earning of marks to reach the fourth stage.
4. *Ticket of leave*, a conditional release for the remainder of the sentence, and the first use of parole as it is known today. The police supervised offenders in rural Ireland, but Dublin had a civilian employee who worked with the police, but also secured employment for the released prisoners, visited their homes, and had them report to him. If they disobeyed the rules, the ticket of leave could be revoked.

These ideas and stages worked well. A report regarding 557 prisoners released during the 1850s noted that only seventeen had their tickets of leave revoked.[5] These stages of release and subsequent supervision in the community are the forerunners of the modern indeterminate sentence, parole officer supervision, and focus on finding employment as a key criterion for success. The Irish system was well received internationally, and many U.S. penologists were soon campaigning to bring these ideas and procedures to the United States.

Parole Begins in the United States

With parole and indeterminate sentences still decades away, the idea of rewarding good behavior with reductions in the time served was initiated in 1817, when the New York legislature authored the first "good time" statute, allowing up to a 25 percent reduction in time served for good behavior and industrious work. Over the next fifty years, twenty-three states passed similar statutes authorizing the use of good time, which was seen as important in encouraging good behavior and preparing for successful release.[6]

Zebulon R. Brockway

a leading U.S. penologist in the mid-1800s who was a proponent of adopting the Irish system in the United States and who became the first superintendent of the Elmira Reformatory

In 1869, New York passed an Act to build a reformatory in Elmira for youthful offenders, which would use indeterminate sentences and hold offenders until "reformed." In 1870, the American Prison Association was formed and held its first meeting in Cincinnati, Ohio. The major discussion was about the use of indeterminate sentences and the Irish parole system. One of the leading U.S. penologists, **Zebulon R. Brockway** of Michigan, presented a paper on the Irish system. The association adopted a Declaration of Principles, promoting the use of the Irish system, parole, good time, and assistance to released prisoners in the United States. These reforms, when made public, were well received across the country. When the **Elmira Reformatory** opened in 1876, Brockway was appointed its superintendent. A system of classification allowing inmates to earn privileges for their work and behavior was implemented, and the reformatory was organized so that inmates spent much of their day in education programs and learning trades. Once inmates demonstrated reformation, prison administrators had the authority to conditionally release them to be supervised by state agents in the community.[7]

Over the next several decades, the use of parole increased, with many states adopting prison programs similar to those of the Elmira Reformatory. By 1900, twenty states had begun to use indeterminate sentences and to have correctional officials determine dates of inmate release by parole. In 1930, New York was the first state to develop an independent parole authority to make release decisions separate from the state department of corrections.[8] Even though the idea was solidly supported, the Great Depression was the real impetus for expansion of parole, as unemployment and Prohibition created a crime wave resulting in an increasing number of people being sent to prison. As prison populations grew and prisons became more overcrowded, states could not afford their operation and looked to parole as a less expensive way to manage offenders. The number of offenders released annually on parole increased from 21,632 in 1923 to 37,794 in 1936.[9] By 1944, all states had adopted the use of parole and indeterminate sentences.[10]

Rehabilitative programs with conditional release were a key element of the operation of the Elmira Reformatory under superintendent Zebulon Brockway. Bettmann/Getty Images.

Elmira Reformatory
the first reformatory in the United States; it opened in 1876 and used the principles of the Irish system, indeterminate sentences, and parole

As reformatories were opened, they stressed education of youthful offenders. Courtesy of the Ohio Department of Rehabilitation and Correction.

Parole and the Medical Model

As indicated in Chapter 1, after World War II, the country began to recognize the value of the scientific approach to solving problems and incorporated this model into dealing with crime and criminals. The medical model of corrections was adopted as the dominant theory influencing prison practices. The medical model assumed that offenders were afflicted with an environmental or psychosocial condition that was the underlying reason for their criminality. Under the belief that offenders were sick, when they were sentenced to prison, their problems were diagnosed and a treatment plan was developed by prison officials who were experts in a variety of areas, such as education, vocational training, and mental health issues. The prison treatment continued until another group of experts (the parole board) determined that the "patient" could no longer benefit from institutional treatment and was ready for release and return to the community.

The medical model perfectly fit the use of indeterminate sentences and parole. Offenders were sentenced to open-ended sentences, with the minimum term determined to meet society's need for punishment, deterrence, and incapacitation. After they met this threshold level of the sentence term, their release depended on how well their treatment plan worked to remedy their deficiencies and prepare them for successful return to the community. A parole board of rehabilitative experts was believed well suited to determine when inmates' treatments were complete and what would be optimal times for release from prison and supervision in the community. In most cases, treatment continued in the community under the supervision of parole officers.

Under this indeterminate sentencing structure, parole served many positive functions. First, dangerous inmates could be incarcerated for longer periods of time than if they had a determinate sentence, which would usually be shorter than the maximum time allowable under an indeterminate sentence. Parole boards regularly require dangerous, high-risk inmates to serve the maximum sentence. Colorado abolished parole as a release mechanism in 1979, but reinstated it after finding out that the length of prison sentences served was decreasing, particularly for high-risk offenders. Second, parole boards act as gatekeepers to ensure that inmates have sound release plans for their return to the community. For inmates to be released they must have a place to live and must address their possibilities of finding a job. If they have no community contacts, inmates are often released to a halfway house or given more time to develop a release plan. However, when a determinate sentence ends, there is usually no way to delay a release due to an insufficient plan.

Third, the fact that a parole board will review inmates is an incentive for good behavior and program participation by inmates. Opponents of parole criticize program participation that is done to impress the parole board and suggest that program participation with no implied coercion will be more effective. Halleck argued that it was almost impossible to distinguish between fully

With the medical model of corrections, classification of inmates involved many professionals to evaluate the inmate and plan a treatment program. Courtesy of the Federal Bureau of Prisons.

voluntary and coercive treatment participation, especially in a correctional setting in which decisions affecting offenders' parole considered such participation.[11] Morris, in *The Future of Imprisonment*, asserted that rehabilitation is a valuable correctional goal, yet it could not be effective if seen as coercive by offenders, or if they saw it as an element of the punishment they were receiving for their criminal offenses.[12] And Irwin argued that inmates viewed decisions of the parole board as arbitrary, capricious, prejudicial, unpredictable, and not subject to review by an external body.[13] However, there has been no evidence that nonvoluntary program participation was less effective than participation with some coercion.

A final positive function of parole is that consideration for release begins the process and creates guidelines for supervision and treatment needs in the community. Parole boards consider inmates' levels of risk and chances for success and create conditions for supervision and treatment to respond to these risks and needs. Without parole, even with mandatory supervision following determinate sentencing release, supervision is often less individualized and based primarily on risk rather than need. Abadinsky suggests that the medical model is based on two questionable assumptions:

- Criminals are "sick" and can thus benefit from treatment/therapy.
- The behavioral sciences can provide the necessary treatment/therapeutic methods.[14]

Attacks on the Medical Model and Parole

The above assumptions and many other aspects of the medical model came under attack during the early 1970s, partly precipitated after Robert Martinson and his colleagues attempted to determine what worked in correctional treatment. They reviewed 231 studies of correctional treatment programs and, although they found a few isolated correlations between a treatment program and a reduction in recidivism, there were no consistent findings of the effect of any single treatment program significantly reducing recidivism.[15] Therefore, the Martinson review concluded, "nothing works," which was just the support that opponents of the medical model and parole were looking for. For public officials desiring to reduce costs and make corrections more punitive, this study provided statistical support, and their arguments for a return to determinate sentences gained momentum.

New models for sentencing and release to replace parole began to be proposed by a variety of individuals with varied philosophical rationales. In 1975, David Fogel, a liberal former correctional official, argued that treatment in prison was a myth, and parole board discretion was unpredictable and unfair to inmates. He proposed the **justice model** as an alternative, in which he suggested the following:

justice model
the model for sentencing proposed by Fogel that would use flat, determinate sentences, eliminate parole boards, and make all treatment voluntary

- A return to flat, determinate sentences, with procedural rules to limit sentencing discretion
- The elimination of parole boards and parole agencies
- Making all treatment programs strictly voluntary[16]

In 1976, conservative Andrew von Hirsch proposed the **just deserts model**, with a return to the classical model of criminology, letting the punishment fit the seriousness of the crime.[17] In this model, indeterminate sentences would be replaced with fixed sentences based solely on the severity of the crime and not on any individual offender characteristics. Also in 1976, the Twentieth Century Task Force on Sentencing proposed presumptive sentencing.[18] A presumptive sentencing

just deserts model
a model for sentencing proposed by von Hirsch that had fixed sentences for each crime so that the punishment fits the crime

system provides a sentence for each category of crime that would be imposed for a typical first-time offender (similar to the just deserts model). However, with this model, the sentencing judge has limited discretion to consider mitigating and aggravating circumstances that would reduce or increase the presumptive sentence.

The "nothing works" findings of Martinson and the criticism of parole by both the political right (for being too soft on crime) and left (for unpredictability and unfairness) created momentum toward abolishing parole and indeterminate sentences. In 1977, the use of parole reached its peak as more than 70 percent of prisoners were released on discretionary parole.[19] Over the next two decades, fifteen states and the federal government ended the use of indeterminate sentencing and **discretionary parole**, in which the decision to release the offender is made by a parole board (see Table 6.1). Twenty other states severely limited the parole-eligible population. Only fifteen states still have full discretionary parole for inmates. The move to determinate sentences was a primary reason why the prison population grew more rapidly than in any other period in the history of prisons.[20] From 1980 to 1996, the number of prisoners in state and federal prisons went from 330,000 to 1,054,000, a threefold increase,[21] and then peaked at over 1.6 million by 2009,[22] before it began to decline.

Parole has gone through several changes and transitions in its support, operations, and processes. Today there are at least three major methods (or statuses) in which inmates are released from prison. No consistent terminology is used to describe the three release statuses from jurisdiction to jurisdiction. The first is the use of discretionary parole, or release from prison to community supervision by the decision of a parole board, after completing the minimum portion of an indeterminate sentence. Parolees are required to meet certain conditions as a stipulation of their release and are subject to being returned to prison if they violate the conditions or commit another offense. A second status of

discretionary parole

release of inmates in which the decision to release is made by a parole board

TABLE 6.1	Abolition of Discretionary Parole
Jurisdiction abolishing parole	**Year abolished**
Maine	1975
Indiana	1977
Illinois	1978
Minnesota	1980
Florida	1983
Washington	1984
Federal government	1984
Oregon	1989
Delaware	1990
Kansas	1993
Arizona	1994
North Carolina	1994
Mississippi	1995
Virginia	1995
Ohio	1996
Wisconsin	1999

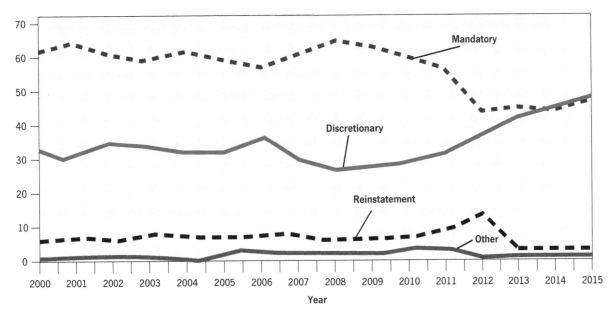

FIGURE 6.1 Entries to Parole, by Type of Entry, 2000–2015   Source: Adapted from data in "Probation and Parole in the United States, selected years," *BJS Bulletin* (Washington, D.C.: U.S. Department of Justice, Bureau of Justice Statistics, 2013 through 2016).

inmate release is **supervised mandatory release** (also referred to as mandatory parole), the release of inmates after they have served a determinate sentence, but with a period of supervision in the community. Supervised mandatory release is a conditional release, as there are still requirements and conditions that must be met or fulfilled or offenders can be returned to prison. Finally, inmates can serve the full portion of their sentence, pay their full "debt to society," and have no supervision after release from prison. This status is often referred to as **unconditional mandatory release** or expiration of sentence.

The Bureau of Justice Statistics reports that the percentage of releases from state prisons on discretionary parole (other than mandatory parole or expiration of sentence) has continued to decline since 1980, but has begun to climb over the past five years. In 2016, there were 626,024 releases from prison, of which 426,755 (68 percent) were conditional and 168,752 (22 percent) were unconditional.[23] Of those released from prison, only 30 percent of inmates were released on discretionary parole, and another 30 percent were released on mandatory parole after a determinate sentence but with supervision.[24] Figure 6.1 illustrates the percent of offenders entering parole each year from 2000 to 2015. Entries to parole from supervised mandatory releases from prison have declined while the percent of discretionary entries to parole have increased. While this is good news for discretionary parole advocates, it is not a major change in policy or return to full discretionary parole by many jurisdictions, but indicates a higher granting of parole rates by those jurisdictions still using discretionary parole.

New Models for Release Decisions

The major emphasis of the move away from parole and indeterminate sentencing has been to limit discretion and to focus sentences more on offender accountability than on rehabilitation. Many of the states maintaining parole created mechanisms to ensure the consideration of community safety in parole board decisions. **Parole guidelines** were created as a means to reduce disparity and make decision

supervised mandatory release
a type of release in which inmates serve a determinate sentence and are then released, but with a period of supervision to follow

unconditional mandatory release
a type of release in which inmates serve the full portion of their sentence and have no supervision after release from prison

parole guidelines
similar to sentencing guidelines, these use predictive factors to determine the offenders' risk to the community and chance for success; guidelines prescribe a presumptive time to be served based on the seriousness of the crime and the factors predictive of success for each inmate

making more understandable to the public and inmates. Parole guidelines, like sentencing guidelines, use predictive factors to determine the offenders' risk to the community and chance for success. Guidelines are then used to prescribe a presumptive time to be served based on the seriousness of the crime and the factors predictive of success for each inmate. The guidelines suggest a projected parole date after the inmate has served a set number of months, assuming good behavior during the prison term. Since guidelines are based on the severity of the sentence as well as factors predicting success, they focus on the "just deserts" form of sentencing.

The U.S. Parole Commission was the first to investigate the possibility of using guidelines during the mid-1970s and was required to use guidelines beginning in 1976 by the Parole Commission and Reorganization Act (Public Law 94–233). To develop the guidelines, the commission hired a group of researchers to identify the factors available to parole board members that are most salient to success on parole. The researchers found several factors regarding the history of offenses that are most predictive of success (or failure) after release. These factors are combined to find the **salient factor score** for inmates. The salient factors have been continually reviewed and validated. Figure 6.2 illustrates the most recent listing of six elements used to predict success. Each inmate is scored on the list of salient factors. The sum of the six factors is the score predicting success, with higher scores indicating a lower probability of recidivism.

salient factor score

a point determination for each inmate for use with parole guidelines; the score is based on factors predictive of success on parole

SALIENT FACTOR SCORE (SFS 98)

Item A. **PRIOR CONVICTIONS/ADJUDICATIONS *(ADULT OR JUVENILE)***...............

None = 3; One = 2; Two or three = 1; Four or more = 0

Item B. **PRIOR COMMITMENT(S) OF MORE THAN 30 DAYS *(ADULT/JUVENILE)***.........

None = 2; One or two = 1; Three or more = 0

Item C. **AGE AT CURRENT OFFENSE/PRIOR COMMITMENTS** ....

26 years or more	Three or fewer prior commitments = 3
	Four prior commitments = 2
	Five or more commitments = 1
22–25 years	Three or fewer prior commitments = 2
	Four prior commitments = 1
	Five or more commitments = 0
20–21 years	Three or fewer prior commitments = 1
	Four prior commitments = 0
19 years or less	Any number of prior commitments = 0

Item D. **RECENT COMMITMENT FREE PERIOD *(THREE YEARS)***....................

No prior commitment of more than 30 days (adult or juvenile) or released to the community from last such commitment at least 3 years prior to the commencement of the current offense = 1; Otherwise = 0

Item E. **PROBATION/PAROLE/CONFINEMENT/ESCAPE STATUS VIOLATOR THIS TIME** ...

Neither on probation, parole, confinement, or escape status at the time of the current offense; nor committed as a probation, parole, confinement, or escape status violator this time = 1; Otherwise = 0

Item F. **OLDER OFFENDERS** ....

If the offender was 41 years of age or more at the commencement of the current offense (and the total score from Items A–E above is 9 or less) = 1; Otherwise = 0

TOTAL SCORE ....

FIGURE 6.2 U.S. Parole Commission Salient Factor Score Sheet Source: U.S. Parole Commission, *Rules and Procedures Manual* (Washington, D.C.: U.S. Department of Justice, 2010).

The salient factor score is then inserted into the guidelines table (Figure 6.3). The categories of offenses are based on the severity of the crime. The combination of the offense severity and parole prognosis (salient factor score) then gives a guideline range for the number of months that should be served before release. As an example, for an offender in Category Five (which includes bank robbery and

GUIDELINES FOR DECISION MAKING
[Guidelines for Decision Making, Customary Total Time to Be Served Before Release (Including Jail Time)]

OFFENSE CHARACTERISTICS	OFFENDER CHARACTERISTICS: Parole Prognosis (Salient Factor Score 1998)			
Severity of Offense Behavior	Very Good (10–8)	Good (7–6)	Fair (5–4)	Poor (3–0)
Category One	Guideline Range <= 4 months	<= 8 months	8–12 months	12–16 months
Category Two	Guideline Range <= 6 months	<= 10 months	12–16 months	16–22 months
Category Three	Guideline Range <<= 10 months	12–16 months	18–24 months	24–32 months
Category Four	Guideline Range 12–18 months	20–26 months	26–34 months	34–44 months
Category Five	Guideline Range 24–36 months	36–48 months	48–60 months	60–72 months
Category Six	Guideline Range 40–52 months	52–64 months	64–78 months	78–100 months
Category Seven	Guideline Range 52–80 months	64–92 months	78–110 months	100–148 months
Category Eight*	Guideline Range 100++ months	120++ months	150++ months	180++ months

*Note: For Category Eight, no upper limits are specified due to the extreme variability of the cases within this category.

FIGURE 6.3 U.S. Parole Commission Guidelines for Decision Making   Source: U.S. Parole Commission, *Rules and Procedures Manual* (Washington, D.C.: U.S. Department of Justice, 2010).

intent to sell hard drugs) who had a salient factor score of six, the guidelines suggest a range of thirty-six to forty-eight months served before release. The parole board can consider other mitigating or aggravating circumstances of the offense or offender to set the release date within the guideline range.

After the federal government developed and began using guidelines, many states adopted similar guidelines for their parole decision making. When I was director of corrections in Ohio, we worked with the state legislature to create similar guidelines for the Ohio parole board release decisions. After a period of criticism by the public and some elected officials regarding decisions by the parole board, the guidelines were a positive reform as they provided both understanding and clarity for the public as well as inmates regarding parole decisions.

Problems with Moving Away from Indeterminate Sentences

Although there are some valid reasons to adopt determinate sentences, there are also many problems with moving away from discretionary parole and indeterminate sentences, which are often a poor fit between theory and practice in regard to "getting tough on criminals." These include the following:

1. With determinate sentences, inmates often serve shorter sentences and smaller portions of the sentence than with parole. Parole boards consider the dangerousness of offenders and often hold them in prison well beyond their minimum eligibility for parole.
2. Without parole, there are few ways to hold inmates accountable for misconduct in prison. Prison administrators miss the control and emphasis on prison discipline that resulted from inmates trying to have a good record to take before the parole board.
3. Elimination of parole does reduce discretionary release decisions, but prosecutorial discretion is just substituted for correctional discretion. One problem with prosecutorial discretion is that it is exercised in private, and there is no review or public consideration of the use of plea bargaining.
4. One advantage of the use of parole boards is that they can reduce disparity in sentencing decisions by individual judges if there are no sentencing guidelines.
5. Parole boards, although they do not admit to consciously trying to do so, can act as a safety valve for prison overcrowding. In more formal ways, parole boards have been used to identify the most deserving inmates for release when there is a need to do so due to prison crowding.
6. In some states (such as Maine), abolishing parole has also included abolishing supervision after release.

Current Status of Parole in the United States

Parole and community supervision are still very important functions in several states. In fact, as illustrated in Figure 6.4, the number of offenders under state parole or mandatory release supervision at year-end 2015 was 870,500, which was more than a fourfold increase in the number of parolees or other postrelease

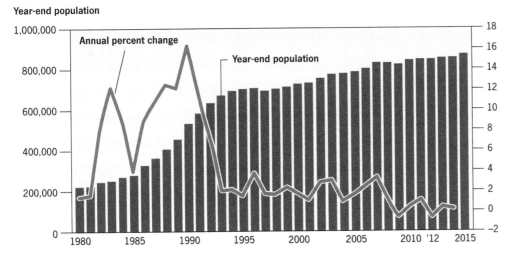

FIGURE 6.4 Adults on Parole at Year-End, 1980–2015   Sources: Data from Lauren E. Glaze and Thomas P. Bonczar, "Probation and Parole in the United States, 2010," and Danielle Kaeble and Thomas P. Bonczar, "Probation and Parole in the United States, 2015," *BJS Bulletins* (Washington, D.C.: U.S. Department of Justice, 2011 and 2016).

supervision offenders in 1980. Nearly all these offenders (94 percent) had been convicted of a felony and sentenced to incarceration of more than one year. Thirty-two percent were serving a sentence for a violent offense, 21 percent for property offenses, 31 percent for a drug offense, 4 percent for a weapons offense, and 13 percent for some other offense. Similar to the makeup of the adult prison population, a high percentage of minorities are under community supervision, with approximately 44 percent of parolees white, 38 percent black, and 18 percent Hispanic at the end of 2015. And 13 percent of the parole population was female, a rate that has remained relatively stable for the past two decades.[25]

The number of offenders under parole supervision has changed significantly over the past three decades. During the 1980s, the number of parolees increased by an average of 8.1 percent per year. During the 1990s, the population on parole increased only 3.3 percent per year. And from 2000 to 2008, it increased 1.7 percent per year before declining 0.7 percent during 2009. Since then, it has increased a small percent each year, except for 2012, when there was a 0.6 percent decline in the number of parolees.[26] Driving changes in population are changes in entry and exits onto parole. Table 6.2 illustrates the number of adults on parole, the entries and exits, the percent change during 2015, and the number of parolees per 100,000 population in state and federal jurisdictions during 2015.

Operations of Parole

The sentencing and release processes for discretionary parole include three major steps: (1) an indeterminate sentence with a minimum time to serve before parole eligibility and a maximum term to be served if not paroled, (2) consideration of release by a parole board authorized to conditionally release offenders, and (3) supervision in the community under specific conditions. When inmates complete their minimum term, there is no guarantee that they will be released from prison. In fact, in the 1979 case of *Greenholtz v. Inmates of the Nebraska Penal and*

TABLE 6.2 Adults on Parole, 2015

Jurisdiction	Parole population, January 1, 2015	Entries Reported	Entries Imputed[a]	Exits Reported	Exits Imputed[a]	Parole population, December 31, 2015	December 31, 2015 Number	December 31, 2015 Percent	Number on parole per 100,000 U.S. adult residents, December 31, 2015[b]
United States total	857,858	431,695	475,200	420,291	463,700	870,526	12668	1.5%	350
Federal	109,365	49,988	49,988	46,315	46,315	114,471	5106	4.7%	46
State	748,493	381,707	425,200	373,976	417,400	756,055	7562	1.0%	304
Alabama	8,065	2,360	2,360	2,287	2,287	8,138	73	0.9	216
Alaska	..	..	..	..	..	..	..	..	..
Arizona	7,502	11,946	11,946	12,069	12,069	7,379	−123	−1.6	141
Arkansas	21,745	10,497	10,497	9,213	9,213	23,093	1348	6.2	1,012
California[c]	87,111	29,614	55,100	31,502	56,200	86,053	−1058	−1.2	285
Colorado	10,067	8,369	8,369	8,167	8,167	10,269	202	2.0	242
Connecticut	2,564	2,487	2,487	2,112	2,112	2,939	375	14.6	104
Delaware	676	31	31	282	282	425	−251	−37.1	57
District of Columbia	5,125	1,465	1,465	1,996	1,996	4,594	−531	−10.4	822
Florida	4,526	6,325	6,325	6,240	6,240	4,611	85	1.9	28
Georgia	25,577	10,249	10,249	11,696	11,696	24,130	−1447	−5.7	311
Hawaii	1,545	667	667	897	897	1,540	−5	−0.3	137
Idaho	4,217	2,695	2,695	2,037	2,037	4,875	658	15.6	396
Illinois	29,644	23,830	23,830	24,328	24,328	29,146	−498	−1.7	294
Indiana	9,481	7,829	7,829	7,876	7,876	9,434	−47	−0.5	187
Iowa	5,741	3,588	3,588	3,411	3,411	5,918	177	3.1	246
Kansas	4,051	3,957	3,957	3,677	3,677	4,331	280	6.9	197
Kentucky	16,731	11,249	11,249	11,417	11,417	16,563	−168	−1.0	484
Louisiana	29,619	17,158	17,158	15,590	15,590	31,187	1568	5.3	874
Maine	20	1	1	0	0	21	1	5.0	2
Maryland	11,537	4,690	4,690	5,340	5,340	10,887	−650	−5.6	233
Massachusetts	1,914	2,318	2,318	2,254	2,254	1,978	64	3.3	36
Michigan	18,413	10,621	10,621	11,125	11,125	17,909	−504	−2.7	232
Minnesota	6,644	6,346	6,346	6,182	6,182	6,808	164	2.5	161
Mississippi	9,883	5,923	5,923	7,382	7,382	8,424	−1459	−14.8	371
Missouri	18,489	12,991	12,991	13,786	13,786	17,694	−795	−4.3	376
Montana	1,094	584	584	586	586	1,092	−2	−0.2	135
Nebraska	1,067	1,430	1,430	1,454	1,454	1,043	−24	−2.2	73
Nevada	5,927	4,502	4,502	4,922	4,922	5,507	−420	−7.1	246
New Hampshire	2,385	1,503	1,503	1,437	1,437	2,451	66	2.8	229
New Jersey	14,889	5,877	5,877	5,586	5,586	15,180	291	2.0	217

TABLE 6.2 (Continued)

Jurisdiction	Parole popula-tion, January 1, 2015	Entries Reported	Entries Imputed[a]	Exits Reported	Exits Imputed[a]	Parole popula-tion, December 31, 2015	December 31, 2015 Number	December 31, 2015 Percent	Number on parole per 100,000 U.S. adult residents, December 31, 2015[b]
New Mexico	2,255	1,577	1,577	944	944	2,888	633	28.1	182
New York	44,889	19,922	19,922	20,249	20,249	44,562	−327	−0.7	285
North Carolina	10,025	12,856	12,856	10,905	10,905	11,744	1719	17.1	151
North Dakota	564	1,269	1,269	1,189	1,189	644	80	14.2	109
Ohio	17,321	7,777	7,777	6,814	6,814	18,284	963	5.6	203
Oklahoma	2,560	345	345	789	789	2,116	−444	−17.3	71
Oregon	..	..	..	..	..	..	..	..	..
Pennsylvania	104,629	70,985	70,985	63,263	63,263	112,351	7722	7.4	1,109
Rhode Island	383	254	254	204	204	433	50	13.1	51
South Carolina	5,177	2,485	2,485	2,641	2,641	5,021	−156	−3.0	131
South Dakota	2,608	1,616	1,616	1,572	1,572	2,652	44	1.7	408
Tennessee	13,606	4,060	4,060	4,573	4,573	13,093	−513	−3.8	255
Texas	111,412	35,834	35,834	35,354	35,354	111,892	480	0.4	547
Utah	3,301	2,263	2,263	2,058	2,058	3,506	205	6.2	167
Vermont	1,090	..	600	..	600	1,090	0	−	215
Virginia	1,732	511	511	667	667	1,576	−156	−9.0	24
Washington	10,926	6,254	6,254	5,725	5,725	11,198	272	2.5	200
West Virginia	2,749	2,028	2,028	1,654	1,654	3,123	374	13.6	213
Wisconsin[d]	20,141	..	6,500	65	7,200	19,453	−688	−3.4	434
Wyoming	702	569	569	459	459	812	110	15.7	181

Note: Due to nonresponse or incomplete data, the parole population for some jurisdictions on December 31, 2015, does not equal the population on January 1, 2015, plus entries, minus exits. Counts may not be actual as reporting agencies may provide estimates on some or all detailed data.

−Less than 0.05%.

..Not known.

[a] Reflects reported data except for jurisdictions in which data were not available. Detail may not sum to total due to rounding.

[b] Rates were computed using the estimated U.S. adult resident population in each jurisdiction on January 1, 2016.

[c] Includes Post-Release Community Supervision and Mandatory Supervision parolees: 46,575 on January 1, 2015; and 29,614 entries, 31,502 exits, and 44,687 on December 31, 2015.

[d] The only exits reported were deaths.

Source: Danielle Kaeble and Thomas P. Bonczar, "Probation and Parole in the United States, 2015," *BJS Bulletin* (Washington, D.C.: U.S. Department of Justice, 2016), pp. 20–21.

Correctional Complex, the U.S. Supreme Court determined that parole was legally considered a privilege and not a right, and full due process rights need not be afforded.[27] If offenders are not granted parole at their first eligibility, the parole board continues them until a later time, when they will again receive a hearing and consideration of release. This process can be repeated until an inmate either is paroled or reaches the maximum sentence term.

The Organization of Parole Boards

Parole authorities can cover either or both of the two major parole functions: the release decision and postrelease supervision. In some states, two separate agencies are responsible for each of these parole functions. In others, the state department of corrections assumes responsibility for both functions. A third model is a separate parole decision-making authority, with parolees supervised by the state department of corrections. An important feature in the organization of parole decision making is that the parole board is independent from the administrators of the prisons. This can create problems if parole board members do not understand the programs provided within the prisons and what certain actions by prison officials may mean regarding an inmate's behavior and readiness for release. However, it would be a much greater problem if the parole board were overly influenced by prison staff opinions of the inmate. Boards are to independently consider the seriousness of the crime, the risk to the community, the chance for success, and institutional conduct and program participation as elements of their decisions.

For the past several decades, almost all parole boards consist of full-time employees of the state, and in most states the governor appoints parole board members. The size of the parole board can vary from two members in Minnesota to nineteen in New York.[28] Historically, governors appointed experts in criminology, social work, or community reintegration to best determine when offenders were rehabilitated and able to return to the community. In fact, the 1967 report of the President's Crime Commission recommended the appointment of parole board members on merit, including qualifications for prospective members of "broad academic background, especially in the behavioral sciences."[29] However, with the era of "tough on crime" attitudes and offender accountability, this has changed, and over the past twenty years the appointment of parole board members has become much more of a political decision.

As a result of parolees committing highly publicized crimes in the community, governors became very concerned about the impression of being soft on crime and letting dangerous criminals out of prison too early. Therefore, they often began to appoint less qualified (in terms of having a background in corrections or rehabilitation), yet politically connected individuals who can represent the governor's views on crime and community safety, rather than focusing on inmate preparation for release. Although this may be perceived as very reasonable, the practical problem is that there is no guarantee that any offender will be successful and avoid further criminality, and therefore every parole decision represents a political and community safety risk. As a result of the change in philosophy by parole boards, they are less likely to approve offenders for parole, and the average sentence served has increased as a result.

The Parole Hearing

hearing officers
officials who are not appointed parole board members, yet they hold parole hearings and make recommendations to the parole board regarding inmates' release

In some states, the actual parole board members hold parole hearings in the prisons, whereas in other states **hearing officers** conduct the hearings and recommend decisions to the parole board, which confirms or modifies the decision. Recently, many parole hearings are by video communications, which saves the members or officers from traveling so much. A few weeks after the hearing, the parole decision is communicated to the inmate in writing through the prison staff. It is unusual to have the final decision made and announced to the inmate at the hearing, but some procedures allow the hearing officers or board members conducting the hearing to immediately inform the inmate of their recommendation.

The hearing procedures vary by state. Although inmates are not provided full due process during a parole hearing, a few states allow inmates to have legal representation. At the beginning of the hearing, the board members or hearing officers review the file or records regarding the inmate and complete the parole guidelines if they are used in the jurisdiction. The prison staff usually provides a summary report of the inmate's background, criminal history, and performance while in prison. However, in most states, they do not make a recommendation regarding parole. The board also considers outside opinions from the inmate's family, law enforcement professionals, or victims regarding the inmate's parole. Some states allow victims to appear at the hearing, and others provide victims the chance to provide input in writing or through a personal meeting with board members prior to the parole hearing.

During hearings, inmates are asked to provide some background as to why they committed the crime, what they have done while in prison, and why they believe they are now ready to return to the community as productive and law-abiding citizens. The board also reviews and questions inmates regarding their release plans. The board is primarily interested in the inmates' plans for housing, employment, and continued participation in necessary treatment programs. Prior to the hearing, prison staff members assist inmates in developing release plans, and these plans are forwarded to field parole offices for investigation into the validity of the plan. A parole hearing of O. J. Simpson in Nevada in 2017 garnered considerable public interest and it was telecast live in many jurisdictions. Simpson had served nine years of a nine- to thirty-three-year sentence for armed robbery and kidnapping. So the general public saw the way parole board members questioned Simpson and the way he responded and made his plea that he had served his time well and was ready for release. Simpson told the Board, "I've done my time. I've done it as well and as respectfully as I think anyone can."[30] The Nevada Parole Board graded Simpson a "low risk to reoffend," and the four members unanimously voted to grant Simpson his release.

After reviewing all material, hearing from the inmate, and receiving any outside input, parole boards decide whether to grant inmates parole at that time or to "continue" them (to serve a longer period of time) until a later date. Some parole boards give presumptive parole dates at the first hearing in many states; they hold the first hearing shortly after the inmate's incarceration, even before parole eligibility. A **presumptive parole date** is a date the inmate can expect to be released on parole, even if it is several years later than the hearing. The presumption is that if inmates have good institutional conduct and program participation they will be granted parole at that date. As the date nears, the prison staff members provide the parole board a report as to the inmate's conduct and program participation. If the behavior and programming are as expected, the board confirms the date in writing without another hearing. If the board has some concerns regarding the inmate's prison performance, it may schedule a hearing and thereafter make a decision as to whether to parole

presumptive parole date
a date the inmate can expect to be released on parole, even if it is five or ten years later than the hearing

In 2017, O.J. Simpson appeared before the Nevada parole board, and after pleading his readiness for release, was granted parole.
Jason Bean/UPI/Newscom.

or continue the inmate. If performance has been poor, the board may do a continuance without a hearing and either reset another presumptive date or set a date for a later hearing.

Decisions regarding parole are seldom simple. The "You Make the Decision" box at the end of this chapter illustrates this point.

Supervision and Conditions of Parole

If the board grants parole (or if the inmate is granted supervised mandatory release), the inmate will also receive a list of conditions that must be followed during the period of supervision in the community. The list of conditions is similar to a contract between the parole board and the inmate. Inmates meeting the conditions can expect to be released from supervision successfully. However, if they violate conditions of supervision, they can expect to receive additional conditions or be returned to prison to serve more time on their sentence. There are two general types of parole conditions: *standard conditions* that are applicable to all parolees and *special conditions* pertaining to a particular parolee. Standard conditions of parole are usually the same as the standard conditions for probation described in Chapter 4, including reporting to their parole officers and keeping them informed of any changes in employment, residence, or other status. Figure 6.5 represents the conditions for community supervision for the state of Ohio for offenders released after serving a term in prison. After the statement of conditions, there is a brief statement of the supervision plan or activities required during the period of supervision. At the bottom of the form, releasees sign the conditions, indicating that they have received and understand the expectations of their supervision.

Special conditions of parole are again similar to special conditions of probation, such as a requirement for drug or alcohol counseling and testing, vocational training, mental health counseling, or other treatment programs; avoiding a particular person or group of people; residing in a halfway house; or being placed under electronic monitoring. The parole board considers the specific characteristics of each inmate when imposing special conditions that can add to the monitoring of the parolee, improve his or her rehabilitation and chance for success, or increase community safety.

Once offenders begin their terms of supervision, they are classified to determine their risk and needed frequency of contacts with their parole officer, the types of programs in which they should be involved, and any specific monitoring (such as intensive caseload or electronic monitoring) requirements. The purpose of classification is to assess the risk of the offender to commit further crimes and the need for treatment programs to improve the offender's chance for success. Most states and the federal government use some type of objective classification instrument as a guide for supervision strategies. Figure 6.6 is an example of risk assessment for community supervision and the variety of characteristics regarding history of crime, employment, and alcohol or drug use that affects classification. Each characteristic is scored, and the total score then determines the classification level. A serious history of substance abuse, mental illness, or some other treatment need may result in an immediate designation to an intensive caseload.[31] Otherwise, the supervision level is based on the assessment score as follows:

Basic high	Risk score of 28 and above
Basic medium	Risk score of 11–27
Basic low	Risk score of 10 or below

STATE OF OHIO
Department of Rehabilitation and Correction
Adult Parole Authority

CONDITIONS OF SUPERVISION

In consideration of having been granted supervision on _____.

1. I will obey federal, state and local laws and ordinances, including those related to illegal drug use and registration with authorities. I will have no contact with the victim of my current offense(s).

2. I will follow all orders given to me by my supervising officer or other authorized representatives or the Court of the Department of Rehabilitation and Correction, including, but not limited to obtaining permission from my supervising officer before changing my residence and submitting to drug testing. I will report my supervising officer in person by the next business day following my release from custody.

3. I will obtain a written travel permit from the Adult Parole Authority before leaving the State of Ohio.

4. I will not purchase, possess, own, use or have under my control, any firearms, ammunition, dangerous ordnance, devices used to immobilize or deadly weapons. I will obtain written permission from the Adult Parole Authority prior to residing in a residence where these items are securely located.

5. I agree to fully participate in, and comply with, Special Conditions that will include programming/intervention to address very high, high, and moderate domains if indicated by a validated risk tool selected by DRC and any other special conditions imposed by the Parole Board, Court, or Interstate Compact:

NOTICE

1. I understand that if I am arrested outside the State of Ohio, my signature as witnessed at the end of the page will be deemed to be a waiver of extradition and that no other formalities will be required for an authorized agent of the State of Ohio to bring about my return.

2. Pursuant to section 2951.02 and/or 2967.131, I am subject to warrantless searches.

3. If I am a Parole/PRC/Interstate Compact offender, I will be required to pay supervision fees in the amount of $20.00 per month unless waived by the Adult Parole Authority. If I am a Community Control/Judicial Release/Treatment in Lieu offender, I will be required to pay financial obligations as determined by the Court and/or as specified in the journal entry(ies).

I have read or had read to me the conditions of my _____. I fully understand these conditions and I agree to follow them. I understand that violation of any of these conditions may result in the revocation of my_____ which may result in additional imposed sanctions, including imprisonment. In addition, I understand that I must follow these conditions until notified by my supervising officer. By my signature I acknowledge that I have received a copy of these conditions of supervision.

Print Witness Name:		Print Offender Name:		Inmate #:
Witness Signature:	Date:	Offender Signature:		Date:

Staff Assistance Required:	☐ Yes ☐ No
Language: _____	ADA Accommodations--Type: _____
Literacy: _____	Other: _____
Staff Providing Assistance:	Date:

DRC 3019 (Rev. 09/2014)

FIGURE 6.5 Conditions of Supervision, Ohio Department of Rehabilitation and Correction   Source: Ohio Department of Rehabilitation and Correction, Policy Manual 3019, revised 2014. Reprinted with Permission.

ASSESSMENT OF OFFENDER RISK

Offender Name:		Offender #:
Date:	F.U. Date:	Unit Location:
Officer (Last, First):		

Select the appropriate answer and enter the associated weight in the score column. Total all scores to arrive at the risk assessment score.

SCORE

Number of Prior Felony Convictions: . . . .
(or Juvenile Adjudications)

   0 None
   2 One
   4 Two or more   _____

Arrested Within Five (5) Years Prior to Arrest . . . .
for Current Offense (Exclude Traffic):

   0 None
   4 Yes   _____

Age at Arrest Leading to First Felony Conviction: . . . .
(or Juvenile Adjudications)

   0 24 and over
   2 20–23
   4 19 and under   _____

Amount of Time Employed in the Last 12 Months:
(Prior to Incarceration for Parolees/PRC Offenders) . . . . .

   0 More than 7 months
   1 5 to 7 months
   2 Less than 5 months
   0 Not applicable   _____

Alcohol Usage Problems (Prior to Incarceration
for Parolees/PRC Offenders): . . . .

   0 No interference
      with functioning
   2 Occasional abuse;
      some disruption
      of functioning
   4 Frequent abuse;
      serious disruption;
      needs treatment   _____

Other Drug Usage Problems (Prior to Incarceration
for Parolees/PRC Offenders): . . . .

   0 No interference
      with functioning
   2 Occasional abuse;
      some disruption
      of functioning
   4 Frequent abuse;
      serious disruption;
      needs treatment   _____

Number of Prior Adult Incarcerations in a State
or Federal Institution: . . . .

   0 0
   3 1–2
   6 3 and above   _____

Age at Admission to Institution or Probation/Community
Control for Current Offense: . . . .

   0 30 and over
   3 18–29
   6 17 and under   _____

Number of Prior *Adult* Supervisions: . . . .

   0 None
   4 One or more   _____

Number of Prior Probation/Community Control/Parole/
PRC Revocations Resulting in Imprisonment
(Adult or Juvenile): . . . .

   0 None
   4 One or more   _____

                            TOTAL: _____

CLASSIFICATION CODE:
_____

1 INTENSIVE
2 BASIC HIGH (28 & above)
3 BASIC MEDIUM (11–27)
4 BASIC LOW (10 & below)
5 MONITORED TIME

OVERRIDE CODE:
_____

1 HIGHER
2 LOWER
3 NONE

IF OVERRIDE, SUPERVISOR'S
INITIALS:
_____

DRC 3001 (7/97)   DISTRIBUTION: WHITE–Central Records   CANARY–District File

FIGURE 6.6 Assessment of Offender Risk   Source: Ohio Department of Rehabilitation and Correction, Policy Manual 3019, revised July 1997. Reprinted with Permission.

Based on the classification level, supervision policy often requires a certain minimum frequency of contacts, but additional contacts can be required if they are deemed necessary to meet the supervision needs of the individual offender:

Intensive: Five contacts per month, with at least one positive contact. For substance abusers, there should also be four drug tests per month.

Basic High: Three contacts per month with at least one positive contact. Substance abusers should be tested three times per month.

Basic Medium: One contact per month. Substance abusers should be tested twice per month.

Basic Low: No contacts required, but the offender completes and submits a form listing his or her activities related to jobs, residences, and so on. For substance abusers, there is one drug test per month.[32]

A **positive contact** is a face-to-face contact with the offender by the officer, and other contacts are those in which significant information is collected (from the offender or an ancillary service such as a treatment provider or employer). Currently, however, many parole agencies no longer specify a set number of contacts per risk level. Instead, the parole officer develops a supervision plan unique to the individual needs of the offender. In 2015, agencies reported that 83 percent of parolees were on active supervision, with weekly or monthly face-to-face contact with their supervision officer. Only 5 percent were on inactive or administrative supervision. The rest were either absconders (6 percent), or some other status.[33]

A somewhat recent development to further aligning risk assessment with intensity of supervision has been created by the Administrative Office of the U.S. Courts, which oversees the operations of the federal probation, parole, and pretrial services. The Administrative Office contracted to develop the post-conviction risk assessment (PCRA).[34] The PCRA has a section completed by the supervision officer (Officer Assessment) and an offender self-assessment based on the Psychological Inventory of Criminal Thinking Styles (PICTS), which was developed by staff of the Federal Bureau of Prisons. The PICTS is verified reliable and valid instrument to assess criminal thinking by offenders. Together, these two segments score items in the following seven categories:

- Criminal History
- Education and Employment
- Substance Abuse
- Social Networks
- Cognitions
- Other (Housing, Finances, Recreation)
- Responsivity Factors

positive contact
face-to-face contact between a parole officer and an offender

After creation, follow-up and continued monitoring of the effectiveness of the PCRA indicate that the results validate the prediction of risk and criminogenic needs. In comparing revocation rates by risk and need score, there was a very strong correlation between items.[35] The U.S. Courts now use this instrument to create supervision levels, determine frequency and intensity of supervision based on the risk to re-offend, and target resources toward those with the highest risk-need levels. Supervision offices also contract with local providers to create and deliver programs to improve offender skills and reduce criminogenic needs. These may include cognitive and criminal thinking classes, employability training, improving social networks, and managing finances and other life skill developments.

TABLE 6.3	Recommended Caseload per Officer by Type of Caseload
Case type	**Cases to staff ratio**
Intensive	20:1
Moderate to High Risk	50:1
Low Risk	200:1
Administrative[a]	No limit? 1,000?

[a] Administrative caseloads require no contact and are just on supervision "on paper." If they have no criminal charges or arrests, there is no action needed by the supervision authority.

Source: Data from Bill Burrell, *Caseload Standards for Probation and Parole* (Lexington, KY: American Probation and Parole Association, 2006), p. 6.

Similar to probation, parolees are placed on a special caseload, regular caseload, or intensive caseload. Special caseloads are for offenders with a special treatment need, such as mental health, substance abuse, or sex offenses. Intensive caseloads are also for offenders with a special treatment need; however, they are more commonly used for offenders with a high level of risk of reoffending. In addition, some states use electronic monitoring for a small portion of their parolees. In most jurisdictions, those under electronic monitoring are placed on a caseload with others under electronic monitoring.

Table 6.3 lists the size of caseload by type of caseload as recommended by the American Probation and Parole Association (APPA). The APPA has no authority and jurisdictions do not have to follow them. However, APPA is a professional organization made up of practicing parole and probation professionals and their reports and recommendations are often supported. As expected, the higher the risk of the offenders, the lower the recommended caseload. "Your Career in Corrections" box describes the job of parole officers.

Terminating Parole Supervision

The length of parole supervision following release from prison can vary from six months to several years. Parolees can either successfully or unsuccessfully terminate their period of supervision. A Bureau of Justice Bulletin reveals that of the 388,789 parolees who exited supervision in 2015, 62 percent successfully completed their term of supervision or were discharged early. Only 28 percent were returned to incarceration, and another 4 percent were either absconders or had another unsatisfactory completion of supervision. Only 7.5 percent of the total exits returned with a new sentence and 17 percent had their supervision revoked for technical violations.[37] Most states allow for release from supervision before the end of the supervision period and before the date that ends the full maximum term of the inmate's sentence. For this to occur, the parole officer must write a recommendation detailing why the supervision should be terminated; the report is considered by the full board, which can agree and terminate supervision or disagree and continue the parolee's supervision. Table 6.4 illustrates the percentage of successful parole discharges by various characteristics of the parolees. Overall, the rate of successful discharges remained steady from 2000 to 2006 but

Your Career in Corrections

Parole Officers

Parole officers are the line-level employees responsible for supervising parolees in the community from the time of their release until they either successfully leave supervision or have their parole revoked. Even though many states have abolished parole, almost all states still provide supervision after release. If not on parole, supervised offenders are often called mandatory releasees, and the supervision (by whatever the supervising officer is called) is the same as if on parole. The only difference is that the authority over the offender during supervision is usually held by the sentencing court, rather than by the parole board.

Officers usually have two primary tasks, supervision and investigations, with supervision making up approximately 80 percent of their responsibilities. Investigations determine the adequacy of the proposed release plans. A prison staff member transmits the proposed plan (including residence, job possibilities, program needs) to the officer, who interviews the person the inmate proposes to live with, prospective employers, and potential program providers. A report on the plan is then sent to the parole board. If the plan is not satisfactory, the parole officer usually suggests an alternative plan (such as living at a halfway house) to allow the inmate to have an adequate plan upon release.

In many jurisdictions, supervision of both parolees and probationers is done jointly by the same agency and many times by the same officers. Supervision entails scheduling offenders for office visits, visiting them in the community at their residence or job/program site, and interviewing significant individuals regarding offenders' progress and conduct. Officers may also place offenders into needed programs, such as substance abuse, parenting classes, or vocational training, and some officers run counseling groups. If offenders violate the conditions of their supervision, the officer must begin the revocation process by preparing a report of the violation and possibly an arrest warrant. Later in the process, the officer may have to testify at a revocation hearing regarding offenders' behavior during supervision.

According to the Bureau of Labor Statistics, in 2016, there are approximately 91,700 probation and parole officers nationwide, and the median salary is $50,160 per year.[36] Although a forty-hour week is standard, parole officers are on-call twenty-four hours per day, and almost all officers work and receive overtime pay or compensatory time for hours in excess of the normal workweek. Most states require a college degree, but no specific major is usually designated. Parole officer jobs are challenging, yet can be very rewarding. There is considerable flexibility in hours worked and significant autonomy on how the job is done. Officers can have a major impact on the success of a parolee in the community. Many officers enjoy their jobs and maintain them throughout their working career, but others see their jobs as great work experience and use them to move into other criminal justice career tracks.

successful completions increased to 58 percent by 2012 and 62 percent in 2015. This is likely again the result of tight budgets and an emphasis on not violating without a notable cause.

Revoking Parole

If offenders do not meet the required conditions of their parole or mandatory release supervision, the violations will be reported to the parole board, which will consider what action to take. For released prisoners under mandatory release supervision, some states have created an authority similar to a parole board to review success during supervision; in other states the sentencing court continues to have jurisdiction during postprison supervision. There are two types of parole violations: technical violations of a standard or special condition and new-crime violations when a conviction of a new crime occurs. When offenders commit a new crime, they can be prosecuted and sentenced for the crime, it is considered a violation of their original conditional release, and they can be processed as a parole violator in addition to the prosecution for the new offense.

| TABLE 6.4 | Characteristics of Adults on Parole, 2000, 2006, 2012, and 2015 |

	Percent of adults exiting parole			
Type of exit	2000	2006	2012	2015
Completions	43%	44%	58%	62%
Returned to incarceration	42	39	25	28
With new sentence	11	11	9	7.5
With revocation	30	26	14	17
Other/unknown	1	2	3	3.5
Absconder	9	11	10	2.4
Other unsatisfactory	2	2	2	1.4
Transferred	1	1	2	0.5
Death	1	1	2	1.5
Other	2	3	2	3
Total estimated exits	459,400	519,200	496,100	388,789

Sources: Lauren E. Glaze and Thomas P. Bonczar, Probation and Parole in the United States, 2010, and Laura M. Maruschak and Thomas P. Bonczar, "Probation and Parole in the United States, 2012," and Danielle Kaeble and Thomas P. Bonczar, "Probation and Parole in the United States, 2015," *BJS Bulletin* (Washington, D.C.: U.S. Department of Justice, 2011, 2013, and 2016), p. 9, p. 9, and p. 24.

When either type of violation occurs, a formal revocation process begins, which includes several steps: (1) determining that there is a violation, (2) a possible stipulated agreement, (3) notice of violation, (4) possible warrant for arrest and custody, (5) preliminary revocation hearing, (6) full revocation hearing, and (7) either reprimand/modification of conditions with return to supervision or violation and return to prison. Obviously, the first step is for the parole officer to determine that there is a **violation**, or failure to follow conditions of supervision. If the offender has committed a new crime, the officer usually receives a notice of arrest and charges from the local police and prosecutor. For technical violations, the officer must make the *determination of a violation*. Violations may be obvious, in that the offender fails a drug test or does not report to the officer as required; the officer may also determine a violation through his or her own investigation, such as if the offender has failed to maintain employment or has moved without notifying the officer.

The second step is authorized in most jurisdictions. If the violation is considered minor, yet does deem that action be taken, the parole officer may discuss the violation with the offender and propose a modification of the conditions of supervision with a continuation of parole. If the offender agrees, the officer writes a report that is referred to as a *stipulated agreement* in many states. In the federal system, it is referred to as an *action with consent and waiver*. In either case, since the offender agrees to the modification, the officer merely files the report with the parole board or supervising court. If the offender does not agree, the officer requests a hearing by the board or the court with a recommendation to modify the conditions.

When a violation occurs and the offender does not cooperate or absconds from supervision and cannot be found, the officer writes a *notice of violation* to the supervising authority and may request a *warrant for arrest and custody* if the officer believes that the offender should be taken into custody. The authority then schedules a preliminary hearing. The offender receives a notice of the violation, with a

violation

failure to follow conditions of parole supervision

listing of the alleged violations and date of the preliminary hearing (usually required within fifteen days of notice of violation or arrest warrant). The purpose of the preliminary hearing is to determine whether *probable cause* exists to believe that the offender has committed the violation. This is particularly important if offenders have been taken into custody, as the preliminary hearing allows a timely determination of whether they should continue to be held pending the full revocation hearing. Offenders may waive the preliminary hearing and proceed to the revocation hearing. If they choose to have the hearing, the officer presents the evidence of the violation before a hearing officer, usually an attorney employed full time by the authority to conduct such hearings. At the hearing, offenders have limited due process rights to have legal representation, challenge the evidence, confront witnesses, and present evidence on their behalf. If the hearing officer determines that there is probable cause, the parolee is held in custody until the full revocation hearing.

The *full revocation hearing* is similar to the preliminary hearing, except that it is more comprehensive. It is held within ninety days of the preliminary hearing, and its purpose is to determine whether a violation of parole is serious enough to warrant a return to prison. The hearing is presided over by parole board members or the sentencing court for mandatory release violators. All activities during the supervision of the offender are reviewed, to include positive adjustment as well as the violation. The board or court can take one of three actions if they determine that the offender violated conditions of release. First, they can return the offender to supervision with no modification of conditions. This is unlikely; if the violation was serious enough to warrant a revocation hearing, there is probably the need to modify the conditions. Second, the offender can be returned to supervision with a modification of conditions. Finally, the offender's conditional release can be revoked and the offender returned to prison to serve additional time.

In many jurisdictions, parole officers and parolees can agree on a stipulated agreement to modify conditions, as a way to respond to minor violations by the parolee. Photo by Richard P. Seiter.

Legal Issues Regarding Revocation

The principal case regarding parole revocation was the 1972 U.S. Supreme Court decision in **Morrissey v. Brewer**.[38] While recognizing the Greenholtz decision that parole is a privilege and not a right and that full due process is not required, the Court noted that once parole is granted a liberty interest is created, and offenders must have certain due process rights in actions to revoke that liberty. The limited due process that must be followed in the revocation process includes the following:

Morrissey v. Brewer
a 1972 U.S. Supreme Court decision that once parole is granted, a liberty interest is created and offenders must have certain due process rights to revoke that liberty

- The parolee is provided advance written notice of the alleged violation and the evidence of the violation.
- The parolee must have the opportunity to attend the hearing and present witnesses and documentary evidence.
- The parolee has the right to confront and cross-examine adverse witnesses.
- A neutral and detached body must hold the hearing.
- The parolee must receive a written decision of the hearing body, as well as the evidence relied upon to revoke the parole.

The *Morrissey* case did not, however, establish the right to counsel during the revocation process. In 1973, in *Gagnon v. Scarpelli*, the U.S. Supreme Court did extend the *Morrissey* due process rights to probationers during revocation proceedings and established that parolees have a limited right to counsel and that the hearing body must determine whether counsel shall be provided to the offender.[39] These two cases are the primary ones that influenced the required process for parole revocations described previously.

Effectiveness of Parole

Views on the effectiveness of parole vary. Parole is often criticized for the wrong reasons, primarily because the public believes that parole is a lenient approach to incarceration and lets dangerous criminals out of prison early. In reality (or at least by design), when indeterminate sentences are created in the penal codes by state legislatures, the minimum time is the term determined to hold offenders accountable for their crimes and satisfy the sentencing goals of punishment, deterrence, and incapacitation. Release at any time after the minimum then considers the individual characteristics of offenders, such as any aggravating circumstances of their crime, dangerousness, and potential for rehabilitation.

To examine the effectiveness of parole, a definition of effectiveness must first be agreed on, although several definitions are often used. First, effectiveness can be defined in terms of how many (or what percentage of) offenders successfully complete their terms of supervision. As noted above, of 388,789 parolees discharged from supervision in 2015, 62 percent had successfully met the conditions of their supervision and 28 percent had been returned to incarceration because of either a rule violation or a new offense. An additional 2.4 percent had absconded and 1.4 percent failed to successfully meet the conditions of supervision but were discharged without incarceration.[40] As illustrated in Table 6.4 above, the rate of successful completion has significantly increased over the past ten years.

A second definition of effectiveness considers the percentage of offenders who do (or do not) recidivate by committing new crimes or being returned to prison. A thorough review of recidivism by Langan and Levin in 2002 states, "Of the two-thirds persons released from prisons in 15 states in 1994, an estimated 67.5 percent were rearrested for a felony or serious misdemeanor within three years, 46.9 percent were reconvicted, and 51.8 percent returned to prison or jail."[41] The findings also indicate that rearrest rates were the highest during the first year (see Table 6.5). And according to the results of a survey conducted by the Pew Center on the States, 45.4 percent of people released from prison in thirty-three states in 1999 and 43.3 percent of those released from prison in forty-one states in 2004 were returned to prison within three years either for commission of a new crime or for violating supervision conditions of their release.[42] However, the study points out how important sentencing policies (determinate and truth in sentencing) and community supervision approaches (such as length of time under supervision and intensity of supervision determined by caseload sizes or use of GPS) can influence the rates of recidivism, especially prison return because of a technical parole violation. The Pew study also examined success on reducing returns to prison for technical violations in three states (Oregon, Michigan, and Missouri). The common result was that the number of technical violations could be reduced significantly if evidence-based supervision was practiced, emphasizing probation and parole officers' work with offenders to address their criminogenic needs and not rush to punishment by revoking offenders but using return to prison as the last resort.[43]

TABLE 6.5	Recidivism Rates of Prisoners Released in 1994 from Prisons in Fifteen States, by Time after Release

	Cumulative percent of released prisoners who were:		
Time after release	Rearrested	Reconvicted[a]	Returned to prison with new sentence[b]
6 months	29.9%	10.6%	5.0%
1 year	44.1	21.5	10.4
2 years	59.2	36.4	18.8
3 years	67.5	46.9	25.4

[a]Because of missing data, prisoners released in Ohio were excluded from the calculation of percent reconvicted.

[b]"New sentence" includes sentence to state or federal prisons, but not to local jails. Because of missing data, prisoners released in Ohio and Virginia were excluded from the calculation of "Percent returned to prison with a new prison sentence."

Source: Data from Patrick A. Langan and David J. Levin, *Recidivism of Prisoners Released in 1994* (Washington, D.C.: U.S. Department of Justice, Bureau of Justice Statistics, 2002), p. 3.

The third and perhaps the most valid measure of effectiveness is how parole and the supervision following discretionary release compare to unconditional mandatory release without parole or supervision. In a dated but still significant study by Sacks and Logan to determine the effect of supervision after release, parolees who received supervision were compared to a group of court-ordered prison releasees who received no supervision in terms of recidivism defined as conviction of a new felony or misdemeanor. After three years, the parole group recidivated at a rate of 77 percent, whereas the group receiving no supervision recidivated at a rate of 85 percent.[44] In addition, a federal study compared prison releasees who received supervision with those receiving no supervision after release. In a review of those who recidivated and were returned to prison, the average time remaining in the community before return to prison was seventeen months for those receiving supervision and only thirteen months for those without supervision.[45] An evaluation of a New Jersey Statutory Early Release (SER) program to require inmates to be released six months before the end of their sentence onto parole was compared against unconditionally released inmates with no parole supervision. The study found that even six months of supervision was better than nothing, as the SER group had significantly reduced rearrest rates than the unconditionally released offenders.[46]

A 2006 study used the same data and releasees as Langan and Levin analyzed recidivism by type of release, identifying three groups: those with discretionary parole release, those with mandatory release from prison but with supervision to follow (mandatory parole), and those unconditionally released from prison with no required supervision. When controlling for differences between the groups, there were only minor differences, as both 61 percent of the mandatory parolees and unconditional releasees were rearrested within two years, and 57 percent of the discretionary parolees were arrested within two years.[47] As well, the Bureau of Justice Statistics compares the percentage of successful discharges from parole by method of release (see Table 6.6). In each year from 1990 to 1999, inmates released under discretionary parole (by the decision of a parole board) were more successful than those under mandatory parole (those released after serving a determinate sentence with supervision to follow).

In the "A Question of Policy" box, consider the issue of the future of parole.

TABLE 6.6	Percentage of Successful State Parole Discharges, by Method of Release

Year	All discharges	Method of release	
		Discretionary parole	**Mandatory parole**
1990	44.6%	51.6%	23.8%
1991	46.8	52.6	24.9
1992	48.6	50.7	29.8
1993	46.9	54.8	33.5
1994	44.3	52.2	30.4
1995	44.3	54.3	28.0
1996	45.2	55.9	30.2
1997	43.4	55.8	30.8
1998	43.8	55.3	32.2
1999	41.9	54.1	33.1

Source: Data from Timothy A. Hughes, Doris James Wilson, and Allen J. Beck, *Trends in State Parole, 1990–2000* (Washington, D.C.: U.S. Department of Justice, Bureau of Justice Statistics, October 2001), p. 11.

A Question of Policy

Should Parole Be Saved?

Parole has been commonly acknowledged to aid prisoner reentry in several ways, and with the indeterminate sentencing structure, parole served many positive functions. First, extremely dangerous inmates were often detained in prisons longer than they would have been under a determinate sentence structure. Determinate sentences are usually shorter than indeterminate sentences, and parole boards regularly require dangerous, high-risk inmates to serve the maximum sentence. The state of Colorado abolished parole as a release mechanism in 1979, but reinstated it after finding out that the length of prison sentences served was decreasing, particularly for high-risk offenders.

Second, parole boards do act as a gatekeeper to ensure that inmates have solid release plans when they return to the community. Parole boards always ask inmates questions such as, "Where will you live when you get out of prison?" and "What job opportunities are available to you?" The boards also have reports available to them from parole officers who have investigated the inmates' release plans. Third, the existence of parole is an incentive for good behavior by inmates and an incentive for program participation that can be beneficial, even if not truly voluntary. There is no evidence that nonvoluntary program participation is less effective than participation with some coercion, and recent data indicate the benefit of participation in a variety of prison programs (cognitive skills training, drug treatment programs, education and work programs, and treatment of sex offenders) on reducing recidivism.[48]

Finally, parole consideration sets the framework for supervision and treatment needs following release. Parole boards create conditions under which parolees must be supervised and attend treatment programs from which they would benefit. Without parole, supervision is less individualized and based on risk rather than need, setting supervision levels based primarily on offenders' history of criminal behavior.

With these issues in mind, students should struggle with the policy question of whether parole should be continued in the states that still have it or reestablished in states that have abolished it. There is no question that the abolition of indeterminate sentences and parole has affected the increase in the number of prisoners. Yet there are many valid reasons why determinate sentences are seen as advantageous. List the pros and cons of parole, and decide whether you think it should be saved.

Prisoner Reentry: A Changing Phenomenon

The prison population in the United States has grown tremendously, with over 1.5 million prisoners currently in federal and state prisons. With so much attention on the number of offenders in prison, less attention has been paid to the fact that many more offenders are also leaving prison and returning to the community than at any time in history. During 2015, adult prisons released 641,027 prisoners, an increase of more than 100,000 since 2000.[49]

This high number of offenders returning to their communities, and some with no supervision, has created new issues regarding **prisoner reentry**. Early in the concern about reentry, the Vera Institute of Justice examined issues facing offenders leaving prison and identified the following as serious obstacles: finding housing, lack of ties with family and friends, finding a job, alcohol and drug abuse, continued involvement in crime, and the impact of parole supervision.[50] In addition, Petersilia identified six collateral consequences of imprisonment: (1) community cohesion, (2) employment and economic well-being, (3) democratic participation and political alienation, (4) family stabilization and childhood development, (5) mental and physical health, and (6) homelessness. These are the result of recycling parolees in and out of families and communities.[51] These issues remain today, and make it difficult for ex-inmates to avoid a return to crime. Therefore, it is critical that prisons have programs to prepare inmates for what they will face upon release and communities and social service agencies are able to support them in their return to the communities.

prisoner reentry
the process of an inmate leaving prison and returning to the community

The world of prisons is very different from the world inmates face when they are released, and the transition from prison to the community often seems surreal to offenders. One ex-offender characterized his experience in leaving prison and returning to the community as "like entering Disneyland" and further describes his release:

> *Leaving prison after all those years was like entering a strange new world. Inside I was a respected convict. I knew where I stood with others, how to act, and what to expect. Once outside in the "free world," everything changed. Moreover, my self-concept and orientation got flipped on its head.*[52]

Prisoners have been released from prison for more than 200 years, yet reentry today is very different from only a few decades ago. These differences include the following:

1. Many more offenders are released from prisons than in the past.
2. Many prisoners are released after serving a determinate sentence, and some have no supervision requirements after release.
3. Prisoners are serving significantly longer prison terms.
4. Only a small percentage of inmates receive the benefit of extensive rehabilitation or prerelease programs.
5. The communities to which prisoners return are more disorganized, their families are less likely to be supportive, and they find fewer social services available to them in the community.
6. With reduced tolerance for risk, a larger number of releasees are returned to prison for commission of new crimes or for violating the technical conditions of their parole or release supervision.

Learning a skill and developing good work habits is part of an effective program for successful reentry to the community from prison. Courtesy of CoreCivic.

These differences result from many factors, including a "tough on crime" attitude, reduced funding for prison programs and community social services, a weakening of the traditional support structures within communities and neighborhoods, and less (sometimes zero) tolerance for lapses by prison releasees under official supervision. The changing nature of prisoner reentry has made successful transitions from prison to community more difficult. For much of the twentieth century, preparation for release was an important part of the prison experience, and all states used indeterminate sentences with release by parole boards to assist in determining offenders' release preparation. The medical model emphasized that prisons should provide programs to prepare inmates for release. Educational and vocational programs, substance abuse and other counseling programs, therapeutic communities and other residential programs, and prison industry work programs were important parts of prison operations.

When prisoners were nearing release, extensive efforts were made to ease their transition to the community. Parole boards closely reviewed inmates' release plans in consideration of parole, and community parole officers investigated the plans and reported on their acceptability to the parole board. If there were not acceptable plans, inmates were usually released through a halfway house so they could be assisted with issues of housing, employment, family relationships, and mental health or substance abuse counseling. Correctional officials recognized the difficulty in the prison-to-community transition, and reintegrative programs were expanded and developed to ease the transition. There was experimentation with specialized caseloads, the use of volunteers in parole, and even ex-offenders as parole officer aides. Inmates' return to the community was intensely supervised. Parole officers' primary responsibility was to guide offenders to programs and services and supervise their successful completion of parole.

Changes Over the Past Three Decades

Over the past three decades, however, this traditional process began to deteriorate. The demise of the medical model, the "tough on crime" attitude of the public and elected officials, the belief that rehabilitation did not work, the reduced funding for prison and transitional programs, and the change in parole supervision from casework to surveillance changed the model of release used until the 1980s. The current model of prison operations and prisoner reentry focuses less on inmate rehabilitation and preparation for release than on punishment, deterrence, and incapacitation. Most offenders serve a determinate sentence that is much longer than in the past. Inmates are seen as making a conscious decision to commit crimes, and punishment is believed important to produce a proper deterrent effect. Prison programs are considered valuable to keep inmates busy and maintain order, more than for release preparation. Without parole boards in many states, there is no gatekeeper to review the inmate's preparation and release plans. After release, if the offender is under supervision, there has been little tolerance for drug use, violations of supervision, and minor criminal behavior, and many offenders are returned to prison for only technical violations.

Most inmates face serious problems, and there are not enough programs within prison to deal with them. Many inmates have long histories of criminal involvement and substance abuse, are gang members, and have few marketable skills. With the closing of state hospitals for people with mental illness, a greater number of mentally ill people end up in prisons and jails, and nearly one in five U.S. prisoners report having a mental illness.[53] And 60–80 percent of offenders under correctional supervision have a substance abuse problem.[54] Yet only 9.9 percent of parolees with a substance abuse problem have received treatment while in prison.[55]

With an emphasis on evidence-based programming, there is much data to indicate which programs are effective in improving prisoner reentry, such as work and prison industry programs, substance abuse counseling, sex offender programs, and release from prison through a halfway house. However, these programs are available only to small numbers of inmates.[56] Yet as of December 30, 2005, only 31 percent of all prisons offered prison industries, 28 percent offered work release, 36 percent offered sex offender programs, and 74 percent offered drug or alcohol dependency counseling.[57] And less than 10 percent of released inmates are placed in halfway houses.[58]

Issues Faced by Offenders Returning to the Community

Many obvious issues face offenders after they serve long sentences in prison and then try to return to their communities, find jobs, support their families, and have a crime-free lifestyle. Simply finding a suitable place to live is difficult. Most ex-offenders have few financial resources when they leave prison, cannot afford high monthly rents or the required deposits of first and last months' rent, and therefore must look for public housing. Unfortunately, some public laws allow providers of federally assisted housing to exclude individuals with a criminal record from receiving public housing.[59]

Offenders also face many collateral consequences as a part of their being found guilty of commission of a crime. **Collateral consequences** are those adverse effects on the offender that stem from a criminal conviction but are not included in the sentence imposed by the court. Common are those that prohibit offenders from voting, holding certain types of jobs, living in public housing, or in some cases reuniting with a child. From a study by the American Bar Association, the National Inventory of Collateral Consequences of Conviction (NICCC) was created that lists more than 45,000 such disqualifications and civil disabilities that adversely impact ex-offenders.[60] Over the past few years, forty-two states and the District of Columbia have enacted reforms of these consequences, to include the "ban the box" prohibition against employers asking someone applying for a job about their criminal history during the application process. Other states have expanded ways ex-offenders can have their criminal records expunged or sealed. And finally, other states have made "certificates of relief" available to allow ex-offenders to avoid collateral consequences under a "forgiving" rather than "forgetting" approach.[61]

collateral consequences
adverse effects on the offender that stem from a criminal conviction but are not included in the sentence imposed by the court

Incarceration also disrupts relationships with offenders and their families. In a three-year study of the incarceration of males in the District of Columbia (of which 10 percent of African American men between ages eighteen and thirty-five were imprisoned), findings indicate that a result of the extensive use of incarceration was "injuring the families of prisoners often as much as and sometimes more than criminal offenders themselves."[62] The incarceration not only affected the ability of the offender to support the family and provide child care, but also diminished the relationship between husband and wife and father and children. Most males in prison are fathers and maintain monthly contact with their children.[63] However, these men fail to offer support as a parent or serve as a positive role model for their children. Incarceration further strains these relationships and makes it difficult for families to stay together even after the prisoner is released.

Finally, it is not easy for ex-inmates to find suitable employment, particularly in the current difficult economic times. In these conditions, employers are less likely to hire ex-offenders, and a larger percentage of former prisoners are unable to find and keep jobs. In the "get tough on criminals" movement, legislatures place more statutory restrictions on ex-offenders. In many states, ex-prisoners are restricted from working in the professions of law, real estate, medicine, nursing, physical therapy, education, dentistry, engineering, and pharmacology.[64] Uggen and Staff summarized the research that illustrates the critical importance of work as a turning point for offenders, while noting the research indicating a relationship between work and crime and that the quality of employment is important for reducing recidivism.[65] An effective program to address the challenge of employment has been developed by the Indiana Department of Corrections and the Department of Workforce Development. They created the Hoosier Initiative for Re-Entry (HIRE) to assist released offenders in finding and keeping employment. From the program initiation until September 2014, they placed more than 2,700 offenders in employment. Indiana has a 35.8 percent recidivism rate (return to prison after three years). However, offenders participating in this program recidivate at the rate of 24.5 percent.[66]

The potentials for obtaining quality work, finding suitable housing, and maintaining strong family relationships are all negatively affected by long terms of imprisonment. A 2008 survey illustrated the critical nature of release planning and identified seven basic needs that should be addressed for inmates before they leave prison. These include transportation, clothing and food, financial resources, housing, employment and education, health care, and support systems.[67] Reentry programs must address these collateral consequences to improve offenders' chances for successful and crime-free lives.

Recent Progress in Prisoner Reentry

Stating the problem of prisoner reentry is easy; it is more difficult to identify what to do about it that lessens the negative effect of incarceration on inmates returning to the community or provides services after release that can reduce recidivism. Over the past few years, many attempts have been made to better understand reentry issues and to improve successful reentry. The Urban Institute launched a "policy conversation" by hosting an ongoing forum of academics, correctional practitioners, community leaders, policymakers, advocates, and former prisoners, and published several reports as a result of these discussions. Soon thereafter, the Re-Entry Policy Council—a bipartisan collection of nearly 100 elected officials, policymakers, and practitioners—was formed. In 2005, they released a comprehensive set of recommendations to reduce recidivism and help ex-offenders succeed in their communities.[68]

These recommendations received strong support and were the impetus for President George W. Bush including the issue of prisoner reentry in his 2005 State of the Union. In the address, he proposed a four-year $300 million prisoner re-entry initiative to expand job training and placement services, to provide transitional housing, and to help newly released prisoners get mentoring. In 2007, the Second Chance Act (H.R. 1593/S. 1060) had broad bipartisan support with ninety-two cosponsors in the House and thirty-three cosponsors in the Senate. It was passed and signed into law in 2008 to ease the reentry process for individuals leaving prison by providing funding for prisoner mentoring programs, job training, and rehabilitative treatment designed to protect public safety and reduce recidivism rates. The bill's provisions initially authorized $362 million to expand assistance for people currently incarcerated, those returning to their communities after incarceration, and children with parents in prison. Each year since the passing of the act, the federal government has made funding available to states or local government to improve transition services.[69] The services to be funded under the bill include the following:

- mentoring programs for adults and juveniles leaving prison;
- drug treatment during and after incarceration, including family-based treatment for incarcerated parents;
- education and job training in prison;
- alternatives to incarceration for parents convicted of nonviolent drug offenses;
- supportive programming for children of incarcerated parents; and
- early release for certain elderly prisoners convicted of nonviolent offenses.[70]

The Second Chance Act funding allows the states to apply and create their own programs that are believed to improve reentry and reduce recidivism. One approach used by many states is to provide residential substance abuse treatment (RSAT) programs. States that received funds under RSAT are required to also provide aftercare services, including case management and other support services. Most RSAT funds are used to support treatment services in correctional settings. Just over one-fifth of RSAT-funded programs provide step-down treatment or aftercare services.[71] Another demonstration project in seven states used risk and needs assessments of offenders to do reentry or transitional planning and guide the delivery of services to participants.[72] And other programs provide an array of pre- and postrelease services, including education and literacy programs, job placement, housing services, and mental health substance abuse treatment.[73]

Another example of progress in prisoner reentry is the development of specialized reentry courts. **Reentry courts** are specialized courts using judicial oversight to monitor offenders' transition to the community and reduce recidivism. As such, they function similarly to drug courts in that their purpose is to oversee a prisoner's reentry to the community, review their plans and progress, order (when necessary) participation in treatment and reintegration programs, use drug and alcohol testing to monitor compliance, and provide graduated sanctions in lieu of a violation and return to prison. This approach is very different from the past, and the involvement by the court ended at sentencing to prison. To test reentry courts, the U.S. Department of Justice Office of Justice Programs awarded grants to nine states to set up courts and track their success. While research of reentry courts shows promising outcomes, results are still inconclusive with mixed results,[74] but reentry courts continue to be studied and modified to improve operations.

reentry courts
specialized courts that use judicial oversight to monitor offenders' transition to the community and reduce recidivism

The focus on work as critical for reentry success is also commonly accepted. Surveys show that about one-third of prison inmates were jobless at their time of incarcerations,[75] and upon release from prison, they are out of work about half the time and earn on average only around $9,000 per year (in 2006 dollars).[76] Therefore, there have been efforts to improve employment among ex-offenders to include transitional employment programs. The transitional employment programs provide subsidized work to former prisoners with close supervision, mentoring, and on-the-job training. While some evaluations of these programs have shown improved employment records correlated with reductions in recidivism,[77] other studies have not shown stable employment reduced criminal activity among serious and violent offenders.[78] A recent review of overall services and their effect on prisoner reentry found that participation in reentry programs is associated with longer time to arrest and fewer arrests.[79]

It is critical that focus and innovation continue in prisoner reentry. We cannot afford to simply recycle criminals through prison to the community and back to prison. We must invest in successful programs that have proven to work in prisoner reentry. The following section presents a guideline on what can be done to improve prisoner reentry.

What Else Can Be Done to Improve Prisoner Reentry?

One of the most important elements to improving the success of prisoner reentry is to build on what we know works. In a review of research regarding prisoner reentry programs, Seiter and Kadela identified several programs that work to reduce the recidivism of released prisoners.[80] The authors first created the following definition of prisoner reentry programs:

- All correctional programs that focus on the transition from prison to community (prerelease, work release, halfway houses, or specific reentry programs), or
- Programs that have initiated treatment (substance abuse, life skills, education, cognitive/behavioral, sex/violent offender) in a prison setting and have linked with a community program to provide continuity of care.

The method to then identify whether a category of program was successful used the *Maryland Scale of Scientific Methods* (MSSM), developed by Sherman and colleagues for the National Institute of Justice, to identify crime prevention programs that work. This scale ranks research studies from one (weakest) to five (strongest) on overall internal validity. Seiter and Kadela identified thirty-two studies that fit the definition of prisoner reentry. Each study was placed into an MSSM level, and evaluations of similar programs have been grouped into (1) vocational training and work, (2) drug rehabilitation, (3) educational programs, (4) sex/violent offender programs, (5) halfway house programs, and (6) prison prerelease programs.

The next step was to determine whether any of these six categories of prison reentry programs were effective, using the Sherman framework definitions. For a program to be considered to be working, at least two level 3 evaluations with statistical significance tests must indicate that the intervention was effective and the preponderance of the remaining evidence must support that conclusion. For a program to be coded as *not working*, at least two level 3 evaluations with statistical significance must indicate the ineffectiveness of the program and the preponderance of the remaining evidence must support the same conclusion. Programs for which the level of certainty from available evidence is too low to support generalizable conclusions were defined as *promising*. Any program not classified in one of these three categories is defined as having unknown effects.

Results indicate a positive result for vocational training and work release programs (found effective in reducing recidivism rates as well as improving job readiness skills for ex-offenders), for drug rehabilitation (graduates of treatment programs were less likely than other parolees and noncompleters to have been arrested, commit a drug-related offense, continue drug use, or have a parole violation), to some extent for education programs (only to increase educational achievement scores, but not to decrease recidivism), for halfway house programs (found effective in reducing the frequency and severity of future crimes), and for prerelease programs (effective in reducing recidivism rates of ex-offenders). In

Idleness in prison makes prison management more difficult and does nothing to prepare inmates for release to the community.
Photo by Richard P. Seiter.

addition, there are promising results for sex and violent offender programs.

Even with the problems resulting from the changes over the past two decades, this analysis of prisoner reentry programs has identified several categories of programs in which there is evidence of success. Public officials should take note of these programs; implement or expand the use of vocational training and/or work release programs, drug rehabilitation programs, education programs, halfway house programs, and prerelease programs that have proved successful; and expand the use of sex and violent offender programs that show promise. These programs can be expanded significantly with only a small portion of funding that is currently used for imprisoning offenders.

The nation has invested billions of dollars in locking up offenders. Policies concerning reentry have become increasingly an avoidance of risk. As a result, we have created a revolving door of offenders who will be committed to prison again and again as they fail in the community. This is not only a failure by the inmate, but also a failure of release and reentry policies. This analysis has pointed out that certain programs can improve prisoner reentry and reduce the revolving-door syndrome. With billions of dollars focused on imprisonment, it is only fitting that a few million more be focused on their return to the community.

A Systems Approach to Prisoner Reentry

In the review of prisoner reentry discussed above, you have seen the changes over the past two decades (longer sentences, fewer community ties, inmates with more serious problems) that have caused more problems for inmates attempting to leave prison and successfully reenter society. You have seen the types of prison programs that have been identified as contributing to successful reentry, yet the low percentage of inmates that participate in these programs. And you have seen the issues in postincarceration community supervision in terms of large caseloads and a surveillance style of supervising offenders that often results in technical violations and return to prison. What you have not seen is a model for addressing these challenges in a systemic and comprehensive manner.

This section presents the State of Washington Department of Corrections plan for a reentry-focused correctional system.[81] This plan created a total focus toward successful return of inmates to the community. This plan begins with the question of whether a reentry-focused correctional system is necessary (see Figure 6.7) and is significant for several reasons. It addresses what experts believe is key to successful reentry: that the reentry process begins at reception. It highlights the many needs that offenders have when they enter a prison that must be addressed while they are serving their sentence. It recognizes the important link between prison programming and the transition to community-based services for continuity of care. It focuses on the reduction of recidivism. And by reducing recidivism, it has a goal of reducing the need for prison beds and the long-term costs to the correctional system. From this review, Washington decided that it needed to refocus its entire correctional system on improving the reentry of inmates to the community.

Department of Corrections
OFFENDER RE-ENTRY

Does Washington need a re-entry focused correctional system?

A re-entry focused correctional system is designed to:

- **Reduce offender deficits correlating to criminal behavior:**
  - 83% of females and 71% of males enter DOC with less than a 9th grade level education
  - 75% of prison offenders have previously been in a country juvenile system
  - 50% of male children whose parents have been incarcerated will end up incarcerated
  - 73% of females and 55% of males in prison have mental health problems
  - 62% of females and 56% of males in prison reported using drugs the month before their offense

- **Increase community participation in supporting offender re-entry**
  - 97% of prison inmates re-enter communities
  - DOC has on average only 21 months to work with each offender
  - Offenders are community members before and after they are with DOC

- **Reduce recidivism**
  - Washington's rate has climbed from 31% to 37% over the last 10 years
  - Estimating over 3,500 offenders releasing in 2006 will commit new crimes by 2011

- **Reduce demand for prison beds**
  - 2006 demand exceeds supply by about 1,600 beds
  - 2017 demand is estimated to exceed supply by about 4,000 beds

A public safety focused Washington needs:

- DOC's re-entry focused correctional system
            AND
- A systemic and collaborative approach from state and local agencies
  - to reduce deficits that precede crime
  - to increase community capacity for successful offender re-entry

FIGURE 6.7   Does Washington Need a Reentry-Focused Correctional System?   Source: Washington Department of Corrections, *A Re-Entry Focused Correctional System* (Olympia, Wash.: Government Management, Accountability, and Performance Forum, November 2006).

A Reentry-Focused Correctional System

ASSESS	PLAN	MANAGE	MONITOR	RESPOND	IMPROVE

Increased Public Safety

DOC's Contribution to Reducing Re-Offense Behavior

Assess and Plan	**Manage and Monitor**	**Respond and Improve**
Reception Diagnostic Center • Reception and Orientation • Assessments • Diagnosis • Personalized Plan From Jail to Community Supervision • Assessments • Personalized Plan	Prisons • Focusing on Behavior and being held accountable for their actions • Step Down through programs and custody levels • Targeted Programs based on individual needs identified in their Personalized Plan • Focused Reentry Programming Facilities Community Participation • Collaborative Partnerships with other Agencies, Communities and Stakeholders • Enhanced Family Connections	Community Corrections • Targeted Programs based on Personalized Plan • Focused Reentry Programs in Community Justice Centers • Increased investments in Work Releases Community Participation • Collaborative Partnerships with other Agencies, Communities and Stakeholders • Enhanced Family Connections
Personalized Plan	**Accountable Behavior**	**Responsibility/Community**
Assessment Components	**Targeted Programs**	**Targeted Programs**
Initial Interview, Personality Assessment Inventory, Educational Assessment, Vocational Assessment, Sex Offender Risk/Treatment Assessment, Chemical Dependency Screening, Risk/Needs, Self Reported Information, Custody Designation, Criminal History, Medical, Mental Health, and Dental Assessment.	Basic Education, English as a 2nd Language, Long-term Vocational Technology Life Skills, Anger Stress Management, Violence Reduction, Cognitive Behavioral Therapy, Correctional Industries, Off-site Work Crews, Department of Natural Resources, Primary Work Programs supporting facility operations, Work Release, Sex Offender Treatment, Long-term Chemical Dependency Treatment, Therapeutic Community, Family Connections, Mental Health Services	Long-term Chemical Dependency Treatment, Cognitive Behavioral Therapy, Sex Offender Treatment, Employment and Job Training, Vocational Programming, Work Crews, Work Release, Therapeutic Community, Family Connections, Mental Health Services

FIGURE 6.8 A Reentry-Focused Correctional System   Source: Washington Department of Corrections, *A Re-Entry Focused Correctional System* (Olympia, Wash.: Government Management, Accountability, and Performance Forum, November 2006).

The next chart (Figure 6.8) is the result of their planning efforts. This comprehensive restructure and alignment of activities is extremely unusual, and the Washington Department of Corrections is to be commended for it. The plan begins with an assessment of inmates at the reception center to determine their needs and create a personalized plan for addressing these needs. The next stage has programs provided within prisons that target the individual needs, while expecting good behavior and rewarding inmates with a step-down of security levels for positive behaviors and program completions. There is also a focus on inmates rebuilding their ties with their families and building relationships with community agencies and other stakeholders. And finally, there is the move to the community using Community Justice Centers and work release, and managing the personalized plan for offenders to complete their programs and live a crime-free and productive lifestyle.

Chapter Review

Summary

During much of the history of corrections, indeterminate sentences and discretionary parole were a cornerstone of both theory and practice. The minimum term of an indeterminate sentence satisfied the punishment, deterrence, and incapacitation sentencing goals, and a parole board of experts then examined the individual offender characteristics to determine when the goal of rehabilitation was maximized and the offender was best prepared for release to the community. However, this model came under attack and was completely abandoned in a third of the states and seriously compromised in another third. The use of determinate sentences that were longer than the minimum indeterminate sentence term developed in its place in an effort to make the punishment fit the crime and to hold offenders accountable for their criminal acts. Unfortunately, punishment, deterrence, and incapacitation became so predominant that rehabilitation was often ignored or seriously reduced in emphasis.

Several problems have resulted from these changes in philosophy, policy, and practice. There has been a fivefold increase in the number of prison inmates, at a tremendous cost to society and, many argue, with little benefit in the reduction of crime or successful return of offenders to the community. With criminal offenders now predominantly receiving determinate sentences, there is no parole board to act as gatekeepers between the prison and community. Some high-risk offenders actually serve shorter sentences than when a parole board could deny parole and continue them even until their maximum sentence term was met. Without a parole board, there is no review of release plans, and there is very little incentive for good behavior while in prison. Almost 80 percent of inmates were released on discretionary parole only twenty-five years ago, yet just over 30 percent are now similarly released. Another 30 percent of prison releasees still receive supervision as a postprison requirement, and violation of conditions results in the possibility of returning to prison. However, approximately 27 percent of prison releasees go into the community with no requirement for supervision.

Prisoner reentry has become a much more significant issue than it was twenty years ago. As pointed out by Jeremy Travis, former director of the National Institute of Justice, in referring to the recent interest and problem of prisoner reentry, "they all come back."[82] Inmates are serving longer periods of time, are older when released, are more prisonized from serving longer times in prison, are less likely to participate in prison rehabilitative programs, and enter communities that are more disorganized and unable to provide them services and assistance. Fortunately, some reentry programs have been found to help prisoners return to the community. It is critical that public policymakers build on these findings and fund and expand those programs proved successful, while hopefully ending the negative cycle of crime–prison–release–crime.

Key Terms

parole	Sir Walter Crofton	just deserts model
Alexander Maconochie	Zebulon R. Brockway	discretionary parole
mark system	Elmira Reformatory	supervised mandatory release
ticket of leave	justice model	unconditional mandatory release

parole guidelines

salient factor score

hearing officers

presumptive parole date

positive contact

violation

Morrissey v. Brewer

prisoner reentry

collateral consequences

reentry courts

Review Questions

1. Describe the four stages of the system of release implemented by Alexander Maconochie on the Norfolk Island penal colony.

2. Describe the four stages of release implemented by Sir Walter Crofton in the Irish system.

3. How did the Elmira Reformatory move toward the implementation of a system of parole in the United States?

4. How did the Martinson findings of "nothing works" influence the use of parole and the medical model?

5. Describe some of the suggested models to replace the medical model of corrections.

6. Compare and contrast parole, supervised mandatory release, and unconditional mandatory release.

7. What two factors do parole guidelines attempt to predict?

8. What are the driving factors in the change in the parole population over the past three decades?

9. Name and describe the two types of parole conditions.

10. What are the two types of parole violations?

11. Describe the process for revoking parole.

12. List the due process rights prescribed by the *Morrissey v. Brewer* decision.

13. List some of the ways in which issues facing prisoners reentering the community are different than they were in the past.

14. Describe Seiter and Kadela's findings regarding the effectiveness of prisoner reentry programs.

▸ You Make the Decision ...

Parole or Not?

The following scenarios represent the types of cases that can come before a parole board. Students should consider the situation in each case and determine what decision they would make regarding the individual's parole.[83]

Inmate A was convicted of vehicular manslaughter and received a sentence of seven years. He killed two teenagers in a head-on collision. He had been drinking, but his blood-alcohol content was below the limit. The inmate has never been arrested for any other offenses. He is twenty-one years old and was a senior in college when the offense occurred. He has been an excellent inmate and is a tutor in school. The victims' families are opposing parole. He has served ten months on the sentence. The minimum time he must serve is thirteen months. His conditional release date is fifty-six months. How much time should he serve?

Inmate B is a thirty-one-year-old male who committed two burglaries and received two ten-year sentences running concurrently. He has two prior prison incarcerations. One is for stealing and the other for first-degree burglary. He is a severe drug addict who has strong family ties. He has received his GED while incarcerated. His minimum mandatory prison term is five years, and he has served three years. His conditional release date is at seven years. How much time should he serve in all?

Inmate C is a nineteen-year-old female who has sold a large quantity of cocaine with no prior incarcerations. She has a prior probation for possession of drugs and is pregnant. She indicated that she is not a drug user but sold drugs because she needed money. She has a ninth-grade education and is going to school to get her GED (General Equivalency Diploma). She has a five-year sentence with a minimum eligibility of twenty months. The conditional release date is at forty months and she has served six months. How much time should she serve in all?

Inmate D has a five-year sentence for felony DWI (Driving while Intoxicated). He has two prior convictions and served time in jail for one of the offenses. He was on probation for DWI and this probation was revoked for the commission of this present DWI. He is thirty-five years old, married with two children. He works steadily when he is in the community. He has been in an inpatient alcohol treatment program before and also attends Alcoholics Anonymous in prison. He states that he had been sober for one year when this present DWI occurred. He is illiterate, is attending school, but is having a difficult time grasping the work. He has served six months and his minimum eligibility is nine months. The conditional release date is at forty months. How much time should he serve in all?

Inmate E has a ten-year sentence for rape after being found guilty by a jury. He has never been in trouble before, and the victim of the offense was a woman that he took out on a date and then raped. He denies it was rape and indicated that

(Continued)

she consented. He is divorced with two children. He has never been in trouble before and is in business for himself. His family is taking care of his business. He has had difficulty adjusting in prison and has had a few minor violations. He has a tenth-grade education. He refuses to go to school. He has served six years and has a minimum eligibility of eight and a half years. How much time should he serve?

Inmate F has a thirty-year sentence for killing her husband. She states that her husband had beaten her during their fifteen-year marriage, and there was some evidence that she had called the police and stated her husband had hit her, but denied the accusations when the police came. She is thirty-four years old and has three children, who are being cared for by relatives. She has a college education. She has no prior arrests and no indication of prior assaultive behavior. She has served eight years and the minimum eligibility is ten years. There is opposition by the victim's family. Her conditional release date is at twenty-five years. How much time should she serve in all?

Inmate G has a twenty-five-year sentence for first-degree robbery. He was sixteen years old when the offense occurred and was certified as an adult. He has a juvenile record and was in a juvenile institution for assaultive behavior for six months. He does not use drugs and there is family support. He has received his GED while incarcerated and is working in the furniture factory. He has had some minor violations and two major violations for assault. He has served ten years and his minimum eligibility has passed. His conditional release date is at twenty years. How much time should he serve in all?

Inmate H has a ten-year sentence for child molestation and the victim was his son. He was on probation for this offense, which he violated when he failed to obtain treatment. He is married and has the support of his wife, who is not the mother of his son. He is a high school graduate and is working in food service. He has served three years and his conditional release date is at seven years. How much time should he serve?

CHAPTER 7

The Clients of Adult Correctional Agencies

Courtesy of CoreCivic

After reading this chapter, you should be able to:

1. Explain the trends in the number, gender, race, ethnicity, and age of offenders in recent decades.

2. Describe the characteristics, classification, and issues of male offenders.

3. Describe the characteristics, classification, and issues of female offenders.

Introduction

In Chapters 2 through 6, we covered the scope of the correctional process, including pretrial services, sentencing, probation and intermediate sanctions, imprisonment, and release and reentry to the community. Each of these process descriptions included historical developments, theoretical basis for the evolution of policy and practice, and an explanation of how the process currently operates. In Part III of this textbook, we move to the clients of corrections and address topics of gender, age, and race distinctions of clients, as well as the operations of the juvenile justice system as separate from the criminal justice system, and the management of special offender groups.

In this chapter, we begin with identifying and providing a basic understanding of the clients of adult correctional systems. Questions asked include the following: What categories of clients do correctional agencies serve? What theoretical underpinnings are the bases of past and current operations? What are the backgrounds and characteristics of the different categories of correctional clients? What might make them unique and require special processing, handling, or management? Has anything in their background contributed to their criminality? For each group, characteristics that make them distinctive and influence how they are handled and managed are described. The chapter begins with an overview of offenders who make up the adult correctional system, including the numbers under supervision and their makeup by gender, offense category, and race and ethnicity. Particular note is made of the increasing number of offenders under correctional supervision and especially the significant increase in the number in state and federal prisons over the past three decades.

The prison population today is very large and much more diverse than in the past. A great deal of the prison growth resulted from the incarceration of many property and drug offenders who previously received probation rather than a sentence to prison. The prison population is increasingly black and brown, as white offenders are a continually smaller proportion of the prison population. And the prison population is no longer "middle crime age" (age twenty-five to thirty-five) and physically and emotionally healthy. It is not uncommon for juveniles to be tried as adults and sentenced to adult prisons, the percentage of elderly offenders is increasing, mental illness among inmates is a challenging problem, and inmates experience a variety of severe health problems. This chapter identifies characteristics of the unique groups of offenders and some of the activities, policies, and programs that are used to respond to their special situations.

The clients of corrections are what corrections is all about. Corrections is not a manufacturing operation with products being spewed off an assembly line. Corrections is not information technology, with hardware and software to make work more efficient. Corrections is about people managing correctional clients. All too often, students of corrections study, analyze, and consider the strengths and weaknesses of the *process* rather than the *people* the process is designed to manage. This chapter provides many facts and figures that may seem impersonal and inconsistent with this admonishment to consider the people. However, using these facts and figures as a beginning point, students can then work to understand the issues that must be considered as government and correctional officials develop policies and operations to meet public safety, offender rehabilitation, and inmate security goals for various criminal sanctions and the variety of criminal offenders. It is important for students to have a clear understanding of the situations and issues that face correctional clients and therefore how specific policies and operations will affect them. Armed with this perspective, students have both the background and sensitivity to better understand and critically assess issues described in later chapters detailing security, inmate programs, the prison environment, and management of special offenders.

Overview of Adult Offenders

The number of adults under correctional supervision (individuals on probation, in jail, in prison, or on parole) has grown dramatically over the past three decades. As indicated in Table 7.1, only 1.8 million adults were on probation and parole and in jail and prison in 1980. This number had doubled in only eight years by 1988, grew to over 7.3 million in 2007, and then began to decline. However, by 2015, there were 6.741,400 adults under the supervision of correctional agencies in the United States. Most private companies and even public agencies would welcome an increase in clients, as there is no group, business, or clients served by government agencies that have grown at anywhere near this rate over the same period of time.

As illustrated in Table 7.1, a significant part of the growth in the number of adults under correctional supervision comes from growth in the prison population. The use

TABLE 7.1	Number of Persons under Correctional Supervision, Selected Years 1980–2015				
	Probation	**Jail**	**Prison**	**Parole**	**Total**[a]
1980	1,118,097	183,988	319,598	220,438	1,842,100
1985	1,968,712	256,615	487,593	300,203	3,013,100
1990	2,670,234	405,320	743,382	531,407	4,350,300
1995	3,077,861	507,044	1,078,542	679,421	5,342,900
2000	3,839,532	621,149	1,316,333	725,527	6,460,000
2005	4,162,495	747,529	1,525,900	784,354	7,051,300
2006	4,237,023	765,819	1,568,700	798,202	7,202,100
2007	4,293,163	780,174	1,596,800	826,097	7,337,900
2008	4,270,917	785,533	1,608,300	828,169	7,312,400
2009	4,203,967	767,434	1,615,500	819,308	7,232,800
2010	4,055,514	748,728	1,613,800	840,676	7,076,200
2011	3,971,300	735,600	1,599,000	853,900	6,978,500
2012	3,942,800	744,500	1,570,400	851,200	6,937,600
2013	3,912,900	731,200	1,577,000	849,500	6,899,700
2014	3,868,400	744,600	1,562,300	857,700	6,856,900
2015	3,789,800	728,200	1,526,800	870,500	6,741,400

[a]Because some offenders may have multiple statuses (i.e., held in a prison or jail but remain under the jurisdiction of a probation or parole authority), totals in 2000 exclude probationers held in jail or prison; totals in 2005 exclude probationers and parolees held in jail or prison; and the total in 2007 excludes probationers and parolees held in jail or prison, probationers who were also under parole supervision, and parolees who were also under probation supervision. For these reasons, details do not sum to total.

[b]The 2003 probation and parole counts were estimated and may differ from previously published numbers.

Source: Data from 1980 to 2000: Bureau of Justice Statistics, "Correctional Populations," updated with Danielle Kaeble and Lauren E. Glaze, "Correctional Populations in the United States, 2015," *BJS Bulletin* (Washington, D.C.: U.S. Department of Justice, 2016), p. 2.

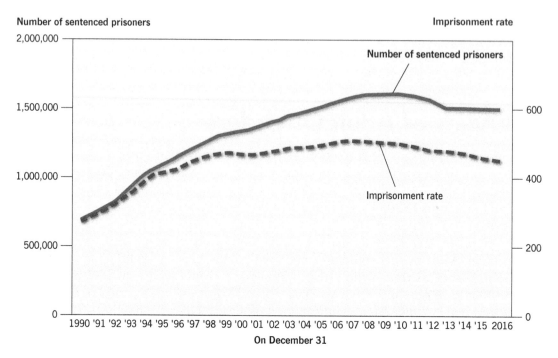

Number of sentenced prisoners

Imprisonment rate

FIGURE 7.1   Number and Imprisonment Rate of Sentenced Prisoners under State Jurisdiction, 1990–2015   Source: Data from E. Ann Carson, "Prisoners in 2016," *BJS Bulletin* (Washington, D.C.: U.S. Department of Justice, 2018), pp. 3 and 8.

of incarceration as a criminal sanction skyrocketed from 1980 until 2009, when it began to slowly decline. In 1980, the rate of sentenced inmates incarcerated per 100,000 population was only 139.[1] By 2016, the rate of sentenced adults incarcerated per 100,000 population had reached 450.[2] The incarceration rate has increased every year from 1980 to 2008, but the rate of increase slowed from 2000 to 2008, and actually declined each year since then. Figure 7.1 illustrates the growth and then decline in the number of prisoners and the incarceration rates since 1990. On December 31, 2016, the states reporting the highest incarceration rates per 100,000 population were Louisiana, 760; Oklahoma, 673; Mississippi, 624; Arizona, 585; Arkansas, 583; Alabama, 571; and Texas, 563. Those reporting the lowest incarceration rates were Maine, 137; Massachusetts, 156; Minnesota, 191; Rhode Island, 192; and Vermont, 201.[3]

Gender, Race, and Ethnicity

In addition to the tremendous growth in the number of individuals in prison, there has been a change in the makeup of this population by gender, race, and ethnicity. First, the rate for females under all types of correctional supervision has grown more rapidly than the number of males under supervision. The Bureau of Justice Statistics reported in 1999, "Women represent about 21 percent of those on probation, 11 percent of those in local jails, just under 6 percent of those in prisons, and 12 percent of those on parole."[4] Although the proportion of the prison population that is female is relatively small, by the end of 2016, females were 7.2 percent of the prison population. The average growth of female prisoners from 2005 to 2014 was 0.5 percent compared to an annual growth of 0.2 percent for male inmates.[5] In 2015, 13 percent of the 870,500 parolees in the United States were females, and of the 3.8 million U.S. probationers, 25 percent were females.[6] Table 7.2 illustrates the number of women in prison from 2000 to 2016 by state. Four of the largest

| TABLE 7.2 | Sentenced Prisoners Under the Jurisdiction of State or Federal Correctional Authorities by Sex, December 31, 2015 and 2016 | | | | | | | | |

Jurisdiction	2015			2016			Percent change, 2015–2016		
	Total	Male	Female	Total	Male	Female	Total	Male	Female
U.S. total[a]	1,476,847	1,371,879	104,968	1,458,173	1,352,684	105,489	−1.3%	−1.4%	0.5%
Federal[b]	178,688	167,080	11,608	171,482	160,090	11,392	−4.0%	−4.2%	−1.9%
State[a]	1,298,159	1,204,799	93,360	1,286,691	1,192,594	94,097	−0.9%	−1.0%	0.8%
Alabama	29,762	27,329	2,433	27,799	25,593	2,206	−6.6	−6.4	−9.3
Alaska[c]	2,261	2,086	175	2,089	1,982	107	−7.6	−5.0	−38.9
Arizona	40,952	37,314	3,638	40,849	37,131	3,718	−0.3	−0.5	2.2
Arkansas	17,656	16,268	1,388	17,476	16,111	1,365	−1.0	−1.0	−1.7
California	129,205	123,474	5,731	130,340	124,443	5,897	0.9	0.8	2.9
Colorado	20,041	18,199	1,842	19,862	17,963	1,899	−0.9	−1.3	3.1
Connecticut[c]	11,220	10,643	577	10,365	9,804	561	−7.6	−7.9	−2.8
Delaware[c]	4,188	3,963	225	4,090	3,889	201	−2.3	−1.9	−10.7
Florida	101,424	94,481	6,943	99,974	93,111	6,863	−1.4	−1.5	−1.2
Georgia	51,700	48,127	3,573	53,064	49,324	3,740	2.6	2.5	4.7
Hawaii[c]	3,769	3,414	355	3,629	3,271	358	−3.7	−4.2	0.8
Idaho	7,255	6,327	928	7,376	6,416	960	1.7	1.4	3.4
Illinois[d]	46,240	43,565	2,675	43,657	41,044	2,613	:	:	:
Indiana	27,334	24,794	2,540	25,530	23,325	2,205	−6.6	−5.9	−13.2
Iowa	8,816	8,016	800	8,998	8,181	817	2.1	2.1	2.1
Kansas	9,578	8,801	777	9,628	8,831	797	0.5	0.3	2.6
Kentucky	21,697	19,110	2,587	23,018	20,077	2,941	6.1	5.1	13.7
Louisiana	36,347	34,301	2,046	35,646	33,665	1,981	−1.9	−1.9	−3.2
Maine	1,754	1,622	132	1,828	1,675	153	4.2	3.3	15.9
Maryland	20,408	19,540	868	19,821	19,010	811	−2.9	−2.7	−6.6
Massachusetts	8,954	8,549	405	8,494	8,140	354	−5.1	−4.8	−12.6
Michigan	42,628	40,355	2,273	41,122	38,880	2,242	−3.5	−3.7	−1.4
Minnesota	10,798	10,027	771	10,592	9,818	774	−1.9	−2.1	0.4
Mississippi	18,236	17,032	1,204	18,666	17,397	1,269	2.4	2.1	5.4
Missouri	32,328	29,061	3,267	32,461	29,124	3,337	0.4	0.2	2.1
Montana	3,685	3,295	390	3,814	3,405	409	3.5	3.3	4.9
Nebraska	5,312	4,893	419	5,235	4,825	410	−1.4	−1.4	−2.1
Nevada[e]	12,944	11,778	1,166	13,637	12,403	1,234	:	:	:
New Hampshire[f]	2,897	2,661	236	2,818	2,591	227	−2.7	−2.6	−3.8
New Jersey	20,489	19,581	908	19,786	18,952	834	−3.4	−3.2	−8.1
New Mexico	6,994	6,301	693	6,972	6,276	696	−0.3	−0.4	0.4
New York	51,606	49,271	2,335	50,620	48,356	2,264	−1.9	−1.9	−3.0
North Carolina	35,523	33,026	2,497	34,596	32,085	2,511	−2.6	−2.8	0.6
North Dakota[g]	1,783	1,577	206	1,779	1,568	211	:	:	:
Ohio	52,233	47,803	4,430	52,175	47,581	4,594	−0.1	−0.5	3.7
Oklahoma	28,114	25,119	2,995	26,486	23,527	2,959	−5.8	−6.3	−1.2
Oregon[h]	15,230	13,923	1,307	15,150	13,846	1,304	:	:	:
Pennsylvania	49,578	46,824	2,754	49,000	46,188	2,812	−1.2	−1.4	2.1
Rhode Island[c]	2,156	2,094	62	2,030	1,962	68	−5.8	−6.3	9.7

TABLE 7.2	(Continued)								
	2015			**2016**			**Percent change, 2015–2016**		
Jurisdiction	**Total**	**Male**	**Female**	**Total**	**Male**	**Female**	**Total**	**Male**	**Female**
South Carolina	20,392	19,129	1,263	20,371	18,981	1,390	–0.1	–0.8	10.1
South Dakota	3,558	3,144	414	3,820	3,323	497	7.4	5.7	20.0
Tennessee	28,172	25,532	2,640	28,203	25,481	2,722	0.1	–0.2	3.1
Texas	157,251	144,508	12,743	157,903	144,928	12,975	0.4	0.3	1.8
Utah[f]	6,488	5,973	515	6,181	5,776	405	–4.7	–3.3	–21.4
Vermont[c]	1,290	1,207	83	1,229	1,146	83	–4.7	–5.1	0.0
Virginia	38,403	35,167	3,236	37,813	34,704	3,109	–1.5	–1.3	–3.9
Washington	18,205	16,756	1,449	19,019	17,377	1,642	4.5	3.7	13.3
West Virginia	7,118	6,253	865	7,162	6,286	876	0.6	0.5	1.3
Wisconsin	21,763	20,429	1,334	22,144	20,734	1,410	1.8	1.5	5.7
Wyoming	2,424	2,157	267	2,374	2,088	286	–2.1	–3.2	7.1

Note: Jurisdiction refers to the legal authority of state or federal correctional officials over a prisoner, regardless of where the prisoner is held. Counts are based on prisoners with sentences of more than one year.

: Not calculated.

[a]Total and state estimates include imputed counts for North Dakota and Oregon, which did not submit 2016 NPS data. See *Methodology*.

[b]Includes prisoners held in nonsecure, privately operated community corrections facilities and juveniles held in contract facilities.

[c]Prisons and jails form one integrated system. Data include total jail and prison populations.

[d]Counts from 2016 are not comparable to counts from prior years due to a change in reporting methodology. See *Jurisdiction notes*.

[e]State did not submit 2015 NPS data. Counts were imputed for 2015 and should not be compared to 2016 counts.

[f]State submitted updated 2015 population counts.

[g]State did not submit 2016 NPS data. Counts were imputed. See *Methodology*.

[h]State did not submit 2015 or 2016 NPS data. Counts were imputed. See *Methodology*.

Sources: Data from Heather C. West and William J. Sabol, "Prisoners in 210," Appendix Table 8, p. 21; and E. Ann Carson, "Prisoners in 2016," *BJS Bulletin* (Washington, D.C.: U.S. Department of Justice, 2018), p. 6.

jurisdictions (Texas, the federal system, Florida, and California) hold more than one-third of all the female prisoners. It is interesting to note the wide variation in the growth among jurisdictions between 2000 and 2015. The overall growth in female prisoners was 23.4 percent from 2000 to 2015, the federal system grew 38 percent, and the states female population grew 22 percent. Seven states more than doubled their female prison populations, and ten states had reductions in their population.

Similarly, there has been a shift in the racial makeup of adults under correctional supervision. Whites made up a majority (65 percent) of the correctional population in 1986. However, by 1997, whites represented only 60 percent of all adult offenders under supervision.[7] A majority of the prison population are minorities. At the end of 2016, the population of state and federal prisons was 30.2 percent white, 33.3 percent black, and 23.3 percent Hispanic.[8] And of the individuals whose race was known under probation supervision at the end of 2015, 55 percent were whites, 30 percent were black, and 13 percent were Hispanics.[9] The fact that white offenders make up 55 percent of probationers, yet only 30.2 percent of prisoners raises further concern.

The rate of growth in the number of female offenders is even greater than that of males. Dean Hanson/ZUMA Press Inc/Alamy Stock Photo.

And the 2016 incarceration rates per 100,000 individuals in state and federal prison for whites was 274, for blacks was 1,608 (six times whites), and for Hispanics was 856 (almost three times whites), again illustrating a large racial disparity.[10]

This issue of the vast **racial disparity** within the makeup of the U.S. correctional population merits an examination of whether criminal justice and correctional policies are in some way discriminatory. It is important to examine how race (separate from social class, level of poverty, drug use, and other issues) affects discretionary decisions by police, prosecutors, judges, prison officials, and parole board members. The National Urban League reports in 2009 that "Ironically, even as an African American man holds the highest office in the country, African Americans remain twice as likely as whites to be unemployed, three times more likely to live in poverty and more than six times as likely to be incarcerated."[11]

But why are these numbers disproportionate to the racial and ethnic makeup of the U.S. population? Wilbanks, in *The Myth of a Racist Criminal Justice System*, proposed that the "perception of the criminal justice system as racist is a myth," in that while there are incidents of individual racism, most studies do not show sufficient evidence of racism; he concludes that prejudice and racism are not systematic.[12] In turn, many researchers argue that the disproportion results from the fact that minorities are disproportionately involved in crime, especially violent crime, both as the perpetrators and as the victims. Minorities in poverty-stricken, urban neighborhoods are most likely to be victims of violent crime. In 2015, the Uniform Crime Report noted that the homicide and nonnegligent manslaughter arrest rates were 45.9 percent for whites and 51.1 percent for blacks.[13]

It is difficult to explain the reasons for racial disparity throughout the correctional process. We know that crime is also closely linked to poverty, drug use, and lack of opportunity for legitimate approaches to economic success. With crime more prevalent in neighborhoods where African Americans and Hispanics reside, it is not surprising that they are arrested at a higher rate than that of whites. Law

racial disparity
the fact that minorities make up a greater percentage of those under correctional supervision than their makeup in the U.S. population

enforcement efforts are always more intense in urban areas with high crime rates and high drug use. A study of how the police responded to the war on drugs noted that arrests for drug use and possession usually occur in the city rather than the suburbs and "have had a disproportionate effect on African Americans."[14] For whatever the causes of disproportionate numbers of minorities under correctional supervision, this disparity creates a perception of racism and challenges to the management of correctional agencies.

A study by the Sentencing Project identifies three "believed to be" causes of disparity, to include policies and practices, implicit bias, and structural disadvantage.[15]

- **Policies and practices:** Throughout the criminal justice process, disparities mount the further along into the system from arrest to incarceration. Harsh drug laws enacted from the late 1980s through the 1990s that lengthened prison sentences more seriously impacted blacks, who are four times more likely to be arrested than whites for drug offenses. Because of income inequality, blacks are more likely to be detained prior to trial than whites. Crime seriousness and prior record impacts sentencing, as does initial charges by prosecutors, and evidence is that these decisions are also unequal according to race.

- **Implicit bias:** Research indicates that beliefs about dangerousness and threat to public safety are more likely correlated to people of color. And other research found that the public knowledge of racial disparities of the prison population actually increases the belief that there must be tough sentencing practices.

- **Structural disadvantage:** The social and economic disadvantages (poverty, unemployment, housing, high school dropout rates, and family issues) of minorities before they are involved in crime contribute to the higher rates of crime in minority communities. These reduce people's ability to desist from crime, begin with involvement in juvenile delinquency, and continue to involve with the criminal justice system.[16]

And another very thorough review of past studies and data by Travis, Western, and Redburn lends further guidance. The review examined the impact of both arrest patterns by race and disparities in sentencing and case processing. Their review found that the early analysis of racial disparity by Blumstein in using 1979 and 1991 data found that arrest patterns by race explained most of the disparities of imprisonment.[17] These studies were seen as conclusive that racial bias was not the primary cause of racial disparities in imprisonment. However, changes in criminal sentencing statutes in the 1980s and 1990s seem to have changed this conclusion. Using the same methods as Blumstein with data from 2004 and 2008, racial imprisonment disparities became much worse, and the causes that could be explained by arrest patterns declined. Tonry and Melewski analyzed 2004 data and could not explain 39 percent of racial disparities in prison by arrest patterns.[18] And Baumer using 2008 data found that large percentages of serious crimes (murder—40 percent, robbery—45 percent, aggravated assault—55 percent, and drug offenses—66 percent) were the result of other than arrest patterns.[19] The conclusion by Travis, et al. was that racial disparities in prison result from "severe sentencing laws enacted in the 1980s and 1990s," which increased prison sentences for violent and drug crimes, both of which have high proportions of arrests of blacks.[20] So while the general conclusion held over the years that the criminal justice system and individual decisions are not racist is likely still true, even small disparities at each level (police targeting of crimes, whether bail is granted or not, sentencing decisions) can have a large cumulative effect and greatly influence the racial disparity in prisons.

Age of Offenders

Another factor that has changed over the years is the age of the typical prisoner in the United States. Historically, adult criminals began their criminal behavior between ages eighteen and twenty-one and were first incarcerated between ages twenty-five and thirty. Most prisoners were age thirty to forty, with very few young or old inmates. However, the bell-shaped age curve of the prison population is leveling out (see Figure 7.2). In 2000, only 3.5 percent of inmates were over age fifty-five, but on December 31, 2016, 19.8 percent (almost 300,000 inmates) were fifty or older.[21]

Three phenomena contribute to the aging of the prison population. First, the overall U.S. population is aging, as Americans over age fifty constituted only 26 percent of the population in 1992,[22] but this figure grew to 33.9 percent by 2014.[23] Second, inmates are serving longer sentences and therefore stay in prison until they are older. Finally, mandatory sentences and sentencing guidelines take away the discretion of judges who may have kept older offenders in the community on probation rather than sending them to prison, as they are not believed to be a risk to the community. Current sentencing approaches are "age blind," and offenders who may have been allowed to remain in the community because of their advanced age are now sent to prison if their crime severity warrants it. The large proportion of older offenders in prison has different treatment, medical, and reentry needs than younger inmates, causing new problems for correctional administrators.[24] A recent report by the Pew Charitable Trusts identifies some of the issues faced by older inmates and the challenges of correctional managers to deal with extensive and expensive health care and need for hospice programs, lack of mobility to get up stairs or across large open prison yards, and being preyed upon by younger and aggressive inmates.[25]

Over the past two decades, there has been an ebb and flow in the number of offenders under age eighteen in state and federal prisons. In the late 1980s and early 1990s, juveniles committed many high-publicity and serious crimes, and

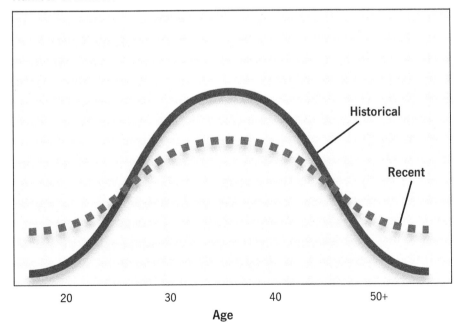

FIGURE 7.2 The Leveling Out of Prison Population by Age

Prisons are now housing a much larger number of elderly offenders, many with serious health problems. Photo by Richard P. Seiter.

many states enacted legislation to prosecute serious juvenile offenders as adults, with a sanction of imprisonment in adult correctional facilities. On December 31, 1997, there were 5,400 offenders in state prisons (less than 1 percent of the total prison population) were under age eighteen. However, the number of juvenile offenders admitted to prison each year more than doubled, from 3,400 in 1985 to 7,400 in 1997.[26] Since 1997, however, the number of juveniles under age eighteen in adult correctional facilities has declined. As of the end of 2016, there were only 956 juveniles in state prisons and none in federal prisons.[27] The use of adult prisons for serious juvenile offenders was an approach with little support by correctional administrators, and fortunately, legislators, prosecutors, and judges all agreed. Only the most serious juveniles are now prosecuted as adults and face imprisonment in adult facilities.

Types of Offenses and Lengths of Confinements

In addition to the preceding changes in offender populations, the types of offenses for which individuals are under correctional supervision have changed. As Table 7.3 indicates, there has been a growth in the relative number of offenders who have committed the most serious crimes from 1980 to 2014. The number

TABLE 7.3	Number of Sentenced Prisoners in Custody of State Correctional Authorities by Most Serious Offense, Selected Years 1980–2015			
Year	**Violent**	**Property**	**Drug**	**Public Order**
1980	173,300	89,300	19,000	12,400
1985	246,200	140,100	38,900	23,000
1990	313,600	173,700	148,600	45,500
1995	459,600	226,600	212,800	86,500
2000	589,100	238,500	251,100	124,600
2005	687,700	248,900	253,300	98,700
2010	715,900	263,400	255,700	116,100
2013	707,500	247,100	210,200	140,200
2014	696,380	250,118	206,676	152,703
2015	707,497	233,669	197,320	150,586

Source: Data from *Correctional Populations in the United States, 1997* (Washington, D.C.: U.S. Department of Justice, 1998); *Prisoners in 2002*; *Prisoners in 2004*; *Prisoners in 2007*; *Prisoners in 2010*; *Prisoners in 2013*; and *Prisoners in 2016* (Washington, D.C.: U.S. Department of Justice, 2003, 2005, 2008, 2011, 2014, and 2018), p. 10, p. 21, and p. 18.

of people in custody for committing violent offenses increased 402 percent (from 173,300 to 696,380), and the number of those committing property offenses increased by 280 percent (from 89,300 to 250,118). The number of violent crimes in the United States has declined since the early 1990s; however, sentence lengths have increased dramatically, and offenders with violent crimes therefore now make up 52.9 percent of the prison population. When there were only 173,300 violent offenders in prison, they were much easier to manage. But today, with almost 700,000 violent offenders, prison officials have their hands full with managing safe prisons for staff and inmates. The policies and practices they use to create an environment that is safe and allows inmates to participate in programs for self-improvement is the focus of Chapters 10 and 13.

Even though there has been a modest reduction in the overall prison population over the past few years, the most significant reduction has been for those sentenced for committing drug offenses. In 1980, **drug offenders** made up only 6.5 percent of the imprisoned population. However, the number of drug offenders in prison increased dramatically from the 1980s into the first decade of the twenty-first century, primarily as a result of the "war on drugs," as the federal government and many states instituted mandatory sentences based on maximizing the deterrent and incapacitative effects of incarceration. By 2010, drug offenders made up 18.9 percent of the prison population. Since that time, at least seventeen states have passed drug sentencing reforms, as jurisdictions strapped by tight budgets began to rethink the benefits and costs of their drug sentencing policies.[28] And in 2014, the U.S. Sentencing Commission modified federal drug sentencing guidelines, making over 40,000 federal prisoners eligible for consideration of a sentence reduction.[29] And as noted in Table 7.3, from 2010 to 2015, there was an almost 23 percent decrease in the number of drug offenders in prison.

drug offenders
those convicted of crimes regarding the possession or sale of drugs

Sentences increased through many "tough on crime" statutes that were passed since 1980. In an effort to alleviate public fear of crime, elected officials have vowed to "lock'em up and throw away the key" for any criminal who commits serious crimes. The average length of incarceration (determined by the number of months served by all prison releasees during any specific year) was 23.7 months for 1990 releases from prison and increased by more than 25 percent to 30 months in 1996, but has declined to approximately 25 months in 2010. Some of this is due to budget challenges, but the increase in the number of inmates continues to drive an increase in correctional costs. Sentencing policies resulting in reduction in sentence times were targeted toward nonviolent offenders. Offenders convicted of murder or nonnegligent manslaughter and released in 2012 had a median time serviced of 153 months, compared to 102 months for those released in 2002. And 2012 releases of those convicted of sexual assault served forty-eight months before release compared to thirty-eight months for those released in 2002.[30]

Male Offenders

As is well known, males commit the largest proportion of crimes and make up the largest proportion of the correctional population under supervision. During 2015, males made up 73 percent of all arrests by law enforcement agencies,[31] yet in 2015, males made approximately 92.5 percent and females only 7.5 percent of the population of state and federal prisons.[32] When the general public thinks of criminals or inmates in prisons, they have a picture in mind of a large, tough-looking male, not a small female. Even though crime rates have been

male offenders

men who are convicted and sentenced; they constitute almost 93 percent of all prison inmates

decreasing over the past few years, the role and scope of corrections in managing **male offenders** continue to increase. Some pertinent facts include the following:

- 1,395,975 male inmates were under the jurisdiction of state and federal departments of corrections on December 31, 2016.[33]
- Males represented 75 percent of all probationers and 87 percent of all parolees under active supervision status on December 31, 2015.[34]

Male Offenders and Violence

Male offenders are much more linked to violence than are female offenders. In 2015, males represented 73 percent of arrests in the United States and 79.8 percent of arrests for violent crime.[35] While violent crime has been decreasing for more than two decades, violent crimes have driven the increase in the prison population. Even with violent crime committed by both males and females on the decline, males are still predominantly involved in the commission (illustrated by the arrest totals) of violent crimes. Table 7.4 illustrates the number of violent crimes committed by males as a percentage of the total of such crimes by both male and female adults. Even though they are a minority of the population of the United States, adult males represented 88.1 percent of the murder and nonnegligent manslaughter arrests and 85.3 percent of all robbery arrests. Only for larceny-theft are a relatively high proportion of the arrests for females, which make up 43.6 percent of arrests for that crime.

With the violent background of so many male offenders, violence is much more likely in male prisons than in female prisons. In 2015, 55.9 percent of adult males sentenced to state prisons were committed for violent offenses, 17.3 percent for property offenses, 14.4 percent for drug offenses, and 11.7 percent for public-order offenses.[36] Table 7.5 illustrates the percentages of sentenced prisoners under state

TABLE 7.4	**Total Arrests of Males in 2015 for All Index Crimes**		
	Number of persons arrested		
Offense charged	**Total**	**Male**	**Percent male**
Total—all offenses	**6,734,363**	**4,913,199**	**72.9%**
Murder and nonnegligent manslaughter	6,201	5,463	88.1
Forcible rape	13,945	13,536	97.1
Robbery	54,003	46,060	85.3
Aggravated assault	231,828	179,138	77.3
Burglary	136,465	110,416	80.9
Larceny-theft	753,665	424,952	56.4
Motor vehicle theft	46,463	36,177	77.9
Arson	5,737	4,633	80.7

Source: Data from Federal Bureau of Investigation, "Ten-Year Arrest Trends, by Sex," *Crime in the United States, 2015*, Table 35 (Washington, D.C.: U.S. Department of Justice, 2016).

TABLE 7.5	Estimated Percent of Sentenced Prisoners under State Jurisdiction, by Offense and Gender, Year-End 2015		
Most serious offense	**All prisoners[a]**	**Male**	**Female**
Total	100%	100%	100%
Violent	54.5%	55.9%	37.0%
Murder[b]	13.7	13.8	11.6
Manslaughter	1.3	1.3	2.4
Rape or *sexual assault*	12.5	13.3	2.4
Robbery	13.2	13.6	8.1
Aggravated or simple assault	10.5	10.6	8.6
Other	3.4	3.3	3.9
Property	18.0%	17.3%	26.9%
Burglary	9.7	9.9	7.3
Larceny-theft	3.7	3.3	8.8
Motor vehicle theft	0.7	0.7	0.8
Fraud	1.9	1.5	7.1
Other	2.0	1.9	3.0
Drug	15.2%	14.4%	24.9%
Drug possession	3.4	3.2	6.8
Other[c]	11.7	11.3	18.1
Public order	11.6%	11.7%	10.2%
Weapons	3.9	4.1	1.7
DUI	1.9	1.9	2.6
Other[d]	5.7	5.7	5.9
Other/unspecified[e]	0.7%	0.7%	1.0%
Total number of sentenced prisoners	1,298,159	1,204,799	93,360

Note: Jurisdiction refers to the legal authority of state or federal correctional officials over a prisoner, regardless of where the prisoner is held. Estimates are based on state prisoners with a sentence of more than one year. Detail may not sum to total due to rounding and missing offense data. See *Methodology*.

[a]Includes American Indians and Alaska Natives; Asians, Native Hawaiians, or Other Pacific Islanders; and persons of two or more races.

[b]Includes nonnegligent manslaughter.

[c]Includes trafficking and other drug offenses.

[d]Includes court offenses; commercialized vice, morals, and decency offenses; liquor law violations; and other public order offenses.

[e]Includes juvenile offenses and other unspecified offense categories.

Source: E. Ann Carson, "Prisoners in 2016," *BJS Bulletin* (Washington, D.C.: U.S. Department of Justice, 2018), Table 912, p. 18.

jurisdiction by offense and gender in 2015. Over 166,000 male inmates were convicted of murder, another 136,000 were convicted of rape or other sexual assault, almost 164,000 were convicted of robbery, and more than 127,000 were convicted of assault. Within all state prisons, 673,500 male inmates are serving time for violent offenses. With so many violent inmates in prisons, there is no question that staff must work in situations that can result in assault or even death.

Male Prisoners

Prison systems are predominantly planned and administered around the management of male inmates. The state and federal prison systems have subcomponents of groups of offenders, including women, juveniles serving time in adult prisons, Inmates with mental illness, substance abusers, and other groups that are housed and managed separately. However, the majority of adult prisons hold normal, male inmates (often referred to as the **general population**) without a particular designation requiring special housing or management. Male inmates in the general population are received into the prison systems, assessed, and classified to one of the various security-level prisons to serve their sentence. Security levels of prisons are designed to match physical security, staff resources, programs, and prison operations with the risk of violence and escape by male inmates assigned to each level.

The various states and federal government use differing titles and definitions of prison security level, such as intake, community, minimum, medium, high/close, maximum, or multiple custody. When the most recent prison census was completed in 2005, the 1,821 state and federal prisons held 1,427,316 inmates. Of these, 21.6 percent were classified as minimum security inmates (to include minimum or low), 42.4 percent were medium security inmates, and 35.9 percent were maximum (includes close and high) security inmates.[37] Each increasing level of security has more physical security to reduce the potential for escapes, a higher staff member-to-inmate ratio, more restrictions on inmate movement, more emphasis on security, and less emphasis on inmate programs. The overall goal of inmate security classification is to maintain homogeneity of inmates by risk of violence and escape and therefore ensure that they are placed in prisons that are physically designed to meet these risks. Housing high-security inmates in a facility that is low or minimum security creates the danger of escape, predatory behavior, or violence against staff or other inmates.

To ensure that inmates are in the proper security level and to plan for their participation in work and programs, prison caseworkers and counselors oversee the classification and program process. The "Your Career in Corrections" box describes the role of these staff members.

Males are much more involved in violent crimes than females and represent more than 80 percent of the arrests for violent crimes. Photofusion/Universal Images Group/Getty Images.

general population
inmates in prison who do not have any specific designation as a special type of offender

Female Offenders

female offenders
women who are convicted and sentenced; 7 percent of prison inmates are females

In 2015, women made up about 27.1 percent of all arrests by law enforcement agencies, an increase from 23.9 percent in 2006 and approximately 22 percent in 2001.[39] As women's involvement in crime has increased, the growth in the number of **female offenders** under correctional supervision has also grown. Most of the detailed information available regarding female offenders is from Greenfeld and Snell's 1999 publication, *Women Offenders*. This study indicated

Your Career in Corrections

Caseworkers and Counselors

A common entry-level job for recent college or community college graduates is that of counselor or caseworker (sometimes called a social worker in some agencies). These professionals work directly with inmates, with the primary responsibility of classifying offenders and creating and monitoring plans for program and work participation. The plans continue throughout the period of confinement and build to the preparation for release.

A key component of the caseworker's job is security and treatment classification of an inmate. When inmates are sent to prison, they must first be classified to determine the security level of the prison in which they will be placed. The caseworker reviews the presentence investigation and any other informational documents to determine criminal and social history, sentence information, medical and psychological needs, education and work history, and other relevant preincarceration information. From this review, the caseworker usually completes an objective classification form to determine whether the inmate will be minimum, medium, or maximum security. The caseworker must continue to update the classification instrument with new information (such as prison behavior and time left to serve) to see if the security classification changes. The classification plan also assists with the assignment of work and program participation to meet identified inmate needs.

In describing the role played by these staff persons, Carlson suggests,

> Case management focuses on the provision of social support programs to an inmate population, and case management staff maintain the official classification documents....These staff members are not only responsible for determining the prisoner's custody and security needs, but charged with helping the inmates plan their institution-based work and program assignments.[38]

Caseworkers often perform as a team with prison educators, mental health professionals, and substance abuse counselors to create treatment plans and monitor inmates' progress toward their goals. Some caseworkers actually perform counseling, but in most state and federal prisons, their principal role is to guide inmates through all aspects of their prison sentence, including the legal sanction and expectation for release, an understanding of their individual treatment needs, and the availability of prison programs to meet these needs. Caseworkers can also assist inmates with services outside the prison (job assistance, family counseling, or halfway house agencies) that will aid in their transition from prison to community.

Jobs as a caseworker require good interpersonal, decision-making, and writing skills. Most states require that applicants for these jobs have a college degree (often in the social sciences), but a few states do not require a degree if the person has experience. The type of college degree may vary with the specific job requirements of the position. If caseworkers perform therapeutic treatment themselves, they may be required to possess a clinical degree in mental health or social work. While the salary for most state or federal caseworker jobs is usually 15 percent to 20 percent higher than the starting pay for a correctional officer, caseworkers usually have less opportunity to earn additional overtime pay, and the annual earnings may actually end up being about the same. However, these are excellent jobs, providing the broad experience, the challenge of interaction with inmates, the need for planning ahead, and the ability to have an important impact on the future lives of criminal offenders.

that the number of women under correctional supervision increased at a greater rate (118 percent) than that of the number of males (70 percent) under supervision between 1986 and 1997, and in 1998, women constituted approximately 16 percent of the total correctional population, including 21 percent of the probation population, 11 percent of those in jails, 6 percent of prisoners, and 12 percent of parolees.[40] These numbers changed little as in 2015, female offenders were 25 percent of adults on probation, 14.3 percent of jail inmates, 7.3 percent of prison inmates, and 13 percent of adults on parole.[41]

Once sentenced, women have historically been given lesser sentences than men. However, during the 1980s, as a result of sentencing guidelines and mandatory prison sentences, judges have less discretion and are now treating women more similarly to men than in the past. Chesney-Lind reports, "Twenty years ago, nearly two-thirds of the women convicted of federal felonies were granted

TABLE 7.6	Characteristics of Adult Women under Correctional Supervision			
Characteristics of women	Probation	Local jails	State prisons	Federal prisons
Race/Hispanic origin				
White	62%	36%	33%	29%
Black	27	44	48	35
Hispanic	10	15	15	32
Other	1	5	4	4
Age				
24 or younger	20%	21%	12%	9%
25–34	39	46	43	35
35–44	30	27	34	32
45–54	10	5	9	18
55 or older	1	1	2	6
Median age	32 years	31 years	33 years	36 years
Marital status				
Married	26%	15%	17%	29%
Widowed	2	4	6	6
Separated	10	13	10	21
Divorced	20	20	20	10
Never married	42	48	47	34
Education				
Eighth grade or less	5%	12%	7%	8%
Some high school	35	33	37	19
High school graduate/GED	39	39	39	44
Some college or more	21	16	17	29

Source: Lawrence A. Greenfeld and Tracey L. Snell, *Women Offenders* (Washington, D.C.: U.S. Department of Justice, 1999), p. 7.

probation, but in 1991, only 28 percent were given straight probation."[42] By the late 1990s, female offenders under correctional supervision had traits similar to those of male offenders. As illustrated in Table 7.6, although nearly two-thirds of women on probation are white, almost two-thirds of women in jail or prison are minorities. Women in prison are older than those on probation or in jail. This simply indicates the influencing factor of criminal history in sentencing decisions. As offenders grow older and accumulate a more extensive offense history, they are more likely to receive a prison sentence. Women under correctional supervision are more likely than the general population to have never been married, and the majority of female offenders have completed high school.

In terms of recidivism, rates for female offenders are high, yet are thought to be less than recidivism rates for comparable male offenders. In a 1983 study of 6,400 women (and more than 100,000 men) released from prison in eleven states, 52 percent of the women were rearrested, 39 percent were reconvicted, and 33 percent were returned to prison during a three-year follow-up.[43] A 2002 study noted similar results, as women had lower recidivism rates than the rates for men, as within three years after release, 17.3 percent of females returned to prison for a new offense (compared to 26.2 percent of males), and 39.4 percent of females were returned to prison without a new prison sentence (compared to 53 percent of males).[44] This continues as a 2010 publication reports that 47 percent of the women in the study were reconvicted or reincarcerated within two years after release.[45] And a 2014 study of patterns of recidivism found that overall, 49.7 percent of all releasees in 2005 were returned to prison within three years, and that within three years, 69 percent of males and 58.5 percent of females were arrested at least once.[46]

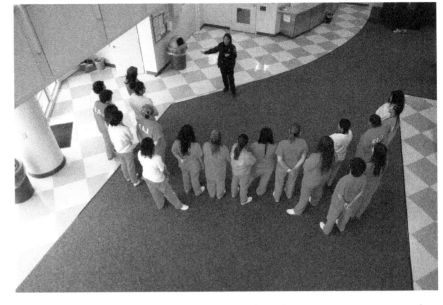

Females are committing more crimes and are being sent to prison rather than receiving probation. Marmaduke St. John/Alamy Stock Photo.

Women in Prison

In 1925, only 3,438 women were in prison, representing 3.7 percent of the national prison population. This percentage of women in the overall prison population remained relatively stable until the 1980s, when it began to rise as many states implemented sentencing guidelines and mandatory prison sentences. The percentage of women in the prison population increased to 5.7 percent by 1990.[47] On December 31, 2016, there were 1,505,397 prisoners in state and federal prisons, of which 111,422 (7.4 percent) were women.[48] As with male offenders, much of the increase in the number of women incarcerated resulted from the war on drugs and expansion of arrests and prosecutions for drug offenses. In 2015, 24.9 percent of all women in state prisons and 56.4 percent in federal prisons had been convicted of drug offenses.[49]

The imprisonment rate of men versus women is dramatically different, with men having an imprisonment rate of 847 per 100,000 population and women 64 per 100,000 on December 31, 2016.[50] And women serve considerably less time than men. As noted in Table 7.7, female inmates serve fewer months for every category of crime. Some would argue that this indicates that women still receive less severe sentences than men. However, it is more likely the result of the fact that men in prison have more extensive criminal careers than women and commit a greater proportion of violent and serious crimes. As noted above, women accounted for 19.7 percent of all arrests for violent crimes in 2012,[51] but only 4.7 percent of state prisoners that were convicted of violent crimes.[52] Even though they still make up a small percentage of all prisoners in the United States, when women go to prison, they have many issues and needs that are different from those of male offenders and create challenges for correctional administrators.

Special Issues and Needs of Female Inmates

Some issues facing female inmates that are different from those of male inmates include health care, vocational training and work opportunities, potential of sexual abuse from staff, alcohol and drug use, and problems relating to their children. Approximately 60 percent of women in state prisons experienced physical or sexual abuses prior to their incarceration.[53] The Bureau of Justice Statistics estimated that 60 percent of incarcerated women are mothers, and almost all have minor

TABLE 7.7	Median Time Served by Released Inmates by Sex and Offense, 2012			

| | Released in 2012 | | | |
Most serious offense	Number of releases	All inmates	Male	Female
Violent	117,400	28 mos.	29 mos.	20 mos.
Murder[a]	6,900	153	158	103
Manslaughter	3,200	42	44	35
Rape/sexual assault	21,800	48	48	29
Robbery	32,300	34	35	25
Aggravated or simple assault	43,100	17	18	16
Other violent	10,100	17	17	14
Property	111,500	12 mos.	12 mos.	10 mos.
Burglary	46,200	15	15	11
Larceny-theft	26,700	11	11	10
Motor vehicle theft	6,000	11	12	10
Fraud	17,600	11	11	10
Other property	14,900	10	11	8
Drug	105,900	13 mos.	14 mos.	10 mos.
Drug possession	33,300	10	11	8
Other drug[b]	72,600	15	16	11
Public order[c]	71,100	12 mos.	13 mos.	9 mos.
Other/unspecified[d]	4,200	12 mos.	13 mos.	10 mos.
Total number of releasees[e]	413,400		364,700	48,700

Note: Estimates based on prisoners with a sentence of more than one year who entered prison on a new court commitment. Detail may not sum to total due to rounding and missing offense data. Offense distributions are based on the thirty-five states that submitted to both the 2002 and 2012 National Corrections Reporting Program (NCRP) data collection, while estimated counts of releases represent data for all states based on NPS. See *Methodology*.

[a]Includes nonnegligent manslaughter.

[b]Includes trafficking, possession, and other drug offenses.

[c]Includes weapons, drunk driving, and court offenses; commercialized vice, morals, and decency offenses; and liquor law violations and other public-order offenses.

[d]Includes juvenile offenses and other unspecified offense categories.

[e]Excludes transfers, AWOLs, and escapes. See *Methodology*.

Sources: E. Ann Carson, "Prisoners in 2013," *BJS Bulletin* (Washington, D.C.: U.S. Department of Justice, 2014), p. 18; Bureau of Justice Statistics, National Prisoner Statistics Program, and National Corrections Reporting Program, 2002 and 2012.

children.[54] As mothers, female inmates often feel guilt for abandoning their children and must ask other family members to care for their children during incarceration. Because a small percentage of inmates are women, there are fewer female than male prisons. Therefore, the distance from home for female offenders is usually greater than for males, making it more difficult for family and the children to visit.

Many states have created innovative programs that they believe are particularly effective in responding to the special needs of female inmates. A survey of these programs in several states identified the following innovations. The number of programs that are operational in each category in all states is shown in parentheses.

Psychological programs (90): substance abuse, mental health counseling, and domestic violence counseling

Work programs (48): work training, prison industry programs, and other work-related programs

Parenting programs (42): child visitation, parent education, and other parenting programs

Other programs (62): transition and aftercare programs, education programs, health programs (including HIV/AIDS education), and life skills programs[55]

Some of the specific issues that confront incarcerated women are described below. As a prelude to these issues, the following "An Interview With" box illustrates the many challenges faced by women who become a part of the correctional system.

An Interview With . . .

A Female Offender

Christine Wideman. Pearson Education

Christine Wideman was originally from Detroit. At age nineteen, she moved to Texas to get away from home and be far enough away that she couldn't "go running home" to Daddy. She was doing pretty well, got a job, and had an apartment. She met her ex-husband and her troubles started. She had five children and has epilepsy. This interview was held in the fast-food restaurant where Christine worked for several months. Before sitting down, Christine went to the regulars, greeted them, and gave many of them hugs. During the interview, two others came by the table to say hello. The following interview illustrates some of her challenges, which are often typical of the lives of women offenders.[56]

Question: Christine, how did you begin to get in trouble and involved in drugs and crime?

Christine: When I moved to Texas, I met and married my husband. He was one of those "bad boys" working in construction who moved around a lot. We lived in several cities in the Southwest looking for work. My husband got hooked on crack, and to get money for his drugs, he prostituted me. He was abusive and beat me regularly. He would beat me if I was gone for too long or didn't come home from prostituting with enough money. Many beatings were so bad that I had seizures.

I also got involved in drugs and became an addict. He would give me some of his drugs as my reward for bringing home money. That became the only thing I looked forward to. By that time, I had three children; they were in foster care. We were homeless, living off what I earned. I got pregnant again and tried to wean myself off drugs. Eventually, I decided to hide from my husband. People on the street saw what was happening. Other prostitutes and my drug dealer helped me hide when my husband started looking for me. My husband threatened to kill me and my family if I left with the kids. And he said if he couldn't find me, he would find and kill my family.

I was arrested several times for prostitution and later was arrested for neglect and prostitution and was sentenced to jail for six and a half months. At that time, I was pregnant with my youngest child. The day I was arrested, it was the only day I didn't cry as I had every other time. I just hated my life. I realized God had answered my prayers, and prison would keep me safe and cured of drugs. I knew my children were safe in foster care, my husband couldn't hurt me or the kids, and I would have access to treatment. Overall, I was in and out of jail several times.

In jail, I wasn't diagnosed and was denied medication for epilepsy until I had a dozen grand mal seizures and was hospitalized. While in jail, I had my fourth baby, and I participated in a drug recovery program. I put my fourth child in temporary custody with a couple, with the agreement that when I got out of jail and was back on my feet, I would get her back. When I was released from jail, I tried to contact them to see her and found out that the couple had already started the paperwork to adopt her. After an almost two-year court battle, I agreed to let them adopt my child.

(Continued)

Question: What type of drug abuse programs did you participate in while in jail?

Christine: "Chances" was the name of the drug program that helped me while in jail. I credit this program with helping me develop a strong desire to recover from drugs. After completing the program, I had the option to transfer out of the drug program or stay there and counsel others as a "big sister." I stayed in the program and was so good at counseling them, I was assigned five little sisters when we were only supposed to have two.

While I was in jail, a caseworker with the Magdalene program came to visit and told me about their two-year recovery program. It sounded good, so I enrolled. When I got out of jail that time, I waited tables to earn a living. I became pregnant with my fifth child, but the strain of pregnancy increased the frequency of my seizures. I had to quit working and continued to live at Magdalene House until the birth of my daughter.

For about a year, I went to the "John" school to talk to other addicts. It's a weeklong program that men, who have been arrested for soliciting, pay $250 (which went to Magdalene House) to attend in order to avoid arrest. I told them about the dangers of soliciting, such as "tag teaming," when one prostitute would go with a man and another would come over and beat and rob the man.

Now, I attend AA, which is a requirement of Dr. Hazel's program. Dr. Hazel runs the recovery program at Magdalene.

Question: You have had a tough life. What are some of the concerns of other female inmates?

Christine: Quite frankly, many seemed concerned with their kids but not "that" concerned. They seemed to be more concerned about getting out of jail. Some of their families took care of their kids; others were in foster care. I had three boys and one girl from my first marriage. At the beginning of my stay in prison, a social worker brought my three boys to see me. The oldest, which refused to be adopted, was placed in guardianship. The next two boys were adopted by different families in different cities. Like I've already said, my daughter was adopted by a couple.

I was actually lucky. My family was normal, my parents were married, I had five siblings, and there was no abuse or alcoholism in our history. My parents tried to obtain custody of my children while I was incarcerated, but they couldn't do it, even though I would have granted it.

Question: What was it like to get visits from your kids while incarcerated?

Christine: It was horrible. I remember the only time the boys came to visit about a month after I went to prison. The oldest understood a little about what was going on, but the others didn't understand why I was there. I told them I was sick and was staying there to get better. My daughter, who was born while I was in jail, was the only one who visited on a somewhat regular basis.

The next time they visited was after I was released. I continued to see them in foster care throughout that period and was fighting for their custody. I went for scheduled visits at DCS (Department of Children's Services) after I was released from jail and was fighting for their custody.

Question: Is there a lot of drug use in prison?

Christine: If you want it, you can get it. I was in minimum security, and it was easy to recognize when people were on drugs because they were dazed and acted very secretive.

Question: How was your medical care in prison?

Christine: It was pretty good after they recognized I was an epileptic. I received the medication I needed. I also had a baby in Meharry (Metro General) Hospital under a physician's care. They treated me well there.

Question: How is your life coming now?

Christine: Pretty good. I have been in a relationship with a man for seven years, with whom I have another daughter. My oldest child is twenty-one and he lives with us, as does our daughter.

But, I will always have a place in my life for all my kids. Even the ones who were adopted. I want to be ready in case they come home. On their birthdays, I always prepare each one's favorite meal so that if they come home, they will know I remembered them. I try to put all this behind me, but there are some things I never will forget.

Words of wisdom (my take on life): One day, when my son and I had the same day off, we decided to make the most of it by walking around and window shopping. During our travels, he started telling me how, when every time life starts looking up for him, something happens and things go downhill. His question: "Mom, why is this always happening to me?" My reply was simple: "Some people like to think that God puts the 'downhill' times in your life so you'll appreciate the ups." My son, at the "ripe old age" of twenty-one, still looked confused and unsatisfied with my response. I elaborated. Chris, you are young, and life is a rollercoaster ride. When you're born, you start out at the top. The ups and downs are your learning experiences, some downs are deeper than others, but you have to keep in mind that the rollercoaster will go up again, and the ride will be exhilarating! No matter how many "downs" you have on this rollercoaster ride called life, the ride ALWAYS lets you off at the top.[57]

Separation from Family and Children

In a way very different than that of male inmates, women inmates suffer from the separation from their family and children and feel helpless in their child-raising role. Approximately 62 percent of women held in state prisons have children under age eighteen and report an average of 2.38 children per inmate. About two-thirds of these women (compared to 42 percent of male inmates) lived with their young children before entering prison.[58] Most children of female offenders end up with their maternal grandmothers, and the remainder are placed in foster homes. This is because the inmate's husband who is also the father of her children is usually also incarcerated. By contrast, almost 90 percent of children of male inmates live with the children's mothers. This placement seems to be the most acceptable to female inmates and gives them the most peace of mind about how their children are being treated and the ease of getting their children back after release.[59] Female offenders know that their criminal involvement has caused a hardship for and separation from their children and feel shame and guilt for their own actions, as well as anger and bitterness with the criminal justice system for their situation. Children with parents in prison create a long-term issue, as approximately one-half of a sample of inmates reported having had a parent in prison or jail.[60] And children with a parent incarcerated are more likely involved in the juvenile justice system or later incarcerated in adult prisons.[61]

With such a large proportion of women inmates having children, visiting in prison is particularly important. However, elderly parents of inmates caring for children often have a difficult time making the trip to visit regularly. Visits are also problematic due to the long distance between the inmates' homes and the prisons in which they are incarcerated. Female prisoners make up a relatively small portion of the nation's prison population, and most states have several male prisons, but only one or two female prisons. Therefore, women are often placed farther from their homes than men. It is interesting that wives of male inmates regularly bring children to visit their fathers. However, when mothers end up in prison, they receive fewer visits with children due to the distances and the logistical problems those giving child care have in making visits.

Many prisons have added a room for children to play in or for parents to read to them so that there is some semblance of normalcy as children visit their parents in prison. Courtesy of the Ohio Department of Rehabilitation and Correction.

Unfortunately, when women receive visits from their children, prison visiting room conditions are not conducive to fostering a parent–child relationship. Prison visiting areas usually provide seating similar to that in an airport waiting area, although many now provide a small room or area of the larger visiting room for small children with a television, videos, and books or toys for children to play with. To improve the parental relationship between women inmates and their children, many prisons have established **parenting programs**. These programs often include training classes to improve parenting skills and suggest methods to "parent" from prison. One example is how to play the role of mother as teacher, by emphasizing the mother reading to children (sometimes on audiotape) and helping children with their school homework during visits. A few programs include special visiting situations where children may be able to spend extended time or even overnight with their mothers and may include special use (separate from other inmates) of the prison recreation or dining areas. A great example of an outstanding program is "PS, I Love You," a family literacy program in the New Mexico Women's Correctional Facility. This program videotapes inmates who are mothers reading a book that is then sent to their children.

Another unique program to assist inmate mothers in staying connected to their children is **Girl Scouts Beyond Bars**. This program was previously Girl Scouts Behind Bars, but now has continued programming both in and out of prisons and jails. Some female prisons have established Girl Scout chapters, have meetings with female inmates and their daughters in the visiting room, and get the inmate mothers involved in "den mother" activities, such as planning meetings or providing snacks. The Girl Scout chapters are usually linked to a chapter in the community so that the children can also be involved in normal Girl Scouts activities. This program also encourages the continued involvement of mothers and daughters in Girl Scouts after the mothers' release from prison.[62]

parenting programs
prison programs to assist inmates to improve their parenting skills, even while in prison

Girl Scouts Beyond Bars
Girl Scout troops that have their chapter based in a prison so inmates with children can participate as Scout parents

Alcohol and Substance Abuse

Many women offenders have a serious history and problem with alcohol and substance abuse, often even more serious and more involved in their criminality than men. Almost half (49 percent) of incarcerated women reported daily use of drugs in the thirty days prior to incarceration and 14 percent reported using three to six times a week.[63] Another study found that 59 percent of female state prisoners were using drugs within the month before their offense, 17 percent of females inmates (compared to 10 percent of men) used methamphetamines in the month before their offense,[64] and 40 percent of women (compared to 32 percent of men) were under the influence of drugs at the time of their crime.[65] Also, "[n]early 1 in 3 women serving time in State prisons said they had committed the offense which brought them to prison in order to obtain money to support their need for drugs."[66] The Center for Substance Abuse Treatment reported that almost 80 percent of the women in state prisons have "severe, long-standing substance abuse problems,"[67] and the high rates of female prisoners with substance abuse, mental health issues, and trauma have been further documented.[68] Unquestionably, women offenders are in need of programs and services to reduce their dependence on alcohol and drugs.

Unfortunately, the need for substance abuse treatment in prison is generally not satisfactorily met. Although 74 percent of all prisons offered drug or alcohol counseling in 2005,[69] in 2002, only 12.9 percent of the prison populations participated in drug treatment programs. Of these, 63,960 were in either individual or group treatment and the remainder were in separate drug treatment units.[70] Twenty percent of women offenders report receiving drug or alcohol treatment

Many female offenders have a need for substance abuse treatment. Marmaduke St. John/Alamy Stock Photo.

during the period of their incarceration.[71] This is still not improved satisfactorily, and even though women are more likely to participate in substance abuse programming in prison than men,[72] the availability of prison substance abuse programs is insufficient to meet the reentry needs of women.[73]

It is important to increase the overall number of **substance abuse programs** and particularly the number of those for female inmates. Also, the women's programs should focus on the specific issues around the reasons for female drug abuse and special circumstances around their postincarceration needs. Chesney-Lind suggests,

> *Women's programs must, first and foremost, give participants strategies to deal with their profound substance abuse problems. They must also be gender-sensitive in additional ways: they must understand that most women take drugs as a form of self-medication, and they must be sensitive to women's unique circumstances (by providing such services as child care and transportation).*[74]

substance abuse programs
programs for offenders to reduce their likelihood of further abuse of alcohol or drugs

Need for Medical Care

Medical care is very difficult to provide in a quality fashion within a prison. Moore suggests, "Problems in providing care to the incarcerated fall into two broad categories: health status of the inmate population and deficiencies in the delivery of medical care,"[75] and identifies six factors inherent in correctional settings that hamper the provision of health services:

1. not a priority of the correctional institution;
2. limited financial resources;
3. difficulties in staff recruitment;
4. absence of a current manual of health care policies and procedures;
5. isolation of the institution from community health care; and
6. lack of a constituency for inmate health services.[76]

Although all inmate medical care is difficult to provide, female inmates have more serious health problems than male inmates. This results not only from the need for gynecological care, but from a history of poverty, drug and alcohol abuse, poor diet and nutrition, and past neglect and lack of health care.[77] Women, of course, also have medical issues around pregnancy. Greenfeld and Snell report that 5 percent of women admitted to state prisons are pregnant, and although 90 percent of these had received a gynecological exam since their admission, only 4 percent had received prenatal care since their admission.[78]

The delivery of correctional health care has improved over the past two decades. However, there is a serious need for correctional administrators to continue to make improvements and, specifically, to address the challenges in providing health care for women prisoners. In describing these challenges for correctional administrators, Seiter notes,

> [T]here are unanswered philosophical questions about the quality and quantity of medical care that should be provided incarcerated felons. Costs of inmate health care continue to rise, and there is constant pressure on administrators to reduce medical spending. Prisons have never been an attractive recruiting ground for medical personnel, and competition for providers has intensified over the past decade. All of these issues require prison administrators to look for new ways to solve serious problems. Yet, there are few states that would suggest they have found the answers, and are comfortable with the cost and quality of the medical care provided in their prisons.[79]

Classification Systems for Female Offenders

One concern that has come to light is that objective classification systems that have been historically developed for male offenders often tend to "overclassify" female offenders, and a survey of state classification systems found that many states have not validated their classification and risk assessments for gender differences.[80] **Overclassification** is the placement of offenders in prisons more secure than needed for their level of risk. Women have different pathways to crime than do men, and their criminality is often related to their connections with others.[81] It is therefore important to recalibrate objective classification instruments with gender-informed assessments, as instruments developed using predominantly male offender examples do not take into account the specific variables that reduced the risk posed by women.

Overclassification
the placement of offenders in prisons more secure than needed for their level of risk

In the 1990s, the Federal Bureau of Prisons (BOP) reviewed its classification system based on these gender issues. The BOP found that it was placing female offenders at a higher level of physical security prisons than their risk of escape or tendency for violence warranted. In most cases, women's criminal involvement was as accomplices to men, and if the crime included the use of a weapon or violence, male offenders actually handled the weapon or resorted to violence. Also, a previously unconsidered factor was that female inmates often had children and close ties in the community. And these were important factors in predicting escape. Therefore, the BOP administratively reduced the number of points assigned for certain types of crimes (such as crimes of violence or use of a weapon during the offense) committed by women and was able to move a large percentage of the female inmate population to less secure prisons. Since that time, many states have also updated their classification in recognition of the gender differences in risk among offenders.

Other Issues for Female Offenders

In addition to the above, women offenders also have a more difficult time finding and maintaining employment than male offenders.[82] Women face employment barriers such as being the sole custodial parent for their children. As a result, women need more intensive programming regarding education and vocational training; employment assistance programs; time management skills; and assistance with child care, housing, and health care.

Another serious problem for female offenders is mental health, as female offenders suffer from mental illness at a higher rate than their male counterparts.[83] James and Glaze report that 73 percent of women prisoners exhibit mental health issues compared to 55 percent of men.[84] And unsurprisingly, mental health issues are interrelated to other issues such as substance abuse.[85]

The "A Look Into" box describes the issues and challenges that prison staff members have in dealing with female inmates.

Female offenders have developed some of the same habits as male offenders (such as adding tattoos), and the courts have declared that they deserve parity with male offenders in programs and services. Photo by Richard P. Seiter.

A Look Into...

Working with Female Inmates

One interesting point regarding female offenders is the differences in them as inmates from their male counterparts. I have worked as a case manager and a unit manager for female inmates. To develop this case study, I talked to someone who has recently been a case manager for a male and a female caseload. It is interesting to see the differences he describes in working with the two populations.

- Females need more contact with agencies outside of the prison. More women are filing for divorce and need contact with the family courts. More women have children issues and must contact the division of family services. These types of contacts often require telephone calls, as they cannot be completed only through the mail.

- Sentences for women overall are less than for men, so the turnaround is greater. More women are referred to halfway houses, and staff members have to move more quickly to get referrals completed.

- Medical and mental health issues are different and more intense. Female inmates are sometimes pregnant while in prison and need prenatal care. Mental health issues seem more pronounced for female inmates, they need more psychological services, and a higher percentage seems to be on antidepressants.

- Women stay much more attached to the community than men, who seem to divorce themselves from their families and community ties. Female inmates take more responsibility with regard to their children and family, especially their

(Continued)

parents, and are continually more stressed out about their problems in the community.

- Female inmates are very different in regard to their relationships with staff and other inmates. Women seem to need someone to talk to and will talk more freely than men to staff about their problems. They are also much more open about their sexual relationships (in prison) than men. They may have a girlfriend; they may have a breakup; and there is more fighting about these sexual relationships. A higher percentage of women seem to participate in homosexuality, or they hide it less. Men get involved in homosexual activity more for the sexual gratification, whereas women get involved for the emotional relationship.
- Women are more interested in being involved in programs. There is a high demand for drug programs, and they are more willing to confront their drug use as a problem that needs attention. They work better with staff and are more willing to take orders and follow instructions.
- One interesting issue concerns property. Men want food or snacks, but women try to accumulate hobby or craft items, to create more of a "homey" atmosphere in their cell or dormitory area than men. They try to get jewelry and often have visitors bring them things that are not allowed.

They have different demands of the commissary; they desire hair dye, skin care products, and other personal cosmetic items.

- Race is not as much of an issue as with men. Female inmates seem less concerned about race and do not self-segregate nearly as much. In male dining rooms, inmates often sit at tables with only their race, whereas women are much less concerned about this.
- Women have fewer disciplinary issues than men. They just seem to accept their incarceration without breaking the rules as much.
- Female inmates, however, are far more manipulative with staff than male inmates. They are more likely to exaggerate or outright lie about a problem at home that requires immediate attention or a crisis phone call home.
- In general, women have many more demands and take much more staff time than men. They realistically have more issues, particularly related to home, and desire immediate attention from staff. When case managers need to talk to male inmates to prepare a progress report, they almost have to order them to come in to talk and discuss their community plans. Women are lined up at the door to talk about issues at home.

The Franklin County Prerelease Center in Ohio is a facility to which women inmates move in their last few months of incarceration to prepare for release to the community.
Courtesy of the Ohio Department of Rehabilitation and Correction.

Legal Issues Regarding Parity for Female Inmates

Over the past ten years, correctional agencies have made many improvements in responding to the specific needs of women in prison. Many of these developments have resulted from the intervention of federal courts, noting the disparate treatment received and conditions faced by female offenders. As early as 1974, a federal court in the case of **Barefield v. Leach** found that the state of New Mexico was not providing parity in vocational training and work opportunity for female inmates and ruled that such disparity could not be justified just because the smaller number of female inmates made it more costly to provide parity in these programs.[86] In *Butler v. Reno*, female plaintiffs who were federal inmates claimed gender discrimination due to denial of access to facilities, programs, and services available to similarly situated male federal inmates. The U.S. District Court for the District of Columbia agreed with the plaintiffs, and the parties entered into a stipulated order of settlement in 1995. In the order, the BOP agreed to provide programs, services, and facilities for female inmates that were comparable to those offered to male inmates. This included placing minimum-security female inmates in camps with limited physical security; maintaining similar staff member–inmate ratios; providing work, education, parent–child, and recreation program opportunities; and providing health care comparable to that in male prisons.

In the 1995 case of **Pargo v. Elliott**, the Eighth Circuit Court found that just the fact that there are differences in programs between male and female prisons is not necessarily a violation of the equal protection clause of the Constitution. The Court suggested that five criteria should be used to examine whether differences in prison programs are discriminatory: the number of inmates in a prison, the prison security level, the crimes committed by inmates, the length of sentences being served by inmates, and any other special characteristics that could be identified by the prison as reasons for program differences.[87] It is recognized that women will look for different types of jobs after release from prison and that many need training in parenting and child-care issues that are not as critical for men.

The solution to the problem of parity has been lessened with the growth in the number of female inmates. Rafter reports that, although only two to three new female prisons were opened every decade between 1930 and 1950, during the 1980s more than thirty-four new women's prisons were opened, by 1990 there were seventy-one women's prisons, and in 1995 there were 104 prisons designated for female offenders.[88] The 2000 Census of State and Federal Correctional Facilities reports that of 1668 correctional facilities, 156 house female prisoners only and 225 house both male and female prisoners.[89] With 111,422 women in state and federal prisons at the end of 2016,[90] many new prisons have opened for women and most have been expanded. This allows for greater economies of scale to provide additional categories of vocational training or other treatment programs for women inmates. New prisons also provide the opportunity to begin new types of educational, vocational, and work programs, focusing on the nontraditional roles of women offenders and providing parity with male programs. Finally, additional prisons scattered across states enable women to be more likely housed closer to their homes than when a state had only one female prison.

Now that students have learned the issues that face women convicted of a crime and have considered the potential for alternatives to incarceration, it is time to struggle with the challenging question of whether women should face justice for their crimes just as men do. Consider this issue in the "You Make the Decision" box at the end of the chapter.

Barefield v. Leach
a 1974 federal court decision that a disparity of programs for female inmates could not be justified because the smaller number of female inmates made it more costly to provide program parity

Pargo v. Elliott
the 1995 Eighth Circuit Court case that allowed that differences in programs between male and female prisons does not necessarily violate the equal protection clause of the Constitution

Chapter Review

Summary

In the last twenty-five years, the number of adults under correctional supervision has increased from just over 1.3 million to over 6.7 million, and the number of prison inmates grew from just over 300,000 to over 1.5 million offenders. These increases have resulted from several factors, including the war on drugs and a tremendous increase in the number of arrests for drug offenses; toughened sentencing statutes that lengthened the time offenders serve in prison, on probation, and on postprison supervision; sentencing guidelines and mandatory minimum sentences that took discretion away from judges and resulted in more female offenders being sent to prison; and a lower tolerance for risk, resulting in an increased number of parole and probation revocations.

Even though the gender makeup of offenders throughout the criminal justice system is still predominantly male, female offenders are "catching up" in that their rate of growth in most areas is greater than that of male offenders. In 2015, women made up 20.2 percent of all arrests for violent offenses, 38.9 percent of arrests for property offenses, and 22.9 percent of arrests for drug offenses. Much of the attention and study of the criminal justice system, offenders, and their characteristics have been historically directed toward male criminals. However, with the increasing number of women offenders, the impact of gender differences on the correctional system is now an important area of study.

Although much of the increase in women's criminal involvement has been linked to drug crimes, women also commit over one-fifth of all violent offenses, and as a result, many are serving long prison terms. Women in prison face a variety of different problems and therefore have different needs for programs and services. Their family ties and separation from their children make visiting and parenting programs even more critical for female than male prisoners. Many women suffer from long-term and serious substance abuse histories, which are unfortunately not being addressed in prison. Their medical needs are much greater than those of men. And the recent implementations of objective classification systems have tended to overclassify them to prisons with a higher emphasis on security than is necessary.

This chapter has set the groundwork for a further and more detailed examination of the makeup of the correctional population in the United States. The next chapter examines the handling of juvenile offenders; following that, the many special groups of offenders who require handling or management are described. As noted in the introduction to this chapter, offenders are what corrections is all about. Corrections is not simply policy, operations, or laws. It is the management of people and the various considerations that must be taken into account as we attempt to manage a diverse group of people in an environment that is safe and secure and contributes to the long-term safety of the public.

Key Terms

racial disparity	female offenders	*Barefield v. Leach*
drug offenders	parenting programs	*Pargo v. Elliott*
male offenders	Girl Scouts Beyond Bars	Overclassification
general population	substance abuse programs	

Review Questions

1. What has been the primary factor in the growth in the number of individuals under correctional supervision over the past twenty years?

2. Compare the increase in females versus males in terms of the number under correctional supervision.

3. What does Wilbanks say about the presence of racism in the criminal justice system and what do most researchers believe is the reason for the disproportionate number of minorities under correctional supervision?

4. How has the age of offenders changed?

5. What percentage of people arrested for violent felonies are male?

6. What is the "general population" within a prison?

7. What is the overall goal of a prison classification system?

8. Why are women now sentenced similarly to male offenders?

9. How does the recidivism rate for women offenders compare to that for men?

10. What percentage of the prison population is female?

11. List the special problems faced by female inmates.

12. What programs do prisons have to deal with the parenting needs of female prisoners?

13. How do female inmate classification systems differ from those for men?

14. Describe the impact that the case *Barefield v. Leach* has had on the operation of female prisons.

▶ You Make the Decision...

Should Women Go to Prison Just Like Men?

In 1925, women represented only 3.7 percent of the national prison population, but in the 1980s this percentage began to climb. By 1990, it had increased to 5.7 percent, and by December 31, 2015, 7.3 percent of the prisoners in state and federal prisons were women. Historically, judges gave female offenders a break by often granting them probation instead of incarceration, thinking that they were not a risk to society and most of their crimes were as accomplices to men. With the war on drugs, the imposition of mandatory prison sentences, and the use of sentencing guidelines, women now receive a prison sentence in almost equal proportion to men. However, the average sentence served by women is still significantly less than that served by men (in 2012, men released from prison had served a median time longer than women in all offense categories).

As noted in this chapter, women face different issues than men do when they go to prison. Eighty percent of incarcerated women are mothers, one-fourth of the women who enter prison are either pregnant or have given birth within the past twelve months, and 65 percent of women held in state prisons have children under age eighteen. About two-thirds of these women (compared to 44 percent of male inmates) lived with their young children before entering prison. More female inmates have a link between their criminality and substance abuse than male inmates. Approximately one-third of women inmates committed the offense that brought them to prison to obtain money to support their need for drugs.

It is not difficult to argue that female offenders are not as dangerous or as serious a risk as their male counterparts. In terms of recidivism, rates for female offenders are high, yet thought to be less than recidivism rates for comparable male offenders. Female offenders are less likely to be involved in violent crimes, and the consequences of male violence are usually more serious for the victim. The facts that there is a significant increase in the number of women in prison, they have many collateral consequences associated with their incarceration, and they are less dangerous to society suggest the need to reconsider the "one size fits all" sentencing approach. Consider all these issues and decide whether women should be sentenced differently than men, or whether there should be more discretion for judges to consider individual factors and sentence women to community alternatives instead of prison.

CHAPTER 8

The Juvenile Correctional System

Courtesy of CoreCivic.

After reading this chapter, you should be able to:

1. Summarize the problem of and trends in juvenile crime.
2. Describe the development of the juvenile justice system, the concept of *parens patriae*, and how juveniles may be transferred to adult courts.
3. Summarize the categories of juvenile offenders.
4. Outline the steps in the juvenile justice process and compare them with similar steps in the adult justice process.
5. Describe juvenile residential facilities and the treatment programs in them.
6. Identify and specify the result of key federal court cases affecting the rights of juvenile offenders.
7. Summarize issues in juvenile corrections, including the challenges associated with juvenile gangs.

Introduction

When I was director of adult corrections for Ohio, I used to tell my colleague who was director of the juvenile correctional system, "I am glad I do not have your job." Our mission was much clearer in dealing with adult sanctions. We supervised and incarcerated adult felons so that society is protected. We built secure prisons and knew how to manage inmates. But my colleague's mission was far less clear. Some people want to treat serious juvenile offenders just as we treat adults. Others argue that these offenders are still children and should not be punished as criminals, but treated as delinquents who need to be led back on the right path to becoming mature and responsible adults. In the juvenile system, there is ongoing debate about whether correctional institutions are prisons or training schools, whether offenders are inmates or students, or whether clients and society are better off with them in institutions or maintained in the community. The juvenile justice system was originally created to deal with delinquent acts committed by individuals under age eighteen (in most states), in a separate system designed to deal differently with juveniles than with adults. Over the years, however, the juvenile justice system has suffered from a lack of consistency and agreement on the mission and approach.

This chapter describes the problem of juvenile crime, the history and creation of the juvenile justice system, and recent developments to ensure that the system can respond to modern challenges of criminal and delinquent behavior by youth. Issues regarding developing case law, drug crimes by youth, and juvenile gang membership are also described.

The Problem of Juvenile Crime

Similar to adult crimes, juvenile crime rates and trends fluctuate over time, yet there is often a disconnect between actual crime data and public perception and justice policies. It regularly appears that media coverage of crimes and criminal activity by juveniles has more influence on policy than actual trends in the data. The Federal Bureau of Investigation (FBI) collects both juvenile and adult crime data in the annual *Uniform Crime Reports* (UCR). Serious and violent crime trends are reviewed by monitoring four crimes in the UCR (murder and non-negligent manslaughter, forcible rape, robbery, and aggravated assault) and the Violent Crime Index.

Over the past three decades, the high number of juveniles involved in crimes has been a serious concern even though the overall juvenile arrest rates have been declining since 1996. As illustrated in Figure 8.1, between 1980 and 1996 there was a continuous increase in the arrest rates for juveniles. However, the overall juvenile arrest rate since 1996 has declined 68 percent since that year until 2015. Of most concern was juvenile involvement in serious violent crimes, and public attention and concern regarding the problem of juvenile violent crime increased. However, juvenile violent crime has also declined. From 1980 through the peak year of 1994, juveniles arrested for violent crimes increased 68 percent. However, the number of arrests began to decline in 1994, and from 2006 to 2015, arrests of juveniles for violent crimes continued to decline from 56,938 to 30,130 (47.1 percent).[1]

Several theories suggest the reasons for the increase in juvenile violent crime from 1988 to 1994. The first is that, as in crime statistics regarding adults, the emergence of crack cocaine and the violence around its use and sale caused an

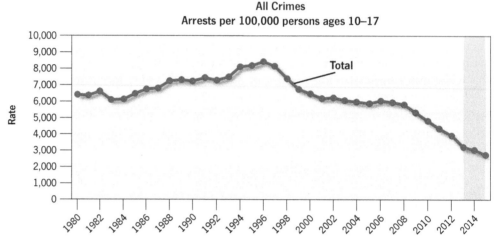

All Crimes
Arrests per 100,000 persons ages 10–17

Note: Rates are arrests of persons ages 10–17 per 100,000 persons ages 10–17 in the resident population.

FIGURE 8.1   The Juvenile Arrest Rate for All Crimes, 1980–2015   Source: Data from Office of Juvenile Justice and Delinquency Prevention, "Juvenile Arrest Rate Trends," *Statistical Briefing Book*, available at https://www.ojjdp.gov/ojstatbb/crime/JAR_Display.asp?ID=qa05200 (accessed September 8, 2017).

increase in juvenile violent crime. Crack cocaine is an extremely addictive drug and can result in violent behavior by those using it. Crack cocaine is also considerably less expensive than powder cocaine, and its emergence created a new drug of choice in urban, poverty-ridden areas. Violent confrontations between various factions of drug sellers occurred as groups attempted to control areas of drug sales for their own group or individual profit.

Second, the expansion of juvenile gang membership during this period resulted in expanded juvenile violence. Gangs lead to violence in a variety of ways. Gangs use violence to get attention, show their toughness, and recruit new members. Violence is also a way that gangs show that they are in control of an area, other gangs should stay out, and nongang youths should join them to be a member of the dominant group and avoid becoming victims themselves. Gang violence also occurs between gangs. Gangs will fight rather than let any other gang gain members or take control of their area. The proliferation of weapons in the possession of juveniles also led to an increase in violence. The number of juvenile arrests for weapons charges increased 103 percent from 1985 to 1994; eleven large cities reported that approximately 40 percent of their juvenile males were in possession of a weapon at some time,[2] and there has been a noted increase in the use of guns by juveniles who participate in the illegal drug market.[3] However, from 2003 to 2012, the percentage of juvenile arrests for weapons charges has declined by 58 percent.[4]

Table 8.1 illustrates the overall numbers of juveniles arrested for all categories of offenses in both 2006 and 2015. The good news is that the overall volume of juveniles arrested declined from 1.28 million in 2006 to 578,638 in 2015 (54.8 percent). Of the total number of juvenile arrests, 70.1 percent were of males, and 29.9 percent were of females.[5] And there has also been a large decrease in the number of arrests for liquor laws (from 94,729 to 29,530) and curfew and loitering (from 60,669 to 19,454). Each of these two categories is an example of a **status offense**, an act that is considered a violation of law for juveniles but not for adults.

Public concern is about not only juveniles' involvement in violent crimes, but also the percent of crime that is being committed by juveniles. The proportion of violent crimes cleared by juvenile arrests averaged about 9 percent of all violent crimes during the late 1980s, climbed to 14 percent of all violent crimes in 1994,

status offense

an activity that is considered a crime only because the offender is under the age of eighteen and would not be a crime if committed by an adult; includes acts such as running away from home, ungovernability, truancy, or underage drinking

TABLE 8.1   Arrests of Juveniles by Offense in 2006 and 2015

Offense charged	Number of persons arrested		
	2006	**2015**	**Percent change**
TOTAL[1]	**1,280,195**	**578,538**	**–54.8**
Murder and nonnegligent manslaughter	642	421	–34.4
Rape[2]	2,111	2,239	–
Robbery	18,201	9,753	–46.4
Aggravated assault	35,984	17,717	–50.8
Burglary	51,953	22,056	–57.5
Larceny-theft	180,623	101,898	–43.6
Motor vehicle theft	17,651	7,547	–57.2
Arson	5,223	1,811	–65.3
Violent crime[3]	56,938	30,130	–47.1
Property crime[3]	255,450	133,312	–47.8
Other assaults	152,396	83,689	–45.1
Forgery and counterfeiting	2,288	632	–72.4
Fraud	5,090	2,776	–45.5
Embezzlement	949	391	–58.8
Stolen property; buying, receiving, possessing	14,032	6,600	–53.0
Vandalism	76,202	27,793	–63.5
Weapons; carrying, possessing, etc.	27,707	11,614	–58.1
Prostitution and commercialized vice	733	269	–63.3
Sex offenses (except rape and prostitution)	9,948	5,643	–43.3
Drug abuse violations	113,132	63,035	–44.3
Gambling	292	133	–54.5
Offenses against the family and children	3,348	2,208	–34.1
Driving under the influence	12,947	4,294	–66.8
Liquor laws	94,729	29,530	–68.8
Drunkenness	11,093	3,528	–68.2
Disorderly conduct	129,948	45,659	–64.9
Vagrancy	3,475	598	–82.8
All other offenses (except traffic)	248,829	107,250	–56.9
Suspicion	203	127	–37.4
Curfew and loitering law violations	60,669	19,454	–67.9

[1]Does not include suspicion.

[2]The 2006 rape figures are based on the legacy definition, and the 2015 rape figures are aggregate totals based on both the legacy and revised *Uniform Crime Reports* definitions. For this reason, a percent change is not provided.

[3]Violent crimes are offenses of murder and nonnegligent manslaughter, rape, robbery, and aggravated assault. Property crimes are offenses of burglary, larceny-theft, motor vehicle theft, and arson.

Source: Federal Bureau of Investigation, "Ten Year Arrest Trends, 2006–2015," *Crime in the United States*, available at https://ucr.fbi.gov/crime-in-the-u.s/2015/crime-in-the-u.s.-2015/tables/table-32 (accessed September 10, 2017).

Refuge Period

a period from 1824 to 1899 when delinquent or neglected children were placed in a home for training and discipline

juvenile justice system

a system to handle juveniles separate from adult offenders, based on the concept of *parens patriae*, which was used as the basis for giving the court the authority to take over supervision of children when their parents failed to provide proper care and guidance

parens patriae

means "parents of the nation," established in 1601 to allow officials to take change of delinquent children and place them in poorhouses or orphanages to gain control of them; in more modern times, this doctrine was expanded as the basis for juvenile court and correctional systems to take responsibility for educating and nurturing delinquents, with an emphasis on reform and rehabilitation

but from 1997 to 2006, the percentage of violent crimes committed by juveniles began to decline. In 2015, the percentage of violent crimes committed by juveniles had dropped to 9.8 percent.[6] We now turn to how we have responded to juvenile crime over the past several years.

Development of the Juvenile Justice System

In the late eighteenth century, as the American colonies were establishing systems of government and courts, juveniles under age seven were seen as below the age of reason and thereby incapable of the formation of criminal intent. However, those over age seven were handled in the criminal justice system, the same as adults. Soon thereafter, recognition of the need to deal separately with delinquent or neglected children developed. As a result, between 1824 and 1899, the **Refuge Period** developed. Houses of Refuge were created to house, train, educate, and provide good habits for these wayward children through strict discipline.[7] These houses were usually operated by charitable or religious organizations, they had few controls or standards, and the attempt to change the behavior of delinquents often resulted in harsh and brutal conditions. As the need for reform of the entire approach to managing juveniles was recognized, the Society for the Prevention of Juvenile Delinquency began to advocate for reforms to include a separation of juveniles from the adult system as early as 1825.

When John Augustus, the Boston shoemaker regarded as the "father of probation," began to bail criminals out of jail in the middle 1800s, he also persuaded judges to place wayward youth under his supervision, and he brought the distinctions between juvenile and adult offenders to the courts' attention. However, the **juvenile justice system** was not created until Illinois passed the Juvenile Court Act, and the first juvenile court was established in Cook County (Chicago) in 1899. By creating a separate juvenile court, the concept of ***parens patriae*** was recognized as the basis for giving the court the authority to take over supervision of children when their parents failed to provide proper care and guidance. The

During the 1800s, Houses of Refuge were operated to house wayward youths and provide them with structure and discipline. T.A. Carlson/Library of Congress/Corbis Historical/ Getty Images.

concept of *parens patriae* means "parents of the nation" and was first established in England with the 1601 Elizabethan Poor Laws, which allowed officials to take charge of delinquent children and place them in poorhouses or orphanages to gain control of them. In more modern times, this doctrine was expanded as the basis for juvenile court and correctional systems to take responsibility for educating and nurturing delinquents, with an emphasis on reform and rehabilitation.

The use of a separate juvenile court, initiated in Cook County, proved to be popular, and by 1925, all but two states had established juvenile courts or probation departments separate from their adult systems.[8] Even though the concept of *parens patriae* is no longer fully applicable in juvenile courts, the theory of nurturing and reforming juveniles continued, and mission statements for most juvenile courts still stress the benevolent nature of the system and emphasize rehabilitating rather than punishing youthful offenders. With this underlying concept, the juvenile system was much less formal and less reliant on legal precedent and due process than the adult system. Hearings were not adversarial proceedings but attempts by the court to determine what actions were in the best interest of the juvenile and society.

By 1960, these philosophies and processes began to be questioned because of concern for the impact they had on the juvenile offender. There was apprehension that the juvenile system's emphasis on treatment could result in the indefinite institutionalization of delinquents until treatment was deemed complete. There was a belief that juveniles, even for benevolent reasons, were often pulled into the system, removed from their family and community, and put into juvenile institutions without a clear ability to treat and return them in a better state. Therefore, there was a move to formalize the court processes, include more due process, and use the criminal standard of proof *beyond a reasonable doubt*, rather than *by a preponderance of evidence*.

There were also efforts to remove status offenders not charged with criminal conduct from the juvenile court system. In the Juvenile Justice and Delinquency Prevention Act of 1974, the U.S. Congress required assessments of the juvenile justice system to identify youth who were victimized, rather than helped, by placement in juvenile facilities.[9] The juvenile institutions, which had been considered a positive environment for youths while emphasizing education and training, began to be seen as an overly aggressive sanction. Advocates for juveniles believed that they should be diverted from the justice system and could better be treated in the community. The highlight of the movement to **deinstitutionalize** juvenile correctional facilities came when Jerome Miller, commissioner of the Massachusetts Department of Youth Services, closed most of that state's juvenile institutions and placed the youths in community programs. Miller believed that institutions were more damaging to juveniles than helpful and that they could be better treated in the community.

Since the early 1980s, however, another reform of the juvenile justice system has prevailed. This reform was prompted by concern not for the juvenile offender, but for community safety. Just as public sentiment regarding adult offenders supported punishment and offender accountability over treatment and rehabilitation, there was a similar swing in attitudes regarding juveniles. The increases in juvenile violent crime created a fear by the public of dangerous, marauding gangs of juveniles creating havoc and violence throughout the urban landscape. During the early 1990s, DiIulio even coined the term **superpredator** in warning of a coming generation of violent youths who practiced almost indiscriminate violence on the streets.[10] Over the next decade, there has been what some call an "**adultification**" of the juvenile system. By this, there have been moves toward making the juvenile justice system more punitive and more looking like adult correctional systems. This may include change in staffing to include juvenile correctional officers, placing staff in military-style uniforms, and having juveniles in residential programs wear uniforms.

In addition, many state legislatures enacted laws to respond in a more punitive and public safety conscious manner, re-creating some juvenile court processes to

deinstitutionalize
the move to remove juveniles from correctional institutions and place them in community alternatives

superpredator
a term created by DiIulio to describe a generation of violent youths who practiced almost indiscriminant violence on the streets

adultification
a move to make the juvenile justice system look and operate more like an adult correctional system

parallel the adult courts, establishing mandatory prison sentences for some juvenile offenses, and waiving serious juvenile offenders from the juvenile to the adult court systems. By the end of the twentieth century, all states had passed laws to permit **waiver to adult courts** of serious juvenile offenders. These waivers allow the movement of serious juvenile offenders to adult courts for criminal processing. States use other terms for this process, including *certification*, *remand*, or *bind over*, for criminal prosecution. In Kansas and Vermont, juveniles as young as age ten could be tried as adults, and often prosecutors, rather than judges, had the authority to waive the case and have it transferred to an adult court. Fortunately, this punitive trend has reversed itself over the past ten years.

Waiver of Juvenile Offenders

Transferring juveniles to adult criminal courts is not a new phenomenon, and provisions for such transfer were available in some states even before the 1920s; many other states have permitted transfers since the 1940s. However, state transfer provisions changed extensively between 1992 and 1999, as all fifty states and the District of Columbia modified their transfer provisions. Many of these modifications instituted *mandatory waiver*, or direct assignment of specific crimes committed by juveniles, to be handled in adult courts.[11]

In *discretionary waivers* from juvenile to adult courts, juvenile courts usually decide on a case-by-case basis whether the court will waive the processing of the juvenile and allow prosecution as an adult in the criminal justice system. In this situation, the juvenile court must first find probable cause to believe that the juvenile committed the alleged act and, if so, must also find that it is in the court's best interest to waive its right to handle the case and give jurisdiction to the adult court. The process and how juvenile offenders are managed in adult prisons are described in Chapter 9. As well, the increase and more recent decrease in this waiver process are also described.

Most correctional professionals question the efficacy of serious juvenile offenders being tried and sentenced in adult courts. The American Correctional Association (ACA) standards distinguish the juvenile justice system as having significantly different processes, procedures, and objectives from adult corrections. James A. Gondles, executive director of the ACA, adds, "We will never, in my view, solve our problems on the back end with punishments.... Treating kids as adults solves very little; it's another quick-fix solution to a complex problem that took years to reach and will take years to resolve."[12] In the "You Make the Decision" box at the end of this chapter, you must take a position on this issue.

Categories of Juvenile Offenders

The juvenile justice system defines three categories of offenders: dependent, neglected, and delinquent. **Dependent children** have committed no legal offense but may be without a family (parent or guardian) or without support, possibly because the parent is physically or mentally unable to act in that capacity. **Neglected children** have a family or guardian but are not receiving proper care, or the situation in the home is harmful to them and their upbringing. **Delinquent children** have committed an act that would be considered criminal if committed by an adult. In many jurisdictions, a fourth category is *status offenders*, children who have committed acts that are law violations only if committed by a person of juvenile status.

The five major categories of status offenses include running away from home, ungovernability (being beyond the control of parents or guardians), truancy, curfew law violations, and underage liquor law violations (such as underage drinking, which also applies to young adults up to age twenty-one). When status offenses do

---

waiver to adult courts
because of the serious nature of a juvenile offender's crime, statutory exceptions were granted to allow the movement from juvenile to adult courts for criminal processing

dependent children
children who, although committing no legal offense, may be without a parent or guardian, possibly because the parent is physically or mentally unable to act in that capacity

neglected children
children who have a family or guardian, but are not receiving proper care, or the situation in the home is harmful to them and their upbringing

delinquent children
children who have committed an act that would be considered criminal if committed by an adult

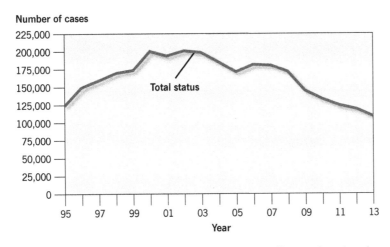

FIGURE 8.2   The Juvenile Court Status Offense Caseloads, 1995–2013   Source: Sarah Hockenberry and Charles Puzzanchera, *Juvenile Court Statistics 2013* (Washington, D.C.: U.S. Department of Justice, 2015), p. 66.

not constitute a separate category of juvenile offenders, states classify them in two other ways. In some states, status offenders are an "incorrigible" subcategory of delinquent children. Other states have moved status offenses from acts of delinquency to the category of dependent children, thereby removing them from the juvenile courts and placing them in a family court or child welfare agency. If the status offense behavior continues, however, the juvenile will be referred to the juvenile court.

As indicated in Figure 8.2, the number of status offenses handled and disposed of by the juvenile courts increased by 61 percent from 1995 until it peaked at over 200,000 in 2002. It then declined by 46 percent by 2013 (the most recent report), when the number of status offenses in the juvenile courts was only 109,000.

As well as the decline in the overall number of status offenses, Table 8.2 indicates a few significant trends in the percentages of each category of status offense cases handled by juvenile courts from 1995 to 2013. The biggest change is in the number of truancy cases resulting in adjudication by the juvenile courts (increasing from 29 percent to 51 percent). In response, runaways dropped from 17 percent to 8 percent, and liquor law violations dropped from 23 percent to 15 percent, and ungovernability declined from 14 percent to 9 percent. Only curfew violations and other miscellaneous offenses remained fairly steady.

TABLE 8.2	Offense Profile of Petitioned Status Offense Cases, 1995, 2004, and 2013		
Most Serious Offense	**1995**	**2004**	**2013**
Total	100%	100%	100%
Running away	17	11	8
Truancy	29	38	51
Curfew violations	10	8	9
Ungovernability	14	11	9
Liquor law violations	23	21	15
Miscellaneous offenses	7	11	8

Sources: Data from Ann L. Stahl, Petitioned, *Status Offense Cases in Juvenile Courts, 2004* (Washington, D.C.: U.S. Department of Justice, Office of Justice Programs, February 2008), p. 1; and Sarah Hockenberry and Charles Puzzanchera, *Juvenile Court Statistics 2013* (Pittsburgh, PA: National Center for Juvenile Justice, 2015), p. 66.

TABLE 8.3	Age of Original Juvenile Court Jurisdiction
Age	**State**
15	New York, North Carolina
16	Connecticut, Georgia, Illinois, Louisiana, Massachusetts, Michigan, Missouri, New Hampshire, South Carolina, Texas, Wisconsin
17	Alabama, Alaska, Arizona, Arkansas, California, Colorado, Delaware, District of Columbia, Florida, Hawaii, Idaho, Indiana, Iowa, Kansas, Kentucky, Maine, Maryland, Minnesota, Mississippi, Montana, Nebraska, Nevada, New Jersey, New Mexico, North Dakota, Ohio, Oklahoma, Oregon, Pennsylvania, Rhode Island, South Dakota, Tennessee, Utah, Vermont, Virginia, Washington, West Virginia, Wyoming

Source: Data from Melissa Sickmund and Charles Puzzanchera, *Juvenile Offenders and Victims: 2014 National Report* (Washington, D.C.: U.S. Department of Justice, Office of Juvenile Justice and Delinquency Prevention, 2014), p. 93.

age of original jurisdiction

the upper or oldest age that a juvenile court will have jurisdiction over categories of offenders

One important factor for each of these offender categories is the **age of original jurisdiction**, the upper or oldest age at which a juvenile court has jurisdiction over categories of offenders (see Table 8.3). Each state defines juveniles by age for the various categories. For status offenses, abuse, neglect, or dependency, the age of original jurisdiction varies and may often go through age twenty. In almost every state, the age of delinquency (for the delinquent category) is under age eighteen at the time of the offense, arrest, or referral to court. However, many states have statutory exceptions to this age criterion and allow exceptions related to the youth's age, alleged offense, and court history. These exceptions (called *statutory exclusions*) can place a youth under the original jurisdiction of the adult criminal court. In other states, these exceptions can place the youth under the original jurisdiction of both the juvenile and criminal courts (called *concurrent jurisdiction*). In concurrent jurisdiction, the prosecutor is given the authority to decide which court will initially handle the case.

By 2000, sixteen states had set an age as the lowest level at which there can be juvenile court jurisdiction over acts of delinquency, because children below that age are presumed incapable of criminal intent. Table 8.4 illustrates these age levels.

TABLE 8.4	Youngest Age for Juvenile Court Jurisdiction over Delinquency Matters
Age	**State**
6	North Carolina
7	Maryland, Massachusetts, New York
8	Arizona
10	Arkansas, Colorado, Kansas, Louisiana, Minnesota, Mississippi. Pennsylvania, South Dakota, Texas, Vermont, Wisconsin

Source: Data from Melissa Sickmund and Charles Puzzanchera, *Juvenile Offenders and Victims: 2014 National Report* (Washington, D.C.: U.S. Department of Justice, Office of Juvenile Justice and Delinquency Prevention, 2014), p. 93.

The Juvenile Justice Process

In many ways, the juvenile justice process is similar to the adult criminal justice process described in Chapter 1. However, as noted in the history of the juvenile justice system, the goals and philosophies in the juvenile justice system differ from those of the criminal justice system. A good example of the differences in the two systems is a comparison of the mission statements of the adult and juvenile correctional agencies in Missouri. The Missouri Department of Corrections states its mission as follows:

> *The Missouri Department of Corrections supervises and provides rehabilitative services to adult offenders in correctional institutions and Missouri communities to enhance public safety.*[13]

The Missouri Department of Social Services, Division of Youth Services lists the following mission statement:

> *The mission of the Division of Youth Services is to enable youth to fulfill their needs in a responsible manner within the context of and with respect for the needs of the family and the community.*[14]

The adult system emphasizes public safety through managing offenders; it mentions supervising and providing rehabilitative services to enhance public safety. This mission gives readers a clear sense of concern about the community as the first priority. The juvenile agency, on the other hand, focuses on enabling youth to fulfill their needs within the context of the family and community. Assessment, care and treatment, and education of youth are seen as the most important functions, and the emphasis in on the youth instead of the community. This example illustrates how most states differentiate their role in dealing with adult criminals versus juvenile delinquents. The language, processes, and steps in each justice process reiterate these differences. In addition, there are several different models of governance for juvenile correctional agencies. From a 2012 survey with forty-nine states responding, in 39 percent of the states, the juvenile agency is a free-standing department within the executive branch of government, 22 percent are a division within child welfare or social service systems, 22 percent are bureaus under human services umbrella systems, and 19 percent are a division within an adult corrections agency.[15]

The juvenile justice process usually begins, just like the adult criminal justice process, with a complaint to the police and a contact between a law enforcement officer and the offender. Table 8.5 illustrates a comparison of the juvenile and the adult criminal justice systems while highlighting the common ground that exists between them.

Steps in the Juvenile Justice Process

As with adults, juveniles begin their entry into or contact with the justice system with a contact with law enforcement, with an investigation after a complaint has been filed that leads to a juvenile as a suspect of a crime, or through police witnessing activity that they believe to be a crime or act of delinquency. However, juveniles can also come into contact with the justice system through

TABLE 8.5	Comparison of Adult and Juvenile Justice Processing	
Juvenile justice system	**Common ground**	**Criminal justice system**
Operating Assumptions		
• Youth behavior is malleable. • Rehabilitation is usually a viable goal. • Youth are in families and not independent.	• Community protection is a primary goal. • Law violators must be held accountable. • Constitutional rights apply.	• Sanctions should be proportional to the offense. • General deterrence works. • Rehabilitation is not a primary goal.
Prevention		
• Many specific delinquency prevention activities (e.g., school, church, recreation) are used. • Prevention is intended to change individual behavior and is often focused on reducing risk factors and increasing protective factors in the individual, family, and community.	• Educational approaches are taken to specific behaviors (drunk driving, drug use).	• Prevention activities are generalized and aimed at deterrence (e.g., Crime Watch).
Law Enforcement		
• Specialized "juvenile" units are used. • Some additional behaviors are prohibited (truancy, running away, curfew violations). • Some limitations are placed on public access to information. • A significant number of youth are diverted away from the juvenile justice system, often into alternative programs.	• Jurisdiction involves the full range of criminal behavior. • Constitutional and procedural safeguards exist. • Both reactive and proactive approaches (targeted at offense types, neighborhoods, etc.) are used. • Community policing strategies are employed.	• Open public access to all information is required. • Law enforcement exercises discretion to divert offenders out of the criminal justice system.
Intake–Prosecution		
• In many instances, juvenile court intake, not the prosecutor, decides what cases to file. • The decision to file a petition for court action is based on both social and legal factors. • A significant portion of cases is diverted from formal case processing. • Intake or the prosecutor diverts cases from formal processing to services operated by the juvenile court, prosecutor's office, or outside agencies.	• Probable cause must be established. • The prosecutor acts on behalf of the state.	• Plea bargaining is common. • The prosecution decision is based largely on legal facts. • Prosecution is valuable in building history for subsequent offenses. • Prosecution exercises discretion to withhold charges or divert offenders out of the criminal justice system.

(Continued)

TABLE 8.5	(Continued)	
Juvenile justice system	**Common ground**	**Criminal justice system**
Detention–Jail/Lockup		
• Juveniles may be detained for their own protection or the community's protection. • Juveniles may not be confined with adults unless there is "sight and sound separation."	• Accused offenders may be held in custody to ensure their appearance in court. • Detention alternatives of home or electronic detention are used.	• Accused individuals have the right to apply for bond/bail release.
Adjudication–Conviction		
• Juvenile court proceedings are "quasi-civil" (not criminal) and may be confidential. • If guilt is established, the youth is adjudicated delinquent regardless of offense. • Right to jury trial is not afforded in all states.	• Standard of "proof beyond a reasonable doubt" is required. • Rights to be represented by an attorney, to confront witnesses, and to remain silent are afforded. • Appeals to a higher court are allowed. • Experimentation with specialized courts (i.e., drug courts, gun).	• Defendants have a constitutional right to a jury trial. • Guilt must be established on individual offenses charged for conviction. • All proceedings are open.
Disposition–Sentencing		
• Disposition decisions are based on individual and social factors, offense severity, and youth's offense history. • Dispositional philosophy includes a significant rehabilitation component. • Many dispositional alternatives are operated by the juvenile court. • Dispositions cover a wide range of community-based and residential services. • Disposition orders may be directed to people other than the offender (e.g., parents). • Disposition may be indeterminate, based on progress demonstrated by the youth.	• Decisions are influenced by current offense, offending history, and social factors. • Decisions hold offenders accountable. • Decisions may give consideration to victims (e.g., restitution and "no contact" orders). • Decisions may not be cruel or unusual.	• Sentencing decisions are bound primarily by the severity of the current offense and by the offender's criminal history. • Sentencing philosophy is based largely on proportionality and punishment. • Sentence is often determinate, based on offense.
Aftercare–Parole		
• Function combines surveillance and reintegration activities (e.g., family, school, work).	• The behavior of individuals released from correctional settings is monitored. • Violation of conditions can result in reincarceration.	• Function is primarily surveillance and reporting to monitor illicit behavior.

Source: Howard N. Snyder and Melissa Sickmund, *Juvenile Offenders and Victims: 1999 National Report* (Washington, D.C.: U.S. Department of Justice, National Center for Juvenile Justice, September 1999), pp. 94–96.

referrals by parents, school officials, or other citizens. In 2013, courts with juvenile jurisdictions handled 1,058,500 delinquency cases, of which law enforcement personnel were the source of 82 percent of delinquency referrals to juvenile court.[16] The police are more likely to divert juvenile offenders or handle them informally than to do so with an adult. It is estimated that approximately one-fourth of juveniles arrested for delinquency are handled informally and released by the police, and about two-thirds of arrests result in referral to the juvenile court.[17] Figure 8.3 is a simplified diagram of the process by which a case travels through the juvenile justice system, although the steps vary from state to state.

Once a juvenile comes in contact with the police, he or she may be detained for a short time to contact a parent or guardian or while awaiting transfer to a juvenile facility. **Juvenile detention**, as defined by the National Council of Crime and Delinquency, is the temporary care of children in physically restricted facilities pending court disposition or transfer to another jurisdiction or agency.[18] In general, juveniles will be detained if they are believed to be a threat to the community, are at risk in the community, may fail to appear for future processing, or if there is a need for an assessment or evaluation of the juvenile. While almost all juveniles arrested for a serious crime against person are detained, only a little more than 20 percent of all cases result in detention.[19] Juveniles detained must be separated from adult offenders and must have a detention hearing within a few days (usually within twenty-four

juvenile detention

the temporary care of children in physically restricted facilities pending court disposition or transfer to another jurisdiction or agency

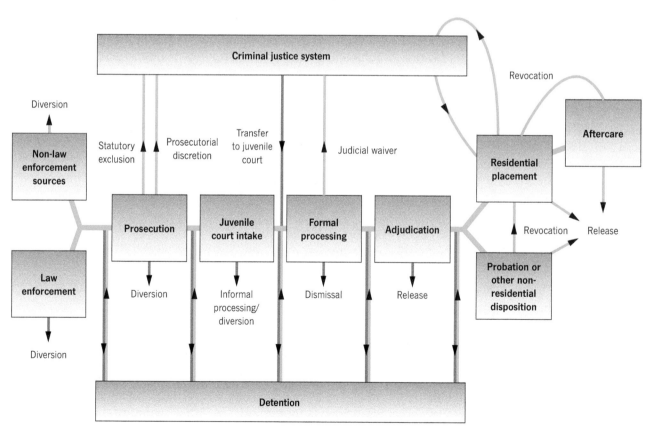

Note: This chart gives a simplified view of case flow through the juvenile justice system. Procedures vary among jurisdictions.

FIGURE 8.3   Stages in the Juvenile Justice Process   Source: Melissa Sickmund and Charles Puzzanchera, *Juveniles and Victims: 2014 National Report* (Washington, D.C.: U.S. Department of Justice, 20014), p. 95.

hours). For serious crimes when juveniles are likely to be charged as an adult, they may be placed in an adult jail. There were 9,500 inmates under the age of 18 in adult jails in 1999. Since then, the number has declined, and was 7,600 in 2010.[20]

The next step in the juvenile justice process is **intake**, carried out by the juvenile probation department or prosecutor's office to determine whether the case should be dismissed, handled informally, or referred to the juvenile court. The purpose of this step is to determine whether sufficient evidence exists to formally process the allegation. At this point, approximately 45 percent of cases are diverted, dismissed, or otherwise handled informally; the other 55 percent are petitioned and continue in a formal manner.[21] With informal handling, the case is often concluded with a **consent decree**, whereby the delinquent juvenile must admit to wrongdoing and agree to specific conditions of behavior (similar to pretrial diversion for adult offenders). This stage is sometimes referred to as *informal probation*. If the juvenile meets all the conditions of the consent decree, the case is dismissed and there is no formal record of delinquent action.

If during intake the determination is to handle the case formally, or the case was originally handled informally and the juvenile does not meet the consent decree conditions, it will be formally handled and a **referral** will be made to the juvenile court. The referral is similar to charging an adult offender with a crime. In the referral, a **delinquency petition** (similar to an indictment for adults) states the delinquent acts the juvenile is alleged to have committed and asks the juvenile court to **adjudicate** (or find the juvenile guilty of the delinquent act) and make the juvenile a ward of the court. A hearing is then scheduled, facts are presented, witnesses may be called, and the court determines whether the juvenile is responsible for the delinquent act. Juveniles do not universally have a right to a hearing before a jury, as do adult felons, yet a few states allow a jury to hear the case.

If the juvenile is found responsible for the delinquent act, the judge must determine what sanction or **order** (similar to the sentence for an adult) should apply. The primary orders for juveniles are for either probation or out-of-home residential placement. In 2013, it was estimated to be 1,058,500 juvenile cases that came to the attention of the juvenile court. As illustrated in Figure 8.4, of this total, 55 percent (582,800) were petitioned or handled formally, and of those, 55 percent (323,300) of juveniles were adjudicated delinquent. The majority (64 percent) received probation and 78,700 (24 percent) were placed outside the home. This number of out-of-home placement was the lowest since 1985. Another 39,900 (12 percent) received another sanction, such as paying restitution or a fine, participating in community service, or entering a treatment or counseling program. Only 4,000 (1 percent) of the cases were waived to the adult courts.

For the past few years, the percentage of the cases receiving probation as the most severe sanction ordered has been fairly consistent. Juvenile probation is similar to adult probation in that there are conditions of supervision and the probation officer plays a dual role of finding appropriate treatment resources and monitoring the juvenile for compliance with conditions. In addition to the types of conditions for adults noted in Chapter 4, juveniles on probation are also required to obey their parents or guardians, attend school regularly, be home at an early hour in the evening, and avoid disreputable companions or other persons on probation.[22] Although adult probation agencies have moved toward a greater emphasis on monitoring compliance, juvenile agencies still primarily focus on rehabilitating

intake
determination if a juvenile case should be dismissed, handled informally, or referred to the juvenile court

consent decree
an informal handling of a juvenile justice case, in which the delinquent juvenile admits to wrongdoing and agrees to specific conditions of behavior; sometimes called informal probation

referral
the formal processing of a juvenile offense through the juvenile court

delinquency petition
a statement of the delinquent acts a juvenile is alleged to have committed; similar to an indictment for adults

adjudicate
to find a juvenile guilty of a delinquent act

order
the sanction for a juvenile found delinquent by juvenile court; similar to the sentence for an adult

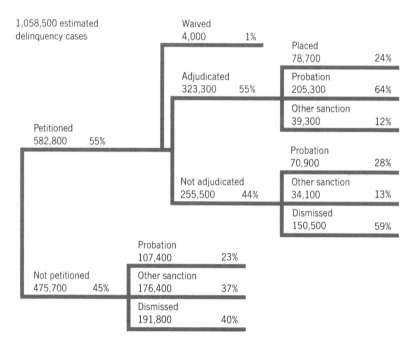

1,058,500 estimated delinquency cases

Waived 4,000 — 1%

Petitioned 582,800 — 55%

Adjudicated 323,300 — 55%

Placed 78,700 — 24%

Probation 205,300 — 64%

Other sanction 39,300 — 12%

Not adjudicated 255,500 — 44%

Probation 70,900 — 28%

Other sanction 34,100 — 13%

Dismissed 150,500 — 59%

Not petitioned 475,700 — 45%

Probation 107,400 — 23%

Other sanction 176,400 — 37%

Dismissed 191,800 — 40%

FIGURE 8.4   Juvenile Case Processing Overview, 2013   Source: Sarah Hockenberry and Charles Puzzanchera, *Juvenile Court Statistics 2013* (Pittsburgh, PA: National Center for Juvenile Justice, 2015), p. 52.

delinquents. The juvenile justice system has very few intermediate sanctions between probation and incarceration, but many jurisdictions have initiated intensive probation supervision programs that are operated very much like such programs for adults.

If the juvenile is not granted probation, the judge may elect to remove the offender from the community and place him or her under the supervision of the state department of youth services. As noted in Figure 8.4, in approximately one in four cases, the court ordered juveniles to out-of-home residential placement such as training school, boot camp, drug treatment, a group home, or some other correctional facility. These residential placements may be in a secure correctional facility (such as a training school or reform school) or a nonsecure group home, depending on the severity of the act and the background of the juvenile. In some states, the sanction is for an open-ended period of time (indeterminate sentence), and the decision to release is the responsibility of the department of youth services. In other states, the judge sanctions the juvenile for a set period of time (determinate sentence) until release back to the community. What is interesting is that out-of-home placement seems not to be a function of the severity of offense, but more likely the situation (past problems, home environment) of the juvenile. Of the 78,700 out-of-home placements in 2013, 29 percent were for person, 33 percent for property, 8 percent for drug, and 31 percent for public order offenses.[23]

aftercare

supervision of a juvenile in the community after serving time in a juvenile correctional institution; similar to parole for adults

After release, the juvenile is on **aftercare** supervision, much like adult parole, with specific conditions that must be followed. If these conditions are not met, the juvenile may be returned to the residential placement or placed in a more secure facility to serve additional time. The process for juveniles is similar to the adult criminal justice system. However, the terminology is distinct. Table 8.6 compares the terminology used in the juvenile and adult justice systems.

The juvenile justice process provides the opportunity for many career choices, including detention staff, juvenile court workers, probation and aftercare staff, and social service staff that works in juvenile correctional institutions. The "Your Career in Corrections" box describes the work of juvenile social service workers.

TABLE 8.6	Terminology in the Juvenile and Adult Justice Systems	
Juvenile justice system	**Activity**	**Adult justice system**
Delinquent	Violator of laws	Offender
Detention	Holding offenders by police	Arrest
Intake	Determination to handle case	Preliminary hearing
Consent decree	Informal handling with conditions	Pretrial diversion
Referred to court	Formal processing by the court	Charges filed
Delinquency petition	Statement of the allegations	Indictment
Respondent	Individual alleged guilty	Defendant
Adjudicate	Find responsible for act	Convict
Hearing	Review of factual issues	Trial
Responsible	Committed the act	Guilty
Order	Court determination of sanction	Sentence
Probation	Supervision in the community	Probation
Commitment	Placed in a correctional facility	Incarcerated
Resident or youth	Institutionalized individual	Inmate
Residential placement	Correctional facility	Prison
Superintendent	Title of facility administrator	Warden
Aftercare	Supervision after release	Parole

▷ Your Career in Corrections

Juvenile Social Service Workers

Juvenile social service workers are staff members who work in juvenile correctional institutions. In many agencies, these individuals fill a dual role of case managers and correctional officers in adult prisons. They usually supervise delinquents, develop treatment plans, and help them prepare for release. Until the 1950s, most juvenile institutions had "house parents" who lived in the institution housing complex with the delinquents and acted as parents would in counseling, guiding, rewarding, and punishing the residents under their care. Today, the role is much more professional, usually requiring a two- or four-year college degree, some training in counseling, and much more adherence to policy rather than individual discretion. In juvenile agencies that have moved more toward the "adultification" of juvenile corrections, there may be a separation of the two roles, and positions of juvenile correctional officers (who focus more on security) and juvenile social workers (who plan programs and counsel youth) both exist.

Juvenile social service workers have challenging yet rewarding jobs. First, even when there are correctional officers to do some of the purely security functions, they must still be sensitive to security issues and maintain control and order of residents. However, they also are often responsible for counseling and program planning for residents and therefore have to play a dual role of case manager. Much of their work in this regard consists of creating a responsible living environment with the other residents of the housing unit. An important part of the management of juvenile correctional facilities is the "governing" of the housing unit. Social service workers direct and mentor residents in how to get along with one another and how to work together to reach the unit's goals of sanitation, positive program participation, and good behavior on the part of all residents. Many juvenile facilities use some type of group behavior modification program in which the housing unit as a group receives or loses privileges based on the group's performance.

Juvenile social service worker jobs can be stressful as well. It is difficult to work with sixteen- to eighteen-year-old offenders who do not have a history of responsible behavior or self-control and may resort to violence as a way to get what they want. These positions are entry level and the pay is usually fairly low. However, these are excellent positions in which to learn how to deal with youthful offenders and use personal communication skills to gain compliance and positively influence behavior. From these positions, there are also opportunities for promotion to midlevel management positions throughout the juvenile justice system.

Juvenile Residential Facilities

Juvenile residential facilities are similar to prisons for adult offenders, holding mainly those youths found delinquent and receiving an order of commitment. When juvenile offenders are placed under the residential supervision of a state department of youth services, they usually are temporarily sent to a reception and diagnostic center. At these centers, juveniles receive psychological, educational, and risk assessments to determine the type of facility to which they should be assigned. After a period of processing at the reception centers, they are placed in a long-term confinement facility, often called a training or reform school.

The number of juveniles in residential placement has been declining since 1999, when the number of residential placements peaked at over 109,000. By 2013, the number of residential placements had decreased by 50 percent, and there were only 54,148 juveniles confined in 1,947 public and privately operated facilities across the United States.[24] Most (89 percent) juvenile offenders in long-term confinement are held for juvenile delinquency offenses that would be criminal law violations for adults, and status offenders account for only 4 percent of all residents. Juvenile placements use both public and privately operated facilities, as 68 percent of juvenile placements are in public facilities.[25] Male delinquents make up 86 percent of the residential placement population, and females the other 14 percent.[26]

Since 2000, issues of overcrowding and poor services in facilities forced a change in approach. Austin and colleagues identified that crowding results in dangerous conditions that make facility management difficult, can be detrimental to rehabilitation and treatment of youth, and creates logistical problems such as how to feed, deliver health care, and find places for youth to sleep.[27] Placing delinquents in a residential facility is now usually the last resort, as a common belief is that the most effective interventions come about in the local community, and more money has been channeled for the implementation of community-based programs. A national model is the Ohio Department of Youth Services (DYS) creation in 2003 of RECLAIM Ohio (Reasoned and Equitable Community and Local Alternative to the Incarceration of Minors). RECLAIM is an initiative to reduce the residential population by providing funding to the local level to encourage juvenile courts to develop or contract for a range of community-based options for juvenile offenders that would keep them in the community and avoid incarceration in state juvenile facilities. The "An Interview With" box talks with the then-director of DYS and explains the program.

Juvenile facilities are similar to adult prisons in that security must be the primary emphasis in the medium- and higher-security facilities. No matter what the philosophy of the juvenile agency (more security and punishment versus a focus on developing the youth), there cannot be violence or escapes without the agency losing credibility. However, in juvenile facilities, programs, and development of residents are very important. In most of these facilities, education is the predominant feature of the day's activities, as most juveniles have not completed high school. Although some facilities follow the adult model and offer a general educational development (GED) program, a more common model is of a formal (often year round) school system with middle and high schools looking very much like small schools in the community. Many juvenile residents need special education, and state and federal mandates require individual education plans (IEPs) as a guide to their education program. These IEPs can cause great

An Interview With . . .

The Creator of the RECLAIM Ohio Plan

Geno Natalucci-Persichetti
Courtesy of Gino N. Persichetti

Geno Natalucci-Persichetti had a long history in corrections, beginning his career as a social worker in an adult prison in 1967, working from 1970 to 1973 as a parole officer and supervisor, becoming the director of a halfway house for twelve years, heading up parole and community services for an adult correctional system, and then serving as director of the Ohio Department of Youth Services from 1987 to 2005. Director Geno (he preferred this informal title) is credited with starting a program for diverting youthful offenders from juvenile institutions that has been copied in several states.

Question: What was the impetus for starting RECLAIM Ohio?

Director Geno: Overcrowding was the impetus for us to look at creating a new incentive program. We (DYS) were a "free good" in an economic sense for the juvenile courts. There was no incentive or disincentive for the courts to not send kids convicted of a felony delinquency to DYS. By the summer of 2003, DYS had over 2,600 youth in facilities that had rated bed capacity of around 1,400. Creating RECLAIM gave the courts an incentive (a subsidy for keeping kids in the local community and money to create programs to divert these delinquent youth to local programs).

We began by researching what types of subsidy programs have worked in the past. We went as far back as the first "probation subsidy program" that started in California in the 1970s. We tried to develop incentives for local counties to create programs to monitor and treat offenders in the community, rather than sentencing them to a state facility. We used a formula based on the number of adjudications counties had for the total state courts. Counties would get a percent of the local subsidy budget based on the overall share of the total percent of juveniles adjudicated for felony offenses. After the county got its share of the money, it would go into a checking account they held. For each juvenile sent to a state institution, 75 percent of the per diem cost of the state facility was deducted from the checking account. In this way, the counties could send as many juveniles as they felt necessary, and they had money to

create diversion programs they thought were right for their community.

One component of RECLAIM that we learned of by looking at other subsidy programs was the "public safety bed" concept. To ensure that a court would not waive a juvenile to the adult court because the nature of the offense was a public safety risk (for example, robbery, rape, or manslaughter) and required lengthy incarceration, RECLAIM legislation allowed the court to send the youth to DYS at no cost or no deduction of their subsidy funding.

Question: What are some examples of how the counties set up their diversion programs?

Director Geno: They did everything from developing alternative schools, expanding drug treatment programs, creating mental health programs, and using intensive probation programs, electronic monitoring, and day treatment programs. They could use their money for almost anything other than construction of new beds. We encouraged them to look at the "what works" literature and implement programs that have proved most effective in reducing future criminal behavior among youthful offenders.

Question: How were these programs received by the local counties?

Director Geno: When we first started, the judges were very skeptical. Lt. Governor Mike DeWine invited many of the juvenile court judges to the statehouse, where we all met in the governor's cabinet room. Lt. Governor DeWine encouraged them to trust the process and give it a try. Before RECLAIM, every time I went before a legislative budget committee, it was always "DYS against the judges." They wanted money to fund their pet programs, but with no accountability for how it was spent. I would give my budget presentation, and then the judges followed me and made their own budget presentation. The Ohio General Assembly, being fellow elected officials, made a big show of the judges being there. After RECLAIM, however, the judges and DYS had the best relationship of any state in the country. The judges and department met monthly, they were involved in our strategic planning, and they helped redesign the formula for RECLAIM funding as money got tight and we had to reduce the overall funding for the juvenile justice system. By then, the judges joined me for a budget presentation, and they supported our budget and the RECLAIM portion. In 2004, we were going through another round of budget cuts. I called some of the judges

(Continued)

and told them I needed their help, because I believed these cuts would go too deep. Approximately twenty judges joined me at a Senate hearing, and we told them that some of the money the House cut had to be restored because it would seriously hamper our operation. It was somewhat funny, because when the hearing first started, the vice-chair was chairing the committee. One of the judges had each of the other nineteen judges stand up and introduce themselves. The vice-chair sent word to the chair and all others members to get up to the hearing because of all the judges there. Once they all arrived, there was another round of introductions, the judges received a standing ovation, and all the money originally cut was restored.

Question: How has the program affected the juvenile facilities in Ohio?

Director Geno: When we kicked it off in 1993, there were 2,600 juveniles incarcerated in facilities terribly overcrowded with a rated capacity of 1,400. We were out of bed space and needed a way to avoid building more institutions. As a result of RECLAIM, there are only about 1,700 juveniles now confined in state facilities. This is in a state that has a population of 11.3 million people. We had been second to California in the rate of incarceration of juvenile offenders, and now Ohio is sixth in the rate of incarceration. Note: this population decline has continued, and on September 1, 2017, there were only

505 juveniles in residential placement (437 in juvenile correctional facilities and 68 in alternative placements).[28] And DYS supervises 284 juveniles on parole. In addition to residential placement and parole, DYS funds and supports 664 community programs that serve 88,000 youth per year though the RECLAIM program.

Question: Have there been any studies of the effectiveness of RECLAIM Ohio?

Director Geno: The University of Cincinnati has done two studies and confirmed there has been a reduction in the number of commitments to state facilities. Also, findings were that youth sent to DYS facilities had a lower success rate than comparable offenders maintained in the community under RECLAIM programs.

Question: Has there been interest from other states?

Director Geno: Yes, there has, and we received a Ford Foundation grant to train twenty other states. Each state has done something a little different, but the principle of subsidizing the counties for diverting and keeping juvenile delinquents locally is the basis of most. At this point, RECLAIM Ohio is the longest running subsidy program in the nation. Students can go to the DYS website at www.dys.ohio.gov to find out more about it.[29]

Although the rate of incarceration for juvenile offenders is much lower than that for adults, the institutions are similar.
Rob Carr/AP Images

difficulty to complete when the juvenile is disruptive or even violent in the classroom or education setting. Vocational training is also important, and most facilities offer extensive programs in a variety of skills that can lead to employment after release. Drug and substance abuse programs are also provided in almost every facility, and recreation and religious instruction are also available on a voluntary basis.

Juvenile Offenders in the Community

As noted above, the past two decades have seen a movement to "de-institutionalize" juveniles by putting more resources in the community and using community alternatives to incarceration. A report by Youth Advocate Programs suggests, "Virtually anything that can be done in an institution can be done better in the community."[30] Community alternatives can be used both at the front end of the system as an alternative to out-of-home placement, or at the back end as aftercare to improve the chance of successful reentry to the community. Community alternatives can provide residential care if necessary on a short-term basis, treatment programs to address the underlying causes of delinquency, or community supervision approaches. As with the Ohio RECLAIM program, funds were transferred from institutional to community care. The average cost of keeping a youth incarcerated averaged $240 per day in 2008, and some states spent as much as $667 per day.[31] Reports from several states have identified savings of from $50 million to over $300 million by redirecting juveniles to community rather than residential placement.[32]

How do jurisdictions develop their strategies for moving from a residential to a community supervision approach? Many jurisdictions begin with principles that have proven effective. These include:

1. Juvenile incarceration and residential placement are expensive and ineffective—studies have shown no correlation between juvenile incarceration rates and crime.
2. Use the "risk principle" that supervision and treatment should be correlated with the risk to reoffend—studies have shown that correctional interventions are more effective with higher risk offenders.
3. Using accurate and valid risk-assessment instruments provide the foundation for cost saving alternatives—most states are using risk assessment instruments and their use has proven predictive of behavior.[33]

As well, the National Council of Crime and Delinquency surveyed several jurisdictions and identified very similar common strategies that both redirect youth and save money. In addition to the above, they also noted the importance of partnering with families and community service providers in developing supervision plans for juveniles.[34]

Most juvenile offenders receive a disposition of probation. The Office of Juvenile Justice and Delinquency Prevention identified that of the more than 1 million cases handled by juvenile jurisdictions in 2010, probation was the most likely disposition (61 percent), residential placement was 26 percent, and 13 percent were other sanctions.[35] Juvenile probation is much like adult probation described in Chapter 4. However, in the juvenile system, probation can either be court ordered or voluntary (all court ordered with adults). Some youth who are not adjudicated delinquent voluntarily agree to probation supervision and conditions, somewhat as a diversionary approach, and if they successfully complete their probationary period, their case will be terminated with no formal processing.

Community placement is more cost effective than residential placement out of the family home. A recent study found that community supervision is an effective alternative to residential services. And delaying delinquency (not jumping to the formal juvenile justice process) and increasing families' ability to work with youth who are misbehaving has been shown to reduce the likelihood of escalation through the juvenile justice system.[36] So far, the juvenile justice system has moved aggressively to reduce the intensity of supervision, save money, and reduce reoffending through these approaches, and their progress has been applauded by many.[37] While the adult system is just now "testing these waters," it is hopeful that the juvenile justice success will serve as a model for what is also possible in the adult system.

Legal Issues Affecting the Juvenile Justice System

As in adult correctional systems, federal courts had little involvement in the operation of juvenile correctional agencies until the 1960s. The first major case reviewed by the U.S. Supreme Court was *Kent v. United States* in 1966. In this case, a sixteen-year-old was charged with rape and robbery and the juvenile court waived jurisdiction to the adult court. The juvenile received a sentence of thirty to ninety years in prison as an adult. The Supreme Court acceptance of the case was the first challenge to the *parens patriae* foundation of the juvenile justice system, in that juveniles charged with offenses should not receive less due process just because the system has a greater concern for juveniles and provides a "compensating benefit." The Court ruled that juveniles must have "the essentials of due process," including the right to notice of the charges in time to prepare for trial, the right to counsel, the right to confront and cross-examine accusers, and the privilege against self-incrimination.[38]

In re Gault

a 1967 U.S. Supreme Court case requiring that, in hearings in which a juvenile may be committed to an institution, they must have the right to counsel, to notice of the charges against them, to question witnesses, and to protection against self-incrimination

The next year (1967), the Court accepted and decided **In re Gault**. Gerald Gault, a sixteen-year-old on probation, called a neighbor and made some obscene remarks. Gault did not attend the adjudication hearing and was committed to a juvenile training school for the period of his minority (to age eighteen). If he had been an adult, this act would have been a misdemeanor punishable by a small fine and a two-month jail sentence. The Court rejected the doctrine of *parens patriae* as giving the juvenile court unbridled discretion and required that, in hearings in which juveniles may be committed to an institution, they must have the right to counsel, to notice of the charges against them, to question witnesses, and to protection against self-incrimination.[39]

In the 1970 case of *In re Winship*, the 1971 case of *McKeiver v. Pennsylvania*, and the 1975 case of *Breed v. Jones*, the U.S. Supreme Court further clarified the due process rights of juveniles. In *Winship*, the Court determined that a finding of guilt for juveniles required more than just a preponderance of the evidence, but had to meet the adult standard of *beyond a reasonable doubt*.[40] In *McKeiver*, the Court did not further expand due process provided to juveniles, deciding that jury trials are not a requirement in juvenile courts.[41] In *Breed*, the Court found that waiver to an adult court after an adjudication hearing in juvenile court constitutes double jeopardy.[42] And soon thereafter, two cases dealt with freedom of the press and juvenile right to privacy. In *Oklahoma Publishing Company v. District Court in and for Oklahoma City*, the Court allowed a photograph of a juvenile involved in a court proceeding to be published.[43] And similarly, in *Smith v. Daily Mail Publishing Company*, the Court confirmed that if legally obtained, the media may publish a juvenile defendant's name.[44]

In two later cases, the U.S. Supreme Court indicated that it had perhaps taken the expansion of due process rights for juveniles to a conclusion. In *Fare v. Michael C.* (1979), the Court affirmed the conviction of murder of a juvenile who claimed he had asserted his right to remain silent. Michael C. was arrested for murder and, when advised of his *Miranda* rights, he asked to see his probation officer. The police said the officer would be contacted later, and Michael could talk to the officer then if he desired. The Court ruled that asking for a probation officer is not the same as asking for a lawyer or asserting the right to remain silent.[45] In *Schall v. Martin* (1984), the Supreme Court upheld the use of preventive detention pending trial for juveniles, stating that the protection of both the juvenile and society from pretrial crimes is not intended to punish the juvenile.[46] In addition, the Court did not rule out the importance of *parens patriae* and reasserted the interest of the state in promoting the welfare of children.

In addition to addressing the due process rights of juveniles, the Supreme Court has also addressed the use of the death penalty for juvenile offenders. In 1982, the Court decided *Eddings v. Oklahoma*, declaring that the youthful age of a defendant should be considered a mitigating factor in deciding whether to apply the death penalty during the penalty phase of a capital punishment trial.[47] In *Sanford v. Kentucky* (1989), the Court determined that the minimum age at which a juvenile could receive the death penalty is sixteen.[48] In 2002, the Court refused to accept and hear the case of *In re Sanford*, which asked the Court to again address the issue of capital punishment for juveniles.[49] On January 27, 2003, the Court again declined to accept a case to reconsider the death penalty for Scott Allen Hain, an Oklahoma offender who was seventeen at the time of his crime. Four justices believed that executing juveniles for murder was unconstitutional, as Justices Stevens, Souter, Ginsburg, and Breyer issued a statement that "the practice of executing such offenders is a relic of the past and is inconsistent with evolving standards of decency."[50]

In October 2004, the U.S. Supreme Court heard the case of *Roper v. Simmons*, and on March 1, 2005, the Court, by a 5–4 vote, held "the Eighth and Fourteenth Amendments forbid the imposition of the death penalty on offenders who are under the age of eighteen when their crimes were committed."[51] The Court believed that, because of a lack of maturity and an underdeveloped sense of responsibility, juveniles are vulnerable and susceptible to negative influences and outside pressures, and their character is not as well formed as that of an adult. With this ruling, the Court removed seventy-two juveniles in twelve states from death row, substituted life in prison for execution, and disallowed the death penalty for juvenile offenders. In 2010, in *Graham v. Florida*, the high court banned life without parole for young people whose crimes did not include homicide.[52] Terrance Graham had been convicted of armed robbery at age sixteen, served a twelve-month sentence, and was convicted of armed home robbery six months after release and sentenced to life in prison without parole. The U.S. Supreme Court in this case determined that the imposition of a life sentence without parole on a juvenile convicted of a non-homicide offense violates the Eighth Amendment prohibition of cruel and unusual punishment.

Two cases decided in June of 2012 (*Miller v. Alabama* and *Jackson v. Hobbs*)[53] by the U.S. Supreme Court clarified the issue of whether it is cruel and unusual punishment for young teenagers convicted of killing someone to be locked up for life with no chance of parole. Before *Miller v. Alabama*, twenty-nine states had statutes requiring life without parole for juveniles convicted of murder. In this case, fourteen-year-old Evan Miller beat a man and set fire to his home. In *Jackson v. Hobbs*, fourteen-year-old Kuntrell Jackson in Arkansas was a part of an attempted robbery and a store clerk was killed, although Jackson did not himself shoot the clerk. The Court ruled that the Eighth Amendment prohibits a sentencing scheme that requires life in prison without the possibility of parole for juvenile homicide offenders. At the time of the decision, there were approximately 2,300 people serving life with no chance of parole for crimes they committed before their eighteen birthday. These offenders would be granted an opportunity for resentencing for something other than their original "death-in-prison" sentence.[54] States have now modified their sentencing statutes around these decisions. Figure 8.5 is a good overview of the U.S. Supreme Court decisions regarding juvenile offenders.

As a result of the active role the Supreme Court played in defining the due process rights of juveniles, there is now little difference in the procedural due process requirements between the juvenile and adult justice systems. Juveniles have the right to notice of charges against them, the right to counsel, the right to confront and cross-examine witnesses, the right to avoid self-incrimination, the right to a judicial hearing with full consideration of their individual case before transfer to adult court, and the right to the standard of *beyond a reasonable doubt* to be found responsible for a delinquent act. While *parens patriae* as a foundation of the juvenile court is not applicable as open discretion for actions by the court, the recognition that the court is to act in the best interests of the juvenile is still acknowledged.

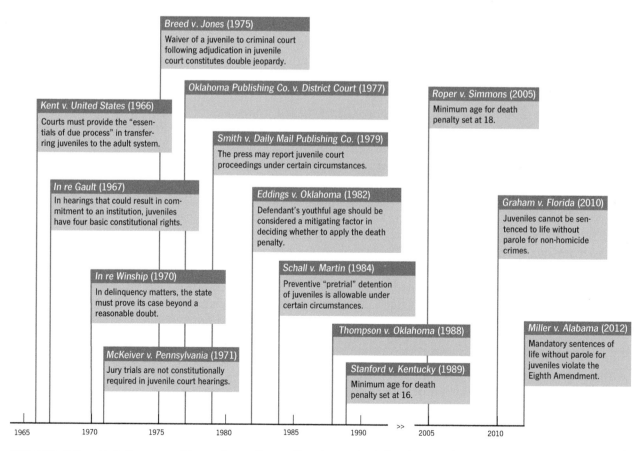

FIGURE 8.5   U.S. Supreme Court Cases Regarding Juvenile Offenders and Courts   Source: *Juvenile Offenders and Victims: 2014 National Report* (Pittsburgh, PA: National Center for Juvenile Justice, 2014), p. 90.

Issues in Juvenile Corrections

Many aspects of the juvenile justice system are similar to those of the adult criminal justice system. These include the role played by juvenile gangs in street crime and the continued influence of these gangs within juvenile correctional institutions. Additionally, a major concern within the juvenile justice system is how to break the cycle of juvenile substance abuse and involvement in drug crimes. Juvenile justice administrators and policymakers attempt to look into the future to determine what new issues will confront juvenile corrections and create new approaches to effectively deal with these issues.

Juvenile Gangs and Juvenile Crime

Over the past twenty-five years there has been a proliferation of juvenile gangs in most large inner cities, and research indicates that gang membership intensifies delinquent behavior. From the earliest to the most recent investigations, criminologists have consistently found that, when compared to youth who do not belong to gangs, gang members are far more involved in delinquency, especially serious and violent delinquency.[55] Gang activities create a fear and perception of danger among most citizens regarding inner-city youth, make neighborhoods unsafe, and prompt a reaction by police to intensify patrolling and arrests of juveniles not only for delinquent acts, but also for loitering and other status offenses.

Juvenile gangs are defined as groups of adolescents or young adults who see themselves as a group and have been involved in enough crime to be of considerable concern to law enforcement and the community.[56] Since 1995, the National Youth Gang Center has gathered annual data from law enforcement agencies from all states about youth gangs. The 2012 survey results show that there were approximately 850,000 gang members from 30,700 active gangs in the United States, indicating a continual increase over the past several years.[57] Most gangs are formed within racial or ethnic groups; law enforcement agencies report gang membership as approximately 35 percent African American and 46 percent Hispanic. Males make up about 92.6 percent of gang membership, and male members commit most gang crime.[58] Gangs are very chauvinistic, and although many male gangs have female auxiliaries, only a few allow female members. Interestingly, new gangs are forming in smaller, more rural communities.

> **juvenile gangs**
> groups of adolescents or young adults who see themselves as a group and have been involved in enough crime to be of considerable concern to law enforcement and the community

Gangs get involved in criminal activities to make money, to intimidate others and protect their turf, and as a part of the structure and role of members. Most gang violence results from their involvement in drug sales, but gangs are regularly involved in all types of index crimes. Survey results for 2012 indicate that youth gang-related homicides increased by 20 percent over the past five-year averages.[59] Gangs have a definite organizational structure. Individuals involved with gangs on a continued and long-term basis are *core members* and are the gang members most regularly involved in crime and violent acts. Some core members are regular or associate members, who actively participate in the gang, and others are fringe members, who are less involved in the gang activities and its criminal acts. The average age of arrested gang members is seventeen or eighteen. The younger individuals who want to join the gang are called "wannabe's," or those being recruited for membership.

Law enforcement officials attempt to control gang activity through suppression and social programs. Sixty-four percent of reporting law enforcement agencies have specialized gang units.[60] These units collect intelligence regarding gang members, their activities, their areas of operation, and their historical activities. Police then target their areas of operation and attempt to disrupt the gang's activities by

Juvenile and adult gangs like to "mark" their territory, warning other gangs to stay away and informing local residents that the gang is in control of the area. Photo by Jeffrey J. Rojek.

patrolling and arresting gang members for loitering, curfew violations, or any crime that can get them off the streets. In addition, some cities have passed ordinances against gang-like activities, and gang members can be arrested and imprisoned for simply hanging out with the gang and violating the ordinances.[61]

Another approach to reduce gang activities is through social programs. In-school education programs inform students of the dangers of gang involvement and how to avoid being forced to enter a gang. One such program is the Gang Resistance Education and Training (GREAT). This evidence-based program has been found effective in discouraging youths from joining gangs.[62] Some of these education programs also provide parents information regarding gang activities and what to watch for to determine whether their child is getting involved in gang activities. Recreational, educational, and vocational programs target potential or even current gang members and get them working or using their leisure time in a noncriminal manner.

Juvenile Competency and Mental Health Issues

Competency refers to an individual's ability to make reasoned decisions that affect his or her behavior. Competency is particularly an issue for youthful offenders due to their level of emotional and intellectual development, immaturity, and inexperience. And this is even more of an issue when the juvenile is waived for processing in adult criminal courts. Competency is considered throughout the juvenile justice process, at questioning by the police, at intake, in the decision to charge, and to decide whether the juvenile can understand the issue to stand trial. Most states, while recognizing that minors achieve varying degrees of maturity and responsibility at different ages, deciding of competency (or capacity) still is based on common law that has been applicable for well over a century.[63] The common law rule of capacity has been known as the Rule of Sevens, and means that if a minor is under the age of seven, there can be no capacity; between seven and fourteen, there is a rebuttable presumption of no capacity; and between fourteen and twenty-one, there is a rebuttable presumption of capacity.

One of the serious challenges confronting police, prosecutors, and judges is that there has been no standard definition of competency for juveniles in regard to their civil rights. At least ten states (Arizona, Colorado, Florida, Georgia, Kansas, Minnesota, Nebraska, Texas, Virginia, and Wisconsin) and the District of Columbia specifically address competency in their juvenile delinquency statutes. Arizona state law suggests that a juvenile does not need to have a mental disease, defect, or disability to be incompetent, as a lack of maturity has been determined to reduce the ability of juveniles to understand proceedings against them. In other states without statutory definitions of competency, courts must determine individual's competency to stand trial in each case.[64]

The issue of competency is closely linked to the serious issue of mental illness among juvenile offenders. Even after processing, treatment in the community or residential placement is critical and necessary just for safe management of these individuals. It has been estimated that as many as 2 million children and adolescents arrested each year in the United States have a mental disorder, and possibly 70 percent of youth in the juvenile system need mental health treatment, and one in five suffer from a mental illness that inhibits their normal development and ability to grow into a responsible adult.[65] A more recent study found similar results, with 66 percent of juveniles who came before the juvenile court had at least one psychiatric disorder and 43 percent had two or more disorders.[66]

Complicating competency issues for juveniles is that mental illness in youth is difficult to identify, and the symptoms vary with age. It is questionable that the juvenile justice system is equipped to address this level of mental health needs by their clients. And even if they receive treatment while in the system, they often are released to a community needing ongoing treatment. However, fragmented and insufficient services in the community can result in a return to delinquency and adult criminality. The issue of competency and effective treatment for these mental health needs is critical to breaking the cycle of delinquency and crime.

Responding to Juvenile Drug Crime

A serious concern regarding juveniles is substance abuse that leads to health problems, undermines family relationships, creates problems in school, and results in delinquency that often continues into adult criminality. The juvenile justice system struggles with how to break this cycle and redirect juveniles into productive and law-abiding patterns of behavior. In the early history of the juvenile justice system, the focus was on the individual juvenile and how he or she could be rehabilitated. Over the past two decades, more emphasis has gone to protecting society and victims while holding delinquents accountable for their behavior, and there is an increased use of incarceration and out-of-the-home placements. With neither rehabilitation nor juvenile accountability proving to be effective in dealing with juvenile drug crime, a blending of both into a balanced and restorative justice (BARJ) perspective has emerged.[67] In a National Institute of Justice document encouraging the use of a balanced approach, the authors note,

> *Specifically, the model strikes a balance among offender accountability (making amends to the victim and community), competency development (changing behaviors and improving functional skills), and community safety (protecting the community by carefully monitoring the juvenile's behavior).*[68]

As indicated in Figure 8.6, BARJ integrates the goals of public safety and rehabilitation, using graduated sanctions to reward good behavior and increased punishments for improper behavior, collaboration with the juvenile justice system

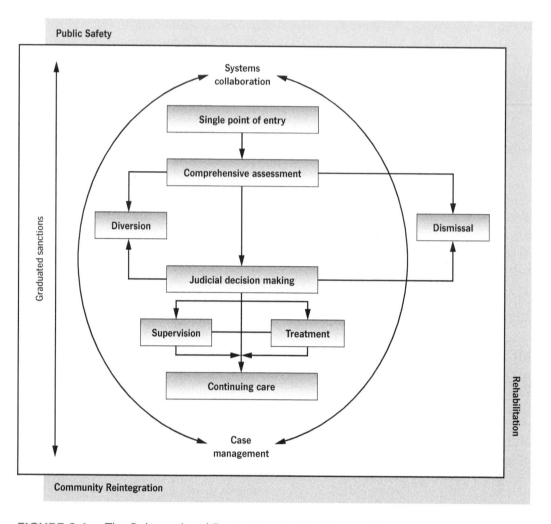

FIGURE 8.6   The Balanced and Restorative Justice Perspective   Source: Data from Curtis C. VanderWaal, Duane C. McBride, Yvonne M. Terry-McElrath, and Holly VanBuren, *Breaking the Juvenile Drug-Crime Cycle: A Guide for Practitioners and Policymakers* (Washington, D.C.: U.S. Department of Justice, 2001), p. 5.

and other community resources such as substance abuse treatment providers, and a case management approach identifying and using community services to build on each juvenile's strengths and talents. Figure 8.6 illustrates the continuous process of entry, assessment, judicial decision making, supervision and treatment, and continuing care to move delinquents from substance abuse to successful community reintegration.

In many ways, the BARJ approach is similar to that used in adult drug courts. BARJ emphasizes collaborative (rather than adversarial) efforts by all parties within the juvenile justice system to focus on the outcome of reducing juveniles' substance abuse and criminal involvement. The model is multidimensional, in that it uses treatment, punishment, and psychological, social, and cultural factors to work toward freedom from drugs for juveniles. Although the system must continue to deal with criminal and delinquent activity by juveniles, the model focuses on the underlying problem of substance abuse as a cause, more than as an effect (involvement in illegal behavior).

The approach of the BARJ model is also consistent with the approach of using evidence-based treatment models. Throughout both the adult and juvenile systems, agencies are examining research as the basis for their program efforts.

A Case Study

Is the Juvenile Justice System "Just"?

A recent case handled in the juvenile justice system is a good example of the challenges faced by either the juvenile or criminal justice system regarding its ability to create a "just" outcome for some cases. A group of teenagers was at a church picnic, horsing around as teenagers do. A thirteen-year-old was bragging about how tough he was and how he could take a blow to the head. He had his skateboard with him and hit himself over the head with it, laughingly telling his friends that it did not hurt. He then challenged any of them to hit him over the head with it to show how tough he was.

Another fourteen-year-old, but one who was much bigger and stronger than the first youth, took up the challenge. He took the skateboard and walloped his friend over the head with it. The youth fell to the ground, began to convulse, and was rushed to the hospital, where he subsequently died. The friend who hit him was taken into custody and charged in juvenile court with murder. A few months later, he pleaded guilty to involuntary manslaughter and received a sentence of one year in a juvenile detention center. There was no indication that this juvenile was a bully or had ever before been violent, and all the facts supported that he had grown up in a typical middle-class family with no serious problems.

The case received considerable media attention, and debate raged about whether justice was served for either party.

The victim had been tragically killed, and nothing could bring him back to life or provide his parents any comfort regarding their loss. The youth who hit him had to live with the fact he had killed his friend. Taking him out of his home and away from his family would not help and probably make it more difficult for him to deal with the result of his actions. Placing him in a juvenile correctional institution illustrated that he had to be responsible and be held accountable for his act of stupidity. Even those who argued for a strong punishment had to admit that incarceration was probably going to make it even more difficult, if not impossible, to get his own life back together. This event and the subsequent sentence will probably result in the loss of two promising lives.

Some argued that if the boy had been in adult court, with the opportunity to go before a jury, and the prosecutor required to prove guilt beyond a reasonable doubt, he might have been able to argue for a lesser sentence. Some also suggested that he was too accepting of responsibility for the act, and that he should have been giving probation and allowed to stay in his parents' home, while receiving counseling and treatment. The one thing most people agreed on is that there seemed to be no "good" sentence for the individual in this case, and they questioned the ability of the juvenile justice system to provide a just outcome.

Especially during these difficult budget times, agencies want to address offender needs through programs that have been proven effective. As we began this chapter, we discussed the mixed missions and challenges of "adultification" of the juvenile justice system. BARJ is a balance between punitive and restorative approaches that continue to challenge the juvenile justice system.

As we end this chapter and the many issues facing juvenile justice, the following "A Case Study" box is an illustration of how many cases in the juvenile justice system seem to result in an unsatisfactory outcome for all involved parties.

Chapter Review

Summary

The juvenile justice system has a long and distinguished history. Formed to protect children who needed society's assistance and to keep juvenile delinquents separate from adult criminals, the juvenile justice system has played a valuable role in the treatment and rehabilitation of generations of the nation's youth. However, during the past two decades, this "kinder and gentler" approach has come under attack, and fear of dangerous and violent juvenile offenders has forced the

U.S. Congress and state legislatures to push for reforms and make the juvenile court similar to adult courts in terms of its goals, processes, and punishments. Although it is difficult to argue with the point that victims don't much care whether their vicious assailant is seventeen or nineteen and that the increase in violent crime does require new methods, it is only normal to think that perhaps we have thrown out the baby with the bathwater and lost some of the rational arguments for the original creation and organization of the juvenile justice system.

The juvenile justice system has had these mixed missions and inconsistent approaches for several decades, and the issues seem to get more confused rather than clearer. Crimes committed by offenders under age eighteen are getting more serious. Some juvenile offenders are now bound over to adult courts and correctional systems for incarceration. Urban youths are joining gangs that encourage violence and a life of crime. Some experts think there should not be a juvenile justice system at all—that all criminals should be treated the same, regardless of their age. Yet others recognize that immaturity leads to mistakes of judgment that require considerations of age, and most people do not want to give up on youthful offenders and accept that they cannot be reformed and made into productive and law-abiding citizens.

The next decade will be an interesting time for the juvenile justice system. Will it continue in the trend toward adversarial judicial processes, waiver from juvenile to adult courts for a growing number of delinquents, and more harsh punishments to include incarceration of juveniles with adult offenders? Or will there be a realization that intervention with rehabilitation and treatment approaches is still the best opportunity society has to correct delinquent behavior and push juveniles back to an acceptable lifestyle? Most likely, the BARJ model, emphasizing a balance between a punitive and restorative approach, will be accepted and implemented in many local and state jurisdictions.

Key Terms

status offense
Refuge Period
juvenile justice system
parens patriae
deinstitutionalize
superpredator
adultification
waiver to adult courts

dependent children
neglected children
delinquent children
age of original jurisdiction
juvenile detention
intake
consent decree
referral

delinquency petition
adjudicate
order
aftercare
In re Gault
juvenile gangs

Review Questions

1. What trends have resulted from the rates of juvenile crime over the past decade?

2. What is a status offense and how are delinquents with status offenses handled?

3. What was the Refuge Period?

4. Define the concept of *parens patriae*.

5. How did the term *superpredator* develop, and what does it mean for the future of juvenile violent crime?

6. What is a waiver to adult courts, and why are some juvenile offenders handled in adult criminal courts rather than juvenile courts?

7. What are the four categories of juvenile offenders and how is each managed in the juvenile justice system?

8. How does the typical mission of a juvenile justice agency differ from the mission of an adult correctional agency?

9. Describe the process followed as a juvenile moves through the juvenile justice system and compare it to the adult criminal justice system.

10. What are the two primary court orders (sentences) for juvenile offenders, and approximately what percentage of juveniles receive each?

11. What has been the trend in the numbers of juveniles receiving an order of commitment to a residential facility?

12. What was the most significant outcome of the U.S. Supreme Court decision in *In re Gault*?

13. Describe and list the most important court decisions regarding sentencing juveniles to the death penalty. What is the current legal position on this issue?

14. How do juvenile street gangs contribute to street crime and what two approaches are taken to control gang behavior?

15. What is the BARJ model for juvenile justice and how does it work?

◤ You Make the Decision...

Should Juveniles Be Tried as Adults?

More juveniles arrested for serious crimes are being bound over to adult courts to be tried as adults and, if convicted, will serve an adult sentence. Since serious crimes are those handled in the criminal justice system, the sanctions usually include imprisonment. Three models of incarceration of juveniles tried and convicted as adults are used. Most states place these juvenile offenders in adult prisons with adult inmates. A few states house juveniles with adults, but require them to be housed and programmed separately. And some states place juveniles in juvenile institutions until they reach age eighteen, and they then are transferred to adult prisons.

There has been a significant reduction from the early years to waiving juveniles to the adult system which resulted in them serving time in adult prisons. From 1985 to 1997, the number of juveniles serving a sentence in an adult prison increased from 2,300 to 5,400.[69] This number then began to decline, and by 2015, there were only 993 inmates under age eighteen

held in adult prisons, a over 80 percent decrease since 1997. Almost all (97 percent) were males, and 63 percent of the total were held in the six states: Arizona, Florida, Georgia, Michigan, New York, and North Carolina.[70] Sixteen states and the Federal Prison System hold no one under the age of eighteen. The original punitive attitude of the late 1990s has lessened, and many people are reconsidering the prosecution of juvenile offenders as adults.

You are to decide whether it is good public policy to try and punish juvenile offenders as adults. Either individually or in a small group, list the pros and cons for juveniles being waived to adult courts. Be sure to address issues such as cost, long-term impact on the juveniles, impact on the various sentencing goals, and protection of the public. You will find this is not an easy issue to agree on, and there are many good arguments on both sides. Once you list and discuss the pros and cons, decide if this is good public policy.

CHAPTER 9

Special Offenders

Courtesy of CoreCivic.

After reading this chapter, you should be able to:

1. Summarize the issues regarding juvenile offenders in adult criminal courts.

2. Summarize the issues regarding drug offenders, and identify the types of substance abuse programs prisons provide for inmates.

3. Describe the impact of the deinstitutionalization of people with mental illness on the criminal justice system.

4. Summarize the issues and needs regarding aging offenders and transgender inmates.

5. Explain the concerns about inmate violence in prisons, and suggest reasons for and against the use of supermax prisons.

6. Describe the types of sex offenders and summarize issues regarding them.

7. Identify types of infectious diseases common with criminal offenders and the issues facing them while under correctional supervision.

Introduction

Correctional agencies have become "all things to all people." Historically, the typical offender was young, was in good mental and physical health, was convicted of property crimes, and did not require unusual handling or management. There were only "standard" caseloads for probation and parole agencies until the 1960s, because all inmates under supervision in the community were handled similarly. Prisons built during the early 1900s were extremely large, with extensive factory space, in order to house prisoners inexpensively, while they produced goods that the prison could sell to help support itself. These standard approaches were fine until the makeup of the offender population began to diversify and the need for special management of certain offenders was recognized.

This change in the management of smaller groups of the correctional population based on their characteristics and needs is referred to as differential handling of special offenders. **Special offenders** are those offenders whose circumstances, conditions, or behaviors require management or treatment outside the normal approach to supervision. This may be the result of some physical problem or infectious disease, a mental disorder, a tendency for violence, a history of sexual assaults, age (juvenile or elderly), or serious substance abuse. All these circumstances required correctional officials to create special methods of managing, handling, or treating these offenders.

special offenders
offenders whose circumstances, conditions, or behaviors require management or treatment outside of the normal approach to supervision

This chapter describes the circumstances and management approaches that result from the individual needs of a variety of special offenders. Included are offenders under age eighteen who are waived from jurisdiction of the juvenile court to adult court and correctional systems, as well as offenders who have serious drug problems or a mental illness. In addition, the chapter includes descriptions of the needs and management of aging offenders (older than fifty), offenders who exhibit violent and dangerous tendencies, and those convicted and sentenced for a sexual offense. Finally, the particular management and treatment of offenders with infectious diseases such as HIV/AIDS and tuberculosis are described. This chapter provides students with an understanding of the challenges and difficulties in attempting to manage all these special populations within a correctional environment.

Juvenile Offenders in Adult Criminal Courts

As noted in Chapter 8, over the past twenty years, there has been a tendency to waive jurisdiction from juvenile to adult court for juveniles who commit what would be serious felony offenses if they were over eighteen. States had historically limited the opportunities for such waivers and protected the authority of the juvenile court to determine whether to waive jurisdiction to allow a delinquent to be prosecuted as an adult, thereby continuing to emphasize the juvenile court philosophy of rehabilitation and providing young offenders the chance to make positive changes in their lives. However, the "tough on crime and tough on the criminals" philosophy invaded the juvenile as well as the adult systems, and currently, all states allow juveniles who commit serious offenses to be waived from the juvenile court and be prosecuted in the adult criminal court system.[1] Forty-five states have waiver provisions that allow judges discretion to move juveniles to adult courts, and fifteen have presumptive laws identifying certain categories of crimes to be moved to adult courts.[2] States have added statutory exclusions, expanded the list of offenses for which transfer is allowable, or lowered the minimum age for which a juvenile may be transferred to adult court.

The legal process for transferring juveniles to the adult court system varies from state to state, primarily focusing on who has the discretion to make the transfer or waiver decision. An Office of Juvenile Justice and Delinquency Prevention report outlines the three variations of how this can occur.

1. *Waiver.* The juvenile court judge is the decision maker and determines whether the offender is waived from the juvenile justice system to adult criminal court. Waivers are usually limited by age (must be above a certain age) and by offense criteria. Some states provide juvenile court judges with guidelines on the types of criteria to consider (such as the juvenile's potential for rehabilitation), whereas others reduce judicial discretion by presuming that the juvenile will be waived for certain types of cases.
2. *Direct file.* Fifteen states have concurrent original jurisdiction, in that the prosecutor has the discretion to file charges in either the juvenile justice or criminal justice system. In these states, the prosecutors' discretion is limited by specific age and offense criteria.
3. *Statutory exclusion.* Twenty-eight states have mandatory waiver to adult courts for specific age and offense criteria. If a juvenile is above the minimum age specified and commits a serious offense designated by statute, judges and prosecutors have no discretion; the case must be prosecuted in adult criminal court.[3]

blended sentencing

a middle ground between juvenile and adult sentences that allows judges to choose from a broad array of both juvenile and adult sanctions

In addition, twenty-two states allow **blended sentencing**, whereby the courts can impose juvenile or adult sentences on certain juvenile offenders.[4] In some states, the authority to blend sentences lies with the juvenile court; in other states, it lies with the adult court. Blended sentences are a middle ground between juvenile and adult sentences in that judges can choose from a broad array of both juvenile and adult sanctions. At times these offenders are given a juvenile sentence as a last chance to avoid an adult sanction.

With a concern for dealing with serious juvenile offenders in a punitive and public safety-oriented approach and with the expansion of authority to move juveniles into the adult court and correctional process, there was initially an increase in the number of waivers to adult courts, but the number then began to decline. The number of delinquency cases judicially waived to criminal court peaked in 1994 with 12,100 cases, a 51 percent increase over the number of cases waived in 1989 (8,000). The number declined, was just over 7,200 in 2006, and then declined more dramatically to just over 4,000 cases in 2014.[5] The decline in the number of cases waived may be the result of many states passing legislation excluding certain types of serious offenses from juvenile court jurisdiction, and therefore they go directly to adult criminal court. Cases most likely (just over one-half) to be waived to adult courts are crimes against persons.[6]

As the waiver laws increased over the last two decades of the twentieth century, the number of people younger than eighteen held in state prisons increased, and from 1985 to 1997, the number grew from 2,300 to 5,400.[7] As indicated in Figure 9.1, the juvenile population then began to decline, and by 2016, there were only 956 inmates under age eighteen held in state prisons. Of these, almost 97 percent were males. States with the largest population of juveniles are Florida (143), Massachusetts (85), Arizona (76), North Carolina (72), New York (68), Georgia (67), and Connecticut (63). The Bureau of Prisons (BOP) population has also been declining, and the BOP housed 49 offenders under age eighteen at the end of 2016, but all of these are in separate contract facilities and are not in adult facilities.[8]

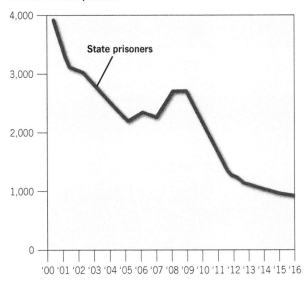

Number of state prisoners

FIGURE 9.1   Inmates Age 17 or Younger Held in Adult State Prison Facilities, 2000–2016   Source: E. Ann Carson, "Prisoners in 2013," *BJS Bulletin* (Washington, D.C.: U.S. Department of Justice, 2014), p. 19. Updated with data from *Prisoners in 2014, 2015, and 2016.*

There are three approaches for housing offenders under age eighteen in state correctional systems. **Straight adult incarceration** places juveniles in adult prisons, with no separate housing or differentiation in programming or job assignment. Although all but six states allow juvenile inmates to be housed in prisons with adult inmates, most separate them from adults to some extent, most often in separate housing units or in separate program assignments. **Graduated incarceration**, used in twelve states, initially places inmates under age eighteen in juvenile facilities. Once they reach a certain age (usually eighteen), they are then transferred to an adult prison to complete their sentence. Finally, eight states use **segregated incarceration**, in which inmates under age eighteen are constantly separated from adults, even though they are housed in the same facility. The juvenile prisoners are housed separately and placed in specialized educational, vocational, life skills training, and substance abuse programs that cater to their age and needs.[9]

Many correctional officials are opposed to housing offenders under age eighteen in prisons with older adult felons, and even most states that allow integration of juvenile prisoners with adults prefer to maintain some type of separation. This is sometimes difficult, especially in states that have only a handful of juvenile offenders. With small numbers, it is almost impossible to keep juveniles separate from adults, yet provide a full range of program offerings. In states with large numbers of juveniles in adult prisons, the administrative problems are less burdensome, as an entire prison can be dedicated to the youthful offenders and specialized programs developed to meet their needs. Unfortunately, there does not appear to be an approach fully supportive for housing juvenile offenders in adult facilities, and there is evidence that this may not be working satisfactorily.

A review of the behavior of juveniles in adult prisons found that the prevalence and frequency of misconduct and violence among juveniles housed in adult prisons were higher than those of comparison groups. The study further found that age was the most consistent and strongest determinant of prison violence, as the juveniles are far more likely than adult offenders to be involved in prison violence

straight adult incarceration

a form of incarceration in which juveniles handled by adult courts are placed in adult prisons with no separate housing or differentiation in programming or job assignments

graduated incarceration

a system in which juveniles handled by adult courts are placed in juvenile facilities until they reach the age of eighteen; they are then transferred to an adult prison to complete the sentence

segregated incarceration

a form of incarceration in which juveniles handled by adult courts are assigned to an adult prison, yet they are housed separately and placed in specialized educational, vocational, life skills training, and substance abuse programs that meet their age and needs

The waiver of juveniles to adult systems and incarceration in adult prisons causes difficult problems for correctional administrators who try to provide proper programs while maintaining the juveniles' safety. Photo by Richard P. Seiter.

and misconduct.[10] There is also evidence that juveniles processed in adult courts have lower recidivism rates than those processed in juvenile courts.[11] And, a review of waiver laws discovered that laws that ease transfer of youth to the adult court system have little or no general deterrent effect in that they do not prevent youth from criminal behavior.[12]

Prisoners with Substance Abuse Needs

One commonly held belief is that drug use leads to criminality. With the initiation of the war on drugs in the late 1980s, the U.S. criminal justice system began targeting and increasing the number of people arrested and punished for selling or using illegal drugs. The war on drugs provided substantial dollars for stopping drugs from entering the United States, prosecuting and punishing those who commit drug offenses, and treating drug addicts. From fiscal year 2007 to 2009, the federal drug control budget was $13.7 billion, of which 36.5 percent was for demand reduction, 27.8 percent for domestic law enforcement, 12.2 percent for international supply reduction, and 23.5 percent for interdiction.[13] The Obama administration has recognized the need for increasing this budget, and their fiscal year 2016 budget climbed to $30.6 billion, of which supply reduction (domestic law enforcement, interdiction, and international programs) was about the same as 2007 at $15.8 billion, while the treatment and prevention was increased to $14.7 billion.[14]

arrestee drug abuse monitoring

gathers data within forty-eight hours of their arrest from individuals regarding their substance abuse

Over the past several years, the U.S. Department of Justice has continued to conduct drug use forecasting and then **arrestee drug abuse monitoring** studies, which all report a strong relationship between drug use and crime. The Arrestee Drug Abuse Monitoring (ADAM) program gathers data within forty-eight hours of their arrest from individuals regarding their substance abuse. The National Institute of Justice did this using drug use forecasting up until 2000, and ADAM I conducted a similar information-gathering survey in thirty-five counties across the country until 2003. From then on, ADAM II has been conducting an annual survey in five counties, and is now administered by the Office of Drug Control Policy.

In the 2013 survey of arrested individuals, it was discovered that between 63 and 83 percent of those booked on criminal charges tested positive for some illicit drug at the time of their arrest.[15] Marijuana is the most commonly detected drug in these tests, as between 34 and 59 percent of arrestees tested positive for this drug. Cocaine is the next commonly detected drug, followed by heroin and other opiates, and then methamphetamine. Of concern is that the number of positive tests for both heroin and methamphetamine has increased since 2000.[16]

In a 2017 report by the Bureau of Justice Statistics, more than two-thirds of sentenced jail inmates and 58 percent of state prisoners were determined to be dependent on or to abuse drugs, while only 5 percent of adults in the United States met this criterion.[17] And 12.3 percent of adult offenders under community supervision also reported a drug dependence.[18] Table 9.1 illustrates the percentage of offenders

TABLE 9.1	Percentage of Prisoners Who Committed Offense to Get Money for Drugs, 2007–2009	
Most serious offense	**State prisoners**	**Sentenced jail inmates**
All inmates	21.3%	20.8%
Violent	14.6	14.0
Property	39.4	36.7
Drug	29.9	28.8
DWI/DUI	1.0	1.9
Other public order	8.7	7.5

Source: Jennifer Bronson and Jessica Stroop, "Drug Use, Dependence, and Abuse Among State Prisoners and Jail Inmates, 2007–2009," *Bureau of Justice Statistics Special Report* (Washington, D.C.: U.S. Department of Justice, 2017), p. 6.

by offense who committed their crimes to get money to buy drugs for their own use. Although the overall drug use by state prisoners has changed little over the past decade, there has been an increase in the reported use of stimulants (primarily methamphetamines), as use in the month before the offense increased from 9 percent in 1997 to 12 percent in 2004,[19] with regular use (at least once a week for at least a month) by 23.4 percent of state prisoners in 2007–2009. And 16.6 percent of this population also reported regular use of heroin or other opiates. [20]

There are also a large proportion of state and federal prisoners serving a sentence for a drug offense. In 2015, 15.2 percent of offenders in state prisons (over 197,000) were convicted of a drug offense.[21] In federal prisons, drug offenses constituted the largest group of inmates, as approximately 92,000 (47.5 percent) of federal prisoners were serving a sentence for a drug offense in 2016.[22] Not all drug offenders are drug users, as some are merely involved to make money and will not personally use drugs. Although the United States has targeted a tremendous amount of resources toward the arrest, prosecution, and punishment of drug offenders, the relationship between drug and alcohol use and crime is complex and lacks a cohesive conclusion. The *National Household Survey on Drug Abuse* (NHSDA) has tracked patterns of licit and illicit drug use among the general U.S. population since 1971. Findings indicate that illegal drug use, as measured by the number of people using an illicit drug in the previous month, steadily declined from 1979 to 1992, and although there has been a leveling off of the decline until about 2008, data on the use of illicit drugs from 2008 until 2015 demonstrate a slight upward trend.[23]

With such a high number of drug offenders in prison, it does not seem they should be in a category of "special offenders." However, what makes at least some of them special is that if their addiction is the basis of their criminality, there must be programs and management approaches in prisons that deal with their substance abuse, or the deterrent effect of their punishment will have no impact. It is therefore critical that prisons offer drug abuse programs (DAPs). Table 9.2 illustrates the percentage of state prison and jail inmates who were involved in various types of drug treatment programs. These programs include residential units with a total environment directed toward dealing with the addictions.

As noted in Table 9.2, 9.5 percent of state prisoners have participated in a residential treatment program. These are the most intensive, and generally considered

TABLE 9.2 Participation in Drug Treatment Programs since Admission among State Prisoners and Sentenced Jail Inmates Who Met Drug Dependence or Abuse Criteria, 2007–2009

Type of drug treatment program	State prisoners	Sentenced jail inmates
Any drug treatment program	28.5%	22.2%
Treatment	14.9%	13.9%
Residential facility or unit	9.5	7.6
Counseling by a professional	6.3	6.1
Detoxification unit	1.3	2.0
Maintenance drug	0.4	0.9
Other programs	25.2%	16.5%
Self-help group/peer counseling	18.9	11.7
Education program	15.3	8.4

Source: Jennifer Bronson and Jessica Stroop, "Drug Use, Dependence, and Abuse Among State Prisoners and Jail Inmates, 2007–2009," *Bureau of Justice Statistics Special Report* (Washington, D.C.: U.S. Department of Justice, 2017), p. 13.

the most effective. However, they are also the most costly. This is why Congress enacted the Violent Crime Control and Law Enforcement Act of 1994, which included funding for Residential Substance Abuse Treatment (RSAT) to provide funds to U.S. states and territories to establish or expand substance abuse treatment in state prisons and local jails. Funding began with $27 million in 1996, climbed to over $60 million in 2002, but then declined to about $10 million from 2012 to 2014.[24]

One of the early RSAT programs was in the BOP. The BOP has separate units in several prisons with the same staffing, structure, length of treatment, and programs provided. Inmate participants in the 500-hour program reside in a treatment unit separate from the prison general inmate population. The program requires offenders to assume responsibility for their behavior and to make a conscious decision to avoid engaging in drug taking and criminal behavior. The treatment model is "bio-psycho-social," emphasizing a comprehensive lifestyle change, with issues of physical well-being, family relationships, and criminality all targeted for change while participants acquire positive life skills as a vehicle to avoid future drug use.[25]

The BOP program has a five-part treatment strategy: (1) orientation screening and referral, (2) drug abuse education, (3) nonresidential drug abuse treatment services, (4) residential drug abuse treatment, and (5) transitional services. Specific unit-based drug treatment is typically delivered no less than four hours a day, five days a week, supplemented by other complementary programs such as education, work skills training, recreation, disease prevention, and health promotion instruction. The BOP, in conjunction with the National Institute of Drug Abuse, is conducting an ongoing evaluation of the effectiveness of the program.

In an early review of outcomes, findings indicate that in high-security prisons, misconduct among inmates who completed the residential drug abuse treatment program was reduced by 50 percent. For the first six months after release from custody, inmates who completed the residential drug abuse treatment program were 73 percent less likely to be rearrested for a new offense than those who did not participate in a residential drug abuse treatment program and were 44 percent less likely to use drugs or alcohol than those who did not participate in a residential drug abuse treatment program.[26] Other studies have also shown prison drug treatment programs to be effective. In a 2007 meta-analysis of 66 program evaluations, it was discovered that participation in drug treatment programs significantly reduced future drug use and criminal reoffending.[27]

Although it is critical to offer DAPs to inmates, it may be even more important to provide drug treatment to offenders on probation and hope that through treatment they can avoid further criminality resulting in a prison sentence. As noted in Chapter 2, there are approximately 3,400 drug courts across the United States. These courts monitor offenders in the community, and almost always require participation in drug treatment programs. Participants had fewer re-arrests compared to non-drug court offenders, and had less drug use (56 percent compared to 76 percent) than comparable offenders.[28] And most probation and parole agencies identify and manage offenders with substance abuse needs in special units. In New York City, the Department of Probation manages probationers with a history of drug abuse through a combination of specialized supervision caseloads and contracts for outpatient treatment programs. The specialized units have smaller than normal caseloads, supervising about 65 probationers, compared with the approximately 175 probationers in regular caseloads. The department contracts with an outside provider for a twelve-month outpatient treatment program that provides counseling services while working closely with offenders and reporting their progress to probation staff. Probationers receive a mandatory urinalysis within the first two weeks of entry to the program, a second urinalysis within two weeks after the first, and then random monthly testing thereafter.

These inmates are participating in a residential drug program. Photo by Richard P. Seiter.

Research indicates that the program is effective because probationers who receive the drug treatment have significant reductions in recidivism, "with the greatest reduction in recidivism among those clients who were appropriately matched to outpatient drug treatment on the basis of the severity of their drug use."[29] Substance abuse treatment provided in the community is more cost-effective than imprisonment. A Justice Policy Institute report found that "Treatment delivered in the community is one of the most cost-effective ways to prevent such crimes and costs approximately $20,000 less than incarceration per person per year."[30]

As is obvious, with the high level of correctional clients that do have substance abuse problems, it is critical that correctional agencies provide substantial opportunities for involvement in substance abuse treatment programs. These have proven to be cost-effective. However, the economic downturn and less tax revenue for states have resulted in some funding reductions for states. And as indicated, federal funding for RSAT programs has also declined significantly in the last fifteen years. Drug treatment is effective, and agencies must find a way to continue funding and reach a higher percent of offenders than the less than one-third of state prisoners and less than one-fourth of sentenced jail inmates that have participated in treatment programs.

Offenders with Mental Illness

antipsychotic drugs

drugs administered to mentally ill individuals to counteract the symptoms of their mental illness, often allowing them to live successfully in the community rather than needing to be institutionalized

During the past half century, the United States has made tremendous progress in the treatment and management of people with mental illness. Unfortunately, reforms and improvements in the mental health field have also caused issues and problems for corrections. **Antipsychotic drugs** were invented in the 1960s, and they helped many people with mental illness remain in the community rather than be placed in mental hospitals. These drugs provided a humane alternative to the deleterious placement of patients in the old state mental hospitals, where patients often had little to do and received minimal treatment. Taking antipsychotic drugs can help most mental health patients stay in the community, and many state mental hospitals closed during the latter half of the twentieth century. In fact, the number of patients in state mental institutions went from a high of 559,000 in 1955 to 69,000 by 1995,[31] and to only 35,000 by 2012.[32]

However, with minimal monitoring, some patients in the community stop taking their medication, as they may not like the uncomfortable side effects, think they are doing better, or just decide to stop taking the medicine. Or they may lose their insurance coverage and cannot afford to buy the medicine. Without their medication, the symptoms of the mental illness return, and many such people with mental illness do not receive treatment, their behavior deteriorates, they end up committing crimes, and they become clients of the criminal justice system rather than patients of the mental health system. A recent report by the Bureau of Justice Statistics estimated that during 2011 and 2012, 14 percent of state and federal prisoners and 26 percent of jail inmates met the threshold for serious psychological distress (SPD), and 37 percent of prisoners and 44 percent of jail inmates had a mental disorder.[33] Another recent report identified 356,268 inmates with severe mental illness in prisons and jails.[34] New York City estimated that 40 percent of their jail inmates had a mental illness, 67 percent had a mental health "need," and 21 percent were affected by serious mental illness.[35]

Treatment for people with mental illness in prisons generally falls into three categories: (1) screening inmates at intake for mental health conditions, (2) therapy or counseling, and (3) psychotropic medications. When inmates are received in prison or jail, they are initially screened for mental illness. The screening is primarily a self-report by inmates as to whether they have ever experienced a mental health problem. If identified with a mental condition, psychologists and social workers determine the type, level, and frequency of treatment. Most inmates with mental health issues receive outpatient counseling by trained and certified staff. A high percent also are referred to a psychiatrist who can prescribe psychotropic medication. And the most serious need inmates can be placed in a residential program with a treatment milieu and treatment program to meet their level of needs. Table 9.3 illustrates the level of mental health care by inmates with a mental health problem, ever in their past, since admission to a prison or jail, or currently receiving treatment. Unfortunately, of those with serious psychological distress, just over one-half of prisoners and one-third of jail inmates received any type of treatment after admission.

It is critical that inmates with mental health concerns are identified and managed in jails and prisons, as they create a dual problem of control and treatment. Since they have committed a criminal act and almost one-half of state prison inmates with mental problems have committed a violent crime,[36] they may require a high-security institutional placement, resulting in their often being housed with non–mentally ill offenders who have also committed serious offenses and are serving equally long sentences. Their behavior and potential

TABLE 9.3	Mental Health Treatment Received by Inmates Who Had a Mental Health Problem, 2011–2012			
	Serious psychological distress		History of a mental health problem	
Time period and treatment type	Prisoners	Jail inmates	Prisoners	Jail inmates
Ever received mental health treatment during lifetime	74.2%	72.7%	88.1%	90.3%
Ever overnight hospital stay	41.8	43.1	44.8	51.3
Ever taken prescription medication	62.8	61.3	76.4	80.4
Ever had counseling/therapy from trained professional	60.9	54.9	74.6	73.9
Mental health treatment since admission	54.3%	35.0%	63.0%	44.5%
Prescription medication	45.8	30.0	52.6	38.3
Counseling/therapy from trained professional	42.2	17.8	48.9	23.5
Prescription medication and counseling/therapy	33.9	12.9	38.7	17.5
Currently treated for a mental health problem	35.6%	29.7%	37.0%	37.8%
Prescription medication	29.1	25.7	29.9	33.0
Counseling/therapy from trained professional	25.8	12.6	26.7	16.4
Prescription medication and counseling/therapy	19.5	8.7	19.7	11.8

Source: Jennifer Bronson and Marcus Berzofsky, "Indicators of Mental Health Problems Reported by Prisoners and Jail Inmates, 2011–2012," *Bureau of Justice Statistics Special Report* (Washington, D.C.: U.S. Department of Justice, 2017), p. 8.

violence must first be controlled, and then they must also receive treatment for their mental illness and be protected from other violent and dangerous inmates.

Inmates with mental illness are more likely than other inmates to have disciplinary problems while in prison. It has been found that 11.6 percent of state prison inmates with a history of mental health problems, compared to 4.1 percent of inmates without a mental health problem, had been charged with an assault of another inmate or staff. Among jail inmates, 9.9 percent of those with a mental health problem compared to 4.2 percent of inmates without a mental health problem had been charged with an assault.[37] And almost 60 percent of state prison inmates with mental illness had been formally charged with breaking prison rules at some point since their admission to prison.[38]

In addition, a recent survey reported that prisoners with mental illness:

- Remain incarcerated longer than regular prisoners;
- Are disproportionately abused, beaten, and/or raped;
- Become much sicker while incarcerated, especially if not being treated;
- Are much more likely to spend time in solitary confinement;
- Are disproportionately more likely to commit suicide;
- Are more likely to be returned to prison following release; and
- Are more expensive to house in prison or jail.[39]

While on probation or postprison community supervision, people with mental illness have similar problems. As a condition of their community supervision, offenders must often maintain employment, submit to drug testing, or participate in treatment. Managing offenders in the community creates unique problems, and only recently have most probation and parole agencies created special caseloads for managing people with mental illness. These caseloads require patience, treatment expertise, and control by the officers in charge. Offenders must have a treatment program developed, must receive counseling for their mental illness, must be encouraged to continue to take their medication, and require much more time and patience in supervising than the typical criminal offender. Probation officers responsible for such caseloads require specialized training to be able to address the difficult dilemma created by the overlap of criminality and mental illness.

Inmates with mental illness are not only challenging to manage while in prison or under community supervision, but also they are more likely to have a history of violence and to recidivate than are other offenders. Table 9.4 illustrates the current offense of prisoners and jail inmates as well as how many times those with histories of mental health issues have been arrested and time served in prison or jail. Of those with any history of mental health problem, over 40 percent of prisoners and almost 48 percent of jail inmates were serving time for a violent offense. And similarly, almost one-half of prisoners and over one-half of jail inmates had been arrested eleven times or more.

Over the past several years, most research into prison-based mental health programs has shown little positive impact on reducing recidivism.[40] However, one approach that seems to have success is the Offender Reentry Community Safety Program in Washington State. This program focuses on a continuum of care from the prison to the community, following a therapeutic community model in the prison with community mental health as well as substance abuse

TABLE 9.4	Indicators of Mental Health Problems, by Offense, Criminal History, and Prior Time Served in a Correctional Facility, 2011–2012

Offense and time served	Serious psychological distress		History of a mental health problem	
	Prisoners	**Jail inmates**	**Prisoners**	**Jail inmates**
Most serious offense				
Violent	16.6%	29.2%	41.7%	47.9%
Property	15.6	27.1	41.4	49.8
Drug	10.2	24.6	26.8	39.8
DWI/DUI	14.0	23.5	32.4	37.9
Other public order	13.2	25.9	35.6	45.4
Number of times arrested (lifetime)				
1 time	12.1%	23.4%	27.0%	30.8%
2–3 times	13.5	23.8	32.0	36.7
4–10 times	14.6	23.2	39.6	46.7
11 times or more	18.1	25.3	48.9	55.9
Total time in a correctional facility prior to current facility				
None	13.4%	24.6%	28.7%	35.1%
1–5 months	14.3	24.1	35.4	41.0
6–11 months	13.7	23.9	37.0	45.4
1–4 years	13.4	22.5	37.8	46.9
5 years or more	16.5	24.9	42.6	54.0

Source: Jennifer Bronson and Marcus Berzofsky, "Indicators of Mental Health Problems Reported by Prisoners and Jail Inmates, 2011–2012," *Bureau of Justice Statistics Special Report* (Washington, D.C.: U.S. Department of Justice, 2017), pp. 6 and 7.

treatment, housing, medical services, and other support services. Studies conclude that the program reduced recidivism by 42 percent (and 36 percent for violent crimes).[41]

Managing offenders with mental illness in the community and in prison is a difficult challenge. These offenders are not deterred by typical punishment. They may understand that they have received a long prison sentence for their crimes, yet may not be able to use that punishment as an incentive to discontinue criminal activities. While they are supervised in the community, their commission of crimes is not the result of a simple decision to recidivate, but is more likely a result of their inability to manage themselves, to maintain the use of their psychotropic medication, and to deal responsibly with problems regarding housing, employment, or relationships.

In prisons, the responsibility of assessing and treating inmates with mental illness falls to correctional psychologists. The "Your Career in Corrections" box illustrates the types of jobs available to psychologists in a prison setting.

Your Career in Corrections

Correctional Psychologists

Correctional psychologists do all the things associated with clinical psychology; only they do them in a correctional setting. Correctional psychology has some subspecialties, such as forensic psychology (conducting evaluations to establish competency and responsibility for crimes or doing judicial evaluations that may influence sentencing), or specialty programming, such as drug or sex offender treatment. The first thing that staff psychologists working in a prison do with new inmates is conduct an intake screening to look for histories of mental health treatment, determine current mental health status, and make program recommendations. They then conduct both individual or group counseling, advise managers on how to best manage inmates, and may be involved in the employee assistance program. They sometimes must respond to and assist with emergency situations and may have special duties such as hostage negotiations, confrontation avoidance (trying to talk an inmate out of an action to avoid a calculated use of force), crisis interventions for inmates or staff (such as an inmate finding out that he or she has an unfaithful spouse), and working closely with medical staff to monitor inmates' compliance in taking medications.

Not everyone is suited for working as a correctional psychologist. Those considering such jobs should be able to work in a paramilitary situation in which psychology and

mental health evaluations may not be the primary factor in action taken. They must also recognize that they will work in what could become an unsafe environment with the potential for violence. However, training that psychologists receive and use in a nonprison clinical practice is very similar for correctional psychologists. The correctional psychologist will treat a greater number of individuals with depression and anxiety and will see more cases of serious mental illnesses such as schizophrenia.

For most states and the federal government, a doctoral degree is required, although some states require only a master's degree in psychology. On an individual basis, a correctional psychologist must have emotional security to work in a prison and be able to work within the structure of an organization focused on security and order. Pay, benefits, and working conditions for correctional psychologists are similar to those of other institutional settings (such as Veterans Administration hospitals or state mental hospitals). On the other hand, many individuals find that career opportunities for correctional psychologists are greater than for an outside clinical psychological practice, since working for a large organization provides not only a more extensive career ladder but also opportunities outside psychology.[42]

Aging Offenders

The prison population in the United States is getting older. Part of the reason for this is that the general population of the United States is also aging. Older Americans represent the fastest growing age group in the United States; in 2012, there were 79.5 million Americans age fifty-five and older (25.7 percent of all Americans) and 40.15 million individuals age sixty-five and older.[43] By July 1, 2016, 15.2 percent of the U.S. population (approximately 49.1 million) were over age sixty-five, an increase from 13 percent of the U.S. population on April 1, 2010.[44] And the number of inmates over age fifty-five is expected to reach 400,000 by 2030.[45] A second reason for the increase in elderly offenders is the changes in the models of sentencing, as sentencing guidelines and mandatory sentencing take away sentencing judges' discretion to consider age, health issues, and risk to the community. Previously, judges would consider these factors and often grant older offenders probation for crimes and criminal backgrounds that would result in a prison sentence for younger offenders. But with an older offender in poor health, judges often opted for a community sanction.[46]

Finally, as a result of lengthening prison sentences for almost every crime, offenders sentenced to prison stay a longer time. And three-strikes and habitual-offender laws often can mandate a sentence of life without parole. These prisoners naturally age while serving their sentence and end up dying while in prison. These factors increase the average age of the U.S. prison population. In 1995, only 6.1 percent of the inmates in state and federal prisons were age fifty or older,[47] and on December 31, 2016, there were almost 289,000 inmates older than age fifty, representing 19.8 percent of the prison population, and just under 39,000 (2.6 percent) prisoners over age sixty-five.[48] And the median age of state prisoners in 1993 was thirty, but by 2013, the median age was thirty-six.[49]

This increase in the average age and number of older offenders creates many management, resource, and programmatic issues for correctional administrators. Prisons and jails are designed and operational processes created to hold young and physically active inmates. The architecture, recreation facilities, and types of housing are usually designed with little consideration of older inmates. Simple problems, such as difficulty in getting around in wheelchairs or inability to walk long distances, result from the campus-style prison architecture emphasizing space to spread out inmates over as much area as possible. Recreation programs such as basketball, jogging, and weight lifting do not meet the needs or interests of the elderly. Few work opportunities can be assigned to older inmates.

Housing and bed arrangements often cause problems for older inmates. Most correctional facilities have bunk beds. Many older inmates cannot get into upper bunks, and assignment to lower bunks due to age causes morale problems among younger inmates who believe they deserve these beds due to their good behavior and time served in prison (the criteria usually considered for preferred assignments). Most prisons and jails have two inmates assigned to each cell. Many older and younger inmates do not want to share a cell because they have different habits and interests in radio or television stations. Younger inmates may have little tolerance for older inmates getting up to go to the bathroom several times per night, resulting in tension and requests for prison managers to change housing and bed assignments. Finally, correctional administrators may need to protect older inmates from being victimized by younger and stronger predators, who find older inmates easy victims from whom to steal or extort money. These officials are constantly challenged with finding solutions to these problems, which have no easy or clear answers.

To remedy these problems, most facilities make allowances in standard policies for cell and bed assignments, or even for inmate movement, and let older inmates begin moving from one building to another before younger inmates. Some correctional agencies even use entire housing units to house older inmates and create counseling programs and recreation that meet their needs. They also try to identify specific jobs that can be done by older inmates and have recreation departments create leisure activities such as stretching classes or table-game tournaments to occupy these inmates and meet their special needs.

Perhaps the most critical, expensive, and difficult issue is increased health care needs. Many illnesses and general health problems result from the aging process and years of risky lifestyle choices, such as tobacco use, extensive drug and alcohol use, and high-risk sexual behavior. As a result, older inmates have increased risk of major diseases, and a greater need for regular medical care for issues associated with aging such as hearing and vision problems, arthritis, hypertension, and dementia. An article in the *Journal of the American Medical Association* notes that *inmates* older than fifty-five have an average of three chronic conditions and one in five have a mental illness.[50] The annual cost for incarceration and health care of inmates age fifty-five and older is two to three times that of other inmates.[51] And average costs per year for older inmates can easily exceed $100,000,[52] and it is estimated that the United States currently spends more than $1.6 billion annually caring for aging inmates.[53] The health problems of the elderly are not only more severe than those of younger offenders, but very different from them, and prison medical clinics are usually not prepared to deal with the depression, sexually transmitted diseases, tuberculosis and other infectious diseases, heart problems, and reduced circulation that occur in older inmates.

And many states are creating specialty units to help in meeting the need of elderly inmates. Washington State opened an assisted living facility in 2010, and the Louisiana State Penitentiary operates a hospice program for dying inmates that is staffed by fellow inmates. A Massachusetts master plan proposes new facilities designated for aging inmates who need significant assistance with their daily living. And Montana created plans to build a 120 bed facility for elderly inmates to provide specialty care to meet their needs.[54]

An interesting development in caring for aging and end-of-life inmates is the move to use Medicaid coverage to reduce the costs of health care for elderly inmates. When Medicaid was created in 1965, prison inmates were not eligible. However, since 1997, it has been determined that when inmates are placed in outside nursing homes or hospitals, Medicaid would pay their bills. Therefore, several states are opting to, instead of building and operating nursing care units in prisons, contract with private nursing homes to care for elderly and disabled inmates under "**medical parole**," which allows them to live outside the prison while still serving their sentence. There is little or no risk of further criminality for these inmates, and nursing homes are much better equipped to care for them than units in prisons. In addition, dying inmates can be granted "compassionate release" to allow them to live their final few days in the community.[55]

These are the issues faced and approaches used by correctional administrators to address the needs of an aging prison population. The following "A Case Study" box illustrates these and other issues that result as older inmates are sentenced to prison.

medical parole

placing aging or disabled inmates in a nursing home or hospital to receive care while still serving their sentence, and costs being covered by Medicaid

A Case Study

Senior Citizen Inmates

The discussion about current issues in corrections that includes the aging of the prison population creates a question of whether all these inmates should come to prison and whether they should stay for their full sentence if their health puts them in danger of dying in prison. An interesting case involved the sentence received by a male offender in his sixties. This person had been a law enforcement officer for more than thirty years, rising to the executive level of two different law enforcement departments. He was respected in his community and spent several hours a week serving his community.

Surprisingly, this person had another life. He had been molesting his grandchildren for the past several years. As the story became public, most people who knew him were shocked, because he did not seem like someone who would do this, and they knew the good he did for the community. However, all his built-up goodwill was not enough to keep him from getting a lengthy prison sentence for his offenses. Even his closest allies and friends could not argue against his receiving a term in prison for molesting his grandchildren.

After the sentence, his life became very difficult. He had a double problem as an inmate. Although inmates do not usually physically abuse child molesters, as had been the case in the past, molesters are held in contempt and are subject to continual harassment by the inmate population. Also, as a past and

well-known law enforcement officer, this person had personally arrested many offenders and put them in prison. Prison administrators had to make intense efforts to protect his safety, including placing him in a prison far away from his home with a population that was less likely to assault him. At times, he had to be placed in administrative detention for his own protection. His punishment of imprisonment was much greater than that of a "normal" inmate.

As time went on, the inmate's health worsened, and it became apparent that he was going to die in the next few years, even though he still had several years to serve on his sentence. The state in which he was incarcerated had a policy that allowed emergency release of a dying inmate. However, due to the nature of his crime, there was little sentiment by anyone that he should be released. So, in effect, his sentence became a life sentence rather than a multiyear sentence.

The issue that surfaces in this situation is how a regular sentence for older offenders can become a life (some may say death) sentence for aging inmates. Yet with mandatory sentences and sentencing guidelines, a judge often cannot consider the age or medical condition of an offender. The other side of the issue is whether someone should receive a lesser sentence for the same crime due to age or infirmity. Unfortunately, there is no easy solution to this dilemma, and aging offenders cause unique problems for correctional administrators.

Transgender Inmates

While many transgender issues in society have been or are being addressed, the management of transgender individuals in U.S. prisons is still very inconsistent and much less developed. Transgender inmates are one of the most vulnerable populations in a correctional facility, and are likely to be marginalized if the many issues around their management are not identified and dealt with proactively. In a 2010 meeting of the American Jail Association, jail risk consultant Donald L. Leach noted, "As gender identity becomes more recognized as a legitimate concern that individuals have, you are going to see more of it in corrections."[56] Yet, most agencies have been slow to react, policies and practices vary among jails and prison systems, and there are no "standards of accepted practice" that have been adopted throughout corrections. A 2015 review of policies across states found that while many are passing statutes or creating policy guidelines for transgender inmates, there were still many states "lagging behind" creating of professional standards for medical or management issues.[57] And in 2015, the editorial board of the *New York Times* opined that "In the United States, transgender people are routinely subjected to harassment, but few are as powerless as those in prison."[58]

There are a multitude of issues that complicate the management of this population in America's prisons and jail. These include assignment to either male or female facilities, classification, housing, health care, mental health treatment programs, inmate searches, clothing and commissary or canteen items, pronouns and names used for an inmate, and terminology. Over the past few years, these challenges and issues have begun and continue to be addressed. And many correctional agencies have established a group of professionals (some inside and some outside the agency) with expertise in transgender issues to advise the jurisdiction regarding specific issues. And while progress is being made, there are still many questions to answer and much work to be done.

The first issue is what gender of prison to assign a transgender inmate. The BOP published their *Transgender Offender Manual* in 2017 to address this issue.[59] The BOP has incorporated the Prison Rape Elimination Act (PREA) regulations into their program statements:

> *In deciding whether to assign a transgender or intersex inmate to a facility for male or female inmates...the agency shall consider on a case-by-case basis whether a placement would ensure the inmate's health and safety, and whether the placement would present management or security problems.[60]*

The BOP has created a Transgender Executive Council (TEC) to offer advice and guidance on unique measures related to the treatment and management of transgender inmates. Upon receipt of a transgender inmate, prison staff contact the TEC for advice on the designation. The TEC considers the inmate security level, past criminal and disciplinary histories, current gender expression, medical and mental health issues, and risk of sexual victimization. The housing decision within the assigned prison is also on a case-by-case basis, with the emphasis on not jeopardizing the offenders' health or safety.

Most states make the original designation decision in this manner, although there are others that have a clearer policy regarding initial assignment. In a discussion regarding transgender inmate management at the Association of State Correctional Administrators meeting in August 2017, some heads of state departments of corrections stated they assign all offenders to a prison based on the gender listed on their birth certificate, and others stated they assign them to a prison based on their current gender identification.[61]

Another issue is the use of the proper pronoun and name when prison staff address an inmate. The official name under which an inmate is committed to prison is usually the accepted name of the inmate. However, some jurisdictions allow a different gender preferred name for an inmate to be added to their record as an "alias," and staff are allowed to use that first name if they are comfortable with it. If staff prefer, they can address the inmate by "inmate" last name, such as "Inmate Smith," without using a gender-identified first name.

Every prison has a policy as to whether only a same-sex staff member can conduct a "pat search" or an unclothed visual search of an inmate. And most jurisdictions state that inmates for purposes of searches will be in accordance of the policy for the gender of the facility or housing unit in which they are assigned. Some jurisdictions allow an inmate to request an exception to policy, and those can be considered and approved on a case-by-case basis. Other facilities allow a transgender inmate to state a preference on gender of staff searches, and they focus on clear communications at the time or a documented preference in the inmate's records. This both acknowledges the inmate's preference and protects staff if the inmate alleges victimization.

Physical and mental health care is also made more difficult for transgender inmates. The National Commission on Correctional Health Care (NCCHC) has adopted a position statement that "Because jails, prisons, and juvenile confinement facilities have a responsibility to ensure the physical and mental health and well-being of inmates in their custody, correctional health staff should manage transgender patients in a manner that respects their biomedical and psychological needs."[62] NCCHC suggests that correctional facilities follow standards developed by professionals with expertise in transgender health, but that most treatment necessary is considered on a case-by-case basis. This is because transgender individuals coming into a correctional environment may be at different stages of both physical and mental health care.

Clothing and commissary items are also a consideration. When jurisdictions assign inmates to an institution other than based on their birth certificate–identified gender, they often allow flexibility in terms of clothing and purchase and use of commissary items. As an example, they may allow transgender inmates to possess and wear undergarments of their identified gender, even when not housed with that identified gender.

The following case study describes how some of the above issues are addressed by the Oregon Department of Corrections (ODOC). Oregon is seen as a very progressive correctional agency regarding many management and program areas. While they note they are still developing many of their approaches and policies regarding transgender inmates, they are looked to by other correctional agencies for leadership on this issue. At the time of this interview, ODOC has just over forty inmates that have identified themselves as transgender.[63]

A Case Study

Oregon's Management of Transgender Inmates

Oregon's recognition of the needs of transgender inmates essentially begins when an offender arrives at the intake center. When a transgender inmate is received, they are initially housed in the infirmary. This is the only unit in the intake center that houses both men and women. In addition, physicians and psychiatrists have close access to them. The offenders go through psychological evaluations and staff monitor their behavior to see if it matches their gender identify. Staff review records and interview the inmate in order to determine their history, background, and medical status. All of this is to be completed within two weeks if possible. The department recognizes this as an anxious and scary time for inmates; they do not know what to expect in terms of their situation and where they will be housed. So they attempt to make these decisions and let the inmate know as soon as possible.

After all the information is gathered, it is presented to the Transgender and Intersex Inmate Committee, which is a multidisciplinary group of ten individuals from across the department. The committee is made up of upper-level department executives, and was created to provide guidance and make some decisions regarding placement of inmates and policies for management of transgender inmates. It includes the institution superintendent of the intake center (Coffee Creek Correctional Facility), the assistant director for Offender Management and Administration, the ODOC PREA administrator, and several other medical and mental health staff. The committee then determines the initial housing assignment, considering where inmates want to live, as well as their need for medical care, their safety, the safety of other inmates, and the overall totality of the case. At this point of time, there are no transgender men (someone assigned female at birth) inmates in male facilities, as all the inmates and the committee believe they would be safer in a female facility. There are, however, transgender women in Oregon's only-female prison. There are some inmates who do not identify as transgender when they arrive at intake, but later identify as transgender. In those cases, the same process of evaluation and decision-making is used.

The ODOC has worked closely with an advocacy group (Basic Rights Oregon) to advise them and provide training to staff. Basic Rights Oregon is a nonprofit advocacy, education, and political organization working to end discrimination based on sexual orientation and gender identity in Oregon. Their guidance is helpful with even basic issues of terminology, which changes all the time. With the help of Basic Rights Oregon, the ODOC delivers training (called Transgender 101) to staff as an overview of managing and communicating with transgender inmates. In 2017, it was a part of in-service training for every ODOC employee. The training includes the decision process to assign transgender inmates to facilities and the correct use of terminology. But most importantly, it includes the expectations of all ODOC staff in working with this population. It is made clear that

(no different than for any other inmate), they are to be treated with respect and a harassment-free environment is to be created. It is often confusing for staff to determine the proper use of pronouns. The ODOC approach is to use the pronoun that inmates want them to use. If staff feel uncomfortable doing that, they may use the gender-neutral "inmate Last Name." It is understood that mistakes may be made, but staff are not expected to purposefully use a pronoun that the inmate finds offensive.

After assignment to an institution, the inmate housing (what cell or dormitory space) assignment is the same process as for any other inmate. Oregon uses an automated and random system for housing assignments. If, however, for mental health or safety reasons, an inmate needs a single cell assignment, this can be considered. Transgender inmates are encouraged to participate in any program that helps meet their need in preparing for release, which could include mental health programming. There are no specific "support groups," regarding their transgender status, but the department may add them at a later time.

Another very important consideration for transgender inmates are the medical protocols used for them. The department has a Therapeutic Levels of Care committee that specifically staffs the needs of transgender inmates. This committee determines medically necessary care for transgender inmates. ODOC contracts with an outside physician who has expertise in treating transgender individuals. This person is also a nonvoting member on the Therapeutic Levels of Care committee. Inmates may be received into prison at any stage of transition. Some are on hormone therapy and others have had some type of surgical procedures. Some do not want to have surgery, and others may want to begin or continue hormone therapy and move toward sex affirming surgery. To consider treatment for each inmate, the committee looks at a number of factors including if it is considered medically necessary, how long the inmate has identified as transgender, their medical history, and the time left to serve before release. Time left to serve is important because ODOC does not want the inmate to go through a surgical procedure and not have enough time to recover before their release date. To receive any type of treatment, inmates must have a gender dysphoria diagnosis, a mental health diagnosis due to distress a person experiences as a result of the sex and gender they were assigned at birth. The distress can become so severe that it leads to depression, self-harm, and even suicide. When treatment is considered medically necessary, the department pays for it.

And a final, yet still important, issue for transgender inmates involves products they can purchase in the prison canteen (sometimes called commissary). Products such as undergarments or makeup may be desired by transwomen living in male facilities. Oregon has solved this problem by having a gender-neutral canteen list, whereby any inmate can order anything from this list.

Alcatraz. Perhaps the most famous and mysterious prison in the history of corrections. Photo by Riffi O'Brien.

Violent Offenders

Many violent individuals are under correctional supervision and particularly in prison. At year-end 2015, 49 percent of all adults sentenced to state prisons were convicted for violent offenses.[64] However, a much smaller number and percentage of inmates are truly violent and predatory and continue violent acts even while in prison. These violent and predatory inmates think nothing of assaulting, raping, or killing other inmates, and correctional officials must take extraordinary actions to protect both staff and other inmates. The standard inmate disciplinary process described later in Chapters 10 and 15 is the procedure used to respond to inmate violence. However, some inmates who exhibit extremely violent behavior in prison are not deterred by standard inmate discipline and cannot be allowed to remain in even high- or maximum-security prisons without being a threat to security.

supermax prisons

either freestanding or distinct units within other prisons that provide for the management and secure control of inmates designated as violent or seriously disruptive in other prisons

For these inmates, many states and the BOP developed **supermax prisons**. Supermax prisons had their historical beginning with Alcatraz, the most famous prison in the world. During the crime wave that swept across the United States during the Great Depression of the 1930s, correctional administrators were first challenged with how to handle offenders with serious criminal histories of violence. As a result, in 1934 the federal government opened Alcatraz Island as the most supermaximum prison ever created in the United States. Alcatraz was designated to handle the most notorious and dangerous criminals of the era, using strict regimens of control and tight security.

However, Alcatraz was very expensive to operate, with no freshwater wells and all supplies needing to be ferried across the water from San Francisco. As a result of cost, Alcatraz closed in 1963, and was replaced with the United States Penitentiary (USP) in Marion, Illinois.

USP Marion had problems adjusting to this mission to control the nation's most dangerous offenders. As a result of continuously tightening security, inmates in 1980 staged a work strike, and the BOP permanently closed Marion's prison factory and terminated all classes. Tensions increased between prison officials and inmates, and on October 22, 1983, two inmates separately killed two correctional officers. Four days later, a prisoner was found murdered in his cell. Marion was placed on emergency status and implemented a twenty-four-hour lockdown of prisoners in solitary cells.[65] Inmates were allowed out of their cells only five hours per week for recreation, showers, and visits with family members. Inmate programs were

Warden James A. Johnson served as the first warden of Alcatraz. Courtesy of the Federal Bureau of Prisons.

USP Marion served as the supermax prison for the U.S. Bureau of Prisons from the closing of Alcatraz in 1963 until 1994, when ADX Florence, Colorado, became the only BOP supermax prison. Courtesy of the Federal Bureau of Prisons.

eliminated, except those provided over video on in-cell television sets or by program staff (such as chaplains) coming to the inmates in their cells. In 1985, inmates filed suit against the lockdown. In the case of **Bruscino v. Carlson**, a federal judge denied their motion, stating, "the Court is of the firm conviction that this litigation was conceived by a small group of hard-core inmates who are bent on the disruption of the prison system in general and of USP Marion in particular."[66] The U.S. Court of Appeals upheld that decision in 1988, claiming that the conditions were not a violation of the Constitution, and in 1989, the U.S. Supreme Court let that decision stand. Marion was then free to continue the lockdown and became the model for supermax prisons that has since been copied by almost every state.

The following "An Interview With" box presents the interview with the warden of USP Marion during the *Bruscino v. Carlson* trial, which opened the door for establishing supermax prisons across the United States.

Bruscino v. Carlson
a 1985 federal court decision that the lockdown of inmates at the U.S. Penitentiary in Marion, Illinois, was not a violation of the Constitution

An Interview With...

A Supermax Prison Warden

Jerry T. Williford. Pearson Education.

Jerry T. Williford had a distinguished career in corrections. He worked for over twenty years for the BOP, was the warden of three prisons, and was a regional director in charge of fifteen prisons. He later became the chief federal probation officer in Atlanta, Georgia. Williford was warden of the United States Penitentiary (USP) in Marion, Illinois, then labeled the "toughest prison in America." Marion represented the first supermax prison in the United States, and during the time he was warden the federal courts decided the case of *Bruscino v. Carlson*. In a decision in favor of Marion and the BOP, the door was opened to other supermax prisons, and several states soon opened their own version of USP Marion.

Question: Could you describe the federal prison in Marion, Illinois, at the time you were warden.

Warden Williford: USP Marion housed about 300 maximum-security inmates and about 120 inmates in a minimum-security camp. The maximum-security inmates were seldom allowed out of their cells, so the minimum-security inmates did the work to maintain the outside grounds and the front of the prison, but came in no contact with the max inmates. I came to the prison as warden shortly after inmates murdered two

(Continued)

correctional officers on the same day, and we started a lock-down that ended up as the model for future supermax prisons.

Question: What was the philosophy under which Marion operated as a supermax?

Warden Williford: The overall philosophy was one of total security and control. Inmates sent to Marion were the worst in the federal prison system. They were sent there based on their misconduct in other maximum-security prisons or they were considered extremely high escape risks because of previous escape attempts or a belief that they were serious escape risks. The inmates sent there for misbehavior almost always were sent for serious violence. In many cases, they had a history of several serious assaults or multiple murders at other prisons. Just being a murderer on the street would not get you sent to Marion. We had two inmates that had both murdered four people while in prison. These inmates were violent and dangerous and had to be in a controlled setting. A study by the University of Minnesota found that inmates at Marion were seven times more dangerous than inmates at Alcatraz.

Question: What were the cells like at Marion?

Warden Williford: The cells at Marion were approximately seven by ten, and housed one inmate. The walls were concrete and the front was open bars. Originally, inmates had metal beds, but they began to use the metal to make weapons, so we took out the metal beds and poured concrete a foot high with a thirty-inch-wide mattress on it. The cell had a toilet and wash basin, but nothing else.

Question: What was the procedure for controlling inmate behavior?

Warden Williford: When inmates first arrived at Marion, they were in a total lockdown status. They were in their cells all the time except an hour per day for recreation time and once every other day for a shower. They were allowed to participate in minimal in-cell programs. They had televisions in their cells on which they could watch regular programming or religious or education programming created by our religious and education departments. If inmates desired, a chaplain would go to their cells to talk to them. They were brought books from the library. Most of their time was spent just lying in bed with the opportunity to contemplate their wrongdoing. They may stay in this first phase at least a year. If during the year, they had no misconduct reports, they could be considered for movement to the second phase. However, we had some extremely violent inmates and gang leaders that were never allowed to move to the second phase, even if they did not misbehave.

The second phase was pretty much like the first phase, but inmates were allowed out of their cells into the center of the cellblock to eat their meals with a small group of other inmates (no more than fifteen). They could also come out of their cells for recreation in these same small groups. We tried to separate known enemies and gang members from gangs that were at war and would kill each other if given the opportunity.

The final phase was called the honor unit. Inmates were out of their cells most of the day and got to work in the prison industries program. They went to the prison dining room to eat their meals. They had to keep at least a year of good conduct in this unit to be considered for release from Marion. If they had misconduct, they were sent back and had to start their control program at the beginning. Those released from Marion were sent to a regular maximum-security federal prison.

Question: What was Marion like when you first arrived as warden?

Warden Williford: I arrived in Marion just months after the two correctional officers were murdered on the same day. As warden, my first focus was to rebuild the confidence of staff and show them that they could be safe in their work. In the early days, I think staff were scared, and some responded by overreaction to inmate violence and with too much bravado. As they felt safer, they realized they could still control inmates and the facility through sound security procedures, rather than to respond to violence with violence. As staff became more confident and calm, the inmates also seemed to relax some as well.

For a long time, the media was very critical of our staff and portrayed them as the aggressors and the inmates as the victims. I tried to open the prison more to the media so that they would see the professionalism of our staff.

About six months after I arrived, the trial for *Bruscino v. Carlson* started, with court held in a prison courtroom. This was so inmates could testify without having to be taken to the federal courthouse. I think the inmates believed they would win the lawsuit and be released from Marion, or at least the lockdown would have to end. There was much tension and hostility between inmates and staff during this time. Whenever I walked the prison, inmates would make catcalls and were extremely disrespectful of staff and myself. After a three-month trial, we won the lawsuit and were allowed to continue to operate Marion on a lockdown status. Once we won, the inmates realized the only way to get out of Marion was to behave, and they started treating staff with respect and worked to try to get out of Marion the right way.

Question: Can you tell us some of the things that went on while you were at Marion?

Warden Williford: While I was there, we had two murders of inmates by other inmates. In both, the murder did not include the use of a weapon and occurred during a one-on-one fight. In one case, an inmate beat the other inmate's head on the concrete floor. In the other, one inmate got the other inmate down on the ground and kicked him in the head until he died.

I spend a lot of time walking the cellblocks, talking to staff, and being accessible to inmates. I would often talk to inmates at the front of their cells. However, an inmate I had known for a while told me there was a "hit" on my life and I should step back from the cell fronts. I took him at his word and, while I still walked the tiers and talked to inmates, I stood back an arm length and protected myself.

Question: Who were some of the more notorious inmates at Marion?

Warden Williford: One of the best-known inmates there was Christopher Boyce, who was convicted of treason and had escaped from another federal maximum-security prison. There was a movie called *The Falcon and the Snowman*, the nicknames for Boyce and his codefendant. Timothy Hutton played the Falcon, based on the Christopher Boyce character. Hutton came to Marion to view the movie with Boyce. Boyce first said he would not see Hutton unless he could do it without being handcuffed. We refused, and Mr. Hutton agreed with our position. So Boyce changed his mind and agreed to watch the movie with Mr. Hutton while handcuffed.

Jack Abbott was another notorious inmate. Norman Mailer helped him get released on parole after he left Marion. Abbot's letters to Mailer were used as the basis for a play called In the Belly of the Beast, about being in prison, killing other inmates, and what it took to commit a murder in prison.

Garrett Trapnell was another well-publicized inmate. Dan Rather interviewed him and Trapnell told him he would escape within a year. Trapnell had formed a relationship with a woman who started to correspond with him while in prison. She hijacked a helicopter and tried to use it to help him escape. She forced the pilot at gunpoint to fly from St. Louis to the prison. Just before landing in the prison yard, the pilot was able to wrestle the gun from the woman and shot her dead. During the fight over the gun, the helicopter crash landed on the prison grounds.

Question: It sounds like a fascinating time, yet it had to be a challenging job.

Warden Williford: It was both. I will never forget the courage and professionalism of the Marion staff. Without their hard work, we would have not won the lawsuit, and there might not be any supermax prisons today.[67]

Operation and Controversies of Supermax Prisons

A supermax prison is defined as follows:

> *A freestanding facility, or distinct unit within a facility, that provides for the management and secure control of inmates who have been officially designated as exhibiting violent or seriously disruptive behavior while incarcerated. Such inmates have been determined to be a threat to safety and security in traditional high-security facilities, and their behavior can be controlled by separation, restricted movement, and limited access to staff and other inmates.*[68]

Security is the dominant feature of the supermax prison. All aspects of maintaining the prison, including structure of the building, education and programs, human contact, medical services, food service, property, and policies and procedures, revolve around proper security measures. When inmates do come out of their cells, they are handcuffed, often placed in leg irons, and escorted by at least two correctional officers. Human contact in a supermax prison is very limited, as inmates have minimum (or no) contact with other inmates, and have contact with medical staff, clergy, or counselors only when these staff members visit their cells. Inmates are almost always alone in solitary cells and generally eat, recreate, and participate in programs (via video) by themselves.

A supermax cell. All the materials in the cell are built to be indestructible and are not able to be used as weapons. Courtesy of the Ohio Department of Rehabilitation and Correction.

Supermax prisons were created for inmates who exhibited violent and predatory behavior in other prisons. However, the use of supermax prisons has expanded; in some states, to reduce gang activity and related violence in other prisons, identified prison gang members are also removed from general-population prisons and placed in a supermax prison, even if they have not committed a violent act while in prison. California in 1989 and Connecticut in the early 1990s were two of the first states to move gang members and leaders to a supermax prison. The only way for gang members to get out of the lockdown situation is to refute their membership and debrief or tell correctional officials everything they know about the gang operations and membership. Once they do tell officials about the gang activities, they would not be welcome back into the gang and would probably be assaulted or killed by other gang members if given the chance. Since the first identification of prison gangs, California has had the most gang members and the most problems and now uses a similar strategy: All gang leaders are placed in the supermax prison at Pelican Bay, are kept in a single-person cell, and recreate by themselves.

The purpose of the solitary isolation and extraordinary security within a supermax prison is to prevent extremely violent and dangerous inmates from harming others. Supermax prisons serve two functions in this regard. First, they control very violent and dangerous inmates. With constant diligence, security, and caution, these inmates have very limited opportunity to harm others. As inmates comply with security rules and show less intent to be disruptive, they usually earn small additional privileges, such as added time out of their cells or the opportunity to recreate or eat with a small number of other inmates. Over two or three years, if they continue to behave, supermax inmates can progress in privileges and work their way out of the supermax to a traditional maximum-security prison. The second function of supermax prisons is to discourage violent behavior in general-population prisons. Correctional administrators point out that the presence of supermax prisons is an incentive for good behavior, because inmates want to avoid being sent to this type of lockdown confinement. The efficacy of these assumptions is, however, in debate. A recent and very thorough analysis of the impact of incapacitation through a concentration of violent inmates and focusing on security reduces violent acts. Wooldredge and Steiner in 2015 examined rates of assault in 247 prisons in forty states, and found that there was actually more violence in these high security prisons.[69] And there is also a questionable outcome for deterrence in behaviors of other inmates who want to avoid supermax assignments.

In a supermax prison, inmates often can recreate out of their cells only in a small caged area with a small number of other inmates. Photo by Richard P. Seiter.

Studies of behavior after assignment to administrative segregation found little or no reduction in violent acts and other misbehavior.[70]

While these supermax prisons were created for what many consider the "right" reason (to protect other inmates), they have been the center of controversy since their establishment. Advocates point out that the presence of supermax prisons is a deterrent and incentive for good behavior, because inmates want to avoid this type of lockdown confinement. However, opponents of solitary confinement assert that the lack of human contact, the absence of work, and the deficiency of intellectual stimulation are human rights violations and have negative consequences on individuals.[71] The most common argument against supermax prisons was that the isolation would result in a deterioration of the mental health of inmates, and would be especially damaging for inmates who already had a mental illness at their time of placement.[72] However, a study in Colorado found no deterioration in mental health as the result of placement in administrative segregation.[73] Even the authors of the report note that findings were unexpected, due to the commonly cited argument that long-term confinement is detrimental to inmates. Advocates of solitary confinement cite the study as evidence in the benefits of supermax facilities. Yet opponents argue that the design of the study and reliance on self-reports by inmates make the findings questionable and at least should not be generalized to long-term solitary confinement in other states.

There are many controversies in regard to supermax prisons. Some of these and the developments around administrative segregation, or restrictive status housing are further presented in Chapter 16. The "You Make the Decision" box at the end of the chapter asks you to decide whether you support the use of supermax prisons.

Sex Offenders

Over the past twenty-five years, as a result of two major factors, the number of sex offenders under correctional supervision has risen significantly. First, public education regarding sex offenses has led to more victims reporting the sexual offense to police. Victims had previously been very hesitant to make their allegations public, fearing that they would not be believed, would be humiliated, and might suffer reprisal. The criminal justice system is better prepared to respond to the allegations of sex offenses, and DNA testing and other advances in forensic science have made some of them easier to prove. Second, legislatures have passed laws to support and aid victims, to clarify definitions of sex offenses that aid in the prosecution of such crimes, and to toughen sanctions for such offenses. Legislation has basically focused on punishment and deterrence, and included longer sentences, registration and notification, involuntary civil commitments, and lifetime probation and parole.[74] As a result, at the end of 2015, 12.5 percent of sentenced offenders in state prisons were serving a sentence for rape or sexual assault.[75]

Sex offenders are commonly defined as those who commit a legally prohibited sexual act or, in some states, any offender who commits any crime that is "sexually motivated." For instance, an assault that was an unsuccessful rape attempt may still be classified as a sex offense. The term *sex offender* usually includes offenders convicted of rape or sexual assault. Sexual assault includes the crimes of statutory rape, forcible sodomy, lewd acts with children, and other offenses relating to fondling, molestation, or indecent practices. **Pedophile** is the term for someone who is sexually attracted to and molests children.

Females are the primary victims of sexual assaults, although both male and female children are more equally molested by pedophiles. According to national crime reports, there were 130,603 rapes in 2016.[76] Female victims accounted for 82 percent

sex offenders
offenders who have committed a legally prohibited sexual act or in some states any offender who commits any crime that was statutorily defined as sexually motivated

pedophile
someone who is sexually attracted to and molests children

of all rapes and sexual assaults, and 69 percent of victims were white.[77] The following illustrates other facts regarding the victims of rape or other sexual assault:

- Victims are primarily white.
- 45 percent of sexual assaults are of children age twelve or younger.
- Over one-third of sexual assaults are by a family member to the victim.[78]
- Data on characteristics of offenders imprisoned for rape and sexual assault indicate that almost 99 percent are males, and 52 percent of rape and 74 percent of sexual assault offenders are white.
- The average age at the time of their arrest for this offense was thirty-four.
- And 22 percent were married, 28 percent (rape) and 35 percent (sexual assault) offenders were divorced, and 52 percent (rape) and 37 percent (sexual assault) offenders had never been married.[79]

Most sex offenders are supervised in the community. In 2016, there were 861,837 registered offenders across the United States.[80] Offenders convicted of rape and sexual offenses receive anything from probation to imprisonment. The number of imprisoned sex offenders is growing. In 1980, only 20,500 sex offenders were in state prisons; by 1994, this number had climbed to 88,100,[81] and by the end of 2015, there were 161,900 inmates sentenced for rape or sexual assault in state prisons.[82] Once in prison, sex offenders serve longer periods of time. In 1990, offenders convicted of rape were serving an average of sixty-two months in prison, and those convicted of other sexual offenses were serving thirty-six months. In the most recent report, for felons sentenced for rape, the average prison sentence was 162 months, the average jail sentence was eight months, and for those receiving probation, the probation period was sixty months. For sexual assault (includes offenses such as statutory rape and incest with a minor) felons, the average prison sentence was ninety-eight months, jail was eight months, and probation was fifty-seven months.[83]

Treatment and Management of Sex Offenders

Even with the toughening of laws to heighten punishment and deterrence of sex crimes, the focus to lower recidivism has been sex offender treatment programming. Sex offenders present a difficult challenge for management in both community and institutional settings. Not all sex offenders share similar characteristics, and the most effective management and treatment come from creating a program that relates to the individual characteristics of the offender. A National Institute of Justice survey of state supervision of sex offenders in the community identified a five-part containment process that "seeks to hold offenders accountable through the combined use of both offenders' internal controls and external control measures (such as the use of the polygraph and relapse prevention plans)."[84] This **containment model** is designed to use a "triangle" of supervision: "treatment to teach sex offenders to develop internal control over deviant thoughts; supervision and surveillance to control offenders' external behaviors; and polygraph examinations to help design, and to monitor conformance to, treatment plans and supervision conditions."[85] And research has identified reductions in recidivism with the containment model.[86] The five components of the model are as follows:

1. An overall philosophy and goal of community and victim safety
2. An individualized case management system of sex offender specific containment tailored to the needs of the sex offender

containment model
an approach to managing sex offenders that includes treatment to develop internal control over deviant thoughts, supervision and surveillance to control external behaviors, and polygraph examinations to monitor conformance to treatment plans and supervision conditions

3. A multidisciplinary approach of collaboration among teams of law enforcement, probation and parole, treatment providers, and prison personnel to manage the offender

4. Consistent public policies reflecting the latest knowledge regarding effective management of sex offenders

5. A quality-control component to monitor whether policies are being implemented as intended and that they are producing the desired impact

In addition to the containment approach, there are other treatment and management approaches for sex offenders in both institutional and community settings.[87] The Center for Sex Offender Management proposes what they call a "comprehensive approach."[88] The comprehensive approach includes the following:

- Victim centeredness—the impact of sexual victimization on the victim and communities must be paramount to any strategy.

- Specialized knowledge—persons working in managing sex offenders must have specialized knowledge of characteristics of sex offenders, their victims, and effective intervention.

- Awareness and information—increasing public awareness and providing the public with accurate information about sex offenders is central to successful prevention and management efforts.

- Monitoring and evaluation—these should be aligned with the most recent evidence-based programs.

- Collaboration—this is a complex issue and all stakeholders must work together to ensure their resources and capabilities are brought to bear on this problem.

Sex Offender Recidivism

Although sex offenders are a difficult group to rehabilitate, the recidivism rates generally attributed to sex offenders are not as high as many people think. In examining sex offender inmates in state prisons in 1991 who were recidivists, an estimated 24 percent of those serving time for rape and 19 percent of those serving time for sexual assault had been on probation or parole at the time of the offense for which they were incarcerated.[89] In a study by the Bureau of Justice Statistics of recidivism by probationers, rapists on probation were found to have a lower rate of rearrest for new felonies (19.5 percent) than other violent probationers (41 percent) over the three-year follow-up.[90] And a study of recidivism over thirteen years for offenders convicted of child sexual abuse reports that 61 of the 447 (13.6 percent) had recidivism of any felony, and only 41 of the 447 (9.2 percent) had recidivism for another sex crime (sex crime is a broader category than child sexual abuse).[91]

There have been several meta-analysis completed on the recidivism rates of sex offenders, all with fairly similar results. Outcomes found lower levels of recidivism for further sexual criminality, and higher recidivism for any offense. And treatment was effective in reducing recidivism. Table 9.5 illustrates the comparative data for recidivism of sexual offenses and all crimes in three meta-analyses, noting that participation is treatment can reduce the rate of sexual reoffense by 5 to 10 percent.[92] And more recent studies had similar conclusions. Duwe and Goldman (2009) found that participating in treatment reduced rearrest, but up to 27 percent for sexual recidivism. And Losel and Schmucker (2015) reanalyzed previous meta-analyses, and found reduced recidivism rates for treated compared to untreated sex offenders, with a 26 percent reduction in sexual reoffending.[93]

TABLE 9.5	Recidivism Rates of Sex Offenders			
	Average Recidivism Rate (Any Offense)		**Average Sexual Recidivism Rate**	
Study	**Treatment (%)**	**No Treatment (%)**	**Treatment (%)**	**No Treatment (%)**
Hanson (2009)	31.8	48.3	10.9	19.2
Hanson (2002)	27.9	39.2	12.3	16.8
Losel (2005)	22.4	32.5	11.1	17.5

Source: Roger Przybylski, "Adult Sex Offender Recidivism," chapter 5, in *Sex Offender Management Assessment and Planning Initiative* (Washington, D.C.: U.S. Department of Justice, 2014).

The management and treatment of sex offenders are difficult and often unsuccessful, even though offenders convicted of rape and sexual assault have lower recidivism rates than other violent offenders. However, there is little tolerance for sexual offenders under community supervision, as almost two of every five offenders are returned to prison, even when not committing a new crime. Intensive treatment and monitoring in the community, including the use of Global Positioning Satellite (GPS) and polygraph examinations to confirm compliance with treatment and supervision conditions, often lead to revoking supervision as a preventive approach to avoid further criminality.

Civil Commitment of Sexually Violent Predators

civil commitment statutes
laws to involuntarily continue incarceration of sexual predators even after they have completed their maximum criminal sentence

For the past two decades, state legislatures have taken another step in controlling sexual offenders and protecting potential victims (especially children) from them by passing a new type of mental disorder that allows a diagnosis of sex offenders as sexually violent predators (SVPs). While arguing that these laws are to allow for additional treatment, involuntary **civil commitment statutes** really are designed to keep sexual predators out of the community even after they have completed their maximum criminal sentence. When a person is convicted of a sex offense, he or she receives a specific sentence for that crime. Once the inmate serves his or her time and is nearing release, the state files a petition to have him or her involuntarily and indefinitely committed to a mental institution or special correctional setting that is a blend of a prison and a mental institution. The process includes the completion of an evaluation by mental health professionals, and a probable cause hearing is held to determine whether to label the offender a sexually violent predator. Most jurisdictions require that the offender has both a history of engaging in criminal sexual behavior, and a mental abnormality or personality disorder that without treatment makes it likely he or she will continue to commit acts of sexual violence, even though there are no specific professional criteria that can objectively be considered. If so labeled, once finishing the prison sentence, the inmate is confined in the mental health facility until he or she is judged by mental health professionals to no longer be a danger to the community. Twenty states, the District of Columbia, and the federal government have now enacted laws to involuntarily commit SVPs. There are variations in the approaches to these civil commitment laws taken by the states. However, all have four common elements that are considered in the screening process: a history of sexually harmful conduct, a determination of a current mental disorder or abnormality, a finding of risk of future sexually harmful conduct, and a link between the mental abnormality and the risk of future sexual violence.[94]

Even after two decades, the civil commitment and confinement of SVPs is still an evolving process. Beginning with the 1997 U.S. Supreme Court case of *Kansas v. Hendricks* supporting the civil commitment of SVP laws as long as specific requirements are followed, the courts have also confirmed this decision in *Selling v. Young* (2001) and *Kansas v. Crane* (2002).[95] In these decisions, the courts accept that the confinement at issue is civil and not criminal or imposed as punishment. Individuals identified as SVPs are not housed with a prison population. The confinement model is the same as for other involuntary committed clients with mental illness, and as long as the purpose of confinement is to treat the sex offender, the state may commit the offender for an indefinite period as far as the Constitution is concerned. There is an expectation of the following:

- Comprehensive treatment programs that are geared toward eventual release of the resident are required. The treatment provider performs sex offender risk assessment and discharge planning, which entails recommendations concerning continued commitment or release to the community.
- Confinement is a nonpunitive setting, and residents are civil commitments, not criminals.
- There is extensive, ongoing interaction with the court system in providing frequent mental health status reports. Residents are provided hearings at which judges review the residents' progress toward treatment goals and potential release.

However, civil commitments are usually under the jurisdiction of correctional agencies, creating several operational problems for officials that must confine, treat, and recommend release of these offenders. First, the case law is far from settled as to what is adequate treatment. Few standards for providing treatment to SVPs have been shown to work. Second, the indefinite nature of commitment makes it difficult to plan for release. Even after it is determined that an SVP can be released, there is often community opposition to release and, if it is a high-publicity case, communities object to the offender coming to that location. For example, in California, the Department of Corrections was forced to install a trailer outside a prison on state grounds to house a sex offender who could no longer be confined; yet no release plans were acceptable to the local community. Another issue is that the in-between status of these offenders as part prisoner and part mental patient creates confusion in how to operate a facility. The residents may still be violent and be a danger to staff or other residents, but the confinement restrictions against punishment sometimes make it difficult to house them safely. Finally, it is still too early to tell (as very few civil commitments have been released for any period of time) the effect of these statutes in reducing sexual recidivism.[96] The next few years should provide additional experience and case law that gives correctional officials additional guidance on the management of this population.

The following interview with Dr. Adam Deming describes treatment approaches, operations, and civil commitment statutes.

An Interview With...

A Sex Offender Treatment Manager

Adam H Deming, Psy.D.
Courtesy of Adam H Deming.

Dr. Deming is the executive director of the Indiana Sex Offender Management and Monitoring (INSOMM) program. The program provides assessment, treatment, and supervision to both juveniles and adults convicted of a sex crime. It also delivers training relating to the assessment, treatment, and supervision of sexual offenders to multiple entities across the state of Indiana, and conducts quality assurance and research on program outcomes and methods. The program is operated by Liberty Behavioral Health Corporation, under contract with the Indiana Department of Corrections (IDOC).

Question: Dr. Deming, could you please describe the program you oversee in Indiana?

Dr. Deming: The INSOMM Program is an integrated system of sex offender services, which starts with recidivism risk assessment and risk based treatment within Indiana Department of Corrections prison facilities, and continues with sex offender specific re-entry services prior to release, and community based treatment and supervision for sexual offenders in the community under parole. It is a fully integrated continuum of care, providing services to adult males and females, as well as juvenile males, with multiple stakeholders actively engaged and communicating vital information on the progress and risks of each program participant.

Program services begin in one of three IDOC facilities (one for adult male offenders, one for adult female offenders, and one for juvenile offenders). At any given time, there are approximately 200 adult males, 30 adult females, and 50 male juveniles actively engaged in treatment within these facilities. There are approximately 50 community based credentialed treatment providers and polygraph examiners providing services throughout the state, with approximately 750 offenders receiving treatment in the community. All offenders convicted of a sex crime, which could include rape, child molestation, possession of child sexual exploitation materials, or other sexual crimes, are screened for participation in the program. What makes this program unique, and highly successful, is the teamwork and commitment of the Indiana DOC staff and parole agents, the Liberty staff, the community based treatment providers, and other stakeholders that coordinate services.

Question: Please briefly describe your background and how it led you to your work today.

Dr. Deming: I've been a licensed psychologist since 1992. In 1989, during graduate school, I had a roommate who worked in a private practice running sex offender groups for offenders under probation. He was going out of town for a few weeks and asked me to fill in to run the therapy groups while he was gone. I found it to be very interesting and rewarding clinical work, and just continued to stay involved in the field. I have been in my current position for eleven years, working with Liberty Behavioral Health Corporation, under contract to provide these services for the Indiana DOC. I am very proud of the program here in Indiana. There is a wonderful sense of team work among all the professionals that make the program successful. The communication and team work of the Indiana DOC staff and parole agents, and the Liberty staff, is the most collegial, productive, and mutually supportive that I have seen in my professional career. Thanks to the hard work and dedication of these individuals, I believe Indiana has one of best sex offender treatment and management programs in the country.

Question: Are there particular approaches or models you use in the treatment and management of sex offenders?

Dr. Deming: In the field of sex offender treatment, cognitive behavioral treatment approaches, that use group therapy as the primary treatment modality, are the most widely accepted. Within that framework, many programs integrate a number of interventions into their programming, such as relapse prevention, risk-need-responsivity, the Good Lives Model, and others. Our model in Indiana fits that description, and our program is "risk based." Offenders are assessed for recidivism risk using the Static-99R and, based on their risk and treatment needs they are placed into low, moderate, or high treatment groups. Our program requires offenders to take responsibility for the index offense, or the offense to which they have pled guilty. Participants work in therapy to address individual and environmental factors that led to their committing a sexual crime, and to work on strategies for ceasing to engage in sexually unhealthy or illegal behaviors once they return to the community.

Question: What is the daily regimen of the program?

Dr. Deming: The adult offenders come from their housing units to the treatment building for group therapy and attend at least 4–8 hours of programming per week, depending on their risk factors, treatment needs, and date of projected release. For juveniles, it's more of an all-day program, similar to a therapeutic community. They also attend school during the day, and the counselors have much more involvement in their housing unit and school, as well as treatment. With juvenile offenders, we provide individual and family counseling as well.

The program length of treatment for juveniles is between nine months to one year. For adult males, it is somewhere between six months and 18 months, with high risk offenders receiving the most intensive treatment programming. We know when offenders are getting released, so we begin to get them engaged in the assessment and treatment process about 18 months to two years prior to their release date.

Adult males have two types of treatment tracks, to include psycho-educational groups (interpersonal and social skills, emotional management, normative sexuality, etc.) and "core groups," which are specifically and directly related to addressing issues regarding their sex crimes. Also, for adult males, we may include polygraph examination and/or penile plethysmography (PPG). The PPG is a method for measuring sexual interests in which individuals are shown images to assess for sexual arousal. A circumferential gage that the offender places around their flaccid penis assesses even a slight amount of arousal. This assessment is only undertaken when offenders volunteer for it, and typically performed with offenders who only have convictions against adults, deny any sexual interest in children, and are requesting to have visitation with their minor children upon release to parole. As part of a larger assessment and decision making process, the PPG can help rule out their sexual interest in children and may permit them to have contact with their children. Polygraph examination is used with offenders who may have pled guilty and taken a plea bargain for their sexual crime, but subsequently deny the offense. The polygraph exam then, as part of a broader decision making process, can help to determine whether they're appropriate for treatment.

Generally speaking, successful completion of the program is based on an offender's ability to complete both psychoeducational and core group programming, and must have meaningfully participated in and completed a minimum number of hours for their recidivism risk level.

Question: Does Indiana have a civil commitment statute? If not, talk about such statutes in other states.

Dr. Deming: Indiana does not have a civil commitment statute. There are currently about twenty states that have sexually violent predator civil commitment statutes at this time. These statutes typically result in the indefinite civil commitment of a sex offender following their release from the DOC. These programs have been somewhat controversial, with regard to the ethical, legal, and treatment challenges they face, since the first program was legislated in the State of Washington in 1990. In 2005 and 2006 I was very fortunate to work with a great group of other professionals on a steering committee that developed a network for staff working within civil commitment facilities. The network has grown, and now meets annually for a training conference. I think the network has helped provide better clarity to professionals about their roles within these programs and how to manage the myriad of challenges associated with these treatment programs.[97]

Offenders with Infectious Diseases

Criminal offenders are generally a high-risk group for infectious diseases. Many have not had a healthy lifestyle, including poor nutrition, a lack of medical care, high stress, likelihood of involvement in violent acts, shared needles for drug use, and interaction with other high-risk individuals. Reviews have identified that the populations of our nation's jails and prisons account for a higher percentage of the total population who are infected with HIV or AIDS, hepatitis C, and tuberculosis than would be expected.[98] Therefore, the problems of infectious diseases are often greater than in the general U.S. population, and management by correctional officials of infected offenders causes more serious problems in handling offenders and keeping disease from spreading. Infectious diseases most common to and most problematic with correctional populations include HIV/AIDS, tuberculosis, and hepatitis C.

HIV/AIDS

Human immunodeficiency virus (HIV) attacks the body's immune system, increasing the chance of infection and other diseases. The HIV infection can develop into acquired immune deficiency syndrome (AIDS), which usually proves fatal after some period of time. HIV/AIDS is a serious concern for correctional agencies, especially prisons and jails, in which offenders and staff interact regularly; there is the chance of violence and blood spills; and staff and inmates fear

human immunodeficiency virus (HIV)
a virus that attacks the body's immune system, increasing the chance of infection and other diseases

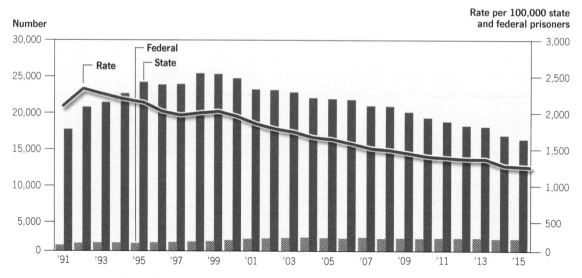

FIGURE 9.2 Number of Inmates in State or Federal Prison Who Had HIV, 1991–2015 Source: Laura M. Maruschak and Jennifer Bronson, "HIV in Prisons - 2015, Statistical Tables," *BJS Statistical Tables* (Washington, D.C.: U.S. Department of Justice, 2017), p. 1.

the transmittal of the disease, even though it is passed only through body fluids (blood, semen, vaginal fluids, and other body fluids) and there is usually little likelihood of individuals contracting the disease through casual or chance contact. In prisons and jails, HIV is usually spread by sexual contact with an infected person or by sharing needles or syringes for drug injection with someone who is infected. HIV/AIDS is a disease that is very difficult and expensive to treat and stresses the ability of staff and availability of dollars for correctional agencies.

It is estimated that in 2014, 1.1 million Americans were living with HIV infection.[99] The overall rate of confirmed AIDS cases among the U.S. prison population was approximately five times the rate in the general U.S. population.[100] While still a serious problem, the incidence of HIV and AIDS in correctional facilities has been reducing. At the end of 2015, state and federal prisons held 17,150 inmates who had HIV or AIDS, down from a high of over 25,000 in 1998. Figure 9.2 illustrates the number and rate of HIV for state and federal prisoners. And the number of inmates who died from AIDS also declined from the high of more than 1,000 in 1995 to a low of 45 deaths in 2015.[101] The percentage of the prison population infected with HIV has also declined over the past few years, from 2.3 percent of the prison population in 1995 to 1.3 percent in 2015.[102]

HIV/AIDS is not distributed evenly throughout the prison population. Ninety-two percent of all prison HIV cases were males. Rates were about the same, as for both males and females, 1.3 percent of prisoners had HIV.[103] Of the forty-five deaths from AIDS in 2015, eighteen were white, twenty-three black, and two Hispanic offenders. And twenty-nine of the deaths were of inmates age forty-five or older.[104]

To determine whether inmates have HIV/AIDS, many states require inmates to have an HIV test. In a 2005 survey, 33 percent of state and federal prison systems reported that they conduct mandatory HIV testing of inmates.[105] However, the Center for Disease Control recommends that prisons allow inmates to "opt out" of testing.[106] Every state and the federal prison system provide educational information to inmates to inform them of the potential for inmates in population to have HIV/AIDS, describe the types of behaviors that can lead to infection, and reduce the fear of infection from other inmates. Once inmates are determined to be positive for HIV, prisons take different approaches to the management of this population. Surprisingly, 80 percent of prison agencies reported that they did not separate inmates testing positive for HIV and 60 percent do not separate those who become symptomatic for AIDS.[107]

Those separated are housed together, some in a medical setting and some in a standard prison housing unit, to reduce concern among other inmates and the potential of transmission to other inmates. Most systems that adopt a nonseparation policy do not divulge the identity of inmates with AIDS to avoid discrimination against them in program and work opportunities and harassment by other inmates and possibly staff. Inmates and staff are told to "take universal precautions," meaning to treat every inmate as HIV positive by avoiding behavior by which HIV could be transmitted and handling inmates or blood spills in a way that avoids the risk of infection (such as by wearing a surgical mask and using rubber gloves when blood is visible).

A controversial issue is to what extent HIV is transmitted inside of prisons. The Centers for Disease Control and Prevention (CDC) suggest "most [inmates] acquired HIV in the community, not while they were incarcerated."[108] In a 2006 study, Krebs found that in a sample of 5,265 male inmates incarcerated as of 1978 and released from prison before 2000, 33 inmates (0.63 percent) contracted HIV infection while in the sampled state prison system.[109] Another 238 inmates released were positive for HIV, but there was no evidence they contracted HIV infection while in prison. These findings are consistent with other studies indicating that most inmates who have HIV are probably infected in the community prior to their incarceration.[110] Hammett notes that "although transmission within correctional facilities has been documented, it does not occur often enough to justify the all-too-commonly used metaphor of correctional facilities as 'breeding grounds' for HIV/AIDS."[111] To reduce the risk of transmission in prisons and jail, another controversial suggestion is to have condom distribution programs. The CDC recommends that this program be "evaluated for use in prisons and jails."[112]

Inmates who are in advanced stages of AIDS require substantial medical care. They are usually hospitalized during the terminal stage of AIDS to provide them treatment and to avoid possible contagious illnesses from other inmates due to their reduced immunity and ability to fight infections. Some prisons have created hostels to provide a sympathetic and dignified setting for inmates who are near death and beyond the ability of medical care to save. Being in prison is difficult for many inmates, but one can only imagine the suffering by inmates who know they are dying and are unable to spend much time with family or friends.

Tuberculosis

Tuberculosis (TB) was a serious medical problem during the early 1900s in the United States, declined, and then resurged in the 1980s and continues to be a problem today. A recent study notes, "At no time in history has tuberculosis (TB) been as prevalence as it is today. More than 9 million new cases occurred in 2006 alone. The increasing world population and other factors, especially HIV infection, have contributed to the increased morbidity."[113] And deaths from TB have also been rising, and it is estimated that there were 1.5 million deaths in 2006.[114] The CDC reports that approximately 4 to 6 percent of all U.S. cases of TB occur among individuals incarcerated at the time of diagnosis, as the incarcerated population contains a high proportion of people at a high risk for TB.[115]

TB is particularly a problem in prisons and jails, as inmates have high rates and risk of TB because of their background of poverty, poor living conditions, substance abuse, and a higher level of HIV/AIDS than the general U.S. population. In addition, close living conditions in correctional facilities increase the potential for transmission of TB among inmates. Early in the 1990s, particular concern was

The Hocking Correctional Facility in Nelsonville, Ohio, was originally a TB hospital. Once TB was able to be treated with medication, those infected were no longer removed from society, and these facilities were available for other uses—such as prisons. Courtesy of the Ohio Department of Rehabilitation and Correction.

raised by various outbreaks of multi-drug-resistant TB in New York State and other jurisdictions. In a 1994 report by the National Institute of Justice regarding TB in prison and jails, the authors write, "Tuberculosis is an airborne disease, transmitted via droplet nuclei (e.g., the dried residue of droplets from sneezes or coughs) from patients who have pulmonary or laryngeal TB and who cough, laugh, spit, or otherwise emit sputum containing the TB bacteria (called *Mycobacterium tuberculosis*). TB can be transmitted through repeated exposure in crowded, poorly ventilated environments; it does not require intimate contact."[116] Although many individuals may test positive for TB infection, the infection may not develop into active TB.

To determine whether inmates have TB, all state and federal prison systems screen inmates at intake to look for signs of TB. In a 2016 survey of state correctional agencies, all respondents noted that they conduct TB tests on all inmates showing signs of TB.[117] The testing is accomplished through a purified protein derivative (PPD) skin test. One problem, both for health care and for detection, is that there can be a false-negative skin test for inmates coinfected with TB and HIV, because the skin test may show negative for TB and the individual does not receive treatment when in fact he or she has both TB and HIV. A review of TB among correctional inmates estimates that 3.8 percent of federal, state, and local prisoner population tests positive for TB.[118]

To avoid the spread of TB in correctional facilities, the Centers for Disease Control recommend the following actions:

- Early identification of persons with TB through entry and periodic follow-up screening;
- Successful treatment of TB disease and latent infection;
- Appropriate use of airborne precautions (infection isolation, environmental controls, and respiratory protection);
- Comprehensive discharge planning; and
- Thorough and efficient contact investigations when a TB case is identified.[119]

An inmate found to have active TB should be immediately removed from the rest of the inmate population, and all effort is made to prevent any staff member or inmate from breathing the contaminated air around him or her. Most prisons have negative pressure isolation rooms in their medical areas and prison hospitals, in which the ventilation system for that room is contained and does not flow into the general ventilation system for the prison. Inmates are placed in these rooms and treated with medication until they prove no longer contagious. They will be regularly screened to detect whether they have returned to an active state. And it is very important to have multiagency and a coordinated approach to dealing with TB. State agencies share data on TB cases and work together to develop and execute communicable-disease control plans.

Hepatitis C

Hepatitis C virus (HCV) is the most common blood-borne illness in the United States and is a serious problem among criminal offenders. It is a serious viral disease that attacks the liver and can result in lifelong infections of the liver, cancer, liver failure, or death. The disease is most commonly spread through the bloodstream as a result of drug users sharing needles when injecting drugs, tattooing, or piercing. In a 2004 publication, a survey with 1,209 prisons responding indicated that almost all facilities test for the disease and of all inmates tested, 17,911 (31 percent) were positive for hepatitis C.[120] HCV infection is much more prevalent in prison inmates than in the general U.S. population, and one estimate is that 17.4 percent of inmates could be infected with Hepatitis C.[121] The CDC estimates are that between 16 percent and 41 percent have ever been infected with HCV and 12–35 percent are chronically infected, compared to 1–1.5 percent of the uninstitutionalized U.S. population.[122]

HCV infection is primarily associated with a history of injection drug use. The Center for Disease Control recommends that inmates be screened regarding past drug use and other risk factors for HCV infection during their admissions for medical evaluations. Those inmates who are determined to have a history of risk should be tested for HCV infection. If they test positive for HCV, they should then receive further medical evaluation to determine if they have chronic infection or liver disease. In a recent survey with forty-five states responding, thirty-six states test at least some incoming prisoners for HCV, three test all prisoners, and twenty-three test those with any clinical indication. Five other states allowed inmates to "opt out" of testing, and two states provided testing for inmates who "opted in."[123]

Hepatitis C was not identified until the mid-1990s, and it is generally accepted that 15–20 percent of those who contract the disease will require no treatment, but in the remainder, the disease will lead to a chronic infection.[124] Treatment with a combination of drugs requires from twenty-four to forty-eight weeks, and many prisoners with relatively short sentences have to defer treatment until they are released to the community. This creates problems upon release both for finding treatment in the community and for community correctional officers who have to work with local medical groups to link offenders to treatment opportunities.[125]

Hepatitis C has quickly become of epidemic proportions and is a serious problem in correctional systems. The ability to identify, diagnose, and treat has improved, but it is often complicated by the simultaneous problems of drug abuse and mental illness among those infected. The long and costly requirement for treatment challenges both prison and community correctional agencies, and it is believed that if treatment options are successful, it can similarly have a positive impact on recidivism. For that reason, researchers and health care officials are calling for a more comprehensive and systemic approach to dealing with criminal offenders with hepatitis C.

Chapter Review

Summary

Most correctional agencies are organized to manage, control, and treat the typical adult offender, who is relatively young, is in good physical and mental health, does not have a serious substance abuse problem, and is not a sex offender. However, it could be argued that when inmates with all these characteristics are removed from the overall group of offenders, very few of those remaining are deemed "typical." Yet groups of offenders with any of these individual issues or needs are defined as special offenders and require specialized treatment, handling, or management. Most community and institutional correctional agencies have unique units (or individuals) trained to deal with these offenders apart from or with different approaches to the mainstream adult offender.

Correctional agencies today face many serious management problems that they did not have in the past as a result of the increasing proportion of the correctional population that may be termed as "special offenders." The increasing number and percentage of the population that are drug offenders, offenders with mental illness, violent offenders, sex offenders, older offenders, or those with an infectious disease create significant problems of control, treatment, and provision of services. Each special group requires additional programs, new policies and procedures, and modified services or even housing arrangements. Such provisions seem difficult enough during times of available budgets and almost impossible during the current times of budgetary constraints.

Another group that is growing in number and in its impact on correctional agencies well beyond the small numbers of prisoners is offenders under age eighteen who have been waived into the adult criminal justice system. Once incarcerated (since most juveniles are waived to adult court for a serious offense, most end up sentenced to prison), correctional agencies struggle with the best way to manage these offenders. Most states attempt to keep juvenile prisoners as separate as possible from adults. Yet when a state has small numbers of prisoners, it is difficult to provide the scope of programs and services that these offenders require, and there seems to be no simple solution to this problem.

Special offenders will continue to be a significant problem for adult correctional agencies. They strain the budgetary resources of an agency, as their management is usually much more expensive per inmate than for nonspecial offenders. They strain the organizational makeup of an agency because they require unique units of specially trained staff to manage, and with so many of these units being created, they take attention away from the central mission and role of most correctional agencies. They also put a strain on staff members, who are under more stress and have greater challenges in dealing with these special groups. Unfortunately, it is not expected that the number of special offenders served by correctional agencies will decline. As this chapter indicates, many more offenders in the correctional population are not being treated or specially managed and require continued expansion of the special services described. Special offenders within prison cause staff members and other inmates serious problems.

Key Terms

special offenders

blended sentencing

straight adult
   incarceration

graduated incarceration

segregated incarceration

arrestee drug abuse monitoring

antipsychotic drugs

medical parole

supermax prisons

Bruscino v. Carlson

sex offenders

pedophile

containment model

civil commitment statutes

human immunodeficiency virus (HIV)

Review Questions

1. What is a special offender, and why do they require special handling while under correctional supervision?

2. What forces encouraged the movement toward the waiver of juveniles into adult courts?

3. In what ways do correctional agencies deal with juveniles under confinement?

4. Explain the distinction between drug offenders and drug addicts.

5. What role have antipsychotic drugs played in the deinstitutionalization of inmates with mental illness?

6. What problems do inmates with mental illness cause?

7. List the reasons for the increased proportion of elderly inmates in the prison population.

8. How do correctional agencies make a gender housing assignment for transgender inmates?

9. Why have supermax prisons become such an attractive option for the management of violent or seriously disruptive inmates?

10. What issues are cited by opponents of supermax prisons?

11. Why do sex offenders present such a difficult challenge for management in both community and institutional settings?

12. What is the containment model of supervising sex offenders?

13. What is civil commitment and who is it used for?

14. Identify the various categories of offenders with infectious diseases.

15. What is the rate of confirmed cases of HIV among inmates, and how does this compare to the rate of those infected with the virus in the nonprison population?

► You Make the Decision...

Should We Use Supermax Prisons?

Over the past two decades, the use of supermax prisons has expanded in corrections, as most states and the federal government have initiated or increased their use of this type of facility. Prison systems have more inmates and many more inmates with histories of violence and gang involvement. With longer sentences and three-strikes laws, many inmates have little hope of ever being released, and they have few disincentives for acting out violently or attempting escape. As a result, prison officials believe supermax prisons are a way to prevent prison violence. If inmates are locked in their cells all but a few hours per week, if programs and services are brought to them instead of them going to the service, and if, when they do come out of cells, they are handcuffed and escorted by staff, they have little opportunity to be violent. Prison officials also believe that the existence of supermax prisons keeps other prisons more peaceful, both because the most violent inmates are in the supermax and because the supermax acts as a disincentive for serious rule violations.

However, there are also many critics of supermax prisons. Opponents express concern that the lack of human contact, the absence of work, and the absence of intellectual stimulation have negative consequences on prisoners. They also argue that physical violence toward inmates may be common in such a controlled atmosphere, and question whether staff working in such a rigid and secure facility will experience problems as well. Supermax prisons are also extremely expensive to build and operate, and several states are reconsidering using them. The requirement for high-security building materials and components, elaborate electrical and technical systems, and the overlay of physical security drives construction costs up to almost double that of a normal medium-security prison. The increased staff member-to-inmate ratio, the need to take services to inmates in a lockdown status, and the absence of inmate workers to carry out many functions also drive up the day-to-day operational costs.

Either individually or in a small group, consider these pros and cons, and decide whether you support the use of supermax prisons. If you do, specify the types of inmates or the acts committed by inmates that would warrant their assignment to a supermax. If you do not, specify how you would handle violent and dangerous offenders.

Courtesy of CoreCivic.

After reading this chapter, you should be able to:

1. Outline the organizational structure of prisons.

2. Describe the various jobs and functions of prison staff, and the functions of custody, treatment, and services in prison.

3. Define unit management and describe the role it plays in the management of a prison.

4. Describe methods for controlling inmate behavior, including classification of inmates and use of a disciplinary system.

5. Suggest ways the staff of a correctional agency can help or hinder a prison accomplishing its mission.

Introduction

What are the essential functions in a prison that make it work effectively? What does it take to accomplish the mission of creating a safe and secure environment and providing inmates the opportunity for program participation that can help them reenter the community? Prisons are complex organizations, based on a tenuous relationship of greatly outnumbered staff controlling potentially violent and dangerous inmates. They must provide all services necessary for their operation in a cost-effective manner and endeavor to change inmates' future behavior through the provision of treatment programs. None of these activities is easy in its own right and trying to accomplish them all can seem like an impossible goal. However, modern prisons do a very good job of meeting these objectives through a combination of organization, methods to control inmate behavior, working through their staff, and taking steps to ensure quality performance of their functions.

The first section in this chapter covers how prisons and their headquarters agencies are organized. The organization of any agency should be designed to enhance the completion of the agency mission. However, in the public sector, the agency must also address many external pressures and interests, which are thus reflected in the agency organization. However, the key components of a headquarters correctional organization are to help the prisons operate effectively and efficiently and to oversee the supervision of offenders in the community. The organizational charts for both a state department of corrections and a state prison are presented to illustrate and explain these functions. Also, the use of unit management as a more efficient method of managing prisons is presented and discussed.

In the second section of this chapter, the methods used to manage inmates and control behavior are addressed. These include the consistent implementation of state-of-the-art policies and procedures, a classification system to match inmate needs and security risks with staff and prison resources, and the use of a fair and equitable system for disciplining inmates who violate rules. There are far fewer prison staff members than inmates at any time in a prison. Therefore, the key to effective management of a prison is to have these types of functions in place to create expectations for staff and inmates, to divide inmates into similar groups of risks and needs so that policies and practices can be tailored to each group, and to reward compliance and punish violation of prison rules by inmates.

Finally, the critical role that staff members play in prison operations is described. No matter how good the physical security of a prison, no matter how thorough the policies, and no matter how well implemented a classification or inmate disciplinary system, if staff members are not competent and professional in carrying out their duties, all these other managerial aspects are undermined. In this regard, this chapter also describes the practices used to recruit and hire quality staff, as well as the role that collective bargaining plays in managing a prison.

The Organization of Prisons

Prisons are organized in a manner that leads toward their ability to carry out their mission of creating a safe and secure environment and providing inmates the opportunity for program participation that can help them reenter the community. Although prisons could, most likely, carry out this mission independently, with no guidance or oversight by a state department of corrections, states and the federal government have found it more effective to have an umbrella agency that oversees prisons, is the link between elected officials and the prisons, and can ensure quality and consistency in the operations of all the prisons within that agency. In Chapter 5, the reasons for and stages of the development of state and the federal correctional agencies were described.

Therefore, to understand the way prisons are organized to carry out their mission, it is also important to understand the role of a state department of corrections and the activities it undertakes to guide and assist in the effective operation of individual prisons. In the following sections, both the organizations of the umbrella agency and individual prisons are presented and described. As of December 31, 2005, the fifty states and the federal government operated 1,821 prisons. The largest correctional agency is the Federal Bureau of Prisons (BOP), which on September 28, 2017, housed 185,740 inmates at its 120 facilities.[1]

State Departments of Corrections

The central organization that oversees state and federal prisons is often called the *central office* or *headquarters*. For much of their history, U.S. prisons were operated independently, governors appointed wardens, state legislatures appropriated the budget for each prison, and wardens ran the prison without interference and in whatever manner they saw fit. As noted in Chapter 5, most of these headquarters organizations have been established over the past thirty years, as states did not previously have a separate agency to oversee the operations of prisons and other correctional components. However, the increasing political and public interest in how states ran their prison systems, the increasing litigation by prisoners regarding conditions of confinement, and the need for quality and efficiency caused the creation of central agencies to ensure consistency of standards and guide the administration of prisons.

As the numbers of prisoners and prisons have grown significantly over the past thirty years, the central headquarters of the state and federal correctional agencies have grown in the number of functions and employees required for overseeing large and complicated organizations and maintaining central control and consistency among prisons. As an example, the table of organization of the central office of the Ohio Department of Rehabilitation and Correction (Figure 10.1) is presented. Ohio has the sixth largest correctional agency in the United States in terms of the number of inmates under supervision, with 52,175 offenders in Ohio prisons on December 31, 2016. The largest correctional agencies in order of number of inmates as of this date were the BOP (189,192), Texas (163,703), California (130,390), Florida (99,974), and Georgia (53,627).[2]

The Ohio Department of Rehabilitation and Correction has responsibility not only for all the state prisons, but also for the parole board and parole supervision, probation services and supervision in some counties, and assistance to counties for jail inspections and developing and funding community sanctions. This department is similar to most state correctional agencies and illustrates the complexity in the management of an agency that operates twenty-seven prisons, has a 2018 budget of $1.8 billion, and in September 2017, employs approximately 12,216 staff members, and supervises 50,257 inmates and 37,405 offenders in the community. The average daily cost per inmate was $72.23, or $26,364.73 per year.[3] Several key functions deserve note in review of the organizational chart for a state department of corrections.

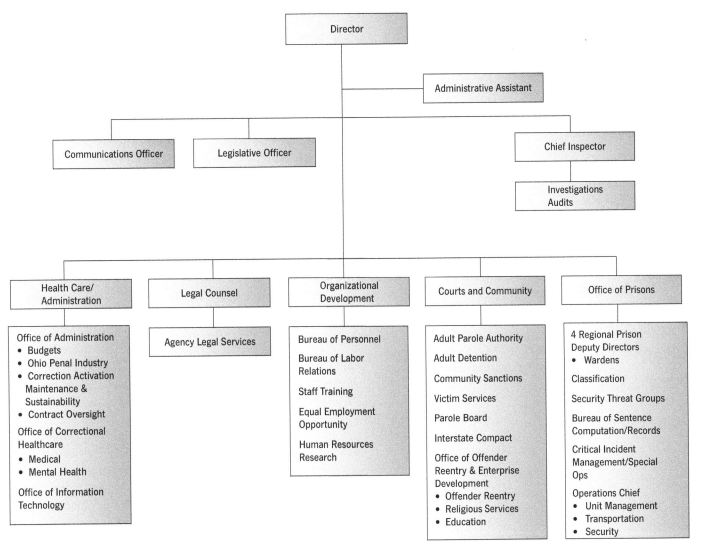

FIGURE 10.1 Table of Organization for the Central Office of the Ohio Department of Rehabilitation and Correction Source: Ohio Department of Rehabilitation and Correction. Reprinted with permission.

Functions of the Office of Director

The chief executive of a state department of corrections is usually called the **director** or secretary of the department. Many functions are attached to the office of the director. Most central correctional agencies organizationally locate the external management functions (legal services, legislative liaison, public affairs, investigations) close to the director and sometimes report to the director. Correctional agencies have found that external management issues are very sensitive and can quickly become political or media crises and, therefore, there should be immediate access to the issue between the staff dealing with it and the person who is the final decision maker. The worst thing that can happen to a correctional agency is for an issue that is potentially sensitive to be misrepresented by lower-level staff members who have not been provided input from the person in charge of the agency.

Directors of correctional agencies often become like managers of professional baseball teams in that, when things go wrong, they get the blame and are replaced. This is not always because they have done a bad job, but because a change is seen as necessary to appease important groups or individuals outside the agency. Directors of state correctional agencies can lose the confidence of their elected supervisors

director
the chief executive officer of a state or federal department of corrections

The director of a state prison system makes regular visits to the prison, talks to the warden and other staff, and clearly communicates expectations. Photo by Richard P. Seiter.

and therefore most often lose their jobs because of the way agency policies are perceived, rather than from an actual failure in the internal management of the agency. Therefore, directors of corrections do not want "surprises" when it comes to developments around sensitive external communications, and they maintain these organizational functions as components of the director's office.

The organizational entities that often reside in the office of the director include communications (public and media affairs), legislative liaison, legal advisors, and chief inspector (internal affairs). As criminal justice and correctional issues have become of great interest to the public, there is a tremendous demand for information from the media. Minor incidents in one prison with local media interest are usually handled at that local prison. However, an issue of state correctional policy or a major incident will usually result in the headquarters public information section responding to requests from the media.

As state correctional agencies have grown to be one of the largest state departments and use a large percentage of the state budget, legislatures have become much more interested in correctional policy and operations, and legislative members regularly have questions about a prison in their district or an issue regarding a constituent. Therefore, correctional agencies usually have an office of legislative affairs, which responds to legislative requests and builds support for the department regarding resources and programs. Staff members of the office of legislative affairs regularly brief staff from legislative offices and committees so that they know the purpose of programs and are not surprised by media reports or bills submitted by the department.

Legal sections within correctional agencies also often report to the director of corrections. Legal offices deal with three general categories of issues: (1) responding to inmate lawsuits, (2) reviewing policy for legal impact, and (3) giving general advice regarding implementation of programs in line with past legal decisions. As described more fully in Chapter 15, with the demise of the hands-off doctrine by federal courts, the floodgates were opened to inmate litigation. In 2016, there was a sharp rise in the number of petitions by prisoners (a total of 73,725; an increase from 52,531 in 2015) filed in U.S. District Courts across the country.[4] Legal staff members of correctional agencies usually do not actually argue the cases in court, as that is the responsibility of the state and federal attorneys general. However, correctional lawyers must often review the lawsuits and initiate investigations to aid in the defense. Also, correctional legal staff members usually review new or changed policy to identify any potential legal concerns.

inspector

a person in a department of corrections who investigates allegations by inmates against staff

The office of the director also will often have an **inspector** or internal affairs division as a part of the organization. In some states, internal affairs may be an independent agency reporting to the governor that investigates any sensitive allegations regarding employees or agencies. The ethical behavior by staff of a correctional agency is a very high priority, and the opportunity for unethical or even illegal behavior is great when staff members are in daily contact with manipulative inmates. Therefore, complaints of a staff member's misconduct by anyone (inmates, other staff members, inmate families, or the general public) are investigated. An objective look by trained investigators is the best defense for staff against untrue allegations, and it is necessary to find cases in which staff members have acted unethically or unprofessionally to maintain a credible and effective operation of prisons.

In addition, many inmate complaints often end up in a lawsuit, so an early investigation of the complaint also creates a documented record for later use (perhaps months or even years later) when the department needs to respond to a legal suit.

State directors of correctional agencies have the opportunity to influence the lives of many people. The "Your Career in Corrections" box describes their roles and responsibilities.

Administration Functions

The administrative section of a correctional agency usually carries out two major functions: budget development and accounting and new prison construction. The central budget division collects information from all the prisons, other divisions, and the governor's office to create a budget that represents desired programs, growth, and continued operations. The corrections budget becomes a part of the entire state budget that the governor presents to the state legislature. Once a budget is approved for a correctional agency, the administrative division maintains accountability of funds and keeps current on spending levels so that the agency does not go beyond its allocated amount.

Your Career in Corrections

Correctional Administrators

There are only fifty-two jobs of this kind in the United States—in the fifty states, the District of Columbia, and the Federal Bureau of Prisons (BOP): director of a correctional agency. How do directors get this job? They have to be appointed by the governor of a state, the mayor of the District of Columbia, or the attorney general of the United States (for the BOP). The people appointed to do these jobs usually have years of correctional experience, but with more sensitivity by elected officials regarding the political impact of correctional policies, people with no correctional experience (but close to the governor or with extensive political experience) have been appointed to these jobs more frequently.

In 2016, the average correctional administrator had responsibility for almost 30,000 prisoners,[5] 8,500 staff members, and average annual budgets (state agencies) of approximately $970 million in 2010.[6] They must oversee the operations of twenty-six prisons (the average in each state); create a politically supported agenda; be responsible for the safety and security of staff, offenders, and the general public; and provide rehabilitative programs to improve the chance of offenders becoming productive and law-abiding citizens. When things go well—there are no prison riots or escapes, no horrible crimes are committed by former clients (offenders under their supervision), and there are no union complaints because of low pay or perceived unsafe working conditions—they are merely doing the job they were hired to perform. However, when bad things happen or when elected officials or the public are upset about specific correctional policies, how they are implemented, or how much they cost, directors get the blame. One would wonder why anyone takes such a job.

Staff members who work in corrections usually do not do so because they are motivated by power or pay. They desire to make a difference, to serve the public, and to assist offenders. They work in corrections for several years and find that they have an affinity for the discipline and management and leadership talent. They see that the individuals in authority have the opportunity to initiate programs and improvements that can benefit staff, offenders, and the public. So as they move into an executive position and the opportunity comes along to be considered for the top administrator position, they do not think of the downside of the position, but only the opportunities it brings.

Pay is not bad for correctional administrators, although similar levels of responsibility in the private sector would pay considerably more. Although the pay has continued to increase, the average salary for directors of adult correctional agencies as of January 1, 2002, was $106,893; however, the average tenure in office at that time was only 4.4 years.[7] Not too many directors stay in the job much longer than this, because with every change of governor, there is often a change in corrections director. Also, the positions are highly stressful, and when things go wrong, there is often a change in leadership.

However, these are great jobs if you enjoy a challenge and having a lot of responsibility. This responsibility is not to be taken lightly, as it can involve the safety of staff and the potential of life-threatening situations. However, the rewards of satisfaction for a job well done, of serving the public, and of helping offenders get their lives in order make this job one worth striving for.

For the past twenty years of tremendous growth in the number of prison inmates, these budget requests have regularly included funds to construct new prisons. In 2001, nine new prisons were opened in the United States at a cost of $387 million; twenty-eight prisons were under construction and fifty-eight existing ones were expanding their capacity at a total cost of $1.5 billion; and funding for capital construction for budget year 2002 was $1.5 billion.[8] From June 30, 2000, to December 30, 2005, 153 new state and federal prisons and 151 new private prisons were constructed and opened.[9] Construction then slowed down, and between 2000 and 2008, another 20,000 state and 3,000 federal beds were added.[10] From 2008 until 2016, both the recession and slowing (sometimes reduction) in state prison populations did not require new construction. However, almost 80,000 beds in capacity were added, even though at least three states reduced their capacities by almost 10,000.[11] The administration division is usually charged with overseeing the design and construction of these new and renovated facilities, including hiring architects, coordinating their design with the departments' correctional experts, overseeing construction, and preparing to open the new facilities.

Human Resources Functions

In some states, the central headquarters performs all human resources activities. In other states, each prison carries out the personnel functions of recruitment, hiring, evaluations, and retirement, whereas the broad human resources functions (labor relations, affirmative action or equal employment opportunity [EEO], and the operation of a central training academy) are carried out by the headquarters human resources division. Many states have a unionized correctional workforce, and negotiating and administering labor contracts are very legalistic and time consuming. Therefore, the central office usually has staff with expertise in labor relations to do the negotiations and advise prison managers on labor contract issues. Although each prison conducts some staff training, almost every state operates a central academy for training new hires and providing specialty training statewide.

Community Supervision Functions

For states that still use indeterminate sentences and parole for release decisions, the parole board and postrelease supervision are usually located within the department of corrections. In some states, the probation functions are also operated by the state rather than the counties (see Chapter 3). Statewide parole and probation functions are organized into geographic regions, districts, or city offices to supervise offenders. In addition, many states carry out intermediate sanctions programs (electronic monitoring, house arrest, intensive supervision, or halfway houses) that are also coordinated by central headquarters. Finally, states sometimes provide assistance to county jails. Assistance may be in the form of grant funds to build new jails or to upgrade policies, procedures, or operations. In addition, every state has statewide jail standards, and department of corrections employees are usually responsible for inspecting jails for compliance with these standards.

Field Operations Functions

Finally, central offices have a division (or geographic regions) that directly supervises prisons. The Ohio system is divided into North, South, and Central regions that supervise the prisons. The role of the central office is to supervise the prison wardens and general operations, to create policy, and to oversee consistent implementation of policy. The following sections describe the organization of a prison and how the prison implements policies prescribed by the central headquarters of a correctional agency.

An interesting link between the headquarters of a correctional agency and the prisons is the personal role of the leaders of the department in overseeing the work of the prison. Although prisons are led and managed by a warden, the director (correctional administrator) of the department sets the tone and should be a role model for managing the correctional institutions. The "An Interview With" box illustrates this role and some ways that correctional administrators keep in contact with what goes on in a prison under their supervision. This interview is with myself, when I was director of the Ohio Department of Rehabilitation and Correction.

An Interview With...

A Correctional Administrator

Richard P. Seiter.

This is an interview with Richard P. Seiter, who served as director of the Ohio Department of Rehabilitation and Correction from 1983 to 1988. He had been previously a warden for the Federal Bureau of Prisons and chief of the National Academy of Corrections. He was thirty-four years old when he was appointed director, the youngest person ever appointed director of this Ohio department.

Question: I understand that you regularly visit the prisons in the state and that these visits are "from dawn to dusk," covering every area and talking to every staff member in the prison. I also understand that when you are there, you do a thorough sanitation inspection, looking, as I am told, "for dust in every corner and on every ledge, for soap grime in the bathroom sinks, and at every fire extinguisher for the monthly inspection documentation." First of all, why do you make such regular and extensive visits to the prisons?

Director Seiter: Well, the problem with working in a headquarters of an agency is that you get removed from the day-to-day working of the agency and its people. So, I do it so I do not forget what it is like, how hard the jobs are, and to hear from our staff firsthand how they are doing and what issues are on their mind. But, as much as anything, I do it because I enjoy it. This may sound pretty strange, but I really get a kick out of being in the prisons, and interacting with staff and inmates.

Question: Let's discuss that in more detail. Talk more about the danger of getting too far removed from the day-to-day operations of the prisons.

Director Seiter: I see my job as primarily to make the job of the staff working in a prison easier. This means many things. First, I need to stay ahead of the issues that are confronting them so that the problems do not get to a point where they are out of control. Every prison has problems in management. That is just the nature of the beast. Inmates are not used to following rules and complying with authority. So, every day, someone will try to avoid compliance, and staff have to deal with each situation—many will not work out as perfectly as planned. They have to take care of those issues by themselves; I can't help them with each situation. But I can understand the forces that create situations and make prison management more difficult. For instance, if we are beginning to have a newly developing friction between some competing gangs, it is important to get on top of it as soon as possible. By being in the prisons, I can get a sense for what is happening from those having to deal with it, gather some intelligence they have picked up, and see what urgency there is to create some system-wide response.

Let me stick to that point for a second. I think an extremely underacknowledged skill of administrators is to understand when an issue has urgency, especially when the administrator is removed from the situation (in his or her prison office or in the state headquarters) and does not feel the intensity of the staff that have to react to it. Not all issues or situations (regardless of how serious they may be—for instance a murder of an inmate by another) have the urgency that requires a system-wide response. Some just need to be handled as best staff can deal with them as they come up. Others need a deliberate and thoughtful response, and the proper response can almost "bubble up" from each sequential incident. Administrators must be careful not to do the wrong thing or create the wrong response, just to react to something before they really understand the cause and underlying issues.

Finally, some issues do have real urgency, and staff are crying out for guidance and policy change or new direction. Let me go back to the example I started to reference about developing

(Continued)

gang tensions. If I hear staff concern about this issue in one prison, it is worth having our gang staff (often called security threat groups) in headquarters survey other prisons to see if they are having similar situations. The fact that I heard about the issue from prison staff firsthand helped me understand the urgency and my responsibility for action. Otherwise, you may just read reports about a variety of incidents in a variety of prisons, and while you sense a link and ask the staff to look into it, you do not do so with the sense that it is critical to the safe management of the prisons. I have talked to my colleagues about issues like this one that have gone on in a state, with staff constantly seeking help on how to deal with it. However, because the top administrators are so tied up with their own issues (budget, the legislature, media pressure about an escape), they don't jump on the importance of this to the prisons. I personally get a better sense of the urgency of an issue by being in the prisons and hearing staff talk about it. One final note: Line staff and even wardens tend to downplay certain things when talking to their bosses; they do not want to give the impression that they can't handle it. So they don't "sound an alarm" themselves and don't often communicate a sense of urgency. That is when your own correctional experience and common sense come into play, and you hear a sense of urgency that is not overtly communicated.

The second way I try to make the job of prison staff easier is to show them that I support them, appreciate them, and respect the job they are doing. Correctional administrators can do this in a variety of ways. They can provide an adequate level of funding for employee awards programs to recognize staff that do a good job. They can urge managers to use incentive awards and can create special awards to recognize the behaviors they think are important at any particular time. They can send notes to employees who have done some especially good job or had a significant accomplishment. They can do media interviews and make public statements of support for staff and the jobs they do. However, nothing is more important than giving staff your time, going to them and saying hello, shaking their hands, and showing them you care about them personally. I received feedback from a prison in the town in which I grew up. In fact, it was told to my mother, which really made me feel good. She met a staff member of the local prison, a relative of a friend of hers in her church. The staff member told her he thought I was a pretty good guy, that when many "dignitaries" visited the prison where he worked and came into an area he was working, they often acted as if he were invisible and did not talk to him. The dignitaries just talked to the warden or whoever was showing them around. But the staff member told my mother that whenever I entered the area where he worked, I went straight to him, said hello, and shook his hand. This made him feel that I respected him and thought he was important. Line staff make these kinds of judgments about the administrators they work for, and those interactions are more important than creating the most effective policy and getting the most favorable budgets from the legislature. They do tough jobs and have to know and believe that their bosses acknowledge this and acknowledge them.

Question: Can you talk more about interacting with staff during these tours?

Director Seiter: Another thing I do when I go to the prisons, which I enjoy and I believe that the staff enjoy, is to challenge them. All staff take pride in their work and want it to be recognized. They feel even better if they have to work really hard and are still successful. When I made my first round of visits to all the state prisons, I checked every fire extinguisher for the required monthly inspections. Each has a tag on it showing that it has been inspected every thirty days to ensure that it is ready for action if needed. Every prison probably has 200 or 300 extinguishers and it is easy to miss a few. I always found a few that had not been checked, until I went to one prison that had an extremely dedicated fire and safety officer. I found only one or two extinguishers that had been missed in some month over the past few months that were noted on the tag. I was extremely complimentary of the fire and safety officer, and he responded that he would be sure none were missed for my next visit. So I returned the challenge and assured him that I would check. Each time I returned I would look in one new place that I thought he might have missed—in a security tower guarding the fence or on a farm tractor. Our challenge, his attempt to be sure no fire extinguishers were missed, and my attempt to find one that had been missed became almost legendary at the prison. Staff would follow my prison tour route by radio, trying to anticipate where I would look on this visit. If I found one, everyone knew within minutes, and the fire and safety officer had to live with the ribbing of his fellow staff for days. If he won, he could bask in their still ribbing him about trying to please the boss. I would do the same thing with sanitation issues with all staff, looking for dirt or dust in some of the less obvious places, complimenting them when I found none, and poking fun at them when I found some. Seldom would I find much after the first couple of visits to a prison. Staff enjoyed the challenge and the fact that I pushed them to be better and appreciated them when they did.

Question: You talked about other ways to help prison staff do their jobs.

Director Seiter: I believe I can make their jobs easier by creating a culture with a positive work environment. Prison jobs are tough enough, without administrators second-guessing staff and the decisions they make. I can help with this by not accepting problems or mistakes, but accepting that individuals will make some. I believe in a saying, "Be tough on the issue, but be soft on the staff." Don't accept that things just happen and that nothing can be done to reduce the likelihood that problems will occur. But don't let it be taken personally by the staff that make the error. If they blatantly disregarded policy, they will be disciplined for that. However, if staff make an error of judgment or don't deal with a situation as well as they should, look for ways to improve the likelihood that they will do better next time. This may mean that a particular type of training should be provided. It may mean that a new policy, procedure, or response to a situation needs to be developed. It may mean that causal factors need to be found and dealt with. But it is wrong not to look for underlying issues, ask tough questions of responsible staff, and try to respond appropriately when possible. And it is wrong to overreact to a staff error with discipline of only that staff member and to do nothing to improve all staff members' ability to be successful the next time.

Question: That was a really interesting overview of the role of an administrator in setting a tone and helping staff do their jobs. But you usually don't think of a director of corrections checking toilets for sanitation, checking fire extinguishers, or looking at farm tractors. Why do you spend so much of your prison tour time on these kinds of activities?

Director Seiter: That's really a good question and one I am not surprised you asked. It can seem odd to do these things. But I do this for a couple of reasons. First, when you enter an area of a prison and want to interact with the staff person working in the area, there are limits to what you can focus on. Many line staff working an area rotate regularly and do not have much control over policy or operational procedures. But they do have control over sanitation. So by checking this so thoroughly you can deal with something under their control, and your few minutes with them will be focused on their work, rather than something they have no control over.

But the most important reason is for the staff and me to pay attention to detail. In corrections, there is a saying that "if you pay attention to detail, the big issues will be worked out." As strange as that seems, it is very true in this environment. Prisons work on routine and consistent following of policy and procedures. Staff and inmates come to expect certain things to happen in certain ways. Inmates also watch staff that shortcut the way they do their jobs, which often results in a security breakdown that observant inmates will take advantage of. If every staff member pays attention to detail and makes sure that each step of a procedure is done the right way every time, there are no security breaches or breaks in routine that can undermine the safe and secure environment you are trying to accomplish. There will be fewer resulting problems and therefore fewer big issues.

When staff see how much attention I pay to detail, they realize the importance of it. I don't just check sanitation; I check the details of the policy. I look at log books to see that they are used as required, I note how staff lock doors behind them, even if they know they are going to have to unlock the door thirty seconds later. I check how we control and keep inventories of syringes in the hospital. Staff have come to expect me to look at the details of how they do their jobs, and they know that these things are important to me. I have seen an improvement in their attention to detail since I have been doing this. I seldom find the same thing twice in a visit to a prison. So I combine a concern for them personally with a challenge for them to do their jobs right every time. Through those two things, I send the messages I want to send and do what I can to help establish the environment in the prisons that I think is necessary.

Prison Staff Organization

Prisons are organized in a manner to carry out the mission of operating a safe and secure environment and providing offenders an opportunity for program participation that can help them after release. Figure 10.2 is the table of organization for the Lebanon (Ohio) Correctional Institution. The chief executive officer of a prison is usually called a warden, although in some states, he or she is called a superintendent. Reporting to the warden are deputy (as in Ohio), associate, or assistant wardens. The general functions supervised by these individuals usually fall into three categories:

1. **Custody**—all the functions that come under the security activities within a prison; includes all uniformed employees, such as correctional officers and correctional supervisors
2. **Treatment**—all of the rehabilitative functions focused on keeping inmates productively engaged and preparing them for release, including counseling, religious services, substance abuse programs, or education
3. **Services**—all the functions that are required to operate the prison, such as budget and finance; maintenance of the facility; human resources management; and those that provide basic services to inmates, such as food and health services, work programs, commissary, and laundry operations

custody
the functions within a prison that come under the security activities; includes all "uniformed" employees such as correctional officers and correctional supervisors

treatment
the creation of an environment and provision of rehabilitative programs that encourage inmates to accept responsibility and to address personal disorders that make success in the community more difficult

services
the functions required to operate a prison such as budget and financial, maintenance, human resource management, food and health services, work programs, commissary function, and laundry operations

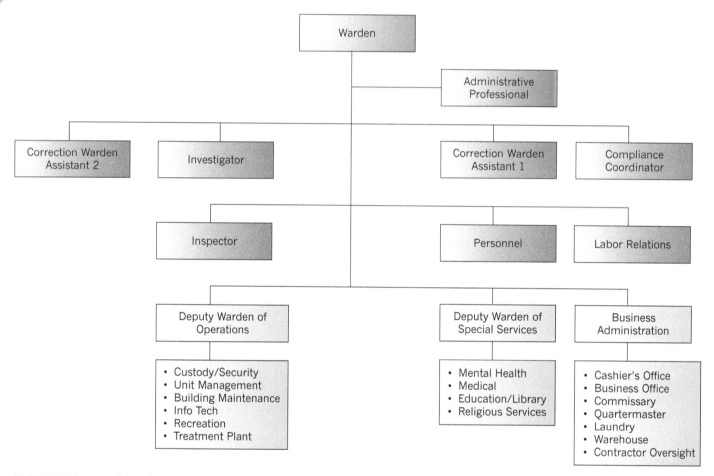

FIGURE 10.2 Table of Organization for the Lebanon (Ohio) Correctional Institution Source: Ohio Department of Rehabilitation and Correction. Reprinted with permission.

The organization of modern prisons is almost as complicated as that of the central headquarters. Although the mission of prisons has changed little over the past fifty years, the organizational structure has changed considerably. Organizational entities that internally control and manage staff and inmates are very much the same, but (similar to central headquarters) functional entities have been added to respond to external management needs. Included in the organization of the warden's office in Figure 10.2 are an inspector of institutional services, an institutional investigator, labor relations, and a compliance coordinator (to focus on maintaining quality). None of these functions was part of a prison table of organization a few decades ago, but changing times require changing organizational focus. Inmate complaints against staff must be promptly and thoroughly investigated, and prisons often have inspectors or investigators to carry out this function. Since collective bargaining and labor relations are prevalent in many correctional agencies, there is often a staff person dedicated to managing the local prison collective-bargaining agreement and dealing with grievances by union members. The general components of a prison organization are presented next.

Custody and Security Functions

The custody and security component is often referred to as *correctional services* and encompasses all the security activities within a prison, including the duties of the security staff, the operations of the special housing unit (SHU), inmate transportation, and the inmate disciplinary process. Correctional services departments are sometimes also referred to as *uniformed staff*; they are paramilitary in organization, rank, and dress (wearing uniforms that are similar to military dress uniforms). The rank of major is usually the highest-ranking uniformed officer, who supervises the security department. Captains run each eight-hour shift and coordinate security operations during that period. Lieutenants are responsible for an area of the prison, such as recreation or the SHU, and sergeants are supervisory correctional staff members who either supervise a smaller area than that of lieutenants or are senior correctional officers assigned to work the most difficult posts.

Correctional services is the largest department (in number of staff members) in a prison, ranging from 50 percent to almost 70 percent of all staff, depending on the state. In many state and federal prisons, no correctional officers are assigned to certain areas of the prison, such as education or prison industries. The non-uniformed staff members who work in those areas (such as teachers and industrial specialists) carry out the security functions, as well as their specialty functions. In other states, correctional officers do more than the pure security functions and may supervise recreation areas such as the gym or yard, oversee inmate leisure-time activities, or even direct inmates who work in prison industries or maintenance departments.

Correctional officers in most states are organized in a paramilitary fashion, wear uniforms, and have ranks of sergeant, lieutenant, and captain. Photo by Richard P. Seiter.

Treatment Functions

The departments within a prison that are labeled as treatment or programs include education and vocational training, recreation, mental health programs, religious services, and substance abuse or recovery services. These functions serve the second part of the mission of a prison: to provide programs to inmates that can help them prepare for reentry to the community. In other words, they provide the rehabilitative activities within a prison. Staff members who work in these departments are sometimes referred to as *professional staff*, because most of the jobs within these disciplines require a college education and specific preparation or certification to perform.

Education departments operate academic teaching, vocational training, library services, and sometimes recreation programs for inmates. These departments are managed similarly to a community elementary or high school. In a few states, the prison system is actually an accredited "school district." Teachers must be certified, but teach a general topic (math, English, or science), rather than a grade. As inmates enter prison, they are tested for academic competence and work toward completion of a GED (general equivalency diploma) at their own pace under the guidance of a teacher, who usually has a class of fifteen to twenty inmates. Vocational programs include carpentry or general building maintenance, landscape or horticulture, food service, and office skills. In many states and the BOP, recreation is also a part of the education department; however, in the Ohio prison organization, recreation is a separate department. Recreation staff members are assigned to areas such as the gymnasium or the recreation yard and not only supervise the area, but also plan and schedule leisure-time activities to try to involve the largest possible number of inmates.

Teachers are very important to the management of a prison. They provide inmates with counseling and instruction in educational areas that are critical to inmates' future lives. Photo by Richard P. Seiter.

Mental health programs are provided in every prison, since (as discussed in Chapter 9) approximately 16 percent of prison and jail inmates have a mental illness. Mental health departments usually employ one or two Ph.D. psychologists to assess and counsel inmates. There may also be counselors with master's degrees to provide counseling programs. Few prisons have a full-time psychiatrist, but usually contract with one for a few hours per week to see the most ill patients who require psychotropic medication. Substance abuse or recovery programs that provide counseling for alcohol and drug abuse are sometimes a part of the mental health department; in other states they are a separate department. Another critical treatment area within a prison is religious services. Prisons usually employ one or two full-time chaplains (often a Catholic priest and a Protestant minister) who hold religious services and coordinate other programs. Since all inmates have a right to practice the true tenets of their religious faith, prisons contract with clergy of other faiths (Muslim, Buddhist, Native American, or Jewish) to provide religious services and counseling to these inmates.

Service Functions

Service functions within a prison are those that deal with staff or facility issues (budget and finance, maintenance, human resources management) and those that provide services to inmates such as food and health services, work programs, commissary, and laundry operations. The functions of operating a business office and human resources department are very similar to those of other government organizations. The budget office has accountants to maintain control and record budget allocations, purchasing agents to buy necessary supplies and equipment, and financial managers to prepare budget needs and do budget projections. The human resources department follows overall government requirements for accepting and scoring applications for employment, going through the hiring process, and training new employees to prepare them for work in the prison. This department also oversees the **employee awards program** to recognize and reward staff members who perform well, the evaluation of staff by supervisors each year, and the labor relations program to monitor compliance with collective-bargaining contracts and respond to labor union issues.

employee awards program
a program to recognize and reward staff members who perform beyond their expected level

The components of the organization that provide services to inmates are also similar to those that would be in place on any military base or Veterans Administration hospital. Whenever there is a relatively isolated group of individuals, basic services of food, health care, laundry, commissary, and maintenance of the facility must be provided. Staff roles in the food and health care areas are described in Chapter 12. Unique in prisons, compared to other public or private agencies, is the work program for inmates. Work programs serve several purposes. They benefit inmates as a rehabilitative tool; inmates learn how to work for a supervisor, follow instructions, and develop positive work habits. Work programs benefit prison administrators by keeping inmates busy and assisting in maintaining control of the prison environment. And work programs benefit the public, by selling prison products and performing other work to reduce the cost of incarceration.

Work programs in a prison are unique in how they are supervised and organized. Each area of work assignment (prison industries, building maintenance, sanitation, food services) has full-time staff members who are experts in the area, but instead of doing the work themselves, they supervise inmate crews to perform the tasks. A good example is how a plumbing shop in a prison operates. There will be one or two plumbers who know how to do all the required plumbing tasks. The plumbers will be assigned a crew of approximately ten to fifteen inmates. The plumbers organize

Maintenance workers supervise inmates in several trade areas that both maintain the prison and develop beneficial skills for inmates. Photo by Richard P. Seiter.

work in the shop for inmates to do (such as repairing damaged equipment) and take inmates into areas of the prison to do maintenance and repair work as necessary. These employees seldom are assigned inmates who are experienced or able to perform these duties without training. Therefore, the staff members have to train inmates as well as supervise them in performing these tasks.

Unit Management

Unit management is a way to organize a prison into smaller components, decentralize the authority to manage the inmate population, and make staff more accessible to the inmate population. Unit management was first established in 1966 by the BOP at the National Training School for Boys, to decentralize the management of the prison and enhance communication between staff and inmates, and has been implemented at every federal prison since that time.[12] The BOP states the mission of unit management is to determine inmate program needs, and monitor participation to encourage prosocial institution and community behaviors that benefit inmates, staff, victims, and society. This is accomplished through functional unit management and effective interaction with inmates.[13] Unit management also operates in a semi-autonomous fashion within the larger prison. The average prison holds approximately 1,000 inmates, and many prisons have as many as 3,000 inmates. Managing such a large inmate population is difficult, so unit management breaks the prison into more manageable units (between 200 inmates and 400 inmates) based on housing assignments. Casework and other unit staff members are assigned and located within the housing unit to be accessible and deal directly with inmates and are given the authority to make decisions and manage the unit.

Unit management enhances staff and inmate communication. The BOP program statement on unit management notes that it "places inmates in close proximity to staff...enhances the quality of relationships between staff and inmates by providing: increased frequency of contact, direct observation of inmate behavior and potential problems, and increase inmate access to the staff who make

unit management
organizing a prison into smaller components by decentralizing the authority to manage the inmate population while making staff more accessible to inmates

Unit management offices are located in the inmate housing areas (see window in lower center of picture) so that staff members are accessible to inmates. Photo by Richard P. Seiter.

primary decisions about them."[14] Unit staff offices are located in the housing unit to not only make them more accessible to inmates, but also to monitor inmate activities and see how each inmate behaves on a daily basis. Staff, by being accessible to and knowledgeable of inmate behaviors, can identify issues as they are developing, and address them as small problems before they become big problems. The "A Case Study" box is a good illustration of the practical impact that unit management can have in enhancing prison security.

The unit team reviews each inmate's background, evaluates his or her needs, and determines appropriate program and job assignments. Upon their arrival, new inmates meet with their team to develop a plan for their work and program activities and then meet with their team every six months to review

A Case Study

The Effectiveness of Unit Management

When I worked at the U.S. Penitentiary in Leavenworth, Kansas, two incidents occurred that illustrated the positive impact unit management can have on the operations of a prison. When I first arrived at Leavenworth, it was not operated under the unit management concept. There were correctional counselors, but instead of being assigned to housing units, they were assigned to areas of the prison, such as industries, the dining room, the main corridor, the recreation yard, and the segregation building. Their duties were to be accessible to inmates in those areas and help out in the management as necessary.

About a year after I began working there, we had a work strike. Several inmates were upset with a change in the telephone policy (how they were allowed to make telephone calls) and decided to organize a work strike to get the attention of the administration and try to force a change in the policy. Early on a Monday morning, when inmates were on their way to work, groups of inmates blocked them in some of the main work areas, showing knives or other prison-made weapons and threatening inmates who did not comply with their demands to go back to their cells and not work.

We quickly discovered what was going on and to avoid putting inmates in danger, we ordered all inmates to return to their cells. We locked down the prison and began to try to identify the organizers of the work strike. We began by interviewing inmates and called all the correctional counselors together to see whether they had an idea of which inmates were behind the

work strike. Unfortunately, we discovered the counselors did not really know the inmates and could not put together a credible list of suspects.

About six months later, we implemented unit management at Leavenworth and assigned unit managers, case managers, and correctional counselors to each housing unit. Their offices were in the housing units, and they spent most of their day observing and talking to inmates. A few months after implementation, there was a serious stabbing in one of the cell houses, and the inmate who was assaulted died a few hours later. When he was being carried out of the cell house on a stretcher, a counselor asked him who stabbed him. The inmate did not know the full name of his assailant (the cell house had about 400 inmates living in it); he just said, "Tommy from California."

The unit staff members quickly got together to see whether they knew who this might be. They had recently noticed some Aryan Brotherhood inmates who appeared to be talking and planning something together, and they knew that one of its leaders was named Tommy and was from California. They immediately went to his cell, found bloody clothes he had not yet gotten rid of, and found him in the shower washing off blood and evidence. Tommy was charged with and convicted of the inmate's murder. In this case, the fact that the unit staff knew the inmates, their names, and their habits led to the staff's ability to bring justice to a killer, whereas the previous management model for the prison was unsuccessful in identifying the organizers of a work strike.

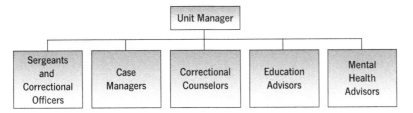

FIGURE 10.3   Table of Organization for a Unit Management Department in a Prison

progress and adjust the plan. Figure 10.3 illustrates the organization of a unit team. The team includes staff from a variety of disciplines and departments within the prison. Units are directed by a **unit manager**, and include case managers and correctional counselors. **Case managers** (called *social workers* or *caseworkers* in some states) have a caseload of 100–150 inmates and are responsible for developing the program of work and rehabilitation for each inmate and writing progress reports that release (parole) authorities or classification staff can use when considering an inmate for a program or transfer to another prison. **Correctional counselors** are promoted from the ranks of correctional officers and still wear officers' uniforms. Correctional counselors work with inmates on the daily issues that confront them while in prison, such as creating a visiting or telephone list, correcting an error on their account of finances held by the prison, or learning how to find a prison job or get along with other inmates. Because these staff members wear officer uniforms, the stereotype that all security personnel do regarding inmates is enforce rules and give them orders is diluted.

There are also correctional staff members (sergeants and officers) who work in the housing unit. In some states, these staff members report to and are evaluated by the unit manager, whereas in others they report to security supervisors, and the unit manager provides input for their performance evaluations. Also considered a part of the unit team, but usually not reporting to the unit manager, are education and mental health specialists. They evaluate inmate needs and help the unit team create appropriate programs for education, vocational training, substance abuse counseling, and psychological assistance. Although a goal of unit management is to enhance communication between staff and inmates, it has a secondary benefit of enhancing communication between these various groups of staff as they work together on the unit team.

Over the past two decades, most states have decided to implement unit management. Although it is generally recognized as a positive way to manage prisons, when a prison decides to implement it, there are still many questions and concerns from staff members regarding the impact on them and the types of positions that are available. Unit management can also be costly, because there may be additional positions for unit counselors and unit managers that were not in the prison prior to the unit management implementation. But these staff positions can often allow for reductions in other areas, such as fewer correctional officers in the housing units, since unit staff are also there. In Ohio, we were able to reduce the costs of perimeter security to fund unit management, but making this decision and change was still difficult.

unit manager
the staff person who is in charge of the unit, including housing, security, and treatment issues

case manager
sometimes called social worker or caseworker; responsible for developing the program of work and rehabilitation for inmates assigned to him or her

correctional counselor
a former correctional officer who works with inmates on prison issues such as creating a visiting or telephone list or getting a prison job assignment

Controlling Inmate Behavior

The mission of a correctional institution includes creating a safe and secure environment, yet because inmates tremendously outnumber staff members, they cannot control behavior (over the long term) through threats, intimidation, and physical dominance. Many activities are key in the management of prisons, contribute to the ability of staff to control inmate behavior, and move toward accomplishing the mission of safety and security. These activities include the consistent implementation of prison policies and procedures, the use of classification to match inmate risks and needs to the appropriate prison, and an inmate disciplinary system to encourage adherence to prison rules and punish inmates who fail to comply with these rules.

Policies and Procedures

One key to controlling inmates' behavior is to have clearly written, well-communicated, and consistently implemented policies and procedures. Every organization uses fairly detailed policies and procedures to guide staff on how to perform and provide clients an understanding of what to expect from the organization. Such guidance and expectations for performance are especially critical within a prison, in which inmates are likely to sue staff members for performing their duties in a way that they believe negatively affects them and in which inmates must be held accountable for following the rules and policies of the prison. Although it is almost impossible to imagine an agency not having written policies and procedures for almost any occurrence or situation, fifty years ago many prisons did not have written policy manuals or consistent implementation of procedures.

At least four conditions are necessary for prison policies and procedures to effectively contribute to the overall prison mission. First, policies must be consistent with professional standards and be written and authorized by the prison administration. The **American Correctional Association (ACA)**, the major professional organization for corrections in the United States, publishes standards manuals for all types of correctional practices. These policies and practices were created through a rigorous development, review, and approval process conducted by national correctional experts. Similar to the American Medical Association or the American Bar Association, ACA standards are created by practicing professionals in the field and are used to guide and evaluate acceptable modes of operation.

Second, for policies and procedures to be effective in managing and controlling inmate behavior, they must be clearly communicated to staff and inmates. A few security policies give details of how staff shall respond during a riot or other emergency situations and are not communicated to inmates, but most policies are made available to inmates. Usually, these policies are available for review in the inmate library so that inmates will understand what is expected of both them and staff. The third element of effective policy is to have procedures consistently carried out. If one correctional officer follows all policies in detail, and another officer follows only those that seem most important, it makes enforcement of the policy difficult and can cause confusion and tension among inmates and between inmates and staff. Inmates realize the need for policy and almost welcome it. Their whole life revolves around the activities within the prison. They recognize the importance of routine in a correctional environment and want to know what they and other inmates have to do in each situation. Inmates also recognize that if policies are not consistently implemented or staff members are not diligent in their monitoring and enforcement, some inmates will take advantage of the complacency, violate the policy, and compromise the overall safe environment for inmates as well as staff. The fourth component of effective policy is to ensure its consistent implementation in a quality fashion. The next section describes some of the quality-assurance practices used in correctional institutions.

American Correctional Association
the largest professional organization for corrections in the United States

Quality Assurance of Policy

Two activities used to ensure consistent implementation of prison policies are monitoring policy compliance and ACA accreditation. The method most commonly used to monitor policy compliance by staff is an active auditing program to determine the extent to which policy is effectively carried out and contributes to the mission of the prison. Prisons use a variety of auditing procedures to monitor compliance with operational policies. One of these, a **policy audit**, determines whether broad agency policy is in place at the prison. Policy audits match agency-required policy with local prison implementation procedures to ensure that procedures are in place at each prison to address each agency policy. In most states, the central headquarters dictates broad policy with which each prison in the state must comply. An example of a statewide policy regarding keeping contraband from entering the prison is that "all vehicles, carts, and boxes or packages must be thoroughly inspected before being allowed to enter or exit a prison." Each prison is required to develop and implement operational procedures to affect the required statewide policy. In this example, the prison describes how it will inspect the vehicles, carts, and boxes or packages, including where it will be done, who will do it, and what equipment will be necessary. A policy audit is valuable to begin an overall review of security operations, but only identifies whether the required scope of written, authorized, and mandated policies at the prison exists. It does not determine compliance with implementation, consistency in practice, or thoroughness of procedures.

policy audit
a review to ascertain whether broad agency policy is in place at the prison

Compliance with policy is determined by a **policy implementation audit**, which identifies whether procedures are consistently being carried out by staff in their daily duties. The policy audit is a review of written documents, whereas the policy implementation audit is a review of actual operations. It is completed by a team of knowledgeable staff from outside the prison who observe the methods by which staff members carry out their assignments and identify any lack of compliance with established policy. Even though staff members are aware that their behavior is being observed during an audit and will be sure to follow the policy as they know it, the audit still identifies weaknesses in compliance resulting from failure to train staff, improper procedures, or a misunderstanding about the policy requirements. And if staff would normally take shortcuts in following policy, the audit reminds them of the importance of following procedures.

policy implementation audit
a review to identify whether the procedures prescribed by policy are consistently being carried out by staff members in their daily duties

The second method of ensuring compliance with policy is **ACA accreditation**. In the early 1970s, corrections improved its ability to be seen as professional through adopting the acknowledged approaches associated with a profession: (1) a systematic body of theoretical knowledge acquired through lengthy academic study and not possessed by those outside the profession, (2) community interests rather than self-interest as a motivator of professional behavior, (3) self- regulation, and (4) a system of rewards.[15] Corrections made many progressive strides to be recognized as meeting these components, especially creating a body of knowledge (standards) of acceptable performance and a system of self-regulation. The ACA formed the Commission of Accreditation for Corrections (CAC), and standards identifying state-of-the-art practices were developed. Agencies that implement and meet these standards may then apply for consideration to be accredited by the ACA. According to the ACA, the benefits of this accreditation process are as follows:

ACA accreditation
a process to promote and recognize improvement in the management of correctional agencies through the administration of voluntary standards

- Safeguarding the life, health, and safety of the public, staff, and offenders.
- Providing a systematic evaluation of all areas of agency administration and operation.
- Improving management through the creation or refinement of written policies and procedures for all areas of agency operation.

- Providing all staff the opportunity to work together to assess needs and develop solutions.
- Providing evidence demonstrating compliance with exemplary practices for correctional agencies.
- Giving recognition for achievement, improving staff morale, and demonstrating accountability to the public.
- Aiding in the defense of potential lawsuits.
- Improving outcomes for strategies to successfully reintegrate offenders back into society.
- Identifying strengths, as well as weaknesses, on an ongoing basis.[16]

When a prison applies to be accredited, ACA conducts an audit to determine whether it meets the required standards. The audits are completed by a team of objective ACA-trained auditors who spend one week at the prison, review written policy, and observe procedures. If all standards identified as "life safety" and 90 percent of others are met, ACA will accredit the prison, meaning that it meets acknowledged standards of professional operations. Not every correctional administrator supports accreditation, arguing that ACA accreditation means nothing and requires a considerable amount of work to complete. Yet most recognize that it gives a professional credibility to those outside corrections (the courts, the public, elected officials), and the process is an excellent reminder and confirms the importance of consistent implementation of policy by staff.

Inmate Classification

Another essential prison management device for controlling inmate behavior is inmate classification. Prison classification systems help control inmate behavior in three ways. First, classification is used to determine the appropriate prison security level to which an inmate should be assigned. When inmates are initially sentenced, the correctional agency does an assessment to determine their risk of escape and potential for violence. By matching inmates' risk of escape and violence to prison physical security, security policies and procedures, and staff allocations, the agency reduces the potential for escape or violence. Second, once inmates are assigned to a prison, classification systems are used (in some states) to determine the type of housing assignment within a prison (single cell, multiple-inmate cell, or dormitory) that is most suitable for each inmate. Finally, the reclassification of inmates after they are assigned to a prison acts as a motivator for good behavior. Inmates' behavior is regularly reviewed and can lead to a reassignment to a higher-security prison with tighter restrictions and fewer privileges or to a lower-security prison.

Until the 1970s, most states used a clinical classification process, in which a team of experienced correctional staff interviewed inmates and reviewed their criminal, medical, psychological, and social histories. They would then decide what type of prison housing, work assignment, and treatment programs would be best for the inmate. Currently, most states use an objective classification system—an actuarial risk assessment—to determine an inmate's initial assignment to a prison. This initial classification is based predominantly on offense history and sentence length. In describing the need for these actuarial systems, as states were converting to objective systems, Dallao wrote, "Instead of assigning offenders to certain security levels based on gut reaction and subjective discussion, this new system provided an orderly and objective way of separating violent from nonviolent inmates."[17]

The BOP was the first correctional agency to implement such a system; in the mid-1970s it assigned a team of specialists to design a classification system that was more predictive of behavior than the early clinical approaches. The team initially identified ninety-six factors that were considered important for classification purposes and sought the opinion of correctional professionals across the country on these factors. The original list was pared to forty-seven factors, and later to six: history of escape or attempted escape, detainers, types of prior commitments, history of violence, severity of offense, and length of sentence. These factors focus on public risk by using acts that occurred prior to sentencing. Brennan suggests that these security classifications emphasize "legal variables, history of criminality, seriousness of current offense, and past escape attempts."[18]

To make the initial assignment of an inmate to a prison, a BOP staff member reviews the background of the offender and assigns a score for each of the six areas. Figure 10.4 shows the form used to determine security designations for each inmate. Inmates are assigned the points indicated on the Security Designation form, and the total points are then used to determine the security level of the prison to which the inmate is assigned. The following security point totals (for males and females) result in placement in the corresponding security level of federal prison:

Security Point Totals		Prison Security Level
Males	Females	
0–11	0–15	Minimum
12–15	16–30	Low
16–23*		Medium
24+	31+	High

Since the adoption of this system by the BOP, almost every state has developed objective classification systems to assign the levels of prison security for inmates. In the last census of adult prisons, 20.4 percent of all prisons were classified for maximum-security inmates, 26.3 percent of all prisons were classified for medium-security inmates, and 53.2 percent of all prisons were classified for minimum-security inmates.[19] Objective classifications reduce the tendency to overclassify that often resulted from clinical systems. As example, to compare with the above percentages, in 1978, 51 percent of prisoners were in maximum-security, 38 percent in medium-security, and 11 percent in minimum-security prisons.[20]

The classification process also is useful in determining the type of housing assignment within a prison that is most suitable for each inmate. Many prisons have a variety of housing areas for inmates, which may be either individual or multi-person cells or dormitory-style housing with several (possibly hundreds of) inmates in an open area without any physical security to separate them from each other or from staff. **Internal classification systems** are instruments used to assign inmates to housing or programs after they are placed in a particular prison. However, most prisons still make these decisions based on clinical judgments or make housing assignments only on the availability of space.

The most widely used internal classification system is the Adult Internal Management System (AIMS) developed by Herbert Quay, which classifies inmates on the analysis of life history records and a correctional adjustment checklist. These factors identify inmates who are likely to be violent and aggressive or likely to be victimized and therefore allow staff to separate likely victims from likely aggressors. Another system developed by the state of Illinois uses an internal classification system to make assignments within its maximum-security prisons. The Illinois system makes housing, work, and program assignments by using some past criminal behavior factors from the external classification system and adding prison disciplinary conduct and history of gang activities to predict a level of institutional aggression.

internal classification system
instruments used to assign inmates to housing or programs after they are placed in a particular prison

INMATE LOAD DATA

1. REGISTER NUMBER :				
2. LAST NAME		3. FIRST NAME	4. MIDDLE	5. SUFFIX
6. RACE	7. SEX	8. ETHNIC ORIGIN	9. DATE OF BIRTH	

10. OFFENSE/SENTENCE

11. FBI NUMBER	12. SSN NUMBER
13. STATE OF BIRTH	14. OR COUNTRY OF BIRTH	15. CITIZENSHIP

16. ADDRESS-STREET

17. CITY	18. STATE	19. ZIP	20. OR FOREIGN COUNTRY
21. HEIGHT FT IN	22. WEIGHT LBS	23. HAIR COLOR	24. EYE COLOR

25. ARS ASSIGNMENT:

SECURITY DESIGNATION DATA

1. JUDGE	2. REC FACILITY	3. REC PROGRAM	4. USM OFFICE

5. VOLUNTARY SURRENDER STATUS   0 = NO   (–3) = YES

    IF YES, MUST INDICATE :   5a.   VOLUNTARY SURRENDER DATE :

                          5b.   VOLUNTARY SURRENDER LOCATION :

6. MONTHS TO RELEASE :

7. SEVERITY OF CURRENT OFFENSE	0 = LOWEST 1 = LOW MODERATE	3 = MODERATE 5 = HIGH	7 = GREATEST

8. CRIMINAL HISTORY SCORE	0 = 0–1 2 = 2–3	4 = 4–6 6 = 7–9	8 = 10–12 10 = 13 +

8a. SOURCE OF DOCUMENTED   – PRESENTENCE INVESTIGATION REPORT or   – NCIC III

9. HISTORY OF VIOLENCE		NONE	> 15 YEARS	10–15 YEARS	5–10 YEARS	< 5 YEARS
	MINOR	0	1	1	3	5
	SERIOUS	0	2	4	6	7

10. HISTORY OF ESCAPE OR ATTEMPTS		NONE	> 15 YEARS	> 10 YEARS	5–10 YEARS	< 5 YEARS
	MINOR	0	1	1	2	3
	SERIOUS	0	3 (S)	3 (S)	3 (S)	3 (S)

11. TYPE OF DETAINER	0 = NONE 1 = LOWEST/LOW MODERATE	3 = MODERATE 5 = HIGH	7 = GREATEST

12. AGE	0 = 55 and over 2 = 36 through 54	4 = 25 through 35 8 = 24 or less

13. EDUCATION LEVEL   0 = Verified High School Degree or GED
                          1 = Enrolled in and making satisfactory progress in GED Program
                          2 = No Verified High School Degree/GED and not participating in GED Program

13.a HIGHEST GRADE COMPLETED

14. DRUG/ALCOHOL ABUSE   0 = NEVER/>5 Years   1 = <5 Years

15. SECURITY POINT TOTAL

16. PUBLIC SAFETY FACTORS	A - NONE B - DISRUPTIVE GROUP (males only) C - GREATEST SEVERITY OFFENSE (males only) F - SEX OFFENDER G - THREAT TO GOVERNMENT OFFICIALS H - DEPORTABLE ALIEN	I - SENTENCE LENGTH (males only) K - VIOLENT BEHAVIOUR (females only) L - SERIOUS ESCAPE M - PRISON DISTURBANCE N - JUVENILE VIOLENCE O - SERIOUS TELEPHONE ABUSE

17. REMARKS

18. OMDT REFERRAL (YES/NO)

FIGURE 10.4   Inmate Load and Security Designation Form (BP-337)   Source: Federal Bureau of Prisons, *Security Designation and Custody Classification*, Policy P5100.08, chapter 4 (Washington, D.C.: U.S. Department of Justice, 2006), p. 16.

Classification is an incentive for good behavior by inmates because it is used to guide inter-institutional transfers due to security or treatment purposes. Inmates seldom stay at the prison to which they were originally assigned throughout their entire term of incarceration. Their time served and institutional behavior change their predicted risk of violence and escape. Correctional agencies regularly reclassify and move inmates to higher- or lower-security prisons based on these changes. Objective classification systems make it very clear to inmates what they need to do to have their security level reduced or what behavior will result in an increase in security. Most inmates strive to get to lower-security prisons throughout their term of imprisonment and therefore work for good behavior to reduce their level of security and increase their freedom and opportunity for program involvement.

Inmates strive to work their way down to minimum-security prisons, which are often less restrictive of their movements and often have additional programs available. Photo by Richard P. Seiter.

The reclassification review is scheduled at regular intervals (often three or six months). At the reclassification review, an inmate's behavior and the percentage of his or her sentence served are combined into the classification score system. If behavior is good and as the inmate reaches certain stages in his or her sentence (so many months served or a certain percentage of the sentence completed), it may result in a lowered security score and corresponding prison assignment. Serious misbehavior by inmates can also result in reclassification, as it indicates that the inmate cannot be controlled in the current security level. An inmate who commits a serious disciplinary infraction or continues to commit less severe infractions receives extra points on the security instrument and may be upgraded to a higher-security prison.

Figure 10.5 shows the Colorado Department of Corrections Reclassification Custody Rating. Unfavorable and favorable behavior scores are combined to recalculate an inmate's classification score. Unfavorable factors include institutional violence, escape history, and serious disciplinary reports. Favorable behaviors include program participation and work evaluations. Inmates are reviewed every six months or whenever there is a serious rule violation.

The goal of initial classification is to have similar-risk inmates assigned to appropriate security-level prisons, and the goal of reclassification is to maintain homogeneity of inmates by security level. Both overclassifying and underclassifying inmates can cause problems: housing high-security inmates in a low- or minimum-security facility increases the potential for escape, predatory behavior, or other types of violence, whereas housing low- or minimum-security inmates in high-security prisons places them in danger of violence and intimidation and wastes correctional resources, because high-security prisons cost three to four times as much to build and operate as do minimum-security prisons.

Inmate Discipline

Another key to controlling inmate behavior is a system of disincentives and punishment for violation of prison rules. Prisons create and use an **inmate disciplinary system** to respond to violation of prison rules by inmates. The disciplinary process includes

inmate disciplinary system
a policy that clearly prescribes the process required to find that an inmate committed a proscribed act and identifies allowable punishments for each act; a key to controlling inmate behavior

COLORADO
Department of Corrections

AR Form 600-1C (05/01/16)

Offender Reclassification Custody Rating
Facility: _____

| Offender Name | _____ | DOC # | _____ | PMD/PED | _____ |
| Case Manager | _____ | Last Custody Level | _____ | Scoring Date | _____ |

1. HISTORY OF INSTITUTIONAL VIOLENCE (Review individual's entire background of incarceration for 7 years prior to admission date.)
   None... 0
   Assault and Battery not involving weapon; no serious injury (exclude fighting)............................ 3
   Assault and Battery involving use of weapon or serious injury.. 10
   Assault against staff or visitors... 10 _____

2. SEVERITY OF CURRENT CONVICTION (Score most serious conviction)
   Low...................... 1   Low Moderate.......................... 2   Moderate.................... 3
   High...................... 5   Highest................................ 7 _____

3. SEVERITY OF PRIOR CONVICTION (Score most serious in adult history)
   None, Low, or Low Moderate...............................0   Moderate.......................... 1
   High...3   Highest........................... 4 _____

4. ESCAPE HISTORY (Rate last three (3) years of incarceration.)
   An escape/attempted escape/abscond resulting in administrative action........................... 3
   An escape/attempted escape from Level II facility or below (no violence)............................ 4
   An escape/attempted escape from Level III facility or above (no violence)........................... 6
   An escape/attempted escape from any facility with violence.. 10 _____

SCORE PART A: (Add items 1 through 4)   PART A SCORE: _____
_____

5. TYPE OF MOST SERIOUS DISCIPLINARY REPORT – PAST 12 MONTHS
   None.. −1Class II b>.. 3
   Class II a... 5Class I (past 18 months)..................... 7 .... _____

6. FREQUENCY OF DISCIPLINARY REPORTS (CLASS I AND II ONLY) – PAST 12 MONTHS
   None.. −11...................................0
   2...13... 3
   4 or more.......................................5 _____

7. PROGRAM PARTICIPATION (Over the past six (6) months, including GED/ABE)
   Noncompliance with recommended programs.........0On waitlist or participation for recommended program............−1..
   No recommended programs or completion of recommended programs...−2 _____

8. WORK EVALUATIONS (Over the last six (6) months)
   Maintained satisfactory employment...−2
   Medically unassigned or actively seeking employment...0
   Unsatisfactory termination, refusal to work, or not actively seeking employment................................2 _____

9. CURRENT AGE
   27 yrs or younger......... 2   28 – 37 yrs............. 0   38 – 60 yrs............−1   61 yrs & older...............−2 _____

Determine Scored Custody Level Indicated by Scale Below
TOTAL CUSTODY SCORE (items 1 – 9)
   15 or more points = Close _____   13 to 14 = Medium _____   3 to 12 points = Minimum R _____   2 or fewer points = Minimum _____

Attachment C
page 1 of 2

FIGURE 10.5 The Colorado Department of Corrections Reclassification Custody Rating Source: Policy 4-4502: Offender Classification, May 1, 2016 (Colorado Springs, CO: Colorado Department of Corrections, 2017), p. 21.

Inmates may violate prison rules and therefore must be punished using the inmate discipline policy. Courtesy of CoreCivic.

an accusation of the violation, investigation of the incident, a hearing to determine guilt, and imposition of a sanction if found guilty. Inmate disciplinary systems usually include (1) a written policy documenting prohibited behavior, which is provided to all inmates, (2) a fair and equitable set of corresponding sanctions increasing with the severity of the rule violation and a process to appeal those sanctions, (3) a way to separate inmates accused of rule violations from the general inmate population when the security of the prison could be threatened, and (4) provisions for long-term separation or special security handling for inmates who continuously threaten institutional security or against whom a serious threat of violence exists.

The first component of an inmate disciplinary system is a written policy of specific prohibited behavior. The policy also explains the process used to determine guilt and the range of punishments that result from rule violations. One of the principles of the BOP policy regarding inmate discipline is stated as follows:

> *Staff take disciplinary action at such times and to the degree necessary to regulate an inmate's behavior within Bureau rules and institution guidelines and to promote a safe and orderly institution environment.*[21]

Correctional agencies provide a copy of the inmate discipline policy to every inmate upon the inmate's arrival at a prison, and inmates sign that they have received, read, and understood the policy. Informing inmates and ensuring that they understand prohibited acts not only is fair, but also reduces the potential for successful appeals of inmate disciplinary actions before a federal court. Most correctional systems categorize prohibited acts by severity. The BOP policy lists four categories of prohibited acts: greatest, high, moderate, and low moderate,[22] with a specific range of sanctions authorized for each category of prohibited act. The BOP provides for a two-stage disciplinary process, with minor violations handled in a less formal manner than serious infractions, and time frames are associated with each step in the process so that the inmate knows the time available for collecting evidence or seeking assistance. Figure 10.6 illustrates the disciplinary process and time limits for each step in the BOP policy.

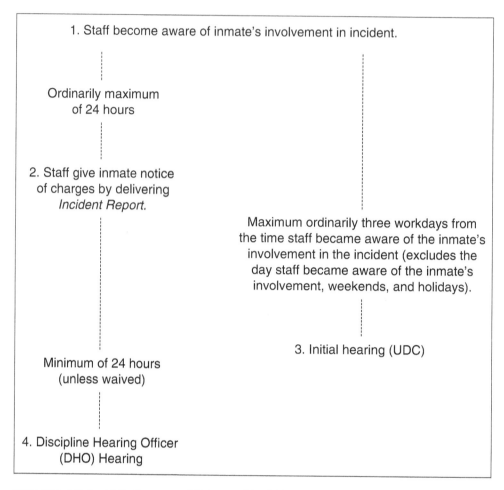

FIGURE 10.6 U.S. Bureau of Prisons Disciplinary Process Source: Based on the Federal Bureau of Prisons, *Inmate Discipline Program*, Policy Statement #5270.09 (Washington, D.C.: U.S. Department of Justice, August 1, 2011), p. 38.

According to the BOP policy, once an incident report is issued to an inmate, an initial hearing must occur within three workdays. If the infraction is minor, the hearing panel (referred to as the Unit Disciplinary Committee or UDC) can determine guilt and impose minor sanctions, such as a loss of privileges. If the violation is more serious and could result in loss of good time, disciplinary transfer to another prison, or disciplinary isolation from the general inmate population, the UDC will refer the case to an upper-level hearing panel, a Discipline Hearing Officer (DHO), who is not a staff member of the prison in which the incident took place and is therefore seen as impartial. Most states have a similar two-tiered system to handle inmate discipline.

Sanctions for commission of prohibited acts can be minor, such as restriction from privileges, or serious, such as transfer to a supermax prison. The following list describes the types of sanctions in order of severity used by most correctional systems:

Warning: Some jurisdictions allow a temporary suspension of disciplinary action, with an inmate receiving a warning. If there are no further violations during the period of suspension, the rule violation may be expunged from the inmate's record.

Reprimand: A reprimand is a written admonishment against the behavior with no other sanction or punishment.

Assignment of extra duty: Assignment of additional work for an inmate, usually for a specific number of hours.

Restriction to quarters: Restriction to quarters requires the inmate to remain in the housing location for a specific period of time (such as one week) whenever he or she is not at work, meals, or an assigned program.

Impoundment of personal property: Inmates may have their personal property confiscated or impounded, and either it will be held or the inmate will have to pay to send it out of the prison.

Loss of job: When the infraction has something to do with the job assignment, inmates may lose their job and have to find or be assigned another less favored job.

Removal from program or group activity: Similar to the loss of a job, an inmate may be removed from a program or group activity if the infraction is related to a program or activity.

Change of quarters: Inmates may be required to move from one housing unit to another.

Loss of privileges: Inmates may be restricted from specific privileges, such as participation in recreation or loss of the use of the prison commissary.

Monetary restitution: If the infraction included damaging government property or another inmate's property, the violating inmate may be required to pay for the damage.

Withholding of good time: Correctional sentences allow inmates to earn a certain number of days off their sentence for each month of good behavior, and if a violation of prison rules is serious, good time may not be granted, lengthening the term of the sentence.

Disciplinary segregation: Inmates may have to serve a sentence in segregation, in a facility separate from the general inmate population, with little time out of their cell.

Disciplinary transfer: Inmates who continually violate prison rules or commit a serious violation can be transferred to a higher-security prison.

Placement in a supermax prison: Supermax prisons (described in Chapter 9) house the most violent and dangerous inmates, and inmates who have shown an inability to follow rules in a standard prison may be transferred to a supermax prison for an indeterminate period of time.

Once there is a finding of guilt and imposition of a sanction, correctional agencies usually provide an **administrative appeals process** to allow inmates to appeal a disciplinary sanction or to seek to remedy any other injustice they believe they have received at the hands of correctional officials. Having an appeals process promotes acceptance by inmates and avoids expensive and burdensome review of disciplinary decisions by federal courts. Administrative appeals usually have at least two levels: first a reconsideration by the warden, and if the inmate is not satisfied with the response, a second level of reconsideration by the agency headquarters. For disciplinary processes, the inmate appeal cannot dispute a finding of fact, but is limited to procedural and due process rights. Inmates usually have thirty days after notice of the decision to appeal. In describing the review process, Cripe writes,

administrative appeals process
an informal process for inmates to appeal a disciplinary sanction or to seek remedy of any other injustice they feel they have received at the hands of correctional officials

> The records (the disciplinary offense report, the investigation report, and the written report of the hearing officer or committee) are examined, to be sure that the procedures required by the agency's disciplinary policy have been followed. The facts of the case and the sanction imposed are summarily reviewed. There must be some evidence to support the finding of the disciplinary authority. The reviewer ensures that the sanction imposed is within the range of punishments authorized for that offense. There is a legal requirement that the hearing officer or committee record the evidence relied on to support the conclusion reached, and that the reasons for the sanction(s) imposed be given.[23]

The Role of Staff in a Prison

Everyone who works for a correctional agency recognizes that the staff is the agency's most valuable resource. Corrections is a business in which people are more important than the bars and fences, prison cells, or available technology. Correctional staff members supervise offenders, monitoring and guiding their behavior toward the development of a crime-free and productive lifestyle. In 2012, local, state, and federal correctional agencies employed 749,418 staff members and approximately 85 percent of a correctional agency budget is spent on staff salaries.[24]

Historically, the role of correctional staff that worked in prisons was very narrowly defined, and there was little effort to recruit, develop, or retain the most educated and professional staff. Line prison staff (such as correctional officers) had minimal discretion or decision-making authority. In 1965, Cressey wrote, "Most guards have nothing to do but stand guard; they do not use inmates productively any more than they themselves are used productively by prison managers."[25] Over the next three decades, this changed and resulted in the ACA in 1993 to pass a resolution to encourage the use of the term "correctional officer" instead of "guard," because it better describes their responsibilities of custody and control, which "require extensive interpersonal skill, special training and education, and...correctional personnel are skilled professionals."[26] Prompted by the emphasis on rehabilitation during the 1960s, the type and scope of prison staff expanded considerably. As a part of this transformation, new professional staff members, including psychologists, educators, and administrators, were brought into prisons, and the importance of the overall prison experience in inmate rehabilitation was recognized.

In addition, with the dramatic increases in the number of prisoners during the 1980s and 1990s, most prisons became overcrowded, and correctional staff often felt overworked and frustrated and feared losing control. Totally outnumbered, correctional officials recognized that the authoritarian style of inmate supervision was ineffective, and that skill in interpersonal communications was more effective to gain the compliance of inmates and maintain order. Correctional officials moved aggressively to recruit educated individuals trained in supervising and communicating with others. Many states and the BOP require candidates for correctional officer positions to have either a bachelor's degree or at least two years' experience working in a correctional or law enforcement setting. Corrections began to recognize the critical value of all staff members, not just those delivering treatment programs, in accomplishing their mission.

Recruiting, Hiring, and Retention of Correctional Staff

Recruiting for prisons in the past was done very haphazardly or not at all. Prisons usually relied on recruitment through encouragement by relatives or friends who already worked at the prison. There was no plan by which characteristics of successful employees were identified, organizational needs considered, and an aggressive recruitment effort implemented, and correctional agencies usually accepted the hiring of a nondiverse workforce with little experience or academic preparation. Most correctional agency recruitment was all too often like that described here regarding the state of Massachusetts:

> *Massachusetts in the 1970s had a depressed economy with high unemployment. At the same time, the Massachusetts prison system had a high turnover rate among officers and a chronic need for new*

officers. Yet...corrections with its similar salary and benefits (to police and fire departments) was in reality a "walk-in" job. Screening and selection were largely limited to investigation of possible criminal records of applicants. The prison officer recruit was largely self-selected.[27]

Line staff members such as correctional officers are critical to the success of a prison, but only if they are properly trained, supervised, guided, and managed. Management of prisons in the mid-1900s was much simpler than it is today. An autocratic warden cannot just create and enforce rules to maintain control and punish staff members who did not follow the leader's directives. Prison order has more to do with fairness and equity, with leadership and empowerment, and with organization and management. DiIulio suggests that the "quality of prison life varies according to the quality of prison management."[28]

Prompted by high turnover and the challenge of a growing workforce, correctional agencies' recruitment is now much more sophisticated. Correctional recruiters have found that there are several rich targets for recruiting future correctional workers. First, the military is a significant recruitment opportunity, as individuals leaving the military make outstanding correctional workers. Their history of working in large organizations with a clear chain of command and being on a team with a diverse group of individuals, and having a focus on accomplishing the organization mission makes the career transition to corrections fairly easy. Second, correctional agencies recruit from both public and private social service agencies. Many staff with this type of work background have knowledge of community resources and have worked with disadvantaged clients with a variety of needs.

Correctional agencies also successfully recruit from community and four-year colleges. One of the fastest growing college majors is criminal justice, and with this course of study, graduates understand the way correctional systems are organized to meet their mission and roles. Probation and parole agencies regularly recruit candidates for parole and probation officer positions from college campuses. Prisons now recruit college graduates for entry-level correctional officer jobs. Some college graduates have the perception that correctional officer jobs are "below" their educational accomplishments. However, as they learn more during the recruitment process, they often understand how working as a correctional officer is excellent experience for developing skills in security and managing inmates. These proficiencies are an important foundation for success in other corrections jobs that the individual may later acquire.

Even with the more sophisticated approach to recruitment, the most effective recruitment is still by referral of current employees. Correctional administrators hope and expect that their employees would be good ambassadors and encourage friends and associates to apply at the agency. But even this "informal" recruitment must be done properly. Employees need to be educated as to the type of people the agency desires, they need to know the minimum qualifications, and they need to be able to explain and "sell" the prospect of working in corrections. Etter suggests that while most correctional employees do not see themselves as salespeople, when recruiting, that is exactly what they are doing. He writes that "You are selling your customers (potential applicants) on your job and on your jail as a good place to work."[29] Yet, you also cannot oversell. Osborne describes the need to be consistent in the message, and "Inform them on what your agency's requirements are and what it can offer. Don't sell them a bill of goods that you cannot deliver."[30]

But it is never an easy sell to entice employees to corrections. Baker and Carrera note, "Recruiting for correctional facilities is unique because of the stigma and false information associated with such employment."[31] Therefore, correctional recruiting requires breaking stereotypes and educating people about the realities of working in a prison, jail, or community corrections environment. And there are many positive factors that can be reinforced about correctional work. In a survey of jail employees, primary reasons people accepted their job included job security (67 percent) and salary and benefit packages (62 percent), and these are often strong points for working in corrections.[32] And correctional agencies focus on "relationship-based recruiting," or talking one-to-one to individuals or small groups.

Even with quality recruiting generating a large pool of qualified applicants, there still must be effective hiring practices to screen and select the most qualified individuals from this pool. Correctional agencies identify the areas of competence that they want in prison employees and create a screening process to rate applicants' abilities. Some of the traits and abilities identified to be a successful correctional worker are the following:

- Good interpersonal skills (both oral and written)
- Ability to make sound decisions
- Lack of prejudice toward criminal offenders
- Understanding of the need to treat all clients or inmates in a fair and consistent manner
- Ability to "think on one's feet"
- Ability to supervise others
- Good presentation of oneself

Correctional agencies use several screening and rating mechanisms to screen and hire staff. Candidates must not only complete a fairly extensive application (including past education, military, and job experience), but also provide examples of how these past experiences are indicative of the identified traits and abilities. After the agency identifies the best group of candidates from the applications, screening usually includes a personal interview, review of a writing sample to determine their ability to communicate in writing, and one of the most important screening mechanisms, the **integrity interview**. During the personal interview, interviewers present candidates with difficult and stressful scenarios, have them describe how they would handle them, and then rate how desirable the candidate's response would be in a correctional environment working with inmates. Since correctional staff members are continually confronted with opportunities to personally benefit from giving offenders favored treatment, integrity interviews are used to determine whether candidates have issues such as financial problems, past employment problems, current drug or alcohol abuse, or other conditions that could put them in a compromising situation or make them more likely to accept a bribe to show favored treatment to an inmate.

After these screening processes, the candidate rated the highest is usually offered employment, although it is usually a "conditional offer," contingent on their passing a physical examination, passing a test for drug use, or completing mandatory training. Over the past decade, more agencies are requiring candidates for employment to take a test to determine recent drug use. Almost all correctional agencies now require correctional staff to pass a drug test before hiring. The medical exam may be only to determine if the candidate has no serious medical problems, but many agencies also require a physical performance test during the training phase. The test replicates the types of requirements for the job (ability to walk/run a mile within a certain time, requirement to carry a heavy bag for a certain distance, and ability to use a weapon satisfactorily and safely). If candidates pass the physical exam and the drug screening, they are officially hired and a date is set to begin their employment.

integrity interview
interviews of candidates for correctional employment used to determine if candidates have issues or conditions that could put them in a compromising situation or make them more likely to accept a bribe to show favored treatment to an inmate

Turnover of staff is a problem for all correctional agencies. A survey by the ACA found that the average national turnover of correctional officers was 16.1 percent, and noncompetitive compensation was the most frequently cited reason for recruitment difficulty and the second most cited reason for retention. Low job satisfaction impacts turnover,[33] and demanding work hours, stress and burnout, and employees not understanding and finding they were not suited for the job were other factors in turnover.[34] Another reason for high turnover rate is the stressful and dangerous nature of correctional jobs. Both institution and community correctional workers must work with difficult clients and (even though the incidents are infrequent) risk assault and potential serious injury. Even with these challenges, a 2013 study found that the majority of 1,924 staff surveyed were satisfied with their jobs and did not intend to resign.[35]

A survey by the Association of State Correctional Administrators (ASCA) identified several enticements to successful recruitment and retention, to include fair salaries and promotional opportunities, training for improved supervision by mid-level managers, and a focus on employee satisfactory as important in recruitment and retention.[36] Pay for correctional workers has always been relatively low. Yet, over the past five years, the economic slowdown and rising unemployment rates are making more people consider working as a correctional, probation, or parole officer. And Delaware, Louisiana, North Dakota, Vermont, Virginia, and West Virginia have raised pay for correctional officers to make them more comparable to law enforcement officers. Delaware reported that after raising pay by 18 percent, their vacancy rate was the lowest in five years. In the past few years, the Texas prison system increased correctional officer starting pay by 10 percent and also provided a $1,500 recruiting bonus if an applicant agrees to work at one of four designated understaffed correctional institutions.

Another way correctional agencies are improving recruitment and retention is positively changing the culture of their organizations. In a case study of Florida and Pennsylvania departments of corrections, it was noted that assessing and enhancing the workplace could reduce staff turnover.[37] Corrections Corporation of America (now CoreCivic), the largest U.S. private prison company with over 17,000 staff, conducted interviews with staff to determine workplace satisfaction, and identified that the way correctional officers were treated by their first-line supervisors had a major impact on turnover. As a result, the company implemented a values-based training program for supervisors and has seen their retention rates improve as a result.[38] Similarly, a recent study identified the correlation of participation in decision making by line staff with perceived supervisor and organizational support.[39]

Although recruitment and retention are improving among many correctional agencies as a result of thoughtful improvements in pay, culture, and working conditions, the biggest impact on reduced turnover is the recession. With severe economic times come layoffs and high unemployment. During these times, individuals look for what they consider to be more stable employers, and correctional agencies are perceived to be "recession proof." And many workers are putting off retirement due to the economy and staying in the correctional workforce.[40] What remains to be seen is whether the improvements made by these agencies will help in retaining employees as the economy improves and jobs in noncorrectional agencies are again available.

An extremely important factor within the operation of correctional agencies is **staff diversity**. Having a staff that is diverse in terms of gender, race, and ethnicity is important for many reasons. First, having women within a correctional workforce brings a calming and normalized influence to men's prisons and doubles the available pool for recruiting talented individuals. Second, with such a large percentage of offenders under correctional supervision being minorities, race and ethnic diversities aid in the management of prisons and community correctional

staff diversity
the representation of a wide variety (in gender, race, and ethnicity) of people working for a correctional agency

agencies. Whites now make up only about one-third, blacks over 35 percent, and Hispanics over 21 percent of the prison population. This disproportionate number of minorities in prison and jails makes it important that correctional agencies aggressively recruit minority staff in order to have the staff be somewhat representative of the offender makeup. In response, correctional agencies have created **affirmative action programs** to recruit and develop a workforce that mirrors, to some extent, the client base. Although race and ethnicity do not have to be a barrier to communication between inmates and staff, a diverse workforce enhances the potential for positive communication by reducing the perception by offenders that the system is racist.

The efforts by correctional agencies to increase the number and percentages of minority staff members have not always come easy. Irwin points out that when minority staff members were first recruited to rural prisons with predominantly white staff, some white staff members felt that the nonwhite, urban officers would be more pro-inmate and less trustworthy and might undermine security and did not easily accept them.[41] Some studies have suggested that nonwhite correctional officers experience more stress than their white counterparts, and black officers are more likely to quit their jobs than white officers, primarily because of conflicts with their supervisors.[42] Just as inmates become bitter and perceive many actions as racist when there is not a diverse workforce, minority staff members can have some of the same feelings when they represent a small minority of the staff and do not feel fully accepted into their workplace.

Collective Bargaining within Correctional Agencies

Although a few states (Connecticut in the 1940s and New York and Washington in the 1960s) have had public employee unions for some time, collective bargaining is relatively new to most state correctional agencies. By the 1970s, more than twenty states had formally authorized collective bargaining by public employees, and by the end of the twentieth century, more than half of the states had collective bargaining for at least some correctional employees. Due to the mission of safety and security and the role of supervising felony offenders, collective bargaining is more complex for correctional agencies than for many other public and private organizations.

Collective bargaining is the formal recognition of employee organizations and their right to negotiate with management regarding conditions of the workplace. The purposes of collective bargaining are as follows:

To establish and protect employees' rights
To improve working conditions and benefits
To establish and maintain more harmonious employer-employee relationships
To establish a participative role for employees in management decisions that affect employees[43]

Even though the purposes seem nonconfrontational and in line with the mission of a prison, many correctional administrators have feared that they would diminish their management authority and undermine prison security. One important point of debate is the role in which **seniority** of staff is considered in such things as work schedules, post assignment, and promotion. Union officials usually desire seniority to be key in determining employees' work assignments, days off, shift schedules, and even promotions. Correctional management officials want to have as much discretion as possible to place staff members with unique abilities in the positions that require their strengths and create schedules to meet

affirmative action programs
activities to aggressively recruit and provide opportunities for employment to women and minorities

collective bargaining
the formal recognition of employee organizations and their right to negotiate with management regarding workplace issues

seniority
the use of the length of employment to determine an employee's assignment, days off, or other job-related functions

security needs. Over the years in which correctional agencies have used collective bargaining, the fears that it would jeopardize an agency mission have not materialized, and input by the unions representing line staff has usually resulted in improved decision making and higher morale.

Overall, union membership has been declining. In 1983, 20.1 percent (17.7 million) of all workers in the United States were union members. In 2015, only 11.1 percent (14.8 million) of salary and wage workers were union members. And only 6.7 percent of private sector workers were union members. The public sector has a much higher percentage of union membership, with 35.2 percent of public sector employees belonging to a union.[44] Many national labor organizations represent public-sector and correctional employees, including the AFL-CIO, AFSFME (the American Federation of State, Federal and Municipal Employees), and the International Brotherhood of Teamsters. In some states, several different organizations represent different groups of correctional employees (correctional officers, nurses, professional staff), and in others employees elect a single labor union to represent all of them. The labor organization that represents employees is able to negotiate issues of pay and benefits for public employees and sometimes other issues, such as how staff members are selected for overtime, the type of clothing provided to staff by the agency, and the number and areas of coverage by correctional officers. Collective bargaining is well entrenched in many prisons and correctional agencies and has a major impact on policy and practice, and there is usually a harmonious relationship between management and labor.

Also a concern by both parties has been the right to strike. Most public-safety organizations are not allowed to strike, which takes away a major union tactic to get management to accept labor's negotiating demands. Although a crisis could occur if police or correctional officers were allowed to strike, unions representing these groups sometimes sanction informal job actions (the "blue flu") to get the attention of management. In the past, there have also been illegal strikes by correctional officers. In New York state, even with the Taylor Law penalties whereby strikers lose two days' salary for each day they are on strike,[45] a strike of New York state correctional officers occurred in 1979. An analysis of the strike found that collective bargaining was not well suited to resolve the problems in this situation (officers believed they had lost status and authority, and racial tension existed within the officer ranks and between officers and inmates) and may have even aggravated them.[46]

Another concern regarding collective bargaining is its impact on security and correctional efforts toward rehabilitation. During the 1960s and 1970s, the rehabilitative movement created a fear by officers that the interest in helping inmates would lead to a reduction of authority for correctional officers, and unionization gained strength within prisons. However, many labor and correctional officials recognize that interests of prisoners and officers are intertwined, and both groups stand to benefit from the rehabilitative philosophy. As rehabilitative programs improve inmate morale, reduce idleness, and enhance security, the workplace situation improves for prison staff.

And a key issue is the influence of union officials on correctional policy and staff performance. Most correctional agencies do (some are required to by contract) ask union officials to review new policy before it is issued to determine if it has any negative impacts on employees or is counter to the contract provisions. And beyond this, some large correctional unions donate money to political campaigns, and elected officials give them access and take their suggestions in addition to those of correctional administrators. An often-cited example is the California Correctional Peace Officers Association (CCPOA), the state correctional union with over 30,000 members and dues are over $2 million per year.

CCPOA is usually large donors to California governor and state legislator elections, and also lobby for bills both favorable to union members and that lengthen prison terms. Another concern is whether unions act to protect unprofessional staff. An article in the *New York Times* in December 2014 states that the head of the New York City correctional officer union "has come to exert extraordinary control over the Correction Department, consulting with commissioners on key appointments, forging alliances with high-ranking uniformed correction leaders and, more recently, speaking regularly with Mayor Bill de Blasio about department policy. His influence has paid enormous dividends for his members, but it has also fed a culture of violence and corruption at Rikers (referring to the city prisons)."[47] If these allegations are true, the situation is not what was intended as jurisdictions institute collective bargaining statutes.

Several states still do not authorize collective bargaining for correctional employees, fearing it will undermine security and the authority and flexibility for management to effectively operate prisons. In the "You Make the Decision" box at the end of the chapter, students are to read through the information, weigh the pros and cons, and decide (if they had the authority) whether they would implement collective bargaining in a state.

Chapter Review

Summary

Many questions were asked at the beginning of this chapter regarding how prisons are managed. These include how a prison manages staff and inmates to accomplish its mission, how a greatly outnumbered staff controls potentially violent and dangerous inmates, how prisons ensure quality performance of their functions, and what role staff members play in the accomplishment of the mission. In this chapter, these questions have been addressed and we hope answered to students' satisfaction. Prisons and their oversight agencies must first organize themselves in a way to manage the staff and resources provided to have a safe and secure environment while offering programs that help inmates return to their communities as successful and law-abiding citizens. Since prisons have become such big businesses and use such a large percentage of state taxpayer dollars, there is much more interest from the public and elected officials in how they perform than ever before. Therefore, these agencies must organize to manage both internal and external environments in the prisons.

The various methods for managing inmates have also been described. Prisons must begin with professional policies and implementation procedures, communicate these to staff and inmates, and consistently carry them out. Since there is a considerable difference in the methods and expense of handling maximum- and minimum-security inmates, an effective classification instrument to separate inmates by needs and risks is beneficial. Prisons must have a fair and equitable disciplinary process to punish violation of prison rules, control misbehavior, and maintain order.

Finally, this chapter describes how important correctional staff members are to the management of a prison. Prisons are sometimes referred to as a "people business," meaning that they are all about people managing other people. Even though prisons must have sufficient physical security, they must also have well-developed and state-of-the-art policies, and they must consistently implement these policies; the accomplishment of their mission is impossible without dedicated and committed professional staff. This chapter has provided information regarding how prisons recruit, hire, and manage staff, including when a collective-bargaining agreement exists between management and labor. Prisons are complex organizations and require the utmost in management and leadership.

Key Terms

director

inspector

custody

treatment

services

employee awards program

unit management

unit manager

case manager

correctional counselor

American Correctional Association

policy audit

policy implementation audit

ACA accreditation

internal classification system

inmate disciplinary system

administrative appeals process

integrity interview

staff diversity

affirmative action programs

collective bargaining

seniority

Review Questions

1. Why are entities such as public and media affairs, legislative liaison, legal advisors, and internal affairs often organizationally located in the office of the director?

2. What is the role of an inspector in a department of corrections or prison?

3. Describe the three functions of custody, treatment, and services within a prison organization.

4. What is unit management and how does it contribute to the management of a prison?

5. Name the three common staff titles working in unit management.

6. Why is it important to consistently implement policies and procedures within a prison?

7. What processes are used to determine whether policies and procedures within a prison are being consistently applied?

8. What is an objective classification system?

9. What is an internal classification system, and what function does it play in a prison?

10. How can a classification process assist in gaining inmate compliance?

11. Define an inmate disciplinary system.

12. List five sanctions that can be taken against inmates for failure to abide by prison rules.

13. What processes are available for inmates to appeal a disciplinary decision or seek to redress wrongs done them by prison staff?

14. Why are staff members so important to the functioning of a prison?

15. Why is staff recruitment and hiring so important to the accomplishment of the mission of a prison?

16. Define collective bargaining and describe its history in corrections.

You Make the Decision...

Implement Collective Bargaining?

When a state or local government authorizes public employees to organize and engage in collective bargaining, the first step is for the employees to select a labor organization to represent them. A key decision in the collective-bargaining process is how to align employee groups for representation. For instance, will all correctional employees be represented by one labor organization, or will employees be clustered into logical groups (all correctional officers, all trade employees, all treatment staff) to be represented by a union? After the employees are grouped for representation, they vote to select the labor organization (such as the AFL-CIO; the American Federation of State, Federal and Municipal Employees; or the International Brotherhood of Teamsters) that will represent them in negotiations and contract management.

The election process can be extremely highly contested and difficult for both management and employees, as competing unions want to find issues and convince staff that they can best represent their interests. One state director of corrections noted the following:

The organizing and election process was horrible. We are a large state, and our employees would end up being several thousand union members. I thought management had a really good relationship with staff, and I personally spent a lot of time with line staff whenever I visited the prisons. I know they appreciated it and respected me for my concern and leadership. All of a sudden, the three national unions vying to represent them were campaigning and trying to find issues to get employee attention. Since there really were no major issues regarding safety or prison management, they had
to make things up. It was a personal affront to me with some of the things they came up with. I couldn't believe some of the nefarious schemes they came up with to suggest why we made certain decisions.

After selection of the union, the parties prepare for negotiations. One of the most important issues is how seniority will be used. It may be used for assignments, promotion, or pay. After the contract is negotiated, the parties must live with it and use it daily. Unfortunately, there are always questions that come into dispute about the true meaning of the contract. When in dispute, management can make a decision, and the union can file a grievance against it. A grievance is a formal complaint that the action taken by management is not within the language or intent of the labor contract, and the grievance then goes through a formal process for resolution. One thing is clear in a collective-bargaining environment: If either or both parties want to be confrontational and argue almost every minor contract issue, they will spend a tremendous amount of time and money to resolve their disputes.

Many people believe that collective bargaining has more positive than negative implications. It certainly can work if both management and labor communicate and listen to each other and are reasonable in their positions. However, when the parties in collective bargaining stop listening, let the issues get personal, and become overly adversarial in the relationship, collective bargaining makes a difficult workplace even more tense and stressful.

You must now decide if you think a state without it should implement collective bargaining. Consider the positives and the negatives, and remember that once the decision is made to implement, it is unlikely it can ever be changed.

CHAPTER 11
Prison Life for Inmates

Photo by Richard P. Seiter.

After reading this chapter, you should be able to:

1. Describe the activities within correctional institutions that Goffman suggested make it more difficult for prisoners to successfully return and adapt to community living.

2. Define the concept of prisonization and explain its impact on inmates both while serving a prison sentence and as they return to the community.

3. Describe the different types of violent acts that occur within prisons, the forces that increase the likelihood of violence, and methods prison staff use to identify and control gang behavior.

4. Summarize issues associated with inmate sexual behavior and describe the focus of the Prison Rape Elimination Act.

5. Identify the ways that illegal drugs come into prisons and evaluate the potential of various methods to limit their availability within prisons.

6. Outline the history of women's prisons.

7. Describe the culture in women's prisons, including the function of pseudofamilies, and compare it to the culture in men's prisons.

Introduction

Now that we have covered the organization, functions, and models used to manage prisons, we move to a look at life for both inmates and staff within a prison environment. From the next two chapters, students will not only assimilate information and facts, but also get a feel for what it is like to be in the closed environment of a prison; the unique relationships among inmates and between inmates and staff; and matters such as material possessions, routines, privileges, and interpersonal communications that take on much more importance in prison than in normal society. The prison world is a social realm of its own, and although it is difficult to describe to those who have not seen or experienced it, it has some structure and organization that need to be considered and understood.

In Chapter 7, characteristics of the clients of correctional agencies, as well as certain activities, policies, and programs related to these characteristics, were described. This chapter addresses the world in which inmates live and the issues of violence, inmate culture, drugs, gang activity, and homosexuality that inmates face. The chapter presents the prison environment for both male and female inmates, because institutions for each have many unique characteristics in terms of the culture, inmate relationships, and potential for violence. The male inmate's world is based more on survival, watching one's back, and getting along without creating problems that can result in assaults or other serious problems. Male inmates adapt to incarceration by isolating themselves; they try to do their time independently and avoid being involved in other inmate problems or issues. However, the existence of prison gangs often requires them to group together and protect themselves or avoid intimidation or coercion for sex or money. However, male inmates (whether in a gang or not) see these groupings only as a value for strength or financial benefit.

Female inmates, on the other hand, adjust to imprisonment by forming close relationships to other inmates, seeking relationships to provide a support structure. With less concern for personal safety than male inmates, women in prison desire a family relationship similar to what they experience outside prison, with specific roles of parent, child, or partner. They also do not mentally separate themselves from their families on the outside as men do, and their lives stay integrated into those of their outside family. The potential for abuse by staff is more of an issue with women inmates, however, and female inmate treatment programs are usually different in terms of their goals and operations than many of those in male institutions. At the end of this chapter, students should understand how inmates adapt to the culture of a prison and how the inmate and staff structures affect their life in prison and influence their life when they return to outside society.

Prison Life for Male Offenders

Prisons strive to provide a balanced approach to accomplishing the multiple goals of corrections. By merely holding offenders against their will and taking away their freedoms, prisons inflict punishment. At the same time, they attempt to create a positive and interactive environment, providing rehabilitative programs to help offenders prepare for release and their return to their communities. However, the somewhat isolated nature of prisons through their location and separation from normal society can easily result in a punitive atmosphere in which inmates lose their identity and ability to make decisions for themselves.

In 1961, Erving Goffman was one of the first to describe the impact a prison environment could have on those housed within the institution. Goffman described the concept of **total institution** as a setting isolating people from the rest of society and unnecessarily manipulating them through the actions of the administrative staff.[1] He suggests that certain characteristics of such institutions result in isolation and inability to act for oneself:

- Staff members supervise all spheres of daily life, such as where inmates eat, work, and sleep.
- The environment is highly standardized, with one set of activities for everyone.
- Rules and schedules dictate how inmates perform all aspects of their daily routine.

Prisons take on these characteristics for controlling and managing inmates' behavior and, through the use of rewards and punishments, attempt to *resocialize* inmates to a law-abiding lifestyle. However, Goffman warns that, although institutions can bring about the desired change in some inmates, others become confused, hostile, and bitter and that extended periods of institutional living can actually reduce an individual's capacity for independent living.

Goffman argues that institutional activities such as making new inmates publicly strip, wear degrading striped uniforms, and shave their heads fail to resocialize inmates. Most of these actions have been recognized as problematic and have been changed in most prison systems. However, subtler, yet perhaps even more important, is the effect of the prison environment resulting from the tone set by interactions between staff and inmates. Staff members are charged with consistent enforcement of rules and maintenance of control. Yet they are not to do so in a punitive or derogatory manner. This balance is sometimes difficult to carry out.

The challenge in creating and continuing positive interactions between staff and inmates is illustrated in Zimbardo's classic experiment.[2] To test the ways in which prisons change human behavior, Zimbardo constructed a mock prison in the basement of a building at Stanford University and used students in one of his

Some aspects of prison life can take away inmates' self-concept and ability to act for themselves, making a successful adjustment back to the community more difficult. Reed Saxon/AP Images.

The experiment by Zimbardo at Stanford University illustrates how hostility can develop between staff and inmates within a prison setting. Courtesy of Philip G. Zimbardo, Inc.

college classes to play the roles of staff and inmates. Twenty-four male students were then randomly assigned to roles as either guards or prisoners. For two weeks, the prisoners were to spend time in the "Stanford County Prison," with the guards responsible for operating the prison. Soon after the experiment began, guards and prisoners became hostile toward each other; guards humiliated and yelled at prisoners, and prisoners resisted and insulted guards. The situation deteriorated to the point that after the first week Zimbardo had to cancel the remaining week of the experiment. Zimbardo wrote that "some boys (guards) treat others as if they were despicable animals, taking pleasure in cruelty, while other boys (prisoners) became servile, dehumanized robots who thought only of escape, of their own individual survival and of their mounting hatred for the guards."[3] This experiment illustrates the type of relationship that can easily develop between staff and prison inmates; constant diligence and strong leadership by prison administrators are needed to avoid such a situation.

Prison Culture and the Inmate Code

inmate code

the expected rules and behaviors represented by the model prisoner and reflecting the values and norms of prison society

prisonization

the process whereby inmates take on the folkways, mores, customs, and general culture of the penitentiary

To the student of corrections, nothing seems more fascinating than the formation of a separate and unique culture within prisons. For many reasons, and in a way that has changed over time, inmates construct a culture with unique values, traditions, roles, expectations, language, and customs while in prison. This culture is called the **inmate code**, the expected rules and behaviors represented by the model prisoner that reflect the values and norms of prison society. What factors influence the creation of a prison culture and inmate code, the extent to which prisonization (inmates accepting and adapting to the prison culture) occurs, and whether the inmate code still exists are topics of continued study and debate.

More than sixty years ago, Clemmer studied prisons and was one of the first to identify the special adaptation that inmates make as they spend time together in prison. He coined the term **prisonization** to describe the process by which inmates "[take] on in greater or lesser degree the folkways, mores, customs, and general culture of the penitentiary."[4] Clemmer suggested that inmates learn the behaviors of being in prison (dressing, working, new language, dependence on others, degradation of status) and that this process of prisonization leads to an increased identification with criminal lifestyles and more difficulty in successfully returning and adapting to the community after release.

Over the next two decades, others who studied the effects of being in prison identified many aspects of the inmate code. The code is how those who want respect as a "con" act and behave. As a philosophy, it emphasizes loyalty to convicts and distrust of correctional

Younger inmates don't respect the code that was followed by older inmates. Photo by Richard P. Seiter.

officers (*hacks* or *screws*), being trustworthy, and not getting involved in other inmates' business. From the work of Sykes in the 1950s[5] and Irwin and Cressey in the 1960s,[6] several behaviors have been identified that are elements of the inmate code:

- Do your own time (don't get involved in the business of other inmates)
- Be a stand-up guy (be someone that other inmates can count on)
- Don't rat on other inmates (do not tell staff what other inmates have done or are doing—don't be a "snitch")
- Don't trust the guards (don't become overly friendly with staff, don't show them respect, and talk to them only when you have to)
- Don't exploit other inmates (don't take advantage of others or their problems or steal from them)
- Maintain dignity and respect (don't show staff a weakness and show respect to other inmates)
- Settle conflict between inmates (don't go to staff with problems between inmates, settle it yourself)
- Respect the real "cons" (the inmates who have done a lot of time, know the system, and live the inmate code deserve respect)

There are two theories on how the inmate culture becomes a part of prison life. The first is that the culture is *indigenous* to prisons; Clemmer believed that it develops as a result of the environment in which inmates find themselves. Sykes believed that the norms arise specifically in response to the deprivations and loss of liberty inherent in incarceration. The other theory is that the culture is *imported* or brought in with the values of the inmates from the outside world. Irwin and Cressey identified three types of offenders that bring characteristics to the prison setting, and the blending of these characteristics creates the prisoner subculture. **Convicts** are long-term inmates, probably beginning with youths who were in foster homes, reform schools, and then prisons. They become used to the single-sex, masculine society and find a way to live in this environment with a minimal amount of problems and disruptions. **Thieves** have adopted a career of crime and are just doing their time in prison until they can get out and hit the "big score." **Square johns** are probably first-time offenders and have more identification with straight society and the norms of noncriminals.

Today, many people believe that the inmate code is dead or at least ignored by most inmates. The older inmates talk of "young punks," inmates who are always out to exploit others, don't respect the old-timers, constantly cause trouble that brings greater supervision from staff, and use muscle and not brains to get through their prison experience. The change in adhering to the inmate culture comes from at least several developments. The first is that, with a greater reliance on prison than on probation for many offenders, there are more square johns in prison, and even though they serve short sentences and turn over rapidly, they represent a larger

convicts
long-term inmates who become used to the prison society and find a way to live in this environment with a minimal amount of problems and disruptions

thieves
inmates who have adopted a career of crime and are doing their prison time until they can get out and hit the "big score"

square johns
inmates who are usually first-time offenders and have more identification with "straight" society and norms of the noncriminals

The availability of telephones and other ways to communicate with the world outside the prison is thought to be one reason why the inmate code is dying. Photo by Richard P. Seiter.

percentage of inmates who do not adhere to the inmate culture. Second, there are many young and impulsive inmates who respect only physical power or intimidation. Finally, the fact that prisons are not as isolated as in the past undermines the solidarity and formation of the inmate code. Today, inmates talk to their family and friends on the telephone on a regular basis, they have visitors several times per week, and they read newspapers and magazines and stay attuned to what is occurring in the outside world. And a recent development is the use of e-messaging by inmates. A few states are beginning to allow electronic messages to be sent and received by inmates. Jurisdictions create kiosks in the prisons by which inmates can send e-letters out through a secure system, so they do not have access to the Internet. These systems improve security, reduce staff time, do not cost money as the rates charged pay for the system, and increase the contact between inmates and their families.[7]

Even though the inmate code has not been seen as a valued commodity by many prison staff, most staff and inmates who have been around for several years regret its demise. They feel that at least the inmate code provided an expected order, organization, and understanding of how the prison would informally work and how inmates would behave toward staff and other inmates.

As with any culture or society, a special language develops. The "A Look Into" box contains a glossary of prison terms and slang.[8]

A Look Into...

A Glossary of Prison Slang

A&P	Inmate store, commissary	Cop out	To confess; inmates claim it is unwise to cop out to anything
Bad Mammy Jammy	Good-looking female visitor	Crib	Inmate's bunk or cell
Bird bath	Taking a sponge bath in the sink in the cell	Crow	An inmate who watches out for officers while other inmates violate the rules
Blow	Cigarette	Dirty dog	Sorry, no-good inmate
To blow	To get mad	Double trouble	When an inmate borrows something and must pay back twice the amount borrowed
Bo-hog	An inmate who bosses other inmates around and preys on weaker inmates		
Bomb	Letter denying parole; also refers to rolled-up toilet paper used for cooking in a cell	Fishing line	Bag and rope tied together to reach something under the cell door
Bricks	Life outside prison; a person hits the bricks when he or she leaves prison	Free worlder	Anyone who is not an inmate
		Front	To pretend to be tough
Bull	Correctional officer or police officer	Ghetto penthouse	Top tier in the cellblock
Bull sisters	A gang of predatory homosexual inmates	Goon squad	Officers who dress in riot gear to quell inmate riots or extract resistant inmates from their cells
Bust a nut	Relief by masturbation		
Buzzard	An inmate who looks out for officers on patrol		
Carry a lunch pail	To hold a routine 9–5 job on the outside; something many inmates despise	Hardcastle	Warden or any officer who acts tough
		Hard stuff	Heroin or opium
Cellie	Cellmate	Head up	One-on-one fight
Convict	A tough prisoner who has proved himself in multiple encounters over the years; also referred to as a *regular, solid,* or *right guy*	Hold your mud	Not backing down in the prison setting
		Hole	Isolation cell

Home boy	Inmate from your neighborhood	Pruno	Prison-made booze concocted from yeast, fruit juices, bread, or potatoes; doesn't taste good, but does cause a buzz
House	Cell		
Hugging the bars	Refers to someone who wants to get out of prison quickly or doesn't want to get involved in an incident		
		Pumping iron	Lifting weights
Jamming	Fist fighting	Punk	Someone who submits sexually to a stronger inmate
Joint	Prison or jail		
Joint converted	Inmate who finds religion	Put it on ice	Don't give up information
Juice	Power; an inmate who can make things happen	Rabbit	Escaped inmate
		Railroad	To get blamed for something you didn't do
Keister stashed	Contraband inserted into the rectum		
Kite	A letter from home, or an informant's tip to the authorities	Reruns	Inmates who return after being released
Lowlife rouger	Someone who steals other inmates' belongings	Road dog	Inmate who roams the yard looking for trouble
The Man	Correctional officer	Screw	Correctional officer
Mud water	Cell-brewed coffee	Shank or shiv	Prison-made knife
Mule	Free person who transports contraband into and out of the prison for inmates	Silent beef	Crimes suspected but not proved in court; the parole board often considers these offenses in deciding on parole
Off someone	To kill a person		
On the Rio	Not joking, serious	Snitch	An inmate who informs on other inmates in return for favors from the prison officials
P.C.	Protective custody		
Peckerwood	In Georgia, refers to a white correctional officer and is an insult; in California, refers to a high-status inmate and is something to be attained		
		Speeding ticket	Minor write-up, disciplinary report
		Throw down	Fight
		Tunk	An inmate card game
		Went for a rib	Provoked an inmate into doing something
Pimp slap	Slap across the face		

Violence in Prisons

As noted in Chapter 7, a large percentage of male inmates have a lengthy history of violence. At the end of 2015, 52.9 percent of adults sentenced to state prisons were committed for violent offenses.[9] With such a large proportion of inmates previously involved in violent acts, it is not surprising, therefore, that violent behavior is a way of life within prisons. Many inmates just resort to violence as their normal reaction to frustration, disagreements, or lack of power. Those who are not prone to violence are constantly watchful to avoid situations that could lead to violent confrontations. A study of inmate-on-inmate violence in thirty prisons confirmed what is called the "importation" theory, or that violent inmates bring their violent ways into prison with them.[10]

Studies have found that approximately one in four inmates are victims of nonsexual violence in prisons.[11] Overcrowded prison conditions;[12] tensions between inmate gangs;[13] the powerlessness, boredom, and sexual frustration of inmates;[14] and the importation of street cultures of "face to face rivalries, retaliation, machismo, disrespect, and drunkenness"[15] have all been suggested as reasons for violent acts in prisons. The simple conclusion as to why there is a high level of violence within prisons is that prisons hold violent people who act out in violent ways, and the prison culture and environment add to the tension and threat of violence by inmates.

Hassine suggests another reason for prison violence: inmate avoidance of the reality of their incarceration. He writes,

Violence in Graterford (a state prison in Pennsylvania) had also become a form of escape for many inmates. In creating and maintaining a predatory environment, these men were able to avoid the reality of imprisonment by focusing all their attention on fighting one another. The more hostile the environment, the more they saw themselves as victims and the less responsible they felt for their own action.[16]

interpersonal violence

prison violence that occurs between two or more individual inmates; the reason for the violence is a personal issue between the individuals

collective violence

prison violence that is between, and initiated by, groups of inmates and includes prison riots and disturbances; it can be groups of inmates against staff or against one another, as this violence stems from the fundamental difference in values and positions of the two groups

In an early review of prison violence, Braswell and colleagues distinguish between interpersonal violence and collective violence.[17] **Interpersonal violence** occurs between two or more individual inmates, and the reason for the violence is a personal issue between the individuals. **Collective violence** is between, and initiated by, groups of inmates and includes prison riots and disturbances. Although collective violence is usually by inmates against prison staff and administration, large-scale gang conflicts also come under this category. Collective violence stems from the fundamental difference in values and positions of the two groups, rather than an individual conflict.

The threat of interpersonal violence causes the constant fear and tension of individual inmates in a correctional environment. Some inmates are always looking for a reason to violently act out, and others are always worried that they may be that reason. Johnson, in describing life in prison, writes,

The convict world is populated by men who doubt their worth as human beings and who feel they must constantly find occasions to "prove" themselves.... The convict world is a world of continuing—and generally escalating—conflict. Aggrieved parties cannot afford to back down, for then they are seen as weak and hence vulnerable to more abuse. Violence in the convict world establishes one's competence as a man who can survive in a human jungle.[18]

Terry, in *The Fellas: Overcoming Prison and Addiction*, uses interviews with inmates and ex-inmates to paint a similar view of the constant problem of violence in prisons. He notes that violence in prison is rampant and likely to continue for some time. He points out how violence occurs, even though inmates may try to avoid it. He quotes some of the "fellas" as follows:

Doing your own time, minding your own business or staying away from trouble while serving a prison sentence...may be next to impossible...what it comes down to is this—I don't care how much you try to stay out of it—nowadays, as crazy as it is, you're gonna be involved some way, some how.[19]

After experiencing an increasing level of violence within federal prisons, officials attempted to identify the types of inmates more likely to commit violent acts. Innes and Verdeyen write that there are three general categories of inmates who resort to violence:

1. *Antisocial offenders* have developed the habit of using force and coercion to get what they want. This group has used violence on the streets, and even though they have the competencies and skills to act in prosocial ways, they have found that violence works successfully for them.

2. *Special-needs offenders* are those with physical or mental deficiencies. As a result of their impairments, they are unable to function satisfactorily in a prison environment and often react to situations violently.
3. *Psychopathic offenders* are predatory, cold, and calculating, and usually act violently for no good reason. They do not feel compassion and will be violent simply for their own enjoyment.[20]

Male inmates live in an environment with the constant threat and potential for violence. Not only are many violent people in prison, but the environment and culture create a breeding ground for violence, with the need to act tough and not back down; a prevalence of gang members and gang activities; pressure for homosexual sex from some inmates; and conflicts that result from the sale and use of drugs. Even though homicide rates dropped from 1980 to 2002, they have been climbing ever since, and in 2012, there were eighty-five homicides in state prisons.[21]

A recent study identified characteristics that are predictive of risk of violent victimization while in prison. The factors associated with such victimization include:

1. *Offense History:* sex offenders are at a greater risk of victimization;
2. *Institutional History:* inmates that antagonize others are at a greater risk of victimization. This can be from preying on other inmates (retaliation for such), instigating institutional misconduct, or having been placed in segregation for punishment;
3. *Personality Characteristics:* offenders with mental disorders or substance abuse, and those with a poor regard for others (their disrespect for others results in retaliation).[22]

Unfortunately, violence in prisons, especially in high-security prisons, is a common event. There are days without fights or serious assaults, but a prison administrator with his or her eyes open and an understanding of the environment knows that inmates are pressured and extorted every day. Prisons are full of individuals who have lived their lives violently and try to intimidate others to get what they want. It is not possible for prison administrators to stop all this from happening; their focus is (1) to provide a situation that allows inmates to protect themselves (in nonviolent ways and using legitimate means) and (2) to do everything possible to isolate the predators from potential victims.

Even with the high possibility of violence, there are relatively few homicides in prison, although any is too many. In 2013, there were 90 homicides in state prisons, and 762 homicides from 2001 to 2013. The rate per 100,000 has been relatively stable, as there were either 3 or 4 per 100,000 from 2001 until 2009. Since then, the mortality rate has climbed, and was 7 per 100,000 in 2012 and 2013.[23] Another danger for prisoners is suicide. Long sentences with little hope for release, the drudgery of service time, a high level of mental illness, and the continuous stress of being in prison make the prison population at high risk for suicide. From 2001 to 2013, there have been 2,577 suicides in state prisons, with a low of 168 in 2001 and 2002, rising to a high of 219 in 2006, and then dropping to 192 in 2013.[24] The prison suicide rate has remained about the same, with 14 per 100,000 inmates in 2001 and 15 per 100,000 inmates in 2013. The approach to preventing suicides in prison is the same as in jails, which was described in Chapter 3.

Gangs in Prisons

Prison gangs not only are disruptive within a prison environment, but also contribute greatly to acts of violence and the resulting tension. A ten-year review by the Bureau of Justice Statistics found that gang members committed 6 percent of violent crimes (or 373,000 per year).[25] And in the 2015 *National Gang Report*, over one-half of jurisdictions surveyed indicated that crime by gangs increased over the past few years.[26] The most recent National Gang Threat Assessment estimates that there are approximately 1.4 million gang members belonging to more than 33,000 gangs active in the United States in 2011, and gangs are responsible for an average of 48 percent of violent crime in most jurisdictions and up to 90 percent in several others.[27] As would be expected, these gang members continue their predatory, violent ways in prison. Gang members stick together to intimidate other inmates, control drug sales and prostitution, and gain power and influence. In a study of the relationship between gang affiliation and violent acts in federal prisons, researchers found that both specific and generic gang indicators were statistically related to violence and misconduct[28] and concluded that controlling gang activities has great potential to reduce tension and violence within prisons.

prison gangs

groups that form in prison and use the threat of violence to intimidate other inmates, control drug sales and prostitution, and gain power and influence

Prison gangs were first identified in California in the early 1960s, when prison administrators realized that many of their problems—violence, intimidation of staff and inmates, and introduction of drugs—were being controlled and coordinated by organized groups of inmates. A Department of Justice report on the early development of gangs and their prison activities notes, "Their organization was so firmly entrenched (in California) before authorities understood the danger confronting them that control of the institutions was seriously threatened. This phenomenon has been repeated in numerous jurisdictions as the presence and influence of gangs have spread throughout the country."[29]

Since that time, prison gangs have continued to grow in number and influence in the nations' prisons. A national survey in 1985 identified more than a hundred gangs, with a total membership of approximately 13,000.[30] An American Correctional Association 1993 survey identified thirty-nine different, major gangs in the nation's prisons and estimated that 6 percent of prisoners were members of a gang.[31] In the most recent survey, state and federal prisons reported that of their total male population, 24.8 percent were prison gang members and 4.09 percent of the female population were gang members.[32] Gang membership is thought to have continued to increase since that survey.[33] And the National Gang Intelligence Center estimated there were 230,000 gang members in prison.[34]

Gang members in prisons usually have a more extensive history of crime than nongang members, get in more trouble in prison, participate in fewer prison programs, and are more likely to have a substance abuse problem.[35] A study of gangs in prison found that the higher the percentage of gang members in a prison, the greater the incidence of inmate-on-inmate violence.[36] Several authors suggest that gangs are a natural outgrowth of large groups of criminals placed together in a prison setting. Scott suggests, "The prison gang, as both a process and an organization, facilitates the adaptation of inmates to life in the prison and, more locally, the cell block."[37] Sykes, describing the prison environment in the 1950s, noted that inmates find ways to cope with their confinement and the deprivations they encounter.[38] However, other authors describe modern prison gangs as more hedonistic than social phenomena and note that through money and power, gang members can avoid the

The existence of prison gangs results in intimidation of staff and inmates and leads to tension and violence within prisons.

Rich Pedroncelli/AP Images.

deprivation of property, freedom, and influence that a prison tries to accomplish. Fleisher and Decker suggest, "Motivated by a desire to make money and be at the top of an institution's inmate power structure, prison gangs exploit the inherent weaknesses resulting from overcrowded, understaffed mega-prisons."[39] Prison gangs today are primarily to control and carry out criminal activities (such as sale of drugs or prostitution) and gain power and influence over both inmates and staff. And as would be expected, gang members have high rates of recidivism after release from prison.[40]

Fortunately, correctional agencies have gained sophistication in understanding prison gangs, and much more is currently known about their operations, membership, and organization. In an issue of *Correctional Management Quarterly* devoted entirely to the threat of prison gangs, Seiter writes, "Correctional administrators can never hesitate, stop gathering intelligence, or fail to stay ahead of the gangs' operations....For the individual correctional staff involved, their will to further the correctional mission—to provide a safe environment for staff and inmates—cannot waiver."[41]

Many prison gangs started as an extension of street gangs. When such groups as Bloods and Crips found that many of their street gang members ended up in prison, it was only natural that they continue their criminal activities while recruiting membership, intimidating other inmates, and attempting to control the drug dealing in prison. Other gangs, such as the Mexican Mafia, Dirty White Boys, and Black Guerilla Family, originated in prison as ethnic and racial groups of inmates began to band together for strength and support. They discovered that such alliances could lead to control over other prisoners, create funds, and provide members power to gain advantages in prison they might otherwise not have. The following list describes some of the current major prison gangs.

- *Aryan Brotherhood (AB):* The Aryan Brotherhood started in 1967 in San Quentin Prison, is limited to Caucasians, and is a Nazi-oriented, antiblack gang that dislikes authority and adheres to violence to gain prestige. They have no hesitancy to kill to keep their membership and organization secure and once had a rule of "making one's bones" to get in, meaning that prospective members had to kill for the gang to show their worth. It was also said that the only way to get out of the gang was to die. The AB has been aligned with many street motorcycle gangs and has extensive prison and street networks for dealing drugs. They also have alliances with other white supremacist gangs to gain numbers and power in prison. They have (from time to time) had an association with the Mexican Mafia to expand their drug dealing and ability to perform contract killings.

- *Mexican Mafia (MM):* The Mexican Mafia is a Hispanic gang that requires members to take an oath of "blood in, blood out," meaning that prospective members must assault someone for the gang to prove themselves and are badly beaten or even killed to get out of the gang. It originated in the Deuel Vocational Institution (California) in 1958; it has since become one of the most powerful prison gangs in the country. Forming from the Mexican Mafia are **Sureños,** now one of the largest prison gangs in the world. Formed in the Southern California prisons, the term *Sureños* means "Southerner" in Spanish. Gang members are required to align with other members when they arrive in a prison. Sureños can be found in more than twenty states. The gang is focused on committing crimes to support its members in prison. The leaders organize the entire criminal activity and often rob banks to gain funds to support their prison activities.

Sureños
formed from the Mexican Mafia; Sureños means "Southerner" in Spanish and is one of the largest and most violent prison gangs in America

- *Black Guerilla Family (BGF):* The Black Guerilla Family also started in San Quentin Prison, and its first leader was George Jackson, the Black Panther who was killed in a 1971 escape attempt. They follow a politically charged revolutionary philosophy intent on destruction of the "white establishment" and overthrow of the government. They hope to coalesce all black inmates so they can "control their own destiny."

- *La Nuestra Familia (NF):* The NF ("our family") was established in the late 1960s in Soledad Prison (California), primarily by Chicano inmates from Northern California, to protect themselves from the Southern California–based Mexican Mafia. They have been at war with the Mexican Mafia (and the Aryan Brotherhood) for most of their existence, but more recently have tried to have a peace agreement. In their battles against these two gangs, they often form an alliance with the Black Guerilla Family. A board of directors, known as *La Mesa*, controls them. Rank in the gang depends on the number of killings accomplished for the gang.

- *Mexikanemi (EME):* This gang, also known as the Texas Mexican Mafia, started in the Texas prison system in 1984. They have spread rapidly in federal prisons across the country and are also in other southwestern states. Gang members are very violent and kill enemies in and outside prison. They usually act alone, but have aligned with the Texas Syndicate to fight the Mexican Mafia. They also are organized in military fashion with generals, lieutenants, sergeants, and soldiers. Members work their way up the organization within the prison they are in and are elected to positions based on their leadership. If transferred to another prison, they lose their rank unless reelected there.

- *Texas Syndicate (TS):* This is another California-originated prison gang; it was started by inmates who had migrated to California from Texas. Instead of joining one of the two California Hispanic gangs, they formed their own to maintain their Texas heritage and band together to protect Texas inmates from other gangs. The TS is well organized and has a national president, with appointed chairmen at each prison. There are vice-chairmen, captains, lieutenants, sergeants at arms, and soldiers. When the early gang members were released from California prisons, they returned to Texas and established the TS in Texas and other southwestern prisons. Their primary agenda is drug trafficking and selling protection to other inmates. They have a reputation for violence and are feared by other inmates.

Prison Gang Control Strategies

To control the activities and violence of gangs, correctional staff members focus on a variety of strategies. These include early detection of gang activities, identification of leaders and members, surveillance of gang activity, denial of gang turf or wearing of gang colors and symbols, separating gang members from other prisoners, and a variety of gang control tactics. Lesce identifies six measures to control prison gangs:

1. Transferring gang members to maximum-security prisons
2. Limiting inmates' access to money, which often plays a critical role in inmates' underground economy
3. Placing the most violence-prone gang members in special facilities
4. Developing gang intelligence
5. Recruiting informers
6. Observing inmates' daily routine activities to identify patterns of activities and associations of gang members[42]

Byrne and Hummer suggest one of the most important actions that prison staff can take to control gangs is classification and early detection of gang activities.[43] Correctional staff members are informed of gangs' organization, activities, and known membership at a prison and are asked to report any intelligence regarding gang member activities. Once identified, individuals are then labeled as leaders, hard-core members, and marginal members, or other terms to identify levels of gang involvement are *member, associate*, or *suspect*. A **gang validation process** requiring several identifiers of gang activity is used to confirm individuals' gang involvement level. Five or six different items are needed to validate an inmate as a *member*, three or four items may substantiate an inmate as an *associate*, and one or two identify an inmate as just a *suspect*. Gang validation identifiers include inmate self-admission that he or she is a gang member; information from a presentence investigation report that the inmate has participated in street gang activities; confiscated gang documents, such as membership lists, photographs, or correspondence from other gang members; violation of prison rules that indicates involvement in gang activities, such as drug trafficking, gambling, extortion, or strong-arming other inmates; involvement with known gang members; or tattoos indicating gang signs.

gang validation process
an identification of the number of identifiers of gang activity used to confirm individuals' gang involvement level

The next gang control strategy is surveillance of gang activities. After gang members are identified, their activities are closely monitored and recorded. The National Major Gang Task Force of the U.S. Department of Justice recommends the following actions to monitor gang members:

- *Posted picture file:* A centralized photo and data file on significant gang members, suspects, and associates should be maintained.
- *Confidential reports:* All staff members should report gang-related grouping activity on the daily confidential reports.
- *Gang communications:* There should be a priority with prison staff to intercept notes passed between gang members.

Gang members like to flaunt their power by showing displays of membership and group strength, such as tattoos, hand signs, staking out turf, or wearing clothes a certain way. Jan Sochor/Alamy Stock Photo.

- *Identify gang visitors:* Visitors of gang members should be identified and their names shared with other prisons. Often visitors of gang inmates at multiple institutions pass along gang information and "hit contracts."
- *Gang control efforts:* Staff should watch for efforts by gangs to dominate any physical area of the institution or access to any inmate program.[44]

Another important activity to control prison gangs is to keep them from showing their power. Gangs like to show their strength to recruit members, tout themselves as controlling activities or areas, and show willingness to be violent against their enemies. To do this, gangs try to flaunt colors, hand signs, and symbols; wear clothing a certain way; and stake out turf. Prison staff members need to be aware of the meaning of the different signs or colors and prohibit inmates from wearing or showing them.

Some jurisdictions, once they identify inmates as gang members, isolate them by moving them either to a high-security prison or to a supermax prison in lockdown status. The Federal Bureau of Prisons (BOP) policy requires that validated members (not associates or suspects) be assigned to a maximum-security prison. And the BOP has recently started gang units to house them in secure and separate units. These units replicate units started in California and Connecticut in the 1990s, and now used by many other states, in which they moved gang members and leaders to a high-security prison in lockdown status, similar to disciplinary segregation or a supermax prison. The only way for members to get out of the lockdown situation is to renounce their membership and **debrief** or tell correctional officials everything they know about the gang operations and membership. Once inmates debrief, they can never be accepted back into the gang and, in fact, become an enemy of the gang.

Over a decade ago, the California Department of Corrections and Rehabilitation (CDCR) began to racially segregate prisoners for up to sixty days each time they enter a new correctional facility in order to identify gang members and keep them separate to reduce violence. CDCR asserted that this prevented violence because most of their gang violence was race based. However, inmate Johnson, an African American, alleged that the policy violated his Fourteenth Amendment right to equal protection. The federal District Court of Northern California initially granted (and affirmed by the Ninth Circuit) the CDCR summary judgment on grounds that they were entitled to qualified immunity. However, the U.S. Supreme Court in 2005 reversed and remanded the Ninth Circuit decision and, while not deciding if the policy violates Johnson's right to equal protection, required the district court to rehear the case and use a test that must narrowly tailor any racial segregation and prove it serves a compelling state interest.[45] California is still trying to find ways to not segregate inmates during admission without increasing the likelihood of violence.

Gangs are a danger to staff and other inmates within a prison, and correctional staff members spend considerable time and effort to identify gang members and control their activity. If they do not, the gangs gain power, other inmates feel compelled to join a gang for their own protection, and prisons become a "war zone" rather than a secure and safe place in which inmates who desire to participate in self-improvement programs can do so. To break the cycle of crime and have any chance of returning prisoners to their communities as law-abiding citizens, prisons must control gang activities and limit potential violence. The "Your Career in Corrections" box describes the role of gang intelligence officers.

debrief
gang members tell correctional officials everything they know about the gang operations and membership; once inmates debrief, they become an enemy of the gang

Your Career in Corrections

Gang Intelligence Officers

For students who like the idea of working in a prison, are fascinated with investigative strategies, and are challenged by the idea of trying to keep ahead of the "bad guys," gang intelligence officer might just be the job to have. Most prisons and large correctional agencies have staff members who act as **gang intelligence officers** (the title varies by jurisdiction). These staff members collect intelligence and advise administrators regarding strategies to manage and contain prison gang activity. As prisons have implemented gang control strategies, gangs are increasingly becoming more secret and try to hide their illegal and strong-arm tactics from detection. Prisons do not specifically recruit and hire gang intelligence officers, but select promising individuals from their internal employee ranks and train them for these jobs. The positions are usually midlevel managers in the prison security departments, but act rather independently, as they are not in the traditional chain of command.

The primary function of gang intelligence officers is to collect and organize intelligence regarding gang activities and members. First, officers train prison staff regarding the types of behavior, dress, or other activities that could indicate gang functioning and how to report it to be included as intelligence information. Second, officers organize the information they

collect to identify specific gangs and specific individuals who may be involved in the gang. Third, officers use this information to designate individuals as gang members, associates, or suspects. Once gang members are identified, staff can pay particular attention to the activities and associations of these inmates. Finally, gang intelligence officers use this information to anticipate gang activities and proactively move to thwart their implementation.

The second function served by gang intelligence officers is the development of comprehensive gang control strategies. The information they gather can be used for control or discovery of gang activities by individuals or small numbers of gang members. It can also be used to develop broader strategies that may be implemented agency-wide to subvert the formation and illegal behavior of gangs. For instance, states such as Connecticut and California have decided to place all identified gang members in a lockdown situation and not let them off lockdown unless they debrief by telling officers all that they know about the gang, its operations, and its members and leaders. Gang intelligence officers, through their experience and knowledge, are the key staff members who develop such strategies to control gang activities to make prison safe for other inmates and staff.

Homosexual Behavior in Male Prisons

A problem that results from the operation of any single-sex prison is homosexual behavior, whether forced or consensual. It is difficult to identify the actual amount of homosexual activity in prisons; inmates are hesitant to admit such involvement and therefore staff members are not aware of the full extent of involvement. A well-designed study by the federal prison system in the early 1980s surveyed more than 300 inmates regarding their sexual activity in prison and found that more than 30 percent admitted some type of homosexual experience.[46] However, less than 1 percent admitted that they were forced into such activities, and 7 percent stated that inmates who were nice to them or gave them gifts later seduced them.

All prisons have a rule against any type of sexual behavior between inmates; if caught, inmates are punished for even consensual homosexual acts. Even though homosexual relationships are accepted in society, they are still not allowed in prisons, because there is no way to ensure that relationships are really consensual. A stronger inmate may actually be forcing a weaker inmate to have sex, while threatening to have him beaten or killed if he tells correctional staff about it. Also, many fights and stabbings in prisons result from **sexual triangles** in which two inmates become jealous and fight over another one. Most inmates who admit homosexual relationships

gang intelligence officers
prison staff charged with collecting intelligence and advising administrators regarding strategies to manage and contain prison gang activity

sexual triangles
two inmates become jealous and fight over another one

while in prison state that they are heterosexual, but due to long periods of sexual deprivation, they get involved in homosexual activity for sexual release.

Prisons do have a problem with forced sex acts or rape. Although some rapes are strictly for sexual gratification, Hassine reports that most sexual assaults (rapes) in prison are committed to "generate fear and to maintain power over the general population."[47] The most likely targets of such assaults are inmates who are young, physically small, and seen as weak and easily intimidated.[48] Inmates often watch for the newly arrived inmates ("fish") to identify likely targets of sexual aggression and then take advantage of them while they are feeling alone and do not yet understand the avenues they can take to protect themselves from assault. These inmates are led to believe that they can later report this sexual pressure and be protected by staff.

However, there does not have to be an acceptance that inmates will be raped in prison, and in 2003, the U.S. Congress passed the Prison Rape Elimination Act (PREA). The Act required the collection of information on the incidence and prevalence of sexual assault within correctional facilities and the development of national standards for the prevention, detection, and reduction of sexual violence in prison. A survey was conducted of jails and prisons to identify the level of sexual violence reported to the correctional agency. The results were an estimated continued increases, with 5,386 alleged incidents of sexual violence during 2004, 6,528 in 2006, 7,444 in 2008, and 8,763 for 2011.[49] The Bureau of Justice Statistics in 2012 continued the survey, and estimated that there were 80,600 inmates in jails and prisons who experienced an incident of sexual victimization.[50] Figure 11.1 illustrates the continual increase in allegations of sexual violence from 2005 to 2011.

The U.S. Department of Justice has also conducted three self-administered and anonymous inmate surveys, the most recent one for 2001–2012. Results were that an estimated 4.0 percent of state and federal prisoners and 3.2 percent of jail inmates experienced one or more incidents of sexual victimization. The differences in the three surveys were not statistically significant. Of the state and federal inmates 2.0 percent reported an incident involving another inmate and 2.4 percent reported an incident involving staff (some reported both). Among jail inmates, 1.6 percent reported an incident involving another inmate and 1.8 percent involving staff.[51]

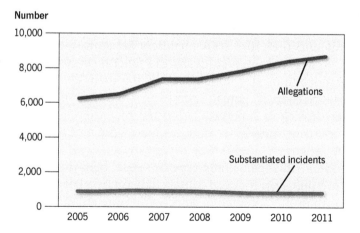

FIGURE 11.1   National Estimates of Allegations and Substantiated Incidents of Sexual Victimization, 2005–11

Source: Allen J. Beck and Ramona R. Rantala, "Victimization Reported by Adult Correctional Authorities, 2005–11," *BJS Special Report* (Washington, D.C.: U.S. Department of Justice, 2014), p. 1.

Of victims of inmate-on-inmate sexual assault, 44 percent were the result of physical force or threat of force, 12 percent were talked into it, and 5 percent were bribed or given alcohol or drugs to engage in the sexual act. The victims of inmate-on-inmate sexual assault were 78 percent male and 22 percent female. Of victims of staff-on-inmate sexual assault, female inmates represented 33 percent of the victims. Female staff committed more than one-half of incidents of staff sexual misconduct and a quarter of staff sexual harassment incidents. While physical force, pressure or abuse of power were identified in 20 percent of the incidents, the sexual relationships "appeared to be willing" in 84 percent when female staff were involved and 37 percent when male staff were involved.[52] This is due to the fact that even "consensual" sexual contact by male inmates and female staff is still against the law and considered sexual assault. And sexual victimization rates were higher among inmates with a history of mental health problems. Among inmates who stayed overnight in a hospital for mental or emotional problems, 5.7 percent of prison inmates and 4.4 percent of jail inmates said another inmate victimized them, and 4.9 percent of prison inmates and 3.4 percent of jail inmates said facility staff victimized them.[53]

In response to PREA and the frequency of reported acts, almost all states formed special task forces or steering committees to implement best practices identified throughout the states to prevent sexual violence.[54] Dimensions that are targeted to impact sexual violence are staff training, inmate education, classification at intake, zero tolerance, reporting procedures, investigative protocols, mandatory separation, and inmate victim aftercare.[55] To try to reduce the number of sexual assaults in prisons, correctional staff members use several preventive and reactionary measures. First, they advise inmates during the reception process that sexual assault is a possibility and that they have the option of telling staff and being separated from the aggressors. Second, staff members watch for signs of such aggressive acts and question potential targets about such pressure. Finally, staff members investigate every allegation of sexual pressure or assault and will separate the inmates from one another as a precautionary measure. Even though most allegations cannot be proved because they become one inmate's word against another's, if staff members fail to act to protect victims once an issue is brought to their attention, they could be held legally liable for any injury or psychological trauma that later results.

Prison wardens were surveyed to determine their beliefs on the best methods to prevent prison rape and sexual assault. Although they believed that good policies and procedures could be somewhat effective (69 percent) and that good staff training was also somewhat effective (52 percent), the most favored method was that increased and enhanced supervision by staff could be "completely effective" (71 percent).[56] The real key to prevention is changing the culture rather than training staff and implementing procedures after a sexual violent act occurs. Culture change includes positive interaction and communications between staff and inmates along with inmate education, so that inmates feel comfortable reporting any beginning pressure for sex well before it develops into a forced sexual act.[57]

One controversial approach to reducing the degree of homosexual activity in prison is to allow **conjugal visiting**, sometimes referred to as family visiting. Conjugal visiting is private visiting between inmates and their spouses, and it is expected that they will engage in sexual relations. Only six states (California, Connecticut, Mississippi, New Mexico, New York, and Washington) permit conjugal visits.[58] Supporters of conjugal visiting argue that it provides a normal

conjugal visiting
sometimes referred to as family visiting, these are private visiting opportunities between inmates and their spouses, and it is expected that they will engage in sexual relations

release of sexual tension, is an incentive for good behavior as only inmates with good records earn such a visit, and reduces homosexual activity in prison. Opponents believe it can only be provided to a small number of inmates and therefore has little impact on homosexual activity. Also, it creates issues such as discriminating against inmates who are not legally married and degrades women in that the visit becomes more sexually oriented than family- or social-oriented. There are many arguments for and against implementing conjugal visiting. In the "You Make the Decision" box at the end of this chapter, you have to decide regarding its implementation.

Drugs in Prisons

There are thousands of drug offenders in state and federal prisons, and a high proportion of inmates have a history of drug or alcohol abuse. In *Prisoners in 2015*, the authors stated that 47.5 percent (81,900 inmates) of federal inmates and 15.2 percent (197,200 inmates) of state inmates were serving a sentence for a drug offense.[59] A Bureau of Justice Statistics report found that 32 percent of state inmates and 26 percent of federal inmates were under the influence of drugs at the time of their offense, and 56 percent of state prisoners and 50 percent of federal prisoners reported drug use in the month before the offense.[60] Therefore, as expected, drug use is a serious problem in the nation's prisons.

Prison inmates that are desirous to use drugs are always scheming to find avenues to bring drugs into prisons. They look for opportunities through the mail, by bribing or paying staff to bring in drugs, by getting their visitors to bring in drugs, and through any other weakness they discover in a prison's security procedures. Once the drugs are inside, inmates sell them at a tremendous profit. The price of drugs depends on their availability, and when prison officials are doing a good job of keeping drugs out of prison, the price gets very high and inmates get much more desperate for ways to bring drugs into prisons. Money is not allowed in prison, so inmate sellers require their buyers to get family or friends to pay the seller's outside contact. If payment is not made, violence usually results. Because of the opportunity for huge profits, prison gangs usually try to control the drug trade. Dealing drugs in prison perfectly fits the gangs' desires to make money, have power, and use violence to enforce payment of debts.

Prison officials attempt to reduce the availability and use of drugs in several ways. First, they try to keep drugs from being brought into the prison by visitors or staff. Inmates are stripped and searched when they leave after any contact visit, and mail and packages are

Random drug tests, in which an inmate's urine is sent to a lab to be tested, are a good way to deter and detect the use of drugs in prison. Photo by Richard P. Seiter.

checked for contraband before they are given to inmates. In addition, most state and federal prisons search staff as they enter the prison for duty. Second, prison staff members continuously search both inmates and areas of the prison, especially inmates' cells and other living areas. Finally, the federal prison system and forty-seven states do **random drug testing** of inmates for drug use, and all do testing if an inmate exhibits traits of being under the influence of drugs. On average, agencies test 22 percent of all inmates annually. For the forty-three state and federal jurisdictions reporting on the most recent data on these drug tests, of more than 2 million tests completed, 3.5 percent of the tests were positive for drug use.[61]

Prisons also provide drug and other substance abuse programs. Chapter 14 describes the types of treatment programs provided in prisons. Substance abuse is an important program in light of the high number and percentage of inmates with prior drug use. Table 11.1 indicates the percentage of inmates who have participated in drug treatment and other types of drug abuse programs since their admission to prison. Although the need for drug treatment far exceeds the provision, from 1997 to 2004 the percentage of inmates participating in drug treatment increased from 34.3 percent to 39.2 percent for state offenders and 38.8 percent to 45.3 percent for federal offenders. A recent review of data from the National Criminal Justice Treatment Practices survey found that prison drug abuse programs most often provided drug education and group counseling. However, these programs only had the capacity to serve approximately 10 percent of offenders, even though one-third were identified as having a severe dependency on drugs or alcohol.[62] Another study of participation found that females were significantly more likely to participate in

random drug testing
randomly selecting a percentage of inmates to urine test to see whether they have used any drug recently; a good deterrent to and source of data about prisoner drug use

TABLE 11.1 Drug Treatment or Program Participation since Admission among State and Federal Prisoners Who Used Drugs in the Month before the Offense, 1997 and 2004

Type of drug treatment or program since admission	Percent of prisoners meeting criteria for drug dependence or abuse			
	State		**Federal**	
	2004 in %	**1997 in %**	**2004 in %**	**1997 in%**
Any drug treatment or programs	39.2	34.3	45.3	38.8
Treatment	14.1	14.6	15.2	15.4
Residential facility or unit	9.2	8.8	8.7	10.9
Counseling by a professional	6.0	6.0	6.8	5.5
Detoxification unit	0.9	1.0	0.8	0.3
Maintenance drug	0.3	0.3	0.2	0.4
Other programs	33.7	28.3	38.8	31.7
Self-help group/peer counseling	26.9	23.1	20.8	15.8
Education program	17.0	14.1	28.1	23.8

Source: Data from Christopher J. Mumola and Jennifer C. Karberg, *Drug Use and Dependence, State and Federal Prisoners, 2004* (Washington, D.C.: U.S. Department of Justice, October 2006), p. 9.

prison drug treatment than males.[63] It is clear that substance abuse programming is important to preparing offenders to successfully return to the community, and more resources need to be directed toward providing treatment to prison inmates.

The Function of Humor in Prison

One interesting note regarding prison life for inmates is the function of humor. Charles Terry, who served lengthy prison sentences in both California and Oregon, writes regarding the use of humor by inmates to negotiate the gap between a normal and a convict identity.[64] Sociologists have used humor to study the cultures of various societies for years, yet its importance in the inmate culture has been less a focus of analysis. Other authors have described how humor in prisons is unique to that environment. Goffman has described inmates' use of humorous "sad tales" to account for their troubled past and reasons for failure.[65] Ungar builds on the use of humor in telling sad tales in describing inmates' use of "self-mockery."[66] And Terry suggests that inmates regularly use humor to "denigrate the system" and blame it for the conditions in which inmates find themselves.

Humor in prison serves many purposes. Male inmates live in an environment that makes it difficult to express their true feelings; they constantly have to show masculinity and toughness. Through humor, they have the opportunity to show real human feelings without showing vulnerability. And, oddly enough, humor allows inmates to achieve control. Terry notes that this is accomplished in two ways:

> It is the only social mechanism within the prison environment that allows feelings to be expressed and authorities cannot control its expression.... It (humor) acts as proof of their power and their release from domination.[67]

The world in which inmates live is very different from the world of normal society in many ways, yet in a few ways is very similar. Humor in prison, just as in society, lets one convey a sad story in a way that does not show weakness. It allows inmates, just as in society, to put themselves down, both to make others laugh and to make an excuse for certain conditions or lack of success. Yet humor in prison is in some ways a chance to get back at the correctional staff members who control inmates' lives in almost every way. By laughing, perhaps much louder and longer than the story or joke deserves, in front of correctional staff, inmates in some ways think that they are annoying staff or showing that their imprisonment won't dampen their spirits. Humor is one legitimate way inmates can show staff that, although their actions are controlled, their emotions are not.

All the activities related to crimes, prison culture, gang membership, and homosexuality are different for male offenders than for female offenders. The next section describes the parallel profiles of women who commit crimes and go to prison. Even though they have several similar issues, there are varying ways that female prisoners group together, look for emotional support, deal with and shape the prison culture, and participate in programs and attempt to prepare for return to the community.

As an illustration of the real world facing prison inmates, the following "An Interview With" is presented.

An Interview With...

An Ex-Con

Clark E. Porter. Courtesy of Clark E. Porter.

Clark E. Porter is now a Program Support Specialist with the United States District Court Probation Office in St. Louis, Missouri. He has worked for this agency since 2009. His job is to help offenders on probation and parole to get resources that can help them avoid crime. He designs and delivers cognitive programming. He gets guys connected to community resources. And he finds training for them that can help them find and keep a job. Clark knows what these guys are thinking and what they need, because he is also an ex-con. After serving fifteen years in federal prisons, he was paroled in 2001. As you will see from the interview below, he was not your model inmate. But he did, when he got out, decide he wanted to better educate himself. He first got an Associate Degree, then got a bachelor's degree in Psychology from Washington University. He then received his Masters of Social Work from the University of Missouri, St. Louis. He held menial jobs such as restaurant cook, nursery school worker, and janitor. As a student, he moved into better jobs as a tutor in the writing lab and doing research for UMSL. But his journey to where he is today was not without challenges.

Question: What were your crimes that sent you to prison, and how long did you serve?

Clark: I committed an armed robbery in 1986 when I robbed a post office with a shotgun. I received a thirty-five-year sentence and was sent to the Federal Bureau of Prisons (BOP). I was first assigned to a medium security prison in Oxford, Wisconsin. I was there two and one-half years and then hit a guy over the head with a pipe and was sent to maximum security in Leavenworth, Kansas. I was there one year, and then stabbed a guy and was sent to another maximum prison in Lompoc, California. After a year, I stabbed another guy, and was sent to supermax in Marion, Illinois. When the new federal supermax opened in Florence, Colorado, I was sent there and stayed in supermax until I was paroled.

Question: You obviously got involved in violent acts. Can you describe why most acts of violence occur in prisons, and how inmates avoid threats to their safety?

Clark: Well, at minimum and even medium security, most of the time inmates do not feel threatened. We call doing time in medium as "play time." By that I mean that you can pretty much go about doing your time, watch TV, even horseplay, and not have reprisals for acts that violate the convict code. The only thing you have to worry about is getting into a physical altercation that is no more than a fist fight. But in maximum security, play time is over. You can't be a weak inmate or just avoid trouble. Trouble has a way of finding you, so you have to have some fortitude and ability to keep inmates from picking on you. You have to be a man. There are four things in a max prison that will lead to violence: homosexuality, drugs, gambling, and disrespect. Disrespect always depends on the situation; if you respond in the wrong way, the fight is on. Disrespect is taking a chair and sitting in it when it is obvious it was someone else's. And it is all about the perception of the person being disrespected; even if you don't think it is. For instance, if a guy always watches the same TV program at the same time every day, and he comes into the TV room and someone has on a different channel. That is disrespect, and the person feels challenged and will respond with violence.

Question: Can you describe the violent acts that got you sent to higher security prisons?

Clark: When I acted out with violence, it was because I felt disrespected and/or had something on my mind that was troubling me. In other words, tension built up and I was just looking for an excuse to act out. With the first incident at Oxford, I was just having a bad day. I was tired of being in prison; bored, and worried about how long my sentence was. Also, I just did not like the guy, and I was looking to score some points for my prison rep (reputation). So, I said something to the guy that was disrespectful, and knew he would have to come back at me. When he did, I was prepared and had the pipe. So when he came at me, I hit him over the head. That got me sent to Leavenworth.

The stabbing incident at Leavenworth involved my co-defendant. He was also at Leavenworth, started gambling, and got caught cheating at the table. He was being choked out and the guy almost killed him. Another of our homies stepped in and stopped it. But my co-defendant wanted some get back. So, when things calmed down, he and I went into a TV room and waited for the guy who choked him. When he came in, we turned off the lights, and I stabbed him while my co-defendant kept watch. The guy was not hurt too bad because the knife was made of plastic. I learned an important lesson. The lesson was don't use a plastic knife. It was dull, and didn't do the job. When I got to Lompoc, my cellie taught me how to make knives; by sharpening metal on a concrete floor after you put Ajax on the floor to make it rough. Ice picks were used for most of the knives at Lompoc. The good thing about an ice pick is that it is easy to make. The bad thing is that you have

(Continued)

to hit the guy in the right place to put him down. With ice pick stabbings, if you don't hit the guy in the right place, he won't be hurt bad enough to stop fighting until he starts to bleed out. He may be hurt pretty bad, but it still takes a while before the fight goes out of him.

Question: So what started the fight in Lompoc?

Clark: This guy told me I had a pretty ass. I was only twenty two at the time, and I tried to give the guy an out, and told him I was not into homosexuality. But the guy did not back down and apologize, so I had to act. I always kept a knife close by: I had one at work, in my cell, and on the exercise yard. I was at work in the kitchen, so I went into dish room, got the knife and stabbed him. He was hurt really bad; I hit him just below neck, in the back, and somewhere else. Since it was an ice pick, he did not fall right away, so we tussled for a minute, and then he fell. Then I backed off. We were in the dining hall when I did it, and a guard was right there. He pushed deuces (an emergency signal used in the BOP), but I would not put the knife down until I was sure I was safe. That was a big dude I hit, he was a Samoan. I had to be sure he would not come back at me. After there were plenty of staff there and they took him out on a stretcher, then I gave them my knife. After that, I was sent to supermax, and for the next ten years, was on lock-down twenty-two hours a day.

Question: What did you do to pass the time and avoid the boredom while you were in supermax?

Clark: We each had a TV, and we got movies piped in. So I watched a lot of movies. We had the latest movies, and watched them a lot. Every Friday night, the list of new movies came out, and they played all weekend. We got to see soft porn on the institution channel. We watched the exercise videos with women exercising nude. We had an educational channel and a religious channel. The religions services were broadcast on the religious channel. You could take a correspondence course on the educational channel. It broke up time reading. I was into religion and race relations, so I studied all types of religions and race relations. We got magazines and passed them around. We got a *USA Today* newspaper we passed around to keep up with current events. Some of us in supermax traded porn. Every guy had to form his own routine based on what he was in to. The artists got paint supplies to do artwork. John Gotti was there and he was a gambler. Guys made up gambling tickets, and they bet on sports games. Some guys were readers. Other guys were porn guys. Whatever group of interest you were in, the guys worked together and passed around what they had. We got out of our cell for either outside or inside rec. You had to be careful going to rec, as you were handcuffed when you moved. You were most vulnerable at that time, and never wanted to be in handcuffs when other guys had their hands free. In Marion, you were put into the rec cage with a few other guys. The understanding was that there would be no one around you when getting uncuffed. At Florence, we were

between two gates when getting uncuffed, so it was safer. But the tradition continued and no one would be near the second gate until you got uncuffed and were inside the gate.

Question: How do the gangs act in prison, and what do inmates who are not gang members have to do to avoid getting at odds with gangs?

Clark: Gangs are pretty prevalent in prison. I was anti-gang; I felt a man stands on his own. But the gangs were different in terms of threats to other inmates. The most dangerous ones were those with "blood in blood out" gangs. The Crips and Bloods were not so organized in prison, so they weren't so dangerous. But if you got into it with the Aryan Brotherhood (AB), you had a problem. If you get into a conflict with one of them, you better kill him. Same with the Mexican Mafia. These were blood in, blood out gangs, and if you crossed one guy, the entire gang was your enemy. The rest of the gangs could be managed. A lot of guys were in clicks, and whatever click you were in, that's who you rolled with throughout your bit. If your click was weak you were weak. Clicks were more a threat than some gangs. Clicks are the people you run with. They were often a group of guys from the same hometown or area of a town. Being in gang could be more dangerous than being out. The majority of murders by gangs were within their own gang. There were always issues of gang politics, jealously and who slighted who, or who was in control. Who is in favor with the leader. I always kept a healthy distance from the gangs and never trusted them. It was interesting, as I am black, and the AB's are predicated on racism, but most of the AB's were not as racist as they appeared to be. They followed the convict code first, and would help out another inmate (even black) if he needed it. But they did not want the rest of the AB gang to know it. In supermax, I often walked yard with Barry Mills, the leader of the AB, because we had the same rec time. I could carry on a conversation with him. He was an AB, but a convict first, and you dealt with him as a man before race.

Question: How prevalent are drugs in prison? How do inmates get and hide drugs or avoid detection from officials?

Clark: Drugs are plentiful in prison. I could stay high as much as I wanted. Guards, girlfriends, other people were bringing in drugs all the time. Drugs are not so much in medium prisons, when people have a lot to lose and want to get out without trouble. But in max prisons where everybody is doing long times, there are plenty of drugs. Gangs were involved in the drug trade. Blood in Blood out gangs have ranks, and the lowest level is the soldier. Bringing in drugs and money and putting in work is how you moved up in the gang ranks. You can't sell dope in prison by yourself; you have to do it with a gang or a strong click. Otherwise guys would just take it away from you if not protected. I have seen guys bring in dope and then get extorted for it. Only the strongest survive.

Everything is predicated on the drug trade. In prison, everyone has to have a "hustle." (Hustle is a way to make money.)

You can't depend on family for money. Whatever your family sends is extra. When you have long time in prison, you lose your relationship with family. Anything in the penitentiary can be a hustle. A few guys get to work in the prison factory to make money, but everyone else has to hustle. An artist may do portraits of guys' girlfriend or kids. Wherever you work you may be able to get things for people. Some inmates may play poker or be a gambler or bookmaker. Some guys were loan sharks. Others were into extortion. My hustle was working in the kitchen, and making wine or making and selling chicken sandwiches. I ran a store; you paid two back for whatever you got. So one pack of cigarettes cost you two packs. I was also good at making knives, but I only made knives for homeys. If I was clicking with you, I would be sure you had one. But I never sold knives and I would not give one to anyone who would not use it. I would never give someone a knife unless I knew he would use it because the other guy's homies would come after me too, so someone had to be carried out on a stretcher.

Question: How prevalent is homosexuality and rape in prison?

Clark: Homosexuality is prevalent in prison; young dudes are always preyed on. In prison, you have openly gay guys; closet gay guys, and those who are threatened or extorted into homosexuality. Guys got turned out (involved in homosexuality) in two ways, and when people know you have been turned out, others will take advantage of it. They may put a guy in a chock hold and make him pull his pants down. Then there is a subtler turning out. They test guys to see how they react. They may bump into a guy and not say excuse me. If the guy does nothing, then they befriend him and then move him into a cell together. If bumped, an inmate must demand an apology, or everyone will know you are weak. You must be aggressive when you know you are being tested. Old guy may look out for younger guys. I was only eighteen when I first went to prison,

and some older guys told me how it would work. It is the same thing in dealing with gangs. You have to be as aggressive. For instance, one day when working in the kitchen an AB went by me and tested me. So I got the guy alone in the kitchen and made sure he knew not to push me. Bitting (doing time) is an art—an art of violence and aggression, or the "dance" of aggression. You have to know how to handle it and you can't turn it on or off. The gangs had different approaches to homosexuality. The Mexican Mafia was against it, and gang members will be killed if they engage in homosexuality. AB members often had a homosexual partner, but they did it for power and sex. They would not walk the yard with a punk, and would stay away from them until they wanted them.

Question: What do inmates think about getting involved in prison programs?

Clark: Prison programs are a part of your bit. If you are sitting on a twenty-year bit, you use programs to pass the time and stay out of the way. Some guys try to use programs to help them for when they get out, but others just to pass the time. Some guys get involved in education because they want it and think it is a way to keep sharp mentally. Most inmates think cognitive programs are bullshit. Cognitive programs and life skills seem unreal for guys in prison. Also the issue they may have to deal with may be more complex than merely knowing how to hold down a job and budget money. Many inmates think the basic stuff is good, but the cognitive stuff is a waste of time. Trades classes are often really not useful in the real world, as you don't learn enough to get certified and can't get jobs with it. They are only good to get a foundation and later follow up with an accredited program once released. Guys have to be realistic when coming out with trade. The trade classes are just a start. Many guys don't participate in programs they know won't get them a job.[68]

Prison Life for Female Offenders

In many ways, women's prisons have many of the same situations, issues, and relationships that occur in male prisons. The history of women's prisons is very similar to that of men's prisons; however, there was a time lag of several decades before reforms spread from men's to women's prisons. Much of that was due to the gender-related policies that resulted in operating women's prisons to reinforce gender stereotypes by providing programming to prepare women for domestic housekeeping and parenting roles. It was more than seventy-five years after the invention of the prison in the United States before the first separate women's facility was opened. And it was almost another century before women received vocational training in areas other than cooking, sewing, and cleaning. However, modern prison environments for women have caught up to some extent. Facilities for both men and women are similar, there is drug abuse and homosexuality in prisons for both sexes, and prisons are not the best situation for preparing to return to the community

The History of Women's Prisons

Male and female offenders were housed in the same facilities in early U.S. jails. Although women were separated in different cells, the institutions were not designed to provide specific security or programs to meet the special needs of female offenders. Both male and female prisoners were under the supervision of male staff, and it was not uncommon for female prisoners to be raped by their guards. The need to separate male and female offenders was a concern of the Quakers, who devised and opened the first prison in a portion of the Walnut Street Jail in the late 1700s, and women were then housed in a separate section. However, while male inmates were housed in single cells and kept separate from other male inmates, female inmates did not receive the same separation and were housed together in large cells within the jail.[69]

Over the next several decades, it was recognized that female prisoners should be housed and dealt with separately. The first of these reforms for female prisoners was prompted by an English woman named **Elizabeth Fry**, a Quaker who formed the Ladies Society for Promoting the Reformation of Female Prisoners in 1816 and tried to convince officials that the special needs of women required hiring female guards and making other reforms.[70] Her efforts finally resulted in Parliament's passing three of Fry's requests, but not until some thirty years after she made them. The suggestions included (1) segregation of prisoners by sex, (2) using female guards to supervise female prisoners, and (3) decreasing the amount of hard labor required of female prisoners.[71] Soon after Parliament passed these Acts, the first prison for housing only female offenders was opened in England.[72]

Fry traveled to the United States and pushed for similar reforms for female prisoners there as well. Partly as a result of her efforts, the New York House of Refuge was opened in 1825 with a totally separate building to house female juvenile offenders, who were to be supervised by female staff. A major step forward in the treatment of female offenders occurred in 1863, when Zebulon Brockway, then-superintendent of the Detroit House of Correction, opened a separate unit for women and hired women as guards or matrons. Brockway also divided the inmates into small family groups, used the matrons as role models for the women, and provided domestic training. He used the concepts of the reformatory movement described in Chapter 1 in creating programs for women. The emphasis was on education and training to prepare inmates for release and successful return to society.

The reformatory model continued for women (and for youthful male offenders) for the next hundred years and continues today for many women's prisons.[73] The Indiana Reformatory for Women and Girls, opened in 1873, was the first separate state prison for women. Soon thereafter, Massachusetts and New York opened reformatories for women, and other states gradually followed their lead and had totally separate facilities for female prisoners.

The design of the reformatories for women was different from the prisons for men; it used a **cottage-style architecture**, with several small housing units holding approximately thirty inmates, and each cottage included kitchens, living rooms, and sometimes nurseries for inmates with children. The design was created as a basis to train women prisoners in the female role of domesticity, through vocational training in cooking, sewing, and cleaning.[74] These types of prisons for women continued into the middle of the twentieth century, when the continuation of promoting gender stereotypes in vocational training and the management of women's prisons was questioned, although some authors suggest that these gender stereotypes continued to influence the operation of women's prisons even into the 1980s.[75]

Elizabeth Fry

a Quaker who formed the Ladies Society for Promoting the Reformation of Female Prisoners in 1816; she tried to convince officials that women prisoners should be separated from male prisoners and that female guards should be hired to supervise them

cottage-style architecture

a style of prison design used for women's prisons, with several small housing units holding approximately thirty inmates; each cottage included kitchens, living rooms, and sometimes nurseries for inmates with children

The Federal Reformatory for Women in Alderson, West Virginia, opened in 1927, and was one of the first prisons created for women and originally had no fence or other perimeter security.
Courtesy of the Federal Bureau of Prisons.

Over the past thirty years, women's prisons have begun to look like and be operated in a manner very similar to men's prisons. The cottage design is no longer used, although campus-style prisons (for both men and women) have housing buildings separate from other program and service buildings. Physical security has increased as well. Many early women's reformatories did not have a secure fence to keep inmates from escaping, relying instead on the inmates' being trustworthy and not a risk to the community if they did escape. Today, prisons for women have the same perimeter security, with fences, razor ribbon, and electronic detection devices to reduce escape attempts. Modern women's prisons also are built with program space to accommodate nontraditional vocational training programs such as carpentry and electronics. They also include special housing units to separate and manage disorderly and potentially violent inmates from the remainder of the population. And most states also house female inmates on death row.

Culture in Women's Prisons

The culture in a women's prison is considerably different from that in a men's prison, with a different style of inmate communications with each other and with staff.[76] Most studies report that women also have an inmate code, emphasizing similar guidelines for women as for men, such as "do your own time" and "don't rat (tell) on other inmates." However, the code is not as important to women as to men. There are two important differences between male and female inmate culture and the inmate code. The first is that female inmates are not hesitant to talk to staff and there is little concern that inmates are "snitches" if they are seen talking to staff. The second difference is in the relationships that women form. Male inmates stay as independent and isolated as possible and avoid any emotional or personal relationships. Female prisoners, on the other hand, seek close personal and emotional relationships with other inmates.

Much of the culture of a women's prison has to do with the fact that approximately 65 percent of female inmates are mothers, and much of their thoughts while in prison are about release and reestablishing their family and role as mothers. A major difference between male and female inmates is the stress and depression they feel due to separation from their children.[77] Owens notes that the importance of women's relationships with their children "has an impact on the values shaping prison culture in several ways, such as making conversations about children sacred, acknowledging the intensity and grief attached to these relationships, sanctioning those with histories of hurting children, and other child-specific cultural beliefs or behaviors."[78]

Both because women enjoy and need the support resulting from sharing personal facts regarding their children and lives with others and because they have been socialized to play a specific role within a family structure, female inmates often tend to form what are called **pseudofamilies**. In these organizations, inmates play actual roles of parents and children. Some but not all pseudofamilies have a romantic dyad or a couple that acts as parents; there may be two mothers or a father and a mother. Parents are usually the older and more prisonwise inmates, and younger inmates take the role of children. The parental partners in these prison families are not always sexual in nature. Propper suggests that they are based on asexual pairing and do not present a greater likelihood of homosexual activity.[79] Pollock-Byrne, in describing these families, suggests that most prison lesbian relationships are based not so much on actual sexual activity as on affection with a sexual connotation.[80] And a study in Texas prisons confirms women join families for support and sexual relationships.[81]

pseudofamilies

family organizations formed by female inmates who have roles of parents and children

Female inmates often form pseudofamilies, in which each inmate plays a role as mother, father, children, and even nieces.
Pat Sullivan/AP Images.

These pseudofamilies become the focus of much of the activity for family members. Family members make a great effort to try to live in the same housing unit, work together on the same jobs, and recreate together. The parents act as mentors for the younger inmates, protect them, and maintain a discipline of order and control. The families also provide mutual support and protection, an aid network, and an opportunity for fun and laughter.[82] Although most of the younger (children) inmates take on the role of daughters, some "women who take on the 'butch' or the aggressive role may be a dad, a son, or a brother, yet these designations can often be fluid."[83] Diaz-Cotto contends that these family relationships are now in decline in many prisons, primarily because inmates have more access to family, friends, and others outside prison and therefore do not have to invest as much in prison-developed relationships.[84]

The sexual relationships that develop in a women's prison are also much different from the homosexuality that occurs in men's prisons. Men must continually show their masculinity through sexual conquest of weaker inmates, and the risk of rape is much greater in men's prisons. The male sexual aggressor is not interested in a relationship, but simply in sexual gratification, power, and dominance. Sexuality for female offenders is altogether different in that it is a search for affection, emotional support, and sharing. The desire for power and dominance and the potential for rape are minimal, and "butches" in women's prisons are sought after by women who want to play a woman's role in a relationship.[85] Early research indicated that one out of four female inmates reports involvement in a lesbian relationship,[86] but it has more recently been estimated that "between 30 and 60 percent of incarcerated women are in lesbian relationships."[87]

In response to the Prison Rape Elimination Act, surveys indicate a significant difference in sexual activity between female and male inmates. In the 2008–2009 and the 2011–12 PREA survey of inmates, women had twice as high a rate of inmate-on-inmate sexual victimization compared to men, yet a lower rate of staff sexual misconduct.[88] And an examination of sexual violence that occurs in female prisons and how if differs from that which occurs in male prisons found that violence between female inmates was part of the "constellation of overlapping individual, relational, institutional, and societal factors," and that violence occurs on a continuum ranging from verbal intimidation to homicide (extremely rare).[89] The report confirmed that violence in women's prisons is not as severe or prevalent as in men's prisons. Women described sexual victimization as ranging from sexual comments and touching to sexual assault by aggressors. Although their threat of unanticipated sexual violence appears to be less likely than in men's prisons, it related more to a build up of the types of relationships described above and can be the result of the relationship going bad through disrespect or jealousy.

The world in which women live in prison is, in many ways, similar to that faced by male inmates. Their special needs, situations, and characteristics create unique management challenges and lead to the development of different cultures within prisons for female inmates. As described by Fleisher and colleagues, after a review of the development of culture within a new women's prison, "A key issue in the development of gender-based distinctions in organizational culture is learning how to create, implement, and then perpetuate a set of organizational values and beliefs that meets women's programming needs and styles of interpersonal interaction."[90]

Chapter Review

Summary

The society of a prison has a unique culture. Few, if any, other environments are so isolated from normal living and society that they result in such a distinct culture. This results from the forced stay, the need for routine and control by staff, the adaptation to living with many other people and many heterogeneous groups, the interdependence between inmates, and the anger and bitterness that inmates feel as a response to their situation. As prison culture has developed over the past two centuries; in some ways it has changed little, whereas in other ways it has changed dramatically.

Prisons still operate with at least a cursory understanding of and sensitivity to an inmate code, particularly the tenets to "be tough" and "don't trust the guards." However, the trusted old con, who lived by the code and was respected by other inmates, is a thing of the past. Younger inmates, many of whom are gang members whose loyalty is to the gang and who follow gang requirements over the inmate code, deal with issues through strength rather than guile and do not respect the "old con," whom they see as weak and not willing to take what they want. Women's prisons have more of an accepted respect and hierarchy related to both how long and how well time is served. However, for women, the status associated with this comes not so much from adherence to the inmate code, but from knowledge and relationships and the ability to mentor and protect younger inmates.

As much as prison staff members want to be aware and in control of everything within a prison, much occurs in the life of prison inmates that staff members do not understand and have little influence over. An example of this is prison "currency" or what inmates use as exchange for goods and services. Prison currency is covered in the following Case Study. Although staff members do not ignore drug use, gang activity and violence, or homosexuality, many honestly admit that they cannot totally control or prevent these activities. In fact, staff members never find out about all the drug use, violent acts, and homosexual activity. Well-managed institutions are said to be "controlled by staff, and not by inmates." Even though this is true, the actions and relationships of inmates usually have a much greater influence on the development of prison culture than the policies and procedures of staff.

Key Terms

total institution
inmate code
prisonization
convicts
thieves
square johns
interpersonal violence

collective violence
prison gangs
Sureños
gang validation process
debrief
gang intelligence officers
sexual triangle

conjugal visiting
random drug testing
Elizabeth Fry
cottage-style architecture
pseudofamilies

A Case Study

Currency in Prisons

An interesting phenomenon in prisons is the underground economy that exists, and what inmates use as currency to fund this economy. Inmates are not allowed to possess money, so prisons allow them to have an account they can contribute to and draw on for purchases. This is the "legitimate" economy that is managed by prison officials. In that situation, an inmate can have family or friends send money (usually by a money order) to put in the inmate's account. The account is then debited when inmates buy commissary items (toiletries, snacks, or workout clothes) or stamps. Inmates are sometimes paid for prison jobs, and that money is also credited to their account. However, as you would expect, inmates use a variety of things to trade for services, drugs, gamble, or other prohibited items from other inmates.

Historically, prisoners used cigarettes as their main underground currency. However, most prisons have now banned smoking altogether, and inmates do not have easy access to cigarettes. Therefore, new currencies have had to come about. A very common item is to use postage stamps as currency. Stamps are small, easy to hide, and make great poker chips for gambling.[91] However, most prison systems limit how many stamps inmates can buy or possess, and, therefore, a need for some other form of "currency" developed. As a result, items that inmates can buy from the prison commissary are often traded or loaned with expected payback plus interest. Commissary is not constantly available to inmates; they often go one time per week. Some inmate hustlers run their own commissary, and collect items to sell to inmates who need something before their commissary day or who do not have money to buy from the commissary. They must then borrow from the "store man" who charges a 50 percent fee on the loaned value.[92] Other items used as currency include mackerel (legitimately bought in the commissary for $1.40 and comes in a 3.5-ounce pouch) or instant coffee (4-ounce bag that sells in the commissary for $3.35) that can be used as tipping for laundry service, cell cleanup, or a haircut.[93]

A former federal inmate describes how he typically used packages of mackerel as prison currency, stating, "At my prison, a packet of mackerel was sold for $1.05 in the commissary." Stamps were not the common currency in my prison, and that probably was because there was a low limit (I think ten) of stamps you could buy per week. Our common and well understood (by staff and inmates) currency was mackerel. The commissary also sold salmon and tuna that also came packaged the same as mackerel. However, those were not used as currency, as they sold for much more, and with mackerel selling for close to a dollar per pack, it was easy to calculate the value of an exchange.

In prison, I was responsible to laundering all my own clothing items. I could do my own bedding (sheets, blankets, and pillowcase) or to take to the prison laundry to have them exchanged. I kept my own pillowcase and towel and had it done, but I exchanged my sheets and blankets. There were washing machines and dryers in the housing unit, and inmates could use them at no charge, but you had to buy your own detergent. But in my prison, there were guys who would do you laundry for a charge. I paid to have my laundry done twice per week, and initially it cost me one mackerel for each bag that I had done. Later, my guy came to me and said the market was going up, and he asked me to pay him four mackerel per week. We settled on three per week. I was very impressed with the quality of the service done on my laundry. It was folded and rolled and came back in really good shape, professionally done like in a retail laundry. I also paid one mackerel as a tip to the barber for a haircut. It was not mandatory, and I did not feel I would get a bad haircut if I did not tip, but it was not uncommon for inmates to tip. I also had one other instance where my audio ear buds stopped working, and I paid a guy 3 "macks" to get them fixed. Seldom did people use anything other than the term "mack." When I got to prison, other inmates filled me in on how things worked and the currency that was used. Macks were also used for gambling, both playing cards and betting on sporting events.

There were guys in the prison who ran commissary stores. They had extra commissary items; if guys got hungry or needed anything, they would sell you items. My bunkmate ran a store of food items he smuggled out of the kitchen. Inmates got a piece of fruit every day, and would want to take them back to their dorms, but staff regularly searched inmates and would frisk them and not allow them to take fruit out of food service. There were always extra apples, oranges, and bananas that were not eaten at a meal, and some inmates would then sneak them out. My bunkmate would get them out and either sell or exchange them for mackerels or other commissary items. Two or three pieces of fruit would be worth a mackerel. We finished dinner about 4:30, so by the end of the evening, people got hungry and would trade a mack for some fruit. My bunkmate was also able to get some fresh vegetables out of the kitchen, such as a tomato or pepper. He even got extra meat that was served at that day's meal, and trade or sell them. He would sometimes get things uncooked and take them to the dorms and later cook them in the microwaves (available in the dorms). Guys would steal flower and cake mix and even bake cakes in the dorms and sell them later.

Review Questions

1. Define what Goffman meant with the concept of "total institutions."

2. Describe the Zimbardo experiment and its results.

3. What are the two theories regarding how inmate culture becomes a part of prison life?

4. How has following the inmate culture in a prison changed, and what are the potential reasons for the change?

5. List five reasons for violence in prisons.

6. What methods do correctional agencies use to control prison gangs?

7. List three of the major gangs in prisons today.

8. Why, does Hassine suggest, do most prison sexual assaults occur?

9. What do correctional officials do to prevent sexual assaults in prison?

10. What is the Prison Rape Elimination Act (PREA) and what types of sexual assault occur in prison?

11. What percentage of inmates in state and federal prisons are serving sentences for drug offenses?

12. How do drugs get into prisons?

13. What role does Terry suggest that humor plays in a prison environment?

14. What were the major reforms that led to the current operation of prisons for women?

15. How does the inmate culture in a women's prison differ from that in a prison for men?

16. According to PREA surveys, how is sexual assault for female inmates different than for males?

▶ You Make the Decision...

Implement Conjugal Visiting?

There are several pros and cons regarding conjugal visiting. When I worked for the Federal Bureau of Prisons (BOP), it became a topic of heavy discussion during one administration. The deputy attorney general (number two in command in the Department of Justice) favored conjugal visits for the BOP and asked Director Norman Carlson to consider it. The BOP had always taken the approach that conjugal visits in prisons were not a normal situation, and the BOP preferred extensive, furlough programs to allow inmates to earn the privilege of going home for a weekend to have a more natural setting and time for a relationship with their spouse. There was also the concern that since only married inmates were allowed conjugal visits in states, it would discriminate against unmarried and homosexual inmates and that there would likely be "jailhouse" marriages (those done out of convenience rather than for a long-term loving situation) just to get the chance for conjugal visits.

However, the deputy attorney general countered that the BOP often expressed concern for the level of violence in prisons, and some of the violence resulted from forced homosexual activities and fights between sexual triangles. It was difficult to counter the bosses' argument, but the leadership of the BOP was against their implementation. They decided to conduct a study, but before it was completed, there was a change in leadership in the Department of Justice, and the deputy left his position. The BOP did not pursue the issue with his replacement, and it was never raised again.

In this "You Make the Decision," decide whether you will implement conjugal visiting. In doing so, consider the pros and cons and try to imagine the logistical problems that would be encountered by the implementation of such a program. But then decide, either by yourself or in a small classroom group, whether you favor or oppose the implementation of conjugal visiting.

CHAPTER 12

The World of Prison Staff

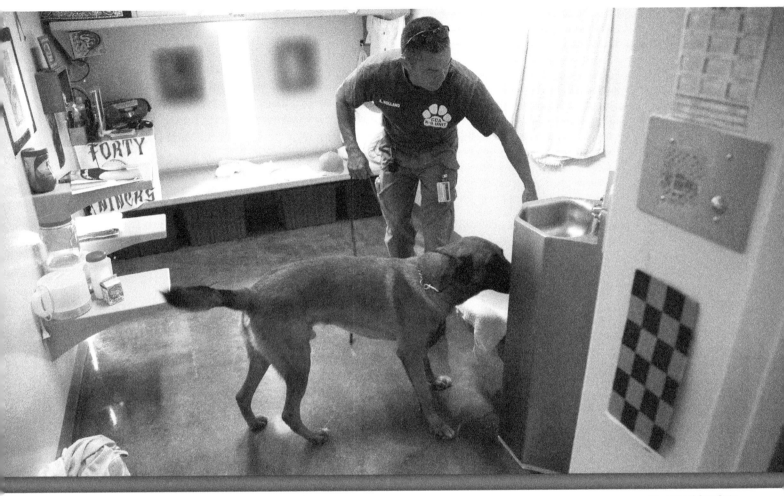

Courtesy of CoreCivic.

After reading this chapter, you should be able to:

1. Describe the various jobs and functions of prison staff.
2. Outline the organizational structure of prisons.
3. Explain the leadership role of a prison warden, including setting and reinforcing the prison's organizational culture.
4. Understand the correctional officer's role and daily activities, and consider the pros and cons of this job for you.
5. Describe the role of treatment and services staff within a prison.
6. Summarize prison culture for staff.
7. Describe the unique challenges and issues faced by female correctional officers.

Introduction

Just as there is a definite culture and hierarchy of status for prison inmates, there is also a culture and organizational hierarchy for prison staff. Some penologists would argue that prison staff members are also influenced by the prison environment and become even more "prisonized" than inmates. That argument does not seem all that unreasonable. Most career prison staff members spend more time "behind bars" than all but a small percentage of inmates. A correctional officer, who works for twenty-five years prior to retirement, 2,080 hours (forty hours for fifty-two weeks) per year, spends a total of 52,000 hours in the prison. This is almost six full years in prison, and the impact of this time on the officer personally is extended over twenty-five years before he or she leaves the prison for good.

Consider also that most staff members in prison interact extensively with inmates, to a much greater proportion than they do with other staff members. Their job is to gain control and compliance without the use of weapons, threats, or intimidation. To do this requires adaptation to (not cooptation by) the prison environment and understanding the most efficient way to maintain control over inmates. The world of prisons is unlike any other social organization. Words and deeds have different meanings inside prisons than outside, and due to the need for constant interaction and communication, there is no hiding anyone's real personality or approach to the job. Inmates quickly see through staff members who try to take on a demeanor that is not really theirs.

In a prison there is considerable and continuous stress, the threat of assault and injury, and the need to never let down one's guard or fail to be attentive to the detail of one's work assignment. Most people on their jobs can have a "bad day at the office," be unproductive, or lose their temper or handle some issue poorly or unprofessionally. However, serious problems can result from having a similar bad day when working in a prison. When your work consists of supervising and maintaining control over possibly a hundred offenders, who are not the most cooperative and likable people in the world and who look for staff weaknesses and take advantage of improper behavior, having a bad day at work can put people at risk or undermine the security of a prison. Prison staff members have to be professional, use their interpersonal skills, rely on one another to do their jobs well, leave the prison environment no worse than they found it, and be prepared to come back the next day to begin their eight-hour shift all over again.

In Chapter 10 the organization of a prison was described, and the elements of the organization that make a prison operate effectively were presented. This chapter focuses on the people rather than the organization: the world in which prison staff members work, the issues they face, the ways they handle them, and the culture that develops as a result of stressful and challenging working conditions. Descriptions and functions of some of the primary prison staff positions are described, but the chapter focuses on the environment and culture that result from working in a prison setting.

There may be no more demanding job than working in a prison. I spent more than thirty-five years working for correctional agencies, was assigned to four different prisons, was warden of two prisons, was responsible for more than 30,000 inmates and 7,000 staff members as director of a state prison system, oversaw a prison industry program that employed 15,000 inmates and sold $400 million in products each year, and supervised the operation of sixty-five correctional facilities with 80,000 inmates and 17,000 staff members for a private prison company. From this work, I have a great appreciation for those staff members who every day enter the world of imprisoned felons, serve the public in difficult and underappreciated positions, face uncertainty and danger, and maintain a professional approach to their jobs, the inmates, and the agencies for which they work.

The Jobs of Prison Staff

When most people think of prison staff, they think of wardens and correctional officers. However, many different positions make up the complement of prison staff. Some of these are listed here:

Chaplain	Industrial supervisor
Counselor or case manager	Laundry supervisor
Computer specialist	Psychologist
Institution administrator	Personnel manager
Substance abuse counselor	Recreation specialist
Employee development specialist	Safety manager
Facility maintenance worker	Secretary/clerical worker
Financial manager	Classification specialist
Food service worker	Teacher
Health care worker (physician or nurse)	Staff training instructor

In many ways, a prison is like a small city, requiring many of the same services and employees. Just like cities, prisons have schools, lodging accommodations, jails, eating establishments, convenience stores, places of worship, recreation facilities, sewer/sanitation/street service departments, facility and vehicle maintenance departments, barbershops, generators or electrical and power resources, laundry services, financial institutions, and administrative offices. All the types of employees that are often found in a small community (except for many retail shops) are found in a prison, because prisons must be fairly self-sustaining and able to provide for themselves in most situations.

Each of these jobs requires specialists, both to manage the functions and to provide the service. Prisons have teachers certified to teach in the public school systems and education supervisors who are usually accredited by the state as school principals. These supervisors carry out many of the functions of a principal

Prison staff includes a variety of positions, such as correctional officer, administrator, medical person, and counselor. Photo by Richard P. Seiter.

in creating a learning environment, supervising teachers, and maintaining discipline of students. Food services administrators must prepare menus, order food, and oversee the preparation of meals, and food service workers oversee inmates preparing and serving food. Prison physicians provide patient care and manage prison infirmaries that are very similar in operations to a typical general-practice doctor's office. In many ways, the jobs within a prison setting are very similar to the same functions carried out in the community, except that they are within a secure environment and all the clients are incarcerated felons.

The Organization of Prisons

The organization and administration of prisons are in some ways very simple, and in other ways very complex. They are simple in that there is a very clear and military-like chain of command. Yet prisons are very complex organizations in that they rely on most staff members operating individually, while following the same policies and, hopefully, subscribing to the same operational values and principles of the organization as a whole. Modern prison operations have moved well beyond the past years' emphasis on "lock them up, work them, and feed them." Expansion of inmate rights, the inclusion of rehabilitative programs, and many more prison service options have broadened the internal management puzzle for administrators to piece together. In addition, the interest of the public, the media, and other government agencies has required that prison administrators manage the "external environment" as well as they manage within the prison. Political and public interests in corrections put additional demands on administrators, both for their time and for their sensitivity to what they do and how they do it.

closed systems

prison systems that consist of only the internal environment, under the direct control of the warden, and without much interest or any interference from external groups

From their inception in the early 1800s until approximately the 1960s, prisons were closed systems. **Closed systems** consist of only the internal environment and, for prisons, this meant what happened within the walls or fences, under the direct control of the warden and without much interest or any interference from external groups. The organization of a closed system, often with autocratic leadership, is usually very simple, and the mission and goals of the organization are determined and the leader enforces compliance. However, as a result of

Prison staff and prison operations have changed since these staff members worked at the U.S. Penitentiary in Leavenworth, Kansas, c. 1895.
Courtesy of the Federal Bureau of Prisons.

the external interest in the management of prisons and the fact that no modern entity operates by itself and without interacting with many others, correctional agencies have changed from closed systems to open systems. **Open systems** have frequent interactions between the organization and other groups to obtain resources, gain support, and accomplish goals. Open systems of prisons receive numerous inputs from external government units and are held accountable for certain expected outputs from taxpayers and elected officials. Prisons today interact with the local community; with their headquarters organization; with interest groups of employees, citizens, vendors, and other public agencies; and with other providers of correctional or counseling services to offenders.

open systems

prison systems that have frequent interactions between the organization and other groups, in order to obtain resources, gain support, and accomplish goals

Prison Chain of Command

Chain of command and unity of command are very critical to every organization, especially a paramilitary organization such as a prison. The chain of command in military organizations has ranks of individuals (privates, sergeants, lieutenants) relating to their place in the chain of command. The **chain of command** represents the vertical hierarchy in an organization, is identified in terms of authority, and is the order through which people receive directives from the person immediately above them and pass these directives to the person immediately below them. Most prisons have a military chain of command and use ranks such as sergeant, lieutenant, and captain. Figure 12.1 illustrates a simple prison chain of command from a warden to a correctional officer.

In a pure chain of command, wardens give orders to the associate warden in charge of security, who passes them on to the chief of security, who passes them on to security supervisors, who pass them on to correctional officers. Although prisons are adopting more modern management practices such as staff empowerment and participatory management, they are still (and will always remain to a great extent) very structured in the use of a chain of command; one of the most revered management practices within a prison is to use and not circumvent the chain of command. Wardens certainly interact with all levels of staff and seek their input on a variety of issues. However, prison operations rely on everyone completing their responsibilities in a consistent manner, and all levels of supervision must know what others are doing. Therefore, wardens would not directly instruct a correctional officer to carry out some function without advising or passing the instruction through correctional supervisors.

In a much more complex sense, prison administrators realize that policies and orders cannot cover every act and decision that must be made by a correctional officer or the way they react to a new experience not covered by policy. Therefore, wardens attempt to instill in all levels of the organization the important principles and values that should be considered when staff members act independently. Through this *empowerment*, staff members do not just receive orders continuously through the chain of command. While they are trained in and follow policy, they are also informed about the reasoning behind the policy and understand the underlying philosophy for carrying out their duties. Therefore, staff perform their duties and make decisions consistent with the philosophy and reasoning behind the policy.

chain of command

the vertical hierarchy in an organization, identified in terms of authority, and the order through which persons receive directives from the person immediately above them and pass these directives to the person immediately below them

The Warden

The earlier era of autonomous wardens running their prisons as they desired and answering to almost no one is over. However, most people still associate that style with the role of a warden, primarily as a result of the way wardens are

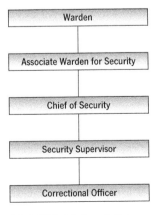

FIGURE 12.1   A Prison Chain of Command

portrayed in movies and on television. In the classic description of the rule of a strong warden in *Stateville: The Penitentiary in Mass Society*, Jacobs described the way Warden Joseph Ragen ran that prison for more than thirty years until the 1960s.[1] Stateville is a maximum-security prison in northern Illinois, and in the middle 1900s, it held almost 4,000 inmates in a space designed for 1,600. The prison was filled with violent inmates and had a reputation as one of the toughest prisons in the United States.

Ragen ruled the prison with an iron fist and demanded strict adherence to rules by both staff and inmates. He maintained the prison as clean and spotless, made inmates march in straight lines when moving about the prison, and prohibited staff and inmate communication.[2] A 1996 book by Kantrowitz regarding Stateville and Warden Ragen further describes how Ragen meted out severe punishment to staff and inmates who violated his rules. Kantrowitz notes that Ragen believed his function was to synchronize men and their behavior in time and space, so the prison ran smoothly daily.[3] Jacobs further describes how Ragen was one of the last of the warden "village chieftains" who vanish as their society modernizes.

Ragen ran the overcrowded prison with an iron fist, answering to no one and representing a management style long gone in the governing of prisons. When Ragen retired, Stateville moved to a more modern management style, forced partly by federal court interventions, and shifted from discipline to rehabilitation. Unfortunately, the change was too much and too fast for the prison, and the education programs that replaced the work programs were not enough to keep inmates productively busy. By 1978, conditions had deteriorated to utter anarchy; inmate gangs ran the prison, declaring certain areas of the prison off-limits to other inmates and staff under threat of death. It took several years to get Stateville orderly, clean, and under the control of staff again. This description is not to support an authoritarian style of prison management as under Ragen, but to point out how fragile the control and authority of staff can be in prison, how inmate groups will quickly move forward to fill any void in leadership and control, and how careful wardens and administrators must be as they attempt to change the culture of such a complex organization.

The Role of Modern Wardens

Today, there are no Warden Ragens, and that type of management and strict adherence to discipline would no longer work. Staff controls prisons, but not

Warden Joseph Ragen "ruled" over the penitentiary at Stateville (Illinois). One unusual thing about it is the panopticon or circular cell houses, which was first proposed by Jeremy Benthum. Bettmann/Getty Images.

through threats and intimidation. Control in modern prisons is maintained through a fair and just disciplinary system holding inmates accountable for their behavior, physical security and use of technology, work and treatment programs to keep inmates busy, consistent operations according to policy, and professional staff communication with inmates.

The move away from autonomous operations of each individual prison to more of a centralization of authority has greatly influenced the organization and operation of prisons. Freeman characterizes this development as the "era of bureaucratic wardens," in which wardens must now take responsibility for maintaining a safe, secure, humane prison environment in accordance with accepted standards (constitutional mandates, centralized policies, accreditation standards of professional organizations, and so on), and suggests several specific activities for the bureaucratic warden:

1. Development of the mission statement for the organization
2. Coordination of the budget process
3. Strategic evaluation and emergency planning
4. Management of daily activities
5. Management of labor relations
6. Formulation of policy
7. Supervision and professional development of staff[4]

The modern **warden** is a manager of resources, a role model for staff, and a juggler of priorities; he or she balances custody and treatment, is firm but fair, and knows how to manage the environment external to the prison as well as that within. When people would ask me what it is like to be a warden, I used to kiddingly say, "It is simple, all you have to do is know how to say no." Seriously, however, the role of a modern warden is one of the most complex management jobs in today's society, and one of the most critical in terms of how the warden personally shows leadership and guides the culture of the prison.

warden
the chief executive officer of a prison, responsible for the day-to-day operations

Currently, the public has much more interest in and much higher expectations for corrections than in the past. This requires new roles for wardens in terms of how they provide leadership to their agency. Historically, wardens had much greater control over the *internal* operations of the prison and very little *external* interference. Traditional wardens were very autocratic, not just because they wanted to be, but because processes and procedures were not spelled out in a step-by-step manner by a centralized bureaucracy. In the early years of correctional administration, there were few written policies, and wardens were often left to their own devices and whims as to what should be accomplished and how it should be done. Today there are rules and regulations for every activity, from hiring staff to spending a budget to supervising an offender.

Previously, wardens had few demands on them to be *external managers* because corrections was of little interest to elected officials, the courts, or the media. Now prison administration is of interest to everyone. Crime is an important domestic priority, and the fact that we have so many prisons that require a large percentage of the annual state budgets means that their operation is of great interest to the public and elected officials. Only a few decades ago, federal courts would not get involved in correctional management issues. Today, they are regularly and intensively involved in corrections and have even taken over and dictated how some correctional agencies must be managed. Media sources seldom report on activities or occurrences in a prison. However, print and television media now regularly have stories about criminal justice and prison programs and operations.

These changes require wardens to have different skills and different leadership styles than in the past. Wardens were leaders at the top of their organizations who exercised power by giving orders and making decisions. Wardens maintained control by offering rewards and resources to staff in exchange for assistance in reaching the organization's goals and punished those who did not assist. James MacGregor Burns defined this type of leadership as "transactional," involving exchange relationships between leaders and followers.[5] **Transactional leaders** were the traditional authorities: those with position, power, and knowledge of a substantive area. They were able to provide answers and give direction for any issue the agency confronted. Staff respected them and looked to them for guidance and direction. Transactional leadership worked well in a prison with a relatively stable environment and with routine situations within the experience of the leader.

However, the challenges of modern times within a prison are not so routine, and the environment is not so stable. Change and changing situations are more the "routine," and it is impossible to have policies to guide how to deal with every new issue. Therefore, wardens cannot be the substantive experts for everything that goes on in the prison, because there are always new issues to confront that they have never experienced before. These factors require wardens to be less transactional and more like **transformational leaders**. Transformational leadership is much broader than transactional leadership. It is based on principles rather than practice and on motivating people to jointly address challenges and find solutions to new problems. Transformational leaders emphasize the set of values and principles to be used as guidelines in responding to issues. They help staff and the organization to learn and to work through problems in an adaptive manner. They involve staff in finding creative and innovative solutions to new problems. Wardens as transformational leaders must encourage managers and line staff to work together and must empower staff to be able to adapt to change and deal with new challenges and issues.[6] Kotter describes how effective leaders empower employees with the authority to manage their own work groups.[7] And results from a study of attitudes of 929 correctional officers demonstrates that having a say in decisions and belief that management leads through motivation and encouragement significantly increases correctional officers' perceptions of procedural justice.[8]

Critical to the role of a warden's leadership is to help set, define, and reinforce the desired culture of the prison. **Organizational culture** includes the values, beliefs, and behaviors that form the way of life within the organization. From the first day of recruiting a prospective staff member and throughout the basic training employees receive before they begin work in a prison, correctional agencies instill the desired organizational culture. For effective correctional agencies, the culture includes being professional, striving to meet high standards, being ethical, positively interacting with inmates, rewarding staff for good performance, and using state-of-the-art correctional practices. The manner in which wardens themselves lead and act play critical roles in setting and reinforcing the organizational culture. Wardens are the role models for how to put the organizational culture in effect in the workplace. Staff

transactional leaders
traditional authorities within an organization who were involved in exchange relationships between leaders and followers; they provided answers and direction for any issue the agency confronted

transformational leaders
organizational leadership based on principles, while motivating staff to jointly address challenges and find solutions to new problems

organizational culture
the values, beliefs, and behaviors that form the way of life within that organization

Transformational leaders communicate constantly with staff members, help them to learn and understand the values of the organization, and seek their input on policies and procedures. Photo by Richard P. Seiter.

members take their cues on meeting standards, communicating with inmates, and rewarding excellence from the warden.

It is sometimes thought that with all the court intervention, political oversight, centralized control from the state department of corrections, and extensive policies and procedures, the role of a warden as a leader has been watered down, and wardens do not have as much impact today as in the past. However, one thing that never changes about organizations is that they reflect the personality of the leader. The warden sets the tone for a prison, defines professional expectations, creates the level of standards for performance, and has a tremendous impact on the morale of staff and inmates. DiIulio, in *Governing Prisons*, writes, "The individual who heads a prison, or a prison system, can shape the organization in ways that help to determine the quality of prison life."[9]

When I was a warden, I was regularly reminded of the attention that inmates and staff pay to the warden: his or her mannerisms, behaviors, tone of voice, and way of speaking. Staff and inmates watch where a warden goes and what he or she does. As I walked around the prison yard and buildings, staff monitored where I was going. I would regularly overhear on someone's communications radio (I did not carry one), "Number 1 [call sign for the warden] on his way to the recreation yard." Staff members closely watch what the warden does and says. On one occasion, a correctional officer asked me, "Are you feeling okay today? You don't seem to be walking with the speed and bounce you usually have." In prisons (similar to other organizations), the leader sets the tone and contributes to the culture. But prisons, probably more than most other organizations, genuinely reflect the personality and professionalism of the warden. Prison culture and setting the tone are addressed later in this chapter.

Life for a Correctional Officer

The role of **correctional officers** is critical within a prison and perhaps unique to prisons and jails. Their role is unlike other law enforcement jobs and unlike the treatment, services, or administrative functions within a prison. As reported in the 2005 census of prisons, there were 295,261 correctional officers working in state and federal prisons in the United States.[10] The *Bureau of Justice Statistics, Expenditure and Employment Extracts 2010* reports there were 785,650 correctional staff working at the federal, state, and local levels in the United States in 2010.[11] Correctional officers and supervisors make up approximately two-thirds of all staff members in state and federal prisons. Of correctional officers in state prisons, 74 percent were male.[12] Between 2000 and 2005, the number of inmates grew at a rate that was greater than that of the number of correctional officers, and the ratio of inmates to correctional officers increased from 4.8 to 1 in 2000 to 5.1 to 1 in 2005.[13] The Bureau of Labor Statistics reported that in 2016, there were 431,600 correctional officers and jailers working in state and federal prisons and local jails in the United States.[14] The percent of female correctional officers has increased, as 27.2 percent of correctional officers in 2013 were women.[15]

The job of a correctional officer is to assist in the accomplishment of the mission of the prison by maintaining control and order within the prison. While prisons and jails have a considerably different mission, there is relatively little difference in the role that correctional officers play in the two types of facilities. Correctional officers are responsible for constant supervision of inmates and implementation of security procedures within a prison. Their world is both highly technical (in that security procedures require strict adherence to policy and attention to detail)

correctional officer
staff person in a prison or jail who accomplishes the institution's mission by maintaining control and order within the prison

Correctional officers and supervisors make up 60 percent of prison staff. Their role of maintaining order and control is basic to accomplishing the prison's mission. Photo by Richard P. Seiter.

and highly interactive (through personal communications) with inmates.

Officers have to be a variety of things to a variety of people. Their bosses expect them to be exact in performing their security duties, while being professional in their interaction with inmates. Their peers expect them to support each other and not show any weakness in how they do their job and supervise inmates. And inmates expect them to be fair and not hassle them for minor things that don't make a difference. Prout and Ross write,

The most successful [correctional officers] have a genuine interest in their work and a real desire to serve the needs of the correctional system, on the one hand, and the requirements of the inmates on the other...They recognize the social and political position of the prison in the larger society beyond the prison walls.[16]

The Daily Grind

The job of correctional officer can become a daily grind of routine duties, while dealing with stressful and possibly dangerous situations. Routine is not a negative in a prison; in fact, it is very important to the successful operation of a correctional facility. Routine in a prison environment is the consistent, scheduled, and expected activities that make up the day within a prison. Officers have to be consistent in the performance of required functions, and inmates have to know what is required of them in terms of such routines as count, locking down in cells, work call, and going to meals.

Correctional officers receive a specific assignment in a prison that can be anything from supervising inmates on a work crew or in a housing area to a noninmate contact job in a tower or control center. Lombardo lists seven different categories of correctional officer assignments:

1. Living units—officers assigned to supervise housing areas
2. Work detail supervisors—officers who oversee work details such as sanitation or lawn maintenance details
3. Industrial shop and school officers—those who provide security and inmate accountability in these areas
4. Yard officers—the patrol and supervision of inmate movement in the compound or center yard of a prison
5. Administration building assignments—checking in visitors or working in the prison control center (opening doors, watching camera monitors, and maintaining radio communications)
6. Perimeter security—the armed posts of perimeter towers or mobile patrol vehicles
7. Relief officers—those who fill in a variety of assignments for officers who are sick or on a day off[17]

Each specific assignment has **post orders**, a detailed description of the activities that are required to be performed throughout the day that often includes the time at which they are to occur. Post orders are different from general policies that spell out how to do an activity (such as handling security keys or conducting an inmate count) in that they are specific to the assignment and detail what to do rather than how to do it. As an example, the post orders for a housing unit officer on the day watch may include a schedule similar to the following list:

post orders
the detailed description of the activities that are required to be performed throughout the day, often including the time they are to occur

- 7:00 A.M.—Report for duty and read the logbook of the prior shift's activities.
- 7:30 A.M.—Open the housing unit doors for ten minutes to let inmates go to work.
- 8:00 A.M.—Start sanitation assignment by inmate crew.
- 10:30 A.M.—Open the housing unit doors for inmates returning from work.
- 11:00 A.M. to noon—Allow inmates to go to the dining room for lunch.
- 12:30 P.M.—Open housing unit door for ten minutes for inmates to go to afternoon work call.
- 1:00 P.M.—Do a census count. Inmates who are off duty may be allowed to go to recreation yard.
- 3:00 P.M.—Enter day's activities into the logbook, and sign over housing unit keys to evening shift officer.

The typical day for a correctional officer is a mix of routine activities and constant communication with inmates. Correctional officers' routine is described as follows: "One minute an officer is handing out toilet paper, the next he is explaining court papers. An officer is joking with two inmates playing checkers, and in an instant he is ordering everyone to their cells."[18] Even with a regular routine of activities, there is constant tension and uncertainty as well. An officer in the Nassau County Jail thinks of his role as the following: "One unarmed correction officer and sixty inmates, the jailer and the jailed, warily taking each other's measure, sparring for control."[19] Farkas and Manning suggest that correctional work is at times routine and monotonous, and at other times it is risky and unpredictable.[20]

Although most correctional officers enjoy the challenge of their jobs and have a considerable amount of pride in and loyalty for the correctional agency for which they work, there are always officers who are bitter and feel at odds with the mission of their agency. They may feel that their agency does not appreciate them, they may have been passed over for promotion, or they just may not be happy in their job. A good example of this is described in the book *The Keepers of the Keys*, in which Dickenson expresses the view of many activities within a prison from the eyes

Correctional officers must be consistent and follow policy in the performance of their required security duties. Photo by Richard P. Seiter.

of a line correctional officer. He makes fun of the word PRIDE, the corrections department motto that stands for Professionalism, Respect, Integrity, Dignity, and Excellence. Dickenson sarcastically suggests that a better application of this motto is Perfunctory, Reaction, Indecision, Deny, and Excuse.[21]

Stress and Danger

Stress is common among law enforcement personnel and particularly among correctional officers. This is not surprising because correctional officers must supervise individuals who are confined, yet do not want to be, and who constantly try to manipulate staff to make their confinement as interesting (many inmates enjoy the challenge of manipulating staff) and tolerable as possible. Stress results from many elements of the correctional officers' working situation. In a recent review, the National Institute of Justice found three categories of danger and stress: work-related (demanding work requirements and work-related family conflicts), institution-related (gang threats and finding contraband), and psycho-social risks (mental health issues and poor work performance due to burnout).[22] Similarly, Finn found the following causes of stress among correctional officers:[23]

- Organizational sources of stress include understaffing, overtime, shift work, and supervisor demands. Understaffing results from high turnover or officers taking excessive sick leave and forces too much work on correctional officers in too little time, apprehension about the supervision of large numbers of inmates without potential backup support, and an inability to get time off for special occasions or family crises. Many officers say they welcome the extra pay of overtime, but too much overtime work quickly burns out staff. Officers in many states have to rotate the shifts they work (going from day to evening to night shifts), and this causes havoc with family life and problems of fatigue. And officers report that their supervisors are "always on you to do the job right, but you can't do it right [because of staff shortages]."[24] And for women working in male prisons, stress can also come from conflicts with supervisors, peers, and role conflict.[25]

- Work-related sources of stress include the threat of violence, inmate demands and manipulations, and problems with co workers. While the number of assaults is still relatively low (a 2011 article found that there were fifty-three assaults on correctional staff for every 100,000 inmates),[26] there is still the chance of serious injury and even death. Data from the Correctional Peace Officers Foundation (an organization created to support surviving families of correctional officers slain in the line of duty at the hands of incarcerated felons) shows there were fourteen deaths between 1965 and 1979, twenty-seven between 1980 and 1989, ninety-eight between 1990 and 1999, and 176 between 2000 and 2016.[27] The Federal Bureau of Prisons (BOP) found that from 2000 through 2010, assaults on staff increased from 1,188 to 1,696, and the number of inmates per BOP staff member increased from 4.13 in 2000 to 4.82 in 2010. For this reason and because of staff concerns for their personal safety, the BOP decided to issue all staff protective vests that would provide protection against stabbings.[28]

- The constant challenge by inmates to correctional officer authority also causes stress. Problems with co workers include competition for promotion and choice assignments, sexist attitudes from male to female officers, and concern for other officers' inappropriate or unprofessional behavior.

- There is stress from outside the system such as poor public image and poor pay. Many officers feel that their work is not understood or appreciated by the public, and low pay causes financial stress even for officers who enjoy their jobs and would like to make corrections a career. And a study of job satisfaction found they were less satisfied than the average American worker.[29]

Ferdik and Smith did a review of articles regarding stress and wellness for correctional officers since 2000, and also discovered the overall environment with difficult work conditions and dangers contribute to CO stress.[30] Although stress is never going to be removed from staff working in a prison, some methods and programs have been identified to reduce the damage that stress can have on both employees and their families. Those believed most successful are staff training on stress reduction, family counseling services, and post-incident counseling. Pittaro suggests that officer stress can be reduced by the leadership style of their supervisors, in that "Correctional administrators need to adopt a transformational leadership approach which has proven successful in reducing officer turnover, improving morale, and job satisfaction."[31]

The Oregon Department of Corrections (ODOC) is one agency that is tackling the health of their employees head on. After partnering with Portand State University and Oregon Health & Science University, their study found that one in three ODOC staff had symptoms of post-traumatic stress disorder, that the staff was overweight, and officers had high cholesterol and triglycerides. And the higher the security level of prisons, correctional officers had higher levels of stress, alcohol abuse, and missed workdays. So they put in place a twelve-week health and safety program to address nutrition, body weight, exercise and strength training, and stress management. And initial results are very positive.[32]

Most correctional agencies conduct training for staff on the causes of stress, how to attempt to avoid stressful situations, and techniques for managing your own stress levels. Staff members learn the benefits of an overall healthy lifestyle of diet, exercise, and seeking stability in financial and family issues and are trained in stress reduction techniques such as breathing exercises. Many agencies provide counseling and services for families, so that they can both better understand the work environment of the officer and deal with stressful home situations that result in adding stress to the employee. Finally, after a critical incident such as an assault on a staff member, immediate and follow-up counseling is provided to employees to give them the opportunity to recognize and manage the natural stress that results from such an incident.

Correctional Officer Careers

Many college students do not think about a career in corrections or seriously consider becoming a correctional officer after graduation, but a job as correctional officer is a tremendous experience and can provide a valuable foundation for future career opportunities. In fact, many states and the federal prison system expect staff members to begin their prison employment as a correctional officer, and officers with a college degree may later move into a job as a counselor or case manager. However, the skills in security, interacting with inmates, and understanding the overall functioning of the prison that are gained in a correctional officer job make employees more valuable in any other role. The "Your Career in Corrections" box describes the role and functions of a correctional officer.

Your Career in Corrections

Correctional Officers

Correctional officers are the front line of prisons, jails, and other correctional facilities. Long ago, the term guard was used for the people in charge of overseeing inmates in prisons and jails. The role of guards, also referred to as turnkeys or hacks, was to simply guard inmates, unlock and lock their cells when necessary, march inmates from the cell houses to another location for work or eating, and brutally enforce rules and discipline. The role of custodial staff members in modern prisons has changed considerably, even to the point to which it is now a misnomer to refer to them as merely "custodial" staff members. The contemporary term of correctional officer is used to describe the complex role of staff members who carry out security functions within a prison. In 1993, the American Correctional Association (ACA) passed a resolution to encourage the use of the term correctional officer, because it much better describes their responsibilities of custody and control, which "require extensive interpersonal skills, special training and educations, and ... correctional personnel are skilled professionals."[33]

Correctional officers (COs) are responsible for overseeing individuals who are detained in jail while awaiting trial or who have been convicted of a crime and are serving a sentence in prison. Their basic responsibility is to maintain order and contribute to the secure operation of the institution. They oversee various sections of an institution, such as a housing unit, yard or compound, perimeter fence, or inmate work or program area. Many tedious custodial functions must be carried out by COs for the maintenance of security and order. They must control doors and grills and lock and unlock them to allow only approved inmate movement. They must search inmates and areas, being alert for contraband such as drugs and weapons that can endanger staff and inmates. They also must conduct inmate counts to maintain inmate accountability and prevent escapes. They make inmates obey the rules and initiate disciplinary action. They often oversee inmate work crews, such as those assigned sanitation responsibilities, and ensure that the inmate crew performs the work at the accepted standard.

Even though some of the details of the CO job may seem unexciting and uninteresting, they are basics that must be accomplished. There are also many challenging roles for correctional officers. Officers must mediate between inmates, educate inmates about rules and procedures, and be a link between the inmate culture and staff management of a prison. COs cannot show favoritism in handing out discipline or enforcing prison rules or policy. Yet they also must use understanding and communication, while recognizing the individualism of every inmate. A major challenge of their role is that correctional officers must maintain order and gain compliance from offenders who are incarcerated against their will and who have a natural inclination to resent those who try to control them. If COs have to force inmates to comply with rules by using disciplinary actions or using force on a regular basis, prisons become the tense, violent, and dangerous world that people envision. Effective correctional officers gain compliance by communicating expectations, fairly enforcing rules, and treating inmates with respect and dignity.

Correctional officers also contribute to the rehabilitation of inmates in three ways: (1) by contributing to an environment of control without threats and tension, (2) by communicating with inmates in a relaxed and professional manner, and (3) by providing human services such as overseeing the feeding of inmates, referring sick inmates to medical staff, or assisting with recreational programs. COs do not have to be counselors or treatment specialists, but they contribute to rehabilitation through the manner in which they conduct themselves. While correctional officers maintain order and provide security, the manner in which they perform their tasks and communicate with inmates has a major impact on the overall prison environment. A brusque and harsh manner, an unwillingness to recognize genuine inmate issues, or a lack of respect for inmates creates an environment with constant tension between inmates and staff. But fair and impartial upholding of prison rules, a pleasant personality, respect for individual dignity, and understanding of the correctional officers' role in prisoner rehabilitation contribute to a relaxed environment with positive interaction between staff and inmates. The role of correctional officer has moved well beyond that of guarding inmates and now requires knowledge, training, good interpersonal communications, and sound decision making.

In 2016, there were 431,600 correctional officers and jailers working in state and federal prisons and local jails in the United States, and the average annual wage was $46,750.[34] In 2013, 27.2 percent of these positions were filled by women.[35] As an indication of pay ranges, in 2017, annual salaries for correctional officers were $36,228 for Texas to $51,708 for California.[36] In addition, correctional officers also regularly work overtime, and it is not unusual for officers to make an additional 20 percent of their base salary. Most prison systems do not require a college education for officers, but many require either experience or a two- or four-year degree. Many states and the federal prison system use correctional officer jobs as the entry level into the prison system; staff members who are successful as officers gain communications and security skills that serve them well throughout their careers and often help them get promotions and additional career opportunities. Many college students do not think of using their degrees to become correctional officers. However, the job is excellent for gaining experience, developing skills, and beginning a successful career in corrections.

Not everyone will make a good correctional officer, and therefore correctional agencies must thoughtfully recruit, screen, and retain only people who have the talents and characteristics to contribute to the agency mission. It seems reasonable to believe that during good economic times, it is very difficult to recruit and hire outstanding individuals to serve as correctional officers, yet in difficult economic times, the recruitment process would be easier. The reality is that states work hard to recruit correctional officers all the time. Riley and Wilder point out that the key to hiring and retaining qualified officers includes the following: "Agencies must take the time at the beginning of the [hiring] process to identify the characteristics they desire in their staff."[37]

Correctional officers are the positions most critical to the day-to-day management of a prison. They constantly interact with inmates. They carry out the vital security functions that form the basis of safe operations. They set the tone for the prison by how professionally they carry out their duties. And they cannot have an "off" day without it being felt by inmates and other staff members who interact with them throughout the workplace. Their jobs are challenging, stressful, and sometimes dangerous. Yet every day, local, state and federal correctional officers perform their jobs in a quality fashion, serve the public, and contribute to the overall criminal justice system in America.

The following "An Interview With" is a good illustration of how professional correctional officers see and do their jobs.

An Interview With . . .

A Correctional Officer

Gary D. Zavislak. Photo by Richard P. Seiter.

Gary D. Zavislak has been a correctional officer at the St. Louis County Justice Center for nine years. But he has worked in corrections for over two decades. Just out of high school, he took a job in a steel mill, and that made him decide to go to college. He was interested in law enforcement and criminal justice. He talked to a school resource officer he knew, who suggested he look at a police cadet program to get experience and see if he liked the work. So he did it and then became a police officer in Sterling Heights, Michigan. He enjoyed the work, and then in 1982, had an opportunity to be assigned to the new detention facility that had been built. He surprisingly liked the work, and then went to work as a correctional officer in a Michigan state prison (the Huron Valley Center), which was a unique prison designed to house convicted felons with mental illness. He then moved to Florida and went to work for the Broward Sheriff's Office that operates five large jails. There, he primarily worked as a community control supervision specialist in the pre-trial release program as an alternative to incarceration.

Question: Thank you Officer Zavislak for sharing with us information about the role of a correctional officer. Talk about your job here at the Justice Center.

Officer Zavislak: Well, we moved to St. Louis six years ago to be with our children and grandchildren, and I still wanted to work, so I applied for a CO job here. I had never worked in a direct supervision environment, and I was very apprehensive about it. They were going to lock me in a housing unit with sixty-five inmates; some with very violent backgrounds. I could not believe this would work. On any given day, I knew I could not control sixty-five inmates if they wanted to take over the housing unit. I finished training, and was assigned to a unit. In my first unit, we had a lot of young violent offenders (murderers, armed robbers, rapists, car jackers) who had not been to prison before and had a lot to learn about doing their time. They tried to bring their gang mentality into the facility, and had to be acclimated to institutional life.

I've found that you have to wear a lot of hats to be an effective direct supervision officer. My job requires being a lot of different things to a lot of different people. I feel like I am part teacher, part traffic cop, part psychologist, part parent giving direction and help, and part referee. You have to take these different hats and blend them all together. But primarily, you are the authority. Your primary job is "protection," as we protect society from the inmates and keep the inmates safe as well.

During training, we were told to "find your own style" that works. So I decided to approach this like I were teaching a college class, and treat the inmates like they were young students. I tell them, "you guys all know the rules; we are all adults here. I shouldn't have to address this, and remind you of that." That seems to work. They appreciate the fact that I let them police themselves to a certain extent and respect them. What is interesting is that direct supervision works. It took me some time, but I realize how well this approach works.

(Continued)

Question: What are the keys to be successful as a correctional officer?

Officer Zavislak: I think the key to being successful in this type of environment is to be honest and fair. I try to pass this tip on to young or new officers—don't try to be the inmates' friend. Tell them if you can't do something they ask; sorry, it is not the policy or it is against the rules. Be open, and treat everyone the same. There can be no special treatment. Inmates will often try to play the "race card." I love a saying from one of my former supervisors who would always respond to that by saying, "the only color I see in here is Khaki" (which is the color of the inmate uniforms).

Another key to success is simple; you have to be dedicated and come to work every day. You can't just say I will take a day off, because then you are letting others down. The attrition (turnover) rate here is very high. Almost on a weekly basis, people are leaving. Some use this as a stepping stone, but others just aren't committed to it. Some try it and know it is not right for them. You have to have longevity, and over time you find your niche and get comfortable with how you are going to do the job. If you leave before you get to that point, you never get to be successful. You have to give yourself and this job a chance.

Question: What are the things you like and dislike about your job?

Officer Zavislak: Some are the really practical things in that I work in a controlled environment—it is warm in winter and dry when it rains. I never have to worry about the weather. Another is—and this is really important for someone looking at a career path—this is a recession proof job. There is always a need for us; so if you are looking for security, it is a good reason to get into criminal justice. I also like that at the end of the day, I feel that I have done something good for someone—inmates, the public, or my co workers. There is always a new challenge—we have a dynamic flow going through this place. When I see on the news at night that a high profile case has been arrested, I know I am part of it. I like helping people—getting them through a crisis—divorce, illness in the family, whatever. I know that almost all the time, when someone comes to me with a problem, I can direct or send them to someone who can help. What I don't like about the job is that you're never going to get rich at this profession. If you are looking for that, look elsewhere. While the pay is not sky high, you can make a living and the benefits are great.

Also—and it is the nature of the beast, there are some politics involved in any government job. These are not things that necessarily make your life miserable, but, part of what happens in politics filters down to us. You have to keep your mind objective and keep the morale up. Also, I do not like mandatory overtime. In a jail or prison, you may have issues like an "Institutional Lockdown," and every officer is forced to work mandatory overtime. Additionally, if the manpower staffing levels fall below the minimum level, you can and will be forced to work overtime. Some officers like a lot of overtime, but I don't like for it to be mandatory. If it happens at an inopportune time, when you want or need to be home, it can be one of the big things that cause stress on the job.

Question: You work with violent offenders; do you ever feel threatened on the job?

Officer Zavislak: Not so much in a general sense, but the inmate to staff ratio gives me a little apprehension. But I don't feel threatened just by walking into a housing unit with violent inmates. We've had officers assaulted by inmates on occasion, but it's rare. An inmate bit me several years ago. You do have some inmates that you know are violent, and they may tell you that they will see you on the street and do this or that. But you just have to take it with a grain of salt.

One of the real challenges for working in corrections is dealing with inmates with mental illness. My current assignment is in a mental health unit; we call ourselves a Multi-Disciplinary Mental Health Team. Society as a whole has let people with mental illness fall through the cracks. Jails and prisons are seeing a serious increase in the number of inmates with mental illness. This creates a special challenge for COs, and therefore new training for officers. We learn how to recognize signs and symptoms of mental illness. When we see an offender with these symptoms, we get them directed to the mental health team, and they may need to be segregated, get counseling, or be put on medication. It is incumbent on first line staff (officers) to first recognize that the need is there. The inmate's mental illness ends up in their behavior being different; you notice the inmate may be acting unusual for their situation. You talk to the guy, and if it seems necessary, put him in touch with a social worker. The inmate may be experiencing an episode, they may have a chemical imbalance with their medication, or they may be a suicide risk. The bottom-line is, you need to be sensitive to this, and not just ignore it.

Question: What causes stress on your job?

Officer Zavislak: Time management is a big stressor. A lot has to go on and there are so many things an officer has to do—the cleaning ritual, feeding the inmates, getting inmates off to court or to the clinic, setting up the dayroom, prepare for medication being passed, and manage recreation time and visits. You have several different populations—one in recreation, another in the dayroom, and those in their cells. Time management can be stressful. Anything an inmate needs—a bar of soap or toilet paper has to come from the officer. Your supervisors can also be stressors. As an example, I believe the housing unit has to be the domain of the officer. If you get a supervisor that wants to micromanage, look for trouble, or stir the pot, your day can be hell. You need your supervisor to provide help, direction, and support. But not come in and upset the apple cart and then leave. I know that being a supervisor is a tough job. I have never wanted to be a supervisor. I do well what I do, but I do not feel I would like to be a supervisor.

Question: What do you do to deal with the stress?

Officer Zavislak: Sometimes you just need to "take a deep breath." If you are on the job in a housing unit, there is not much else you can do about it. What I tend to do is just try to make the day as least stressful as possible, by taking care of the schedule, setting the right tone, and not creating conflict. And, I try not to take it home with me. One thing I started doing is to go for a walk off the unit during my lunchtime. We get a thirty-minute lunch break—I go for a walk and that helps a lot. I think about things other than work, and it clears my head and gives me exercise as well.

Question: Would you recommend this job to others?

Officer Zavislak: Oh, definitely. I have talked about the pay and benefits. But, corrections is a career that has a lot of room for advancement. There are many upward opportunities, and many noncustody jobs that you can move into. You don't have to go into this assuming you will have the same job, but many people (like myself) do that. But you come into this business, even if not sure what you want to do, and get exposed to many things. You get a feel for what others do and you can find your career path by working as a CO. If you spend time doing this, you will feel a sense of accomplishment.[38]

Recruiting and Retaining Correctional Officers

One of the very difficult challenges faced by correctional agencies is the recruitment of quality individuals as correctional officers who are interested in corrections as a career and committed to giving the job a fair trial to see if it works before quitting. Even though correctional agencies do many things to get the word out about available jobs and the challenges to be faced, the work environment is still not well known. Cornelius and Courtright point out that criminal justice students often do not have a clear understanding of what correctional officers do, nor the stressors, dangers, or difficulties of the job.[39] As noted above, the job of a correctional officer can be stressful, dangerous, and tedious, and there is little positive recognition and pay is often low for the challenge. A New York State correctional officer noted, "Police and firefighters are recognized as heroes. It's not as glamorous to be a correctional officer."[40] And even though agencies have improved their recruitment efforts, two-thirds of correctional staff still heard of the job opening through personal contact or other employees.[41]

Correctional agencies have historically experienced high turnover and low officer morale over the past decade. In 2005, Oklahoma starting pay for a correctional officer was $21,000, and the state prison system had 500 vacant positions. In New York state, correctional officers were paid between $30,000 and $50,000 per year, but this was not adequate to draw qualified applicants in counties near New York City.[42] In 2001, the Texas prison system had 3300 vacancies in its complement of 26,000 correctional officers.[43]

A 2003 survey by the ACA found that the average national turnover of correctional officers was 16.1 percent, and noncompetitive compensation was the most frequently cited reason for recruitment difficulty and the second most cited reason for retention. Demanding work hours, stress and burnout, and employees not understanding and finding they were not suited for the job were other factors in turnover.[44] Another survey of correctional staff in forty-five correctional systems identified recruitment problems as the failure to compete monetarily with law enforcement agencies and the rural location of correctional facilities.[45] The challenge of retention is only getting worse, as projections are that the number of available correctional officer and jailer positions will continue to increase.[46]

As problematic as these issues seem, correctional agencies are addressing the most serious issues to recruitment and retention, and the recession and rising unemployment rates are making more people consider working as a correctional officer. To avoid retention problems and recruit people who want a career, the Michigan correctional system has consistently paid correctional officers higher rates than those in neighboring states. And in recent years, Delaware, Louisiana, North Dakota, Vermont, Virginia, and West Virginia have raised pay for correctional officers to make them more comparable to law enforcement officers. Delaware reported that after raising pay by 18 percent in 2006, their vacancy rate was the lowest in five years.[47]

Another way correctional agencies are improving recruitment and retention is positively changing the culture of their organizations. In a case study of Florida and Pennsylvania departments of corrections, it was noted that assessing and enhancing the workplace could reduce staff turnover.[48] And CoreCivic, the largest private prison company with over 17,000 staff members, conducted interviews with staff to determine workplace satisfaction and identified that the way correctional officers were treated by their first-line supervisors had a major impact on turnover. As a result, the company implemented a values-based training program for supervisors and has seen its retention rates improve as a result.[49] Runde and Rusak identify how conflict (often between employees and supervisors) undermines a positive work environment, and by using a process of conflict resolution, workplace harmony can be improved.[50]

Although recruitment and retention are improving among many correctional agencies as a result of thoughtful improvements in pay, culture, and working conditions, perhaps the biggest impact in reduced turnover is the recession. With severe economic times come layoffs and high unemployment. During these times, individuals look for what they consider to be more stable employers, and correctional agencies are perceived to be "recession proof." What remains to be seen is if the improvements made by these agencies will help in retaining employees as the economy improves and jobs in noncorrectional agencies are again available.

The Roles of Other Prison Staff

As can be seen from the extensive listing of prison jobs given earlier, there are many more than the two positions (warden and correctional officer). The warden provides leadership and sets the tone for the prison, and correctional officers are key to successfully accomplishing day-to-day activities, but many other staff members contribute to the accomplishment of the prison mission. Prison staff members work either in an administrative capacity or in one of the three operational areas of security, programs or treatment, and service. Some of these roles are described next.

Other Security Personnel

Prisons operate using a very clear chain of command, and nowhere in the prison is this clearer than with security or custody personnel. Most prisons (particularly high- and maximum-security prisons) have a deputy, associate, or assistant warden in charge of security. This is such an important part of prison operations and includes such a high number of staff members (50–60 percent of all staff members) that it is important to have a senior manager responsible for these functions. The next level of management is a midlevel manager and the highest-ranking **uniformed staff** person in the prison, often assigned the rank of major. This person supervises all security personnel and is the substantive expert on custodial policies and practices. The next level is the rank of uniformed security staff members who oversee each eight-hour shift of operations in the prison. Staff members who are assigned the rank of captain oversee the daily functioning and routine within the prison, assign work, and ensure that there are the required number of officers to cover all posts or assignments. Lieutenants are usually assigned to some of the most sensitive and explosive areas of the prison, such as the recreation area, industrial complex, and housing complex. Sergeants act either as senior correctional officers who are assigned the most difficult posts or as the direct supervisors of correctional officers who are responsible for ensuring consistency and quality implementation of policies.

uniformed staff
those prison or jail staff members who work in the security or custody department and are responsible for the implementation of security policies and procedures

Treatment and Program Staff

As described in Chapter 14, treatment and program staff members deliver programs (education, vocational, recreation, substance abuse, religious, psychological) to inmates. The following program or treatment departments are found in most prisons.

Psychological services
Vocational training
Substance abuse

Education
Religious services
Recreation

professional staff
prison or jail staff members in a specialty area that requires distinctive training and education and may also require a professional certification to deliver a program

Each department includes midlevel managers who are substantive experts and manage each area and line staff members who are primarily responsible for working with inmates in their specialty areas. The education program has teachers and vocational specialists, the religious programs have chaplains, and the psychological and substance abuse programs have counselors. These are usually specialty areas that require special training and education, and some require professional certification (to do a specific type of drug or mental health counseling) to deliver the programs.

In some prisons, these staff members are called **professional staff**, although correctional administrators would rather call all their staff members *professional* and use *program* or *treatment* to refer to this category of staff. There is also often a deputy/associate/assistant warden of programs or treatment who supervises these functions. The role of the program and treatment staff is to deliver programs that assist inmates in their rehabilitation and preparation for reentry to the community. Inmates may take general education, English as a second language (ESL), or general equivalency diploma (GED) programs from teachers. They may receive individual or group counseling from staff psychologists, participate in substance abuse programs with drug and alcohol counselors, receive a vocational

Chaplains are responsible for making religious worship opportunities available to inmates. They lead services, counsel inmates, and oversee services provided by contract ministers. Photo by Richard P. Seiter.

certificate from a class taught by a certified vocational instructor, or participate in a religious program overseen by a prison chaplain or a contracted priest, imam, rabbi, Protestant minister, or any other religious leader.

Services Staff

The third category of prison staff includes staff members who operate departments providing inmate services within a prison. Included departments are prison industries, facility maintenance, business operations, food services, and medical care. The staff organization for each of these departments is different, but they are usually led by a deputy/associate/ assistant warden for services (or operations). Service departments include the following:

Maintenance workers train and supervise inmates in performing work to maintain the prison. Photo by Richard P. Seiter.

Prison industries	Business administration
Facility maintenance	Human resources
Safety and sanitation	Health services
Staff training and development	Food services

Each department has a midlevel manager who provides substantive expertise and manages the budget, staff, and delivery of services within the department. Prison industries departments have factory managers to oversee the production of goods and several industrial specialists who supervise inmate workers. Similarly, facilities maintenance departments have managers and trades supervisors (electrical, carpentry, plumbing, heating, and air conditioning) who supervise inmate workers. The food services department is organized similarly, with a manager and food service supervisors responsible for overseeing inmates who prepare and serve food. In most prisons, the business offices operate the inmate commissary and laundry and have staff members who supervise inmates in providing these services. Finally, the medical services department has a chief medical officer (physician) as the department head and nurses, pharmacy staff, and other health care delivery personnel to operate the prison infirmary.

These varieties of jobs provide career opportunities for students with many different majors. In the "You Make the Decision" box at the end of this chapter, students must weigh the pros and cons and make a decision as to whether they would consider working in a prison.

The Prison Culture for Staff

Staff and inmates quickly learn the culture of a prison. Staff may say, "That's not the way things are done here," or tell inmates, "You need to forget how things were at your last prison, and get used to our way." They are talking about organizational culture, which is reflected in the way policies and procedures are actually carried out. State correctional agencies require the same policies to be implemented at every prison, yet the way policy is implemented differs based on the culture of the prison. Stojkovic and Farkas correctly suggest that there is a "nexus between prison leadership and prison culture," meaning that the leadership of the prison directly influences the culture of the prison.[51] But in some prisons the culture may have continued so long or be so strong that leadership of the prison fails to affect it without lengthy and aggressive efforts.

Many models of prison organizational culture are based on a single focus, whether it varies by characteristics of officers or whether multiple cultures exist within the different levels of staff.[52] In the latter, a "three-cultures" model is presented by Farkas and Manning, suggesting that values, sentiments, and modes of thinking vary between three organizational levels: the lower participant or officer segment, the middle management segment, and the top command segment.[53] In this model, the perspective from which the group looks at their jobs influences the culture of the job level. The line officer level is influenced by their union or labor organization and most influenced by the internal organization of what occurs as they carry out the daily tasks in the prison. The middle management level identifies with either the line officer or top command level and is influenced by the internal orientation of their jobs and working environment. The top command level is consumed with administrative duties, must respond to and is influenced by external audiences (their agency bosses, the public, politicians), and looks beyond the daily activities to longer term objectives.

Even though all three levels may have a distinct culture, the levels may also influence each other so that there is a merger of cultures, resulting in one blended culture rather than three distinct cultures. This blending is considered a positive development, and strong and visionary leaders work to bring convergence among the cultures of the three levels. A desired result is that the top command influences the other two to see the long-term good (vision) of the agency and prison, rather than reflect that of the day-to-day activities and strictly internal culture of the line officers. The most effective prisons have only one dominant culture, although there is no denying that all individuals and groups are most strongly influenced by what they desire from their job and the way they look at their work.

Two types of culture develop within a prison, one dealing with the management style of command to line staff and one dealing with the relationship between staff and inmates. The style of **management culture** has to do with the way leadership deals and communicates with subordinate staff and falls into a continuum between *autocratic* and *empowered*. The **relationship culture** is the style by which staff members view and communicate with inmates and falls into a continuum between *authoritarian* (gaining compliance by threats and intimidation) and *reasoned* (gaining compliance through incentives and disincentives).[54] Both types of prison culture greatly affect the overall tone in which the prison is operated. Staff and inmates are aware of the culture and adapt and respond as expected, and their behavior therein perpetuates the continuation of the culture.

The management culture of a prison is represented in Figure 12.2. There is no question that the culture of Stateville under Warden Ragen was one of autocratic rule. Staff members never made a decision that was not checked with their

management culture
a culture based on the way prison leadership deals and communicates with subordinate staff; it falls into a continuum between autocratic and empowered

relationship culture
a culture based on how staff members view and communicate with inmates; it falls into a continuum between authoritarian and reasoned

Autocratic	Moderate	Empowered
Staff must follow policy or check with supervisors before making decisions		Staff make decisions with full knowledge and consistent with prison principles and values

FIGURE 12.2 A Continuum of Management Cultures in a Prison

supervisors. In an autocratic prison culture, staff members strictly follow the rules and cannot make decisions to address issues outside of policy. In an empowered culture, employees are knowledgeable about the principles, values, policies, and expected outcomes in the prison, and make decisions consistent with the expected outcome. Seiter writes,

> *Empowerment involves providing employees with the principles and values of the organization, along with the desired outcomes (vision and mission), and allowing them to make decisions and respond to situations that are consistent with the principles and values, and move toward the desired outcomes.*[55]

Throughout history, most prisons have operated toward the autocratic end of the management culture continuum, partly because of their development as paramilitary organizations, but also because of fear that line staff would make mistakes that could result in dire consequences of loss of life, escapes, or riots. However, a style of empowerment is important in modern prisons for several reasons. First, there is continuous change, and correctional agencies have difficulty developing routine procedures that can be counted on to work over time. Second, rapid changes result in situations that have never before been encountered, and no guidelines on how to respond are available. Third, prison employees are better educated and better trained than in the past, have experienced a world of rapid change, and are prepared to meet never before confronted challenges. Finally, today's employees demand to be involved in the organization and cringe at a rigid bureaucracy that expects them to follow orders and carry out prescribed functions without knowing the reasons behind them.

The prison culture reflecting the relationship between staff and inmates is also critical within a prison environment. This cultural continuum is depicted in Figure 12.3. In the authoritarian culture, staff members are threatened by inmates and believe that they cannot maintain control of the prison unless they constantly reinforce their position of authority by threats and intimidation. In such a prison, staff members are seen as "weak" if they are polite or show respect and courtesy to inmates. In the reasoned culture, staff members know that they have the power of sanctioning inmates with disincentives and rewarding inmates with incentives, and they maintain control through fairness in making these decisions. Therefore, they interact with inmates in a relaxed and congenial fashion, without losing authority or appearing weak. Prisons that operate on the more reasoned end of the continuum develop a less stressful and tense long-term environment.

Leaders are responsible for creating the culture within an organization. Wardens set the tone and culture by the management style they adopt and the style of staff–inmate interaction they support. The "A Case Study" box gives a good example of a warden taking a leadership role in creating a positive culture within a prison. It represents a real situation I faced after a riot at a prison where I was the warden.

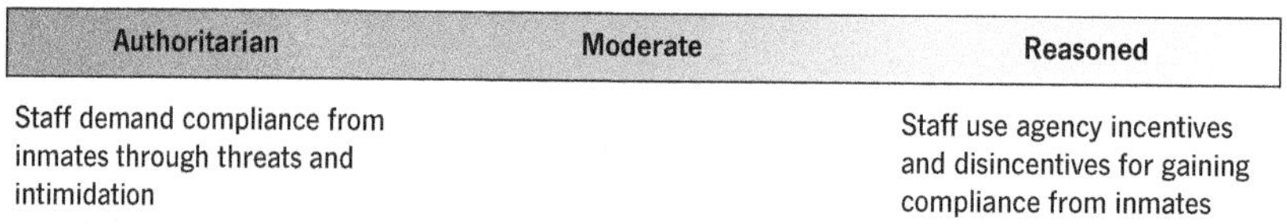

Authoritarian	Moderate	Reasoned
Staff demand compliance from inmates through threats and intimidation		Staff use agency incentives and disincentives for gaining compliance from inmates

FIGURE 12.3 A Continuum of Staff–Inmate Cultures in a Prison

▶ A Case Study

Setting the Tone

After the riot at the prison, the warden observed that staff members were taking a much more authoritative approach in their interactions with inmates. More staff members elevated their voice and took on a tone of discipline when talking to inmates and statements by staff to direct an inmate to change their behavior became more like "barking orders" than reminders of the rules. Although these types of interactions are necessary in certain situations and with certain noncompliant inmates, when they tend to become the regular rather than infrequent method of interaction, it sets a climate of tension and hostility that can make the environment more stressful and less stable for both staff and inmates. The warden felt that this staff behavior was the result of the riot, the fact that staff had witnessed a few inmates destroying property and assaulting staff, and the fact that some staff members were fearful and less confident. As a result, staff began to treat all inmates as violent and dangerous and became more terse and disrespectful in their communications. The warden, in conjunction with his top staff, developed a plan to change this interaction style into one that was more relaxed and positive. First, he initiated activities to directly respond to staff members' fear of further victimization by inmates. This included "hardening" the prison by replacing wooden doors with metal ones and putting bars over windows to create "safe havens" for staff if another dangerous situation broke out. Staff members were trained in disturbance control methods, boosting their confidence that they could handle a violent situation if one occurred.

As staff members felt more comfortable with their personal safety, the warden set out to improve the positive communication between staff and inmates. Additional training was provided to staff regarding positive interactions and proper interpersonal communication. The warden made a video shown to all staff members of him discussing the importance of positive staff–inmate interactions. On the video, the warden explained the reasons for such positive interaction, emphasizing that it was not to be soft on inmates, but that this approach in effect enhanced the security and safety of the institution. As well as reducing tension and lessening the likelihood of an inmate spontaneously responding with violence in a confrontational situation with staff, positive communication opened the door to inmates sharing important intelligence with staff about planned inmate misconduct or potential inmate gang activities. Supervisors were asked to immediately correct communication that did not comply with this approach by line staff and use this as a key discussion point in all staff evaluations. The warden also appealed to line staff members to recognize the problems that inappropriate communication caused and to correct their fellow employees who destabilized the environment and made it more dangerous for everyone else.

These activities worked well over time. Fewer staff members used harsh and authoritative tones of voice when unnecessary. More staff members began to repeat the importance of positive communication and prided themselves on their ability to gain inmate compliance without having to "bark orders" and demand it. As staff members learned that they maintained order more effectively through treating inmates with courtesy and respect, while still consistently and fairly enforcing rules, they operated with increased skill and success. The overall climate of the institution returned to one of positive staff and inmate interaction, a relaxed and less stressful environment, and actually a reduced level of disciplinary infractions for failure to follow orders or insubordination by inmates.

Female Correctional Officers in Men's Prisons

Four decades ago, women were not allowed to work in men's prisons as correctional officers; it was believed they would not be able to perform effectively and safely. The arguments against women working as correctional officers included "(1) women weren't strong enough, (2) their presence would be disruptive to prison operations (inmates would not follow their orders or would fight for their attention) and (3) the privacy of male inmates would have to be violated."[56] The only female employees in men's prisons held jobs with no inmate contact, such as clerks, secretaries, or mailroom workers.

However, Title VII of the 1964 Civil Rights Act, amended in 1972, proscribes employment discrimination on the basis of race, religion, sex, and national origin and therein granted women the legal right to seek employment as correctional officers in men's prisons. Women quickly filed several cases with the Equal

BFOQ

a bona fide occupational qualification reasonably necessary to the normal operation of that particular business or enterprise that may allow for some discriminatory practices to occur

Dothard v. Rawlinson

a 1977 U.S. Supreme Court case regarding a woman who was denied a position as a correctional officer in an Alabama male prison; the Court ruled that a BFOQ against women correctional officers was allowable because of the deplorable conditions of the Alabama prisons and the presence of predatory male sex offenders as inmates

Gunther v. Iowa

a 1979 case in the U.S. District Court of Iowa in which the court determined that inmate privacy was not a valid reason to refuse to hire women as correctional officers; the *Gunther* decision eliminated the major support used for the BFOQ by states in not hiring female correctional officers

Employment Opportunity Commission (EEOC), claiming discrimination on the basis of sex by criminal justice agencies. A provision of Title VII, however, states that some discriminatory practices might be allowed if there is "a bona fide occupational qualification (**BFOQ**) reasonably necessary to the normal operation of that particular business or enterprise."[57] Therefore, correctional agencies hesitated to hire women for correctional officer positions, believing that the risk to security and loss of privacy for inmates would be considered an acceptable BFOQ exception.

In 1977, the U.S. Supreme Court decided the case of ***Dothard v. Rawlinson*** and first addressed the BFOQ exception.[58] Rawlinson was a woman who was denied a position as a correctional officer in an Alabama men's prison because the state prohibited women in any position that would require contact with male inmates. The Court ruled that a BFOQ prohibiting female correctional officers was allowable because of the deplorable conditions of the Alabama prisons and the presence of predatory male sex offenders as inmates. In *Dothard*, however, the Court did not address the issue of privacy for inmates with regard to the presence of female correctional officers. In 1979, in ***Gunther v. Iowa***, the U.S. District Court of Iowa did not find the same predatory environment in a medium-security Iowa prison that was believed to exist in the *Dothard* case within a maximum-security Alabama prison. The court therefore determined that inmate privacy was not a valid reason to refuse to hire women as correctional officers, finding that the state could create staffing and assignment patterns to avoid infringing on inmate privacy.[59] The *Gunther* decision eliminated the major reason that states claimed a BFOQ in not hiring female correctional officers, and most states moved quickly to hire women.

By 1993, women represented 17.3 percent of the approximately 169,000 correctional officers in state and federal prisons; by 2002, 22.7 percent of the 218,000 total U.S. correctional officers were women, and 39,059 (77 percent of the total employed) of these female officers worked in men's prisons.[60] And by 2013, there were approximately 413,000 jobs as bailiffs, correctional officers, and jailers, and 27.2 percent of these positions had women.[61] This progress did not come easily, however, as the historical bias against and assumption that female officers would have different attitudes and carry out their duties differently from their male counterparts persisted. Some of the early negative reaction by male correctional officers to women working as co workers is apparent in the following survey results:

> *Out of a hundred men interviewed, only a handful were at all supportive of [women working as correctional officers]. ... The most frequently voiced reasons for opposing the presence of women were that they impair the security of the institutions as a whole and jeopardize male guards' own safety.*[62]

Early studies found either no or only minor differences in relation to the attitudes and job performance of women compared to men.[63] A study of female correctional officers in California found that women performed as well as men as correctional officers. However, men continued to perceive women as less effective when the situation required physical strength or a violent emergency existed.[64] And a study within the BOP also found no lapse in performance, but did find that female correctional officers experienced hostility and sometimes sexual harassment from male staff and inmates.[65]

Although many women now work as correctional officers in men's prisons, they still face challenges because they are women working in a predominantly male environment. Photo by Riffi O'Brien.

Interesting findings resulted from a survey of male inmates who were asked to rate female correctional officer performance compared to male correctional officers. Cheeseman and colleagues found that higher security inmates were more likely to favorably rate the performance of female officers than lower security inmates. The authors write, "Specifically, prisoners classified as close custody were significantly more likely than minimum or medium custody inmates to agree that female staff performed as well as male staff when responding to stabbings, responding to physical fights, settling verbal disputes among inmates, and preventing riots or disturbances."[66]

In a report of interviews with female jail officers, the findings were that female officers believed that they received paternalistic treatment, were excluded from work socialization opportunities, had higher job stress, and had more limited career prospects.[67] The findings further suggested that female correctional officers experience various problems stemming from sexism and sexual harassment by their male co workers, which could be reduced if the jail administrators demonstrated a commitment to the thorough integration of women within the formal and informal organizational structure. With the passing of time, women have been more openly accepted into male prison environments, and in most states and county jails, women receive the same work and promotional opportunities as men.

In fact, there are many benefits to women working as correctional officers. One is that the style of supervision by female correctional officers of male inmates may bring a calming and normalized influence to a prison. Pollock writes,

Women officers tend to ask inmates to do things rather than tell them. Female correctional officers foster personal interest in the inmate and use the relationships they develop as a technique of control. This relieves some of the tension found in prisons for men and encourages male prisoners to interact with correctional officers rather than cultivating isolation and separate subcultures.[68]

Females now make up a large proportion of prison and jail correctional offices. Courtesy of CoreCivic.

Although modern correctional administrators accept women as able to effectively perform the role of correctional officers in men's prisons, some stereotypes still exist, and women in some correctional facilities are forced to endure a lack of respect that is given to male officers by inmates or even other correctional officers. Even though these attitudes are not based on fact or performance, prisons for male inmates are very male-dominated places, and these stereotypes and perceptions will be difficult to totally overcome. The "A Look Into" box reflects the challenges women still face in a predominantly male environment. A female correctional officer describes the challenges faced in developing the skills to be an effective female officer in a men's prison.

▶ A Look Into . . .

Female Correctional Officers in Male Prisons

Even though there are benefits in having female correctional officers working in prisons housing male inmates, there are naturally challenges to those women who choose to work as officers in this setting. At the time of this interview, Pamela McBride was a correctional officer at the Belmont Correctional Institution (BeCI) in St. Clairsville, Ohio. She has worked at BeCI for almost five years, and provided this look into the work environment and challenges faced by a woman correctional officer. Officer McBride lists some of the issues faced when working with male inmates and in primarily a male work environment.

"I did not originally plan to be a correctional officer. I worked in the legal field for almost seventeen years, and decided to go back to college. I was working toward my Associates degree at Belmont College. I was an older and non-traditional student, and one of my adjunct professors was the warden at BeCI. As a part of the class, she took us on a tour of the prison.

I had no idea what went on in the prison, and all the career opportunities that were available. The warden encouraged me to think about applying for a job, and I am now committed to a career in corrections. I am continuing my education to get my Bachelors in social work, and hope to be licensed and move into that area of corrections. BeCI has approximately 2700 inmates. It is a Level 2 (of 5 levels), making it low to medium level. The average sentence for inmates varies. There are some inmates serving only six months and others are serving twenty or more years. I think there are around four hundred staff, about one-half are correctional officers. I would estimate about twenty to thirty percent of the officers are women."

"Before applying, I was concerned about what the job would be like, and thought about it for a while before I applied. I knew there would be certain risks and concerns. My parents were not happy I was going to work in the prison, as they were fearful of what could happen. While they now accept it, they always tell me to be careful. I went to our training academy before starting at the prison. One of the lessons was that being new, inmates are going to try to test you to see what type of officer you will be; one who does their job by the book or one who lets things slide. Once I started work, I found that the tour, the training, and all the advice, while helpful, cannot totally prepare you for what you feel as a CO working with large numbers of inmates. Other officers and supervisors have been very helpful, and suggest how to handle a variety of situations. They are always there to answer questions."

"Of my five years, I have worked in the same housing unit for almost four years. My partner is a male CO, and the two of us are assigned a general population dormitory with 272 inmates. He had previously worked for the Ohio Department of Youth Services, so had some experience in a correctional environment. I could ask for a reassignment, but we both like knowing where we are working. There is always some stress, and while nothing has ever happened, I know there is a potential for something serious to occur. But we know that things can change very quickly. Our dorm is also where they assign newly arrived inmates for orientation. They stay with us for a while and then rotate to a permanent dorm. So we have inmates that are new to prison, and they are also trying to figure out the routines and how we will treat them. Most inmates are very respectful, but some do have issues with women as authority figures. That is why I like working with a male partner. We handle things very well together, and when there are challenges, your interpersonal communications skills are essential."

"I think the key to being a good officer is to be respectful when dealing with inmates. However, the situation will dictate your response in terms of firmness. It is also important to follow the rules and follow the book. It is ok to feel fearful; if not,

your awareness can be down and you might become complacent. Being a CO can be challenging in many ways. The first time I had to do a standing count (inmates must all stand at the foot of their beds), being new and being a female, walking down each aisle of dozens of male inmates was challenging. It felt like walking the gauntlet. But I found that you just hold your head high, and not show you are nervous. A person's personality is most important; I am a person who demands respect. I think if you are fair but not a pushover, that is most effective. Most of the inmates think I am former military, and they often ask what branch of military was I in. When I take a count, I look each one in the eye. I try to carry myself that way."

"Being proactive as opposed to reactive is crucial in diffusing or eliminating situations and is a good characteristics of an officer. Inmates know if they do not follow the rules, they will receive a rule violation. Depending on the inmate; when you are new they are trying to see if you will always follow the rules or let things slip. They will always try to manipulate you. They start with small things, asking if they can use your pen, or if you will write down the address of another prison for them. Just to get you to do something they request. These things are a definite 'no.' If you begin to let them get by with little things, they will continue to build them into bigger requests."

"But the work is really enjoyable and rewarding, and there is good career potential. It is an occupation where you need a thick skin, but you can promote and work up through the ranks. I was a temporary lieutenant until they hired someone for the job. While I enjoyed that, after finishing my degree, I want to move into a social work position. There are females at every level of our institution and throughout the department. So I know there are opportunities and am looking forward to my career."[69]

Chapter Review

Summary

In this chapter, the people who work in prisons were described and discussed. The goal of the chapter is for students to better understand the challenges these staff members face, the contributions they make, and the environment and culture in which they work. Although most people think of wardens and correctional officers as staff of prisons, there are many more categories of job specialties within a prison. A prison needs almost every category of specialist that it takes to operate a small city. There must be staff to maintain the facility, provide food services and health care to inmates, offer rehabilitative programs, hire and train other staff members, manage the finances and budget, and maintain a secure and safe environment.

At the top of the prison chain of command is the warden. Wardens have become almost mythical individuals in the American culture. Partly because of their challenging job of maintaining order among hundreds or thousands of convicted felons, partly because they must direct a diverse workforce often represented by a union and sometimes at odds with the mission of the agency, and partly because of the way in which they are portrayed in movies and television shows, wardens are usually thought of as autocratic, harsh and insensitive to inmates and staff, and often unethical. However, modern wardens have to be outstanding managers of people and resources and must rely on education, intelligence, and experience more than simply a dominating personality.

Correctional officers make up the line position that is critical to the day-to-day operation of a prison and deals directly with inmates. Their job is not glamorous, not easy, and generally underappreciated. Correctional officers have challenging jobs because inmates are constantly trying to manipulate and challenge them and to avoid following rules. Officers must enforce security procedures, and lapses can cause escapes, assaults, and even riots. Officers are key in setting the tone of interaction between staff and inmates. They can perform their duties in a brusque and authoritative manner or act with more respect and courtesy toward inmates. The latter is much more effective in maintaining a more relaxed and less tense environment, yet requires maturity and confidence by the officers to communicate effectively.

Two key issues in a prison are the overall culture and the role of female correctional officers in men's prisons. The culture is the approach or manner in which policies and procedures are carried out within a prison. A prison adopts a culture regarding how staff members communicate with each other and how they communicate with inmates. The warden and other leadership within a prison are critical to establishing and maintaining a positive organizational culture. The use of women as correctional officers has also become a controversial issue in men's prisons. Although banned from working in men's prisons only thirty-five years ago, female officers are now recognized as valuable employees both in how they perform their jobs and in how they contribute to a positive organizational culture.

Key Terms

closed systems	organizational culture	relationship culture
open systems	correctional officer	BFOQ
chain of command	post orders	*Dothard v. Rawlinson*
warden	uniformed staff	*Gunther v. Iowa*
transactional leaders	professional staff	
transformational leaders	management culture	

Review Questions

1. Prisons have many staff members other than correctional officers. List five other staff positions within a prison.

2. What is a closed and open system of a prison?

3. How does staff empowerment expand the effectiveness of prison operations beyond the traditional use of issuing orders through the chain of command?

4. What is the role of a modern prison warden?

5. How does transformational leadership differ from transactional leadership?

6. What percentage of all prison staff members are correctional officers or correctional supervisors?

7. Describe the job of a correctional officer.

8. What is a post order?

9. What are three causes of stress for correctional officers?

10. How do correctional officers gain the compliance of inmates?

11. List three types of treatment departments within a prison.

12. What are service departments within a prison?

13. What are the two types of culture that can develop within a prison?

14. What did the case of *Gunther v. Iowa* decide, and how did it affect employment of women as correctional officers in men's prisons?

15. Approximately what percentage of state and federal correctional officers is female?

You Make the Decision...

Do I Want to Work in a Prison?

One issue that confronts students considering a career in corrections is whether they want to work in a prison. Often the first reaction is negative. Students think, "I don't want to work in a prison. I didn't get my college degree to work in that type of environment. I want a more professional job." However, if they become more familiar with prisons, their operation, the jobs and roles of various staff, and the quality of the people who work there, they often reconsider their earlier hesitancy to work in a prison.

In this "You Make the Decision," you are to consider the pros and cons of working in a prison. Think of the various roles and issues for staff members who work in a prison described in this chapter. Create a list of all the good things about prison jobs, such as stability, benefits, and opportunities for advancement. Then create a list of the things that are not so positive about working in a prison, such as danger, stress, and relatively low pay.

Once you have created your lists, imagine what it would really be like to work in a prison, and decide (individually or in a group) whether you would take a job working in a prison.

CHAPTER 13

Custody within a Prison

Courtesy of CoreCivic.

After reading this chapter, you should be able to:

1. Summarize the security and custody functions within a correctional facility.

2. Describe how prison officials ensure that inmates are accounted for, including the three types of counts.

3. Explain how contraband comes into the possession of inmates and specify procedures to prevent this from occurring.

4. Describe the two categories of inmate assignments in a special housing unit.

5. Describe the factors that can combine to cause an inmate riot, the stages of a riot, and methods to prevent and control riots.

6. Outline the functions and operations of the three types of emergency teams in a prison.

Introduction

The primary mission of prisons is to create a safe and secure environment, but this must be done in a balanced manner to support the opportunity for inmates to be involved in programs that can help them in their rehabilitation and reentry to the community. We describe the issue of custody in this chapter, and then turn to prison treatment in Chapter 14. To create a safe and secure environment, *custody*, the activities within a prison that control inmate behavior and maintain order, must be accomplished in a way that reduces the likelihood of escape or violence. Prisons must be secure to prevent escapes and must be safe, so that inmates and staff can live and work in the prison without constant fear of assault and injury.

The task of controlling behavior and maintaining order envisions a picture of total and absolute control by correctional officers and an environment in which inmate rights and individual characteristics must be secondary to security. This is not the reality; however, as the challenge for prison management is to prudently balance custody and security with treatment and rehabilitation. In this chapter, the activities prison officials undertake to create a safe and secure environment are described. For prisons to be safe and secure there must be sufficient physical security, consistent implementation of security practices, methods to control behavior and prevent inmates from possessing dangerous items, and preparation to reduce the likelihood of or to respond to inmate unrest. Following are descriptions of how this is done in a modern and professional prison.

Security and Custody within a Prison

What are security and custody within a prison? Most experts would suggest that they include all the activities that provide for the overall control of inmate behavior, in a way that reduces the likelihood of escape or violence. The most immediate goal of prison operators is to have a safe and secure prison. A safe prison is one in which staff and inmates are relatively safe from assaults or other violent acts. A secure prison is one in which inmates are prevented from escaping and unable to get to prohibited areas of the prison.

The question of how to maintain security and custody within a prison is one that many people think should be very simple, because they perceive that inmates are locked in cells most of the time; people believe that when inmates are out of the cells, they are under the close supervision of many correctional staff members. Yet those who work inside correctional institutions recognize that maintaining security and custody is very complicated and requires an integration of several functions and activities within a prison. In reality, inmates are in their cells only a few hours a day and, at other times, they actively participate in work, programs, and leisure activities. Seiter writes:

> There are no simple solutions to creating a safe and secure environment.... Inmates are serving longer sentences, often have little hope for a quick release, and may see few incentives for positive behavior. Long sentences can also create frustration and a sense of bitterness and unfair treatment on the part of inmates toward staff. The increasing percent of the inmate population that are youthful, impulsive and gang affiliated heightens the likelihood of violence.... Maintaining a safe and secure prison involves the integration of several elements within the prison.[1]

The following eight types of activities combine to contribute to the security and custody functions within a prison and are more fully described in this book:

1. *Effective inmate classification systems.* The goal of an inmate classification system is to separate offenders according to risk of violence and escape, and to match offender needs with correctional resources. The physical security of a prison should be designed to match these risks of violence and escape.

2. *Physical security within a prison.* Prisons are categorized as minimum-, medium-, or maximum-security in terms of the physical security provided, including the type of fences and perimeter security, housing, and construction material used. Physical security also includes the use of modern technology and physical barriers to keep inmates in or out of certain locations within the prison. Although many observers tend to over-rely on physical security, more than that is required to have a safe and secure prison, as prison design and technology "cannot substitute for well-trained staff and good security practices."[2]

3. *Consistently implemented security policies and procedures.* The importance of professionally developed and consistently implemented policies and procedures for controlling inmate behavior was noted previously. The performance of sound security practices is one of the most critical elements in accomplishing security and custody within a prison.

4. *Control of inmate movement and accountability.* Inmates are allowed to move from one prison location to another for much of the normal day. Yet these movements must be established in a manner that allows staff to maintain inmate accountability at any time during the day.

5. *Control of contraband items.* There are several items that inmates are not allowed to possess (called contraband), including items that can assist in an escape, are dangerous, can sabotage or subvert prison physical security, or create an unhealthy or unsanitary condition. Custody practices call for thorough procedures to keep such items from falling into inmate hands.

Physical security, such as a secure perimeter fence with razor ribbon, is one of the many elements essential to a safe and secure prison. Photo by Richard P. Seiter.

6. *Implementation of an effective inmate disciplinary system.* Inmates must be told what behaviors are not allowed within a prison and must be punished and held accountable if they commit these acts. An inmate disciplinary system is therefore an important tool for controlling inmate behavior and effecting prison custody and security.

7. *Methods to separate unruly inmates or inmates at risk.* Prisons use special housing units (SHUs) to separate inmates who are being investigated for misconduct, are at risk of being assaulted, or are being punished for violating prison rules. The operation of SHUs is a key activity in the security and custody function within a prison.

8. *Control and reduction of the likelihood of a prison riot or disturbance.* The greatest fear within a prison is that inmates (who outnumber staff members by perhaps twenty to one at any time) will stop following prison policy and rules, act out in a violent manner, injure prison staff, or take over control of the prison. Prison administrators go to great lengths to understand the causes of prison unrest, take action to reduce the likelihood of riots, and prepare to respond to inmate disturbance quickly and efficiently to reduce the potential of serious injury to staff or inmates and the destruction of the prison or government property.

Security and Custody Functions

Many activities are critical security and custody functions within a prison and eight of these have been listed. Four were described earlier in this book, and inmate accountability, control of contraband, management of SHUs, and prevention of and preparation to respond to inmate unrest and prison riots are presented below. Security and custody functions are often tedious and time consuming, yet must be accomplished in a thorough and conscientious fashion in order not to undermine the overall goal of creating a safe and secure prison environment. The following describe the technical and procedural aspects of custody and security within a prison. These are important to understand the underlying activities that go on within a prison. Yet the other aspects described in prior chapters (professional staff, positive staff and inmate communications, security classification, and state of the art policies) as well as the provision of treatment programs described in Chapter 14 are equally important in creating an overall safe and secure prison environment. We begin this chapter with a description of the importance of staff communications and the tone that is set within a prison and how it contributes to security and custody.

Inmate accountability is a principal component of a prison custody operation. Even though physical barriers such as fences, walls, and cells keep inmates in a specific location, the procedures used to account for them during the many hours a day they are out of their cells and involved in work or other programs are perhaps even more important in preventing escapes and maintaining prison order. A prison cannot be safely managed without control of contraband or items that can assist in an escape or be used as dangerous weapons. Prison staff sometimes must separate inmates, either as punishment or for their protection, in SHUs (sometimes thought of as a jail within the prison). And correctional officials can never forget the potential danger that can result from inmates deciding to riot or take control of a prison, and its staff, and can never waver in their efforts to prevent such incidents and prepare in case they do occur.

Staff and Setting the Tone

In Chapter 10, there is a section on the role of staff in a prison. This section goes further in linking staff communications and setting the tone in a prison with the improvement in security and reducing the likelihood of inmate unrest or even disturbances. It is critical to have activities and procedures (such as inmate counts and searching for contraband) that contribute to custody and security, and these must be performed consistently and thoroughly. However, the "manner" in which they are carried out and the tone that is set in a prison can improve or undermine safety and security. Staff have to be trained in and utilize good interpersonal communication skills. They have to treat inmates with courtesy and respect. And they have to understand that you do not rule prisons by authority and threats, but by gaining compliance through policy and communications.

In the "An Interview With" box, former Director George Lombardi of the Missouri Department of Corrections is excellent in describing the importance of these things. He notes how they do checks and audits to insure policy and procedures are carried out. But more importantly, he describes how critical positive staff communications with inmates as well as a way for inmates to air their grievances are to creating a culture with reduced tension and less acting out by inmates. And it is very interesting that Missouri uses restorative justice (requiring inmates to participate in activities to "make right" or "give back" to their communities for their criminal actions). The goal is to give inmates compassion through altruism. All of these things set a tone that makes the Missouri prisons safer and more secure places for inmates to live and for staff to work.

An Interview With...

A Director of Corrections

George Lombardi. Photo courtesy of Tim Bommel, MO House of Representatives Photographer.

George Lombardi was the Director of the Missouri Department of Corrections from 2009 to 2016. He was responsible for twenty adult prisons, seven community supervision centers, two community release centers, and fifty-four parole offices across the state. This included approximately 11,500 staff, 75,000 probationers and parolees, and 30,000 inmates. He is a forty-year veteran of the department, having started as a staff psychologist at the Missouri State Penitentiary in Jefferson City. He quickly rose through the ranks and at age twenty-nine was named Warden at the State Correctional Pre-Release Center in Tifton, Missouri. Prior to becoming director in 2009, he also served as Division Director for Adult Institutions for eighteen years.

Question: Director Lombardi, thank you for taking the time to discuss custody and security in prisons. In your mind, what is the definition of a safe and secure prison?

Director Lombardi: A safe and secure prison is one in which everyone in the facility has a purpose and are busy carrying out that purpose. This includes both staff and inmates. Inmates may be involved in programs or simply participating in recreational activities. Prisons require a lot of communications—up and down, staff to inmates, and inmates to staff. It is very important for staff to, as much as possible, have an understanding of inmate population, and this needs to be available to everyone on every shift. In this way, you limit the potential for surprise and nefarious activity. When communications is extensive, it creates a foundation for which inmate programs and rehabilitation can occur. Prisons have to have organization; everyone has to be organized and understand where they are supposed to be at all times. Obviously, staff must have good training and be as knowledgeable as they can be about custodial policy and procedure as well as human behavior. When I go into a prison and I see staff and inmates busy with a purpose, I know we have the beginning of a safe and secure environment.

Question: As a correctional administrator, what are the two or three prison custody/security situations that most worry you?

Director Lombardi: I think one of the major things I worry about is whether our staff are engaged and are communicating with inmates. This has to occur on all shifts. Our top-level administrators need to make contact on all shifts, on weekends, and at unexpected times. They need to listen, observe, ask questions, and try to determine that the environment is good. I also worry about the quality of our personnel—it only takes one staff member to succumb to temptation, bring in drugs or other contraband, and undermine security. An unethical staff member can turn your facility into chaos. And because as we all know in this business, perception is even stronger than reality (for instance, if inmates perceive the food is bad), we have to go beyond doing things well and right, and also help shape perceptions. Inmates will react to perception even if it is not reality. Inmates need to have the perception that they are treated fairly, and it is really critical that there is a credible avenue to bring their complaints forward to consideration. So I worry about the perception of how inmates believe they are being treated.

Question: What are the types of approaches that can be taken to respond to these concerns?

Director Lombardi: Well, obviously, you need to have your staff adopt the underlying philosophy you espouse—in this case that offenders are treated fairly, and have credible and reasonable avenues to have their complaints heard. You have to have a system of checks and balances to be sure leadership is in touch with line staff and inmates on all shifts. At one time, we required our facility administrators to record those types of contacts, and that they were there on evening shift, or on a Saturday night. This emphasis took hold, and we no longer require the documentation, as that culture is now a part of what we do. When I go into a housing unit, I want to see that the relationship between staff and offenders is open and that they are reasonably polite and respectful. This should be between staff and inmates and inmates and staff. Our goal is for staff to understand that effective communications in this manner is the key to good security. Counter to that, if they communicate in a harsh and abrupt manner, it undermines good security. In this regard, training is really important; as is getting your stars (people who know and understand that) to be mentors to those new to the job. Mentoring and modeling appropriate behavior is really important. Unfortunately, some people that are harsh think they have to be that way to establish their reputation with inmates, but that is so misguided. Being polite—yet firm and do your job—is very important to setting a tone of respect and order. How you treat people impacts the way they treat you back. That is not only a nice thing it is also a necessary thing. We all know that the prison environment is a very artificial one; small things are magnified and become much bigger and seemingly important than what they are. In prisons, many people are overly sensitive, and react to triggers that may not cause any reaction if they were not in the prison setting.

Question: How do you measure the quality of a prison's custody and security record?

Director Lombardi: We do this in three key ways. First, we audit the prison environments. We have a cadre of senior staff to go into each prison and do an audit of the culture and environment. From their experience and understanding of the vision we have for our facilities, they can present to the facility leadership needs for improvement in operations or in training for staff. Second, we do major facility shakedowns either random or after serious events (a stabbing or staff assault) in the prisons. The results of the shakedowns (finding drugs, weapons, or other contraband) tell us how the facility is doing on a day to day basis. Finally, we review the grievances from inmates to see if there are any trends (certain shifts, locations within the prison, staff) that are the source of grievances and can also be targeted for improvement or training.

Question: How is your department organized (staffing or function) to prevent incidents occurring at prisons?

Director Lombardi: We have four division directors (Probation and Parole, Human Services, Rehabilitative Services, and Adult Institutions). Under Adult Institutions, there are three deputy directors that split up the twenty prisons. All three of these people were wardens prior to this job. This helps a lot, as they have the time to get out to the prisons and work with wardens to identify weakness and find solutions. And we also have a Security Chief as well. He, along with the CERT (Correctional Emergency Response Teams) team commanders, does audits and the shakedowns. Every facility has a cadre of CERT members. This department-wide cadre of CERT members can respond to emergencies in other facilities, and we put together a team to complement the CERT members at any one facility when we do the facility shakedowns.

One of things I changed when I became director was to take emergency response issue directly into this office. I wanted to ensure that we were conducting practice exercises on a regular basis to simulate situations (escape, disturbances, Hazmat problems, or major communicable diseases) and be prepared to react to them. The Security Chief and CERT commanders create scenarios that are realistic. We do these at least once a year in each facility, and we include our community partners—the highway patrol, local hospitals, and local law enforcement. From practicing those exercises, we can learn a great deal, and discover where your breakdowns are in knowledge and practice.

As I mentioned, a critical area for us in prevention is the grievance area. We have a cadre of Central Office grievance responders that review wardens' responses to inmate grievances. If they are not satisfied that we responded fully and appropriately, they are empowered to send it back to have it redone. We consider this very serious and very important. We did not always do this well, but set out to improve it. And we went from very bad to very good. When the U.S. Department

(Continued)

of Justice started certifying prison grievance systems, we were the only state that had all prisons certified. Our inmate litigation has dropped dramatically over the years. But more importantly, if inmates believe the grievance process is credible, it helps the safety and security of the facility.

We take this one step further. We have a citizens' advisory committee for the department made up of eight to ten non-corrections people. They meet at a prison every month, so they see all of our prisons regularly. The warden and top staff do a briefing for them, and they tour the prison. And we also give committee members certain types of grievances to look at to see how we respond to them. This also keeps the process credible.

Question: Are there any other things you do to help maintain a safe and secure environment in the prisons?

Director Lombardi: Yes, one thing that is really important and that is part of the core philosophy of what we do is restorative justice. We believe all prisoners have to do something to make things for people in need in the community. This is a way for them to, in some small way, give back for their transgressions to the community. I believe that a quality that is missing among offenders is empathy for others. Either they never had it or it was suppressed because of a childhood trauma. Anything we can do to inculcate compassion in offenders makes for a healthier prison environment and makes them better people when they walk out of the prison door. Altruism makes a difference in so many ways.

As examples, we have dog programs in nineteen of our twenty prisons. The inmates train dogs to be companions for families. We received our first dog from a dog shelter on February 1, 2010, and inmates have now trained and had 2,807 dogs adopted. This program has a tremendous impact on the inmate handlers and the facilities. And it has helped in the relationship between offenders and staff, as prison staff has adopted more than half of the dogs. This program helps inmates feel useful, and they will often articulate that it is the first time they have done anything positive in their lives. An

inmate dog handler recently told me, "You know, when I get up in morning and dog looks me in eye and I know I have to take care of him; I am pretty sure that's how my six year old looked at me. But I was always too drunk to see it."

Our prisons also have gardens; offenders have produced 180 tons of produce that is given to over eighty pantries across the state. We also have a program called Kids Smart, to make supplies and items that can be used in school (like flash cards, coloring books, or learning blocks). Kids Smart is a place where teachers in poor school districts—which can't even afford the basics for kids—can go into the place and take school supplies off shelves. Our offenders have made products valued at over $500,000 over the past ten years. We had major tornados come through Missouri a few years ago. For the residents of Joplin after the tornado, we made quilts, blankets, and cool ties to put around their necks in hot weather. We grew and gave 150 trees to St. Joe when the tornado blew away all the trees in that town. Every facility is involved in something. And a critical part of the program is that whenever we give something to an entity, we require that the entity write a letter telling how it was used so the inmates can understand the impact they had. This adds to their altruism and compassion. This has made a real difference in attitude, hearts, and change in offenders.

Question: Recognizing the importance of professional staff, what do you do to hire and train good correctional officers and other entry-level staff?

Director Lombardi: Obviously, have recruitment done by both our HR department and uniform staff accompanies them. We go out and speak at different events. The recruitment process is tough, we are primarily rural but do have some urban facilities. Missouri is one of the lowest paid states for our correctional officers. But in the rural areas, our pay is competitive and with our benefits, we are often the best job available. But it is much more difficult in the urban areas. Most of our recruiting still is by word of mouth from our current staff. Our people tell others it is a good place to work and they recruit the type of people they want to work with.[4]

Gaining Compliance of Inmates

The most important skill for correctional officers to learn is how to gain compliance from inmates without having to resort to threats, coercion, or taking disciplinary action and without risking the eruption of violence from an inmate refusing to abide by the orders of an officer. It is not easy to gain compliance from inmates already in prison, many of whom rebel against all authority and are serving long sentences with very little to lose. The overall prison disciplinary system creates the backdrop for gaining compliance by listing expected behavior and the penalties for failure to follow prison rules. Inmate classification systems also provide inmates who behave the opportunity to move to less secure prisons with more privileges for inmates. Inmates are aware of these incentives and disincentives and understand that failing to follow orders of staff can result in punishment.

Correctional officers gain inmates' compliance through communication rather than threats and intimidation.
Photo by Richard P. Seiter.

Therefore, staff members do not have to *individually* take responsibility for making inmates follow rules. Correctional officers know they will win any war of wills, because an inmate who continues to refuse to comply with rules or a direct order from staff will be punished through the inmate disciplinary system. This allows correctional officers to be relaxed and confident in dealing with inmates. Effective officers use interpersonal communication skills to simply treat inmates as individuals, or as a work supervisor would treat an employee. Inmates know what they are to do and what the rules of a prison are, and reminding them of their responsibilities usually results in proper behavior.

The "A Case Study" box illustrates a good example of the dos and don'ts of gaining compliance.

Inmate Accountability

In the classic and still accurate publication, Henderson and colleagues define **inmate accountability** as "the staff's ability to locate and identify inmates at any point in time ... the very heart of institution security, from minimum-security camps to maximum-security penitentiaries."[3] It would be simple to know where inmates are at any time if they were always locked in their cells or dormitories. However, inmates are out of their cells almost eighteen hours a day, and therefore policies and procedures must exist to identify where inmates should be, to control their movement, to supervise them to the greatest extent possible, and to have a system of "counting" them to ensure that they are all where they are supposed to be. The following are key components of inmate accountability policies and procedures:

inmate accountability
the staff's ability to locate and identify inmates at any point in time within a prison

- Inmates are assigned to work and programs on a daily basis. These assignments place them under the supervision of staff responsible for that program or work activity.

A Case Study

Gaining Compliance

A new, young, and aggressive correctional officer (Robert Dole) at a high-security prison wants to establish himself as tough and unwilling to take anything from inmates. He is assigned as a yard officer, and as such watches inmates move across the prison compound from one building to another. As a part of his duties, Dole is to randomly pat-search inmates (similar to frisking by the police). With a pat search, officers move their hands over inmates' bodies to search for concealed weapons, drugs, or other contraband under their clothing. One day, Dole sees an inmate (Jones) he wants to pat-search, he points at Jones and calls out, "Hey, you come over here," and tells him, "Hold your arms out for a pat search," in a brusque and terse manner. When finished and finding nothing prohibited, he orders the inmate, "Ok, keep moving."

Jones realizes he will be searched from time to time, but doesn't like the attitude of disrespect he believes that Dole presented. He is angry about it, and when he arrives at his work area, he is confronted by his work supervisor who wants to discuss his recent poor performance with him. Jones is not a very responsible or mature person and reluctantly begins the conversation with his supervisor. When the supervisor asks why he did not complete a task assigned the previous day, Jones angrily responds, "You guys are just looking for me to screw up, and this is a bunch of bullshit." The supervisor tries to calm him down, but Jones just seems to get madder, and starts yelling at the supervisor. Soon, other correctional staff members have to intervene, and while trying to move Jones away, Jones strikes one of them. He is forced to the ground by staff, handcuffed, and taken to the special housing unit.

This incident can happen almost anytime with Jones because of his lack of maturity and responsibility. However, when correctional officer Peter Smith is working as the yard officer, there are fewer such problems. Smith has been working at the prison for a few years and has become comfortable in gaining compliance through courtesy and respect. Smith handles pat searches as follows. When Jones approaches, and Smith decides to pat him down, he looks at Jones and says, "Mr. Jones, could you step over here please, I need to pat you down." When Smith finishes the search without discovering anything, he says, "That's it, Mr. Jones, thank you." Jones is not thrilled with being searched, but leaves feeling that Smith respects him through his courtesy. Both Dole and Smith accomplish their pat-down tasks, yet both create an outcome (Dole's bad, and Smith's good) as a result of how they did their job.

- There is a system of inmate movement from one location to another within the prison that reduces the likelihood that inmates can go to other than their assigned location.
- Staff members provide both casual and direct inmate supervision when inmates are not in their housing units.
- There are counts of inmates at regular and random times to ensure that they are where they are supposed to be within the prison.

Program and Work Assignments

Prison work and program assignments not only aid in inmate rehabilitation, but are also critical security functions in that they keep inmates active, limit time inmates might use to plan an escape or violation of rules, and place inmates under the direct supervision of staff. For example, inmates assigned to participate in an education program are assigned to the classroom of a specific teacher, who checks inmates in as class begins and is responsible for the inmates until the end of the assignment. This contributes to security and custody, because inmates are assigned to a correctional staff member who maintains responsibility for them, supervises them, and knows where they are during that time.

Prison work and program assignments are also an important part of the normal routine of the prison day. The "A Case Study" box illustrates how a routine of work and programs contributes to inmate accountability.

A Case Study

The Daily Routine

The daily routine for a prison is an important part of inmate accountability and contributes greatly to the overall security of a prison. A well understood routine by both staff and inmates is critical. The day begins early and continues late; prison officials desire to have scheduled activities during which inmates are under the direct supervision of staff for as many hours a day as possible. A typical prison workday is presented here.

On workdays, inmates awake between 5:30 A.M. and 6:00 A.M. and leave their cells at 6:00 A.M. to shower and prepare for the workday. They are allowed to go to the dining hall for breakfast from 6:30 to 7:00 and must return to their housing unit by 7:15 A.M. There is a **work call** at 7:30 A.M., and inmates move to their assigned jobs or programs. They are at their assigned location until 10:30, when they are to return to their housing unit, to be released to move to the dining hall for lunch from 11:00 until 12:00 noon.

After lunch, there is an afternoon work call at 12:30 P.M., and inmates remain at their assignments until 3:30. They then return to the housing unit, have a formal "count," and then go to the dining hall for dinner. After dinner, there are evening programs and leisure activities until 8:30, when inmates return to the housing unit and are locked in. They usually have time in the unit until approximately 11:30 P.M., when they are locked in their cells until let out the next morning. The work-and-program routine serves as the foundation for inmate accountability. Both staff and inmates know the schedule and adhere to it. Inmates know and move to where they are to be, and prison staff members know the inmates who are assigned to them and for whom they are responsible. Staff members then directly supervise those inmates and maintain their accountability during the six to eight hours per day of their assignment.

Inmate Movements

As illustrated in the case study, inmates move throughout the prison during the day and evening. How they move and the way these movements are controlled and supervised are another essential element of inmate accountability. Many people imagine that inmates move individually in a prison, with at least one staff person walking with them from one point to another. However, this is not accurate, and inmates usually move in large groups from their housing units to work, meals, or education or recreation programs. To maintain inmate accountability during these mass movements, prisons use a controlled system for inmate moves.

Controlled movement is the procedure used by prisons to maintain accountability for inmates as they move throughout the prison. The most common form of controlled movement is to schedule inmates to move from one point to another at a specific time, according to the daily routine and schedule. For example, at the 7:30 A.M. work call, a controlled movement begins with the unlocking of doors to the housing units and program and work areas. The staff members who unlock the doors stand by the doors and watch inmates exit and enter. Inmates usually have a short time (ten minutes) to move from one location to another. After the ten minutes, inmates are expected to have reached their designated destination, and the doors are all relocked. Inmates who are not in their required location are subject to disciplinary action.

Controlled movement contributes to inmate accountability in that it limits the time in which inmates have freedom to move or walk around the prison and prevents them from standing and communicating with other inmates to organize gang activities or pass information. Efficient controlled movement gives staff both real and perceived control over inmates; it not only maintains accountability, but also has specific policies and procedures to form the habit of inmate compliance with prison rules.

Even with ideal schedules and routines, there are times other than during mass movements when inmates must move individually. They may have a visit from a

work call
the time when inmates move to their assigned jobs or programs assignments

controlled movement
the procedure used by prisons to maintain accountability for inmates as they move throughout the prison

Inmates are out of their cells most of the day and move across the prison compound using a variety of controlled movement methods. Courtesy of CoreCivic.

family member, may have an appointment with the prison doctor or psychologist, or may be required to meet with a staff member who is not their work or program supervisor. These individual movements are usually handled either through the use of a *call out* or a *pass system*. With the **call out**, inmates are scheduled for their appointments at least a day in advance. A schedule of all the appointments and required moves for the day is prepared and distributed to staff, naming the inmate, the time, and the beginning and ending points of the move. Supervising staff members allow inmates to move according to the call-out schedule.

Instead of, or sometimes in addition to, a call-out system, some prisons use a pass system for individual inmate movement. A prison **pass system** is similar to that used in many high schools; an inmate is issued a pass by the work or program supervisor to go to the scheduled appointment. The pass includes a place for staff members to write the time the inmate leaves their supervision and for receiving staff members to write the time the inmate arrives and leaves the appointment. Upon the inmate's return to the work or program supervisor, the time of return is also written on the pass. Staff members are aware of the time it takes to move from one area of the prison to another and recognize any deviation from the expected time to move. If inmates take longer than they should during the move, they are subject to disciplinary action. During the time inmates are walking from one location to another, staff members who see them will often ask to see their pass and double-check that the inmate is in possession of a pass and is moving toward the intended destination. Through the use of controlled mass movements and either a call-out or pass system for individual movement, staff members control inmate movement within the prison without having to escort them.

Casual and Direct Inmate Supervision

Casual and direct supervision of inmates by staff is another critical component of inmate accountability. Work and program supervisors are responsible for inmates during the times of their assignment, and correctional officers are responsible for

call out

a schedule of all the appointments and required moves for a day, including the name and expected times of the moves

pass system

a form of inmate movement in which an inmate is issued a pass by the work or program supervisor to go to a scheduled appointment inmates assigned to areas that they supervise. This supervision is *direct* in that assigned staff can directly see and watch inmates and their activities. In addition to direct supervision, prisons incorporate an approach that aids in security without adding staff or increasing tension. Inmate accountability is also enhanced through *casual* supervision, or supervision by staff members who are not responsible for inmates, but still have the opportunity to see their movements or activities. All prison staff members constantly watch inmates and look for suspicious behavior. Staff members who are walking across the prison compound see inmate movements, and even though they are not directly responsible, they monitor inmate behavior for anything unusual. Staff members working in their offices look out windows and also monitor inmates' movements and activities.

Prison classrooms, staff offices, and program areas often have several large windows so that casual supervision can occur. Photo by Richard P. Seiter.

Modern prison design can aid in the casual supervision of inmates. For example, in the education areas within prisons, education administrators and teachers often have offices with windows with a view into the central compound of the prison and can see inmates move from one area to another. They also have windows between their offices and adjacent classrooms or library areas, so they can casually monitor inmates in those locations and see if any other staff members are having trouble with an inmate. Classrooms have large windows into the corridor, into adjacent classrooms, and on the outside of the building. Not only can teachers see inmates outside their classrooms, but other staff members can also see them and their interactions with inmates in their classrooms. These easy viewing situations provide additional supervision and security and keep staff from feeling isolated, insecure, and unprotected.

Inmate Counts

Another element of inmate accountability is the actual counting of inmates at various locations and times. Counts are done to determine that all inmates are where they should be and that no inmates either are out of bounds (in an unauthorized location) or have escaped. A series of daily counts reduces the amount of time an inmate may be unaccounted for, reducing the opportunity to escape (or quickly finding out if an escape has occurred) or to plan any other act that threatens the secure and orderly operation of a prison. Prisons use three different types of counts: regular, census, and random. **Regular counts** consist of the scheduled counting of inmates in their housing units to ensure that they are in the prison and have not escaped. At these counts, inmates must be in their cell or on their beds, and correctional officers walk by and count how many are in the housing unit. They then call in the number to a central location, at which staff members add up all the counts to be sure that they have the correct number of inmates.

regular counts
the scheduled counting of inmates in their housing units to ensure that they are in the prison and have not escaped

American Correctional Association standards require a minimum of one count per eight-hour correctional shift; however, most agencies have at least five scheduled counts during a twenty-four-hour period. With these many counts, inmates are quickly discovered missing if they have escaped or are trying to escape. Prison

Correctional officers perform counts in prison housing units by going to every cell door and counting the number of inmates to be sure that all are accounted for. Photo by Richard P. Seiter.

regular counts usually occur at midnight, at 3:00 A.M. (when inmates are asleep in their cells), before work call at approximately 7:00 A.M., after return from work for the day (approximately 4:00 P.M.), and when inmates are required to return to their housing units after evening programs or recreation (approximately 9:00 P.M.). The 4:00 P.M. count is often a **stand-up count**, the most formal count of the day, at which inmates must stand at their cell door or by their dormitory bed to be counted and matched to the number of and identification of inmates assigned to each housing area.

A second type of count is a **census count**, a less formal count conducted at program and work assignments by the staff responsible for supervising inmates. They are usually held at the beginning and end of each work period to ensure that the work and program details have the correct number of assigned inmates. A third type of count is a **random count**. Random counts are done at any time and wherever inmates are when the random count is called. The warden or a high-ranking prison official will determine that a random count is needed (just to keep everyone honest) and put out an order for all inmate movement to cease, for all doors to be locked, and for all inmates to be counted where they are at the time. Since inmates know when the regular and census counts are held, random counts keep inmates from planning to leave their assigned area right after a count and give themselves the maximum expected time between regular and census counts.

stand-up count

the most formal count of the day, at which inmates must stand at their cell door or by their dormitory bed to be counted and matched to the number of inmates assigned to each housing area

census counts

a less formal count conducted at program and work assignments by the staff responsible for supervising inmates

random counts

counts done at any time, freezing inmates at whatever location they are in when the random count is called

contraband

any item that inmates are not allowed to possess, including items that can assist in an escape, are dangerous, can undermine prison physical security, or are nuisance items

Control of Contraband

A second component of prison custody and security is to control contraband. **Contraband** is defined simply as any item that inmates are not allowed to possess and can include items that can assist in an escape (ladders or ropes), are dangerous (weapons or drugs), can sabotage or subvert prison physical security (wire cutters that can cut a security fence), or are nuisance items that create unhealthy or unsanitary conditions (unsealed food that can spoil in an inmate cell). Since contraband undermines the safe and secure operation of a prison, custody and security staff members have many specific policies and spend considerable time implementing them to avoid possession of contraband by inmates.

Prisons have policies clearly identifying contraband items, or the limits on the number of items that inmates are allowed to have. Contraband policies also categorize contraband by risk, with the risk levels requiring different methods for storage and use. For example, tools are classified by their risk to prison security. Class A tools are those that can be a weapon, aid in escape, or undermine the security of a prison and include items such as files, knives, saw blades, ladders, ropes, extension cords, lift devices, and grinders. Class A tools are only to be used under the direct supervision of staff and must be placed in a secure storage area when not in use. Class B tools are less risky, and include light pliers, short power cords, or other hand tools that are not likely to be used as a weapon or aid in an escape. They may be stored and used by inmates under less stringent conditions, but must still be controlled and accounted for.[5]

Contraband items may end up in possession of inmates in at least four ways. First, inmates may receive prohibited items hidden in mail or packages. Prisons allow inmates to send and receive letters; sometimes inmates may receive packages with reading material or other allowable items. To keep small items such as drugs from being mailed into a prison, inmate mail is not read, but is opened and searched for contraband items. Hardback books and magazines (in which it is easy to hide drugs or other small contraband) may be purchased and delivered only directly from the publisher, thereby reducing the opportunity for a friend or family member to hide contraband in these publications.

Class A tools such as ladders are a serious security risk in prisons and therefore are locked so that inmates cannot take them to use as an aid in escape. Photo by Richard P. Seiter.

Second, inmate visitors may bring contraband items into the prison and give them to an inmate. Visiting by friends and family is important to maintain inmates' community ties and helps in their successful reintegration upon release. Visiting rooms are designed to allow as relaxed as possible contact and conversation between inmates and their visitors. Also, if there is no reasonable suspicion, visitors may not be searched. Visitors pass through a metal detector upon entry to the prison, and they are permitted to take only limited personal items into the visiting room, such as money and unopened packages of cigarettes. However, in the normal visiting setting, it is difficult to control the introduction of contraband such as drugs. During the visit, correctional staff members monitor the visiting room and the conduct of inmates and visitors. Unfortunately, it is unlikely that staff (unless tipped off by another inmate) will notice passing of small contraband between a visitor and inmate. The best protection against entry of contraband through the visiting room is a thorough search of inmates after the visit and before they return to the general area of the prison. As they leave their visit, inmates are strip-searched, and when all visiting ends for the day, the visiting room is thoroughly searched before any more inmates enter the area.

Third, inmates may gain possession of contraband that is available in the prison, but should not be in possession of inmates without staff supervision. Inmates often attempt to smuggle items out of the allowed area of supervision. Some seemingly nonthreatening examples of such contraband are those that can cause a health and sanitation problem, such as food that is served in the dining room. Inmates try to obtain extra food, hide it, and take it to their housing units, sell it to others, or keep it for their own use at a later time. More serious examples of such contraband are the Class A tools described previously. Inmate food services workers often must be issued knives to prepare food; inmate maintenance workers may sometimes be issued tools that can cut wires or even bars. Prison contraband control procedures reduce the chance of such dangerous tools or utensils falling in an inmate's possession or being removed from the assigned area.

Class A tools and food service knives are hung on a **shadow board**, a light-colored background with the outline of the tool painted on it. This enables staff to quickly identify a missing tool or knife. When a tool or knife is issued to an inmate, a record of the staff member who issued the tool and the inmate to whom it was given is created. Before the end of the work period, all tools must be

shadow board
a light-colored background with the outline of the tool painted on it, allowing for a missing tool or knife to be quickly noticed

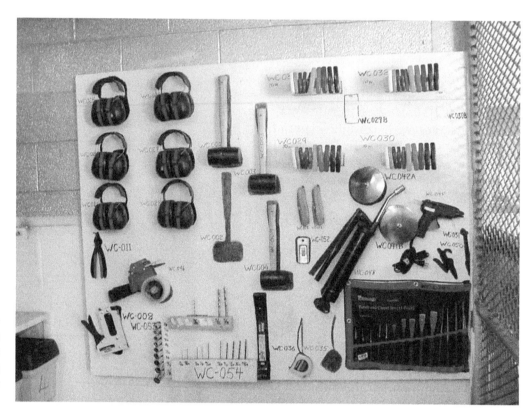

One way to control hazardous tools or knives is to use a shadow board and lock them in a cage so inmates cannot get to them. Photo by Richard P. Seiter.

accounted for and back on the shadow board before inmates may leave the area. And, as inmates are released from a work area that uses such tools or knives, they are searched and, in some situations, must walk through a metal detector.

Finally and unfortunately, unethical staff members may provide contraband items to inmates. Some staff members may do this to make money. Inmates will arrange payment to the staff member by someone in the community if they bring drugs or possibly weapons into the prison. Other naive staff members may do it "to be nice," bringing an inmate only nuisance items such as food or cigarettes that an inmate cannot get in prison. After a staff member has agreed to do this, however, manipulative inmates then threaten to tell prison officials about the staff violation of rules, knowing that the staff member will be punished for violating rules, unless the staff member agrees to bring more serious and dangerous contraband into the prison in exchange for the inmate's silence.

To deter such actions by staff, some prisons search their staff members or require them to walk through metal detectors as they come to work. Since staff members are well aware of these procedures and can easily avoid detection of bringing contraband into a prison, many prisons do not even attempt such searches. Instead, they rely on hiring the right kind of people and treating staff as trusted professionals, while encouraging all staff to share in the responsibility of identifying staff members who may be smuggling items into the prison. Prison training programs for new staff members present the dangers of providing contraband to inmates and how it undermines the safety of all staff. Although these efforts work for most staff members, there is always a staff member who fails to heed the warning and, whether for money or because of poor judgment, is a target for inmates who try to get them to bring contraband into the prison.

A serious problem for prisons has been the use of cell phones by inmates. As cell phones are cheaper and smaller, they are more easily brought into a prison (staff or visitors smuggle them in or they get them mailed in and hidden in other objects), and they are difficult to find and detect. Almost every major correctional jurisdiction has a problem with cell phones smuggled into prisons and detention facilities, with many reporting finding hundreds of contraband cell phones. As example, Florida reported that in searching the cells of two murderers serving life sentences who escaped from prison last fall, they found a cellphone used to help plan the escape. And Florida officials said it was just one of 4,200 cellphones found by correctional staff in the last year.[6] Inmates have been found using cell phones to call elected officials, to plan escapes, to participate in social media and even have Facebook pages, to deal in drugs, and simply to call their family and friends without having to use the prison inmate phone system. Cell phones have been smuggled in by unprofessional staff, been sent in with packages from home, and even bags of them thrown over the perimeter fences to waiting inmates.

Currently, there are four main approaches to keeping cell phones out of prisons. The first is keeping them from coming in through hardening avenues that they get in the prison. The second is using technology to keep inmates from using them. There are systems to detect cell phones when in use, and a technology (managed access) that keeps the cell signal from calling outside of the prison. The third approach is to eliminate the reason inmates have cell phones, that regular phone calls are expensive and inmates are limited in use. The Indiana department of corrections now allows inmates to check out cordless phones for use in their cells, so they can talk as long as they want and in private.[7] And Minnesota reduced the prison phone rates to reduce inmates' desire to have contraband cell phones.[8] And finally, the Federal Communications Commission will not allow prisons to "block" cell phone usage, as the blockage can "leak" beyond the prison walls, and block the legitimate use of cell phones, such as for emergency purposes. Correctional agencies and members of Congress have contacted the FCC and encouraged them to change their position. On October 4, 2017, four U.S. Senators and forty-eight members of Congress signed a letter to the Chair and a Commissioner of the FCC, highlighting the public safety risks of inmate possession of cell phones, and asking the FCC to meet with correctional leaders and come to a collaborative solution.[9] The issue of prevention of inmates using cell phones is far from over.

As noted, contraband can create dangerous situations for staff. Knowing that you can never keep dangerous contraband out of the hands of inmates, correctional agencies often turn to technology to help make prison staff safer. Examples are using body armor to protect staff from stabbings, devises to detect drugs in the mail, and technology to monitor inmate behavior. Corrections has worked with the U.S. Department of Defense to develop the Staff Alarm and Inmate Tracking (SAINT) program to help pinpoint the location and nature of problems such as an assault on an officer within seconds of its occurrence. These systems are a combination of cameras throughout a facility and a duress alarm worn by an officer that can be triggered by the officer or automatically goes off if the officer is knocked down. When triggered, it not only sends an alarm, but also identifies the location on a map of the prison and can direct a pan-and-tilt camera to automatically focus on that spot and begin recording. Technology is also helping prison operations through the improved detection of contraband. Inmates often try to have drugs smuggled into a prison through the mail, by injecting cocaine into the ink of a gel pen, or placing drops of liquid LSD on the envelope glue. A team from the Sandia National Laboratories developed both a hand-portable and a fixed drug detector that can detect trace amounts of drugs and identify them in less than ten seconds.[10] Other technologies develop systems that detect contraband at portals or entries to prisons.[11] And corrections has also been experimenting with body cameras worn by correctional officers.[12] The use of body

Correctional officers regularly frisk search inmates to look for contraband. Courtesy of CoreCivic.

cameras has gotten much more public scrutiny and call for more widespread use after the death of Ferguson Missouri teenager Michael Brown by a policy officer in the summer of 2014.

Prison officials not only take many precautions to prevent contraband from getting into the hands of inmates, but also require regular efforts to search for contraband that an inmate may have acquired. A considerable amount of time every day is devoted to searching areas of the prison or shaking down inmates to find contraband and deter its possession. Correctional officers assigned to housing units have post order requirements to search a certain number of cells every day, and teams of staff may be assigned to an area (such as prison industries or a recreation building) for a complete search. Inmates are randomly selected for shakedowns or frisk searches of their bodies (similar to the standard pat downs performed by police officers on criminal suspects) as they move across the compound. And all inmates leaving work areas where Class A tools are used (food services, maintenance, or industries) are patted down and may walk through a metal detector.

Special Housing Units

special housing unit
a temporary housing assignment for inmates who present a danger to the security of the prison, need protection from other inmates, or are being punished for violating prison rules

A critical security and custody function is to be able to separate certain inmates from the rest of the general inmate population, either for their protection, as punishment, during an investigation, or because they are a threat to the orderly operation of the prison. For these situations, prisons have a **special housing unit** (SHU), similar to the operation of a jail in the community. An SHU is a temporary housing assignment for inmates who present a danger to the security of the prison, need protection from other inmates, or are being punished for violating prison rules. A stay in the SHU can be only a few days or up to a few months. Inmates who need longer separation from a prison's inmate population are either transferred to another prison or placed in a supermax facility. While an SHU is similar in design and operations, it is not the same as a supermax prison described in Chapter 9. Supermax prisons are for inmates determined so violent and predatory;

they cannot remain in a regular prison. An SHU is a temporary placement in a regular prison that can be very short in nature, and for investigative or inmate protection reasons, as well as for punishment and control.

There are two general categories of assignments to the SHU. The first category is **administrative detention** (AD), a "non-punitive confinement used to house inmates whose continued presence in the general population may pose a serious threat to life, property, self, staff, or other inmates, or to the security or orderly running of the institution."[13] Inmates may be placed in AD if they are charged with violating a serious rule in the prison, and allowing them to remain in the general prison population could undermine security or for their own safety. For a minor charge of violating a prison rule, such as the possession of nuisance contraband, inmates remain in the general population pending a disciplinary hearing. However, for more serious violations, such as fighting or possession of a weapon, they are held in AD until the hearing and a determination of guilt and decision regarding punishment.

Inmates may also be placed in AD for their own safety. Inmates who are being threatened or believe they are at risk of being assaulted often notify staff and seek protection, for example, if the inmate has a co-defendant in the prison against whom he or she testified or if the inmate is being pressured to participate in homosexual activity or to have a visitor bring drugs into the prison. In these situations, the inmate is placed in AD, an investigation is completed, and officials decide whether to transfer the inmate to another prison. There is no predetermined time to hold inmates in AD; they remain until the investigation is complete and appropriate action is taken. The "You Make the Decision" box at the end of the chapter illustrates the difficult decision prison staff members have to make regarding inmates potentially at risk in a prison.

The second category of SHU placement is **disciplinary segregation** (DS), a status of punishment after a finding of guilt for a serious prison rule violation. DS is for a set amount of time established by the person or committee that considers the violation. In the Bureau of Prisons disciplinary policy, infractions of greatest severity can result in DS of up to sixty days, infractions of high severity can result in up to thirty days, and those of moderate severity can result in up to fifteen days.[14] Once inmates complete their DS time, they are returned to the general population, unless the disciplinary sanction also included a transfer to another prison.

The SHU is a separate building within a prison, usually located in such a way that inmates in the SHU cannot communicate with general-population inmates. It is physically very secure; cells have metal doors and metal furnishings. Furnishings include a stainless steel toilet and sink and a bed and writing table secured to the floor or walls. Outside but adjacent to the SHU is a small, fenced recreation area in which inmates are allowed to exercise between five and ten hours per week. Operating procedures for the SHU are similar for both statuses. Inmates come out of their cells only when handcuffed and escorted by staff. Meals are brought to each cell. Medical and program (education or religious) staff members visit inmates in the SHU, as all services are brought to the unit. SHU inmates do have access to correspondence, limited reading material, and visiting privileges.

The inside of a cell in the SHU has minimal comforts, and inmates do not like placement there and separation from the rest of the inmate population.
Photo by Richard P. Seiter.

administrative detention
a nonpunitive confinement in SHU used to house inmates whose continued presence in the general population may pose a serious threat to the security or orderly running of the prison

disciplinary segregation
a punitive assignment in SHU after a finding of guilt for a serious prison rule violation; disciplinary segregation is for a set amount of time established by the authorized hearing official

Inmate Riots and Disturbances

The most feared event at a prison is an inmate riot or disturbance. No matter how well staff members follow policy or do their jobs, emergency situations such as riots, escapes, hostage taking, and nonviolent food or work strikes can occur. Therefore, prison officials implement security and custody procedures in prisons to reduce the likelihood of such emergencies and to be prepared if emergencies do occur. Preparation includes developing contingency plans, training staff in their proper response, and creating and training special teams for hostage negotiations and responding to a disturbance.

Inmate disturbances have a devastating impact on a prison, the staff, and even the inmates. The last fifty years have seen several serious riots that received national attention, from the 1971 riot at Attica to a 2009 riot in California.[15] And every year, there are several disturbances that result in deaths of inmates or staff. In September 2017, one inmate was killed and several others injured when a riot broke out in a California prison near San Luis Obispo.[16] The Attica, New York, riot captured the interest of the U.S. citizens, and was one of the first in which a look into prisons and the issues on the inside became public.[17] Tensions had been building at Attica for several months, as inmates complained about poor food and medical service and discrimination by staff. A large proportion of the Attica inmates were African Americans from New York City, whereas staff members were predominantly white and from rural upstate New York. In September 1971, inmates took control of a large section of the prison and held several staff members as hostages. Negotiations between correctional officials and inmates continued for four days until the governor of New York and the director of corrections decided it was time to end the siege. The New York State Police were sent into the prison and authorized to use deadly force to regain control. After they retook the prison, thirty-two inmates and eleven staff members were found killed. The investigation discovered that the state police killed thirty-nine of those during the retaking of the prison.

The Attica (New York) riot in 1971, one of the most deadly in the history of prisons, highlighted many factors that can create tension and increase the potential for disturbances within a prison. Bettmann/Getty Images.

Another riot that was known for its violence and savagery occurred in February 1980, when prisoners took over the entire prison in Santa Fe, New Mexico. Inmates held twelve staff members as hostages, controlled the prison for thirty-six hours, and caused more than $100 million in damage.[18] Inmates got control of other inmates' records and found that some had acted as informants or **inmate snitches**. An "execution squad" of inmates tortured and killed thirty-three inmates they believed to have provided information to staff. Inmates were killed with blowtorches, others' throats were cut, and some were also hanged. The cause of this riot was believed to be because of overcrowding, as 1,136 inmates were in the prison designed for only 900. As well, the prison had several open dormitories, and the lack of cells made it difficult to control high-security inmates. Inmates were also unhappy with what they saw as oppressive conditions and lack of programs.[19]

Another serious riot took place in 1993 at the Southern Ohio Correctional Facility in Lucasville, Ohio. In an article regarding this riot, Ohio correctional executives wrote,

> On Easter Sunday 1993, inmates returning to L-block from recreation at the maximum security Southern Ohio Correctional Facility in rural Lucasville assaulted the entry officer. Minutes later, L-block was over-run, and the longest prison siege in U.S. history where lives were lost was underway. Eleven days later the riot ended. Corrections Officer Robert Vallandingham and nine inmates had been murdered. Thirteen corrections officers had been taken hostage. Five were held for the duration of the disturbance. L-block was virtually destroyed.
>
> As the more than 200 media reporters packed up their cameras and satellite dishes, Ohioans breathed a collective sigh of relief that the carnage was over. But for the 11,000 employees of the Ohio Department of Rehabilitation and Correction, the end of the riot signaled fundamental changes at every level of the operation.[20]

Investigations of inmate riots and disturbances have discovered that most are not planned or precisely initiated by inmate leaders. Disturbances more often result from the coalescing of two types of factors and events. The first are **environmental factors** that create tension and an underlying unrest among inmates. They can include hot weather, reduction in budgets for recreation equipment, prison crowding, poor food service or medical care, a perceived pattern of unfairness in prison management, or poor security procedures that allow inmates to create an unsafe environment. The second is a **precipitating event**, often thought of as the "spark in the haystack," that sets off an inmate riot. It usually takes both the right environmental factors and a precipitating event to create the beginning of a prison riot.

Preventive actions that prison administrators can take to reduce inmate unrest and lessen the chance that a single precipitating event will result in a riot include the following:

- Understanding the importance to both staff and inmates of managerial visibility and approachability.
- Performing effective security audits that discover security deficiencies so they can be corrected before inmates exploit them.
- Consistently enforcing all rules and regulations.
- Maintaining effective communications between inmates and staff, among staff members, and particularly between line and supervisory personnel.

inmate snitches
inmates that provide information to staff about other inmates misconduct or potential problems in the prison such as riots or assaults. Inmate snitches are hated by other inmates.

environmental factors
factors that create tension and an underlying unrest among inmates; they can include hot weather, reduction in budgets for recreation equipment, prison crowding, poor food service or medical care, a perceived pattern of unfairness in the management of the prison, or poor security procedures that allow inmates to create an unsafe environment

precipitating event
the "spark in the haystack" that sets off an inmate riot; usually must be preceded by the right environmental factors before a precipitating event creates the beginning of a prison riot

Rioting inmates at the Southern Ohio Correctional Facility in Lucasville, Ohio, in 1993 did severe damage to the facility and murdered ten people. Courtesy of the Ohio Department of Rehabilitation and Correction.

- Providing appropriate programs and services of all types (food, medical care, and so forth).
- Implementing effective management systems, such as sanitation, safety and security inspections, contraband deterrence and detection, tool and key control, and inmate accountability.
- Developing sensitivity to changes in inmate actions or the institution atmosphere.
- Using risk-assessment programs to identify possible trouble spots and correcting them as soon as possible; such systems may include the use of objective indicators (tests, review of incident data, sick call data) or more subjective elements (staff and inmate interviews) to assign levels of risk to a situation or institution.[21]

The "A Look Into" box gives an example of a riot that occurred while I was the warden of the Federal Correctional Institution in Greenville, Illinois (FCI Greenville). It illustrates how environmental factors and a precipitating event can combine to result in a serious riot culminating in staff injury and major destruction of the prison.

Planning for Emergency Situations

Inmate disturbances can occur in any prison. Knowing this, all prisons develop contingency or emergency plans to identify the responses and procedures to be put in place in case of a disturbance. These plans describe how to prevent disturbances and, if a riot occurs, the initial reactions, communications, staff response, the potential use of firearms and crowd control ordinances, managing the media, and postemergency actions. Emergency plans are a guide for actions in a time when emotions are high, staff and inmates may be in danger or already injured, things seem chaotic and out of control, and the warden and top prison officials

A Look Into . . .

Causes of a Riot

In October 1995, the Federal Correctional Institution in Greenville, Illinois, was a new federal prison. It was constructed using Federal Bureau of Prisons (BOP) standard medium-security guidelines, with solid wood cell doors and card tables and folding chairs used by inmates in the housing units' common areas. The prison first accepted inmates in early 1994. The prison had just over 500 cells, but because of severe overcrowding in other federal prisons, it rapidly filled to twice that capacity to more than 1,000 inmates, with two inmates in every cell and even three inmates in some cells. Most inmates were transferred to Greenville from Southeast and West Coast federal prisons, which were experiencing the most overcrowding. These inmates were moved away from their families and friends, could not receive visits, and did not want to be in southern Illinois.

As is the practice in federal prisons, some experienced staff members are transferred to new prisons, but the majority are hired locally and have no prison experience. Procedures were new, and some were still changing and developing. The newly hired correctional officers and other staff members were learning to deal with medium-security inmates, almost all of whom had been transferred from other prisons and knew how to try to take advantage of new staff members and untried procedures.

Throughout 1995, there was considerable public discussion about changing the federal drug laws regarding crack cocaine. There was a ten-to-one ratio of crack to powder cocaine, meaning that to receive a mandatory ten-year prison sentence, crack cocaine offenders had to possess only one-tenth the amount required for powder cocaine offenders. Since crack cocaine was primarily used in African American communities, more than 95 percent of the crack cocaine offenders at Greenville were African American. This became an issue of racial injustice and was being reconsidered by the U.S. Sentencing Commission. In fact, in the summer of 1995, the commission recommended to Congress that the two drugs should be equalized in their weight and corresponding sentence. Through rumor, African American inmates convicted of crack cocaine trafficking believed that a change would be made, it would be retroactive, and that many would receive an immediate reduction of their sentences.

In the fall of 1995, a report issued by the U.S. Department of Justice, Bureau of Justice Statistics, noted the much higher percentage of black men between ages nineteen and thirty who were incarcerated at a much greater rate compared to their percentage in the overall U.S. population. This also became a rallying cry for racial injustice. Over the summer and fall of 1995, much media attention was given to a call for a "Million Man March" by Minister Louis Farrakhan, the controversial leader of the Nation of Islam. The Million Man March called attention to the need for African American men to take responsibility for their families. However, it also emphasized, especially in the minds of inmates, the issue of racial injustice regarding the disparity between crack and powder cocaine sentencing.

The Million Man March occurred on Monday of the third week of October. On Wednesday evening of the same week, Congress rejected the recommendation by the sentencing commission to reduce the disparity between crack and powder cocaine sentences. The next day riots broke out in federal prisons in Alabama, Tennessee, and Pennsylvania. There was national media coverage of the fires and destruction from these riots, and inmates in Greenville watched these events unfold on television news coverage.

On Friday of that week, the BOP took peremptory action to prevent more riots, ordering a national lockdown of all federal prisons. At Greenville, inmates were called back to their housing units around 3:00 P.M., about one hour earlier than usual. Arriving in the housing units, inmates were told to go into their cells to be locked down. Several inmates refused to go into their cells and began assaulting staff. A riot ensued and resulted in injury of thirteen staff members and massive destruction of two housing units. Four or five other federal prisons also experienced smaller disturbances during the next few weeks.

Environmental factors in this riot included inexperienced staff implementing new procedures. Many inmates were extremely unhappy about being in Greenville. Feelings of racial injustice were heightened by the Million Man March, and there were expectations that the injustice would be ended by congressional action. The congressional action to maintain current sentences was unexpected by prison officials and was disappointing to inmates. The precipitating event was the attempted lockdown, in a time when external (societal) tensions were high. The inmates were extremely upset because they did not know the duration or reasons for the lockdown or even if this action was warranted.

This picture shows the burned-out center of the U.S. Penitentiary in Atlanta, Georgia, after rioting Cuban inmates took over the entire prison and held several staff members as hostages for several days in 1987. Courtesy of the Federal Bureau of Prisons.

may be out of the prison. The plan is detailed to the point that it provides the order of steps to take to respond to certain events. Staff members are required to read the plan and are trained in its implementation in the event of an emergency. Well-coordinated, appropriate, and timely reaction at the beginning of a disturbance is critical. Boin and Van Duin write:

> As prison authorities find themselves confronted with a riot, ... [they] will have to take some sort of action in order to cope with the threat and restore a state of normalcy. It is in this stage that the actions of prison authorities may make the difference between a food strike in an isolated cell block (a riot you will never hear about) and the overtaking of an entire institution (a riot you might never forget).[22]

Emergency Response Teams

In preparation for inmate disturbances, emergency plans require creation, staffing, and training of at least three teams, capable of using all the options available in crisis situations, including negotiation, controlling the disturbance, and use of deadly force. The three teams include a hostage negotiation team, disturbance control team, and special emergency response team. The key is for the decision maker to decide which team to use and how to react. During a disturbance, the tactical priorities include safety of the public (preventing escapes), accountability of inmates (find who is where), and safety of personnel and inmates.[23] However, each incident is different, and the response must always be "contingent on the type of emergency faced."[24]

In some riots, staff members are taken hostage, creating a very difficult and stressful situation that eliminates or delays many of the activities that could be used to respond to a nonhostage emergency. **Hostage negotiation teams** (HNTs) are used to respond to a hostage taking. The HNT is made up of eight to ten prison employees with excellent communication skills and ability to perform under stress. The team's principal role is to open lines of communication with the

hostage negotiation teams

a team of eight to ten prison employees, with excellent communication skills and ability to perform under stress, with the principle role to open lines of communications between staff and hostage takers hostage takers as quickly as possible so that inmates see an option to injuring the hostage and begin to consider how to resolve the situation. The HNT goal is to preserve life and regain control of the prison and inmates. Once they open communication lines, they attempt to slow down the pace of activities, and reduce tension with the hostage takers. The negotiators listen for intelligence that will be of assistance if negotiations fail, and allow hostage takers to express their anger and frustration.[25] Over the period of negotiations, a rapport builds between the negotiators and the hostage takers, and the Stockholm syndrome develops between the captors and the hostages. The Stockholm syndrome is thought to result in the hostages and captors beginning to identify with each other; hostage takers see the hostages as people rather than just objects, and they are therefore less likely to physically harm or kill their hostages.

The second type of emergency team is the **disturbance control team** (DCT). The DCT has a primary mission of controlling inmates during riot situations by using defensive tactics and equipment to move them, isolate them, and get them to give up and stop the disturbance. The team wears helmets, ballistic-resistant vests, and baseball-catcher-style shin guards and carries riot batons, gas masks, handcuffs, chemical agents such as tear and pepper gas, and ordnance such as smoke grenades, stun and flash rounds, and Sting-Ball grenades. The DCT responds to a riot with a deliberate, orderly, and disciplined approach. Through this "show of force," inmates often end the confrontation, recognizing that the DCT is well trained and the inmates are likely to be hurt if they do not capitulate.

Unfortunately, some riots and hostage situations do not end successfully through negotiation or the use of the DCT. In these cases, the third type of team, the **special emergency response team** (SERT), may be called upon. A SERT, similar to a police SWAT team, is trained in the use of weapons, explosives, entry procedures, and snipers. They will be authorized to use lethal force when all else fails to resolve an emergency situation. It is a difficult decision for correctional officials to commit to the use of a SERT assault with deadly force. Hostage takers always give deadlines and threaten to kill hostages if their demands are not

disturbance control team
an emergency team with the primary mission of controlling inmates during riot situations by using defensive tactics and equipment to move, isolate, and get them to give up and stop the disturbance

special emergency response team
an emergency team trained in the use of lethal force when all else fails to resolve an emergency situation

Disturbance control teams are designed to move inmates and often disperse chemical agents. Courtesy of CoreCivic.

SERT members must train regularly with weapons to be used in serious prison emergency situations. Courtesy of the Ohio Department of Rehabilitation and Correction.

met. It is good strategy to have the negotiating team try to talk to hostage takers past deadlines, while hoping that they will not injure hostages. Yet hostage takers may reach a point at which they are about to kill or injure hostages, and the order must be given and the SERT prepared to begin an assault.

Before the SERT assaults, they prepare a detailed plan that must receive the approval of the emergency decision maker. Once the plan is approved, the team moves into position and stays ready to begin the assault upon receiving the "go" order. If force is necessary, it must be overwhelming, but only in the amount necessary to restore order. Prison officials' goal is to develop a tactical action that ensures total control of the inmates as the final outcome so that inmates cannot take the weapons and have SERT members as more hostages.

Chapter Review

Summary

Custody is one of the two key emphases in the mission of prisons (treatment being the other as addressed in Chapter 14). Prisons attempt to create a safe and secure environment through the implementation of professional security policies without undermining the opportunities to provide inmates with program opportunities. As will be noted in Chapter 14, prison administrators must create a culture with a balance of both custody and treatment so that one does not exist at the harm of the other. But it can seem difficult when wondering how a prison can maintain security and order while encouraging inmates to participate in self-improvement programs? Or how can positive programs operate within an environment that must control every inmate activity? However, in other ways, these two emphases seem to complement and support one another, because active programs help develop self-control and encourage inmate good behavior.

In this chapter, the approaches and activities undertaken within prisons to ensure security and custody in prisons are described. Important practices for maintaining security and order include effective classification systems, adequate physical security, consistent implementation of policy and procedure, inmate accountability and control of contraband, a fair and equitable disciplinary system, methods to separate inmates when necessary, and preparation to respond to inmate disturbances and riots.

No one questions the importance of security and custody practices within a prison. Few would doubt the need to control inmate behavior and mandate compliance with rules and policies to create a safe environment for staff and inmates and fashion such habits among inmates. Before anything can be accomplished in a prison (programs or delivery of services or staff development), there must be an environment in which staff and inmates feel safe and can focus on these other areas.

Key Terms

inmate accountability

work call

controlled movement

call out

pass system

regular counts

stand-up count

census count

random count

contraband

shadow board

special housing unit

administrative detention

disciplinary segregation

inmate snitches

environmental factors

precipitating event

hostage negotiation team

disturbance control team

special emergency response team

Review Questions

1. What is the definition of prison custody?

2. List the eight types of activities that contribute to the security and custody functions within a prison.

3. Define inmate accountability and list the key components to maintaining inmate accountability in a prison.

4. What is the difference between controlled movement and a pass system?

5. What is a stand-up count?

6. How do random counts prevent inmates from planning escape around the other two types of counts?

7. What is contraband?

8. List five Class A tools under prison security policies.

9. What is a shadow board and how is it used to control contraband?

10. What is the purpose of an SHU and what are the two categories of assignment to an SHU?

11. What does it take for a precipitating event to cause a prison riot?

12. Name the three types of teams included in prison emergency plans.

13. What is the Stockholm syndrome?

You Make the Decision . . .

Lock Him Up?

Inmates may be placed in administrative detention (AD) if determined a risk to their safety if they remain in general population. The difficult decision is when to lock up inmates, or place them in the SHU, when there is no definite evidence that they are at risk. The following situation is not uncommon.

An inmate comes into the captain's office and tells the officer in charge that he is being pressured to have his wife bring drugs into the prison by a group of inmates. He thinks the inmates are in a gang. He says they told him if he doesn't do it, he will be killed. He will not identify the inmates, because he is afraid that if he does, their fellow gang members will kill him. He won't give any more or any specific information, saying that anything he says that can be traced back to him and result in the other inmates being locked up for investigation will also result in his being killed. None of the security staff members have had previous encounters with this inmate, can vouch for his credibility, or have any information to support his story. His case manager, when contacted, says the inmate had been seeking a transfer to a prison closer to his home where his wife lives. The case manager told the inmate that that prison was very overcrowded and that there was a moratorium on transfers for twelve months.

You could decide to place him in AD to separate him from the threatening inmates and transfer him to another prison. However, two problems can result. First, inmates sometimes create a story like this to get a transfer. They know that if they are at risk, they can expect to be moved to another prison, so they can manipulate the system. Second, just transferring the inmate does nothing to deal with a gang that is pressuring inmates to bring in drugs, and they will just try another inmate if this doesn't work out. So, most prison officials will push the inmate to give more specific information to act on the allegation, but do not want him to be in danger, even if he won't provide any details.

So, what do you do? You have to decide whether you would place him in AD. You do not want to give in to his manipulations for a transfer if he is not telling the truth. If you do, other inmates will do the same thing. Yet you can't ignore his request. Consider this, and decide either individually or in a small classroom group whether to lock him up or not.

CHAPTER 14

Treatment and Programs within a Prison

Courtesy of CoreCivic.

After reading this chapter, you should be able to:

1. Define *rehabilitation* and describe its evolution throughout the history of prisons in the United States.

2. Explain how inmate needs are identified.

3. Describe the various types of education and vocational programs provided in prisons.

4. Explain the scope of mental health needs of inmates and how prisons provide programs that meet these needs.

5. Identify the level of substance abuse among the inmate population and the level of program opportunities provided in prisons.

6. Describe programs for prison work, counseling/therapy, religion, and recreation.

7. Summarize the overall effectiveness of correctional treatment programs.

Introduction

Even during the "get tough on crime (and criminals)" mentality of the past two decades, there is still support for providing treatment and programs within prisons and preparing inmates for successful release and return to the community. As noted in Chapter 13, prisons have a mission with two dominant themes: custody and treatment. Treatment and active programming for inmates not only prepare offenders for reentry, but also aid in custody and order within a prison. Active and positive programs enhance supervision of inmates and improve morale and get them focused on the future rather than their current situation.

Treatment is the creation of an environment and provision of rehabilitative programs that encourage inmates to accept responsibility and to address personal disorders that make success in the community more difficult. The image of treatment within prisons is envisioned as just the opposite of custody. How can prison counselors and treatment staff treat inmates in a "soft and caring" manner, get inmates to acknowledge their weaknesses, and initiate a program of rehabilitation within an environment that is totally controlled and focused on order? The reality is that neither of these suggested images of prisons is accurate. The challenge for prison management is to prudently balance custody and security with treatment and rehabilitation. This balance is not easy to accomplish, and a movement in emphasis to either custody or treatment can upset the balance and lead to serious problems.

In this chapter, we turn from custody to creating an environment to provide inmates the opportunity to address problems and prepare for release. We address some of the issues identified by special offenders (mental illness and substance abuse) in Chapter 9. However, in this chapter, we examine the challenges and manner in which prisons provide treatment programs. Also, the difficulty of maintaining the delicate balance between custody and treatment is explained, and the methods by which prison administrators attempt to maintain a dual emphasis on both are presented. For prisons to provide effective rehabilitative services there must be assessment of needs and provision of a variety of programs (substance abuse, mental health, religious services, education and recreation, and work opportunities) to address these needs and prepare inmates for release. And, for prisons to accomplish their dual mission in a balanced fashion and while maximizing the effectiveness of programs, there must be skilled prison leadership guiding the delicate balance for both security and treatment.

Treatment and Programs within a Prison

As described in Chapter 13, while creating a safe and secure environment, prisons also focus on the part of their mission of providing inmates the opportunity to participate in programs that can help in their rehabilitation and successful reentry to the community. Although it has always been acknowledged that rehabilitation is a valid correctional goal, support for it and the emphasis that rehabilitative programs receive in prisons have ebbed and flowed over the history of U.S. corrections. However, the public continues to support and correctional officials continue to encourage programs that are designed to improve offenders' deficiencies that may have contributed to their past criminality.

Rehabilitation, at that point better termed "redemption," was a primary focus of the first U.S. prison (the Walnut Street Jail), opened in Philadelphia in 1790. Inmates were expected to read the Bible and reflect on their wrongdoings. They were also required to work on trade products in their cells so that these products could be sold to help support the prison. Over the next 150 years, work became the primary program within prisons, although counseling and religious services remained a mainstay of every prison. In the history of U.S. corrections, programs for the rehabilitation of offenders have always been considered important.

The heyday of the goal of rehabilitation came during the middle of the twentieth century when corrections adopted a *medical model*, in which crime was believed to be the result of an underlying pathology of offenders that could be diagnosed and treated. Offenders were considered sick and in need of treatment to prepare them to return to the community as productive, law-abiding citizens. Correctional agencies implemented a variety of treatment programs to improve offenders and to provide them with the tools necessary to be successful members of society. The need for rehabilitation of offenders was emphasized by the Commission on Law Enforcement and the Administration of Justice, appointed by the former president Lyndon Johnson in 1966, which noted a need for "substantial upgrading" of the correctional system and its reorientation "toward integration of offenders into community life."[1]

By the 1980s, however, public support of rehabilitation was declining, partly the result of the publication of an early 1970s study of the effectiveness of correctional treatment. In a review of findings from 231 correctional treatment programs, Lipton and colleagues found no common themes in correctional interventions that consistently reduce recidivism.[2] In an earlier article regarding the review that became known as the "nothing works" conclusion, Martinson stated that "with few and isolated exceptions, the rehabilitative efforts that have been reported so far have had no appreciable effect on recidivism."[3]

During this time, correctional philosophy reverted to Darwinism and the *classical model*, in which offenders are seen as rational individuals with free will who chose to commit and are personally accountable for their crimes. With this philosophy, punishment and deterrence are considered more important as goals than rehabilitation. However, rehabilitative programs have continued in prison and community corrections settings, although medical terms such as *treatment* and *diagnosis* have been replaced with *programming* and *assessment*. In the current era of accountability, offenders must take responsibility for their criminal acts. Although there is recognition of and support for self-improvement of offenders, these programs are often voluntary, prisons provide them as "opportunities" rather than treatment for deficiencies, and offenders are seen not as ill but in need of modifying their willingness to commit crimes.

Currently, the public expects criminals to be punished, yet supports providing rehabilitation programs to inmates. The public wants to be protected, but it also wants the correctional system to improve inmates' likelihood of success upon release. A 2006 public opinion survey indicated that 87 percent of those surveyed favor rehabilitative services for prisoners as opposed to a punishment-only system, and greater than 90 percent of those surveyed rated as "important" that prison inmates receive job training, drug treatment, mental health services, family support, and housing assistance.[4] A 2012 survey found that 60 percent of those surveyed disagreed that efforts to rehabilitate nonviolent criminals is a waste of time and money.[5]

In this textbook, the term *rehabilitation* will continue to be used. Rehabilitation, by definition, means "to return to a previous form." However, for correctional purposes, rehabilitation is to provide programming to address the needs of offenders that can reduce their risk of criminal behavior and improve their chance of success in the community. Prisons offer a variety of programs in education, vocational training, recreation, religion, substance abuse, mental health, work, and a variety of other self-improvement modalities. These programs are valued, not only because they result in the self-improvement of the offender, but also because they have been found to result in less idleness, disruption, and violence within prisons. This more practical than altruistic emphasis continued for crime prevention purposes. Cullen and Applegate have suggested that "the rehabilitative paradigm requires that government invest in lawbreakers. The goal is to improve offenders both as an end in itself and as a means of reducing recidivism and of protecting society."[6]

The following sections describe the process and programs that are ordinarily provided within prisons, which include assessing the program needs of inmates and creating a plan for them to follow during their period of incarceration. These programs can include education and vocational, recreational, substance abuse, mental health, and work programs.

Identifying Inmate Treatment Needs

Once an offender is sentenced to prison, a reception and classification process begins. Many states have correctional reception centers to which inmates are initially assigned to assess their risk of violence and escape and their need for rehabilitative programs. The risk assessment is normally done through the use of objective classification systems, with a determination of the security level of prison (based primarily on the physical security available) to which an inmate will be assigned. The identification of program needs is determined through a combination of assessment instruments, interviews with psychologists or other mental health professionals, and educational and vocational testing.

From these assessments, testing, and interviews, inmate needs for various types of programs are identified. Educational proficiency exams give an indication of an inmate's level of literacy, regardless of the grade completed in school, and indicate whether additional educational programming is needed. Psychological assessments identify any mental illness, suicide proclivity, or need for special mental health placements or programs. And through interviews and review of histories, the need for substance abuse treatment is determined. Since most offenders have limited work histories and poor work skills, the program plan also addresses the types of vocational training or prison work experience that may help the inmate.

Once needs are identified, inmates move from the reception process to the regular incarceration stage of their sentence. If they were originally in a reception center, they are transferred to a prison to begin service of their sentence. Once transferred, inmates meet with the unit management or program team to develop a program plan to follow during their sentence. If the inmates' functional literacy is below a certain level, they are assigned to go to school. If a mental health or substance abuse problem has been identified, they are referred to the mental health department for treatment or placement in a substance abuse program. They will be assigned to a vocational program or prison job to develop work skills. And they will be informed of leisure programs and other programs within the prison believed to be of interest or assistance to them.

The unit or treatment team normally meets with inmates every six months thereafter to review the progress and current status of their program, but if an inmate requests a change in program, the team will schedule a review early. At these reviews, the team examines reports from the various program departments and discusses progress, concerns, or successes with the inmate. Most treatment programs are voluntary, yet the team may strongly suggest the inmate's involvement and commitment. Other programs may be required by statute (in several states and the federal government, inmates testing below a certain literacy level must enroll in school) or as a part of their sentence (some states allow judges to require inmates to participate in a substance abuse program during their sentence).

Types of Prison Programs

Inmates have a variety of needs, and no two inmates are exactly the same. However, there are a few inmate programs that most inmates need and participate in. Approximately half of entering prison inmates have graduated from high school. Nearly 80 percent of state prison inmates have a drug or alcohol problem. Very few inmates have an extensive work history or marketable vocational skills. And approximately 16 percent of incarcerated offenders have a mental illness. Prisons therefore attempt to create programs to meet the general needs of inmates and deal with individual requirements within these programs. Educational and vocational, mental health, substance abuse, work, religious, and recreational programs within prisons are presented next.

Academic and Vocational Programs

Education is recognized as critical to everyone's success in modern U.S. society. The achieved educational level of the general population of the United States has increased steadily in the past few decades, and criminal offenders have consistently been found significantly less educated than their law-abiding peers.[7] The Bureau of Justice Statistics reported that only 18.4 percent of the general population had not completed high school or received a general equivalency diploma (GED), whereas 39.7 percent of state prison inmates, 26.5 percent of federal prison inmates, 46.5 percent of jail inmates, and 30.6 percent of probationers had only some high school or less. A recent report of a survey of prison and jail inmates indicated more than one-half of each group had less than a high school education.[8] And another report indicated that only 43 percent of offenders entering prison had obtained a GED or high school diploma, while a comparison of all households versus all prison inmates showed 82 percent of households and 63 percent of prison inmates had a GED, high school diploma, or postsecondary studies.[9] And of all high school diplomas or equivalencies, more than one in ten come via GED testing.

Since inmates have a significant need for educational programs, most prisons provide these programs. In a survey of adult correctional facilities, 85 percent of all prisons provided educational programs for inmates.[10] Prisons offer a variety of education programs, with secondary education programs to prepare inmates to take the GED the most prevalent. Approximately two-thirds of inmates participate in education programs,[11] and over 80 percent of prisons provide courses that lead to a GED acquisition.[12] While education programs involve more inmates than any other prison programs, there are still unserved inmates who could benefit. Correctional educators suggest several reasons (to aid in reentry, to reduce recidivism, or support employability) to increase prison education programs.[13]

Education has been a part of prison programming for more than a century. One of the most famous U.S. penologists, Zebulon R. Brockway, argued that law-abiding behavior was attainable through legitimate industry and education and advocated it for inmates at the American Prison Association conference in 1870. The current American Correctional Association standard for correctional educational programs states that:

> written policy, procedure, and practice provide for a comprehensive education program, available to all inmates who are eligible, that includes the following: educational philosophy and goals, communications skills, general education, basic academic skills, GED preparation, special education, vocational education, postsecondary education, and other education programs as dictated by the needs of the institutional population.[14]

Historically, most prison education programs have been voluntary; however, many states and the Federal Bureau of Prisons (BOP) now have a requirement of **mandatory prison education** programs. In 1983, the BOP implemented the first mandatory literacy program for inmates who functioned at less than a sixth-grade educational level. The standard was raised to the eighth-grade level in 1986, and in 1991, the Crime Control Act of 1990 (Public Law 101–647) directed the BOP to have a mandatory functional literacy program for all mentally capable inmates, and the BOP raised their educational standard to the twelfth grade. Many states have since adopted such standards, and the mandatory requirement has much to do with the increasing participation over the past few years.

Results have been mixed concerning the impact of correctional education on postrelease recidivism. While there was early evidence that correctional education was not linked to recidivism,[15] there have been several studies indicating a positive relationship between participating in prison education and reduced recidivism.[16] A recent metal-analysis of fifty prior studies by the Rand Corporation of the effectiveness of correctional education in state prisons is the most compelling. The analysis included in the definition of correctional education, studies of adult basic education, secondary education, vocational or technical training, and postsecondary education. In terms of recidivism, the authors write, "across 32 years of empirical studies…on average, the odds of recidivating among inmates receiving correctional education are 64 percent of the odds of recidivating among inmates not receiving correctional education."[17]

In addition to adult basic and secondary education, most prisons also offer vocational training programs to improve inmates' occupational skills. **Vocational training** is specific training in a trade area, such as carpentry, electronics, welding, office equipment and word processing, food services, or horticulture and landscaping. Vocational training has also been shown to be effective in reducing recidivism. Saylor and Gaes found that "those who participated in either vocational or apprenticeship training were 33 percent less likely to recidivate through the observation period," which was as long as twelve years and as short as eight years.[18] And a 2009 study of career and technical education in prisons found that these programs lowered postrelease recidivism rates and

mandatory prison education
many states and the Federal Bureau of Prisons require inmates without a high school diploma or GED to attend school

vocational training
specific training in a trade area to prepare students to work in that trade

Some vocational classes are very traditional and include carpentry and electrical. Andrew Aitchison/Pictures Ltd./Corbis News/Getty Images.

Other vocational training classes teach inmates skills that are current and often high-tech. Courtesy of CoreCivic.

Pell grants

grants for disadvantaged individuals used to cover tuition costs for college courses

parole revocations and improved postrelease employment, and inmates in these programs also had better disciplinary records while in prison.[19]

Unfortunately, few prisons have extensive postsecondary education programs, even though several thousand inmates took college classes and earned college degrees in the past. State and federal prisons previously used **Pell grants** to fund inmate college programs. Pell grants were enacted and funded by Congress in the 1970s as a way for "disadvantaged populations" to receive funds to take college courses. Inmates met the definition of disadvantaged, and most prisons arranged with local colleges to offer courses in the prison and qualify inmates to receive Pell grant funds to pay their tuition. When I was the director of corrections in Ohio, almost every prison had more than 100 inmates attending college classes as full-time students. These college programs were considered a productive use of inmate time and were found to motivate inmates and improve morale.

However, in 1994, after complaints that inmates should not get a "free" college education in prison, Congress specifically eliminated inmates from receiving Pell grants, and many active and proven college programs in prisons were eliminated.[20] Some states were able to provide limited funding and keep college-level programs going on a minimal basis. In 2000, the BOP proposed modifying its own rules to make inmates responsible for all college-degree tuition costs.[21] Prisons now will help inmates arrange to take correspondence courses, but all costs must be borne by the inmate. Even two decades after the end of Pell grants, most correctional educators still bemoan their loss as a step back in correctional education and the ability to encourage inmates to maximize their education potential, at a time when they have little else to do. The loss of Pell grants is even more disappointing when considering that studies have shown that postsecondary education can effectively reduce recidivism. A meta-analysis of ten years of studies during the 1990s demonstrated that there is a positive correlation between postsecondary education and reduced recidivism.[22] And a 2014 study in Minnesota and a 2013 study in New York both found that earning a postsecondary degree significantly reduced recidivism.[23]

The good news for proponents of Pell Grants is a July 31, 2015, announcement by the Obama Administration that they would allow, on a temporary basis, federal grants to be used to cover college costs as a pilot program.[24] In August 2015, the

U.S. Department of Education invited states and colleges to apply for these pilot programs to provide eligible incarcerated offenders Pell Grant funding, and the states that were included in these pilots found them very successful. A good example is the state of Michigan, which had almost 1,500 students enrolled in college courses in 2017. These inmate students had the opportunity to earn degrees that included Associates in General Studies, in Arts, and in Business Administration, as well as Certificates in Business Administration and in Computer Service Technician. The average GPA for these student inmates was 3.63 (on a 4.0 scale). And an amazing result was that of all students who attended Jackson College and were on the Dean's list for academic excellence, 57 percent were incarcerated students.[25] There is hope that the success of these pilot programs will encourage Congress and the Administration to continue allowing inmates to receive Pell grants.

Issues in Educational Delivery in Prisons

Over the years, there has been little change in the traditional delivery of education programs. A staff instructor delivers most academic education in a classroom. Classrooms appear very much like a public school high school. However, there have recently been many issues and changes that have developed in correctional education in prison, just as in the delivery of education to the general public.[26] The resources online that can be used for instruction or testing prompt much of this. But others are a result of the effectiveness of correctional education in reducing recidivism, and the desire by correctional agencies to use education and other evidence-based programs to reduce recidivism and save money.

An important emphasis is the practical use of education programs to help prepare inmates for reentry. The focus of state and federal prisons has been on transiting prison education, vocational training, and even work programs into what is called career development. Career development most commonly refers to examining the local job market, assessing inmate skills, and then creating a way to translate the prison experience into a resume that demonstrates the inmate's preparation and readiness for a job and career. In most correctional agencies, the career development activities are delivered in the education departments. This can be done in a classroom or using a computer lab to conduct prerelease classes on finding a job and life skills.

A recent development has been the selection of curriculum to be used for high school equivalency. Across the country, school districts are using the "Common Core" as a standardized curriculum. This change is controversial, but was developed to have a unified higher standard of what was expected in terms of knowledge and skills for high school graduates. Unfortunately, this standard required additional teacher training and resources, and therefore, many school districts are not supporting the move to the Common Core. Teaching to the Common Core is different and the expected levels of performance (especially for math and writing) are higher than that for the GED. This has caused new curriculum development and training for prison instructors.

In addition, in 2014, the testing for the GED was required to be electronic instead of paper and pencil. In response, each prison had to have (or create) a computer lab and have an instructor certified as the test monitor. In addition, the GED electronic exam was designed to be taken via active Internet connectivity, and prisons have avoided allowing inmates to be on the Internet for fear they will access other sites and even use it to commit financial or other fraudulent crimes. Prisons were able to work with the Electronic GED testing centers to create a way to download the test and then upload the inmate/student scores. During 2014, the total number of students taking the GED exam has declined, as have the successful pass rates due to the increased difficulty of the new test against the Common Core. According to the GED Testing Service, 401,388 people earned a GED in 2012 and about 540,000 in 2013. But as of mid-December 2014, only 55,000 had passed the GED nationally.[27] Most of this is due to the more difficult testing against the Common Core, the fact that it seems more focused on college rather than workforce preparation, and that a large number of adult learners (and prisoners) do not have access to a computer in their home. As a result, thirteen states have adopted one of two other accepted high school equivalency curriculums and tests, to include the Test Assessing Secondary Completion (TASC) and the HiSET high school equivalency test. These two still allow a paper and pencil test for prison inmates.

An interesting development in the delivery of curriculum is through the experimentation with the use of computer tablets. As noted above, prisons have been hesitant to allow inmates on the Internet. However, some private companies have now created a way to download academic curriculum on an Android tablet, meaning it does not need Internet connectivity. These preloaded tablets can be used by inmates to study, do exercises, or even complete practice tests outside of the classroom, and their answers or work products can then be uploaded to staff-controlled computers to monitor their progress. This approach is still in the early experimental stages, but is considered a very positive opportunity to expand the number of students that can participate in education without significantly adding staff or expanding classroom space.

The world of correctional education is very interesting and has been shown to be effective both for prison management and to reduce recidivism. To further describe how education is delivered in a prison, the following "An Interview With" presents the experiences of someone who has spent years organizing, delivering, and overseeing correctional education programs.

▶ An Interview With...

A Correctional Educator

Catherine L. Linaweaver.
Courtesy of Catherine L. Linaweaver.

Catherine L. Linaweaver is a twenty-five-year corrections veteran, having retired recently as a Warden in the Federal Prison System. She began her career as a teacher in 1990 at the U.S. Penitentiary in Leavenworth, Kansas. After six years, she was promoted to Supervisor of Education at the federal prison in Greenville, Illinois. In 1999, she advanced to one of six regional education administrators for the Bureau of Prisons. Pursuing a career in prison administration, she then served as Associate Warden at two federal prisons and later as the Warden of two other federal prisons. She is not only a recognized correctional

educator; she is also a recognized prison administrator. In 2012, she was selected as the North American Association of Wardens and Superintendents (NAAWS) Warden of the Year. This award is selected annually from the over 3,500 Wardens and Superintendents across the United States and Canada.

Question: Ms. Linaweaver, thank you for taking time to discuss correctional education. Will you provide some background in your career in education?

Ms. Linaweaver: Absolutely! Correctional education was my love and career emphasis for fourteen of my twenty-five years in corrections. After graduating from Pittsburg State University (Kansas), I taught speech and English and was the debate coach at Lansing (Kansas) High School. One of my classes was remedial English for freshman and sophomores. The students in my classes were assigned there because of a previous academic failure. Not because they lacked the aptitude to learn, but because they were just not really interested in English. When I saw the ad for a reading specialist at the Leavenworth federal prison, I knew teaching inmates would not be much different from teaching some of the high school students.

I began at Leavenworth as a GED teacher and reading specialist for inmates not able to read. That meant I had the lowest level of educated inmates, many of whom were completely illiterate. I put these inmates into small groups and worked with them on phonetics, spelling, and very basic reading and writing skills. I also taught mainstream GED students. For these inmates, I had classes of twelve to fifteen inmates, functioning at various levels (typically from fifth to eighth grade). Most could read, but few could write an essay. I (as do most prison education programs) used inmate tutors, and they worked with small groups of students, in small groups, almost like a "mini classroom." As a teacher, I knew the level of all my students. The lowest level would learn to spell and link words. The next group knew words and could write a sentence, and we worked to get them to write a paragraph. The advanced guys could get to the point where they could write a three-page essay. You had to be careful never to humiliate the lower level guys, so the tutors and I were the only ones who knew the level of the guys they were working with.

At the time I was a teacher, we were experiencing a tremendous growth in the Hispanic prison population, and need for English as a Second Language (ESL) classes became important, so I also taught an ESL class (even though I did not speak Spanish). One of the things I also enjoyed was developing a curriculum and teaching a parenting class. We made videos and sent them to the inmates' children, which was very unusual for that time at a high security prison.

Question: And what was your job when you were the Supervisor of Education?

Ms. Linaweaver: The Supervisor of Education in a federal prison is like a principal in a public school. You oversee everything that has to do with the quality of programs. I also had responsibility for vocational training, library services, and inmate taught adult continuing education classes (ACE). I had to manage the education budget, and I supervised eleven full-time and four contract education staff. The contract teachers included a test administrator, a substitute teacher, and two vocational instructors. The full-time staff included two vocational instructors, two administrative staff, and seven academic teachers. One teacher specialized in special education (learning needs students), and everyone else taught the GED, ESL, and parenting classes. In a prison, these classes are rarely by subject (this differs from public school), and most are by groupings of pre-GED (below the eighth grade), and GED levels. This is organized very similar to community adult education centers. In public schools, age and grade is important. But for adult education, students are grouped by performance level.

Question: Why is it important for inmates to participate in education while they are in prison?

Ms. Linaweaver: Well, it is easy to say education is the key to success. But, I believe the number one reason education for inmates is important is that it aids in their self-esteem. If a person has poor self-esteem, it is often because they feel inferior. As a result, they create a coping method. Often, they become a bully or the class clown, and this persona allows them to avoid learning. In prison, this inferiority complex can become dangerous, as these inmates already have a history of violence. But getting an education can build self-esteem. I have seen many very violent and dangerous inmates become pretty good inmates after participating in education programs. There's a lot of truth to the old saying, "An idle mind is the devil's workshop."

Secondly, education in a prison for these guys is very different than their experience on the streets. When you think of Maslow's Hierarchy of Needs, if you don't know if you will have anything to eat or a roof over your head at night, you can't learn very well while you're in school. There are people in prison that want to learn, and at least in prison they know their basic needs will be met. They are locked up because they don't abide by society rules. In prison, we give them a substitute society, one in which they have to follow rules, but a safety net to allow them to focus on education and their progress.

Finally, there are many different motivators for inmates. As a teacher, I dealt a lot with inmates doing very long sentences, some who won't ever get out. Even for them, they may want to be a role model for their kids or show their mom or grandmother they can do it (get their GED). But most are going to get out and having a GED will be very important to their finding a job and supporting their families.

Question: Describe prison inmates and how they get involved in education. And why are they now successful when they were not before?

Ms. Linaweaver: Let me describe this in what I call the "Prison Rule of Ten." I believe that if you enroll ten inmates in my class, there will be two that will make it no matter what I do. On the other end, you have two that are not going to make it no matter how much or how well I teach. Education is just not their thing, and there is no "carrot or stick" that is going to work for them. For these two, you just have to keep them from disrupting the others from learning. The key is what you do for the six in the middle. They can go either way based on what the correctional educator does. If they believe you respect them, they will try harder. They watch everything. If they see the two "knuckleheads" getting by the easy way and getting treated the same as the two guys working hard, they will drift to that level. If they think that doing well in school makes their life (inside and/or out of prison) better, they move that way. So every time I got a new group of students, I applied the rule of ten. My goal as a correctional educator was always to focus on those six, and for the most part I was successful with at least four or five, sometimes all six!

(Continued)

Question: What type of vocational programs do prisons offer, and how do they mirror the types of jobs available in the community?

Ms. Linaweaver: Most prisons offer a variety of vocational training (VT) classes. The need for various classes runs a cycle, and changes over time. Twenty years ago, we started off with people taking computer classes. The reality is that most inmates coming to prisons now are computer savvy, and don't need these basic computer classes. The programs I believe are the best and get inmates the best jobs are the trades, such as machine shops, welding, or apprentice programs. I remember driving to my work in Chicago, and hearing on the news that Chicago needed 20,000 welders. I thought, I know where they can find and train 20,000 inmates! We think it is important to send people to college, but the jobs available to inmates are those in the trades. Another example is a new VT program that teaches road resurfacing and how to operate asphalt paving equipment. Inmates that get out of prison with this skill are almost guaranteed a job as the U.S. has so many infrastructure needs.

Correctional educators study the vocational outlook guidelines to see the professions that are forecasted to be a shortage. Prison administrators look at these jobs and then determine which ones can logistically and safely be taught in a prison, and of course, they must be affordable. However, sometimes very good vocational programs are those that make a difference in the inmates, even if not "job relevant." For instance, I am a big supporter of programs where inmates train dogs. This is not just about getting a job, but changing a person. Some training programs focus on inmates improving their attitudes and helping motivate them to do other things. These can in fact be life altering. I don't care if you get a job as a dog trainer, but if you will be a better person after completing something like this. The quality of some programs can't be measured in the jobs or the salary that will result from the certificate they get. Programs like Puppy's Behind Bars are excellent prison programs that help the inmates but, not because every inmate who completes the program will leave prison and be employed as a dog trainer.

Question: Do prisons provide any postsecondary education now without Pell grants available?

Ms. Linaweaver: Very few prisons still provide much in postsecondary education. The ones that do provide programs focus on technical training rather than general college courses. It is difficult to establish a postsecondary program because the inmates must pay for these classes themselves. Therefore, the only option is correspondence courses, which have been replaced by online programs. I believe it is just a matter of time before inmates can take and pay for online classes. The security concerns about inmates on the Internet are not as relevant as they were in the past and are able to be addressed. Some colleges get state funding for full-time students, so in those cases, inmates may be able to take courses and get funding through the colleges. Inmates are still citizens and even though they have been removed from society, the majority of them will return. It may be in our best interest to make some of these funds available to them before they become our next door neighbors again with no job skills.

Question: How does the delivery of correctional education differ from that provided in the community?

Ms. Linaweaver: The primary difference is prison education is based on an adult education model instead of the model used to teach juveniles. Teachers don't go to college to learn to be an adult educator. They learn elementary or high school teaching methods, but being an adult educator is very different. You have to pick this up as you go and it is often, "trial by error." If you teach inmates as you teach high school students, it won't work. You don't lump students together by subject, but by level.

Question: What type of person makes a good correctional educator?

Ms. Linaweaver: First of all, they have to enjoy what they are doing. If someone is unhappy in his or her life, everyone knows it. And you have to believe it is never too late to learn. What's wrong with a fifty-three-year-old person working on their GED? They are going to turn fifty-three regardless, so they might as well have something to show for it! You just have to learn how to motivate someone like this. Motivation for inmates is not the same as motivating a child. Stars and happy faces don't have the same effect on a grown man, and hugs aren't an option in prison! There are very few tangible items you can give an inmate to encourage them, therefore, one of the most important incentives you have available is mutual respect. School may be the only place in prison where inmates get a "How are you doing, good job, or have a good day." Teachers and inmates give mutual respect, and that is very motivating to inmates.[28]

Mental Health Programs

Providing programs for inmates with mental illness represents a very difficult problem within correctional institutions. First, as described in Chapter 9, a relatively high percentage of inmates have mental health problems. Second, the security demands to control these inmates can be obstacles to program efforts. Finally, correctional agencies are not designed to provide mental health programs to the same extent as mental health agencies. Unfortunately, in many states, the link between correctional and mental health agencies is often not as strong as it could be, and some mental health agencies (in many states, the mental health agencies are charged with the responsibility) do not give provision of mental health services within a prison a high priority.

A 2006 U.S. Department of Justice, Bureau of Justice Statistics, survey of prisoners estimated that more than half of all prison and jail inmates experienced a mental health problem within the past twelve months. And, 15 percent of state prisoners and 24 percent of jail inmates reported symptoms classified as psychotic disorders.[29] This is consistent with an earlier estimate that 16.2 percent of all prisoners were identified as having a mental illness,[30] and by 2012, it was estimated that 356,268 inmates with severe mental illness were in prisons and jails while only approximately 35,000 patients with severe mental illness in state psychiatric hospitals.[31] A 2017 report noted that 37 percent of prison and 44 percent of jail inmates had a mental health disorder in the past, and one in seven prisons and one in four jail inmates had a serious psychological distress (SPD). This compares to one in nineteen persons in the U.S. general population that have a serious psychological distress.[32] Table 14.1 illustrates the prevalence of mental health indicators among prisoners and jail inmates during 2011–2012.

TABLE 14.1	Prevalence of Mental Health Indicators Among Prisoners and Jail Inmates, by Type of Indicator, 2011–2012	
Mental Health Indicator	**Prisoners***	**Jail Inmates**
No indication of a mental health problem[a]	49.9%	36.0%**
Current indicator of a mental health problem[b]		
Serious psychological distress[c]	14.5%	26.4%**
History of a mental health problem		
Ever told by mental health professional they had mental disorder	36.9%	44.3%**
Major depressive disorder	24.2	30.6**
Bipolar disorder	17.5	24.9**
Schizophrenia/other psychotic disorder	8.7	11.7**
Post-traumatic stress disorder	12.5	15.9**
Anxiety disorder[d]	11.7	18.4**
Personality disorder[e]	13.0	13.5

Note: See appendix table 4 for standard errors.
*Comparison group.
**Difference with the comparison group is significant at the 95% confidence level.
[a]Includes persons with a score of 7 or less on the K6 scale and who had never been told by a mental health professional they had a mental disorder.
[b]Current at time of the interview.
[c]Includes persons with a score of 13 or more on the K6 scale. See *Methodology*.
[d]Includes panic disorder and obsessive compulsive disorder, and excludes post-traumatic stress disorder.
[e]Includes antisocial and borderline personality disorder.
Source: Jennifer Bronson and Marcus Berzofsky, "Indicators of Mental Health Problems Reported by Prisoners and Jail Inmates, 2011–12," *BJS Special Report* (Washington, D.C.: U.S. Department of Justice, 2017), p. 3.

There are many reasons why so many people with mental illness came under the supervision of criminal justice agencies. First, people with mental illness are more likely to cause public disturbances or nuisances. Second, people with mental illness have a greater risk of developing substance abuse disorders than others. And nearly one-third of the homeless in the United States have serious mental illness.[33] A 2001 Bureau of Justice Statistics report found that while 1,394 of the nation's 1,558 public and private adult prisons were providing mental health services to inmates, only one in eight prisoners was receiving mental health therapy or counseling services.[34] Although still too low, this appears to have marginally improved. A 2006 review indicated that 34 percent of state inmates, 24 percent of federal inmates, and 17 percent of jail inmates received mental health treatment since their admission.[35]

Even though almost all prisons provide outpatient treatment to inmates with mental illness, there are also 155 prisons that were designed for and have an operational mission to provide mental health programming for inmates.[36] Some of these facilities are like psychiatric hospitals and house inmates with mental illness for long periods or throughout their incarceration. Others are used to house and treat inmates who have experienced acute episodes of mental illness for short terms, stabilize them with medication and treatment, and then return them to the general-population prison. A few states have agreements with the state mental health agencies to transfer inmates whose mental illness conditions are the most severe to secure psychiatric hospitals for long-term treatment. In most cases, this requires a probate hearing by a court to determine that the inmate's illness is so acute that he or she must be hospitalized in such a facility.

Table 14.2 illustrates the percentage of prison and jail inmates that had ever received, received since admission to the correctional facility, or were currently receiving treatment for their mental health disorder during the 2011 to 2012 period of the survey. An earlier report of treatment provided to state prisoners indicated that 16,986 state prisoners (1.8 percent) were housed in a mental health unit and received twenty-four-hour care, 12.9 percent of state inmates were receiving mental health therapy or counseling services from a trained professional on a regular basis, and 9.8 percent of all state inmates were receiving psychotropic medications, such as antidepressants, stimulants, sedatives, or tranquilizers.[37]

One key to successfully providing mental health treatment to inmates is a positive partnership between state and local correctional agencies and state and local mental health service agencies. In many states, the correctional agency creates the physical setting for treatment within prisons, and the state mental health department provides staff, training, and other resources to carry out the treatment. In Ohio, a team of individuals from both the correctional and mental health agencies has developed a conceptual model of *holistic health care* that provides the following:

- Integrated medical, psychiatric, psychological, and chemical dependency service delivery.
- Continuity of care within the Department of Rehabilitation and Corrections and upon release.
- An array of services.
- Delivery of services by self-directed multidisciplinary work teams.[38]

continuum of care
provision of mental health programs based on the intensity of needs for each inmate, including as inmates prepare for release to the community

Particularly important is the **continuum of care** to provide various levels of mental health treatment based on the intensity of needs for each inmate as inmates prepare for movement from prison to release to the community. The most

TABLE 14.2	**Mental Health Treatment Received by Prisoners and Jail Inmates with an Indicator of a Mental Health Problem, by Type of Indicator, Time Period, and Treatment Type, 2011–2012**

Time Period and Treatment Type	Serious Psychological Distress[a]		History of a Mental Health Problem[b]	
	Prisoners*	Jail Inmates	Prisoners*	Jail Inmates
Ever received mental health treatment during lifetime	74.2%	72.7%	88.1%	90.3%**
Ever overnight hospital stay[c]	41.8	43.1	44.8	51.3**
Ever taken prescription medication	62.8	61.3	76.4	80.4**
Ever had counseling/therapy from trained professional[d]	60.9	54.9**	74.6	73.9
Mental health treatment since admission	54.3%	35.0%**	63.0%	44.5%**
Prescription medication	45.8	30.0**	52.6	38.3**
Counseling/therapy from trained professional[d]	42.2	17.8**	48.9	23.5**
Prescription medication and counseling/therapy	33.9	12.9**	38.7	17.5**
Currently treated for a mental health problem[e]	35.6%	29.7%**	37.0%	37.8%
Prescription medication	29.1	25.7	29.9	33.0
Counseling/therapy from trained professional[d]	25.8	12.6**	26.7	16.4**
Prescription medication and counseling/therapy	19.5	8.7**	19.7	11.8**

Note: See appendix table 11 for standard errors.

*Comparison group.

**Difference with the comparison group is significant at the 95 percent confidence level.

[a]Includes inmates with a score of 13 or more on the K6 scale. See *Methodology*.

[b]Includes inmates who reported they had ever been told by a mental health professional they had a mental disorder.

[c]Includes inmates who stayed overnight or longer in any type of hospital or other facility to receive treatment or counseling for any problems with their emotions, nerves, or mental health.

[d]Includes a psychiatrist, psychologist, social worker, or nurse.

[e]As of the time of the interview.

Source: Jennifer Bronson and Marcus Berzofsky, "Indicators of Mental Health Problems Reported by Prisoners and Jail Inmates, 2011–12," *BJS Special Report* (Washington, D.C.: U.S. Department of Justice, 2017), p. 8.

intensive level of care is an inpatient prison hospital, in which inmates with acute needs who represent a risk to themselves or others can receive aggressive treatment. For inmates who have severe mental illness symptoms but do not require a hospital setting, short-term crisis units are designed to stabilize their symptoms and return them to a general-population prison. The third level is a residential unit within a general-population prison, in which inmates with mental illness live and receive treatment in a therapeutic milieu, yet interact with other inmates for work, food services, and other program participation. Finally, general-population prisons provide outpatient therapy and counseling for inmates with mental illness who can live and function in a general-population prison.

Mental health programs within prisons are critical to accomplishing the mission of a correctional facility. Without the types of integrative and multileveled programs described here, inmates with mental illness can be disruptive and undermine the safe and secure operation of a prison. Without effective treatment, these inmates will be unable to prepare for release and successfully reenter the community. The final step in an effective correctional mental health program is transition to the community. In preparation for release, prison and postrelease staff contact community mental health programs, identify resources for continuing mental health treatment from prison to the community, and encourage the offender to seek care from these programs. Although prison mental health treatment is essential to prison order, it has generally not been found to conclusively reduce recidivism unless it also targets criminogenic needs. Most experts believe this is because mental illness is concurrent with many other problems (such as substance abuse and antisocial patterns of behavior).[39]

Substance Abuse Programs

Substance abuse treatment programs are also critical activities within prisons because such a high proportion of inmates have a history of drug or alcohol abuse, and it is a major risk factor for recidivism.[40] In a survey of the drug and alcohol abuse patterns of incarcerated offenders, the Bureau of Justice Statistics categorized inmates based on their substance abuse involvement (see Table 14.3). Fifty-three percent of state and 45.5 percent of federal prison inmates were classified as having any dependence or abuse. Of these, most (56 percent of those in state prisons and 50 percent of those in federal prisons) were regular drug users in the month prior to their arrest.[41] In addition, 9 percent of state and 5 percent of federal inmates were determined to have been involved in alcohol abuse at the time of their offense.

Historically, the treatment needs of drug abusing inmates have gone unmet while they are in prison, but the percentages of inmates involved in such programs has increased. Table 14.4 illustrates the types of drug abuse treatment that are provided to state and federal prisoners. In 2004, about 39 percent of state prisoners and 45 percent of federal prisoners who were drug dependent or abusing in the year

TABLE 14.3	**Prevalence of Drug Dependence or Abuse among State and Federal Prisoners, 2004**	
	Percent of Prison Inmates	
Diagnostic Criteria	**State**	**Federal**
Any dependence or abuse	53.4%	45.5%
Dependence and abuse	34.9	27.5
Dependence only	1.2	1.2
Abuse only	17.3	16.8
No dependence or abuse*	46.6	54.5

*Includes inmates who did not use drugs.

Source: Data from Christopher J. Mumola and Jennifer C. Karberg, "Drug Use and Dependence, State and Federal Prisoners, 2004," *Bureau of Justice Statistics Special Report* (Washington, D.C.: U.S. Department of Justice, October 2006), p. 7.

TABLE 14.4	Drug Treatment or Program Participation since Admission among State and Federal Prisoners Who Used Drugs in the Month before the Offense, 1997 and 2004			

	Percent of Prisoners Who Used Drugs in the Month before the Offense			
Type of Drug Treatment or Program since Admission	**State**		**Federal**	
	2004	**1997**	**2004**	**1997**
Any drug treatment or programs	39.2%	34.3%	45.3%	38.8%
Treatment	14.1%	14.6%	15.2%	15.4%
Residential facility or unit	9.2	8.8	8.7	10.9
Counseling by a professional	6.0	6.0	6.8	5.5
Detoxification unit	0.9	1.0	0.8	0.3
Maintenance drug	0.3	0.3	0.2	0.4
Other programs	33.7%	28.3%	38.8%	31.7%
Self-help group/peer counseling	26.9	23.1	20.8	15.8
Education program	17.0	14.1	28.1	23.8

Source: Data from Christopher J. Mumola and Jennifer C. Karberg, "Drug Use and Dependence, State and Federal Prisoners, 2004," *Bureau of Justice Statistics Special Report* (Washington, D.C.: U.S. Department of Justice, October 2006), p. 9.

before their admission to prison took part in a drug abuse program.[42] Substance abuse treatment in prisons is critically important, as the Office of National Drug Control Policy has reported that treatment while in prison and during postincarceration supervision can reduce recidivism by roughly 50 percent.[43]

Other reviews of the effectiveness have also demonstrated the success of drug treatment programs. A 2007 meta-analysis of sixty-six evaluations found that prison treatment programs significantly reduced future drug use and recidivism.[44] Of prison treatment programs, residential treatment is the most intensive, in which inmates live in a unit entirely focused on a substance abuse milieu, and is often considered the most effective treatment for substance abuse. This type of treatment is also the most expensive, and that explains why only 9.2 percent of state and 8.7 percent of federal inmates participate in residential programs. An example of a residential substance abuse program is the Federal Bureau of Prisons' Drug Abuse Programs (DAP), a 500-hour program, during which inmates reside in a treatment unit separate from the rest of the inmate population. The program operates with a philosophy that offenders must assume personal responsibility for their behavior and, despite the influence of environmental conditions and circumstances, the individual must make a conscious decision to avoid engaging in drug taking and criminal behavior. The treatment model is bio-psycho-social and emphasizes comprehensive lifestyle change, with issues of physical well-being, family relationships, and criminality all targeted for change while acquiring positive life skills as a vehicle to avoid future drug use.[45] The five-part treatment strategy includes (1) orientation screening and referral, (2) drug abuse education, (3) nonresidential drug abuse treatment services, (4) residential drug abuse treatment, and (5) transitional services. In a study of BOP residential treatment programs, only 3.3 percent of those receiving treatment (compared to 12.1 percent of a similar group that did not receive treatment) were rearrested in the first six months after release.[46]

Substance abuse inmates participate in group counseling sessions. Marmaduke St. John/Alamy Stock Photo.

In a review of several high-quality studies of drug treatment programs published since 2000, the authors found that a variety of pharmacological treatments were associated with a reduced frequency of drug use.[47] As well, offenders that received contingency management or cognitive-behavior therapy tended to use drugs less frequently. And if individuals participating in treatment also had an aftercare program, drug use and crime was lower. In summary, the reviews found that effective treatment programs:

- Focused on high-risk offenders,
- Provided strong inducements to receive treatment,
- Included several different types of interventions simultaneously,
- Provided intensive treatment, and
- Included an aftercare component.[48]

Other Types of Prison Programs

Prison Work Programs

Just as rehabilitative programs have been an accepted component of prisons throughout their history, so has the importance of work. In the Walnut Street Jail, inmates labored in their cells at spinning, weaving, and shoemaking. Not only was such work considered redemptive for the inmate, but early prison labor also benefited the state, as goods were sold to help prisons be self-sufficient. In the early 1800s, state prisons leased out prisoners to the private sector. Companies would bid for control of the prison and its labor, and the winning leaseholder worked the inmates in their industrial operations and, to maximize profits, spent as little as possible to house and feed the inmates.

The **lease system** ended in the early twentieth century, and states began to operate their own prison industries to keep inmates busy and make a profit from the sale of produced goods.

As prison industry programs expanded during the early 1900s, organized labor began to complain about the unfair competition resulting from prisons' sale of goods using free inmate labor. As a result, Congress passed the Hawes–Cooper Act in 1929, requiring that prison products be subject to the laws of any state to which they were shipped. Opponents of prison-made products argued that this did not go far enough, and in 1935, Congress passed the Ashurst–Sumners Act, mandating that prison products be marked as prison-made goods, and then amended the Act in 1940 to fully prohibit the interstate shipment of prison goods.

These Acts ended the sale of prison products on the open market and, as an alternative, prisons began to produce goods that could be used by the state and federal governments. This **state-use system** resulted in prison industries producing inmate clothing, office furniture, and other products that could be sold to government agencies. In 1934, Congress established Federal Prison Industries (FPI) as a wholly owned government corporation to produce prison goods for sale to the federal government. A description of FPI is presented in Chapter 5. FPI is currently the largest prison industry program and is a major producer of goods for government agencies (primarily the military) with sales of almost $500 million a year.

Although thousands of inmates work in prison industries, the majority works in other areas of prison operations to help run the prison. In most prisons, staff members supervise inmates who actually do the work, such as preparing and serving food, doing laundry, doing electrical or plumbing work to maintain the facility, and cutting grass or doing other landscape work. The public supports prison work programs both to assist in rehabilitation and to prepare inmates for the work environment in the community. Prison officials consider work programs essential for managing a correctional institution, because they keep inmates productively busy and help maintain control and order.

lease system

state prisons accepted bids and leased out prisoners to the private sector, which would work the inmates in their industrial operations

state-use system

only allowing prison-made goods to be sold to and used by the state and federal government agencies

Many prison inmates work in trades areas such as heating and air conditioning, learning skills that can help them find jobs after release. Photo by Richard P. Seiter.

Inmates are assigned to several different areas of the prison. Some work in the prison laundry washing sheets, blankets, and inmate clothing. In food service, inmates prepare food, serve it to the inmate population, and clean dishes and cooking equipment for the next meal. Other inmates work in the prison maintenance department in such areas as plumbing, electrical, heating and air conditioning, carpentry, and maintenance of prison landscaping and grounds. Finally, prisoners are used to constantly clean the prison. Sanitation is very important to prevent unsanitary conditions and the spread of infectious diseases in a prison with such large numbers of people living in congested, overcrowded conditions. Overall, between 75 percent and 90 percent of prisoners work in these types of job assignments to maintain the prison and its daily operations.

A relatively recent type of prison job is for inmates to work in community service projects. Perhaps initiated through an emphasis on restorative justice (discussed in Chapter 1), jails and prisons began using minimum security inmates to go into the community to pick up trash, maintain parks, or paint public buildings. Inmates get to keep busy in work that pays back the community for their offenses, and is seen as enriching and rewarding for them. And the public strongly supports these work programs for the same reason. Almost every correctional agency has work programs whereby prisoners go into the community. In June 2015, the Texas prison system reported handling 197 projects while providing 49,005 offender work hours.[49]

Prison Industries

Even with criticism from labor and trade organizations resulting in restrictions for the markets, prison industries continue to be very important to prison operations and for inmate rehabilitation. Prison industries have several benefits:

1. Industrial work assignments that are similar to private-sector operations provide inmates realistic work experience and instill positive work habits.
2. Work experience can provide valuable training and skill development that inmates can use after release.
3. Inmate earnings can be used to support families, pay fines and restitution, and provide inmates money to purchase their own personal items allowed in prison.
4. Earnings by the industry can be used to offset the cost of incarceration.
5. Industrial work assignments are a positive way to reduce idleness and serve as an incentive for good behavior; therefore, they are valuable for inmate management.[50]

After surviving the challenges presented by the congressional Acts of the 1930s, prison industry programs have grown significantly. In 2002, there were 78,881 inmates (7.8 percent of the prison population) working in prison industries in the fifty states, the District of Columbia, and the BOP. In 2001, these programs had sales of $1.7 billion and profits of nearly $19 million.[51] Inmates work under the supervision of staff, which must maintain a close watch over

Prison industry programs keep inmates productively busy while in prison and have been shown to reduce recidivism after release by inmate participants. Photo by Richard P. Seiter.

security and quality. Some of the most common products produced and sold for state use include garments and textile products, wood furniture, printing services, metal products, and other services such as laundry, warehousing, data entry, and construction. Inmates are paid between $2.63 and $7.64 per day.[52]

In addition to the state-use programs of prison industries, Congress in 1979 passed the Private Sector Prison Industry Enhancement (PIE) Certification Program, which allowed for the sale of prison goods on the open market if the program is certified as meeting several conditions, including the following:

- Paying the inmates wages comparable with similar jobs in the community.
- Consulting with representatives of private industry and organized labor.
- Certifying that the PIE industry does not displace employed workers in the community.
- Collecting funds for a victim assistance program.
- Providing inmates with benefits in the event of injury in the course of employment.
- Ensuring that inmate participation was voluntary.
- Providing a substantial role for the private sector.[53]

Almost two-thirds of the states are involved in the **PIE Program**, in which private companies hire inmates to produce goods inside the prisons. By the end of 2005, 6,555 inmates worked in PIE programs, and more than 70,000 have participated since the program's inception.[54] Another requirement of PIE programs is that a share of the inmates' wages is withheld for fines, victim compensation, room and board, support of families, and payment of taxes. From the beginning of the PIE Program until June 2003, on wages of $264 million, more than $146 million was withheld from pay, of which 48 percent was for room and board, 24 percent for taxes, 17 percent for victim restitution, and 11 percent for family support.[55] And a study of the impact of PIE programs found that PIE participants found jobs faster and maintained them longer than inmates who worked in either traditional prison industries or other work programs. As well, PIE participants had lower rates of rearrest, conviction, and incarceration than offenders in either traditional industries or other work assignments.[56] An evaluation of the PIE programs indicated that participants in these programs had lower rearrest rates and obtained employment sooner after release than inmates who worked in regular prison industries or had other work assignments.[57]

PIE Program
prison industry programs operated by private companies, with prison goods authorized to be sold on the open market if the program is certified as meeting certain conditions

Prison industry programs are assets to prison operations, provide funds to operate, and reduce recidivism. In addition to the above outcome, Saylor and Gaes conducted the Post-Release Employment Project, collecting data on more than 7,000 federal offenders for a four-year period, comparing those participating in prison industries work programs with similar offenders who did not participate in programs. The results demonstrated significant and substantive effects on both in-prison (misconduct reports) and postprison (employment and arrest rates) outcome measures.[58] As beneficial and successful as prison industries are to a prison operation, it is unfortunate that such a low percentage of inmates are able to participate in these programs.

Counseling and Therapy Programs

In addition to the above types of programs, there are many individual and group therapy programs focused on changing behavior of offenders. Some of these that have proven effective in a correctional environment are cognitive behavior therapy, life skills development such as thinking for change, and therapeutic communities.

Cognitive behavior therapy (CBT) is an approach based on the belief that criminal behavior results from dysfunctional thinking and poor decision-making. The therapy is usually provided in group settings, and helps offenders identify how they respond to certain situations, and how their choices in these situations can result in criminal or deviant behaviors. CBT programs allow offenders to identify the triggers (impulsiveness, lack of thinking of consequences, or failure to consider others' perspectives) that often impact their decisions in a negative way. Discussions, role plays, feedback from peers, and other approaches provide inmates better skills to work through situations and find alternative behaviors that do not result in dysfunctional behaviors. CBT programs have been found to effectively reduce recidivism, and the results from several studies and meta-analyses have shown reductions in recidivism of between 20 percent and 30 percent. And when targeting the highest risk offenders and insuring high quality program delivery, it can be even higher.[59]

An often used CBT is Thinking for Change (T4C). It was developed for use with offenders in collaboration with the National Institute of Corrections, and has been implemented in many correctional agencies across the country. Its focus is on building life skills that improve individuals' competences in areas such as financial management or parenting skills, while also enhancing self-esteem. It is delivered through a set of lessons in a workbook that offenders work through both individually and as a group. Evaluations have found that it is also effective in reducing recidivism.[60] And finally, therapeutic communities (TCs) are used in a variety of program deliveries in prisons. Therapeutic communities are created in residential units in prisons, and build a supportive treatment culture that is integrated throughout every aspect of the housing unit. They are often a part of substance abuse programming, but the model can be used for other recovery programs. The inmates and staff work together to change behavior, as members both support positive behavior and confront negative behavior. The community acts as the agent of change to influence behavior in line with the mission and goals of the community.

Religious Programs

Since their inception, prisons have been places for religious reformation. Even though religion used to reform offenders is not the focus in modern prisons that it was in the Walnut Street Jail, religious programming continues to be an important rehabilitative opportunity within prisons. Whether due to the history of prisons or because U.S. society values religion, we will probably never give up the belief that the practice of religion is valuable for inmates and that offenders who develop a foundation of religious beliefs are more likely to be successful upon their return to the community. Today, prisons strive to provide religious programs for any group or individual who wants to worship and follow the tenets of a recognized faith. In a survey of prison chaplains, respondents indicated they lead worship services, hold religious instruction sessions, and provide spiritual counseling. Respondents were also very positive about the impact of their religious programming on inmate discipline.[61]

Most inmates are Muslim, Jewish, Protestant, or Catholic, yet there are dozens of other religious sects and worship groups. In most prisons, religious services and activities are coordinated by one or two full-time chaplains (usually Protestant and Catholic) who contract with ministers of other sects to hold services and provide religious guidance for prisoners of those faith groups. In addition to regular services, activities may include Bible study or religious discussion groups. With usually fifteen to twenty different religious groups, the schedule for religious programs is usually very full, and there are often two or three faith groups meeting on any given night. Volunteers play a particularly important role in providing religious programming; they are used to lead study or discussion groups.

A recent development in prison religious programming is faith-based programs. These are usually residential in nature, as a housing unit is turned into a faith-based program assignment. The programs are usually led by a prison chaplain and extensively utilize volunteers. They do not (and federal law prohibits them from "pervasively sectarian") focus on a particular religion, but allow inmates to study and work on their own religious beliefs, and use an overall emphasis on concern for their fellow man, avoidance of doing injury, and avoiding criminogenic behaviors as change agents. Studies of these types of programs have found reductions in recidivism among program participants, in part due to volunteer mentoring that begins in the prison program and continues into the community.[62] And these programs have also been found to improve inmate behavior in prison.[63]

Recreation Programs

Another important but far more controversial area of prison programming is recreation or leisure activities. It is certainly reasonable to recognize that inmates cannot be in their cells or working the entire day, and therefore some types of organized and supervised activities are important to maintain order. Therefore prisons have gymnasiums, recreation yards, and other leisure time areas to play table games, listen to music, or read. However, the public does not like the image of inmates with too much idle time, watching color television or lifting weights. Therefore, prison officials attempt to have active recreation programs that reduce idleness, promote health and fitness, and allow inmates to "burn off steam" through exercise.

Most inmates are required to work approximately six hours per day, five days per week, but there could be far too much idle time without extensive recreational programming to keep inmates busy. Prison recreation programs include outside sports such as soccer, basketball, or softball; less active recreation such as table games or card playing, billiards, or Ping-Pong; art and craft activities such as painting, leather crafts, or pottery making; and fitness programs such as running or calisthenics. Organized athletic activities, such as intramural teams, also have positive rehabilitative benefits, in that they require inmates to work together, develop teamwork, and follow rules and procedures. Recreational programs are also an incentive for good behavior, because inmates can be disciplined by restriction of their participation in such activities.

Recreation is considered critical to a controlled and orderly prison. Photo by Richard P. Seiter.

The most controversial recreational activity is weight lifting, which has been a staple of prisons for decades. Many state legislatures, county governments, and Congress have recently passed legislation ending or limiting weight lifting in prisons and jails. The first effort to ban weight lifting in prison came after inmates, in a 1993 riot at the Southern Ohio Correctional Facility, used weight equipment to break into rooms in which staff members were hiding and take them hostage. As a result, an Ohio congresswoman proposed legislation to ban weight lifting in prison, arguing that the elimination of weights would protect staff from harm.[64] Along with banning weight lifting, many of these legislative acts have also banned the use of electronic musical instruments, paid programming such as HBO movies, and leisure activities such as pool and billiards.

Opponents of weight lifting in prisons argue that inmates who get stronger represent a danger to correctional and law enforcement personnel who may have to physically control them. They suggest that the public does not like the image of inmates spending their time getting stronger by working out with weights, and this image reinforces the stereotypes of a leisurely prison life that does not serve as a punishment and deterrent to crime. However, most correctional officials oppose any ban on the use of weight equipment, arguing that such exercise is an important incentive for good behavior and that there are very few cases in which staff must physically confront a stronger inmate. They point out that weight-lifting inmates seldom get into trouble; they are usually very self-disciplined and do not want to lose the opportunity to exercise. Also, prison staff members are trained not to attempt to break up a fight or get into a physical confrontation unless they have a definite physical advantage or staff members greatly outnumber inmates.

With the controversy regarding weights in prisons, several prisons have removed weights and replaced them with "dip" bars or other exercise equipment.
Photo by Richard P. Seiter.

Over the past decade, and partially as a result of the ban on weight lifting in many jurisdictions, prisons have started recreation programs focusing on educating inmates regarding health and diet to encourage them to develop healthy lifestyles. Offenders enter prison with histories of poor medical care, nutrition, and eating habits and a lack of understanding of the importance of exercise and aerobic activities to reduce fat and improve heart functioning. As prison sentences lengthen and inmates age while in prison, the costs of medical care increase significantly. Health education programs are a negligible investment in improving the long-term health of offenders and thereby reducing health care costs for inmates in the future.

Even though there is significant opposition to recreation programs for inmates, they will continue to be an important part of prison programming. There is no alternative to increased idleness if inmates have nothing to do with the time they are not at work or participating in a self-improvement program. Prison administrators fear idleness as a precursor of violence and inmate unrest, especially in today's overcrowded prisons, and forcibly argue this point to elected officials, and prisons will continue to have active recreational programs to encourage good behavior and maintain order.

Effectiveness of Treatment Programs

One issue that has created controversy and influenced correctional policy over the past twenty-five years is the evaluation of the outcome of correctional treatment programs. Although the public supports the concept of rehabilitation and correctional officials value treatment programs for the stabilizing effect they have on offender populations, the bottom line is that there is an expectation that these programs will reduce recidivism. Elected officials and advocates and opponents of rehabilitation all agree that, in exchange for the dollars they are spending on such programs, there should be a crime reduction payback.

Corrections is a big business, with billions of dollars directed to the operation of correctional agencies, so it is important that we use evidence-based programs that have been shown to be cost effective and successful. Allen Ault, former commissioner of corrections in three states and former chief of the NIC National Academy of Corrections noted,

> I do not believe that we in corrections will ever be a "profession," or that we in it will ever be considered professionals or listened to by the public or the politicians, until we have our own body of knowledge— the distinction of a profession—that is backed by solid research. We have adapted other knowledge from many other professions and attempted to apply it in the correctional setting, but too often we did not have any research component to consider if it worked or not. It is hard to sell programs when you do not have facts to back up their effectiveness.[65]

Fortunately for those who support the correctional goal to rehabilitate offenders, there has been resurgence in support for rehabilitation programs; one reason being that there is now evidence of success, and agencies and public officials want to implement programs that are **evidence based**. This means there is evidence of success, generally defined as reducing recidivism, and many states require correctional agencies to only fund evidence-based programs.

Support for rehabilitation dwindled after an early 1970s review by Martinson and colleagues of the effectiveness of correctional treatment. While finding a few isolated correlations between a treatment program and a reduction in recidivism, they identified no consistent findings that any single treatment program significantly reduced recidivism.[66] Their conclusion that "nothing works" led to the abandonment of the medical model of corrections and began the momentum for many states to move from indeterminate sentencing with a focus on changing the individual offender to determinant sentencing with an emphasis on deterrence and incapacitation.

There have been many methodological concerns about the early work of Martinson and the ability to actually evaluate correctional treatment programs based on recidivism. Many question the validity of using recidivism as a measure of the effectiveness of correctional programs, considering it unfair to expect correctional treatment to have a long-term impact by reducing recidivism. Recidivism can have varying definitions, including the commission of any new crime, commission of a felony during the period of community supervision, and return to prison. A reasonable length for posttreatment follow-up is also a concern. Can a correctional sanction or program be expected to have an impact on an offender for three or even five years after the termination of the sanction or program? Another concern is that social science research designs often have difficulty controlling for the many external and internal factors that can affect recidivism rates.

evidence based
a focus on provision of programs where there is evidence of success, generally defined as reducing recidivism

meta-analysis

a statistical measure of the average effect an intervention has on recidivism across all studies, while identifying and controlling for various study conditions

In a recent review of the effectiveness of correctional treatment, Cullen and Gendreau point out several limitations in the review by Martinson.[67] First, since the initial study, there have been developments in researchers' abilities to quantitatively synthesize and assess the impact of research findings, particularly through the use of **meta-analysis**. Meta-analysis statistically measures the average effect an intervention has on recidivism across all studies, while identifying and controlling for various conditions such as the characteristics of the offenders treated, the type of setting, and the study methodology. Second, although the review by Lipton and colleagues was comprehensive for that time, there were a limited number of studies per treatment category: "7 for casework/individual counseling; 15 for skill development; 12 for individual psychotherapy; 19 for group methods; and 20 for milieu therapy."[68] Third, the Lipton review did not include cognitive–behavioral therapy programs, which have been found to be successful treatment approaches for offenders.[69] Finally, the review did not consider any impact or outcome other than recidivism, such as prison behavior or educational achievement.

Later studies revisit and question the "nothing works" concept regarding correctional treatment. In 1990, Andrews and colleagues found that of the better-controlled studies, 40 percent found that treatment had a "positive effect."[70] In a 1993 analysis of the impact of correctional treatment, Lipsey and Wilson reviewed ten meta-analyses and identified a 25 percent reduction of recidivism by psychological, educational, and behavioral correctional treatment programs.[71] In 1995, Losel reviewed thirteen meta-analyses and found that the average impact from the treatment intervention would result in a recidivism rate of 45 percent for the treatment group and 55 percent for the control group.[72] More recently, researchers have been examining the "quality" of correctional programs, in terms of leadership, resources, program integrity, and focus on principles of treatment interventions.[73] Treatment programs that are ranked high on quality are more likely to result in reductions of recidivism. And staff quality (as measured in staff characteristics, training and supervision) are also related to program effectiveness.[74]

We now have sound research studies that can show the effectiveness of correctional activities and programs. There is evidence that shows a relationship between drug programming, job readiness classes, and education that link program completion with reduced criminality.[75] We know that a focus only on surveillance does not improve the success or reduce the risk of community offenders reoffending. For correctional administrators to have credibility with the external environment, it is important to know and be able to describe the results of program effectiveness and to be able to use data to argue for correctional programs they believe improve their ability to manage or reduce recidivism.

There has been resurgence in support for rehabilitation programs. Two factors have led to this resurgence. The first is that with tightening government budgets, officials are recognizing that we cannot continue to "recycle" offenders through correctional programs only to have them continue to fail when returned to the community. A second is the interest in finding and implementing programs that are evidence based. This means there is evidence of success, generally defined as reducing recidivism, and many states require correctional agencies to only fund evidence-based programs. A recent publication of recidivism data from 2005 to 2010 in thirty states found that within five years after release, 55.1

Rehabilitative programs are believed to reduce recidivism.
Courtesy of CoreCivic.

percent of 404,638 releasees returned to prison for either a parole or probation violation or commission of a new crime.[76] States recognize that by bringing these high recidivism rates down, they can save money.

An example is Washington state, where after forecasts that the state would need to construct several new prisons in the coming decades, the Washington legislature directed the Washington State Institute for Public Policy to find "evidence-based" options that could reduce recidivism and avoid the need for expensive prison construction. After a review of 571 program evaluations within corrections, the Institute estimated the benefits and costs of them, and created an alternative policy of putting money into effective programs rather than new prison construction. The estimated savings for avoiding prison construction in the state is approximately $2 billion.[77]

In Pennsylvania, the Board of Probation and Parole began providing offenders with a Cognitive Life Skills program to include criminal thinking, decision-making, problem solving, high-risk behaviors, and other criminogenic needs. Results of program participants from 2010 to 2013 had reduced recidivism compared to nonparticipants.[78] And, in an effort to reduce recidivism, Ohio reorganized of all its prisons to a three-tiered system aimed at reducing violence and increasing rehabilitative opportunities for positive change. Inmates participate in evidence-based programs, and Reintegration Units were created to house offenders nearing release and provide community transition services, such as job readiness opportunities. The agency mission has been restated to "reduce recidivism for those we touch."[79] And this focus seems to be working. The Ohio three-year return to prison recidivism rate for offenders released in 2003 was 39.52 percent, for offenders released in 2008 was 31.2 percent, and for those released in 2012 was 29.26 percent.[80]

Chapter Review

Summary

Treatment programs have been a critical part of the mission of prisons since their initiation, and are broadly supported to provide inmates many program opportunities that can aid in their successful reentry to the community. Chapter 13 presented the policies and procedures to create a safe and secure environment in prisons. As might be envisioned, in many ways, custody and treatment may seem in competition with each other. How can a prison maintain security and order while encouraging inmates to participate in self-improvement programs? And how can positive programs operate within an environment that must control every inmate activity? However, in other ways, these two emphases seem to complement and support one another, because active programs help develop self-control and encourage inmate good behavior.

In this chapter, the variety and background of prison programs are presented. There is much discussion regarding the importance of prison programs in terms of their cost and potential to undermine the punitive and deterrent aspects of a prison sentence. Yet prison programs reduce idleness, teach inmates to live and work in groups, open staff-inmate channels of communication, increase the confidence and self-esteem of offenders, encourage them to accept challenges and strive for success, and increase the educational and vocational skills of inmates.

Many correctional programs have proved effective in reducing recidivism. Several studies over the past decade have affirmed the value of prison rehabilitation programs and bode well for their future. Even with an emphasis on "punishment" of criminals, the public expects them to return to the community better prepared to become law-abiding citizens. Rehabilitative programs are a reasonable investment in saving money associated with continued offender criminality. We know that simply enhancing criminal sanctions and increasing the level of punishment do not reduce recidivism. However, correctly classifying offenders and providing them with quality treatment interventions result in a significant reduction in recidivism.

Many students will find the work in delivering treatment programs in prisons as attractive jobs. In that light, the following "Your Career in Corrections" box highlights the role that correctional educators play in prisons.

Your Career in Corrections

Correctional Educators

Correctional educators are the people who teach, oversee, or coordinate education and sometimes vocational training programs within prisons. Education is one of the oldest and largest programs in any prison; most prisons have between five and ten education staff members. Correctional education formed as early as the 1800s, with prison chaplains considered the first "teachers," as they used the Bible (often the only book allowed in early prisons) to teach inmates how to read. As the earliest prison reformers began to push for improvements in the operations of U.S. prisons, one of their first initiatives was to push for more education programs to give inmates the literacy skills seen as critical to success after release.

Correctional education is a nontraditional occupation; it is not an area that people specifically study or prepare for. Not many teachers begin thinking that they want to work in a prison; they seem to fall into it through one way or another. Most find that they love teaching, but are not completely happy with the traditional school system and begin to look for other options. They also don't always plan to make it a career, but often find it a challenging and rewarding job and decide to continue correctional work until retirement.

Correctional educators have a nontraditional setting in that in some ways, it is like a "one-room" school. Teachers are not divided into grades, but have specialty areas such as English, math, or reading, and have students at multiple levels in their classes at one time. Adult learners are tested to determine their proficiency and then work at their own level under the guidance of the teacher. Many correctional educators really like the adult learner approach as well as the structure and order of a prison education program. They find the work very rewarding, as they do not lose students each year (as they move to another grade), but see them continue until they reach a milestone of success (such as getting their GED). Most inmates enroll in school because they see it as their only means of not coming back, and they have a true motivation to learn. They (and their teachers) get almost immediate gratification, because they do not have to wait twelve years to graduate from high school, and they can get their GED in a matter of months in many cases. Another positive factor in many correctional educators' minds is that they do not worry about security in the prison environment; many say they actually feel safer teaching in a prison than in many public schools. They have control over inmates and the inmates face consequences if they misbehave.

There are also some disadvantages and frustrations teaching in a prison. First, inmates have many issues in their own backgrounds that can affect their ability to learn: special learning disorders, family problems, drug addiction, or a long sentence.

One frustrating thing (especially for correctional education administrators) is that teachers are not trained in working with students in a prison environment. Special training and professional development must be provided to teachers until they become accustomed to the special circumstances they will face. Even though many inmates are motivated, others are not, so teachers have to be creative with limited resources. Their students did not succeed in traditional school systems, and correctional educators must get them past this failure and do things differently. Finally, and only partly seriously, correctional educators do not get the summers off. Prison education programs go year round, unlike the traditional school calendar.

Overall, correctional educators are a very satisfied, motivated, and dedicated group of professionals. They do a difficult job, but feel that they are really helping people who understand the importance of their education and generally recognize that they do not have too many more chances to be successful. It can be a good career for those who like to teach and help others.

Key Terms

mandatory prison education
vocational training
Pell grants

continuum of care
lease system
state-use system

PIE Program
evidence based
meta-analysis

Review Questions

1. What is the definition of prison treatment?
2. What are the activities used to identify inmate treatment needs?
3. How does the percent of prison inmates compare to the general U.S. population in terms of completion of high school or receiving a General Equivalency Degree?
4. What are mandatory education programs in prisons?
5. How are mental health programs delivered in prisons and what is the continuum of care?
6. Describe the various types of substance abuse programs in prisons.
7. Define the state-use system for prison industries.
8. Outline the conditions required to be certified as a PIE Program.
9. List the arguments against weight lifting in prison.
10. Define a meta-analysis, and how has its availability changed the early "nothing works" conclusion?

You Make the Decision...

Should Weight Lifting Be Banned in Prisons?

As noted earlier, weight lifting for prison inmates has become very controversial, as many jurisdictions have banned it from prisons and jails. The argument against it is that inmates who get stronger are a danger to prison staff members who may have to physically control them, and perhaps even more important is that they just don't like the image of inmates working out with weights. Most correctional officials argue both for the allowance of weight lifting as an incentive for good behavior and that they just don't experience problems with physically strong inmates.

Now it is your turn to decide. If you were the director of a state prison system, what would you argue? You are to appear before the state legislative committee with jurisdiction over your department. There is a very vocal group of committee members that have been saying that weight lifting is dangerous to staff and taxpayers should not spend money to buy equipment for inmates to get stronger. You know that there are some reasonable members that would support you if you argued to keep weight lifting, but the vote up or down is very undecided at this time. There will also be significant media coverage at the hearing. You are the primary witness. Either individually or in a small classroom group, outline your position and the reason for it, and consider how you will testify at the hearing.

CHAPTER 15

Legal Issues and the Death Penalty

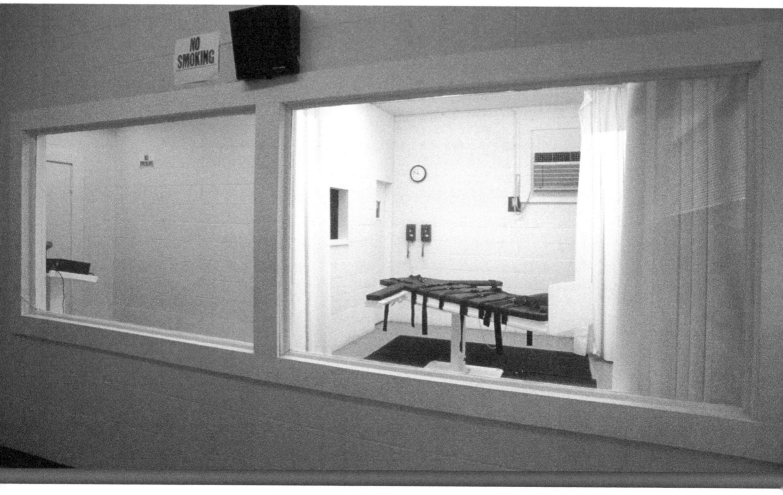

Michele Molinari/Alamy Stock Photo.

After reading this chapter, you should be able to:

1. Outline the development and sources of prisoners' rights as well as the rights they have today.

2. Explain how the First, Fourth, Eighth, and Fourteenth Amendments to the U.S. Constitution create a basis for inmate lawsuits.

3. Specify the legal cases and constitutional standards regarding cruel and unusual punishment, inmate religious practice, delivery of medical care, inmate discipline, and limits on inmates' litigation.

4. Outline the history of capital punishment in the United States and the legal provisions for it.

5. Detail the number of executions each year, how executions are carried out, and the problems associated with them.

6. Summarize the arguments for and against the use of the death penalty.

7. Describe the current and any changes in public attitude regarding the death penalty.

Introduction

This chapter discusses the complex issues of the legal rights of inmates and the use of capital punishment. There are, perhaps, no more emotional topics than these in the overall operations of correctional agencies. Few people would argue that inmates should lose every right they have, as citizens of the United States, as a result of committing a felony and being imprisoned. It is uncomfortable to think about the unfair treatment, torture and excessive use of force, discrimination, and failure to provide basic due process to inmates that has occurred during the history of correctional institutions. Although most agree that inmates do not deserve such treatment, many people also believe that inmates today receive too many rights and unduly burden correctional officials and cost taxpayers money with petty claims, and that the pendulum has swung too far in providing inmates more rights than they should have. The first section of this chapter addresses the evolution of inmate rights, the foundation for prisoner rights provided by the U.S. Constitution, a description of the specific areas of inmate rights, and some movements to limit litigation by inmates against correctional agencies and officials.

The second section of this chapter addresses another emotional issue: the use of capital punishment. Even though our country has a long history of the use of the death penalty as a sanction for serious crimes, the majority of the public supports it, and the U.S. Supreme Court has ruled that capital punishment in itself is not cruel and unusual; there is still deep concern and persevering debate on the topic. The historical use of capital punishment in the United States and the very active consideration of capital punishment laws by the federal courts over the past thirty years are presented. Arguments for and against the need for capital punishment are described, as well as the constant concern about error in conviction and the irrevocability of a sentence of death.

Legal Issues Regarding Inmates

As much as is heard about inmates suing the state, the governor, the prison warden, or any number of other prison staff members, we tend to believe that lawsuits have always been a part of the history of prisons, and inmates have always had, as some people think, more rights than law-abiding citizens. However, that is not the case. The truth is that inmates are still citizens of the United States and therefore come under the protection of the Constitution and the Bill of Rights, just like any other U.S. citizen. However, certain security and safety concerns in the operation of a prison allow prison administrators to limit inmates' full enjoyment of the rights they would have if they were not in prison.

Inmates have not been hesitant to file suits against correctional agencies or prison staff. In 1977, there were only 8,777 petitions filed by inmates in U.S. District Courts for civil rights or prison condition issues. The number increased each year until it peaked in 1996, when there were 41,215 civil rights lawsuits filed by inmates against state and federal correctional agencies. The number of lawsuits began to slow thereafter, and was only 25,110 petitions in 2012, and then increased to 26,444 cases in 2015 and 27,804 in 2016.[1] These drops are more significant considering the number of inmates is much higher than in the decade before.

The Development of Inmate Legal Rights

Historically, until fifty years ago, there was little consideration of the rights of people confined in correctional institutions, as federal courts did not want to intervene in the administration of prisons. This avoidance was primarily the result of the 1871 decision of *Ruffin v. Commonwealth of Virginia*,[2] in which the U.S. Supreme Court enunciated the **slave-of-the-state doctrine** holding that inmates were, for all intents and purposes, slaves of the state and had no rights that were not granted them by the state. With this decision, the Court created what became known as the *hands-off doctrine* and did not accept lawsuits regarding violation of inmates' constitutional rights. The Court believed it good policy to continue this approach due to (1) the Court's lack of expertise in corrections and showing deference to the judgment of prison administrators, (2) the need for separation of powers between the judicial and the executive branches of government, and (3) a concern that accepting prisoner-rights cases would open a Pandora's box of further litigation, and the courts would be flooded with prisoner lawsuits. The hands-off doctrine was supported in the 1948 decision of *Price v. Johnston*, when the Court ruled that convicted inmates must expect that as a part of their punishment they lose the freedoms that free citizens take for granted.[3]

Federal courts adhered to the hands-off doctrine for most of the next two decades. However, after reading complaints by inmates that seemed like a continuing escalation of the violation of basic tenets of the Constitution, the Court decided that it needed to give some guidance to correctional officials. In 1964, it accepted and heard *Cooper v. Pate*,[4] a case regarding religious freedom in prison. Black Muslim inmates claimed that they were not being allowed to congregate, eat their prescribed religious diet, or wear distinctive items of clothing, all of which were basic tenets of their religious practice and therefore a violation of Section 1983 of the Civil Rights Act of 1871. The Court, recognizing the Black Muslim faith as constituting an established religion, ruled that black Muslims should be allowed to follow the prescribed practices of that religion, if those practices did not present a clear and present danger to the security and orderly running of a prison.

With its decision in *Cooper v. Pate*, the Court effectively ended the hands-off doctrine by recognizing that inmates could sue prison officials for violation of their rights under the Constitution. With this decision, the world of inmate lawsuits and legal issues for inmates changed forever. The floodgates were opened; the federal courts spend considerable time and resources handling inmate complaints and correctional administrators must constantly stay attuned to new decisions by the courts and the impact that such decisions have on prison operations. New decisions clarify the rights that are not lost by being convicted of a felony and incarcerated and guide correctional officials in following the earlier court **precedents** and revising policies and procedures to be consistent with such decisions. As a result, instead of the early belief that inmates lose their rights, it is now believed that inmates retain their constitutional rights as citizens when incarcerated unless the necessity for security and order in a prison deems otherwise.

Since the U.S. Supreme Court abandoned the hands-off doctrine, the number of cases filed has increased tremendously. In a 1994 review of the use of litigation by inmates under Section 1983 of the Civil Rights Act, Hanson and Daley note,

> *The Administrative Office of the U.S. Courts counted only 218 cases in 1966, the first year that state prisoners' rights cases were recorded as a specific category of litigation. The number climbed to 26,824 by 1992.... Finally, there is approximately one lawsuit for every thirty state prison inmates.*[5]

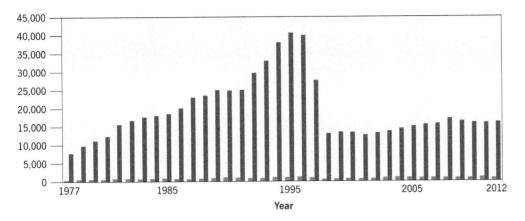

FIGURE 15.1 Petitions Filed in U.S. District Courts by Federal and State Prisoners Source: Data from *Sourcebook of Criminal Justice Statistics*, Table 5.65.2012, available at http://www .albany.edu/sourcebook/pdf/t5652012.pdf (accessed December 5, 2017).

Figure 15.1 is a good illustration of the increase in the number of lawsuits from 1977 until 2012. Following a description of the development of prisoner legal issues in a variety of areas, there is a further explanation of the slowdown of lawsuits by inmates over the past decade.

The Bill of Rights and Congressional Actions Providing Inmate Rights

The source of all inmate rights is the Constitution of the United States (ratified in 1788) and the Bill of Rights (added in 1791), just as they are the source of the rights granted to all citizens of the United States. The primary amendments that are used as a basis of lawsuits by prison inmates are the Eighth (prohibiting cruel and unusual punishment) and the Fourteenth (providing due process to individuals charged with crimes). Other amendments, as well as specific laws passed by Congress, are used less frequently, but are still the basis of many inmate rights.

The **Eighth Amendment** states that no cruel or unusual punishment may be inflicted and is a broad opening for a variety of inmate lawsuits over aspects such as prison overcrowding, life and safety issues, use of force against inmates by staff, or poor food or medical care. It is difficult for a court or correctional administrators to determine what level of restrictions in a prison constitutes "cruel and unusual punishment." Obviously, torture or physical punishment are not allowed, but less obvious allegations of cruel and unusual punishment are more difficult to define specifically because almost every case has individual situations and presents varying facts. Over the past three decades, the federal courts have provided additional guidance in defining cruel and unusual punishment in three major prisoner-rights cases.

In the 1970 case of *Holt v. Sarver*, a federal district court looked at conditions throughout the Arkansas prison system and created a standard of cruel and unusual punishment under the Eighth Amendment. Going beyond the concept of torture or physical punishment, the court found that if people of *reasonable sensitivity* found the treatment shocking or disgusting, it would also be considered cruel and unusual. The court ruled that in general terms, cruel and unusual punishment is that which "amounts to torture, when it is grossly excessive in proportion to the offense for which it is imposed, or that is inherently unfair, or that is unnecessarily degrading, or that is shocking or disgusting to people of reasonable sensitivity."[6]

In the 1979 case of *Bell v. Wolfish*, the Court reviewed conditions and practices at a federal jail for short-term offenders in New York City. Even though the jail was

Eighth Amendment
states that no cruel or unusual punishment may be inflicted

recently constructed, it was already overcrowded, with two inmates held in most cells at the time of the inmates' complaints leading to this decision. Inmates also complained that prohibiting them from receiving hardback books not mailed directly from a publisher, not allowing them to observe searches of their cells, and requiring them to submit to visual searches of body cavities after visits with family members or friends constituted cruel and unusual punishment. The Court ruling adopted the *punitive intent standard*, stating that the case should turn only on whether the practices in question violated detainees' right to be free from punishment, using a standard of whether the individual restrictions were punitive or merely regulatory restraints, whether the practice is reasonably related to a legitimate goal other than punishment, and whether it appears to be excessive in relation to that alternative purpose.[7]

In *Solem v. Helm*, the Court in 1983 developed the *test of proportionality*, declaring the following:

> [W]e hold as a matter of principle that a criminal sentence must be proportionate to the crime for which the defendant has been convicted.... In sum, a court's proportionality analysis... should be guided by objective criteria, including (i) the gravity of the offense and the harshness of the penalty; (ii) the sentences imposed on other criminals in the same jurisdiction; and (iii) the sentences imposed for commission of the same crime in other jurisdictions....[8]

Fourteenth Amendment

no state shall deprive any person of life, liberty, or property without the due process of law; states may not deny any person the equal protection of the law

balancing test

established in *Pell v. Procunier*, finding that prison inmates retain those First Amendment rights that are not inconsistent with their status as prisoner or with legitimate penological objectives

Civil Rights Act of 1871

this act of Congress guaranteed the rights of freed slaves and provided access to federal courts for violations of the act

Section 1983

a section of the Civil Rights Act that prohibits any person acting under the color of any statute, ordinance, or regulation (color of law) from depriving another person of his or her constitutional rights

The **Fourteenth Amendment** asserts that no state shall deprive any person of life, liberty, or property without the due process of law and also prohibits states from denying any person the equal protection of the law. When initially passed, the Constitution and Bill of Rights applied only to the federal courts and federal law in defining the relationship between citizens and government. The Fifth and Sixth Amendments guarantee due process in the course of legal proceedings, and the Fourteenth Amendment expanded these rights to states. Inmates who claim that prison officials have taken action against them for disciplinary reasons without providing them due process or that they have not had access to legal materials and therefore access to the courts often cite the Fourteenth Amendment.

Inmate lawsuits also regularly cite the First Amendment as the basis for their complaints. The First Amendment guarantees that no law shall be enacted that restricts or abridges an individual's freedom of religion, speech, and the press. These were seen by our founding fathers as such basic and fundamental rights (thus, the "First" Amendment) that the federal courts require very compelling reasons for prison officials to deny such freedoms to inmates. In the 1974 case of *Pell v. Procunier*, the U.S. Supreme Court created the **balancing test**, declaring "[a] prison inmate retains those First Amendment rights that are not inconsistent with his status as prisoner or with the *legitimate penological objectives* of a correctional system."[9] The Court recognized that correctional officials have legitimate concerns in trying to provide security and safety within a correctional institution and that these should be weighed (or balanced) against the restriction of rights. In more recent decisions, courts often have required prison officials to make reasonable accommodations to practices and procedures to allow for such rights. Issues under the First Amendment of use of the mail, access to outside publications, and access to the press are described next.

Not every right was anticipated or addressed in the U.S. Constitution or the Bill of Rights. Therefore, over the years, Congress has passed several Acts to protect individuals against discrimination. The earliest was the **Civil Rights Act of 1871**, which guaranteed the rights of freed slaves and provided access to federal courts for violations of the Act. **Section 1983** of the Civil Rights Act prohibits any person, acting under the color of any statute, ordinance, or regulation (color of law), from depriving another person of his or her constitutional rights. The use of Section 1983 of the

Civil Rights Act has expanded beyond the original use intended by Congress, and inmates regularly use it to sue government employees in their individual capacity for restricting religious practice, failing to provide proper medical care, or not protecting an inmate from assault by another inmate.

Another Act of Congress that affects correctional institutions is the **Americans with Disabilities Act (ADA)** of 1990. The ADA prohibits any entity from discriminating against an individual with a disability in regard to employment, public services and transportation, public accommodations, and telecommunications services. The most difficult issues for correctional agencies arise in the sections dealing with employment and accommodation. Many prisons (like most law enforcement agencies) have physical conditions of employment that some disabled individuals cannot meet. And inmates can sue regarding the requirement that all areas of a prison be accessible to people

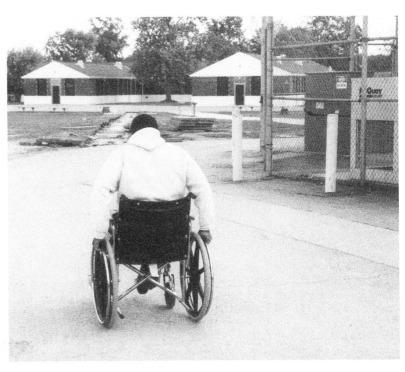

The Americans with Disabilities Act of 1990 requires prisons to make accommodations for inmates with all types of physical disabilities. Photo by Richard P. Seiter.

with disabilities. The courts have continually (against strenuous objections by prison officials and governors from almost every state) held that the ADA applies to correctional institutions as well as other public entities. The states often argue that the ADA was not intended for prisons, but for public buildings, and that prisons, although funded with public money, are not public in that not everyone has access to them. However, in *United States v. Georgia* (2006), the Court unanimously ruled that under Title II of the ADA, the state has a duty to accommodate the needs of disabled persons, and that prisoners whose rights have been violated under the Act may sue for monetary damages if the ADA violation also involves a violation of a prisoner's constitutional rights.[10]

Americans with Disabilities Act
a law that prohibits any entity from discriminating against an individual with a disability in regard to employment, public service and transportation, public accommodations, and telecommunications services

Specific Rights of Prisoners

The Constitution, Bill of Rights, and other Acts of Congress form the basis of rights provided to inmates and guide correctional officials as they struggle to maintain security and order in prisons without violating the basic rights of inmates. The next several sections describe specific areas in which inmate rights are often argued in courts and in which there has been an evolution of practice in correctional facilities. These include overcrowding and overall conditions of confinement, religious freedom, medical care, freedom of speech, use of the mail and receipt of publications, access to the press, access to the courts, privacy and search and seizure, and inmate discipline.

Conditions of Confinement

Inmates often complain about overcrowding and poor overall conditions of confinement (poor food, lack of satisfactory health care, unsanitary conditions) that can

totality-of-conditions test

a test created in *Pugh v. Locke* that examines the aggregate of circumstances in a prison to determine whether cruel and unusual conditions exist

deliberate indifference

as established in *Wilson v. Seiter*, the standard that conditions at prison are not unconstitutional unless prison administrators show deliberate indifference toward inmates' basic needs

result from overcrowding or from simple neglect by prison officials. Courts have used the **totality-of-conditions test** to determine whether the overall conditions within a prison constitute cruel and unusual punishment. The totality-of-conditions test examines the aggregate of circumstances in a prison to determine whether they, as a whole, are cruel and unusual, even if no single condition of the prison is cruel and unusual. This test was first created in *Pugh v. Locke* in 1976, when Alabama prison conditions were found so debilitating that they deprived inmates of the opportunity to rehabilitate themselves or even maintain skills they already possessed.[11]

However, the U.S. Supreme Court clearly determined that overcrowding itself (having more than one person in a cell) is not cruel and unusual punishment in violation of the Eighth Amendment. In *Bell v. Wolfish* in 1979, the Court held that there is no one-person, one-cell guarantee within a prison.[12] Shortly thereafter (in 1981), the Court in *Rhodes v. Chapman* determined that double-celling in itself does not constitute cruel and unusual punishment, in that it does not "inflict unnecessary or wanton pain."[13] And in 1991, the Court in *Wilson v. Seiter* (a significant corrections decision with the author of this text as the named defendant) noted that uncomfortable conditions are a part of the penalty that inmates pay for their criminality and that inmates must prove that conditions are objectively cruel and unusual and that they exist due to the **deliberate indifference** of prison administrators.[14] Deliberate indifference thereafter became the standard for individual liability under conditions of confinement suits brought under Section 1983. The "A Case Study" box illustrates some of the background issues that can lead to the development of inmate lawsuits.

A very interesting case, which could change consideration of conditions of confinement, is *Brown v. Plata*, a case decided by the U.S. Supreme Court in 2011.[15] In consideration was that California's prisons were designed to house a population just under 80,000, but the population was almost double that. The federal courts were frustrated that after twenty years, several lawsuits, appointment of a special master and then receiver, and several injunctions, California had still not improved its delivery of medical and mental health care to the inmate population to a level that the courts believed it did not violate the Eighth Amendment.

The plaintiffs in previous lawsuits believed that a remedy for medical and mental health care could not be achieved without reducing overcrowding, and they moved their respective district courts to convene a three-judge court to order reductions in the prison population. The judges in both previous actions granted the request, and the cases were consolidated before a single three-judge court. After hearing testimony and making extensive findings of fact, the court ordered California to reduce its prison population to 137.5 percent of design capacity within two years, and required the state to formulate a compliance plan and submit it for court approval. California appealed to the U.S. Supreme Court, and the Court in 2011 held that the population limit is constitutionally and statutorily authorized. The Court stated that the three-judge court did not err in finding that crowding was the primary (but not the only) cause of the failure to provide quality medical and mental health care, yet also acknowledged that reducing crowding would not entirely cure the violations.[16]

What is significant is that this use of a population and overcrowding reduction was the first of its kind in several years and may reopen some of the standards resulting from findings in *Rhodes v. Chapman* and *Wilson v. Seiter*. Some suggest that the courts in *Brown* may have developed a "one-bed, one-prisoner" standard, in that arrangements of adding temporary beds or having inmates sleep on the floor due to overcrowding is not acceptable. However, there have been no additional cases since *Plata* to further determine if a new standard for overcrowding and violations of the Eighth Amendment would be created.

A Case Study

The Development of an Inmate Lawsuit

Two significant cases regarding conditions of prison confinement are *Rhodes v. Chapman* and *Wilson v. Seiter*. As director of the Ohio Department of Corrections, I was directly involved in one of these lawsuits; I became director shortly after the U.S. Supreme Court decided *Rhodes v. Chapman*. The following case study illustrates some of the issues that can lead to inmate lawsuits and affect a court decision regarding the cases.

Rhodes v. Chapman involved the Southern Ohio Correctional Institution (SOCF) located in Lucasville, Ohio. SOCF was opened in the early 1970s to replace the century-old Ohio Penitentiary (OP). Its design was to be state of the art in that it would be all single cells in three different sections so that different groups of inmates could be separated. However, the prison opened with a large percentage of new staff members, and some of the worst prisoners from the OP were transferred to the new prison. Too many inmates were transferred to SOCF too fast, and the staff competence and procedures could not keep up with the rapid growth in the number of inmates, many of whom were violent and disruptive.

The prison experienced several problems, including inmate riots, hostage takings, escapes, and staff union strikes. The upper management was changed and while things improved, there were still many problems. Inmate Kelly Chapman and others decided to sue the Ohio Department of Corrections, complaining primarily that the prison held many more inmates than the 1,600 single cells were designed to hold. Prison officials were unconcerned about double-celling, as the cells were fairly large (approximately 80 square feet), and the prison had ample space for programs and services.

The department won the case at the federal district court level, but the inmates appealed and won in the U.S. Court of Appeals. Ohio decided to appeal to the U.S. Supreme Court, believing that one person per cell would not be upheld. The case was won at this level, but only because the "totality of conditions" at SOCF indicated that inmates were out of their cells all but eight hours per day, many programs (education, vocational, and work) kept inmates busy during the day, and services (food services and medical) were adequate.

In *Wilson v. Seiter*, we had opened an old tuberculosis hospital that had been closed for several years as the Hocking Correctional Facility (HCF). Housing was of dormitory style, and the prison had just over 300 inmates. We decided to place older inmates in the prison, as there was limited program and recreation space, believing that these inmates would need less space for such activities. Although the prison seemed to meet our needs, inmates complained that the old facility was too hot (it was not air conditioned) in the summer, and in the winter (due to rows of windows similar to an elementary school), it was not warm enough for the older inmates who lived there.

The case was quickly thrown out at the U.S. District Court level, as the court did not believe that inmate "Pearly" Wilson and others involved in the lawsuit had complained about issues that breached their constitutional rights as prisoners. When the inmates appealed, the upper-level court determined that the lower court had used the wrong standard for determining that we as prison administrators had not violated the constitutional standard against cruel and unusual punishment. The case went to the U.S. Supreme Court not on the conditions that existed at HCF, but on the standard that prison administrators must be held to when conditions that were "uncomfortable" but possibly not "unconstitutional" existed. The decision by the Supreme Court that conditions at a prison are not unconstitutional unless prison administrators show "deliberate indifference" toward inmates' basic needs was a good win and very important for future defenses of inmate lawsuits by correctional agencies.

Religious Freedom

The practice of religious freedom was so fundamental in the founding of the United States that courts hold correctional officials to a high standard in the restriction of the practice of inmates' duly recognized religion. The First Amendment to the Constitution states that "Congress shall make no law respecting an establishment of religion, or prohibiting the free exercise thereof...." In the 1964 case of *Cooper v. Pate*,[17] the Court determined that inmates should be allowed to practice their religion when the following conditions are met: (1) The religion claimed is a duly established religion, (2) the practices desired by inmates are part of the basic tenets of the religion, and (3) the practices do not present a clear and present danger to the security and orderly running of a prison.

Although federal courts initially ruled that prisons must provide sweat lodges for Native American inmates to practice their religious tradition of going into a small lodge (the branches forming an igloo-like structure are covered with blankets), a later decision allowed that if prison officials believe this undermines security, they can prohibit sweat lodges. Photo by Richard P. Seiter.

Several cases since *Cooper v. Pate* have further refined this ruling. In terms of the religion being duly established, it is not for prison officials to determine which religions inmates may practice, yet inmates cannot just create some religion to subvert prison restrictions. In *Cruz v. Beto* (1972), the Supreme Court stated that inmates must be given a "reasonable opportunity" to practice their religion, even if the inmates' faith is not traditional or conventional.[18] Yet when a group of inmates at the Atlanta federal penitentiary attempted to expand the definition of a non-traditional or unconventional religion, by creating a new religion called the Church of the New Song (CONS) and demanding that steak and wine be included on the prison menu, the federal court disagreed (*Theriault v. Silber*, 1977), and found that it was not a religion entitled to First Amendment protection.[19]

If the religion is a valid one, inmates can practice activities that are basic tenets of the religion. For example, Jewish inmates must be provided kosher food as a part of the prison menu (*Kahane v. Carlson*, 1975).[20] Yet the court ruled in *O'Lone v. Estate of Shabazz* (1987) that prison officials do not have to rearrange inmate work schedules to allow a Muslim inmate to attend Friday worship services, even though Jumu'ah is a central part of the Islamic religious faith.[21] Another clarification of what is required for provision of religious activities is how in 1996, the Eighth Circuit ruled that prison officials must provide sweat lodges and the opportunity to use them to Native American inmates (*Hamilton v. Schriro*, 1996).[22] However, this was modified in the Eighth Circuit in 2008 when the court considered the potential future security problems that could occur with sweat lodges and the equipment and materials that go along with it (*Fowler v. Crawford*, 2008).[23] In this case, if prison officials reasonably believe that security and safety are compromised, they do not have to provide a sweat lodge to inmates.

When a religious practice can present a danger to the security and orderly running of a prison is difficult to generalize. In the *O'Lone* case, prison officials were successful partly because they argued that modifying the work schedules for inmates would undermine security. The courts often use a "reasonableness" test, established in the 1987 case of *Turner v. Safley*, in which the restriction of practice must reasonably be related to a legitimate penological interest, such as security or safety, but possibly including conserving resources.[24] And while the court recognized that it is not practical to provide every inmate a member of the clergy (*Gittlemacker v. Prasse*, 1970),[25] Muslim inmates have been allowed to have a special meal to end Ramadan, despite prison officials' argument that provision of special food served after sunset would be cost prohibitive (*Walker v. Blackwell*, 1969).[26]

An attempt to clarify the religious rights of prisoners through legislation came with the passing by Congress of the Religious Land Use and Institutionalized Persons Act (RLUIPA) in 2000. RLUIPA says that for the government to impose a substantial restriction on an inmate's right to exercise religion, it bears the burden to justify that the restriction furthers a compelling government interest and is implemented in the "least restrictive means" of furthering that interest.[27] This was challenged by the state of Ohio, but in *Cutter v. Wilkinson* (2005),[28] the Supreme Court found that RLUIPA did not violate the First Amendment and the least restrictive test continues. The decision of *Fowler v. Crawford* is likely to be further examined by the Supreme Court as to whether it modifies this standard.

An interesting case (*Americans United for Separation of Church and State v. Prison Fellowship Ministries*) decided recently has to do with prisons using public funds to offer faith-based programs to inmates. An Iowa state prison provided inmates a chance to live together and participate in the InnerChange program operated by Prison Fellowship Ministries, which was dominated by Bible study, religious revivals, and church services. In 2006, the Southern District Court of Iowa ruled that the program was "pervasively sectarian" and therefore unconstitutional as it violated the separation of church and state.[29] Inmates in the program received privileges other inmates did not (more privacy, family visits, and computer time), and there were no equivalent nonreligious programs. The Eighth U.S. Circuit Court of Appeals affirmed the district court decision, noting that inmates had "no genuine and independent private choice" to receive rehabilitation services from an organization other than the one run by Prison Fellowship.[30] Another case separating treatment and religion is *Hazle v. Crofoot*, in which a parolee was required to participate in a residential drug treatment program. Hazel was an atheist, and was removed from the program and his parole violated when he refused (as required by the program) to acknowledge a higher power. The Ninth Circuit Court found this unacceptable and required the state of California and its contractor that ran the program to provide Hazel compensatory damages for the additional time he spent in prison.[31]

Medical Care

The provision of adequate medical care is another basic right for inmates, established through court decisions responding to inmate suits alleging that failure to provide such care was a violation of the Eighth Amendment prohibition of cruel and unusual punishment. In 1970, the court looked at conditions throughout the Arkansas prison system, including medical care, and created a test of cruel and unusual punishment within the Eighth Amendment. Instead of including only the concept of torture or physical punishment, the court found that if people of reasonable sensitivity found the treatment shocking or disgusting, it would also be considered cruel and unusual (*Holt v. Sarver*).[32]

In *Estelle v. Gamble* (1976), the Supreme Court determined that prison officials have a duty to provide medical treatment to inmates, since inmates are dependent on them to provide for their medical needs. In this case, the Court prohibited "deliberate indifference" in responding to inmate medical needs, and neither medical staff in responding to needs nor correctional staff by denying, interfering with, or delaying access to medical care can be deliberately indifferent to such needs without the unnecessary or wanton infliction of pain.[33] In *Ramos v. Lamm* (1980), the court further suggested that deliberate indifference can also result from "repeated examples of negligent acts which disclose a pattern of conduct" by the correctional and medical staff.[34] And in 1991, the Court established that medical care in prisons must be "reasonably commensurate with modern medical science and of a quality acceptable within prudent professional standards" (*Fernandez v. United States*, 1991).[35]

The principle of **community standards** seems reasonable in providing medical care, because inmates should expect to get the same quality of treatment for their

community standards
the test established in *Fernandez v. United States* that medical care for inmates must be reasonably commensurate with medical care they would receive if not imprisoned

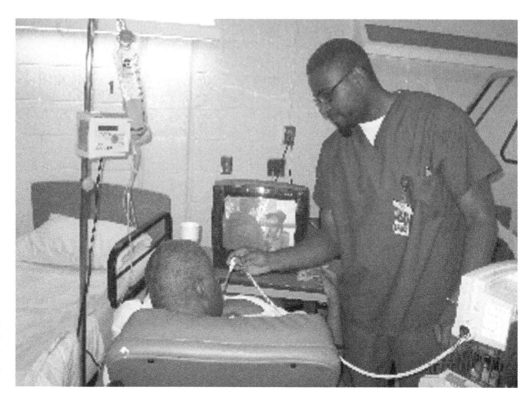

Prison medical care is an area of great sensitivity to inmates, who regularly complain about it. Photo by Richard P. Seiter.

health needs as they would receive if they were in the community. This does not mean that prisons must take every possible step in responding to medical needs, but they cannot deny inmates care that they would have received if not incarcerated. Medical care continues to be the topic that receives the most inmate complaints and suits. In addition to challenging a lack of adequate medical care under the Eighth Amendment, inmates often sue prison officials personally through Section 1983 of the U.S. Code, established in the Civil Rights Act of 1871. Besides the *Brown v. Plata* case mentioned earlier, the only recent medical care case is *Portaltin v. Department of Corrections* (2009). In this case, the department began charging inmates a "copay" for medical care. The court ruled that this does not create a hardship to inmates and is not a violation of the Eighth Amendment.[36]

First Amendment Rights

The First Amendment of the Constitution prohibits Congress from "abridging the freedom of speech, or of the press, or the right of the people peaceably to assemble...." Yet in terms of freedom of speech, almost everyone has heard that "you can't yell fire in the middle of a crowded theater" and recognizes that there are some restrictions to the common citizen's rights to free speech. It is easy to imagine that many such restrictions would apply to free speech, access to the press, or freedom to assemble in a prison environment. The balancing test created in *Pell v. Procunier* is the guideline used in determining the reasonableness of restricting First Amendment rights to inmates.

An example of the use of the balancing test is in the handling of inmate mail. Mail is recognized as important in communicating with family and friends outside prison, and such contact aids in rehabilitation and success after release. However, in the case of *Procunier v. Martinez* (1974), the U.S. Supreme Court acknowledged that there was a valid security interest in prison officials reading inmate mail, but determined that they could not censor it.[37] Prison officials also cannot prevent inmates from writing letters that are vulgar or disparaging about prison staff (*McNamara v. Moody*, 1979).[38] In *Turner v. Safley* (1987), the Supreme Court also allowed prison officials to continue to ban inmates from writing to inmates in other correctional institutions.[39] And in regard to restricting the right of assembly, the Supreme Court in 1977 supported the ban on inmates soliciting other inmates to join an inmate union, having union meetings, and doing bulk mailings regarding the union (*Jones v. North Carolina Prisoners' Labor Union, Inc.*).[40]

Freedom of access to the press as a First Amendment right has also been the subject of many inmate legal cases. In the *Pell v. Procunier* case, California prison officials were allowed to ban press and other media interviews with specific inmates when they believed it could endanger prison security. The Court found that there were alternative channels for inmates to communicate with the media other than in-person interviews. However, most correctional agencies do allow inmates to have interviews with the press, either by telephone or in person. The greater concern regarding media interviews is the inmate's right to privacy, and prison officials usually require that an inmate request such an interview, rather than a media person seek an interview with an inmate through prison officials.

Receipt of publications (magazines and books) is also an issue of First Amendment rights. In the 1971 case of *Sostre v. Otis*, the court created the "clear and present danger" standard.[41] Because there are publications that could detail how to saw prison bars with mess hall utensils, make a bomb, or provoke a prison riot, the court noted that such material could be inflammatory or dangerous, and its presence in a prison could create a clear and present danger. A ban of publications that wardens thought were detrimental to good order and institutional discipline or that might facilitate criminal activity was also upheld in *Thornburgh v. Abbott* (1989).[42] Prison officials are also concerned about publications such as magazines and books that, due to the nature of how they are assembled, could be used to hide small contraband items such as drugs. For that reason, the courts have upheld a restriction that allows inmates to receive such publications only directly from the publisher (*Guajardo v. Estelle*, 1978).[43]

Access to the Courts

Another basic right for U.S. citizens is that they have access to the courts to address any injustice. This holds true for inmates. In 1969, the Supreme Court in *Johnson v. Avery* recognized that inmates, to have full access to the courts, must often have legal assistance.[44] In its decision, the Court ruled that inmates have a right to consult other inmates for legal advice if trained legal advisors are not available. And shortly thereafter, the Court added that prisons must provide sufficient legal materials to enable inmates to conduct legal research in order to have reasonable access to the courts (*Younger v. Gilmore*, 1971).[45] This was further established in 1977, when the Court decided *Bounds v. Smith*, requiring prisons to provide adequate law libraries or adequate assistance from trained legal people.[46]

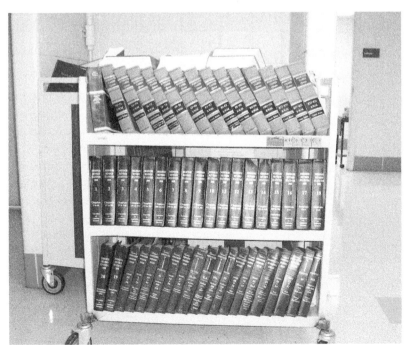

Even in jails or if inmates are held in an SHU, they have access to legal materials. Some institutions deliver legal books to these inmates on a cart. Photo by Richard P. Seiter.

Fourth Amendment Rights

The Fourth Amendment provides that people be secure "against unreasonable searches and seizures." This affects prison officials, who must closely watch inmates, monitor their behavior, and control the importation of dangerous contraband (principally weapons and drugs) to maintain safety and security. As noted in Chapter 13, the practices of searches of inmates, their belongings, and their housing areas are basic to good prison security practices. The legal issue is how much privacy from searches is reasonable within a prison. The courts have clearly ruled that inmates do not have an expectation of privacy while in prison. In *Hudson v. Palmer* (1984), the Supreme Court dismissed the claims of inmate Palmer that searches of his cell were just to harass him and held that "the Fourth Amendment proscription against unreasonable searches does not apply within the confines of the prison cell."[47] Prison officials may do searches randomly and without providing specific justification. However, they are expected to leave inmates' cells orderly (not to trash them in the search), or inmates may sue under the Eighth Amendment for destruction of their property.

Inmates are also personally searched on a regular basis. In *Bell v. Wolfish* (1979), routine strip-searches of inmates were deemed not to be a violation of the Fourth Amendment because they are reasonable to maintain security within a prison.[48] Searches of body cavities are more sensitive than a visual search of an inmate's naked body. However, it is not unusual for inmates to hide drugs, handcuff keys, weapons (bullets for guns), or even hacksaw blades in the rectum to smuggle them into a prison. Therefore, while these searches must be done, the courts require that there must be information that an inmate is hiding contraband in a body cavity, medical staff must conduct the search, and the search must be done in a manner that respects the inmate's dignity and privacy (*Tribble v. Gardner*, 1988).[49]

The courts have also addressed the issue of searches by prison staff of the opposite sex. In *Grummett v. Rushen* (1984), the court agreed with California prison officials that prohibiting female correctional officers from being assigned to housing areas in which inmates could be seen in partial or total nudity did not outweigh the women's equal employment opportunity rights.[50] The need for privacy can easily be accommodated by inmates wearing robes and by installing privacy screens in front of showers that do not totally block the view and therefore reduce security. Additionally, in *Johnson v. Phelan* (1995), the court also allowed searches of inmates by opposite-sex correctional staff, noting how impractical it would be to have only the same sex conduct searches of inmates.[51] However, the courts lecture against searches that may harass, humiliate, or intimidate inmates, and correctional agencies generally use same-sex staff to conduct searches, unless in an emergency.

An important issue for primarily jail administrators is whether you can strip-search non-felons arrested for minor offenses when there is not reasonable suspicion that they are a threat. Jail staff members believe that anyone who will be placed in the general population of a jail should be strip-searched to avoid drugs or weapons from entering the jail. While felon arrestees are presumed to be a threat, other minor crimes are not. The courts have generally ruled you cannot strip-search without reasonable suspicion, and strip-searching of less than felons has resulted in judgments of $5.9 million to settle the claim in *Boone v. City of Philadelphia* (2009)[52] and $33 million to settle claims in *McBean v. City of New York* (2010).[53] However, another 2010 case (*Bull v. City and County of San Francisco*) resulted in the court ruling that strip-searching all arrestees before placement in the jail general population was not a violation of the Fourth Amendment.[54] With these divergent decisions, correctional administrators were very anxious to see the U.S. Supreme

Court 2012 decision in *Florence v. Board of Chosen Freeholders of the County of Burlington.* Florence had been arrested during a traffic stop, when a computer error indicated he had an outstanding warrant. He was stripped searched prior to placement in jail. His lawyers argued that persons arrested for minor offenses cannot have unreasonable searches unless prison officials have reason to suspect concealment of weapons, drugs, or other contraband. The Supreme Court on a 5–4 vote opined that anyone arrested and temporarily detained was subject to a strip-search.[55] The Court gave deference to the expertise by jail and prison administrators that stated allowing anyone into the general population of a facility without a strip-search was dangerous to both staff and inmates.

Inmate Discipline

Inmate disciplinary processes are guided by the Fourteenth Amendment, which states, "No State shall…deprive any person of life, liberty, or property, without due process of law." Due process as it relates to disciplinary processes for inmate misbehavior within the prison was first considered in the 1974 case *Wolff v. McDonnell*, which dealt with a claim that the state of Nebraska disciplinary processes denied inmates due process and were therefore unconstitutional.[56] However, the Supreme Court differentiated between due process required by a defendant at trial and that of a prison inmate. Although prison inmates do not receive all the due process of someone not yet proved guilty, the Court enumerated the steps required for prisoner due process when facing a prison disciplinary hearing:

- The right to receive advance written notice of the alleged infraction
- The right to have sufficient time (at least twenty-four hours) to prepare a defense
- The right to present documentary evidence and to call witnesses on the prisoner's behalf, unless permitting this would be unduly hazardous
- The right to have assistance (by an inmate or staff representative) when the circumstances of the case are complex or if the prisoner is illiterate
- The right to a written statement of the findings of an impartial disciplinary committee of the evidence relied on supporting the finding of fact and the reasons the disciplinary action was taken

A later 1995 Supreme Court case clarified and gave new guidance to inmate disciplinary procedures requiring due process. In *Sandin v. Conner*, the Court, noting that the purpose of prison disciplinary actions is to maintain good prison management and achieve rehabilitative goals, determined that disciplinary actions in pursuit of those goals that do not add to the sentence being served or change the conditions contemplated in the sentence being served do not create a liberty interest and do not require due process.[57] Thus, under *Sandin*, an

Inmates have the right to limited due process in prison inmate disciplinary processes, and hearing officers not from the inmates' prison often decide guilt and punishment. Jessica Hill/Hartford Courant/MCT/tribune News Service/Getty Images inmate who violates a prison rule and receives a punishment of placement in disciplinary segregation for a temporary period does not trigger the need for due process, whereas loss of good time that subsequently extends the sentence (by delaying the release date) does trigger the need for due process. Even with the *Sandin* decision, most prisons find it more efficient and continue to provide the full *Wolff* due process rights for handling inmate discipline.

All these areas regarding inmate rights are constantly developing and practices are changing based on the latest legal precedent. The greatest time of change was from 1965 until 1980, the first fifteen years after the U.S. Supreme Court abandoned the hands-off doctrine. Correctional agencies began to be somewhat more proactive in dealing with issues that often were found to be of concern to federal courts. However, in the early 1990s, public sentiment indicated a frustration and disenchantment with the high number of inmate lawsuits, and Congress took action to limit lawsuits filed by inmates.

Limiting Litigation by Inmates

Over the past two decades, with frustration over the number of court petitions filed by inmates, there have been a number of actions in an attempt to reduce the number (especially for frivolous issues) of these suits. First, some Supreme Court decisions seem to have "turned the tide" of decisions away from inmates and toward support for prison administrators. The beginning of the restrictions on inmates' rights was the 1987 case of *Turner v. Safley*, when the Supreme Court ruled that correctional administrators could restrict inmates' constitutional rights to reasonably further a legitimate penological interest such as security, order, or rehabilitation.[58] The 1991 case of *Wilson v. Seiter* is considered a key decision for correctional agencies; the Court stated that prison conditions, while they may be uncomfortable, are not unconstitutional unless administrators acted with "deliberate indifference" to the basic needs of inmates.[59] Also, the 1995 decision regarding the due process that should be provided to inmates in the disciplinary process in *Sandin v. Conner* considerably lessened the requirements of earlier cases by determining that only disciplinary actions that add to the sentence being served or change the conditions of the sentence require due process.[60]

Second, the courts have moved back toward the hands-off doctrine of allowing prisons to deal with problems themselves, rather than have inmates file lawsuits that are expensive to the correctional agencies and taxpayers. In 1980, Congress revised the Civil Rights of Institutionalized Persons Act, requiring inmates to exhaust their administrative remedies before filing a petition in federal court. If correctional agencies provide an administrative remedy process and give inmates a chance to informally resolve a problem or have a complaint dealt with by prison officials, the courts will require this process to be used before they accept an inmate lawsuit. Many federal courts require inmates to certify that they have exhausted these administrative appeals and include a copy of the response from the agency.

Finally, Congress has acted to make it more difficult for inmates to file successful suits against correctional agencies. In the Violent Crime Control Act of 1994, Congress (1) specified that federal courts find a violation of the Eighth Amendment only if the inmate filing the suit demonstrates that he or she has personally suffered from overcrowding conditions, (2) prohibited federal courts from imposing a population cap on a prison unless the "cruel and unusual punishment" is clearly harming particular identified inmates, and (3) allowed a review of any court orders or consent decrees based on violations of the Eighth Amendment.

In 1996, Congress passed the Prison Litigation Reform Act, requiring inmates filing prison suits to pay a filing fee unless they claim pauper status, limiting awards of attorney fees, punishing inmates with loss of good time for filing frivolous suits, and prohibiting inmates from suing for mental or emotional distress unless they have suffered a physical injury.

Although these actions do not eliminate the filing of lawsuits by inmates, many critics suggest that legitimate inmate cases are being blocked and cite the fact that even with an increase in the number of inmates from 1.5 million to over 2 million, the number of prisoner-initiated lawsuits in federal courts has dropped from over 41,000 in 1996 to less than 17,000 in 2012,[61] and fewer correctional facilities are under court directives than in past years. In 2000, one in five adult prisons were operating under a court order or consent decree, and by 2005, there was only one in eight.[62] The federal courts once were so actively involved in inmate legal actions that they often had to appoint a court monitor or special master to oversee their decisions. Correctional agencies now have the opportunity to thoughtfully address valid inmate claims and do not have to spend so much time and money responding to frivolous claims.

As we conclude this review of legal rights of inmates, the "Your Career in Corrections" box describes the role of correctional attorneys.

Your Career in Corrections

Correctional Attorneys

Although it is not a position that most people think about in a correctional agency, with all the inmate lawsuits it is obvious that correctional agencies need attorneys to advise and represent them. In most state and federal correctional systems, the agencies have full-time staff attorneys who work with staff and administrators, and the office of the attorney general (AG) then handles the actual litigation. The role of the AG is to direct the case and its defense and argue it in court if it goes that far before being dismissed or settled. The staff attorneys who work for the agencies have a very different role.

When an inmate sues a correctional agency, a big part of the function of the staff attorney is fact-finding: digging for documentation, talking to witnesses, and finding out what really happened. It usually takes a combination of finding the right documents and talking to people to discover the true facts. Then the staff attorney works with the AG office to assess the case and determine the legal position of the agency. In most cases, there is no or limited basis for the inmate claim, and the agency takes a position to fight the case and is usually successful in getting it dismissed before it goes to trial. In other cases, there may actually be the potential for liability, and the correctional agency must decide whether to fight the case or settle it (agree to some conditions or payment for the liability). In some cases, an inmate is asking only for a minor amount ($50 for a pair of shoes that were damaged or lost), and even though the agency does not feel responsible, it is more expensive to fight the case. Correctional agencies do not want to settle too many cases on this "nuisance value" situation, as it can encourage other inmates to file similar suits just because the agency will not fight it, but it is sometimes good practice to settle such nuisance cases.

Another role of the staff attorney is preventive, to watch for issues (policies or procedures) that may incur potential legal liabilities and try to get the policy or procedure changed. The staff attorney brings the issue to the decision makers, expresses the legal concerns, and advises them on the potential problems. In a way, the attorney helps administrators determine the most important aspects or outcomes of the policy or procedure and then works to find a more legally defensible way to accomplish what they want.

Correctional attorneys note that the best thing about their job is the variety of issues they address and variety of cases they work. At any time, they may have cases involving use of force, freedom of religion, medical malpractice, or conditions of confinement. In private practice, young attorneys are often pigeonholed into one particular area of the law and do nothing except work on these types of cases. The negative things about the job are that it sometimes seems as though much time is wasted dealing with minor or trivial cases, such as the nuisance value cases noted earlier. Most people do not go to law school thinking about working for a correctional agency. Somehow they fall into the position and, once involved, most people stay with the correctional agency, obviously enjoying the variety and challenge of their work.

Capital Punishment

Many people, in discussing inmate rights, suggest that the ultimate right is to "life, liberty, and the pursuit of happiness." They go on to suggest that no discussion of the rights of inmates should fail to address the issue of *capital punishment*, the legal killing of someone by the government as punishment for serious criminal misconduct. The topic of capital punishment is one of the most hotly debated, emotionally charged, and controversial components of our criminal justice system. Some people oppose it on a moral basis, claiming that government never has the right of retribution by taking someone's life. Others argue that capital punishment is a deterrent and that executing a few people saves many other lives. The practical-minded propose that the overall cost to the criminal justice system should be considered in any decision regarding capital punishment. However, many disagree about whether capital punishment or a sentence of life in prison is less expensive.

In this section, we examine the history of capital punishment in the United States, the legal cases and developments regarding the use of the death penalty, the current status of capital punishment, the number of people on death row, and the methods of execution that are currently used. Also described are issues regarding capital punishment, including the potential for error in the finding of guilt, execution of juveniles, execution of offenders with mental illness, and execution of offenders with intellectual disabilities, the deterrent value, and the cost of capital punishment versus a lengthy prison sentence. Finally, the public's view and opinion of the death penalty are discussed, and the most recent actions by state officials regarding the death penalty are described.

The electric chair has been used throughout the history of capital punishment and is still in use in some states today. Courtesy of the Ohio Department of Rehabilitation and Correction.

The History of Capital Punishment in the United States

As noted in Chapter 1, capital punishment was used extensively in England and in the early American colonies, as many crimes (not just murder) carried a penalty of death. Brutal corporal punishments also regularly resulted in death, as the imposition of such torture so seriously injured the offender as to be a cause of his or her death. Both torture and executions were often carried out in public, as a deterrent to others with the threat of the punishment they would receive if committing similar crimes. Public executions continued until 1936, when several thousand people witnessed the execution by hanging of a black man convicted of raping and murdering a white woman in a small town in Kentucky.

With the creation of the prison as a criminal sanction, the reliance on corporal and capital punishment lessened, and the number and types of crimes that could result in capital punishment were reduced. Even though we believe that the criminal justice system became more "enlightened" and "merciful" during the twentieth century, the 1930s and 1940s still saw more than 150 executions

FIGURE 15.2   Executions, 1930–2015   Source: Tracey L. Snell, "Capital Punishment, 2014–2015," *Bureau of Justice Statistics: Statistical Brief* (Washington, D.C.: U.S. Department of Justice, 2017), p. 1.

per year. However, as indicated in Figure 15.2, the number of executions declined to zero in the late 1960s and did not rise until the late 1970s. Since the mid-1980s, the number of executions has climbed rapidly until 1999, when ninety-eight prisoners were executed in twenty states.[63] Since that time, the number of executions has declined almost every year, and in 2015, only twenty-eight inmates were executed in six states,[64] and in 2016, five states executed twenty inmates.[65]

Legal and Statutory Provisions for the Death Penalty

Figure 15.2 illustrates the dramatic decline in the number of people executed from 1940 to 1967. Peaking at 199 executions in 1935, the graph looks like a mountain range with peaks up and down, but with a consistent decline through the next three decades. Only two executions took place in 1967, and none were performed in 1968 or for the next decade. This decline was primarily the result of the courts' willingness to consider appeals from death row inmates and continued legal challenges to the constitutionality of the death penalty. At this time, the public was not in a retributive mood; we were coming out of a war with a considerable number of fatalities, there was a strong belief in rehabilitation and that people could change, and crime was not a serious concern among the public.

The increasing amount of litigation regarding capital punishment culminated with the 1972 landmark decision by the U.S. Supreme Court in *Furman v. Georgia*.[66] Furman (a twenty-six-year-old black man with a sixth-grade education) was burglarizing a home. When discovered by the homeowner, Furman tried to escape, shot back into the house through a closed door once outside, and killed the homeowner. Before his trial, Furman was committed to a state psychiatric hospital for evaluation. The hospital staff concluded that Furman had a mild to moderate mental deficiency, with psychotic episodes and a convulsive disorder. However, the staff concluded that Furman was not psychotic at the time of his trial, knew right from wrong, and was able to cooperate with his attorney to prepare a defense. Therefore, he was able to stand trial, and the jury found him guilty of first-degree murder and sentenced him to death.

The case was appealed and made its way to the U.S. Supreme Court, at which several critical decisions were made regarding the death penalty. First, the Court did not determine that capital punishment in itself is unconstitutional as cruel and unusual punishment, although two of the justices voted that it was. Without such a determination, the Court's decision did not put an overall ban on capital punishment throughout the United States. Second, in a 5–4 vote, the Court determined that due to the arbitrary, capricious, and unfair manner in which it was applied, the death penalty as then administered was cruel and unusual. However, the Court's decision (even with, or perhaps because of, each justice writing a separate opinion) provided no clear guidance to states as what would be considered not arbitrary and capricious. Within months after the decision, states began to rewrite their death penalty statutes to make them less arbitrary and constitutionally acceptable.

States took two approaches to try to overcome the "arbitrary" concerns of the Supreme Court. The first approach was to adopt mandatory requirements for a sanction of the death penalty when a specific crime was committed, thereby eliminating discretion altogether. Both Louisiana and North Carolina had such mandatory statutes found unconstitutional in the 1976 cases of *Robert v. Louisiana* and *Woodson v. North Carolina*.[67] After that, most states passed guided-discretion statutes that provided for **bifurcated trials**, in which guilt was first established at a traditional trial. If found guilty, the trial moved to a second stage of sentencing, at which the jury would decide between death and life imprisonment, using statutory guidelines to consider both aggravating and mitigating circumstances of the crime. Aggravating circumstances could include the killing of a law enforcement officer, committing murder during commission of another felony such as rape or robbery, previous convictions of murder, or multiple killings. Mitigating circumstances could be emotional stress that impaired decision making, mental deficiencies, playing a secondary or minor role in the murder, or developmental problems that bring sympathy from the jury.

The first case in which a guided-discretion statute was considered and found constitutional by the U.S. Supreme Court was the 1976 case of *Gregg v. Georgia*.[68] Through its decision in this case, the Supreme Court laid out the expected elements of a state's death penalty to pass constitutional muster:

bifurcated trial

used in capital cases, with guilt first established at a traditional trial, and if found guilty, a second stage of sentencing considers between death and life imprisonment

- The death penalty can be considered only for specific and the most serious crimes.

- The trial must be bifurcated into two stages: one to determine guilt and the other to consider the sentence.

- During the sentencing stage, the jury will hear evidence regarding both mitigating and aggravating circumstances surrounding the crime, the victim, and the defendant.

- There must be an automatic appeal and review of the death sentence to consider whether the sentence could have been arbitrary due to prejudice, passion, or some other factor; whether the evidence supports the finding during sentencing of statutory aggravating circumstances; and whether the death penalty has been similarly imposed for similar crimes and similar defendants.

Several other federal court decisions have addressed the death penalty since *Gregg v. Georgia*, some clarifying and addressing the death penalty regarding certain groups of offenders. As noted in *Gregg v. Georgia*, the death penalty can be imposed only for specific, serious crimes, and several cases have dealt with the issue of what is an acceptable crime for which to impose death as a sanction. In *Coker v. Georgia* (1977), the Court said that the death penalty was excessive for rape of an adult.[69] In *Godfrey v. Georgia* (1980), the Court decided that statements of aggravating circumstances that define the crime being "outrageously or wantonly vile, horrible, or inhumane" are too broad and vague.[70] And in 1987, the Court determined that the death penalty could be imposed on offenders who do not specifically intend to kill their victims (*Tison v. Arizona*).[71]

The U.S. Supreme Court has also considered the use of the death penalty for offenders with mental illness, those with intellectual disabilities, and juveniles. In 1986, the Court considered the case of *Ford v. Wainwright* and ruled that people with mental illness cannot be executed.[72] When convicted, Ford was not judged to have a mental illness and not until he was on death row did he display conditions of mental illness. The Court considered the case and concluded that executing a person with mental illness was a violation of the Eighth Amendment, in that the accused must comprehend both the fact that he or she has been sentenced to death and the reason for the sentence.

The Court, in addressing the issue of the death penalty for the intellectually disabled, decided but then reversed itself on this issue. Johnny Paul Penry, who had an IQ of approximately 70, was considered able to stand for trial, and was convicted of murder. In 1989, the Court (in *Penry v. Lynaugh*)[73] decided that the execution of intellectually disabled offenders does not violate the Eighth Amendment; even though at that time, only two states (Maryland and Georgia) prohibited executing the intellectually disabled. However, in 2002, the Court heard the case of *Atkins v. Virginia* and, by a 6–3 vote, determined that executions of intellectually disabled criminals were "cruel and unusual punishment" under the Eighth Amendment.[74] Atkins was convicted of shooting a man for beer money in 1996. At that time, he had an IQ of 59. The majority acknowledged a reversal of *Penry*, but noted that there has been a growing national consensus since 1989 that executions of the intellectually disabled may be unacceptable, even though only eighteen of the thirty-eight states that allow capital punishment had disallowed such executions. With the ruling, inmates on death row who can prove intellectual disability (usually an IQ less than 70) will have their sentences commuted to life imprisonment.

The Supreme Court has also considered the use of the death penalty for juvenile offenders, and there has been an evolution of case law similar to that developed regarding the death penalty for the intellectually disabled. Until recently, juveniles could be executed for capital crimes. In *Eddings v. Oklahoma* (1982), the Court held that the youthful age of a defendant should be considered as a mitigating factor during the sentencing stage of a capital punishment trial.[75] In 1989, the Court ruled in *Stanford v. Kentucky* that the minimum age to impose a death sentence on a juvenile is sixteen.[76] In 2002, the Court refused to consider *In re Stanford*, declining to reconsider the issue of capital punishment for juveniles,[77] and on January 27, 2003, the Court also declined to consider the death penalty for Scott Allen Hain, a seventeen-year-old Oklahoma

In *Atkins v. Virginia*, the U.S. Supreme Court determined that executions of intellectually disabled criminals (like Rodney Atkins) were cruel and unusual punishment under the Eighth Amendment. Sangjib Min/Daily Press/AP Images offender, even though four justices wrote that they believed executing juveniles "is a relic of the past and is inconsistent with evolving standards of decency."[78] At that time, sixteen remained the age for which juvenile offenders could be considered for a sentence of death. In 2004, of the thirty-eight states that allowed the death penalty, only twenty states allowed for the execution of juveniles; six jurisdictions did not specify a minimum age; and fourteen others indicated an age between fourteen and seventeen for which the death penalty could be imposed.[79]

On October 3, 2004, the U.S. Supreme Court heard the case of *Roper v. Simmons*[80] and considered evidence of a national consensus against the death penalty for juveniles that was in some respects parallel to the evidence used in *Atkins* to demonstrate a national consensus against the death penalty for the intellectually disabled. On March 1, 2005, the Court by a 5–4 vote held that "the Eighth and Fourteenth Amendments forbid the imposition of the death penalty on offenders who are under the age of eighteen when their crimes were committed."[81] The Court believed that a lack of maturity and an underdeveloped sense of responsibility are found in youth more often than in adults, juveniles are more vulnerable or susceptible to negative influences and outside pressures, and the character of a juvenile is not as well formed as that of an adult. The Court's ruling removed seventy-two juveniles in twelve states from death row, substituting life in prison for execution.

The most recent case concerning who can be executed was *Kennedy v. Louisiana* (2008),[82] in which the Supreme Court by a 5–4 vote found that a Louisiana state statute allowing persons convicted of raping a child to be sentenced to death violated the Eighth Amendment prohibition against cruel and unusual punishment. The Court recognized the horrific nature of the crime, but questioned whether the death penalty met society's current standards of decency. Using their logic in *Roper* and in *Atkins*, the Court found a societal consensus against the death penalty for child rape, as while nine states still allowed the death penalty as a punishment, there had been no execution for such a crime since 1964. The Court ruled that capital punishment is a violation of the Eighth Amendment unless it is consistent with the current standards of decency, and there is a difference between intentional first-degree murder and non-homicide crimes, including child rape. Although child rape is devastating in harm, it does not compare to murder in its "severity and irrevocability."[83]

By the end of 2017, thirty-one states and the federal government have capital punishment statutes. The District of Columbia and nineteen states (listed in Table 15.1) have either not passed or passed and later abolished death penalty statutes. The current status has come with considerable shuffling over the past

TABLE 15.1	States That Do Not Have the Death Penalty (Year Abolished in Parentheses)	
Alaska (1957)	Minnesota (1911)
Connecticut (2012)	New Jersey (2007)
Delaware (2016)	New Mexico (2009)
Hawaii (1957)	New York (2007)
Illinois (2011)	North Dakota (1973)
Iowa (1965)	Rhode Island (1984)
Maine (1887)	Vermont (1964)
Maryland (2013)	West Virginia (1965)
Massachusetts (1984)	Wisconsin (1853)
Michigan (1846)	

few decades. After the Court's clarification of what was required to have a constitutional death penalty statute, most states did initiate a death penalty statute. However, support for the death penalty has been declining over the past decade (addressed below), and since 2007, seven states have banned capital punishment.

Current Statistics and Methods of Capital Punishment

Death Row Prisoners

At year-end 2015, thirty-three states[84] and the Federal Bureau of Prisons held 2,881 prisoners under sentence of death, which was sixty-one fewer than at year-end 2014.[85] As can be seen in Figure 15.3, the number of inmates on death row declined immediately after the 1972 Supreme Court decision in *Furman v. Georgia*, holding that the death penalty as then administered was unconstitutional. Even with that decision, not every state emptied its death row, so the number did not reduce to zero. Soon thereafter, the number on death row began to climb significantly as the Court in *Gregg v. Georgia* and other cases upheld the revised capital punishment laws.

Of those on death row at year-end 2013, 98 percent were male and 2 percent were female. Fifty-six percent were white and 42 percent were black, and 14 percent were Hispanic, but included in white and black figures. The mean age is forty-seven, and 48 percent have less than a high school diploma or GED.[86] Race and gender ratios have remained relatively unchanged since 2000. Race has been an issue in the capital punishment debate for the past several decades, as minorities continue to be overrepresented among those sentenced to death, on death row, and executed.

This fact has opened the door to arguments of racial bias in the administration of the death penalty. However, in the 1987 case of *McCleskey v. Kemp*,[87] the Supreme Court heard an argument of race discrimination in the death penalty. McCleskey was a black man convicted of murdering a white police officer.

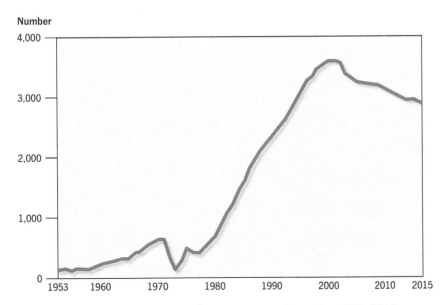

FIGURSE 15.3   Prisoners under Sentence of Death, 1953–2015

Source: Tracey L. Snell, "Capital Punishment, 2014–2015" *Bureau of Justice Statistics: Statistical Briefs* (Washington, D.C.: U.S. Department of Justice, December 2017), p. 1.

McCleskey's attorneys, in their arguments to the Supreme Court, used a study by Baldus, Woodworth, and Pulaski that examined the role of race in the imposition of the death penalty in Georgia. The study found that defendants charged with killing whites were 4.3 times more likely to receive the death penalty than those convicted of killing blacks.[88] The attorneys argued that this disproportionate sentencing to death of killers of whites indicated a denial of the equal protection clause under the Fourteenth Amendment and likely an arbitrary and capricious use of the death penalty in violation of the Eighth Amendment. However, by a 5–4 vote, the Court rejected these claims, noting that a statistical study did not establish discrimination in this particular case.

Executions

As indicated in Figure 15.2, after 1977, the number of executions began to rise, and peaked with ninety-eight persons executed in 1999. Since that time, there has been a steady decline, and in 2015, twenty-eight inmates were executed in six states. Figure 15.4 lists the number of executions by state during 2015. Texas led the way, executing thirteen people, and Missouri executed six people, and Georgia executed five. All of these executions were by **lethal injection**. The most recent data indicates that the average time for those executed in 2013 from sentence to execution was 190 months, which has been increasing over the past twenty-five years, as the average elapsed time was only seventy-four months in 1984.[89]

lethal injection

a method of execution in which drugs are injected into a person's body, making the heart stop and causing death

Overall, from 1977 through 2015, there have been 1,422 executions carried out in the United States. Again, Texas has by far more (531 since 1977) than any other state. Using data available from 1977 until 2013, of the 1,359 executions during that period, 770 (56.6 percent) were of whites, 464 (34.1 percent) were of blacks, 111 (8.2 percent) were of Hispanics, and 14 (1 percent) of other races.[90] Of the 34 states and the federal system that have conducted the 1,422 executions since 1977, almost all (1,247) were by lethal injection, while 158 were by electrocution, 11 by lethal gas, 3 by hanging, and 3 by firing squad.[91] In some states, more than one method of execution is authorized, although currently almost every state authorizes only the use of lethal injection.

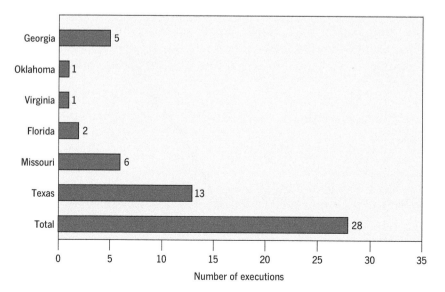

FIGURE 15.4   Counts of Executions by State, 2015   Source: Created from Tracey L. Snell, "Capital Punishment, 2014–2015," *Bureau of Justice Statistics: Statistical Briefs* (Washington, D.C.: U.S. Department of Justice, December 2017), p. 2.

Lethal injection has come under challenge over the past few years. In 2006, death penalty opponents and lawyers for death row inmates began to challenge its use as a violation of the Eighth Amendment prohibiting cruel and unusual punishment. Most states used a three-drug protocol for lethal injection. The three-drug "cocktail" administered uses sodium thiopental to render the person unconscious, pancuronium bromide to paralyze breathing muscles, and potassium chloride to stop the heart. Even though death penalty supporters and attorneys for states using lethal injection argue that no evidence exists, inmate attorneys suggest that the use of the first two drugs may not always fully work, and the inmate can suffer during the process.

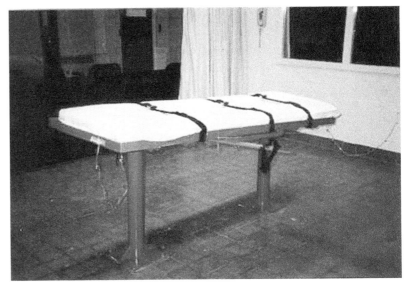

Lethal injection is now the most widely used method of execution.
Courtesy of the Ohio Department of Rehabilitation and Correction.

In 2006, the Eighth U.S. Circuit Court of Appeals delayed the execution of Missouri death row inmate Michael Taylor until a hearing on the issue of whether lethal injection is unconstitutionally cruel and unusual. California (with 650 inmates on death row) had to postpone executions because they could not recruit appropriately trained and licensed medical personnel to mix the drugs and insert intravenous lines into inmates to be executed. This issue also brings up the conflict between the American Medical Association and other medical groups that oppose licensed medical personnel administering drugs to end life and state requirements that such licensed personnel oversee the executions.

This issue of the use of the drug protocol was settled as the U.S. Supreme Court accepted and heard the case of *Baze et al. v. Rees*. The petitioners were convicted murderers sentenced to death in Kentucky. The state trial court held fact-finding hearings and ruled that there was minimal risk of the improper administration of the drug protocol and upheld its use as constitutional. This was affirmed by the Kentucky Supreme Court. On April 16, 2008, the U.S. Supreme Court voted 7–2 to affirm the decision.[92] The Court noted that the inmates conceded that the procedure was "humane" when carried out correctly and failed to prove the incorrect administration of the drugs would violate the Eighth Amendment. However, inmates continue to challenge the lethal injection protocols and their correct use by prison officials.

However, another recent issue is the availability of the drugs used in lethal injections. Drug manufacturers, especially those in Europe that does not support capital punishment, have stopped selling the sedative sodium thiopental, and states have tried a variety of approaches to finding this or a substitute drug. California, Missouri, Oklahoma, and several others have begun to secretly buy these drugs from pharmacies, often using cash, in order to protect the pharmacy.[93] As a result of the shortage of sodium thiopental, states are modifying the three-drug protocol. Texas began using a one-drug protocol in 2012, administering a single lethal dose of pentobarbital. Ohio switched to a two-drug protocol (the first state to use this formula). When the state executed Dennis McGuire, it took twenty-six minutes for him to die, and witnesses reported him as snorting, arching his back, clenching his arms, and gasping for air. His family complained this was cruel and unusual punishment. As a result, Ohio's governor has delayed further executions until they find out what happened.

In March 2014, an Oklahoma federal appeals court delayed the execution of two inmates because they were not convinced the state could carry out the death penalty in a constitutional manner.[94] And in April 2014, a Texas federal district court issued an injunction to the execution of Tommy Lynn Sells, a convicted serial killer, because the Texas Department of Criminal Justice (TDCJ) would not reveal the supplier of pentobarbital to be used in his execution. TDCJ argued that the identity of the supplier must be kept secret to protect the company from threats of violence. However, the fifth Circuit Court of Appeals overturned this, and the decision headed to the U.S. Supreme Court.[95] Later in April 2014, Oklahoma used for the first time a new mixture of drugs and executed Clayton Lockett. Lockett died of a heart attack forty-three minutes after being administered the sedative. Witnesses described how he tried to rise, exhaled loudly, and he twitched and mumbled.[96] An investigative report found that it was the way it was administered (a vein failed as the drugs were being administered) rather than the drugs used. Since then, states began reviewing their drug protocols, and most began to use a one-drug protocol using pentobarbital only. However, the issue of cruel and unusual punishment in the administration of the death penalty is far from resolved.

As a result, many states are considering other methods than lethal injection to carry out executions. Due to the legal challenges and in some cases the inability to get the required drugs for lethal injection, many states have put their executions on hold until there is clarity on the issue. As a result, in 2016, only twenty people were executed in five states (Georgia, Texas, Alabama, Florida, and Missouri).[97] And in 2017, Arkansas executed four inmates in eight days, trying to get the executions completed before their supply of lethal drugs expired at the end of April 2017.[98] In 2017, Mississippi (although they had not executed anyone since 2012) approved using prior methods (the gas chamber, electric chair, or firing squad) in case the lethal injection protocol is not held constitutional. And Alabama, Florida, and Tennessee have also approved using the electric chair for the same reasons.[99]

Most writings about capital punishment take into account the constitutionality and the impact on death row inmates. However, the following "An Interview With" box describes the issues that must be considered and the personal feelings of correctional officials as they plan for and carry out an execution.

Operational Problems

People seldom think about it, but how do you manage offenders who have already proved that they have a propensity for violence and are in prison facing execution? They obviously have little to live for, and correctional administrators can threaten them with no penalty that is worse than what they already face. This creates the dilemma of how to operate death rows. They must be secure to protect staff and other inmates. Yet these prisoners have not (in most cases) violated any prison rule to deserve to be isolated in a special housing unit (SHU-type) situation.

Most administrators decide to err on the safe side and operate a very secure death row, with inmates in single cells most of the time. Death row is operated like an SHU in that all services come to the unit, inmates are in their cells most of the time, and they recreate and do almost everything by themselves. A few states allow inmates on death row to work, and some even have a prison industry as a part of the death row. However, security and safe operations have to be constant at all times.

Reasons for and Against Capital Punishment

Proponents of the death penalty argue for its existence for several reasons, which usually include deterrence, retribution, incapacitation, and cost.

Deterrence

Proponents of the death penalty argue that, by having capital punishment laws, additional murders are prevented through general deterrence. Reflecting back to Bentham's hedonistic calculus that crimes will be prevented if the punishment outweighs the pleasure from the crime, it is difficult to understand how a rational person would commit a murder knowing that he or she will be executed in return. This logic seems to challenge theories of the deterrent effect of the death penalty. It can first be argued that fully rational people do not commit many murders. The results of research on the deterrent impact of the death penalty have been inconclusive and even contradictory. A few early studies found evidence of capital punishment as deterrence. However, some of these have been criticized as methodologically flawed and are not recognized as credible evidence.[100] A more recent study by Mocan and Gittings concludes that there is a deterrent effect of capital punishment. Both their 2003 study and a 2006 study that reexamined the data found that each execution results in five fewer homicides, and commuting a death sentence means five more homicides.[101]

An Interview With...

A Warden Who Oversees Executions

Stephen Huffman. Courtesy of Stephen Huffman

Stephen Huffman is a twenty-five-year veteran of the Ohio Department of Rehabilitation and Correction (DRC). He started his career in the business office at the London Correctional Institution. He rose through the ranks to become assistant warden and became warden of the Southern Ohio Correctional Institution in Lucasville in 1997. Lucasville is a maximum-security prison and has housed the execution chamber since its opening in the 1970s. Mr. Huffman was promoted to regional director of the North Region in 2000 and one year later was assigned as regional director of the South Region, where Lucasville is located. He then became and has since retired as Assistant Director of DRC. As warden at Lucasville, he oversaw the first execution to take place in Ohio in thirty-six years and witnessed nineteen more executions as Southern Regional Director.

Question: Director Huffman, can you describe what you had to do when you had to prepare for the first execution in Ohio to take place in thirty-six years?

Mr. Huffman: When I first arrived at Lucasville as warden, death row inmates had the choice of execution between the electric chair and lethal injection. Forty-eight hours before the execution was scheduled, the inmate had to decide which method of execution he wanted used. All chose lethal injection. Since 2001, inmates do not have a choice, and lethal injection is the sole method now used in Ohio. Because of the choice, we had to prepare for both means of execution. For several years before the first execution, we selected the execution teams, and they would practice quarterly. Within the last month before a scheduled execution, we practiced weekly. The practices were done in as real a situation as possible, with someone in the chair and someone on the table as a part of practice.

(Continued)

Question: What are some of the key things you have to consider and practice for an execution?

Mr. Huffman: For the electric chair, we had several physical and maintenance types of activities. First, we had to make sure there was proper ventilation in the death house. Our electricians and maintenance staff had to make sure the voltage regulator worked properly so that the flow of electrical voltage was regulated at the level specified. We carefully selected people to be on the team, and practice was just like the real thing. We had twelve members and a leader on the team. Each person had a specific assignment. Some staff would monitor the inmate and respond to all requests he had. Others were assigned to death house and had to escort the inmate into the chamber and strap him to the chair or table.

Staff had to volunteer for the assignment, and we were careful to choose only staff that would not be overly sensitive and could not handle the process and were also not overeager to do it. Everyone had to be extremely professional at all times. Since the first execution on February 19, 1999, only one member has asked to be removed from the execution team. Unless you go to the facility and work with these people daily, you do not realize what they do and how well they perform their job. As an example, it is not unusual for families of the executed inmate to write to the warden and thank him for how the staff treated their family member and did their job with such dignity.

Question: What are some of the unexpected issues that come up in preparing for an execution?

Mr. Huffman: One difficulty for the first execution was finding a physician that would participate and pronounce the inmate as dead. At this early time, the American Medical Association had not taken a position on involvement by physicians in an execution, and physicians feared they might lose their license for such involvement.

Another issue arose in the witnesses for the inmate and for the victim. Both the inmate and the victim families get three witnesses at the actual execution. Staff are assigned to each family group. One of the toughest things is to keep the families calm and avoid any animosity between them. They are all in the same small room to witness the execution and, as you can imagine, emotions are quite high. It takes a special person with the right demeanor to deal with both families. The media are also with the families in the witness room. Three media (one radio, one television, and one print journalist) are allowed as witnesses. When the execution is over, both families and the media are given the opportunity to speak to the rest of the media and, almost all the time, all speak to the media.

Question: What is the process up to the execution time?

Mr. Huffman: That depends on the time of the execution. Executions used to be at midnight, then at 9:00 P.M., and they are now at 10:00 A.M. This changed in part so that the attorney general's office has time to work on last-minute appeals. The AG's office must respond if a state or federal judge requests a stay of execution. This is a very sensitive and difficult time, and the AG's office tries to respond quickly so that the execution is not delayed too long. In 1998, an inmate was being transported to the facility and received a stay. This particular inmate had volunteered to be executed, meaning he did not seek any appeals after his sentence. It still took six years before the process was finished and he was executed. When he got the stay, I was being interviewed by the media who told me of the stay and asked me what we would do. I responded something like we had to stay prepared, because the execution "may" still go on. I got in a lot of trouble with my bosses for that comment, because the legal process was responding rapidly with the belief that the sentence was both legal and just and "would" go on.

During the time before the first execution, death row inmates in Ohio were housed at the Mansfield Correctional Institution, where death row had been moved from Lucasville. Death row is now at the Ohio State Penitentiary, our supermax prison. Death row was placed somewhere other than where the execution was to take place to avoid the Stockholm syndrome, where staff begin to get too close and empathize with the inmate. We don't release the date or time that inmates will be transported to Lucasville for the execution. When they are, they are escorted by our special emergency response team (SERT). At Lucasville, they are placed in a cell within the death house with a television, radio, a telephone, or a typewriter. They are dressed in special clothing noting death row. This may seem odd, but the biggest thing for the warden is to give the inmate confidence that you will carry out the execution in a dignified manner and abide by his wishes. Up to the last few hours, the inmate is counting on the warden and focusing on the execution. A few inmates stay awake all night, but most sleep very little and spend time talking to their family or the execution team members. The family of the inmate can visit up to two hours before the execution and then only three (chosen by the inmate) are allowed to stay to witness the execution. We don't call it the last meal, but they get a preferred meal, which can be almost anything we can fix within the prison.

The warden is always going between the victim and the inmate's families to talk to them and be sure their needs are met. You also have to deal with protesters. The Ohio Highway Patrol assists and keeps the protesters separated by those who are for and those who are against the death penalty. There are usually pretty large crowds, although with each execution, the number of protesters and of media is reduced.

Question: Can you describe some personal feelings about an execution?

Mr. Huffman: During one of the early executions that I oversaw, I was standing next to the execution table, and the inmate asked me if he would be able to see his mother and sister while he was on the table. I told him yes, if he turned his head to the left, they would be just a few feet away. He never looked at them, but that is when reality hit me that he was a human being who had a mother and sister who loved him unconditionally, just like the rest of us. His family was a victim of the crime as well.

Question: What is the role of the warden in dealing with the media regarding an execution?

Mr. Huffman: Now, the warden seldom meets with the media. The public information officer does most of it, as it is just too much for the warden to manage the media and the execution. At that first execution in 1999, we had over 200 news media at the institution. There is a lot of pressure on the warden. But some of the news media will only talk to the warden. What is tough is that there is a small percentage of the media that want to paint a negative picture of a "killer squad" or "death squad." I received hate mail from other countries, telling me I was no better than Hitler. When I speak to college students about my job, I tell them the toughest thing is dealing with media that want to paint a picture that is negative of you and your staff. We are just trying to carry out the law and do it professionally.

Personally, I often get asked what my own position is on the death penalty. I just respond that it is the law and I have no problems carrying out the law. What does bother me, however, is that I often see other people not on death row who did not get the death penalty, but who have done as bad or worse acts as those under sentence of death. It just does not seem fair that they will not be executed just because of plea bargaining or whatever else. That is the only thing I have a problem with.

When I was going through that first execution, it was very hard on me personally. It is not easy to be called a Nazi or killer when you are just trying to do what is right and do it with dignity for all involved. I owe a lot to my church, which supported and helped me through all this.

Question: What happens in the rest of the prison during the time of an execution?

Mr. Huffman: On the day of an execution, all inmates are locked down after breakfast. We go under the incident command system with an incident commander in charge of the operation of the prison. That leaves the warden free to concentrate on the execution. We have not had a single incident during an execution. The other inmates stay calm and don't interfere.

The most important thing for everyone, the other prisoners, families, the inmate, and the staff, is to maintain organization and make everything very routine. You must keep that routine with staff so that everyone knows their role and their place. It is a very difficult situation, but I believe that Ohio does a very good job at it.

However, there is other evidence that capital punishment does not deter other murders. A 1984 study by Decker and Kohfeld of homicide rates in Illinois from 1933 to 1980 did not identify any differences in rates depending on whether there was a death penalty allowed, a death penalty was allowed but not used, or the death penalty was abolished.[102] A 2006 research report used "model averaging" to weigh averages of a wide set of possible models of deterrence, and concluded there is little empirical evidence of a deterrent effect from capital punishment.[103] Similarly, Donnohue and Wolfers examined recent statistical studies that claimed to show a deterrent effect from the death penalty, and conclude that estimates claiming that the death penalty saves numerous lives are not credible. The authors used a different methodology and found that it leads to the exact opposite conclusion: that is, that the death penalty actually increases the number of murders.[104] Other studies of homicide rates from various states have also not found a deterrent effect with the death penalty.[105] A 2012 review of past studies concludes, "research to date on the effect of capital punishment on homicide is not informative about whether capital punishment decreases, increases, or has no effect on homicide rates. Therefore, the committee recommends that these studies not be used to inform deliberations requiring judgments about the effect of the death penalty on homicide."[106]

The majority of the general public does not think the death penalty is an effective deterrent. In a 2011 public opinion poll, 32 percent responded "yes" that they "believe the death penalty acts as a deterrent to the commitment of murder, that it lowers the murder rate, or not," 64 percent responded that it "does not," and 4 percent were not sure or refused to answer. It is interesting that this has almost completely reversed in twenty-five years, as in 1985, 62 percent of respondents believed the death penalty a deterrent and 31 percent believed it was not.[107, 108]

Retribution

Most people believe that punishment is important to show that "bad acts result in bad outcomes." People generally do not want criminals to get off without punishment adequately matched to the severity of their crime. The concept of retribution is that offenders get their just deserts, a punishment that fits their crime (an eye for an eye).[109] As described by Bohm in writing of capital punishment and retribution, revenge for taking a life is based on a belief that a killer deserves to be executed.[110] Many people believe that capital punishment is the only just punishment for the taking of a life. However, opponents point out that even with bifurcated trials as a result of *Gregg v. Georgia*, there is still racial and ethnic discrimination in the application of capital punishment,[111] undermining a retributive argument.

Incapacitation

The incapacitation argument regarding capital punishment is that the only sure way to protect the public from a criminal so vicious that he or she would kill someone is to execute the person. However, it is also generally accepted that murderers have very low rates of recidivism. Studies by Sorensen and colleagues and by Vito and Wilson of inmates who had committed murder and then had their death sentences commuted indicate that offenders who commit murder have a very low rate of recidivism, and less than 1 percent later committed another murder.[112] Opponents of the death penalty also argue that life in prison without the chance of parole equally protects society through incapacitation rather than execution. A 2010 poll indicated that 49 percent of people think the death penalty and 46 percent believe life imprisonment without parole is the better penalty for murder.[113] And for all inmates on death row in 2013, 9 percent had prior homicide convictions.[114]

Cost

A common argument when considering the death penalty is cost. Proponents of the death penalty argue that it is less expensive than life imprisonment, whereas opponents point out that the additional costs of a capital trial and appeals make the death penalty more expensive. Depending on the assumptions made, both sides can show evidence to support their position. Bedau[115] and Bohm[116] point out that capital punishment is more expensive due to the high cost of the trial and subsequent litigation. A 1993 study found that capital trials in North Carolina are significantly more costly than noncapital trials and, when comparing the cost of incarceration on death row for ten years, found that it was less costly than regular imprisonment for twenty years.[117] And a review of several state comparisons of the cost of the death penalty compared to life imprisonment reported much greater expense for a death penalty trial and imprisonment than for a life sentence (in New York, $1.4 million compared to $602,000; in Florida, $3.2 million or six times the cost of life imprisonment).[118]

In addition, a 2008 report by the Urban Institute found that in Maryland, the average capital-eligible case in which prosecutors did not seek the death penalty had a lifetime cost of $1.1 million, to include $870,000 for incarceration and $250,000 for adjudication. A capital-eligible case resulting in the death penalty cost approximately $3 million, with prison costs for holding on death row of $1.3 million and $1.7 million for adjudication.[119] Cost was one of the factors cited as Governor Bill Richardson signed legislation repealing the death penalty in New Mexico in early 2009, and when New Jersey abolished its death penalty in 2007.[120]

And many recent studies have found that states facing difficult budget challenges could save money by changing their death penalty laws. A recent Duke University study found that North Carolina could save $11 million a year by substituting life in prison for the death penalty, this following an earlier Duke study that found that death penalty cases cost $2.1 million more than cases seeking life imprisonment. The Tennessee Comptroller recently estimated that death penalty trials cost 48 percent more than those in which prosecutors sought life sentences. A state-sponsored study in Kansas found that death penalty cases cost 70 percent more than murder trials that didn't seek the death penalty. And a Florida study found the state could save $51 million by eliminating the death penalty.[121]

The Potential for Error

One serious concern regarding the death penalty is the potential for error, or the fallibility of the death penalty. We tend to have faith in our justice system and want to believe that it makes very few errors, especially in capital murder trials when the death penalty is a possible sanction. There is considerable debate as to how many mistakes are made in findings of guilt in death penalty trials and whether the potential for a mistake (with the irrevocability of the death penalty) puts in question the use of capital punishment. Proponents of the death penalty suggest that few errors have occurred since *Gregg v. Georgia*, with bifurcated trials and automatic reviews. However, Dieter has reviewed the risk of error and identified several reasons that error still exists:

- *General reasons:* The overall expansion in the authorization of the death penalty and the fact that it has become a political issue
- *Investigative reasons:* The pressure on the police to solve murders and on prosecutors to win trials, along with lack of resources by defense attorneys for investigation
- *Reasons during trial:* The fact that juries are often influenced by publicity, there are mistaken identities, and the heinous nature of many murders increases the likelihood of conviction
- *Plea bargaining and failure to dismiss:* There are more guilty pleas by innocent defendants, and there are fewer dismissals of charges for innocent people[122]

The Death Penalty Information Center reported that since 1973 to October 11, 2017, 160 inmates under sentence of death have been released with evidence of their innocence.[123] In the past three decades, the use of DNA evidence has provided a credible source for review of the guilt of some death row inmates. The use of DNA as evidence was not available at the time of trial for some death row inmates, but can now be used to reconsider questionable cases of guilt. An outstanding and very powerful book entitled *Just Mercy: A Story of Justice and Redemption* is recommended for those desiring to read a real account of the work of a legal rights organization that provided assistance to several innocent death row prisoners.[124]

Perhaps the greatest attention to the fallibility of the death penalty occurred in Illinois. From 1976 to 2000, Illinois executed twelve people and released thirteen from death row due to actual innocence. Death row proponents suggest that this proves that the system and layers of appeals work. Law students at Northwestern and DePaul Universities have for several years been researching death row cases, looking for evidence of innocence. If not for their efforts, most of these death row inmates would not have been freed. In 2000, Governor George H. Ryan declared a moratorium on executions in Illinois over concerns regarding the possible execution of innocent people. In doing so, he created a blue-ribbon task force to examine how death penalty investigations and trials worked in Illinois, and the task force made eighty-five recommendations for improvement in the administration of the death penalty.

On January 11, 2003, Governor Ryan took a dramatic step. Condemning the capital punishment system as fundamentally flawed and unfair, he announced that he was commuting the death sentences of 167 people (163 men and four women), primarily to life in prison. A few days earlier, he had pardoned four death row inmates, freeing them from death row and from prison. Ryan left office as governor on January 13, 2003, just two days after he emptied the state's death row, setting the stage for further debate over potential errors. There were cheers for his actions from many anti-death-penalty groups and the families of those on death row. And almost a decade later, former Illinois governor Pat Quinn signed a bill to abolish the death penalty (effective July 1, 2012) in Illinois. As an interesting aside, in September 2006, former governor Ryan was himself sentenced to 6.5 years in prison for conspiracy and fraud for taking payoffs from political insiders in exchange for state business.

Capital punishment has been a hotly debated topic in the United States for years. Proponents call it just and cite the general support of the public. Opponents call it brutal and immoral and cite the number of innocent defendants who have been convicted and executed. Even though a majority of Americans continue to support its use, there is a softening of support for capital punishment, especially with more information available on potential errors in convicting innocent defendants. This perplexing dilemma is apparent in a recent speech given by Renee Cardwell Hughes, a common pleas judge in Philadelphia, Pennsylvania. Judge Hughes noted, "I am a trial judge and there are two people on death row whose commitment papers bear my signature." However, continuing the speech, Judge Hughes commented that the death penalty "is in fact a cruel and unusual form of punishment which violates the laws which assure equal protection to all of our citizens."[125] After reading the arguments for and against the death penalty, students must now struggle with their own beliefs regarding the death penalty in the "You Make the Decision" box at the end of the chapter.

Public Opinion Regarding the Death Penalty

Over the past forty years, public opinion regarding the death penalty has changed significantly. The lowest levels of support were in the mid-1960s. In surveys of the U.S. public in 1965, the Harris Poll reported that only 38 percent favored the death penalty;[126] and in 1966, the Gallup Poll reported that only 45 percent were in favor of the death penalty for a person convicted of murder.[127] Over the next four decades, public attitudes continuously became more supportive of the use of capital punishment. Support increased, and peaked at 80 percent in 1994, but then began to decline. By 2013, the Gallup Poll reported that 60 percent of those surveyed favored the death penalty for murder convictions.[128] Overall support for the death penalty has declined. A Pew Research Center survey found that support for the death penalty declined from 78 percent in 1996 to 55 percent in 2013.[129] Some of this movement is due to the fact that 95 percent of those polled believed that innocent people are sometimes convicted of murder. Support of the death penalty has consistently varied by the gender and race of those surveyed. In 2012, 67 percent of males and 59 percent of females, 68 percent of whites, 41 percent of nonwhites, and only 28 percent of blacks were in favor of the death penalty.[130]

Chapter Review

Summary

Have we as a society gone too far in recognizing the legal rights of inmates? Many people believe we have, yet few would argue that inmates should lose all protections of the Constitution and Bill of Rights because they have committed a felony and been incarcerated. This chapter has described the emergence and then abandonment of the hands-off doctrine regarding suits by inmates and the evolution of recognition by the courts of specific rights of confined individuals. Many legal decisions have created guidelines for the provision of medical care, opportunity to practice one's religion, conditions of confinement, and due process during inmate disciplinary hearings.

For twenty-five years after the landmark decision of *Cooper v. Pate* opened a Pandora's box of inmate lawsuits, federal court decisions seemed to expand the requirements for prison officials to grant additional privileges and rights for inmates. However, over the past twenty years this trend has reversed somewhat and, in fact, the number of lawsuits by prisoners has actually declined significantly since 1995. Proactive policy implementations by prison administrators, congressional actions, and some court decisions have all contributed to this changing trend.

This chapter has also addressed the complex and emotional issue of the use of capital punishment in the United States. Although long a part of sentencing for serious criminal behavior, the use of capital punishment declined significantly during the 1950s and 1960s and ended for a short period after the Supreme Court ruled in *Furman v. Georgia*. This case did not declare capital punishment in itself as cruel and unusual punishment, but did create general guidelines that must be followed for capital punishment statutes to be considered constitutional. Since *Furman*, thirty-six states and the federal government have reenacted capital punishment statutes, and almost 3,000 prisoners are currently on death rows awaiting execution.

The reasons for support of capital punishment are also addressed. Proponents usually cite the value of capital punishment as a deterrent and provide the need for retribution, protection of society from further crimes, and reduced costs as arguments for their support. However, opponents counter these arguments, and there have been few, if any, conclusive studies on the impact of capital punishment in any of these areas. The biggest concern regarding capital punishment is its fallibility, or the chance of error in finding an innocent person guilty. Recent uses of DNA evidence have led to the exoneration and release of several inmates previously found guilty of murder and sentenced to death. For this reason, public support for capital punishment has diminished, especially when considering an option of life imprisonment without parole.

This chapter brings an end to our look into life in prisons and our examination of the world in which inmates live and prison staff work. We have reviewed the approaches taken by prison administrators to manage prisons and create a safe and secure environment while offering inmates the opportunity to participate in rehabilitative programs. In the final chapter of this book, we turn to recent and developing correctional challenges, including increasing correctional populations, the impact of politics on correctional policy, tightening public budgets, determining effectiveness, and future questions for correctional students and officials to deliberate.

Key Terms

slave-of-the-state doctrine

precedents

Eighth Amendment

Fourteenth Amendment

balancing test

Civil Rights Act of 1871

Section 1983

Americans with Disabilities Act

totality-of-conditions test

deliberate indifference

community standards

bifurcated trial

lethal injection

Review Questions

1. What is the hands-off doctrine, and in what case did the U.S. Supreme Court abandon it?

2. Define *cruel and unusual punishment* of the Eighth Amendment as it relates to prison conditions.

3. What is the *deliberate indifference* test regarding conditions of confinement as established in *Wilson v. Seiter*?

4. How did *Cooper v. Pate* change the reluctance of the federal courts to get involved in prisoner lawsuits?

5. What standards are used to determine whether the level and quality of medical care provided to inmates are constitutionally acceptable?

6. List the due process principles established for inmate discipline in the case of *Wolff v. McDonnell.*

7. How did the Prison Litigation Reform Act of 1996 limit litigation by inmates?

8. Define a bifurcated trial as established by *Furman v. Georgia.*

9. How many states currently have a statute allowing the death penalty?

10. What 2005 case dealt with the death penalty for juveniles under age eighteen, and what was the outcome of the decision?

11. Of all death row inmates, what percentage is white?

12. How many inmates were executed and by what method in 2015, and what state executed the most offenders?

13. Describe the controversy over the drug protocol for executions, and what has occurred as a result.

14. Describe evidence of the deterrent effect of the death penalty.

15. What percentage of the public supports the death penalty?

16. What dramatic step did Governor George Ryan of Illinois take in 2003 while expressing concerns about the fallibility of the death penalty?

▮ You Make the Decision...

Support the Death Penalty?

The reasons for and against capital punishment related to deterrence, retribution, incapacitation, and cost are listed in the preceding sections. Public support and the potential for error are also described. At this time, students must decide, if they do not already have a position, whether they support the death penalty. Even if you have a firm position, go through the exercise of considering all factors and see if it leads you to the same conclusion.

Either by yourself or in a small classroom group, list all the areas that are discussed as reasons for capital punishment.

Then list other factors you think should be considered part of the capital punishment equation. These may be religious or humanistic, desires by the victims' families, or any other factor you think is important. Weigh all these factors and decide whether you support capital punishment. This exercise is much more fun if done in a small group, and students can argue their points and try to convince others of the strength of their positions.

CHAPTER 16

Current and Future Issues in Corrections

Courtesy of CoreCivic.

After reading this chapter, you should be able to:

1. Identify the forces that have caused an increase in the prison population and compare the population growth of the state prisons to that of the federal prisons.

2. Explain the status of state budgets, the impact of funding for corrections, and the approaches states are taking to compensate for budget shortfalls.

3. Identify the negative consequences resulting from mass incarceration, and compare the U.S. incarceration rate with those of other countries.

4. Identify issues debated regarding private operation of prisons, and compare the effectiveness of public versus private prisons.

5. Compare the arguments and the evidence of physical and psychological impact of solitary confinement.

6. Consider whether or not a career in corrections may be right for you.

Introduction

Corrections is a constantly evolving discipline. Although it could be argued that we still do what was done centuries ago (incarcerate criminals and supervise them in the community), it can also be argued that everything has changed (prison architecture and management, styles of community supervision). Something certain about the field of corrections is that things do change. New issues develop. New pressures are brought to bear. New factors enter into old problems. And, quite frankly, old issues or programs reappear, sometimes with a different name or a different "spin." Yet, often it is (as the saying goes) the same old car, just a new wax job.

In this chapter, we review some of the most recent developments, issues, and challenges facing corrections today and tomorrow. First, trends in prison and jail populations are examined. We are seeing a rather unusual phenomenon, as the prison population across the United States has begun to decline for the first time in two decades. What is especially interesting is to speculate as to whether this decline will continue, or whether the prison population will begin to increase again. To examine this requires a look at an increasingly critical issue and its impact on the prison population. Corrections and the operations surrounding it had little public importance in the political agenda just two decades ago. However, with the growth in the number of correctional clients, there has been a tremendous increase in budget allocations to correctional agencies. Yet with the downturn in the economy over the past few years, governments are forced to find ways to reduce correctional spending. The option with the most potential to save is sentencing reforms as discussed in Chapter 2. This chapter also examines these and what states have been doing to reduce budget allocations for corrections.

A critical topic under discussion over the past few years has been "mass incarceration." Many people are looking at the United States use of incarceration in a global comparison, and questioning if we are getting the "bang for the buck" in terms of public safety and prisoner rehabilitation from the large dollar commitment we make to prison growth and operations. One approach to relieve prison and jail overcrowding and to reduce correctional costs is privatization. This move has been very controversial, in terms of not only philosophical issues, but whether privately operated facilities are really less expensive or whether they are as effective as public facilities. These issues are addressed in a section on private prisons. A private prison executive presents his perspective on the controversies around private prisons, and we look at the future prospective for the private prison industry.

Another recent controversy is over the use of "solitary confinement" in prisons. The original intent was to control violent and predatory inmates, enhancing security of prisons and making them safer for staff and other inmates. However, the use of solitary confinement has expanded beyond its original intent, and forces a reexamination of the effects on inmates and whether it does in fact make prisons safer. And finally, we address corrections as a career. It is the desire of this author that students of corrections will seriously consider it as a career. The issues and pros and cons of making corrections a lifelong activity are discussed.

We begin this chapter with an interview with an internationally recognized correctional expert. In the following "An Interview With" box, and as a part of examining the issues that challenge correctional officials, we present some of the general topics that issues that confront corrections today and are likely to continue into the future.

An Interview With...

A Correctional Expert

Reginald A. Wilkinson. Courtesy of Reginald Wilkinson.

The following interview is presented with someone who is truly an expert in corrections today and a visionary into what corrections can be in the future. Dr. Reginald A. Wilkinson was director of the Ohio Department of Rehabilitation and Corrections for more than fifteen years and has served the department in many capacities for more than thirty years until he retired in 2006. He has been the president of the American Correctional Association (ACA), the Association of State Correctional Administrators (ASCA), and the International Association of Reentry, as well as vice-chair for North America of the International Corrections and Prison Association. He is a former chair and current member of the National Institute of Corrections Advisory Board. Wilkinson is, moreover, the chairperson of the U.S. Department of Justice Panel on Prison Rape. He is perhaps the most visible and respected voice regarding corrections in the United States.

Question: Dr. Wilkinson, thank you for taking the time for this interview. To begin, can you describe what you think are some of the most significant developments in corrections over the past ten years?

Dr. Wilkinson: First, I would say that the movement to emphasize prisoner reentry has been huge. When the president of the United States (George H. W. Bush) remarks that "America is the land of the second chance" and mentions the importance of prisoner reentry in his 2004 State of the Union address, this puts major emphasis behind it. In Ohio we espouse that the reentry process begins the day a person arrives at prison, not two or three weeks or months before they are scheduled for release. When we receive someone at a reception center that is when we begin to prepare him or her to go home. Our reentry planning is not a program; instead, it's a way to integrate the reentry of offenders into the basic constructs (muscle memory) of everything we do. Our reentry philosophy has become our operating system (like Windows 2007 for a computer) that is the underpinning of our correctional operations.

Second, the focus on sexual misconduct on American correctional facilities, including jail, juvenile and adult institutions, is having a tremendous impact on correctional operations—and rightfully so. The Prison Rape Elimination Act that became federal law in 2003 is now being enforced. The U.S. Attorney General has approved national standards governing actions by correctional administrations in an attempt to minimize, if not eliminate, sexual misconduct. Administrators are working diligently to conform to and abide by these rigorous standards. As a member of the Prison Rape Review Panel, we hold federal hearing on how well the correctional facilities are addressing efforts to comply with the PREA law.

Consuming time of administrators and clinicians alike, is dealing with persons committed to a correctional agency with a mental illness. Prisons, for the most part, have become the New Asylums. Many state-run hospitals for people with mental illness and those with developmental disabilities are now closed for various reasons: the high cost of their operation and a concentration on community mental health options. A high percentage of inmates and juveniles have a documented history of mental illness. The challenge, of course, is to ensure treatment of mental health problems while still safeguarding the orderly operations of the correctional institution. Although, most agencies are confronting this issue with much success, we still need to improve the quality of mental health care in prions, jails and juvenile facilities.

Finally, I think there has been a broadening of the entire framework upon which we think about corrections work. In fact, I seldom use the phrase "criminal justice," because it is such a misnomer. The criminal element of justice is just a small piece of what is important in our society. Today, we have victims' justice, community justice, and restorative justice. And perhaps most important is the overall focus on social justice, which is more descriptive of what we should be all about. The justice system cannot solve the crime problem or the drug problem alone. Quite frankly, government is not equipped to adequately address these concerns without collaborative relationships. It takes a combination of employers, social service agencies, community leaders, and other nongovernmental agencies in order to be effective. Without involving all these other entities, we will merely be putting Band-Aids on the problems that we have. We have to look differently at what we do.

Question: And what do you think are likely to be some of the most significant developments in the future?

Dr. Wilkinson: From my perspective it's neither a defined activity nor a traditional program. The future success of corrections

(Continued)

work will reside with talented staff that has made this work a career. There are correctional professionals now who are really beginning to "get it." Also, we will continue to do a better job at harnessing best practices and promising programs that work. We will furthermore do much more sharing important data within and between jurisdictions. A good example is the Association of State Correctional Administrator's Performance-Based Measurement System. The PBMS will allow us to compare apples to apples and to define true uniform measures. As a result of improved information technology and data, we will be able to make well-informed decisions. I believe that if you can't measure something, then you shouldn't do it. We will be measuring much more of what we do in the future. Legislators and public officials will not accept anything less than that. Our management will be the result of evidence-based practices.

Question: What types of metrics make sense for monitoring the management of corrections?

Dr. Wilkinson: The first and foremost is money. It used to be that correctional agencies were just a blip on the fiscal radar screen. Nowadays corrections agencies consume large portions of taxpayer dollars. Public officials are extremely interested in how much money we can save without compromising public safety. Another metric will be exactly how effective we are. For instance, rates of recidivism must be reduced. Thus, victimization is reduced. Prisoners must become better prepared to go home "for good." Public officials must understand that rehabilitation is achievable. Another measure is how we manage offenders with special needs, such as people with mental illness. We need to ensure that clinical and social services are available to those who need them. The price of not doing this will mean more crime and more incarceration and, therefore, the need for more correctional funds.

Question: How do you encourage public or elected officials to pay more attention to corrections?

Dr. Wilkinson: This is already happening. For the past several years, my approach has been that correctional administrators should not just be administrators of corrections operations. We must be advocates for what is right and we must help influence the community and public officials as to what we should be doing. We can't just talk about running prisons, but how crime and corrections problems can be solved. We must go well beyond correctional systems' capabilities to solve criminality by truly implementing a social justice movement. We are better prepared today to effect positive change than when I began my corrections career in 1973. At that time in Ohio, we had 7,800 inmates and eight prisons. Today, we have 46,000 inmates in thirty-two prisons. Furthermore, the U.S. Congress has passed laws on prisoner reentry, correctional mental health, sexual

assaults, and more in recent years. Thus, the impact of elected officials should include national and local initiatives.

Question: What can be done to stop the "tough on crime" rhetoric by elected officials?

Dr. Wilkinson: The key is that we in corrections must have credibility with public officials. Correctional administrators must be respected as public servants who want to improve the quality of life of all citizens. We must show them we are good stewards of the public trust and that we care about public safety.

I am proud of and believe we in corrections have had many successes in this area, but we still have many challenges as well. For instance, in Ohio we have 600 people in prison merely for not paying child support. Now, putting them in prison for six months seems meaningless. They aren't going to be paying child support while they sit in prison. We would be better off to assign them to some type of work program so that they can learn job skills and pay their debts. Ohio is one of a few states that are incarcerating these "dead beat dads," and there are many constituent groups that support locking up these types of people. But we have to question whether or not it is good public policy. A success in Ohio is that we have all but stopped sending offenders back to prison solely because they used drugs and had a positive drug use. Again, it would not be cost-effective to send them to prison for a few months and then re-release them no better able to avoid drugs in the community than when they were first released. But to do any of these things, correctional officials must have credibility and a relationship with legislators to get them to take you seriously.

Question: What things do you see regarding corrections that make you most proud of your profession?

Dr. Wilkinson: It is probably that we are employing and promoting better educated persons to run our correctional systems. This is true of staff at all levels. This means there will be continuous improvement in what we do.

The more sophisticated our staff the better decision making will be. Decisions made will not be based on a hunch but on data, experience, and identifying best practices. The more academic we become about our work, the better the choices we will make on how to solve our critical challenges. The notion of workforce development and continuing education for corrections staff is made easier by the advancements in Web-based applications and professional development. Despite the many challenges we face in the justice business, we will continue to improve our processes.[1]

Prison and Jail Populations

At midyear 2002, the population of the nation's prisons and jails for the first time reached 2 million. On December 31, 2015, there were 2,173,800 offenders incarcerated in the fifty states and the District of Columbia, in federal government prisons and local jails. One-third of these offenders were in jails (728,200), and two-thirds were in prison (1,526,800).[2] Even though both prison and jail numbers have grown over the past decade, there has been a declining percentage of growth in the number of people incarcerated in state prisons, federal prisons, and local jails since 2008, when there were 2,310,300. During the 1990s, the inmate population grew an average of 8.7 percent per year.[3] Then from 2000 to 2008, the total incarcerated population increased 2.6 percent per year, with prison populations increasing by 1.6 percent and local jails by 2.4 percent. And from 2008 to 2015, both jails (−7.3 percent) and prisons (−5.1 percent) had a decline in their populations.[4]

Figure 16.1 illustrates the overall growth and then recent reduction in the number of people held in prisons. The state prison population increased rapidly from 1978 until 2009, declined each year until 2012, slightly increased in 2013 (from 1,352,582 to 1,361,084), and then again declined each year to 1,316,205 in 2016. The federal prison population also increased significantly from 1980 until 2012, and then had its first decline (by 1900) during 2013. The population has continued to decline from its high in 2012 of 217,815 to 189,192 in 2016. And these trends have been reflected in the growth and then decline of the imprisonment rate for sentenced prisoners. Between 2003 and 2008, the incarceration rate grew from 483 to 506 per 100,000 U.S. residents.[5] Since then, the incarceration rate has declined each year to 450 per 100,000 in 2016.[6] Figure 16.2 illustrates the same information regarding the jail population. Similar to prisons, the jail population increased from 2000 until 2008, and then declined until 2015, although the population rose and fell marginally throughout that period. These overall declines in incarceration for both jails and prisons over the past few years represent a significant change from the previous thirty years. The most significant reason for the fall in the number of prisoners is addressed in the next section regarding the impact of budgets.

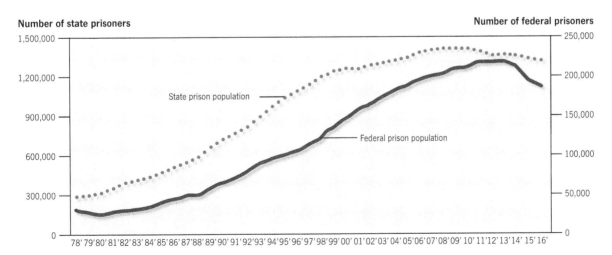

FIGURE 16.1 Total State and Federal Prison Population, 1978–2016 Sources: E. Ann Carson, "Prisoners in 2013," *BJS Bulletin* (Washington, D.C.: U.S. Department of Justice, 2014), p. 1; and "Prisoners in 2016," (2018), p. 3.

Average daily population of inmates

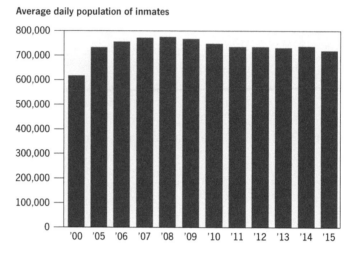

FIGURE 16.2   Average Daily Population of Inmates Confined in Local Jails, 2000 and 2005–2015   Source: Todd D. Minton and Zhen Zeng, "Jail Inmates in 2015," *BJS Bulletin* (Washington, D.C.: U.S. Department of Justice, 2016), p. 1.

An interesting result of the changing prison population has been the impact on private prisons. As indicated in Table 16.1, from 2000 to midyear 2008, the number of inmates held in privately operated prisons increased from 87,369 to

TABLE 16.1	**State and Federal Prisoners in Private Facilities, December 31, 2000–2016**			
	Number of Prisoners in Private Facilities			**Percent of All Prisoners**
Year	**Total**	**Federal**	**State**	
2000	87,369	15,524	71,845	6.3
2001	91,828	19,251	72,577	6.5
2002	93,912	20,274	73,638	6.5
2003	95,707	21,865	73,842	6.5
2004	98,628	24,768	73,860	6.6
2005	107,940	27,046	80,894	7.1
2006	113,697	27,726	85,971	7.2
2007	123,942	31,310	92,632	7.8
2008	129,482	33,162	96,320	8.0
2009	129,333	34,087	95,246	8.0
2010	128,195	33,830	94,365	8.0
2011	130,972	38,546	92,426	8.2
2012	137,220	40,446	96,774	8.7
2013	133,044	41,159	91,885	8.4
2014	131,261	40,017	91,244	8.4
2015	126,272	34,934	91,338	8.3
2016	128,323	34,159	94,164	8.5

Source: "Prisoners in the United States," *Bureau of Justice Statistics* (Washington, D.C.: U.S. Department of Justice, Selected Years).

129,482, an increase of 48 percent over eight years. By 2008, 8 percent of all prisoners were housed in private facilities. What seems to have occurring in those years is that much of the new growth in prison inmates are going into private prisons, most likely because the private companies provide the funding to add capacity without government agencies having to sell bonds and budget all the capital construction money up front. However, since the prison population growth has slowed in the past few years, the number of inmates in private prisons also slowed and then decreased. There was slow growth from 2008 until 2012, when the number of inmates housed in private prisons peaked at 137,220, which was 8.7 percent of the overall prison population. Yet it declined since that time, and was 128,323 at the end of 2016. Just as much of the growth in the overall prison population during the early 2000's went into private prisons, as the prison population declines, inmates are removed from private prisons at a rate greater than the reduction in public prisons. This is consistent with earlier studies of privatization. In one report, the authors projected that "[t]he number of privatized prisons is likely to increase, but not at the pace exhibited during the past decade."[7] And another study suggested that there is evidence that prison privatization is in decline as a result of declining incarceration rates, overbuilding of prison beds, legislation antagonistic to the private prison industry, and a number of well-publicized serious incidents.[8]

There are several reasons for the slowdown in the growth of incarcerated offenders that has continued (seemingly unabated) from the 1980s until the first decade of 2000s. First, it is only natural that after such growth there would be a slowdown at some time. If, as proponents of the use of incarceration argue, incapacitating offenders in prison reduces crime, then at some point a large number of potential criminals will be in jail and prison, and the increase in new admissions will have to slow down. Although reducing the inmate population by shortening sentences or eliminating mandatory prison terms for some offenses does not seem politically popular, recent incarceration trends do note some relief.

After the era of lengthening sentences over the past twenty years, it is difficult to comprehend that legislative bodies will significantly roll back sentencing codes to the "less tough" levels that existed before the mid-1980s. However, most states have a constitutional requirement to balance their budgets and are not allowed to operate at a deficit. Therefore, as addressed in a section below regarding the impact of tightening budgets on correctional policy, there is now a political opportunity to modify statutes to reduce the number of people in prison. In addition, there has been considerable publicity about the questionable merit of tough sentencing laws such as California's three-strikes legislation. In a review of this process, Greenwood and colleagues suggest that legislators who found voting for the legislation politically attractive later reversed themselves and found that voting against funding the Act's implementation was just as politically attractive.[9]

Second, many states have increased their use of alternatives to incarceration, and these efforts are finally having some impact. There has been an increasing concern that continued increases in the use of incarceration have failed to concurrently increase public safety,[10] yet this policy has undoubtedly increased the cost to taxpayers. Therefore, many states have looked for and implemented sanctions between probation and incarceration. Many of these have proved effective and less costly when the risk of offenders is properly identified and matched to correctional sanctions. As well, jail pretrial release programs have been added in many local jurisdictions and have also effectively slowed the increase in the

The inmate population, after years of growth has been slowing and even recently reduced. Courtesy of CoreCivic.

number of jail inmates. The Pretrial Services Resource Center, in a review of methods used to alleviate jail overcrowding conducted for the U.S. Department of Justice, reported,

> In response to increased jail populations, probation agencies are working with other criminal justice agencies to develop alternative programs. Many counties opt for increasing the number of community-based alternatives, instead of the rate of incarceration, because the former is a more cost-effective means of alleviating jail crowding while maintaining public safety.[11]

Finally, the continually increasing costs to government for building and operating correctional facilities challenges a jurisdiction's budget, and the economic downturn beginning in 2008 challenged state and local budgets. Even though some state revenues are improving, the past five years have shown that we can reduce the number of inmates and the cost to house them without reducing public safety. In a report regarding methods to alleviate jail overcrowding (that is also relevant to prisons), the authors noted, "Construction and operation of local jails are extremely expensive propositions. Over the years, the view that a jurisdiction can solve its jail crowding problem through building has proved to be wrong."[12] There are many factors that influence correctional policy, including politics and budgetary challenges. Both of these issues are addressed below.

Corrections policy is at the critical crossroads where tight budgets and politics intersect. It will be interesting to observe whether elected officials who have been willing to reform sentencing to save money will stay with that approach if and when state and local budget coffers improve. Although it is hoped that elected officials will stay away from political rhetoric and emotion and instead use research, analysis, and careful planning to shape our crime policies in the future, which has not been the case in the past.

The Impact of Budgets on Correctional Policy

As noted earlier, the recession and budget challenges at the federal, state, and local levels have had an impact on incarceration rates as governments try to reduce the cost of corrections. The economic downturn over the past few years has resulted in reduced tax receipts by local, state, and the federal governments. As the economy has improved and tax revenue has increased, government budgets are still not strong enough to fund a continuation of the growth of the number of people in prisons and jails that we had seen in the past. When the economy was strong and governments were experiencing budget surpluses, it was an easy decision to expand prison space and other correctional services to meet the burgeoning population under supervision. As budgets tightened, it became a much more complicated decision as to whether to increase taxes, reduce the correctional population, or eliminate some services or supervision to meet budget shortfalls. The increased funding requirements for correctional agencies requires elected officials to encourage correctional administrators to find ways to reduce budget requirements and brings into question many policies and practices that the public believes create unnecessary expenditures.

As noted above, over the past forty years, the number of clients served by adult correctional agencies has grown significantly. As illustrated in Figure 16.3, the population under correctional supervision has risen significantly, and at the end of 2015, 6.7 million individuals were under correctional supervision of probation, prison, jail, or parole.[13] By far, most of the spending is for the operation of prisons. From 1980 until 2015, the U.S. prison population increased from just fewer than 320,000 to 1.527 million.[14] Annual reports by the National Association of State Budget Officers show a continued increase in state general fund spending for prison operations (not including bond costs for capital expansion). As illustrated in Figure 16.4, expenditures for state correctional institutions jumped from approximately $10 billion in 1982 to $51.6 billion in 2016.[15]

Key drivers of increased cost are inmate health care and salaries for staff, as prisons are struggling mightily to keep a full complement of officers on

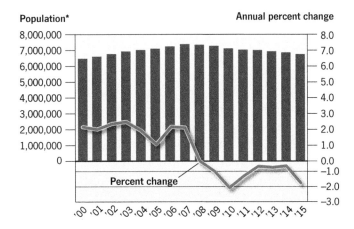

FIGURE 16.3   Total Population under the Supervision of Adult Correctional Systems, 2000–2015   Source: Danielle Kaeble and Lauren E. Glaze, "Correctional Populations in the United States, 2015," *Bureau of Justice Statistics Bulletin* (Washington, D.C.: U.S. Department of Justice, 2016), p. 1.

Dollars (in billions)

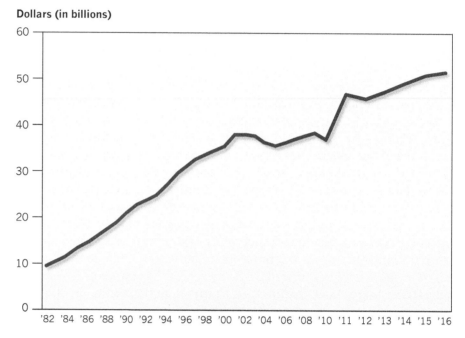

FIGURE 16.4   Change in Institutional Operations Expenditures by State, 1982–2016   Source: Tracey Kyckelhahn, "State Correctional Expenditures, FY 1982–2010" *BJS Bulletin* (Washington, D.C.: U.S. Department of Justice, 2012), p. 5. Expanded to 2016 by National Association of State Budget Officers (NASBO), *State Expenditures Report,* each year, 2011 to 2016 (Washington, D.C.: NASBO, 2017).

staff. A study by the Vera Institute of Justice reports that costs of incarceration are even higher than thought to be. Researchers examined costs beyond the aggregate budgets for the state corrections agencies and found a 13.9 percent additional cost outside corrections budgets for services such as capital construction, funding of employee retirement and health benefits, and inmates health and hospital care. They reported a 2010 average cost per inmate of $31,166, or $85.39 per day.[16]

And states are not able to meet their budget demands. In 2009, states reported over $50 billion shortfalls in revenue to fund their budgets. Over the next three years, the budget gaps lessened, yet for fiscal year 2013, the gap was still $49 billion.[17] And by 2017, only twenty-eight states had fully recovered from the loss of pre-recession (2007) tax revenue.[18] To help budgets stay within revenues, prison operations are a prime target for cuts, as surveys of thirty-four states indicate that nine out of every ten corrections dollars were spent on prisons.[19] Community alternatives are significantly less expensive, and jurisdictions are taking unprecedented approaches to try to reduce the costs of corrections by moving more of the population from prison to community supervision. As noted above, historically, no politician wanted to be painted as "soft on crime." In these tight budget times, however, fiscal issues are beginning to trump politics.

The Pew Report *One in 31* notes, "Some policy makers are questioning the wisdom of devoting an increasingly large slice of the budget pie to incarceration, especially when recidivism rates have remained discouragingly high."[20] As a result, many policy makers are looking to lower correctional costs by considering both the opportunity to divert lawbreakers guilty of nonviolent or less serious crimes and to restructure sentencing to reduce the overall length of stay for a large proportion of the prison population. In a recent report summarizing how states are dealing with the fiscal crisis they face, three areas of activity were highlighted:

1. *Operating Efficiencies:* States are trying to reduce budget expenditures through reducing healthcare services, joining purchasing coops to lower medical and other supplies, reducing the number of staff by instituting hiring freezes, reducing salaries and benefits, consolidating facilities, and reducing offender programs.
2. *Recidivism Reduction:* States are strengthening community corrections programs to reduce parole and probation violations and improving reentry services.
3. *Release Policies:* States are trying to reduce both the number of offenders entering prison and their length of stay in prison. Many states identify groups of people who can be safely released after serving shorter sentences.[21]

There are two ways to divert offenders from prison. The first is to reduce the number of prisoners on the "front end of sentencing" by using more programs to keep offenders in the community rather than in prisons. The second approach is "on the back end" by reducing the revocation rate of offenders on parole or supervision after serving their prison terms. The following examples are what many states are doing to create community alternatives to prison so that offenders can stay in the community rather than being sentenced to prison.

Texas has diverted thousands of inmates from prison to community rehabilitation facilities designed to help them reenter society and has funded new treatment facilities for offenders sentenced for driving while intoxicated (DWI) at which they are provided substance abuse treatment. They have also expanded drug treatment diversion beds in lieu of sending offenders to prison. The goal of this is to reduce the need for construction of costly new prisons. "We have changed the course of the ship substantially in the state of Texas," said Representative Jerry Madden, chairman of the House Corrections Committee and an engineer of the prison plan.[22] Texas estimates they have avoided spending $523 million in building more prison beds by expanding drug treatment and diversion beds, many of them in secure facilities.

An accepted target for diversion is nonviolent offenders with drug addictions. Since 2004, at least thirteen states have adopted legislation creating or expanding community corrections options for nonviolent offenders, including the use of drug courts.[23] As a result, since 2000, the number of state prisoners serving time for drug offenses declined by 8.2 percent.[24] In 2009, New York State repealed the 1970s Rockefeller drug laws that required mandatory prison terms for low-level drug felons. In its place, the state would give judges more authority to send nonviolent drug offenders to community treatment instead of prison.[25] Although treatment in lieu of prison would cost $80 million per year, in the long run, the repeal is expected to save money as the treatment program would be less expensive than the $45,000 it costs per year to confine a prisoner in New York.

Kansas has also enhanced their efforts to save money by diverting offenders from prisons to less expensive community alternatives. The Kansas legislature passed a law to reduce prison admissions by providing counties with financial incentives to create community correctional systems and to provide opportunities for low-risk inmates to reduce their sentences by participating in prison programs. If counties reduce their recidivism rates of probationers and parolees by 20 percent or more, they qualify for grants from the state. The law also allows early release of up to sixty days for qualified offenders who successfully complete education and counseling programs that are expected to decrease their chances of returning to prison.[26] And Wisconsin is using dollars from the 2009 Recovery Act funds (the stimulus bill passed by the Obama administration) to divert offenders from prison, keeping the most serious offenders in prison while increasing supervision for nonviolent and lower-risk offenders in the community. The state believes that additional focus on reentry, community treatment, and diversion programs will reduce recidivism and the number of offenders that must be held in prisons.[27]

On the "back end," some states are considering changing how to deal with those who violate rules of probation and parole. Over the past two decades, there was less tolerance for technical violations of parole (such as failing a drug test or missing an appointment with their parole officer), and parole failures constituted a growing proportion of all new prison admissions. In 2005, parole violators accounted for more than one-third of all prison admissions.[28] In 2005, 45 percent of parolees were successfully terminated from supervision, whereas 38 percent were returned to incarceration. Yet by 2015, 61 percent of parolees successfully completed supervision, and only 26 percent returned to incarceration.[29] The number of new prison admissions that were parole violators peaked to 253,053 in 2008, but by 2015, only 164,626 admissions to prison were parole violators, representing 27 percent of all admissions.[30]

To reduce the number of prison admissions, jurisdictions are opting to punish technical parole violators with community-based sanctions, such as day reporting centers, electronic monitoring systems, and community service. A good example is California, which has a parolee return to prison rate of 66 percent (compared to the national average of 40 percent), representing two-thirds of all admissions to the state prisons. California recognized that they are recycling their inmates, as violators can be returned by the Board of Parole Hearings for no more than twelve months. In a report analyzing this problem, the authors suggested the development of a range of intermediate, community-based sanctions (especially for parolees with substance abuse problems) instead of a return to prison.[31]

The Washington Institute for Public Policy in 2006 published a very important work that reviewed 571 evaluations of correctional programs that had rigorous methodologies and could be used to determine what worked to reduce crime and save taxpayers' money.[32] Their work identified categories of programs that were determined to be "evidence based" in that there were sufficient data to prove that they were effective in reducing crime and were therefore cost effective. Programs found effective included vocational training and education, cognitive behavioral therapy, prison industries, sex offender treatment, and drug treatment for prison inmates. In the community, drug courts, employment training, drug treatment, and intensive supervision with treatment are effective. The conclusion was that states should implement these evidence-based programs to save money while not endangering public safety.

In addition to diversion from prison, jurisdictions are reducing the number of prisoners by restructure sentencing codes, so that prisoners do not stay longer than is necessary for punishment and the opportunity for rehabilitation. Many states are giving inmates the chance to earn more good time in order to reduce the length of sentence served. In Rhode Island, lawmakers expanded good time to move more offenders from prison to postprison supervision. In Kentucky, nonviolent offenders were allowed to serve up to 180 days of their prison sentence at home. In Mississippi, the state passed a measure to make nonviolent inmates eligible for release after serving 25 percent of their sentences. In South Carolina, there was a proposal to abolish parole to slow down the return of parole violators to prison.[33]

In 2011, Ohio passed a sentencing reform that would avoid incarcerating what was then 12,000 inmates in Ohio prisons that were nonviolent and serving less than one year in prison. The biggest change was that instead of having a cost of $26,000 per year in prison for every inmate, the state would reinvest money in local government to provide community alternatives at a cost of approximately $5,500 per inmate per year. Under this bill, first-time property and drug offenders are not going to go to prison; local sentencing judges use local correctional sanctions funded by the state instead of sentencing them to prison. The target was to get the prison population back to the 2008 level and save $46 million by 2015.[34] And in 2017, Ohio again modified their sentencing statute for nonviolent offenders to divert and treat as many as 3,400 in the community rather than sending them to prison.

Many of these state reforms have come about from states' participation in the **Justice Reinvestment Initiative** (JRI), a partnership between the Bureau of Justice Assistance and the Pew Charitable Trusts. From the initiation of the act in 2011 until 2017, over thirty states have begun or completed the reinvestment process.[35] States establish bipartisan groups of officials (legislators, prosecutors, judges, defense attorneys, victim advocates, corrections staff, and law enforcement agencies) to work with criminal justice policy experts and researchers. They examine system wide data to determine the causes of a state's correctional costs, with a focus on reversing an increasing prison population and reducing costs through reinvesting in **evidence-based practices (EBPs)**, programs and policies as community alternatives to prison. In almost every state, these efforts have been effective, especially regarding reductions in "revocation recidivism," which are return to incarceration from probation or parole at between 24 percent and 46 percent.[36] Evidence-based practices that JRI states have implemented include the following:

Justice Reinvestment Initiation
an approach to use evidence-based policies and programs to create community alternatives to prison to both slow the increase or reduce the prison population and save money

evidence-based practices
programs and policies that research finds effective

- Requiring risk and needs assessments
- Implementing problem-solving courts
- Employing intermediate sanctions and incentives
- Requiring the use of EBPs by justice agencies
- Monitoring the effectiveness of new programs.[37]

An example of reform through the JRI is North Carolina. From 2000 until 2010, the state prison population had climbed 27 percent to over 40,000, and the budget had increased by 49 percent to $1.3 billion. Much of the problem was from revocations of supervision, more than one-half of prison admissions in 2009 resulted from failures on probation, with three-quarters for technical violations only. To reduce revocations, North Carolina added options other than when probationers missed appointments, curfews, or failed drug tests. They also trained officers to improve the quality of their interactions with offenders, and also gave officers the authority to immediately place offenders in substance abuse treatment programs or put them under electronic monitoring without waiting for a judicial hearing. As a result of these reforms, the state prison population fell by 3,400 inmates in three years, ten prisons were closed, and the corrections budget was reduced.[38]

The JRI also had positive results in Georgia, which enacted HB 310 in 2015 to reorganize probation and parole, and implemented SB 367 in 2016 to allow drug-related mandatory sentences to be eligible for community supervision. Georgia experienced a 6 percent decrease in the prison population, saving the state $264 million in corrections costs and reinvesting $56 million of those savings into recidivism reduction strategies to include accountability (specialty) courts, add evidence-based programming, and enhance reentry. In 2015, two-thirds of the admissions to prison were for violating probation or parole, so in 2017, SB 174 was enacted to reduce lengthy probation terms, improve probation practices, and reduce high probation officer caseloads.[39] Reform efforts included assessing probationers for risk and need while focusing officer time on the highest risk/need, developing case plans with performance-based objectives, creating an early termination from supervision policy for certain qualifying offenses, and creating administrative caseloads for those who are qualified and have performed well under supervision. As a result, it is projected that by 2022, 44,104 fewer people will be on probation and $7.3 million in spending will be averted.[40]

A unique approach to examining how best to target resources toward correctional supervision and programs is a benefit-cost analysis by the Washington State Institute for Public Policy. The Institute examined forty-four different approaches to managing and treating adult offenders. Some were in the community and could be considered alternatives to incarceration, and some were programs provided in prisons or as a transition to the community. The Institute identified the overall benefit of each program in dollars per participant (could be for reduced crime and processing, impact on victims, or economic benefit to society or the participant), the cost of delivery, and the benefit to cost ratio (for each dollar spent, number of dollars saved when cost is less than benefit). The following lists some of the benefit to cost rations for a sampling of the programs examined.[41] The program name is listed on the left, and the benefit to cost ratio (for every dollar spent, the savings that result) on the right. The savings are based on 2016 dollars.

> Offender Reentry Community Safety (for those with serious mental illness) $1.90
> Correctional education—post-secondary $19.79
> Drug Offender Sentencing Alternative (for drug offenders) $13.91
> Vocational training in prisons $11.89
> Inpatient or intensive outpatient drug treatment during incarceration $10.15
> Correctional education—basic skills $9.67
> Drug courts $2.83
> Therapeutic communities during incarceration for substance abuse $ 5.05
> Risk Need and Responsivity supervision (for high and moderate risk) $6.99
> Cognitive Behavioral Therapy (high and moderate risk individuals) $6.32
> Correctional industries in prison $12.68
> Employment counseling and job training in the community $2.16
> Inpatient or intensive outpatient drug treatment in community $(1.51)
> Community-based correctional facilities (halfway houses) $(0.71)

And perhaps the most surprising sentencing change is coming at the federal level. In October 2015, the U.S. Senate reached agreement to modify legislation that would cut mandatory prison sentences for nonviolent criminals and provide more early release options in order to reduce the financial and societal costs of incarceration. These criminal justice reforms would turn around some of the 1980s and 1990s laws to get tough on drug crime.[42] And following a visit by President Barak Obama to a federal prison (first ever for a sitting president), the U.S. Justice Department announced that it would review and release approximately 6,000 federal prisoners at the end of October 2015. This was to both reduce prison overcrowding and more fairly sentence offenders primarily sentenced for powder cocaine and methamphetamine–related crimes. Apart from the president's visit to the prison, the U.S. Sentencing Commission in July 2015 voted to retroactively change sentencing guidelines for nonviolent drug offenders, a change that could make 46,376 federal prisoners eligible for release.[43] However, the Department of Justice under President Donald Trump has indicated they desire to return to tougher sentencing. Attorney General Jeff Sessions has ordered federal prosecutors to pursue harsh charges against criminal suspects, reversing the Obama administration efforts to ease penalties for some nonviolent drug of-fenders.[44] It will take some time to determine the overall impact of this approach on the prison population.

The question is whether these reforms will continue and if a well-publicized incident is not used to roll them back. Several times in the past three decades, there have been modest efforts to restructure sentences and use more alterna-tives to prison in an effort to either reduce costs or create a system that seems to provide more equity and fairness. However, political reaction has always been strongly negative, and the sponsors of such legislation have backed down with few changes and very little change in policy or budgets. If the current recession deepens and continues, the likelihood that these efforts will this time lead to more significant and longer-lasting change increases.

Mass Incarceration

The growth of the prison and jail population increased dramatically and now ap-pears in decline. The politics of criminal sanctions continue to support the safest option of placing great numbers of offenders in prison. Yet the tight fiscal situa-tion of federal, state, and local governments still force elected officials to look for less expensive options to incarceration. One issue that has continued is what has over the past five years been referred to as **mass incarceration**. Mass incarcera-tion is generally a term used to refer to the fact that the U.S. prison population has grown dramatically over the past forty years, and the United States incarcer-ates a much higher ratio of people than any other country. Of the approximately 9 million people worldwide in prison, one-half is in the United States, Russia, and China.[45] For 2016, the U.S. incarcerated population per 100,000 was 716, the next highest countries were Cuba at 510, Rwanda at 492, the Russian Federation at 475.[46] And when discussing mass incarceration, it often has race and ethnicity overtones in that there is a much higher proportion of Black and Hispanic offend-ers in prison than their make up in the overall U.S. population. But what is the definition of mass incarceration? For this textbook, I will define it as the overuse of prisons and jails for sentencing and detaining offenders beyond what is effec-tive and necessary to protect society and at too great a cost.

Mass incarceration has become a way for researches, authors, and others to communicate the large number of people in the United States that are incarcer-ated, and to advocate for a change in policy resulting in fewer people behind bars and simultaneously spending less money on incarceration and the correctional system. The argument is that there are many alternatives that are as effective (par-ticularly with an analysis of risk) and much more efficient. The sections above illustrate this, as after decades of increasing the incarceration rates, even well after crime began to decline, it took a budget crisis before elected officials would stand up to change policy to increase the use of alternatives instead of prisons and jails. And the American public appears to support these changes. After decades of believing that politicians were on safer ground to enhance punishments with lon-ger criminal sanctions, the public is now saying "enough." After being told that nearly one-half of the federal prison population is incarcerated for drug crimes, 61 percent of people surveyed responded that there are too many drug offend-ers in prison, and that space is best used for people who have committed acts of violence or terrorism.[47] Similarly, three-quarters of those surveyed favor ending federal mandatory minimum sentences, and more than 80 percent support pro-grams and reforms that allow inmates to earn a reduction in their prison terms.[48]

mass incarceration
the overuse of prisons and jails for sentencing and detaining offenders beyond what is effective and necessary to protect society and at too great a cost

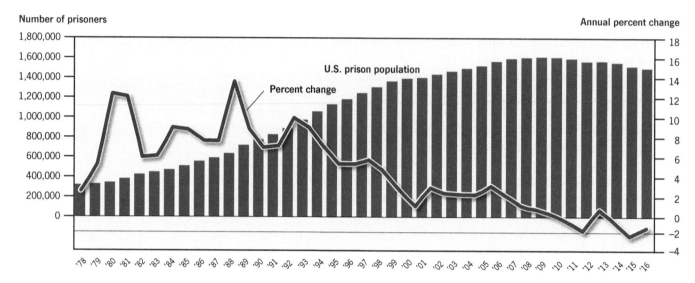

FIGURE 16.5 Prisoners Under the Jurisdiction of State or Federal Correctional Authorities, December 31, 1978–2016   Source: E. Ann Carson and Elizabeth Anderson, "Prisoners in 2015," *BJS Bulletin* (Washington, D.C.: U.S. Department of Justice, 2016), p. 3. Updated with E. Ann Carson, "Prisoners in 2016," *BJS Bulletin* (Washington, D.C.: U.S. Department of Justice, 2018).

So if the prison population is declining and public opinion is more in favor of ending the expensive mass incarceration of offenders, why is this still an issue? Look more closely at the trends of the prison population. In Figure 16.5, we see the dramatic increase in state and federal prisoners from 1978 to 2015. While it has been declining from 2009 through 2015, that was only from 1,613,487 to 1,526,792 (a total of 88,695 or 5.5 percent). Yet from the approximately 350,000 in 1978 to the high of 1.6 million in 2009, we increased by 1.265 million or 360 percent. So while the last six years of decline are encouraging, we still incarcerated over four times the number of people we did forty years ago.

What caused the major increase in incarceration? Travis, Western, and Redburn examined both the causes and consequences of this major increase from 1980 until 2010. They categorized four potential causes or contributions: the number of crimes, the ratio of arrests to crimes, the percentages of prison sentences per arrest, and the time served per prison admission. They found little contribution from the first two. Crime rates began falling for most crimes since the early 1980s. And the ratio of arrests per crimes remained relatively unchanged from 1980 to 2010. They found the growth in the prison population impacted almost equally to the other two. Taken by decade, the 1980s growth in incarceration rate (107 percent) was largely driven by the increase in prison commitments by arrest; in other words, taking discretion away from judges through sentencing guidelines, mandatory minimum sentences, and three strikes laws forced more people into prison that may have otherwise been supervised in the community. And during the 1990s when the incarceration rate increased by 55 percent (from the large ending decade number from the 1980s), the major driver was the length of sentence or time served, as state legislatures and the U.S. Congress continually increased prison sentences for almost every crime. There was little growth in the prison incarceration rate from 2000 until 2010.[49]

There are many negative consequences to mass incarceration. Travis, Western, and Redburn identify the following areas of impact:

• Health and mental health of prisoners;
• Employment and earnings of former inmates;

- Family and children of incarcerated offenders;
- Communities and neighborhoods from where those incarcerated come;
- General impacts on U.S. society, such as collateral consequences affecting those imprisoned, a public impact by increased marginalization of minority and poor populations, and the overall cost of increased use of confinement.[50]

After reviewing and analyzing studies in each area, when possible, conclusions were made. In general, the health and mental health of prisoners created a challenge to correctional officials, and there were generally not adequate amounts or quality of care delivered for most areas of health, mental health, or substance abuse. Former inmates were found to have lower levels of employment and earnings than those not going to prison. The families and children of incarcerated parents were negatively affected. Communities (usually poor and minority) from which large numbers of offenders were removed and incarcerated were disrupted. There are many collateral consequences to those with felony convictions, and they are increasingly marginalized and disenfranchised. And the public costs of corrections have increased dramatically, causing fiscal pressures on all levels of government. As an example, inflation-adjusted state spending on corrections from 1980 until 2009 increased by 400 percent while the number of inmates increased by 475 percent.[51]

Consider what could happen if we decided to incarcerate only as many people now as we did twenty-five years ago (just under one million), still an almost threefold increase from 1978. Assuming the average cost of incarceration is now $35,280 (it was $31,166 in 2010 times 1.132 percent for inflation until 2017),[52] the cost of incarceration would be approximately $35 billion. We know overall we are spending between $70 and $80 billion for corrections. Add to this the cost of community supervision that must be provided for the 4,650,900 offenders under community supervision at the end of 2015,[53] plus another 527,000 that would be in the community instead of in prison. Assuming an estimated cost of $5 per day, the cost of community supervision would therefore be approximately $2.8 billion. In other words, while there are several contingencies not considered in this rough calculation, it is feasible that we could save the U.S. taxpayers $30 to $40 billion per year by reducing our prison population to 1993 levels. We have so many unmet needs in American society; these funds could be used in a much better way than the almost total negative impact we are receiving from our policies contributing to mass incarceration.

Private Prisons

A growing method used by correctional agencies to reduce their costs is to contract some services or the entire operation of prisons to the private sector. Some contracting for services has been done for years by correctional agencies, but some approaches are relatively new. Since the 1950s, halfway houses have served as a transition from prison to the community. Most halfway houses are privately operated, although most are owned by faith-based or not-for-profit charitable organizations. By the 1980s, almost every state had contracts with privately operated halfway houses to provide residential services, supervision, and transitional programs for inmates leaving prison and returning to the community.[54] Also, many states with very small juvenile offender populations have often found it cost-effective to contract with privately operated facilities, rather than to open state-run juvenile facilities. In 1984, it was reported that 65 percent of all juvenile facilities were private, housing approximately 32,000 offenders.[55] During the 1980s, prisons began to contract with private companies to provide food services, medical and mental health care, educational programming, and substance abuse counseling, and by the turn of the century, there were 126 state and federal prisons contracting for food services and 397 for medical care for inmates.[56] Another 300 prisons had private contractors providing mental health services, and 226 prisons contracted for substance abuse services.[57] And more recently, there have also been privatized probation services, to include supervision, drug, testing, and electronic monitoring. While there has been concern over privatizing probation,[58] it does not get the attention that resulted from the privatization of total prison operations.

private prison

any secure correctional facility operated by an organization other than a governmental agency, and usually in a for-profit manner, that contracts with the government to provide security, housing, and programs for adult offenders

These uses of the private sector in corrections have not been controversial. However, when agencies began to contract to house adult prisoners in private for-profit prisons, many ethical and practical questions were raised. A **private prison** is any secure correctional facility operated by an organization other than a governmental agency, and usually in a for-profit manner, that contracts with the government to provide security, housing, and programs for adult offenders. In a private prison, staff that operate the prison are employees of the company that owns and operates the prison. Many government agencies that oversee the contract also maintain one or more full-time employees at the prison to monitor quality. Such prisons can be administered without cumbersome governmental purchasing and personnel policies, although they are still held to the same constitutional standard for treatment of inmates as a public prison.

The first private contract to house adult offenders was in 1984, for a small, 250-bed facility operated by Corrections Corporation of America under contract with Hamilton County, Tennessee. Soon thereafter, additional contracts with the private sector to house illegal aliens (contracted with the U.S. Immigration and Naturalization Service) and youthful offenders (with the Federal Bureau of Prisons) were established. The growth over the next few decades in the privatization of correctional facilities was spurred by the increasing number of inmates and the rapid need to build new prisons, the budgetary challenges required to fund these new prisons, and the Reagan-era support of using the private sector to help downsize the scope of government. There were also many states under litigation in federal courts due to their overcrowded conditions, and they turned to the private sector to add capacity. Welch notes,

> At that time, the prevailing political and economic philosophy encouraged government officials to turn to the private sector to administer public services, such as sanitation, health care, security, fire protection, and education. As a result of the introduction of free-market principles into the administration of public services, ... the privatization of corrections appeared to be a new and novel approach to some old problems (i.e., overcrowding and mounting costs).[59]

By 1990, Logan reported that private prisons held just over 9,000 adult inmates,[60] but by the end of 2016, there were 128,323 state and federal prisoners held in private prisons, accounting for 8.5 percent of all prisoners.[61]

How Private Prisons Function

When a jurisdiction decides to attempt to contract the placement of prisoners in a private prison, a formal legal and contractual process must begin. The first step is to determine the need for housing of inmates, both in terms of the number of inmates and security level required. Second, the correctional agency typically develops a request for proposal (RFP), which outlines in detail the requirements, expectations, and standards to be met by the bidding companies. In the RFP, the agency will usually clarify the geographic area for which they will consider contracting for bed space. It is usually not necessary for the private prison to be located in the same jurisdiction as the correctional agency. It is not unusual for states to contract for bed space in a state some distance away.[62]

The agency makes public the RFP, and any private company that meets the minimum requirements of experience and capabilities may submit a bid. Bids are usually evaluated on both cost and quality of service delivery, often rated by the company's past record and description of how they would operate the prison. The governmental jurisdiction then awards the contract, transports prisoners to the facility, and monitors compliance with contract provisions. These provisions are usually both general in nature, such as requiring the company to comply with American Correctional Association standards, and very specific, such as directing the availability of sick call for inmates or the number of calories per day in meals served.

There are several variations of operations by private companies as they comply with RFPs. First, the RFP may require a private company to own (already or build) a prison to house the inmates. Many times, a private company will build a large prison and then respond to RFPs from many jurisdictions to fill it. Very few problems result from having inmates from a variety of jurisdictions in the same facility. Second, a jurisdiction may already have a prison and may seek a private operator to manage the facility. Some jurisdictions prefer this approach, fearing that if contractual problems result with the private company, they can find another manager. However, if the company owns the prison, they must find available space elsewhere if the contract ends.

Finally, there are some governmental agencies that operate as private firms and respond to RFPs from other jurisdictions. Sechrest and Shichor refer to these as "public proprietary facilities" operated by "small jurisdictions without a strong economic base, thus making the (facilities) a potential source of income and employment."[63] These municipalities or counties pass bonds and build prisons specifically for contracting with other governmental jurisdictions. They often contract with one of the large private prison companies to manage them. However, the fact that they are owned by a governmental agency makes the contracts less bureaucratic to develop, and a response to an RFP can usually be avoided, and a "direct award" to the public proprietary facility is legally allowable.

Issues in Prison Privatization

As noted, privatizing the operation of prisons has been controversial, and there are arguments both for and against private involvement in corrections. These arguments include two general areas of issues: philosophical and pragmatic. The philosophical issues center on the distinction of roles between the private sector profit-making enterprises and government, ethics and corruption, and the larger public interest. The pragmatic arguments include cost effectiveness, quality of service, security and public protection, and liability.

Logan identified the following ten issues that are key to any deliberations regarding the use of private prisons:

1. *The propriety of proprietary prisons*—Can the punishment of offenders be delegated to nonpublic agencies?
2. *Cost and efficiency*—Are private prisons operated less expensively than public prisons?

3. *Quality*—Does the profit motive diminish the drive for delivery of quality services and programs to inmates?
4. *Quantity*—Does the involvement of the private sector to make a profit encourage the expansion of imprisonment beyond what is in the public interest?
5. *Flexibility*—Does the fact that the private sector does not have to follow bureaucratic government policies for purchasing and personnel management increase efficiency?
6. *Security*—Does the fact that an emphasis on profits and cost cutting undermine security for inmates, staff, and the community?
7. *Liability*—What impact does a government contracting with a private firm for housing inmates have on the liability of the government for violation of inmates' constitutional rights?
8. *Accountability and monitoring*—How will the private contractor be monitored to fulfill requirements and be held responsible if they do not?
9. *Corruption*—Without the restraints inherent in government to reduce the likelihood of corruption, will there be an increase in private prisons?
10. *Dependence*—Will the public sector become dependent on the private sector contract, and if so, how does this affect decision making?[64]

The first issue to address is philosophical as to whether private companies should make a profit out of incarcerating criminals. Many individuals and groups (such as the American Civil Liberties Union [ACLU]) argue that taking away an individual's freedom is the responsibility of the government and should not be abdicated to the lowest bidder. At this point, the U.S. Supreme Court has not clearly established whether government can transfer correctional functions to the private sector.[65] Logan notes, however, that the authority of government is derived from the consent of the governed and, therefore, may be delegated further with similar consent.[66]

The issue of whether or to what extent a government agency that contracts with the private sector is able to pass on liability is complex and not yet clearly established through case law. It is generally accepted that the state or local government does not escape liability by simply contracting with a private provider for housing criminal offenders. The government maintains responsibility for the constitutional rights of all citizens, including prisoners. Private prisons act "under the color of the law," or with the power of the government. In general, case law indicates that under the Federal Civil Rights Act (42 USC Section 1983), government liability would not be reduced by contracting with the private sector.[67]

In *Lugar v. Edmonson Oil Co.*, the U.S. Supreme Court determined that a party alleging a violation of its constitutional rights must first show that the violating party was acting under the color of law.[68] When this has been established, both private contracts and the governmental agency can be held liable (See *Medina v. O'Neill*). In *Medina v. O'Neill*,[69] the Immigration and Naturalization Service detained stowaways on a vessel, placed some in a local jail, and placed others in the custody of a private company. When the illegal aliens attempted to escape, a private guard accidentally killed one of them. The Court found both the government and the private company liable for damages in the death.

If it is determined that it is legally and ethically acceptable to contract with the private sector to incarcerate inmates, the next key issue is that of cost efficiency. Several studies have compared the cost of privately operated prisons, but few controlled for comparable security levels for the evaluated prisons. Several studies have compared the cost of privately operated prisons. The earliest review of the Hamilton County, Tennessee, private prison suggested that it saved from 4 percent to 15 percent annually over county-operated penal farm costs.[70] A 1992 study comparing costs for public and private facilities housing parole violators in California found a lower cost per day for private facilities.[71] A study initially funded by private prisons determined that between

1999 and 2004, "states that have some of their prisoners in privately-owned or -operated prisons experience lower growth in the cost of housing their public prisoners."[72] A *Harvard Law Review* article concluded, "what imperfect empirical evidence there is suggests that private prisons cost less than public prisons and that their quality is no worse."[73] A literature review in 2002 by the Reason Foundation identified seventeen studies that measure quality of operations by government and private prisons, and fifteen of those conclude, "the quality at the private facilities is as good or better than at government-run facilities."[74] Yet a 2011 review by the Arizona Department of corrections found that medium security private beds cost $53.02 per day compared to state operated medium security beds at $48.42.[75] Segal and Moore, in a review of the costs of outsourcing correctional services, concluded that "Policymakers should be wary of over-reliance on cost-comparison data in making privatization decisions, and be certain that cost analysts do not take it upon themselves to make policy assumptions in determining cost figures."[76] The Sentencing Project argues that although there are sometimes savings with private prisons, they believe that the structure and demands for for-profit can undermine quality of services.[77] And a 2014 analysis of costs and quality indicated that many other comparisons do not include long-term cost savings (such as public employee retirement benefits or bond issues to build new prisons), and when considered, the private sector is generally lower in cost.[78]

Another reason why correctional agencies turn to privatization is to eliminate having to appropriate funds for the enormous capital outlay required to build prisons. During the period of tremendous growth in the inmate population from the late 1980s through the early 2000s, the private sector was able to fund, build, and provide prison beds more rapidly than the public sector. Austin and Coventry note that, because private companies are not subject to government regulations regarding construction of buildings, the private sector can build prisons for nearly 25 percent less and in half the time compared to the public sector.[79] Culp also notes that some states were approaching their debt ceilings or did not have the time to issue bonds to fund new prison construction.[80] A 2004 analysis of Oklahoma's use of private prisons found that the state succeeded in housing a substantial number of offenders without spending a penny on building new facilities.[81]

There have also been reviews of quality with mixed results. A study comparing costs of public and private prisons in Kentucky and Massachusetts found that private prisons appeared to be better managed than public prisons.[82] Results from a Florida study comparing recidivism of releasees from private and public prisons favored the private prisons. Recidivism of releasees from the private prisons was lower than for those released from public prisons, and of those who reoffended; the crimes were less serious for the private prison releasees.[83] When the General Accounting Office (GAO) conducted a comprehensive review of five outcome studies of private prisons completed since 1991 in Texas, New Mexico, California, Tennessee, and Louisiana, analysts did not believe that three of these studies were sufficiently designed to use results, but found that outcomes from the remaining two indicated minimal or no differences between the public and private prison operations.[84]

Other studies have also failed to find any significant differences between the outcomes of offenders released from public versus private prisons.[85] In a national survey to compare private and public prison operations that analyzed the types of inmates, inmate misconduct, and general characteristics of prisons and their staff, Camp and Gaes concluded that private prisons had higher escape rates and more positive results from drug tests and did not enhance staff or community safety.[86] There has not yet been a sufficient number of "apples to apples" comparisons of quality and cost between public and privately operated prisons to draw decisive conclusions. The most recent and perhaps most comprehensive is a review of the Taft, California, private prison, which found that inmates and staff were provided a safe living and working environment, and the private facility cost less to operate, but it had lower rates of assault, more escapes, higher rates of drug use, and higher rates of inmate grievances.[87]

Perhaps the most difficult issue to address is the one of "quantity." Essentially, the question is whether the involvement of the private sector as a profit-making entity in control of the imprisonment of offenders may somehow push for more, rather than less, incarceration. Sentencing policies and the increasing number of prisoners are always areas of public debate and dispute, and it is reasonable to examine the interest of private prison operators regarding these issues.

Lilly and Knepper investigated the developing private correctional enterprise and compared the commercial pressures for expansion to those that exist in the "military-industrial complex."[88] A 2014 book released detailing the pressures and situations in privatizing prisons in California also provides interesting lessons about demand and supply.[89] There is no doubt that successful private correctional companies have spent millions of dollars lobbying and educating elected officials in their role and performance. Although it is doubtful that private correctional companies would intentionally push for changes in sentencing that would end up sending more offenders to prison simply for the potential business, the private companies certainly could benefit from such laws. However, this issue is more of a perception than reality. There is no evidence that the involvement of private corrections influences overall sentencing policy. The following interview with Damon Hininger, CEO of CoreCivic, provides the private sector's position on some of these controversies.

An Interview With . . .

A Private Prison Executive

Damon Hininger. Courtesy of Damon Hininger.

Damon Hininger was named President and Chief Executive Officer of Corrections Corporation of America (now renamed CoreCivic) in August 2009. Mr. Hininger joined the company nearly twenty years before, as he began his corrections career in 1992 as a Correctional Officer at Leavenworth Detention Center in Kansas. He joined CoreCivic's headquarters team at the Facility Support Center in 1995, served in several different positions, and was appointed Vice President, Federal/Local Customer Relations in 2002, and Senior Vice President, Federal/Local Customer Relations in 2007. Mr. Hininger earned a bachelor's degree in sociology and criminal justice from Kansas State University, and an MBA from the Jack Massey Graduate School of Business at Belmont University in Nashville.

Question: What are the advantages to government contracting with a private prison company that led to the large growth for over thirty years?

Mr. Hininger: I would say that advantages have been the same since day one when the company started; we provide flexible, innovative, and customized solutions for our government customers. This can be either a short- or long-term solution. The private sector has historically helped our government partners meet their prison capacity needs over the rapid growth in the prison population from the 1980s through the early 2000s. Our value proposition has been to use our own capital and balance sheet to meet a customer's needs. In some cases, a jurisdiction only needed capacity for a short term until they were able to fund and build a new facility, and in this situation, we can be a relief valve for them. In other situations, a customer decided they did not want to use their own bond authority and commit large amounts of funds to staff and operate a new prison, and want a longer-term solution. We are flexible and can build capacity to meet the customer needs for a short-term solution, but we look at what the future needs may be for use of that facility after the original customer no longer needs the capacity. We as an industry have done a great job of looking beyond the short-term and making investments in locations that can provide solutions to many different jurisdictions for the long term.

Note: According to the latest data, the growth of inmates in private prisons went from just over 9,000 in 1990, grew rapidly to 90,500 in 2000, and then was at a high of 137,200 in 2012. It then declined each year to 126,272 in 2015, before a 2 percent increase to 128,323 in 2016.[90]

Question: What forces caused the increase and now decline in the number of inmates in private prisons, and what do you see happening now and in the future?

Mr. Hininger: The last forty years you saw a lot of jurisdictions at federal and state levels with tremendous growth in their prison populations, and the private sector has been a valuable relief valve for them. More recently, there have been many reforms resulting in a decline in prison populations. I think this represents the real practical value proposition of the private sector in that as the population declines and jurisdictions no longer need the capacity, they can end their contract with us, and they have not had to commit funds over the long term to build and operate a public prison. As we have seen this decline in prison capacity need, we look at how we can use our expertise to assist in other ways. So one way is that some jurisdictions have older outdated facilities that they would like to replace. In a couple of jurisdictions, we have leased our unused facilities to states that allowed them to update to more modern facilities that can be more efficient and save them money, and can provide a safer environment for staff and a more humane environment for inmates. In another state, we are working on a procurement whereby the state wants to replace a current facility built in the 1860s by having the private sector design and build a new facility right next to the old one. The state estimates that a modern and efficient facility can save them $13 to $15 million per year in operating costs. In this case, the private sector can use our balance sheet and expertise for timely construction to replace their outdated prison.

Question: As you well know, there are ideological and political critics of private prisons. Some of these are simply a philosophy that a company should not profit from the incarceration of individuals. What are your thoughts on this?

Mr. Hininger: Well I have strong views that the private sector does a great job day in and day out, that we not only provide thoughtful and innovative solutions, but that we have helped many people along the way. As an example, over the five years from 2011 to 2016, over 10,000 inmates in CoreCivic facilities were awarded a GED, and another 20,000 inmates were awarded a certification for a vocation such as electrician or mason. These inmates will be better prepared to find employment and support themselves and their families. We are not a silver bullet solution for everyone, but we are a great tool in the toolbox, and we have a good track record of providing that type of service over the last forty years.

Question: And other arguments are that the private sector does not do as good a job as the public sector, as the profit motive undermines quality. How do you counter that point of view?

Mr. Hininger: One thing I would say about this is that we have a very unique business, in that the vast majority of our customers do exactly the same type of work themselves, and they have done this for decades. The point is that they know the quality they expect, and if we are not doing a good job and giving our partner a quality product, they will go somewhere else

or do it themselves. I like to tell various stakeholders that over past six years, we have renewed our customer contracts at over a 90 percent rate. If our customers did not like the quality we are providing, they would not renew these contracts.

Question: How has the private prison industry evolved since its inception? I understand that your company changed its name from CCA to CoreCivic as it diversified its business offerings. Would you describe why the change and what you see as the future benefits to government and impact to the industry?

Mr. Hininger: In 2016, we renamed our company to CoreCivic, with three different business operations. We only did this after analyzing where the customer needs were, touching base with many customers, shareholders, and others, and then rebranding and renaming the company to CoreCivic to better reflect the expertise we have to meet our government customers' current needs. The three entities include CoreCivic Safety, which is our traditional business as owner and operator of prisons, jails, and detention facilities. Through CoreCivic Properties, we provide real estate solutions using our balance sheet and expertise to help jurisdictions meet their needs for updating or adding capacity. Over the past two decades, we have designed and built dozens of prisons, and our partners can use this experience to quickly and efficiently add to or replace their facilities. Our goal is to provide facilities that are safer for staff and more humane for inmates. And CoreCivic Community is the owning and operating (sometimes operating by a third party not-for-profit) community correctional facilities. We started CoreCivic Community in 2013, and now have over thirty of these facilities. This mission resonates with all of us, in that it allows us to extend the programs we provide in the prisons into the community to aid in prisoner reentry. We bring our know-how and standardization of operations to community corrections in a way that can improve quality and continuity throughout the prison to community transition. While we have had a really amazing journey over the past forty years, I feel really good about the future of our company going down this path, and the name change and rebranding allows us to catch up with where the needs are in terms of our business.

Question: Thank you Damon. I think it is always important to have the perspective of all sides to any issue. Is there anything you would like to add?

Mr. Hininger: Let me just say that I am very proud and thankful to have been with CCA (now CoreCivic) for now twenty-five years. I am very proud of the work we do and very thankful for all the people that have worked with our company day in and day out since our inception in 1983. I am grateful for the opportunities I have had, and the chance to work with such a great group of employees and with such a dedicated group of government partners.[91]

The Future of Private Corrections

Although the growth in the number of state and federal prisoners has slowed over the past few years, significant increases in the number of inmates are still expected, and with state and federal revenues down due to the recession, very few jurisdictions are constructing new prisons. Tightening government budgets force public officials to increasingly look for alternatives to the traditional approaches. And the continued lack of public confidence in the public sector leads many citizens to support giving the private sector a chance. Gowdy notes,

> Nonetheless, the public's unsatisfactory view of today's penal system in terms of its costs and high recidivism rates are two factors that are likely to encourage further expansion of the private sector's role.[92]

An interesting result of the changing prison population has been the impact on private prisons. What has occurred is that approximately one-half of the new growth in prison inmates over the past decade was into private prisons, most likely because the private companies provide the funding to add capacity without government agencies having to sell bonds and budget all the capital construction money up front. And since the prison growth slowed and even declined the past few years, the number of inmates in private prisons has held fairly level over the past five years. This is consistent with studies of privatization. In one report, the authors projected that "[t]he number of privatized prisons is likely to increase, but not at the pace exhibited during the past decade."[93] And another study suggested that there is evidence that prison privatization is in decline as a result of declining incarceration rates, overbuilding of prison beds, legislation antagonistic to the private prison industry, and a number of well-publicized serious incidents.[94]

Opponents of the use of private prisons cite the lack of firm data as undermining the argument by the private sector that they can be more effective than their public counterparts. Dolovich questions even the legitimacy of using the private sector, even if private prisons can operate for less money without a drop in quality.[95] Proponents suggest the evidence proves that the private sector can operate prisons at a high quality, and the private sector plays a valuable role as partners to the public sector in providing correctional services. Even without firm cost and quality comparisons, it is expected that the use of contracts by public correctional agencies with the private sector will continue at a substantial level for the foreseeable future.

The "You Make the Decision" box at the end of this chapter asks students to decide whether they would turn to the private sector to house prisoners for their state agency.

Recent Controversies with Solitary Confinement

The issue of "solitary confinement" is one that has developed and changed its focus over the past several years. This issue began with the controversy surrounding supermax prisons (presented in Chapter 9), which identify and assign violent and predatory inmates to a prison in which inmates are locked down in their cells for close to twenty-two hours per day. The argument for this type of confinement is that it controls and prevents violence from these dangerous inmates, and it is an incentive for good behavior in other prisons, as inmates detest the thought of being sent to lockdown confinement. And taking the most violent and predatory inmates out of other prisons keeps general-population institutions more peaceful and orderly. Opponents of supermax prisons assert that the lack of human contact, the absence of work, and the deficiency of intellectual stimulation are human rights violations and have negative consequences on individuals.

But this issue has expanded beyond supermax prisons, and the debate has moved to what is often called **solitary confinement**. Inmates can be held in this status for a variety of reasons, to include protection for themselves, awaiting transfer to another facility, or while awaiting a hearing or as a sanction for violating a facility rule. As well, special populations such as those with medical or mental health needs, death row, or maximum-security inmates can also be placed in a solitary confinement status. There are three separate and distinct populations of people in solitary confinement:

solitary confinement
the practice of isolating inmates in cells for 22–24 hours a day, with limited human contact, usually for several months at a time

1. The first is the traditional use of supermax or administrative segregation for those inmates deems dangerous or predatory and need to be separated from the general population. This placement is usually for an indeterminate period, or when correctional officials believe the inmate is no longer the danger her or she previously was.
2. The second is a more short-term placement in a segregation unit, for the investigation or punishment of a specific violation of prison rules. This is almost always for a determinate period, and is usually called either "administrative detention" or "disciplinary segregation."
3. And the third group refers to restrictive housing for specific categories or classifications of inmates, such as death row, maximum custody inmates, protective custody inmates, or gang members.

Concerns regarding solitary confinement have resulted in much more attention to solitary confinement over the past five years. A 2015 report by the Bureau of Justice Statistics found that on any given day, 4.4 percent of prison inmates and 2.7 percent of jail inmates were held in solitary confinement.[96] This could be as many as 150,000 offenders. The United Nations "Mandela Rules" for international correctional standards suggest that solitary confinement beyond fifteen consecutive days is "prolonged solitary confinement," and prohibit it as "torture or other cruel, inhuman or degrading treatment or punishment."[97] These concerns along with the high cost of their operation have prompted a reconsideration of supermax prisons, and some states have closed them as a result.[98] One example is Mississippi, which closed its "Unit 32" in 2010, saving the state $5 million, and Colorado, Maine, Ohio, and Washington have taken steps to reduce the number of prisoners in long-term isolation.[99] In addition, Illinois decided to close their supermax at Tamms after fourteen years of operation. The state lists the cost at Tamms at about $64,000 per year per inmate, almost twice the cost of a regular maximum-security prison.[100]

The Association of State Correctional Administrators (ASCA) began examining policies and practices to determine those that were most consistently recommended by their members as principles to management of this inmate population.[101] ASCA partnered with the Yale Law School to examine current practices, and found a wide variety of uses and operations of administrative segregation throughout the states.[102] ASCA has since created a set of best practices for managing inmates in this status. They selected the term "restrictive status housing," to attempt to be inclusive of the variety of terminology used across states (isolation, administrative segregation, supermax). **Restrictive status housing** designates the housing for inmates whose continued presence in the general prison population would pose a serious threat to life, property, self, staff or other inmates, or to the security or orderly operation of a correctional facility.[103] These suggested practices included:

restrictive status housing

the housing for inmates whose continued presence in the general prison population would pose a serious threat to life, property, self, staff or other inmates, or to the security or orderly operation of a correctional facility

- A separate and objective decision-making process for assigning inmates to restrictive status housing, with regular reviews of the assignment;
- Mental health assessments within seventy-two hours of placement and periodic assessments thereafter and development of treatment plans when appropriate;
- Progressive levels with increased privileges as incentives for positive behavior and program participation;
- Visiting, exercise, medical, and mental health access;
- Transition planning for return to the general population.[104]

As a result of this reexamination and guidance from ASCA, states have changed their practices to allow inmates more out-of-cell time, the opportunity to interact with other inmates in programs and recreation, and participation in education and cognitive programs. Historically, inmates in this status were locked down 22–23 hours per day. The emphasis is now to have inmates out of their cells for much longer periods of time. Correctional officials believe that this out-of-cell time reduces tension and violent incidents by inmates. In addition, some of this out-of-cell time reduces the very expensive cost of operation of supermax. Previously, all services had to be brought to the inmate cell by staff. Now, inmates may go the commissary, eat some meals in an inmate dining room, and even work jobs to save staff time. In addition, inmates participate in small groups of programming. Since some of these inmates are still potentially very dangerous to staff and other inmates, they often are seated in specially designed chairs in which they may be handcuffed or their legs attached to the chairs while allowing them to take notes and participate in programming.[105] These changes are creating a less problematic and less expensive while still secure option to manage violent and predatory inmates.

California was one of the states that used solitary confinement for a broad array of prisoners, to include any inmate validated as a prison gang member. No state locked up so many nor kept them isolated longer than California. However, in 2015, the state agreed to a federal court settlement of a suit filed on behalf of inmates arguing to restrict the prolonged use of solitary confinement. Under the settlement, prisoners will not be sent to isolation for an indefinite period, nor for their gang affiliation. The state will continue to isolate prisoners found guilty of serious violence or escape attempts. Yet even these inmates will have more out of cell time, the chance to participate in programs, and some small group leisure activities.[106] These reforms in California even received the attention of the television show *60 Minutes*, on a segment hosted by Oprah Winfrey on October 22, 2017.

Over the past few years, the attention to solitary conferment has expanded. In a strong statement condemning the use of solitary confinement, U.S. Supreme Court Justice Anthony Kennedy criticized its use and cited anxiety, panic, withdrawal, and self-mutilation as effects of long-term isolation.[107] And even President Barak Obama has weighed in. The U.S. Department of Justice did a review of the use of solitary confinement by the Bureau of Prisons and other correctional agencies. After the review was completed, in January 2016, the President adopted the DOJ recommendations, and banned solitary confinement for juveniles and as a response to low-level infractions, expanded treatment for people with mental illness, and increased the amount of time inmates in solitary can spend outside their cells, affecting some 10,000 federal prisoners held in this status. And in August of 2016, the American Correctional Association (in partnership with ASCA) approved accreditation standards for Restrictive Housing. These standards will be used whenever a prison applies for ACA accreditation. There were several themes included in the standards:

- Controlling Intake
- Length of Stay
- Conditions of Confinement
- Transitioning to General population
- Staff in Restrictive housing
- Special Populations

Even with all of the controversy, the unanswered question is whether solitary confinement benefits are real, and whether the negative consequences on inmates are serious. A recent review and article by Morgan, Labrecque, Gendreau, Ramler, and Olafsson now moves this issue forward regarding administrative segregation (AS), which is another term for solitary confinement.[108] The often-published argument against administrative segregation is that there are negative physiological and psychological effects on inmates assigned to this status. And it has been believed that offenders with a history of mental illness are more susceptible to increased deleterious effects from AS. Yet the authors point out that the studies used to support these claims are not conclusive. To clarify the impact, the authors undertook two meta-analytic reviews, one to examine the physical and mental health impact on inmates and the other to look at behavioral outcomes such as recidivism. The results of the first meta-analysis indicate a "small detrimental effect upon inmates' mental health and physical functioning."[109] And the study found that beneficial effect on postrelease recidivism as well as a suppressive effect on institutional misconduct. The second meta-analysis found "small effects for social and cognitive impairment and moderate effects for impaired behavioral functioning and physical and mental health functioning."[110] As a result of this study, the authors made several recommendations, to include using AS only in extreme situations for inmates with severe mental illness providing therapeutic step down programs for inmates who serve long terms in AS, and having mental health professional make regular rounds among the AS inmates to identify if decompensation in inmate functioning appears.

These controversies over the use of solitary confinement are far from resolved. There are still many jurisdictions that strongly believe that the best way to manage potentially dangerous prisoners is through "incapacitation" or by removing them from the general prison population and keeping them in a very secure setting. Yet many other jurisdictions as well as outside experts on mental health and behavior argue that this type of setting is deleterious to inmates, do not prevent violence, and do not make staff safer. The next few years will see more developments of this evolving issue.

Corrections as a Career

This text has presented various jobs that are available to those seeking a career in corrections. There have been discussions regarding the pay, working conditions, challenges, benefits, and issues that people face while working in corrections. With this information, it is time for students to consider whether a **career in corrections** is right for them. Correctional jobs are difficult to perform, and not every person who expresses an interest in corrections is suited for this type of work.

It is important to seriously consider the roles and specific duties of these jobs before applying for a job and committing to a career in corrections. Corrections is a people business, meaning that it is not the bars, fences, policies, or equipment that successfully carry out the goals of a correctional sanction. It is the staff. Positive, professional correctional staff can make any program or policy effective. Yet unprofessional, poorly trained, or uncaring staff will cause any policy or program to fail. Because of the mission of corrections, the role of staff in correctional agencies is even more critical than the role of staff in most other public agencies or private-sector companies. Correctional agencies are responsible for protecting the public by limiting offenders' freedoms. This is a serious responsibility. When correctional staff members fail to effectively do their jobs, innocent citizens may be victims of crime. Correctional staff members have considerable discretion in how they carry out their duties and take away offenders' individual freedoms. Therefore, staff members doing these difficult jobs must follow the highest of ethical standards.

It is not unusual for people to apply for and get a job with a correctional agency and then determine that it is not the right type of position for them. This leads to a high turnover of correctional staff, especially during the first

career in corrections
beginning work for a correctional agency with a possibility of working in corrections from now until retirement

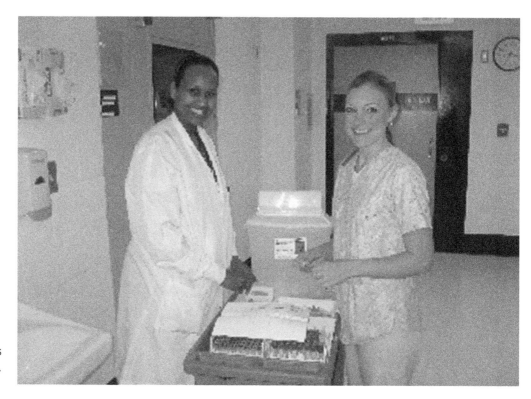

There are several positions in health care in corrections.
Photo by Richard P. Seiter.

few months of employment and especially in the difficult role of correctional officer. However, as noted in Chapter 12, over the past decade, correctional agencies have improved pay, embraced staff empowerment, and increased other benefits to recruit and retain the best people available, and turnover rates are improving.

One reason for a high turnover rate in these and other correctional jobs is the stressful and dangerous nature of the positions. Correctional staff members in prison and the community work with difficult clients who regularly challenge them, attempting to avoid compliance and detection of violations. There is also always the risk of assault and serious injury. Although many job-related functions lead to stress for correctional workers (understaffing, rotating shift work, inmate demands and manipulations, and poor public image), in a survey regarding correctional staff stress, officers mentioned the threat of violence more frequently than any other single feature of their occupation.[111]

Even with these challenges and concerns, there are many reasons to consider corrections as a career. First, there are many available jobs. The *Bureau of Justice Statistics, Expenditure and Employment Extracts 2010* reports there were 801,766 correctional staff members working at the federal, state, and local levels in the United States in 2010.[112] This is a 44 percent increase since 1992, when there were 556,500 correctional employees.[113] Second, these

Correctional officers make up the highest percentage of jail and prison staff members and conduct a variety of custody and security functions. Photo by Richard P. Seiter.

jobs are very stable, and there are many career opportunities. Seldom does a correctional agency have a layoff or have to reduce its number of staff. Staff members with the proper educational requirements who work hard and do a good job will be promoted and given opportunities for advancement. Third, the pay is better than most people believe, and the benefits are very good. Public-sector correctional agencies usually have excellent vacations, days off, and health care coverage. Many have a special retirement system, similar to those of law enforcement agencies, in which employees can retire after twenty-five to thirty years of service at any age. This seems like a long time for students today thinking about a career, but retiring at age fifty or fifty-five is an outstanding benefit.

Finally, corrections is an interesting and enjoyable career. There is seldom a boring day in a correctional job. You deal with people, you face new challenges, and you have to make decisions as you go. Even though corrections is not a career for everyone, it is a career for people who do not want to be desk-bound, who enjoy working with people, who are not afraid of a challenge, and who want to serve the public. People with these characteristics will be making the right choice to select a career in corrections. This textbook was written to provide students a real-life understanding of what corrections is really all about. Students should seriously consider all the issues identified in this book as they consider whether a career in corrections is right for them. But in this author's opinion, corrections is a good career choice. I enjoyed it for more than thirty-five years and would recommend it to anyone.

Your Career in Corrections

Prison and Community Corrections Jobs

As noted in Chapter 1, there has been tremendous growth in the number of clients under the supervision of correctional agencies (on probation, in prison or jail, and on parole), the number of jobs, and the dollars spent on corrections. When I started work in corrections, there were less than two million offenders under supervision, and just over 300,000 in prison. I gave a speech regarding the future of corrections and suggested that we may reach 400,000 prisoners, but that we could not afford to continue the growth beyond that. Yet, by the end of the twentieth century, more than six million offenders were either in prison, in jail, or under supervision in the community.

Expenditures for correctional agencies jumped from approximately $18 billion in the early 1980s to $80 billion today.

As offenders and budgets grew, of course the number of employees climbed as well. As noted above, today there are more than 800,000 employees working in corrections. And as noted in Chapter 1, there are a wide variety of correctional jobs. No matter what your expertise or academic major, there are jobs in corrections that fit your interest and skills. These are challenging, yet can be very rewarding jobs. As we end our study of corrections, please consider the many career opportunities, request an internship, or visit a correctional agency and see if it is right for you.

Chapter Review

Summary

It is interesting to theorize why the growth in the prison population has been slowing. As a result of "tough on crime" legislation to send more offenders to prison for longer times and initiatives such as the war on drugs, the prison population in the United States grew by almost 600 percent in twenty years. Yet several factors now seem to be slowing that trend. Whether it is simply a demographic change with a lower percentage of the nation's population in the high-crime age, a need to find alternatives to incarceration to reduce budget demands, the incapacitative effect of incarcerating so many people, or a combination, for the first time in decades some states are actually experiencing a reduction in their prison population.

One definite truth is that the formation of correctional policies has become much more politicized than in the past. Elected officials (or those seeking office) have been limited in what they believed were approaches to dealing with criminal offenders without endangering society. However, the challenge of tightening budgets may force officials to reconsider the increased use of incarceration as a criminal sanction. A variety of activities (enhancing the use of community alternatives, reducing technical violations of probation or parole, and contracting with the private sector) are being considered to try to reduce the budget crunch in order to fund correctional agencies.

The United States leads the world in the use of incarceration, and we have even coined the phrase "mass incarceration" to explain our appetite for locking people up well beyond the crime reduction benefit that results from this very expensive option. If we were able to return to even a mid-point of the rates of incarceration from forty years ago until today, we could save billions of dollars. A cost-saving approach that is controversial is the use of private prisons. The chapter has included an overview of the issues and information that jurisdictions consider when deciding whether to and to what extent to use private operators for prison management. And we examine the overall impact of a slowdown in the growth of the incarceration rate on the private prison industry.

Another recent correctional controversy is the use of solitary confinement. Correctional agencies began this practice to control violent and predatory inmates and make prisons safer for staff and other inmates. However, there are debates of whether we have gone too far in using solitary confinement and the potential negative physical and psychological impact it can have on inmates in this status. All that is left for readers and students of this book is to determine if corrections is the "right" career for them. There are challenges, but there are also rewards. I have found it a wonderful career, I have made many friends, and I believe I have had a positive influence on the lives of staff and offenders. I ask you to join my colleagues and give corrections a try. I think you will be surprised how much you like it.

Key Terms

Justice Reinvestment Initiative
evidence-based practices
mass incarceration

private prison
solitary confinement

restrictive status housing
career in corrections

Review Questions

1. What has occurred in regard to the size of the state prison population over the past five years?

2. How has the federalization of many crimes affected the populations of state and federal prisons?

3. Describe the status of state budgets.

4. How are states using community alternatives to bring down the cost of corrections?

5. What is mass incarceration and how does the United States compare to other countries in rates of incarceration?

6. How much money could potentially be saved if we moved away from mass incarceration?

7. How many inmates are housed in private prisons?

8. Are private prisons less expensive and more effective than public prisons?

9. Why have the number of inmates housed in private prisons declined over the past few years?

10. What is solitary confinement?

11. What reforms have been made to solitary confinement in the past few years?

12. What are the physical and mental health impacts on inmates from being in solitary confinement?

13. What are the positive and negative factors of working in corrections?

▸ You Make the Decision...

Use the Private Sector to Operate Prisons?

You are the director of a state department of corrections with no history of contracting entire prison operations to the private sector. Several of your fellow state administrators have used the private sector to house their inmates, and no one has expressed a serious concern about price or quality. However, you are aware of several serious incidents (riots, escapes, and inmate brutality) that have occurred in a few private prisons across the country and are sensitive to the negative publicity that these incidents brought. You are also aware of all the studies that are inconclusive in terms of the benefits of the private sector in comparison to the public sector for cost and outcome.

Yet your legislative budget committee is pushing for the state to try privatization. With tightening budgets, they want to find less expensive ways to manage the burgeoning correctional population in the state. You have a good relationship with the labor union representing state correctional officers, and they are firmly opposed to privatization, as they fear the loss

of public, union jobs with privatization. You are caught in the middle of the budget committee and the labor union in regard to whether you will support privatization. You are going to make one of them very unhappy with whatever decision you make.

You have decided to go through the list of ten issues regarding privatization that have been presented in this chapter, weigh these factors as good or bad, and decide whether you will support privatizing a new prison in your state. For this exercise, either by yourself or in a small classroom group, go through each of these ten issues, determine whether they are favorable or unfavorable to the private sector, and then score your overall view either for or against the privatization of prisons. Use this score to decide whether you will support privatizing a state prison and what statement you will make as to your reasons for the decision. Once you make this decision, determine how you will deal with the party (budget committee or labor union) you will anger with your decision.

ENDNOTES

Chapter 1

1. Data adapted from *Sourcebook of Criminal Justice Statistics*, available at http://www.albany.edu/sourcebook (accessed August 6, 2017). Data included in Tables 3.109.2010, 4.7.2010, 5.44.2006, 5.22.2010, 5.47.2006, and 5.25.2008.
2. State and local governments spent $72.5 billion on corrections, The Hamilton Project, *Twelve Facts about Incarceration and Reentry* (Washington, D.C.: the Brookings Institution, 2016), available at http://www.hamilton-project.org/papers/twelve_facts_about_incarceration_and_prisoner_reentry (accessed August 3, 2017), and the Bureau of Prisons budget for 2012 was $6.9 billion. See https://www.justice.gov/sites/default/files/jmd/legacy/2014/02/02/fy13-bop-bud-summary.pdf (accessed August 3, 2017).
3. From Table 1, State Prison Costs per Inmate, in Chris Mai and Ram Subramanian, *The Price of Prisons: Examining State Spending Trends, 2010–2015* (New York, NY: The Vera Institute, 2017).
4. Pew Center on the States, *One in 31* (Washington, D.C.: Pew Center on the States, 2009), p. 12.
5. National Association of State Budget Officers, *State Expenditure Report* (Washington, D.C.: National Association of State Budget Officers, 2017). Also see Tracey Kyckelhahn, "State Correctional Expenditures, 1982–2010," *BJS Bulletin* (Washington, D.C.: U.S. Department of Justice, 2013), p. 1.
6. Bureau of Justice Statistics, *Expenditure Facts at a Glance*, www.ojp.usdoj.gov/bjs/glance/tables/exptyptab.htm (accessed January 17, 2010).
7. See Bureau of Justice Statistics, *Justice Expenditure and Employment Extracts, 2012* (Washington D.C.: U.S. Department of Justice, 2013), p. 3.
8. Bureau of Justice Statistics, *Sourcebook of Criminal Justice Statistics, 1994* (Washington, D.C.: U.S. Department of Justice, 1995), p. 26.
9. Tracey Kychelhahn, *Justice Employment and Expenditure Extracts, 2012, Sourcebook of Criminal Justice Statistics* (Washington, D.C.: U.S. Department of Justice, Bureau of Justice Statistics, 2015), Table 2.
10. U.S. Department of Justice, Federal Bureau of Investigation, *Crime in the United States 2015*, Table 1, available at https://ucr.fbi.gov/crime-in-the-u.s/2015/crime-in-the-u.s.-2015/home (accessed August 7, 2017).
11. Alyssa Davis, In U.S., Concern about Crime Climbs to 15-Year High, Gallup Organization, 2016, available at http://www.gallup.com/poll/190475/americans-concern-crime-climbs-year-high.aspx (accessed August 7, 2017).
12. Harry E. Barnes and Negley K. Teeters, *New Horizons in Criminology*, 3rd ed. (Upper Saddle River, NJ: Prentice Hall, 1959), p. 322.
13. See Richard Louis Dugsdale, *The Jukes: A Study in Crime Pauperism, Disease, and Heredity*, 3rd ed. (New York: G. P. Putnam's Sons, 1985); and Henry Herbert Goddard, *The Kallikak Family: A Study in the Heredity of Feeblemindedness* (New York: Macmillan, 1912).
14. For more information, see Richard Herrnstein, *Crime File: Biology and Crime* (Study Guide) (Washington, D.C.: National Institute of Justice, 1986).
15. For an overview of this issue, see Frank Schmalleger, *Criminology Today: An Integrative Introduction*, 4th ed. (Upper Saddle River, NJ: Pearson Prentice Hall, 2006), p. 152.
16. Gabriel Tarde, *Penal Philosophy*, translated by R. Howell (Boston: Little, Brown, 1912). Originally published in 1890.
17. Randy Martin, Robert J. Mutchnick, and W. Timothy Austin, *Criminological Thought: Pioneers Past and Present* (New York: Macmillan, 1990).
18. A good overview of these theories of crime can be found in Hugh D. Barlow, *Criminal Justice in America* (Upper Saddle River, NJ: Prentice Hall, 2000), pp. 84–117.
19. *The American Prison: From the Beginning... A Pictorial History* (College Park, Md.: American Correctional Association, 1983), p. 16.
20. Ibid., p. 24.
21. Barnes and Teeters, *New Horizons in Criminology.*
22. For the complete list of principles of the 1870 National Prison Association, see Enoch C. Wines, ed., *Transactions of the National Congress on Penitentiary and Reformatory Discipline* (Albany, NY: Argus, 1871).
23. Margaret Cahalan, *Historical Corrections Statistics in the United States: 1850–1984* (Washington, D.C.: U.S. Department of Justice, 1986), p. 36.
24. *The American Prison*, p. 208.
25. Douglas Lipton, Robert Martinson, and Judith Wilks, *The Effectiveness of Correctional Treatment and What Works: A Survey of Treatment Evaluation Studies* (New York: Praeger, 1975).
26. Hutto's speech to North American Wardens and Superintendents Association. Reprinted with Permission.
27. *Bell v. Wolfish*, 441 U.S. 520 (1979).
28. *Solem v. Helm*, 463 U.S. 277 (1983).
29. Todd R. Clear, Michael D. Reisig, and George f. Cole, *American Corrections*, 11th ed. (Boston, MA: Cengage Learning, 2016), p. 74.
30. Norman A. Carlson, Karen M. Hess, and Christine M. H. Orthmann, *Corrections in the 21st Century* (Belmont, Calif.: West/Wadsworth, 1999), p. 16.
31. Alfred Blumstein, "Selective Incapacitation as a Means of Crime Control," *American Behavioral Scientist* 27, no. 1 (1983): 93.
32. Marianne W. Zawitz, ed., *Report to the Nation on Crime and Justice* (Washington, D.C.: U.S. Department of Justice, Bureau of Justice Statistics, 1983), p. 35.
33. Peter Greenwood, *Selective Incapacitation* (Santa Monica, Calif.: RAND Corporation, 1983).
34. Stuart Miller, Simon Dinitz, and John Conrad, *Careers of the Violent* (Lexington, Mass.: Lexington Books, 1982).
35. Michael R. Gottfredson and Travis Hirschi, "The Methodological Adequacy of Longitudinal Research on Crime," *Criminology* 25 (1987): 581–614.
36. Harry E. Allen, Edward J. Latessa, and Bruce S. Ponder, *Corrections in America: An Introduction*, 14th ed. (Boston, MA: Pearson Education, 2016), p. 53.
37. Barry Krisberg and Susan Marchionna, "Attitudes of US Voters toward Prisoners Rehabilitation and Reentry Policies," *Focus: Views from the National Council on Crime and Delinquency* (Washington, D.C.: National Council on Crime and Delinquency, April 2006).
38. Ibid.
39. Robert M. Freeman, *Correctional Organization and Management: Public Policy Challenges, Behavior, and Structure* (Boston: Butterworth-Heinemann, 1999), p. 397.
40. Myron Steele and Thomas J. Quinn, "Restorative Justice: Including Victims in Community Corrections," in *The Dilemmas of Corrections: Contemporary Readings*, edited by Kenneth C. Haas and Geoffrey P. Alpert (Prospect Heights, Ill.: Waveland Press, 1995), p. 530.
41. Alfred Blumstein and Allen J. Beck, "Population Growth in U.S. Prisons: 1980–1996," in *Prisons: A Review of Research*, edited by Michael Tonry and Joan Petersilia (Chicago: University of Chicago Press, 1999), pp. 17–62.
42. Jeremy Travis, Bruce Western, and Steve Redburn, Editors, *The Growth of Incarceration in the United States: Exploring Causes and Consequences* (Washington, D.C.: The National Academies Press, 2014).
43. Sam C. Proband, "Corrections Leads State Budget Increases in FY 1997," *Overcrowded Times* 8, no. 4 (1997): 4.
44. John Irwin and James Austin, *It's about Time: America's Imprisonment Binge* (Belmont, Calif.: Wadsworth, 1994).
45. An Interview With...
    An Elected Official, Attorney General Mike DeWine. Reprinted with Permission.
46. Joan Petersilia, *When Prisoners Come Home: Parole and Prisoner Reentry* (New York: Oxford University Press, 2003), p. 221.
47. As cited in Peter D. Hart Research Associates, *Changing Public Attitudes toward the Criminal Justice System* (New York: Open Society, February 2002).
48. Christopher Hartney and Susan Marchionna, "Attitudes of U.S. Voters toward Non-Serious Offenders and Alternatives to Incarceration," *Focus: Views from the National Council on Crime and Delinquency* (San Francisco, Calif.: NCCD, June 2009).
49. Hart and Associates, op. cit.

Chapter 2

1. National Association of Pretrial Service Agencies, *Promising Practices in Pretrial Diversion* (Washington, D.C.: NAPSA, 2010), p. 5.
2. National Association of Pretrial Services Agencies Diversion Committee, *Pretrial Diversion Abstract: Information Report* (Milwaukee, Wis.: National Association of Pretrial Services Agencies, 1998), available at http://www.napsa.org/publications/diversionabstract.pdf (accessed August 10, 2014), pp. 2–3.
3. Treatment Alternatives to Street Crime, *TASC Annual Report 2013: Thriving in Change* (Chicago, Ill.: TASC, 2014), p. 5.
4. For a discussion of diversion and factors that impact evidence-based practices, see Joseph M. Zlatic, Donna C. Wilkerson, and Shannon M. McAllister, "Pretrial Diversion: The Over-Looked Pretrial Services Evidence-Based Practice," *Federal Probation* 74, no. 1 (June 2010): 28–34.
5. National Association of Pretrial Services Agencies Diversion Committee, *Pretrial Diversion Abstract*, pp. 3–4.
6. A good overview of the risk factors often used can be found in: Pretrial Justice Institute, "Pretrial Risk Assessment 101: Science Provides Guidance on Managing Defendants," *PJI Issue Brief* (Washington, D.C.: Pretrial Justice Institute, 2013).
7. *United States v. Salerno*, 481 U.S. 739 (1987).
8. William Rhodes, Raymond Hyatt, and Paul Scheiman, "Predicting Pretrial Misconduct with Drug Tests of Arrestees," *National Institute of Justice Research in Brief* (Washington, D.C.: National Institute of Justice, 1996), pp. 1–6.
9. Todd D. Minton and Daniela Golinelli, *Jail Inmates at Midyear 2013* (Washington, D.C.: U.S. Department of Justice, 2014).
10. Justice Policy Institute, *Bail Fail: Why the U.S. Should End the Practice of Using Money for Bail* (Washington, D.C.: Justice Policy Institute, 2012), p. 3.
11. Cherise Fanno Burdeen, *Jail Population Management: Elected County Officials' Guide to Pretrial Services* (Washington, D.C.: National Association of Counties, 2009).
12. Mary T. Phillips, "Bail, Detention, and Nonfelony Case Outcomes," *Research Brief*, no. 14 (New York: New York City Criminal Justice Agency, 2007).
13. Michael R. Jones, *Unsecured Bonds: The As Effective and Most Efficient Pretrial Release Option* (Washington, D.C.: Pretrial Justice Institute, 2013), p. 3.
14. Mary T. Phillips, *Commercial Bail Bonds in New York City: Characteristics and Implications* (New York: New York City Criminal Justice Agency, 2011).
15. *Pretrial Diversion in the 21st Century* (Washington, D.C.: National Association of Pretrial Service Agencies, 2009), p. 13.
16. A dated but still accurate description of pretrial supervision programs is, Thomas J. Wolf, "What United States Pretrial Service Officers Do," *Federal Probation* 61, no. 1 (March 1997): 19–24.
17. In Phillips (2007), offense history and arrest charges explained 30 percent of the variations of conviction, and detention decisions explained an additional 6 percent.
18. J. C. Oleson, Christopher T. Lowenkamp, Timothy P. Cadigan, Marie VanNostrand, and John Wooldredge, "The Effect of Peretrial Detention on Sentencing in Two Federal Districts," *Justice Quarterly*, 2014, published online at http://dx.doi.org/10.1080/07418825.2014.959035 (accessed June 28, 2018).
19. Gregory M. Gilchrist, "Plea Bargains, Convictions and Legitimacy," *American Criminal Law Review* 48, no. 1 (Winter 2011): 143–183.
20. *Williams v. New York*, 337 U.S. 241 (1949).
21. *Booth v. Maryland*, 482 U.S. 496 (1987); *Gathers v. South Carolina*, 490 U.S. 805 (1989); *Payne v. Tennessee*, 501 U.S. 808(1991).
22. Robert C. Davis and Barbara E. Smith, "The Effects of Victim Impact Statements on Sentencing Decisions: A Test in an Urban Setting," *Justice Quarterly* 11, no. 3 (September1994): 453–470.
23. As cited in Joan Petersilia, "Parole and Prisoner Reentry in the United States," in *Prisons*, edited by Michael Tonry and Joan Petersilia (Chicago: University of Chicago Press, 1999), pp. 489–490.
24. Paula M. Ditton and Doris J. Wilson, *Truth in Sentencing in State Prisons* (Washington, D.C.: U.S. Department of Justice, Bureau of Justice Statistics, 1999).
25. Timothy A. Hughes, Doris J. Wilson, and Allen J. Beck, *Trends in State Parole, 1990–2000* (Washington, D.C.: U.S. Department of Justice, Bureau of Justice Statistics, October 2001).
26. A description of this is available on the Illinois Department of Corrections website, available at http://www2.illinois.gov/idoc/news/2013/Pages/NewAdministrativeRuleonSentenceCredit.aspx (accessed August 7, 2017).
27. Information current from Bureau of Prisons website, available at https://www.bop.gov/about/statistics/statistics_inmate_offenses.jsp (accessed January 8, 2018).
28. For an overview of three-strikes laws before 2000, see Walter J. Dickey and Pam Hollenhorst, "Three-Strikes Laws: Five Years Later," *Corrections Management Quarterly* 3, no. 3 (1999): 1–18.
29. Emily Bazelon, "Arguing Three Strikes," *New York Times Magazine*, May 21, 2010, available at http://www.nytimes.com/2010/05/23/magazine/23strikes-t.html (accessed August 8, 2017).
30. For a good review of the three-strikes law in California, see Kevin E. Meehan, "California's Three-Strikes Law: The First Six Years," *Corrections Management Quarterly* 4, no. 4 (2000): 22–33.
31. Franklin E. Zimring, Sam Kamin, and Gordon Hawkins, *Crime and Punishment in California* (Berkeley, Calif.: Institute of Government Studies Press, 1999), p. 83.
32. For a discussion of this change, see J. Richard Couzens and Tricia A. Bigelow (Sacramento: CA: California Appellate Court, 2017) available at http://www.courts.ca.gov/documents/Three-Strikes-Amendment-Couzens-Bigelow.pdf (accessed August 8, 2017).
33. For a discussion of the background for adopting sentencing guidelines, see Bureau of Justice Statistics, *Report to the Nation on Crime and Justice*, 2nd ed. (Washington, D.C.: U.S. Department of Justice, 1988), p. 92.
34. *United States v. Booker*, 543 U.S. 220 (2005).
35. Don Stemens and Andres F. Rengifo, "Policies and Imprisonment: The Impact of Structured Sentencing and Determinate Sentencing on State Incarceration Rates, 1978–2004," *Justice Quarterly* 28, no. 1 (February 2011): 174–201.
36. A study by the NC Department of Public Safety found that a study group of 1,198 people who received a "quick dip" between 2013 and 2015 compared to a the same number who did not experience a "quick dip," the study group was about one-third less likely to be revoked to prison than the comparison group. See CSG Justice Center Staff, *North Carolina Reduces Probation Revocations with Short, Swift Sanctions*, April 13, 2017, available at https://csgjusticecenter.org/jr/north-carolina/posts/north-carolina-reduces-probation-revocations-with-swift-sanctions (accessed November 9, 2017).
37. Data from Bureau of Justice Statistics, *Key Facts at a Glance: Imprisonment Rate, 1980–2009*, and E. Ann Carson and Elizabeth Anderson, "Prisoners in 2015," *BJS Bulletin* (Washington, D.C.: U.S. Department of Justice, 2016), p. 8.
38. Don Stemen, Andres Reggifo, and James Wilson, *Of Fragmentation and Ferment: The Impact of State Sentencing Policies on Incarceration Rates, 1975–2004* (Washington, D.C.: U.S. Department of Justice, 2006).
39. *United States v. Booker*, 543 U.S. 220 (2005).
40. U.S. Sentencing Commission, *Report to Congress: Mandatory Minimum Penalties in the Federal Criminal Justice System* (Washington, D.C.: U.S. Sentencing Commission, 2011).
41. Alison Lawrence and Donna Lyons, *Principles of Effective State Sentencing and Corrections Policy: A Report of the NCSL Sentencing and Corrections Policy Work Group* (Washington, D.C.: Nation Conference of State Legislatures, 2011).
42. Kim Steven Hunt and Andrew Peterson, *Recidivism among Offenders Receiving Retroactive Sentence Reductions: The 2007 Crack Cocaine Amendment* (Washington, D.C.: U.S. Sentencing Commission, 2014).
43. Pew Center for the States, *State of Recidivism: The Revolving Door* (Washington, D.C.: Pew Center for the States, 2011), p. 2.
44. *31 States Reform Criminal Justice Policies Through Justice Reinvestment* (Washington, D.C.: Pew Center for the States, 2016).
45. Ram Subramanian and Ruth Delaney, *Playbook for Change? States Reconsider Mandatory Sentences* (New York: Vera Institute for Justice, 2014). Another good overview of reforms in sentencing is The Sentencing Project, *The State of Sentencing 2013: Developments in Policy and Practice* (Washington, D.C.: The Sentencing Project, 2014).

46. The Pew Center and the Mellman Group, *Public Opinion on Sentencing and Correctional Policy in American* (2012), available at http://www.pewtrusts.org/~/media/Assets/2012/03/30/PEW_NationalSurvey-ResearchPaper_FINAL.pdf (accessed June 28, 2018).

47. The Associated Press, "Prisoners Freed Quickly after Voters OK Prop. 47," *Decision 2014*, November 8, 2014, available at www.nbcbayarea.com/news/local/prisones_freed_281986651.html (accessed November 18, 2014).

48. A full description of the process can be seen in an article written by Director Mohr in "Reforming a System: An Inside Perspective on How Ohio Achieved a Record-Low Recidivism Rate," *Council of State Governments Justice Center Newsletter* (March 2012), available at http://csgjusticecenter.org/nrrc/posts/reforming-a-system-an-inside-perspective-on-how-ohio-achieved-a-record-low-recidivism-rate/ (accessed August 9, 2017).

49. Interview: A State Director of Corrections - Director Gary Mohr. Reprinted with Permission.

50. A good overview of the history of drug courts can be found in Authur J. Lurigio, "First 20 Years of Drug Treatment Courts," *Federal Probation* 72, no. 1. (2008): 13–18.

51. Drug Court Programs Office, *Defining Drug Courts: The Key Components* (Washington, D.C.: U.S. Department of Justice, Office of Justice Programs, 1997).

52. National Association of Drug Court Professionals, *Adult Drug Court Best Practice Standards: Volume I* (Alexandria, Va.: National Association of Drug Court Professionals, 2013).

53. C. West Huddleston III, Karen Freeman-Wilson, Douglas B. Marlowe, and Aaron Roussell, "A National Report Card on Drug Courts and Other Problem Solving Court Programs in the United States," *Painting the Current Picture* 2, no. 1 (May 2008).

54. Bureau of Justice Assistance, *Drug Courts* (Washington, D.C.: U.S. Department of Justice, 2011).

55. West Huddleston and Douglas B. Marlowe, *Painting the Current Picture: A National Report on Drug Courts and Other Problem-Solving Court Programs in the United States* (Alexandria, Va.: National Drug Court Institute, 2011).

56. Lenny Bernstein, "White House Opioid Commission Calls for Wide-Ranging Changes to Anti-Drug Policies," *The Washington Post*, November 1, 2017, available at https://www.washingtonpost.com/news/to-your-health/wp/2017/11/01/white-house-opioid-commission-calls-for-wide-ranging-changes-to-anti-drug-policies/?utm_term=.b8a34e6755cc (accessed November 1, 2017).

57. J. S. Goldkamp, "Miami's Treatment Drug Court for Felony Defendants: Some Implications of Assessment Findings," *Prison Journal* 74, no. 2 (1994): 110–157.

58. Roger H. Peters and Mary R. Murrin, "Effectiveness of Treatment-Based Drug Courts in Reducing Criminal Recidivism," *Criminal Justice and Behavior* 27, no. 1 (2000): 72–96.

59. John Roman, Wendy Townsend, and Avinash Singh Bhati, *Recidivism Rates for Drug Court Graduates: Nationally Based Estimates, Final Report* (Washington, D.C.: U.S. Department of Justice, National Institute of Justice, July 2003).

60. Celinda Franco, *Adult Drug Courts: Evidence Indicates Recidivism Reduction and Mixed Results for Other Outcomes* (Washington, D.C.: U.S. Government Accountability Office, February 2005).

61. Denise C. Gottredson, Stacy S. Najka, Brook W. Kearley, and Carlos M. Rocha, "Long-Term Effects of Participation in the Baltimore City Drug Treatment Program: Results from an Experimental Study," *Journal of Experimental Criminology* 2 (2006): 67–98.

62. Michael W. Finigan, Shannon M. Carey, and Anton Clark, *Impact of a Mature Drug Court Over 10 Years of Operation* (Washington, D.C.: U.S. Department of Justice, 2007).

63. Deborah K. Schaffer, Dissertation entitled *Reconsidering Drug Court Effectiveness: A Meta-Analytic Review* (Cincinnati, Ohio: University of Cincinnati, March 2007).

64. Amanda Cissner et al. *Statewide Evaluation of New York's Adult Drug Courts: Identifying Which Policies Work Best* (Washington, D.C.: The Urban Institute, 2013).

65. Lisa M. Shannon, Afton Jackson Jones, Jennifer Newell, and Connie Neal, "Examining the Impact of Prior Criminal Justice History on 2-Year Recidivism Rates: A Comparison of Drug Court Participants and Program Referrals, *International Journal of Offender Therapy and Comparative Criminology* 62, no. 2 (April 2016).

66. Henry J. Steadman, Susan Davidson, and Collie Brown, "Mental Health Courts," *Psychiatric Services* 52 (2001): 457.

67. Council of State Governments, Justice Center, *Mental Health Courts*, available at http://csgjusticecenter.org/mental-health-court-project/ (accessed June 28, 2018).

68. Michelle Andrews, *Mental Health Courts are Popular, But Are They Effective?* National Public Radio, December 16, 2015, available at http://www.npr.org/sections/health-shots/2015/12/16/459823010/mental-health-courts-are-popular-but-are-they-effective (accessed August 9, 2017).

69. Criminal Justice/Mental Health Consensus Project, *Mental Health Courts: A Primer for Policymakers and Practitioners* (New York: Council of State Governments Justice Center, 2008).

70. Eric Trupin, Henry Richards, David Werthheimer, and Carole Bruschi, *Seattle Municipal Court, Mental Health Court: Evaluation Report* (Seattle, Wash.: City of Seattle, 2001); Heidi A. Herinckx, Sandra C. Swart, Shane M. Ama, Cheri D. Dolezal, and Steve King, "Rearrest and Linkage to Mental Health Services among Clients of the Clark County Mental Health Court Program," *Psychiatric Services* 56 (2005): 853–857.

71. Dale E. McNiel and Renee L. Binder, "Effectiveness of a Mental Health Court in Reducing Criminal Recidivism and Violence," *American Journal of Psychiatry* 164 (2007): 1395–1403; Marlee E. Moore and Virginia A. Hiday, "Mental Health Court Outcomes: A Comparison of Re-arrest and Re-arrest Severity between Mental Health Court and Traditional Court Participants," *Law and Human Behavior* 164 (2006): 659–674; and Britany Cross, *Mental Health Courts Effectiveness in Reducing Recidivism and Improving Clinical Outcomes: A Meta-Analysis* (Tampa, Fla.: University of South Florida, 2011).

72. Lauren Almquist and Elizabeth Dodd, *Mental Health Courts: A Guide to Research-Informed Policy and Practice* (New York: Council of State Governments Justice Center, 2009).

73. For an overview of reentry courts, see Christine Lindquist, Jennifer H. Walters, Michael Rempel, and Shannon M. Carey, *National Institute of Justice Evaluation of Adult Reentry Courts* (Washington, D.C.: U.S. Department of Justice, 2013).

74. Office of National Drug Control Policy, *Veteran Treatment Courts* (Washington, D.C.: Office of National Drug Control Policy, 2010).

75. Stephen R. Binder, "Homeless Court Program: Taking the Court to the Streets," *Federal Probation* 65, no. 1 (June 2001): 14–17.

76. William T. Fujioka, *Los Angeles County Homeless Prevention Initiative Status Report*, available at http://ceo.lacounty.gov/sib/pdf/Los%20Angeles%20County%20HPI%20Status%20Report_Board%20Memo_10.27.09.pdf (accessed August 9, 2017).

Chapter 3

1. Todd D. Minton and Zhen Zeng, "Jail Inmates in 2015," *BJS Bulletin* (Washington, D.C.: U.S. Department of Justice, 2016), p. 1.

2. The John Howard Society was formed in the mid-1800s and has dozens of chapters throughout Canada and a few in the United States. As an example of their overall approach, the John Howard Society of Illinois has a stated mission of independently monitoring correctional facilities, policies, and practices, and advancing reforms needed to achieve a fair, humane, and effective criminal justice system, available at http://www.thejha.org (accessed August 10, 2017).

3. David Rothman, *The Discovery of the Asylum: Social Order and Disorder in the New Republic* (Boston: Little, Brown, 1971), p. 56.

4. James Stephan and Georgette Walsh, *Census of Jail Facilities, 2006* (Washington, D.C.: U.S. Department of Justice, December 2011).

5. Minton and Zeng, op. cit., p. 6.

6. Stephan and Walsh, *Census of Jail Facilities*, p. 11.

7. Minton and Zeng, p. 3.

8. *Sourcebook of Criminal Justice Statistics*, Table 6.14.2012, available at www.albany.edu/sourcebook (accessed August 10, 2017).

9. United States Census Bureau, *State and County Quick Facts*, available at http://quickfacts.census.gov/qfd /states/00000.html (accessed August 10, 2017).

10. Todd d. Minton, "Census of Jails: Population Changes, 1999-2013," *BJS Bulletin* (Washington, D.C.: Bureau of Justice Statistics, 2015).

11. Minton and Zeng, p. 4.

12. Doris J. James, "Profile of Jail Inmates," *Bureau of Justice Statistics Special Report* 2002 (Washington, D.C.: U.S. Department of Justice, 2004).

13. James J. Stephan, *Census of Jails, 1999* (Washington, D.C.: U.S. Department of Justice, Bureau of Justice Statistics, 2000), p. 4; and Minton and Zeng, p. 4.

14. E. Ann Carlson and Elizabeth Anderson, "Prisoners in 2015," *Bureau of Justice Statistics Bulletin* (Washington, D.C.: U.S. Department of Justice, 2016), p. 16.

15. Ibid.

16. Todd D. Minton, "Jail Inmates at Mid-Year 2012," *BJS Statistical Tables* (Washington, D.C.: U.S. Department of Justice, 2013), p. 8.

17. Sean Rossenmerkel, Matthew Durose, and Donald Ferole, Jr., "Felony Sentences in State Courts, 2006," *BJS Statistical Tables* (Washington, D.C.: Bureau of Justice Statistics, 2009).

18. Minton and Zeng, pp. 1 and 3.

19. Carlson and Anderson, p. 10.

20. Todd D. Minton, et al., "Census of Jails: Population Changes, 1999–2013," *BJS Bulletin* (Washington, D.C.: Bureau of Justice Statistics, 2015), p. 3.

21. Tim Brennan, "Implementing Organization Change in Criminal Justice: Some Lessons from Jail Classification Systems," *Corrections Management Quarterly* 3, no. 2 (1999): 12.

22. Ibid., p. 14.

23. Minton and Zeng, p. 9.

24. Ibid.

25. As reported in James J. Stephan, *Census of Jails, 1999* (Washington, D.C.: U.S. Department of Justice, 2000), p. 25.

26. Stephan and Walsh, *Census of Jail Facilities*, p. 24.

27. Minton and Zeng, p. 9.

28. Stephan and Walsh, p. 24.

29. Stephan, *Census of Jails, 2001*, p. 26. Also, Minton and Zeng, p. 9.

30. Stephan, *Census of Jails, 2001*, p. 31.

31. Leanne Fiftal Alarid, "Risk Factors for Potential Occupational Exposure to HIV: A Study of Correctional Officers," *Journal of Criminal Justice* 37, no. 2 (March/April 2009): 114–122.

32. As cited in Robert W. Duffy, "City's $101 Million Justice Center Is State-of-the-Art in Jail Design," *St. Louis Post-Dispatch*, November 17, 2002, p. B5.

33. G. J. Bayens, J. Williams, and J. O. Smykla, "Jail Type Makes a Difference: Evaluating the Transition from a Traditional to a Podular Direct Supervision Jail across Ten Years," *American Jails* 11, no. 2 (May/June 1997): 33–39.

34. Interview: A Jail Administrator - Herbert L. Bernsen. Reprinted with Permission.

35. Minton and Zeng, p. 4.

36. Paige M. Harrison and Allen J. Beck, *Prison and Jail Inmates at Mid-year 2004* (Washington, D.C.: U.S. Department of Justice, 2005).

37. Minton and Zeng, p. 4.

38. For a good overview of the issues regarding privatization, see Richard P. Seiter, "Private Prisons: Myths, Realities, & Educational Opportunities for Inmates," *Saint Louis University Public Law Review*, XXXIII, no. 2 (2014): 415–428.

39. Stephan, *Census of Jails, 2011*, p. 6.

40. Stephan and Walsh, *Census of Jail Facilities*, p. 11.

41. *Bell v. Wolfish*, U.S. 520 (1979).

42. Stephan, *Census of Jails, 2011*, p. 5.

43. Stephan and Walsh, *Census of Jail Facilities*, p. 11.

44. William C. Collins, *Legal Issues in Jails—2013* (Washington, D.C.: U.S. Department of Justice, 2013).

45. "Prisons Replace Hospitals for the Nation's Mentally Ill," *New York Times*, March 5, 1998, p. A26.

46. E. Fuller Torrey et al., *The Treatment of Persons with Mental Illness in Prisons and Jails: A State Survey* (Arlington, V.A.: Treatment Advocacy Center, 2014).

47. Doris J. James and Lauren E. Glaze, *Mental Health Problems of Prison and Jail Inmates* (Washington, D.C.: U.S. Department of Justice, Bureau of Justice Statistics, September 2006), p. 1. See also, Henry J. Steadman et al., "Prevalence of Serious Mental Illness among Jail Inmates," *Psychiatric Services* 60, no. 6 (2009): 761–765.

48. Jennifer Bronson and Marcus Berzofsky, *Indicators of Mental Health Problems Reported by Prisoners and Jail Inmates, 2011–12* (Washington, D.C.: U.S. Department of Justice, 2017).

49. See Rise Haneberg, Tony Fabelo, Fred Osher, and Michael Thompson, *Reducing the Number of People with Mental Illnesses in Jails*, available at https://stepuptogether.org/wp-content/uploads/2017/01/Reducing-the-Number-of-People-with-Mental-Illnesses-in-Jail_Six-Questions.pdf (accessed August 14, 2017).

50. See Torrey et al., *The Treatment of Persons with Mental Illness in Prisons and Jails*, p. 17.

51. Ibid.

52. Margaret Noonan, Harley Rohloff, and Scott Ginder, "Mortality in Local Jails and State Prisons, 2000–2013 – Statistical Tables," *BJS Statistical Tables* (Washington, D.C.: U.S. Department of Justice, Bureau of Justice Statistics, 2015), p. 7.

53. Ibid.

54. These include cancer, liver disease, respiratory disease, cerebrovascular disease, influenza, and other natural causes of death.

55. Noonan, et al., p. 7.

56. Maurice Chammah and Tom Meagher, *Why Jails Have More Suicides than Prisons* (New York, NY: The Marshall Project, 2015).

57. Christopher J. Mumola, *Suicide and Homicide in State Prisons and Local Jails* (Washington, D.C.: U.S. Department of Justice, 2005), p. 1.

Chapter 4

1. David Dressler, *Practice of Probation and Parole* (New York: Columbia University Press, 1962).

2. Ibid., p. 18.

3. Joan Petersilia, *Reforming Probation and Parole in the 21st Century* (Lanham, Md.: American Correctional Association, 2002), p. 20.

4. Dressler, op. cit.

5. Danielle Kaeble and Thomas P. Bonczar, "Probation and Parole in the United States, 2015," *BJS Bulletin* (Washington, D.C.: U.S. Department of Justice, 2016), p. 3.

6. Comptroller General of the United States, *State and County Probation: Systems in Crisis, Report to the Congress of the United States* (Washington, D.C.: U.S. Government Printing Office, 1976).

7. Danielle Kaeble and Lauren Glaze, "Correctional Populations in the United States, 2015," *BJS Bulletin* (Washington, D.C.: U.S. Department of Justice, 2016), p. 2.

8. Linda Layton, Dennis, McFarland, and Diane Kincaid, *An Elected Officials Guide to Community Corrections Options*, 2nd. (Lexington, KY: American Probation and Parole Association, 2012), p. 11.

9. Kaeble and Bonczar, p. 3.

10. Kaeble and Glaze, p. 2.

11. Kaeble and Bonczar, p. 4.

12. Ibid., p. 5.

13. Richard P. Seiter and Angela West, "Supervision Styles in Probation and Parole: An Analysis of Activities," *Journal of Offender Rehabilitation* 38, no. 2 (2003): 55–75. Also see Angela D. West and Richard P. Seiter, "Social Worker or Cop? Measuring the Supervision Style of Probation and Parole Officers in Kentucky and Missouri," *Journal of Crime and Justice* 27, no. 2 (2004): 27–57.

14. Jay Whetzel, Mario Paparozzi, Melissa Alexander, and Christopher T. Lowenkamp, "Goodbye to a Worn-Out Dichotomy: Law Enforcement, Social Work, and a Balanced Approach," *Federal Probation* 76, no. 2 (September 2011): 7–12.

15. Camille Graham Camp and George M. Camp, *The 2002 Corrections Yearbook: Adult Corrections* (Middletown, CN: Criminal Justice Institute, 2003), p. 191.

16. Jennifer Eno Louden, Jennifer L. Skeem, Jacqueline Camp, and Elizabeth Christenson, "Supervising Probationers with Mental Disorder: How Do Agencies Respond to Violations?" *Criminal Justice and Behavior* 35, no. 7 (July 2008): 832–847.

17. Lauren C. Babchuk, Authur J. Lurigio, Kelli E. Canada, and Matthew W. Epperson, "Responding to Probationers with Mental Illness," *Federal Probation* 76, no. 2 (September 2012): 41–48.

18. Camp and Camp, *The 2002 Corrections Yearbook*, p. 191.

19. Peter Finn and Sarah Kuck, "Stress Among Probation and Parole Officers and What Can Be Done about It," *NIJ Research for Practice* (Washington, D.C.: U.S. Department of Justice, June 2005).

20. Sarah Kuck Jalbert, William Rhodes, Michael Kane, Elyse Clawson, Bradford Bogue, Chris Flygare, Ryan Kling, and Meaghan Guevara, *A Multi-Site Evaluation of Reduced Probation Caseload Size in an Evidence-Based Practice Setting* (Washington, D.C.: U.S. Department of Justice, 2011).

21. *Bearden v. Georgia*, 461 U.S. 660 (1983).

22. *United States v. Birnbaum*, 421 F.2d 993 (1970).

23. *Mempa v. Rhay*, 389 U.S. 128 (1967).

24. *Morrissey v. Brewer*, 408 U.S. 271 (1972).

25. *Gagnon v. Scarpelli*, 411 U.S. 778 (1973).

26. E. Ann Carson and Elizabeth Anderson, "Prisoners in 2015," *BJS Bulletin* (Washington, D.C.: U.S. Department of Justice, 2016), p. 11.

27. Daniel Glaser, *The Effectiveness of a Prison and Parole System* (New York: Bobbs-Merrill, 1964), p. 423.

28. Paul T. Alberty, *A Study of the Relationship between Styles of Supervision and Parole Officer's Violations Rate* (Master's thesis, University of Missouri, 1969), p. 3.

29. David I. Rothman, *Conscience and Convenience: The Asylum and Its Alternatives in Progressive America* (Boston: Little, Brown, 1980).

30. William Adams and Jeffrey Roth, *Federal Offenders under Community Supervision, 1989–96* (Washington, D.C.: U.S. Department of Justice, Bureau of Justice Statistics, 1998).

31. Camp and Camp, *2002 Corrections Yearbook*, p. 201.

32. In a study of St. Louis parole and probation officers, Seiter and West found that 54.1 percent of respondents majored in criminal justice, 1.1 percent in psychology, 9.0 percent in sociology, and 4.5 percent in social work. Other majors included education, business, art, and history. See Richard P. Seiter and Angela D. West, "Supervision Styles in Probation and Parole: An Analysis of Activities," *Offender Rehabilitation* 38, no. 2 (2003): 57–75.

33. Heather C. West and William J. Sabol, "Prisoners in 2007," *BJS Bulletin* (Washington, D.C.: U.S. Department of Justice, 2008), p. 3.

34. Joan Petersilia, "When Prisoners Return to the Community: Political, Economic, and Social Consequences," *Federal Probation* 65, no. 1 (June 2001): 3–8.

35. Kevin Johnson, "To Save Money on Prisons, States Take a Softer Stance," *USA Today*, March 18, 2009, p. 1.

36. Kelli D. Stevens-Martin, "Tackling the Issue of High-Risk Offenders and Chronic Probation Violators," *Corrections Today* 76, no. 5 (September/October 2014): 74–78.

37. For a description of the RNS model, see D.A Andrews, James Bonta, and J. Stephen Wormith, "Risk-Need-Responsivity (RNR) Model: Does Adding the Good Lives Model Contribute to Effective Crime Prevention?" *Criminal Justice Behavior* 38, no. 7 (July 2011): 735–755.

38. For a good overview, see Guy Bourgon, Leticia Gutierrez, and Jennifer Ashton, "Evolution of Community Supervision Practice: The Transformation from Case Manager to Change Agent," *Federal Probation* 78, no. 2 (September 2012): 27–35.

39. Faye X. Taxman, "No Illusions: Offender and Organizational Change in Maryland's Proactive Community Supervision Efforts," *Criminology and Public Policy* 7, no. 2 (May 2008): 275–302.

40. Richard A. Oppel, Jr. "States Trim Penalties and Prison Roles, Even as Sessions Gets Tough," *The New York Times*, May 18, 2017, available at https://www.nytimes.com/2017/05/18/us/states-prisons-crime-sentences-jeff-sessions.html?mcubz=0&_r=0 (accessed August 22, 2017).

41. The broken windows approach to probation was first described in a report by the Reinventing Probation Council, "'Broken Windows' Probation: The Next Step in Fighting Crime," *Civil Report* 7 (1999): 2.

42. Carson and Anderson, "Prisoners in 2015," p. 11.

43. *Bureau of Justice Statistics National Update* (Washington, D.C.: U.S. Department of Justice, 1994), p. 10.

44. Danielle Kaeble and Thomas P. Bonczar, "Probation and Parole in the United States," *BJS Bulletin* (Washington, D.C.: U.S. Department of Justice, 2015).

45. Todd Clear and Anthony Braga, "Community Corrections," in *Crime*, edited by James Q. Wilson and Joan R. Petersilia (San Francisco, Calif.: Institute for Contemporary Studies, 1995), pp. 421–444.

46. Patrick Langan and Mark A. Cunniff, *Recidivism of Felons on Probation, 1986–89* (Washington, D.C.: U.S. Department of Justice, Bureau of Justice Statistics, 1995).

47. Michael Geerken and Hennessey D. Hayes, "Probation and Parole: Public Risk and the Future of Incarceration Alternatives," *Criminology* 31, no. 4 (1993): 549–564.

48. Joan R. Petersilia and Susan Turner, *Prison Versus Probation in California: Implications for Crime and Offender Recidivism* (Santa Monica, Calif.: RAND, 1986), pp. 27–33.

49. Jalbert, et al. 2011, *A Multi-Site Evaluation of Reduced Probation Caseload Size in an Evidence-Based Practice Setting*.

50. Jennifer L. Skeem and Sarah Manchak, "Back to the Future: From Klockars' Model of Effective Supervision to Evidence-Based Practice in Probation," *Journal of Offender Rehabilitation* 47, no. 3 (2008): 220–247.

51. Laura Barber, "Results-Based Framework for Post-Conviction Supervision Recidivism Analysis," *Federal Probation* 74, no. 3 (December 2010): 5–10.

52. Christian Henrichson and Ruth Delaney, *What Incarceration Costs Taxpayers* (New York: Vera Institute, 2012), p. 9.

53. The Pew Center on the States, Public Safety Project, *One in 31: The Long Reach of American Corrections* (Washington, D.C.: The Pew Charitable Trusts, March 2009), p. 12.

54. Chris Trotter, "Reducing Recidivism Through Probation Supervision: What We Know and Don't Know from Four Decades of Research," *Federal Probation* 77, no. 2 (2013): 43–48.

55. Tony Fabelo, Geraldine Nagy, and Seth Prins, *A Ten-Step Guide to Transforming Probation Departments to Reduce Recidivism* (New York: The Council of State Governments, 2011), p. vii.

56. Justice Center, *Reducing Recidivism: States Delivering Results* (New York: Council of State Governments, 2017).

57. Justice Center, *Justice Reinvestment in North Carolina: Three Years Later* (New York: The Council of State Governments, 2014).

58. Justice Center, *Georgia's Justice Reinvestment Approach: Strengthening Probation and Increasing Public Safety* (New York: Council of State Governments, 2017).

59. Presentation by Justice Michael Boggs of the Georgia Supreme Court, who was co-chair of the Georgia Justice Reinvestment Initiative. Association of State Correctional Administrators meetings, St. Louis, MO, August 19, 2017.

60. Justice Center, *Georgia's Justice Reinvestment Approach*, op. cit.

61. Pew Charitable Trusts, *31 States Reform Criminal Justice Policies Through Justice Reinvestment* (Washington, D.C.: The Pew Charitable Trusts, 2016).

62. General Accounting Office, *State and County Probation Systems in Crisis* (Washington, D.C.: U.S. Government Printing Office, 1976), p. 53.

63. Vincent O'Leary and Todd R. Clear, *Directions for Community Corrections in the 1990s* (Washington, D.C.: U.S. Department of Justice, June 1984), p. 11.

64. Meghan Guevara and Enver Solomon, *Implementing Evidence Based Policy and Practice in Community Corrections*, 2nd ed. (Washington, D.C.: U.S. Department of Justice, October 2009).

65. Ibid., p. xi.

66. Elizabeth Drake, *Predicting Criminal Recidivism: A Systematic Review of Offender Risk Assessments in Washingon State* (Olympia, WA: Washington State University Institute for Public Policy, 2014).

67. For an overview of the T360, see Alisha Shoates James and Ed Welch, "T360: The Tennessee Model of 360 Seamless Supervision," *Corrections Today* (November/December 2017): 38–43.

68. The Pew Center on the States, *One in 31*, p. 2.

69. Joan Petersilia and Susan Turner, "Intensive Probation and Parole," in *Crime and Justice: An Annual Review of Research*, edited by Michael Tonry (Chicago: University of Chicago Press, 1993).

70. Paul Gendreau and Tracy Little, *A Meta-Analysis of the Effectiveness of Sanctions on Offender Recidivism* (University of New Brunswick, 1993).

71. Christopher T. Lowenkamp, Anthony W. Flores, Alexander W. Flores, Alexander M. Holsinger, Matthew D. Makarios, and Edward J. Latessa, "Intensive Supervision Programs: Does Program Philosophy and the Principles of Effective Supervision Matter?" *Journal of Criminal Justice* 38, no. 4 (August 2010): 368–375.

72. Sarah Kuck Jalbert, William Rhodes, Christopher Flygare, and Michael Kane, "Testing Probation Outcomes in an Evidence-Based Practice Setting: Reduced Caseload Size and Intensive Supervision Effectiveness," *Journal of Offender Rehabilitation* 39, no. 4 (May–June 2010): 233–253.

73. Elizabeth K. Drake, Steve Aos, and Marna G. Miller, "Evidence-Based Public Policy Options to Reduce Crime and Criminal Justice Costs: Implications in Washington State," *Victims and Offenders* 4 (2009): 170–196.

74. A good description of the use of electronic monitoring can be seen in Randy R. Gainey and Brian K. Payne, "Understanding the Experience of House Arrest with Electronic Monitoring: An Analysis of Quantitative and Qualitative Data," *International Journal of Offender Therapy and Comparative Criminology* 44, no. 1 (February 2000): 84–96.

75. John K. Roman, Akiva M. Liberman, Sam Taxy, and P. Mitchell Downey, *The Costs and Benefits for Electronic Monitoring for Washington, D.C.* (Washington, D.C.: District of Columbia Crime Policy Institute, 2012), p. 3.

76. William Bales, Karen Mann, Thomas Blomberg, Gerry Gaes, Kelle Barrick, Karla Dhungana, and Brian McManus, *A Quantitative and Qualitative Assessment of Electronic Monitoring* (Washington, D.C.: U.S. Department of Justice, 2010).

77. Pierre du Pont, *Expanding Sentencing Options: A Governor's Perspective* (Washington, D.C.: U.S. National Institute of Justice, 1985).

78. Christian Henrichson and Ruth Delaney, *What Incarceration Costs Taxpayers* (New York: Vera Institute, 2012), p. 9.

79. The Pew Center, p. 145.

80. Interview: A CRC Director - Denise M. Robinson. Reprinted with Permission.

81. 221 were reported in James J. Stephan, "Census of State and Federal Correctional Facilities, 2005," *National Prisoner Statistics Program* (Washington, D.C.: U.S. Department of Justice, October 2008), p. 2.

82. Lauren E. Glaze and Thomas P. Bonczar, "Probation and Parole in the United States, 2010," *BJS Bulletin* (Washington, D.C.: U.S. Department of Justice, November 2011), p. 31.

83. For an overview of evaluations of correctional boot camps, see Jeanne B. Stinchcomb, "Recovering from the Shocking Reality of Shock Incarceration—What Correctional Administrators Can Learn from Boot Camp Failures," *Corrections Management Quarterly* 3, no. 4 (1999): 43–52.

84. U.S. General Accounting Office, *Prison Boot Camps: Short-Term Prison Costs Reduced, but Long-Term Impact Uncertain* (Washington, D.C.: U.S. Government Printing Office, 1993).

85. Cynthia A. Kempinen, "Pennsylvania's Motivational Boot Camp Program: What Have We Learned Over the Last Seventeen Years?" (Harrisburg, PA: Pennsylvania Commmission on Sentencing, 2011).

86. Gennaro Vito, "Developments in Shock Probation: A Review of Research Findings and Policy Implications," *Federal Probation* 50, no. 1 (1985): 23–25.

87. Edward J. Latessa and Harry E. Allen, *Corrections in the Community*, 2nd ed. (Cincinnati, Ohio: Anderson, 1999), pp. 403–404.

88. Joan Petersilia, "A Decade of Experimenting with Intermediate Sanctions: What Have We Learned?" *Corrections Management Quarterly* 3, no. 4 (1999): 23–24.

89. Benedict Carey, "Drug Rehabilitation or Revolving Door?" *New York Times*, December 23, 2008, p. D4.

90. Urban Institute, *Transforming Prisons, Restoring Lives: Final Recommendations of the Charles Colson Task Force on Federal Corrections* (Washington, D.C.: Urban Institute, 2016).

Chapter 5

1. President's Commission on Law Enforcement and Administration of Justice, *The Challenge of Crime in a Free Society* (Washington, D.C.: U.S. Government Printing Office, 1967), p. 165.

2. Ibid.

3. David Shichor, *Punishment for Profit* (Thousand Oaks, Calif.: Sage, 1995), p. 9.

4. E. Ann Carson, "Prisoners in 2016," *BJS Bulletin* (Washington, D.C.: U.S. Department of Justice, 2018), p. 3.

5. *Rhodes v. Chapman*, 29 Cr. L. Rptr. 3061 (1981).

6. *Bruscino v. Carlson* (Civil Action No. 84-4320), D.C.S.D. III (1987).

7. Cisco Lassiter, "Roboprison," *Mother Jones* (September/October 1990): 76.

8. Douglas C. Eadie, "Strategic Management by Design," in *Strategic Planning for Local Government: A Handbook for Officials and Citizens*, edited by Roger L. Kemp (Jefferson, N.C.: McFarland, 1993), p. 85.

9. Federal Bureau of Prisons website, available at www.bop.gov (accessed August 25, 2017).

10. Carson, op. cit.

11. Poll conducted by Gallup regarding crime, October 5-9, 2016, available at http://www.gallup.com/poll/1603/crime.aspx (accessed August 25, 2017).

12. Camille Graham Camp and George M. Camp, *The Corrections Yearbook, 2002* (Middletown, Conn.: Criminal Justice Institute, 2003), p. 39.

13. Carson, "Prisoners in 2013," Table 17, p. 18; the average time served was calculated from this table.

14. Michael Tonry, "Why Are U.S. Incarceration Rates So High?" *Crime and Delinquency* 45, no. 14 (October 1999): 445.

15. Bureau of Justice Statistics, *National Prisoner Statistics* (Washington, D.C.: U.S. Department of Justice, 1977).

16. Ibid.

17. Katherine J. Rosich and Kamala Malik Kane, "Truth in Sentencing and State Sentencing Practices," *NIJ Journal* 25 (July 2005): 18–21.

18. Edward E. Rhine, "Probation and Parole Supervision: In Need of a New Narrative," *Corrections Management Quarterly* 1, no. 2 (1997): 73.

19. Heather C. West, William J Sabol, and Sarah J. Greenman, "Prisoners in 2009," *BJS Bulletin* (Washington, DC: U.S. Department of Justice, 2010), pp. 2 and 5.

20. Lauren E. Glaze and Thomas P. Bonczar, "Probation and Parole in the United States, 2010," *BJS Bulletin* (Washington, D.C.: U.S. Department of Justice, November 2011), pp. 32 and 41.

21. Bureau of Justice Statistics, *Drugs, Crime and the Justice System* (Washington, D.C.: National Institute of Justice, 1993), p. 2.

22. Office of National Drug Control Policy, *National Drug Control Strategy: FY 2005 Budget Summary* (Washington, D.C.: The White House, March 2004), p. 13; Office of National Drug Control Policy, *National Drug Control Strategy: FY 2003 Budget Summary* (Washington, D.C.: Executive Office of the President, 2003), pp. 10–11.

23. According to the Bureau of Prisons website, on July 29, 2017, 46.3 percent of the inmates were serving a sentence for a drug offense. See www.bop.gov (accessed August 26, 2017).

24. Carson, "Prisoners in 2016," p. 8.

25. Pew Center for the States, *Prison and Crime: A Complex Link* (Washington D.C.: Pew Center for the States, 2014).

26. Camille Graham Camp and George M. Camp, *The 2002 Corrections Yearbook: Adult Systems* (Middletown, Conn.: Criminal Justice Institute, 2003), pp. 82–83, 84, 97, 98, 118.

27. James J. Stephan, "Census of State and Federal Correctional Facilities, 2005," *National Prisoner Statistics Program* (Washington, D.C.: U.S. Department of Justice, October 2008), pp. 1–2.

28. Carson, "Prisoners in 2016," p. 22.

29. Ibid., p. 21.

30. Stephan, op. cit.

31. Carson, p. 21.

32. This act was officially known as "An Act for the Erection of United States Prisons and for the Imprisonment of United States Prisoners, and for Other Purposes."

33. The U.S. Penitentiary in Leavenworth was built with convict labor, from inmates housed at the U.S. Disciplinary Barracks for Military Prisoners in Leavenworth, and took several years to complete. While it was not fully finished until 1928, it began housing inmates shortly after the beginning of the twentieth century.

34. BOP website at www.bop.gov (accessed August 26, 2017).

35. There was an acting director from the retirement of Mr. Samuels in 2016 until the appointment of Mr. Inch in 2017.

36. Brian A. Reaves and Lynn M. Bauer, *Federal Law Enforcement Officers, 2002*, NCJ 199995 (Washington, D.C.: U.S. Department of Justice, Bureau of Justice Statistics Bulletin, August 2003), p. 1.

37. Ibid., p. 2.

38. BOP website at www.bop.gov (accessed August 29, 2017).

39. E. Ann Carson, "Prisoners in 2013," *BJS Bulletin* (Washington, DC: U.S. Department of Justice, 2014), p. 2.

40. Bop website at www.bop.gov (accessed January 10, 2018).

41. Ibid.

42. An excellent history of FPI can be found in, Federal Prison Industries, *Factories with Fences: 75 Years of Changing Lives* (Washington, DC: U.S. Department of Justice, 2010), available at https://www.unicor.gov/publications/corporate/CATMC1101_C.pdf (accessed August 28, 2017).

43. Federal Prison Industries, *Fiscal Year 2016: Annual Management Report* (Washington, DC: U.S. Department of Justice, 2016), p. 3.

44. The author, Richard P. Seiter, was Assistant Director of the Bureau of Prisons and Chief Operating Officer of Federal Prisons Industry from 1988 to 1993. The early 1990s were some of the highest points of inmate employment.

45. FPI, *FY 2016 Annual Management Report*, op. cit.

46. William G. Saylor and Gary G. Gaes, "Post Release Employment Project: Prison Work Has Measureable Effect on Post-Release Success," *Federal Prisons Journal* 2, no. 4 (Winter 1992): 32–36.

47. Carson, "Prisoners in 2016," p. 1.

48. Ibid., p. 5.

49. Stephan, *Census of State and Federal Correctional Facilities, 2005,* Appendix Table 1.

50. This number was calculated from data regarding the total number of state and federal prisoners in Danielle Kaeble and Lauren Glaze, "Correctional Populations in the United States, 2015," *BJS Bulletin* (Washington, D.C.: U.S. Department of Justice 2016) and subtracting the BOP population available at bop.gov, Population Statistics (accessed August 29, 2017).

51. Ibid.

52. Prisoners in 2009, p. 2.

53. Ibid.

54. Carson, op. cit., p. 3.

55. Chase Riveland, "The Correctional Leader and Public Policy Skills," *Corrections Management Quarterly* 1, no. 3 (1997): 23.

56. Camp and Camp, 2002 *Corrections Yearbook*, p. 5.

57. Carson, "Prisoners in 2016," p. 4.

58. Ibid.

59. Allen Beck and Darrell Gilliard, *Prisoners in 1994* (Washington, D.C.: U.S. Department of Justice, 1995), p. 10.

60. BOP website, www.bop.gov (accessed August 28, 2017).

61. James J. Stephan, *Census of State and Federal Correctional Facilities, 2005* (Washington, D.C.: U.S. Department of Justice, Bureau of Justice Statistics, October 2008), p. 2.

62. Richard Werner, Effectiveness of the Direct Supervision of Correctional Design and Management: A Review of the Literature," *Criminal Justice and Behavior: An International Journal* 13, no. 3 (June 2006): 392–410.

63. A list of these facilities is available at https://www.ice.gov/detention-facilities (accessed August 30, 2017).

64. *ICE Enforcement and Removal Operations Report: Fiscal Year 2015* (Washington, D.C.: U.S. Immigration and Customs Enforcement, 2015).

65. Carson, op. cit., p. 33.

66. Ibid., p. 31.

67. Ibid., p. 34.

68. Harry Allen, Evelyn Parks, Eric Carlson, and Richard Seiter, *Program Models, Halfway Houses* (Washington, D.C.: U.S. Department of Justice, 1978).

69. Edmund R. McGarrell and Timothy Flanagan, *Sourcebook of Criminal Justice Statistics, 1984* (Washington, D.C.: U.S. Department of Justice, 1985).

70. Michael Welch, *Corrections: A Critical Approach* (New York: McGraw-Hill, 1996), p. 416.

71. Charles Logan, *Private Prisons: Cons and Pros* (New York: Oxford University Press, 1990), p. 20.

72. Carson, "Prisoners in 2016," p. 28.

73. Stephan, op. cit.

Chapter 6

1. William B. Taylor, "Alexander Maconochie and the Revolt against the Penitentiary," *Southern Journal of Justice* 3, no. 1 (1978): 18.

2. Robert Hughes, *The Fatal Shore* (New York: Knopf, 1987), p. 468.

3. As cited in Norval Morris, *Maconochie's Gentlemen: The Story of Norfolk Island and the Roots of Modern Prison Reform* (New York: Oxford University Press, 2002), p. 156.

4. Harry E. Barnes and Negley. K. Teeters, *New Horizons in Criminology* (Upper Saddle River, N.J.: Prentice Hall, 1959).

5. Andrew A. Bruce, *Parole and Indeterminate Sentences* (Springfield: Illinois Parole Board, 1928).

6. Michael S. Sherrill, "Determinate Sentencing: History, Theory, Debate," *Corrections Magazine*, no. 3 (September 1977): 3–13.

7. E. Lindsey, "Historical Origins of the Sanction of Imprisonment for Serious Crimes," *Journal of Criminal Law and Criminology* 16, no. 1 (1925): 9–26.

8. David Dressler, *The Parole Chief* (New York: Viking Press, 1951).

9. Margaret Werner Cahalan, *Historical Corrections Statistics in the United States, 1850–1984* (Washington, D.C.: U.S. Government Printing Office, 1986).

10. Edward J. Latessa and Harry E. Allen, *Corrections in the Community,* 2nd ed. (Cincinnati, Ohio: Anderson, 1999), p. 159.

11. Seymour Halleck, *The Politics of Therapy* (New York: Science House, 1971).

12. Norval Morris, *The Future of Imprisonment* (Chicago: University of Chicago Press, 1974).

13. John Irwin, "Adaptation to Being Corrected: Corrections from the Convict's Perspective," in *Sociology of Corrections*, edited by R. G. Legar and J. R. Stratton (New York: Wiley, 1977), pp. 276–300.

14. Howard Abadinsky, *Probation and Parole: Corrections in the Community*, 13th ed. (Boston, MA: Pearson Education, 2018), p. 141.

15. Douglas Lipton, Robert Martinson, and Judith Wilks, *The Effectiveness of Correctional Treatment and What Works: A Survey of Treatment Evaluation Studies* (New York: Praeger, 1975).

16. David Fogel, *We Are the Living Proof* (Cincinnati, Ohio: Anderson, 1975).

17. Andrew von Hirsch and Kathleen J. Hanrahan, *Abolish Parole?* (Washington, D.C.: U.S. Government Printing Office, 1978).

18. Twentieth Century Task Force on Sentencing, *Fair and Certain Punishment* (New York: McGraw-Hill, 1976).

19. Bureau of Justice Statistics, *National Prisoner Statistics* (Washington, D.C.: U.S. Department of Justice, 1977).

20. Alvin Blumstein, "Prisons: A Policy Challenge," in *Crime: Public Policies for Crime Control*, edited by James Q. Wilson and Joan Petersilia (Oakland, Calif.: Institute for Contemporary Studies, 2002), pp. 451–452.

21. Jill R. Furniss, "The Population Boom," *Corrections Today* 58, no. 1 (1996): 38–43.

22. E. Ann Carson, "Prisoners in 2013," *BJS Bulletin* (Washington, D.C.: U.S. Department of Justice, 2014), Table 1, p. 2.

23. E. Ann Carson, "Prisoners in 2016," *BJS Bulletin* (Washington, DC: U.S. Department of Justice, 2018), p. 11.

24. Calculated using figures from Danielle Kaeble and Thomas P. Bonczar, "Probation and Parole in the United States, 2015," *BJS Bulletin* (Washington, D.C.: U.S. Department of Justice, December 2016), p. 22.

25. Kaeble and Bonczar, op. cit., p. 7.

26. Ibid.

27. *Greenholtz v. Inmates of the Nebraska Penal and Correctional Complex*, 99 S. Ct. 2100 (1979).

28. Edward E. Rhine, William R. Smith, and Ronald W. Jackson, *Paroling Authorities: Recent History and Current Practice* (Laurel, M.d.: American Correctional Association, 1991), p. 54.

29. President's Commission on Law Enforcement and Administration of Justice, *Task Force Report: Corrections* (Washington, D.C.: U.S. Government Printing Office, 1967), p. 67.

30. Eric Levenson, "O.J. Simpson Granted Parole: I've Done My Time," *CNN On Line*, July 21, 2017, available at http://www.cnn.com/2017/07/20/us/oj-simpson-parole-hearing/index.html (accessed September 4, 2017).

31. Ohio Department of Rehabilitation and Correction, "APA Offender Classification," Policy Section 501, Number 28, February 15, 2001, p. 3.

32. Ibid., pp. 5–6.

33. Danielle Kaeble and Thomas P. Bonczar, "Probation and Parole in the United States, 2015," *BJS Bulletin* (Washington, D.C.: U.S. Department of Justice, 2016), p. 7.

34. The development and end result of this process is described in James, L. Johnson, Christopher T. Lowenkamp, Scott W. Vanbenshoten, and Charles R. Robinson, "The Construction and Validation of the Federal Post Conviction Risk Assessment (PCRA)," *Federal Probation* 75, no. 2 (September 2011): 16–29.

35. Erin Harbinson, *Is Corrections "Collar" Blind: Examining the Predictive Validity of a Risk/Need Assessment Tool on White-Collar Offenders* (Washington, D.C.: Administrative Office of the U.S. Courts, 2017).

36. Occupational Handbook Outlook, "Probation Officers and Correctional Treatment Specialists," Bureau of Labor Statistics, available at www.bls.gov/ooh/community-and-social-service/probation-officers-and-correctional-treatment-specialists.htm (accessed September 5, 2017). Note, even though it only lists probation officers, parole officers are also included in this number.

37. Kaeble and Bonczar, p. 24.

38. *Morrissey v. Brewer*, 408 U.S. 471 (1972).

39. *Gagnon v. Scarpelli*, 411 U.S. 778 (1973).

40. Kaeble and Bonczar, p. 24.

41. Patrick A. Langan and David J. Levin, "Recidivism of Prisoners Released in 1994," *Bureau of Justice Statistics Special Report* (Washington, D.C.: U.S. Department of Justice, June 2002), p. 1.

42. Pew Center on the States, *State of Recidivism: The Revolving Door of America's Prisons* (Washington, D.C.: Pew Center on the States, 2011), p. 2.

43. Ibid.

44. Howard R. Sacks and Charles H. Logan, "Does Parole Make a (Lasting) Difference?" in *Criminal Justice: Law and Politics*, 4th ed., edited by George F. Cole (Pacific Grove, Calif.: Brooks/Cole, 1984), pp. 362–378.

45. William J. Sabol, William P. Adams, Barbara Parthasarathy, and Yan Yuan, *Offenders Returning to Federal Prison, 1986–1997* (Washington, D.C.: U.S Department of Justice, 2000), p. 6.

46. Michael Ostermann and Jordan M. Hyatt, "Is Something Better than Nothing? The Effect of Short Terms of Mandatory Parole Supervision," *Justice Quarterly Online* (November 2014), available at http://dx.doi.org/10.1080/07418825.2014.980300 (accessed December 18, 2014).

47. Amy Solomon, "Does Parole Supervision Work: Research Findings and Policy Opportunities," *Perspectives* 30, no. 2 (Spring 2006): 234–251.

48. G. G. Gaes, T. J. Flanagan, L. L. Motiuk, and L. Stewart, "Adult Correctional Treatment," in *Prisons*, edited by Michael Tonry and Joan Petersilia (Chicago: University of Chicago Press, 1999), pp. 361–426.

49. Carson and Anderson, p. 11.

50. Marta Nelson, Perry Deess, and Charlotte Allen, "The First Month Out: Post–Incarceration Experiences in New York City" (Monograph, the Vera Institute, September 1999).

51. Joan Petersilia, "When Prisoners Return to the Community: Political, Economic, and Social Consequences," *Corrections Management Quarterly* 5, no. 3 (2001): 4.

52. Charles M. Terry, "From C-Block to Academic: You Can't Get There from Here," in *Convict Criminology*, edited by Jeffrey Ian Ross and Stephen C. Richards (Belmont, Calif.: Wadsworth, 2003), p. 105.

53. Paula M. Ditton and Doris J. Wilson, *Truth in Sentencing in State Prisons* (Washington, D.C.: U.S. Department of Justice, Bureau of Justice Statistics, 1999).

54. Thomas E. Feucht and Joseph Gfroerer, "Mental and Substance Use Disorders among Adult Men on Probation or Parole: Some Success Against a Persistent Challenge," *The SAMSHA Data Review* (Washington, D.C.: U.S. Department of Justice, 2011), p. 1.

55. Camille Graham Camp and George M. Camp, *The 2001 Corrections Yearbook: Adult Systems* (Middletown, CN: Criminal Justice Institute, 2002), p. 192.

56. For a good review of programs that assist in reentry, see Richard P. Seiter and Karen R. Kadela, "Prisoner Reentry: What Works, What Doesn't, and What's Promising," *Crime and Delinquency* 49, no. 3 (April 2003): 360–388.

57. James J. Stephan, "Census of State and Federal Correctional Facilities, 2005," *Bureau of Justice Statistics: National Prisoner Statistics Program* (Washington, D.C.: U.S. Department of Justice, October 2008), p. 5.

58. From reports from states noted in various years of Camp and Camp.

59. See Gwen Rubenstein and Debbi Mukamal, "Welfare and Housing—Denial of Benefits to Drug Offenders," in *Invisible Punishment: The Collateral Consequences of Mass Imprisonment*, edited by Marc Mauer and Meda Chesney-Lind (New York: New Press, 2002), pp. 37–58.

60. Catherine E. Forrest, *Collateral Consequences of a Criminal Conviction: Impact on Corrections and Reentry* (Washington, D.C.: U.S. Department of Justice, 2016).

61. For a complete update on actions to reform collateral consequences across the United States, see *Four Years of Second Chance Reforms, 2013–2016: Restoration of Rights and Relief from Collateral Consequences* (Washington, D.C.: Collateral Consequences Resource Center, 2017).

62. Donald Burman, "Families and Incarceration," in *Invisible Punishment: The Collateral Consequences of Mass Imprisonment*, edited by Marc Mauer and Meda Chesney-Lind (New York: New Press, 2002), p. 117.

63. Christopher J. Mumola, *Bureau of Justice Statistics Special Report: Incarcerated Parents and Their Children* (Washington, D.C.: U.S. Department of Justice, 2000).

64. A good review of collateral sanctions can be found at Kevin G. Buckler and Lawrence F. Travis, "Reanalyzing the Prevalence and Social Context of Collateral Consequences Statutes," *Journal of Criminal Justice* 31, no. 5 (September/October 2003): 435–453.

65. Christopher Uggen and Jeremy Staff, "Work as a Turning Point for Criminal Offenders," *Corrections Management Quarterly* 5, no. 4 (2001): 1–16.

66. Becky Deeb, "The Indiana Department of Correction an Department of Workforce Development Team Up to Help Ex-Offenders and Indiana Businesses," *Corrections Today* 77, no. 1 (January/February 2015): 56–57.

67. Nancy La Vigne, Elizabeth Davies, Tobi Palmer, and Robin Halberstadt, *Release Planning for Successful Reentry* (Washington, D.C.: Urban Institute Justice Policy Center, September 2008).

68. The Justice Center, *The Report of the Re-Entry Policy Council* (New York: Council of State Governments, 2005).

69. A review of the reported successful program implementation can be found at Christine Linquist, et al., *Second Chance Act Offender Reentry Demonstration Project – Final Implementation Lessons Learned* (Washington, D.C.: Urban Institute, 2007).

70. A good summary of federal assistance of prisoner reentry can be found at Nathan James, *Offender Reentry: Correctional Statistics, Reintegration into the Community, and Recidivism* (Washington, D.C.: Congressional Research Service, 2015).

71. Kristin Stainbrook, Jeanine Hanna, and Amy Salomon, *Residential Substance Abuse Treatment Study: The Characteristics and Components of RSAT Funded Treatment and Aftercare Services* (Sudbury, MA: Advocates for Human Potential, Inc., 2017).

72. Shelli B. Rossman, et al., *Second Chance Act Adult Offender Reentry Demonstration Projects, Evidence-Based Practices: Screening and Assessment* (Washington, D.C.: U.S. Department of Justice, 2016).

73. Christine Linquist, et al., *Second Chance Act Adult Offender Reentry Demonstration Programs: Implementation Challenges and Lessons Learned* (Washington, D.C.: U.S. Department of Justice, 2015).

74. Stephen E. Vance, "Federal Reentry Court Evaluations: A Summary of Recent Evaluations," *Federal Probation* 75, no. 2 (September 2011): 64–73.

75. U.S. Department of Justice, *Survey of Inmates in State and Federal Correctional Facilities* (Ann Arbor, Mich.: Inter-University Consortium for Political and Social Research, 2004).

76. Bruce Western, *Punishment and Inequality in America*, chapter 5 (New York: Russell Sage Foundation, 2006).

77. For a summary of the three evaluations, see Bruce Western, *From Prison to Work: A Proposal for a National Prisoner Reentry Program* (Washington, D.C.: The Brookings Institution, December 2008), pp. 10–11.

78. Nora E. Wikoff, *Labor Force Participation and Crime Among Serious and Violent Former Prisoners*, Dissertation presented at Washington University (St. Louis, MO: Washington University, 2015).

79. Christy A. Visher, Pamela K. Lattimore, Kelle Barrick, and Stephen Tueller, "Evaluating the Long-Term Effects of Prisoner Reentry Services on Recidivism: What Types of Services Matter?" *Justice Quarterly* 34, no. 1 (2017): 136–165.

80. Seiter and Kadela, "Prisoner Reentry."

81. Washington Department of Corrections, *A Re-Entry Focused Correctional System* (Olympia, Wash.: Government Management, Accountability, and Performance Forum, November 2006).

82. Jeremy Travis, "But They All Come Back: Rethinking Prisoner Reentry," *Corrections Management Quarterly* 5, no. 3 (2001): 23–33.

83. Victoria C. Myers, formerly a member of the Missouri Parole Board, developed these scenarios.

Chapter 7

1. Heather C. West and William J. Sabol, *Prison Inmates at Midyear 2008—Statistical Tables* (Washington, D.C.: U.S. Department of Justice, Bureau of Justice Statistics, March 2009), p. 2.

2. E. Ann Carson, "Prisoners in 2016," *BJS Bulletin* (Washington, D.C.: U.S. Department of Justice, 2018), p. 8.

3. Ibid., p. 9.

4. Lawrence A. Greenfeld and Tracy L. Snell, *Women Offenders* (Washington, D.C.: U.S. Department of Justice, Bureau of Justice Statistics, 1999), p. 6.
5. Carson and Anderson, Ibid., and Paul Guerino, Paige M. Harrison, and William J. Sabol, "Prisoners in 2010," *BJS Bulletin* (Washington, D.C.: U.S. Department of Justice, 2011), p. 3.
6. Danielle Kaeble and Thomas P. Bonczar, "Probation and Parole in the United States, 2015," *BJS Bulletin* (Washington, D.C.: U.S. Department of Justice, 2016), pp. 5 and 7.
7. Bureau of Justice Statistics Correctional Surveys (*National Probation Data Survey, National Prisoner Statistics, Survey of Jails, and National Parole Data Survey*) as presented in *Correctional Populations in the United States*, 1997 (Washington, D.C.: U.S. Department of Justice, 1998)
8. Calculated from Carson, "Prisoners in 2016," Table 3, p. 5.
9. Kaeble an Bonczar, op.cit., Table 4, p. 5.
10. Carson, Table 6, p. 8.
11. National Urban League, "State of Black America: Message to the President," *Executive Summary* (Washington, D.C.: National Urban League, 2009), p. 1.
12. William Wilbanks, *The Myth of a Racist Criminal Justice System* (Monterey, Calif.: Brooks/Cole, 1987), pp. 5, 6.
13. *Crime in the United States 2015*, "Arrests by Race and Ethnicity, 2015," Table 43a, available at https://ucr.fbi.gov/crime-in-the-u.s/2015/crime-in-the-u.s.-2015/tables/table-43 (accessed September 6, 2017).
14. John M. Klofas, "Drugs and Justice: The Impact of Drugs on Criminal Justice in a Metropolitan Community," *Crime and Delinquency* 39, no. 2 (1993): 204.
15. Ashley Nellis, *The Color of Justice: Racial and Ethnic Disparity in State Prisons* (Washington, D.C.: The Sentencing Project, 2016).
16. Nelis, Ibid. This report cites several studies that support these conclusions.
17. Alfred Blumstein, "On Racial Disproportionately of the United States' Prison Populations," *Journal of Criminal Law and Criminology* 73, no. 3 (1982): 1259–1281, and Alfred Blumstein, "Racial Disproportionality of US Prison Populations Revisited," *University of Colorado Law Review* 64, no. 3 (1993): 743–760.
18. Michael Tonry and Matthew Melewski, "The Malign Effects of Drug and Crime Control Policies on Black Americans," *Crime and Justice* 37, no. 1 (2008): 1–44.
19. Eric P. Baumer, *Reassessing and Redirecting Research on Race and Sentencing*, Draft manuscript prepared for the Symposium on the Past and Future of Empirical Sentencing Research, University of Albany (Tallahassee, FL: Florida State University, 2010).
20. Jeremy Travis, Bruce Western, and Steve Redburn, Editors, *The Growth of Incarceration in the United States: Exploring Causes and Consequences* (Washington, D.C.: The National Academies Press, 2014).
21. Allen J. Beck and Paige M. Harrison, "Prisoners in 2000," *Bureau of Justice Statistics Bulletin* (Washington, D.C.: U.S. Department of Justice, 2001), p. 10; and Carson, Table 9, p. 15.
22. Kenneth Moritsugu, "Inmate Chronological Age versus Physical Age," in *Long-Term Confinement and the Aging Inmate Population* (Washington, D.C.: Federal Bureau of Prisons, 1990), pp. 22–25.
23. U.S. Census Bureau, U.S. Population by Sex and Age, 2014, available at https://census.gov/data/tables/2014/demo/age-and-sex/2014-age-sex-composition.html (accessed September 7, 2017).
24. Two sources describe these issues well. See Tina Maschi, Mary Beth Morrissey, Russ Immarigeon, and Samantha L. Sutfin, *Aging Prisoners: A Crisis in Need of Intervention* (New York, NY: Fordham University, 2012), and J. Kerbs and Jennifer M. Jolley, *Senior Citizens behind Bars: Challenges for the Criminal Justice System* (Boulder, Colo.: Lynne Rienner Publishers, 2014).
25. Michael Ollove, *Elderly Inmates Burden State Prisons* (Washington, D.C.: Pew Charitable Trusts, 2016).
26. Kevin Strom, *Profile of State Prisoners under Age 18, 1985–1997*, NCJ 176989 (Washington, D.C.: U.S. Department of Justice, Bureau of Justice Statistics, February 2000), p. 1.
27. Carson, p. 16.
28. For a good overview of the reform of mandatory sentencing policies, see Ram Subramanian and Ruth Delaney, *Playbook for Change? States Reconsider Mandatory Sentences* (New York, NY: Very Institute of Justice, 2014).
29. Jerry Markon and Rachel Weiner, "Thousands of Felons Could Have Drug Sentences Lessened," *The Washington Post*, July 18, 2014, available at http://www.washingtonpost.com/politics/thousands-of-felons-could-have-drug-sentences-lessened/2014/07/18/4876209e-0eb1-11e4-8341-b8072b1e7348_story.html?wpisrc=nl_eve?wpisrc=nl_eve.
30. Carson, "Prisoners in 2013," Table 17, p. 18.
31. Federal Bureau of Investigation, "Ten Year Arrest Trends by Sex," *Uniform Crime Reports, 2015* (Washington, D.C.: U.S. Department of Justice, 2016), Table 33, available at https://ucr.fbi.gov/crime-in-the-u.s/2015/crime-in-the-u.s.-2015/tables/table-33 (accessed September 6, 2017).
32. Carson, p. 3.
33. Ibid.
34. Kaeble and Bonczar, pp. 5 and 7.
35. FBI, *Uniform Crime Reports*, op.cit.
36. Carson, p. 18.
37. James J. Stephan, "Census of State and Federal Correctional Facilities, 2005," *National Prisoner Statistics Program* (Washington, D.C.: U.S. Department of Justice, October 2008), Appendix Table 11.
38. Peter M. Carlson, "Inmate Classification," in *Prison and Jail Administration*, 3rd ed., edited by Peter M. Carlson (Burlington, Mass.: Jones and Bartlett Learning, 2015), p. 53.
39. FBI, *Uniform Crime Reports*, op. cit.
40. Lawrence A. Greenfeld and Tracy L. Snell, *Women Offenders* (Washington, D.C.: U.S. Department of Justice, Bureau of Justice Statistics, 1999), p. 5.
41. Kaeble and Bonczar, pp. 5 and 7; Todd Minton and Zhen Zeng, "Jail Inmates in 2015," *BJS Bulletin* (Washington, D.C.: U.S. Department of Justice, 2016), p. 4; and Carson and Anderson, p. 3.
42. Meda Chesney-Lind, "The Forgotten Offender, Women in Prison: From Partial Justice to Vengeful Equity," in *Exploring Corrections: A Book of Readings*, edited by Tara Gray (Boston: Allyn & Bacon, 2002), p. 8.
43. Reported in Greenfeld and Snell, *Women Offenders*, p. 11.
44. Patrick A. Langan and David J. Levin, "Recidivism of Prisoners Released in 1994," *Bureau of Justice Statistics Special Report* (Washington, D.C.: U.S. Department of Justice, 2002), Table 8, p. 7.
45. Beth M. Huebner, Christina DeJong, and Jennifer Cobbina, "Women Coming Home: Long-Term Patterns of Recidivism," *Justice Quarterly* 27, no. 2 (April 2010): 225–254.
46. Matthew R. Durose, Alexia D. Cooper, and Howard N. Snyder, "Recidivism of Prisoners Released in 30 States in 2005: Patterns from 2005 to 2010," *BJS Special Report* (Washington, D.C.: U.S. Department of Justice, 2014), pp. 1 and 11.
47. Allen J. Beck, *Prisoners in 1998* (Washington, D.C.: U.S. Department of Justice, 1999).
48. Carson, "Prisoners in 2016," p. 3.
49. Ibid., pp. 18 and 20.
50. Ibid., p. 8.
51. UCR, op.cit.
52. Carson, "Prisoners in 2013," p. 16.
53. Greenfeld and Snell, *Women Offenders*.
54. Lauren E. Glaze and Laura M. Maruschak, *Parents in Prison and Their Minor Children* (Washington, D.C.: U.S. Department of Justice, Bureau of Justice Statistics, August, 2008), p. 3.
55. Merry Morash, Timothy S. Bynum, and Barbara A. Koons, "Women Offenders: Programming Needs and Promising Approaches," *National Institute of Justice: Research in Brief* (August 1998): 7.
56. Unfortunately, Christine (as a result of her years on the street and as a drug addict) died in 2014. She had remarried, and had another daughter. Her husband also died in 2014, and relatives are now raising her daughter. My wife and I thought of Christine as a friend, and it was always troubling to see her struggle with health, employment, and financial issues. Although she did everything she could to turn her life around, the damage of those years on the street could not be ameliorated.
57. Interview: A Female Offender - Christine Wideman. Reprinted wit Permission.
58. Glaze and Maruschak, *Parents in Prison and Their Minor Children*, pp. 3, 4, and 16.
59. Phyllis Jo Baunach, *Mothers in Prison* (New Brunswick, N.J.: Transaction, 1984).

60. Caitlin M. Novero, Ann Booker Loper, and Janet I. Warren, "Second-Generation Prisoners: Adjustment Patterns for Inmates with a History of Parental Incarceration," *Criminal Justice and Behavior* 38, no. 8 (August 2011): 761–778.

61. Diana DeHart, Cheri Shapiro, and James W. Hardin, *Impact of Incarceration on Families: A Single-Jurisdiction Pilot Study Using Triangulated Administrative Data and Qualitative Interviews* (Washington, D.C.: U.S. Department of Justice, 2017). A good overview is included in Eric Martin, "Hidden Consequences: The Impact of Incarceration on Dependent Children," *NIJ Journal* no. 278 (May 2017): 1–7.

62. For a description of recent Girl Scouts Beyond Bars programs, see the website available at http://www.inmatemoms.org/index.aspx (accessed September 5, 2017). An article describing the origination of such programs is Marilyn C. Moses, "The Girl Scouts behind Bars Program: Keeping Incarcerated Mothers and Their Daughters Together," in *National Institute of Justice Program Focus* (October, 1992): 1–11.

63. Stacy Calhound, Nena Messina, Jerome Cartier, and Stephanie Torres, "Implementing Gender Responsive Treatment for Women in Prison: Client and Staff Perspectives," *Federal Probation* 74, no. 3 (December 2010): 27–33.

64. Christopher C. Mumola and Jennifer C. Karberg, "Drug Use and Dependence, State and Federal Prisoners, 2004," *Bureau of Justice Statistics Special Report* (Washington, D.C.: U.S. Department of Justice, October 2006), p. 3.

65. Greenfeld and Snell, *Women Offenders,* p. 8.

66. Ibid.

67. Center for Substance Abuse Treatment, *Substance Abuse Treatment for Incarcerated Women Offenders: Guide to Promising Practices* (Rockville, Md.: Department of Health and Human Services, Public Health Service, 1997), p. 2.

68. Bonnie L. Green, et al., "Trauma Experiences and Mental Health Among Incarcerated Women," *Psychological Trauma-Theory Research Practice and Policy* 8, no. 4 (July 2016): 455–463.

69. Stephan, "Census of State and Federal Correctional Facilities, 2005," Appendix Table 19.

70. Camille Graham Camp and George M. Camp, *The Corrections Yearbook, 2002* (Middletown, Conn.: Criminal Justice Institute, 2003), p. 136.

71. Jennifer C. Karberg and Doris J. James, *Substance Dependence, Abuse, and Treatment of Jail Inmates, 2002* (Washington, D.C.: U.S. Department of Justice, Bureau of Justice Statistics Bulletin, July 2005), p. 10.

72. Steven Belenko and Kimberly A. Houser, "Gender Differences in Prison-Based Drug Treatment Participation," *International Journal of Offender Therapy and Comparative Criminology* 56, no. 5 (August 2012): 790–810.

73. Jennifer R. Scroggins and Sara Malley, "Reentry and the (Unmet) Needs of Women," *Journal of Offender Rehabilitation* 49, no. 2 (February/March 2010): 146–163.

74. Chesney-Lind, "Forgotten Offender, Women in Prison," p. 11.

75. Jacqueline M. Moore, "Privatization of Inmate Health Care: A New Approach to an Old Problem," *Corrections Management Quarterly* 2, no. 2 (1998): 46.

76. Ibid., p. 47.

77. The special needs of female offenders were identified in Robert R. Ross and Elizabeth A. Fabiano, *Female Offenders: Correctional Afterthoughts* (Jefferson, N.C.: McFarland, 1986), and continue in Kathryn D. Morgan, "Issues in Female Inmate Health: Results from a Southeastern State," *Women & Criminal Justice* 23, no. 2 (April–June 2013): 121–142.

78. Greenfeld and Snell, *Women Offenders,* p. 8.

79. Richard P. Seiter, *Correctional Administration: Integrating Theory and Practice,* 3rd ed. (Columbus, OH: Pearson Education, 2017), pp. 351–352.

80. Patricia L. Hardyman and Patricia Van Voorhis, *Developing Gender-Specific Classification Systems for Women Offenders* (Washington, D.C.: U.S. Department of Justice, 2004).

81. Becky Ney, *Ten Facts About Women in Jails* (Hagerstown, MD: American Jail Association, 2014).

82. An analysis of employment issues is found in Shawn M. Flower, *Employment and Female Offenders: An Update of the Empirical Research* (Washington, D.C.: U.S. Department of Justice, 2010).

83. Peggy Burke, Rochelle Giguere, and Leilah Gilligan, *Special Challenges Facing Parole* (Washington, D.C.: U.S. Department of Justice, 2011).

84. Doris J. James and Lauren Glaze, *Special Report: Mental Health Problems of Prison and Jail Inmates* (Washington, D.C.: U.S. Department of Justice, 2006).

85. Christine M. Sarteschi and Michael G. Vaughn, "Double Jeopardy: A Review of Women Offenders' Mental Health and Substance Abuse Characteristics," *Victims & Offenders* 5, no. 2 (April 2010): 161–182.

86. *Barefield v. Leach*, No. 10282 (D. N.M., 1974), 196.

87. *Pargo v. Elliott*, 49 F.3d 1355 (8th Cir. 1995), 196.

88. Nicole H. Rafter, *Partial Justice: Women, Prison, and Social Control,* 2nd ed. (New Brunswick, N.J.: Transaction, 1990).

89. Jennifer C. Karberg and James J. Stephan, *Census of State and Federal Correctional Facilities, 2000* (Washington, D.C.: U.S. Department of Justice, 2003).

90. Carson, p. 3.

Chapter 8

1. Federal Bureau of Investigation, *Crime in the United States, 2015*, Ten Year Arrest Trends by Age, available at https://ucr.fbi.gov/crime-in-the-u.s/2015/crime-in-the-u.s.-2015/tables/table-32 (accessed September 8, 2017).

   Note: Also look at *Statistical Briefing Book* (Washington, D.C.: U.S. Department of Justice), available at http://www.ojjdp.gov/ojstatbb/crime/JAR_Display.asp?ID=qa05201&text=yes.

2. Howard N. Snyder, Melissa Sickmund, and Eileen Poe-Yamagata, *Juvenile Offenders and Victims: 1996 Update on Violence* (Washington, D.C.: U.S. Department of Justice, 1996), p. 21.

3. Alfred Blumstein, "Youth, Violence, Guns, and the Illicit-Drug Industry," *Journal of Criminal Law and Criminology* 86, no. 1 (1995): 14.

4. Data from FBI, *Crime in the United States,* Ten Year Arrest Trends, by Age, op. cit.

5. Federal Bureau of Investigation, *Crime in the United States, 2015*, Ten Year Arrest Trends by Sex, available at https://ucr.fbi.gov/crime-in-the-u.s/2015/crime-in-the-u.s.-2015/tables/table-33 (accessed September 12, 2017).

6. FBI, Ten Year Arrest Trends by Age, op. cit.

7. A description of the Refuge Period and other developments in the juvenile justice system can be found in Todd R. Clear, George F. Cole, and Michael D. Reisig, *American Corrections,* 10th ed. (Belmont, Calif.: Wadsworth, 2013), pp. 434–439.

8. Howard N. Snyder and Melissa Sickmund, *Juvenile Offenders and Victims: 1999 National Report* (Washington, D.C.: U.S. Department of Justice, National Center for Juvenile Justice, September 1999), p. 86.

9. The Juvenile Justice and Delinquency Prevention Act of 1974 (Public Law 93–415) encouraged removing status offenders from the juvenile court system.

10. John J. DiIulio, Jr., "The Question of Black Crime," *Public Interest* (Fall 1994): 3–12.

11. For a good overview, see Patrick Griffin, Sean Addie, Benjamin Adams, and Kathy Firestine, "Trying Juveniles as Adults: An Analysis of State Transfer Laws and Reporting," *OJJDP National Report Series* (Washington, D.C.: U.S. Department of Justice, 2011).

12. James A. Gondles, Jr., "Kids Are Kids, Not Adults," *Corrections Today* (June 1997): 3.

13. "Mission Statement," Missouri Department of Corrections, available at http://doc.mo.gov/Documents/OD/missionvisionvalues.pdf (accessed September 12, 2017).

14. State of Missouri Department of Social Services, available at http://dss.mo.gov/dys/ (accessed September 12, 2017).

15. Council of Juvenile Correctional Administrators, "Profile of Agencies," *CJCA Yearbook* (Braintree, MA: Council of Juvenile Correctional Administrators, 2013), p. 7.

16. Sarah Hockenberry and CharlesPuzzanchera, *Juvenile Court Statistics 2013* (Pittsburgh, PA: National Center for Juvenile Justice, 2015), pp. 6 and 31.

17. Melissa Sickmund and Charles Puzzanchera, *Juvenile Offenders and Victims: 2014 National Report* (Washington, D.C.: U.S. Department of Justice, 2014), p. 94.
18. National Council on Crime and Delinquency, *Juvenile Justice Policy Statement* (San Francisco: NCCD, 1991).
19. Hockenberry and Puzzanchera, op. cit., p. 32.
20. Sickmond and Puzzanchera, op. cit., p. 220.
21. Op. cit., p. 36.
22. Howard Abadinsky, *Probation and Parole: Corrections in the Community*, 13th edition (Boston, MA: Pearson Education, 2018), p. 52.
23. Op. cit., p. 46.
24. Sarah Hockenberry, "Juveniles in Residential Placement, 2013," *OJJDP National Report Series* (Washington, D.C.: U.S. Department of Justice 2016), p. 3.
25. Ibid.
26. Ibid., p. 11.
27. James Austin, Kelly Dedel Johnson, and Ronald Weitzer, "Alternatives to the Secure Detention and Confinement of Juvenile Offenders," *Juvenile Justice Bulletin* (Washington, D.C.: Office of Juvenile Justice and Delinquency Prevention, 2005).
28. Data from the Ohio Department of Youth Services website, available at http://dys.ohio.gov/Portals/0/PDFs/Statistics/Mfs_2017Sep.pdf (accessed September 12, 2017).
29. Interview with "The Creator of the RECLAIM Ohio Plan" - Geno Natalucci-Persichetti. Reprinted with Permission.
30. Shaena M. Fazal, *Safely Home: Reducing Youth Incarceration and Achieving Positive Youth Outcomes for High and Complex Need Youth through Effective Community-Based Programs* (Washington, D.C.: Youth Advocate Programs Policy & Advocacy Center, 2014), p. iv.
31. Op. cit., p. 5.
32. Robert Wiederstein, "Juvenile Justice Reform: More Bang for the Buck," *Bench and Bar* 77, no. 1 (January 2013): 11–15.
33. Ibid.
34. Antoinette Davis, Angela Irvine, and Jason Ziedenberg, *Supervision Strategies for Justice-Involved Youth* (San Francisco, C.A.: National Council of Crime and Delinquency, 2014).
35. Sickmund and Puzzanchera, op. cit., p. 168.
36. Stephanie Bontrager Ryan, Kristin Winokur Early, Gregory Hand, and Steven Chapman, "Juvenile Justice Interventions: System Escalation and Effective Alternatives to Residential Placement," *Journal of Offender Rehabilitation* 52, no. 5–8 (December 2013): 358–375.
37. The Editorial Board, "Jails and Kids, A Bad Combination," *The New York Times*, Editorial Section, December 28, 2014.
38. *Kent v. United States*, 383 U.S. 541, 86 S. Ct. 1045 (1966).
39. *In re Gault*, 387 U.S. 1, 87 S. Ct. 1428 (1967).
40. *In re Winship*, 397 U.S. 358, 90 S. Ct. 1068 (1970).
41. *McKeiver v. Pennsylvania*, 403 U.S. 528, 91 S. Ct. 1976 (1971).
42. *Breed v. Jones*, U.S. 519, 95 S. Ct. 1779 (1975).
43. *Oklahoma Publishing Company v. District Court in and for Oklahoma City*, 480 U.S. 308, 97 S. Ct. 1045 (1977).
44. *Smith v. Daily Mail Publishing Company*, 443 U.S. 97, 99 S. Ct. 2667 (1979).
45. *Fare v. Michael C.*, 442 U.S. 707 (1979).
46. *Schall v. Martin*, 467 U.S. 253, 104 S. Ct. 2403 (1984).
47. *Eddings v. Oklahoma*, 455 U.S. 104 (1982).
48. *Stanford v. Kentucky*, 492 U.S. 361 (1989).
49. *In re Stanford*, 123 S. Ct. 472 (2002).
50. Quoted in Associated Press, "Supreme Court Appears One Vote Shy of Rejecting Death Penalty for Young Killers," *St. Louis Post Dispatch*, January 28, 2003, p. 2.
51. *Roper v. Simmons*, 000 U.S. 03-633 (2005).
52. *Graham. v. Florida*, 560 U.S (2010).
53. *Miller v. Alabama*, 132 U.S. 548 (2011) and *Jackson v. Hobbs*, U.S. case 10-9647 (2012).
54. The term "death-in-prison" sentence was used for sentences of life without parole in a book I highly recommend regarding a lawyer's work at the Equal Justice Initiative, a legal practice to defend the poor, wrongly convicted, and those unjustly treated by our criminal justice system. The book cite is, Bryan Stevenson, *Just Mercy: A Story of Justice and Redemption* (New York: NY: Spiegel & Grau, 2015).
55. Ronald, C. Huff, "Comparing the Criminal Behavior of Youth Gangs and At-Risk Youth," *National Institute of Justice Research in Brief* (Washington, D.C.: U.S. Department of Justice, 1998). See also, Sarah R. Battin-Pearson, Terence P. Thornberry, J. David Hawkins, and Marvin D. Krohn, *Gang Membership, Delinquent Peers, and Delinquent Behavior* (Washington, D.C.: U.S. Department of Justice, Office of Juvenile Justice and Delinquency Prevention, October 1998), p. 1.
56. C. L. Maxson, K. J. Woods, and M. W. Klein, "Street Gang Migration: How Big a Threat," *National Institute of Justice Journal* 230 (February 1996): 26–31.
57. National Gang Center, *2012 National Youth Gang Survey*, available at https://www.nationalgangcenter.gov/Survey-Analysis/Measuring-the-Extent-of-Gang-Problems#estimatednumbergangs (accessed September 13, 2017).
58. National Gang Center, *2012 National Youth Gang Survey*, available at https://www.nationalgangcenter.gov/Survey-Analysis/Demographics#anchorregm (accessed September 12, 2017).
59. Arlen Egley, Jr., James C. Howell, and Meena Harris, "Highlights of the 2012 National Youth Gang Survey," *OJJDP Juvenile Justice Fact Sheet* (Washington, D.C.: U.S. Department of Justice, 2014), p. 2.
60. Op. cit., p. 3.
61. For a description of how police organize to target the suppression of youth gang activity, see Vincent J. Webb and Charles Katz, "Policing Gangs in an Era of Community Policing," in *Policing Gangs and Youth Violence*, edited by Scott Decker (Belmont, Calif.: Thompson-Wadsworth, 2003), pp. 17–49.
62. Finn-Aage Esbensen et al., *National Evaluation of the Gang Resistance Education and Training (GREAT) Program* (Washington, D.C.: U.S. Department of Justice, 2002).
63. See *The Queen v. Smith*, 1 Cox C.C. 260 (1845); 42 Am.Jur.2d, Infants, §§ 9, 45, 142.
64. A good guide for states is *Competency to Stand Trial in Juvenile Court: Recommendations for Policymakers* (Washington, D.C.: National Juvenile Justice Network, 2012).
65. Sue Hammond, *Mental Health Needs of Juvenile Offenders* (Washington, D.C.: National Conference of State Legislators, 2007), p. 4.
66. Linda Teplin, et al., "The Northwestern Juvenile Project: Overview," *OJJDP Juvenile Justice Bulletin* (Washington, D.C.: U.S. Department of Justice, 2013).
67. This shift is described in Sickmund and Puzzanchera, op. cit., p. 87.
68. Curtis C. VanderWaal, Duane C. McBride, Yvonne M. Terry-McElrath, and Holly VanBuren, *Breaking the Juvenile Drug-Crime Cycle: A Guide for Practitioners and Policymakers* (Washington, D.C.: U.S. Department of Justice, National Institute of Justice, May 2001), p. 2.
69. Kevin J. Strom, *Profile of State Prisoners under Age 18, 1985–97* (Washington, D.C.: U.S. Department of Justice, Bureau of Justice Statistics, February 2000), p. 1.
70. E. Ann Carson and Elizabeth Anderson, "Prisoners in 2015," *BJS Bulletin* (Washington, D.C.: U.S. Department of Justice, 2016), p. 33.

Chapter 9

1. For a good history of this transition, see Howard N. Snyder, Melissa Sickmund, and Eileen Poe-Yamagata, *Juvenile Transfers to Criminal Courts in the 1990s: Lessons Learned from Four Studies* (Washington, D.C.: U.S. Department of Justice, Office of Juvenile Justice and Delinquency Prevention, August 2000), p. xi.
2. Benjamin Adams and Sadie Addie, "Delinquency Cases Waived to Criminal Court, 2009," *Juvenile Offenders and Victims National Report Series* (Washington, D.C.: U.S. Department of Justice, 2012).
3. Patricia Griffin, Sean Addie, Benjamin Adams, and Kathy Firestine, "Trying Juveniles as Adults: An Analysis of State Transfer Laws and Reporting," *Juvenile Offenders and Victims: National Report Series* (Washington, D.C.: U.S. Department of Justice, 2011).

4. A good overview of blended sentencing is found in Jeffrey Rosinek and Steven Weller, "Overview of Juvenile Transfer Laws," in *A Judge's Guide to Juveniles before the Adult Criminal Court*, edited by Steven Weller and Robin E. Wosje (Reno, Nev: The National Judicial College, 2002), pp. 18–19.

5. Sarah Hockenberry and Charles Puzzanchera, *Juvenile Court Statistics 2014* (Washington, D.C.: U.S. Department of Justice, 2017), p. 40.

6. Ibid.

7. Kevin J. Strom, *Profile of State Prisoners under Age 18, 1985–1997* (Washington, D.C.: U.S. Department of Justice, Bureau of Justice Statistics, February 2000), p. 1.

8. E. Ann Carson, "Prisoners in 2016," *BJS Bulletin* (Washington, D.C.: U.S. Department of Justice, 2018), pp. 16–17.

9. James Austin, Kelly Dedel Johnson, and Maria Gregoriou, *Juveniles in Adult Prisons and Jails: A National Assessment* (Washington, D.C.: National Council on Crime and Delinquency, 2000).

10. Attapol Kuanliang, Jon S. Sorensen, and Mark D. Cunningham, "Juvenile Inmates in an Adult Prison System: Rates of Disciplinary Misconduct and Violence," *Criminal Justice and Behavior: An International Journal* 35, no. 9 (September 2008): 1186–1201.

11. Kareem L. Jordan, "Juvenile Transfer and Recidivism: A Propensity Score Matching Approach," *Journal of Crime and Justice* 35, no. 1 (2012): 53–67.

12. Richard E. Redding, *Juvenile Transfer Laws: An Effective Deterrent to Delinquency* (Washington, D.C.: U.S. Department of Justice, 2010).

13. National Drug Control Strategy, *Office of Nation Drug Control Policy, Federal Drug Control Spending by Function, FY 2007–FY 2009* (Washington, D.C.: Office of National Drug Control Policy, 2010), p. 11.

14. Diana C. Maurer, *Office of National Drug Control Policy: Testimony Before the Committee on Homeland Security, U.S. Senate*, May 17, 2016, available at http://www.gao.gov/assets/680/677235.pdf (accessed September 30, 2017).

15. Office of National Drug Control Policy, *ADAM II: 2013 Annual Report* (Washington, D.C.: Executive Office of the President, 2014), p. xiv.

16. Op. cit., pp. xv and xvi.

17. Jennifer Bronson and Jessica Stroop, "Drug Use, Dependence, and Abuse Among State Prisoners and Jail Inmates, 2007–2009," *BJS Special* Report (Washington, D.C.: U.S. Department of Justice, 2017).

18. Ibid.

19. Christopher J. Mumola and Jennifer C. Karberg, "Drug Use and Dependence, State and Federal Prisoners, 2004," *BJS Special Report* (Washington, D.C.: U.S. Department of Justice, 2005).

20. Bronson and Stroop, op. cit.

21. Carson, "Prisoners in 2016," pp. 18–19.

22. Op. cit., p. 20.

23. *Results from the 2015 National Survey on Drug Use and Health: Detailed Tables* (Washington, D.C.: U.S. Department of Health and Human Services, 2016), Table 7.3A.

24. For a description of the RSAT program, see Kristin Stainbrook, Jeanine Hanna, and Amy Salomon, *The Residential Substance Abuse Treatment (RSAT) Study* (Washington, D.C.: U.S. Department of Justice, 2017).

25. Bernadette Pelissier, William Rhodes, William Saylor, Gerry Gaes, Scott D. Camp, Suzy D. Vanyur, and Sue Wallace, "Triad Drug Treatment Project," *Federal Probation* 65, no. 3 (December 2001): 3–7.

26. Edward E. Rhine, ed., Federal Bureau of Prisons, "Drug Treatment Programs in Federal Prisons," *Best Practices: Excellence in Corrections* (Lanham, Md.: American Correctional Association, 1998), pp. 427–430.

27. Ojmarrh Mitchel, David B. Wilson, and Doris L. MacKenzie, "Does Incarceration-Based Drug Treatment Reduce Recidivism? A Meta-analysis Synthesis of the Literature," *Journal of Experimental Criminology* 3 (2007): 353–375.

28. National Institute of Justice, *Drug Courts* (Washington, D.C.: U.S. Department of Justice, 2017).

29. Gregory P. Falkin, Sheila Strauss, and Timothy Bohen, "Matching Drug-Involved Probationers to Appropriate Drug Interventions: A Strategy for Reducing Recidivism," *Federal Probation* 63, no. 1 (June 1999): 4.

30. Amanda Petteruti, Nastassia Walsh, and Tracy Velazquez, *Pruning Prisons: How Cutting Corrections Can Save Money and Protect Public Safety* (Washington, D.C.: The Justice Policy Institute, May 2009), p. 1.

31. Fox Butterfield, "Prisons Replace Hospitals for the Nation's Mentally Ill," *New York Times*, March 5, 1998, p. A-26.

32. E. W. Fuller Torrey, et al., *Treatment of Persons with Mental Illness in Prisons and Jails: A State Survey* (Washington, D.C.: Treatment Advocacy Center, 2014), p. 1.

33. Jennifer Bronson and Marcus Berzofsky, "Indicators of Mental Health Problems Reported by Prisoners and Jail Inmates, 2011–12," *BJS Special Report* (Washington, D.C.: U.S. Department of Justice, 2017).

34. Torrey et al., *Treatment of Persons with Mental Illness in Prisons and Jails*, p. 1.

35. Michael Winerip and Michael Schwirtz, "New York City Plans Focus on Mental Health in Justice System," *New York Times*, December 1, 2014, available at http://www.nytimes.com/2014/12/02/nyregion/new-york-city-to-expand-health-services-for-mentally-ill-inmates.html?smid=nytcore-iphone-share&smprod=nytcore-iphone&_r=0 (accessed December 2, 2014).

36. Op. cit., p. 8.

37. Bronson and Berzofsky, op. cit., p. 9.

38. Doris J. James and Lauren E. Glaze, *Mental Health Problems of Prison and Jail Inmates* (Washington, D.C.: U. S. Department of Justice, 2006), p. 10.

39. Torrey et al., *Treatment of Persons with Mental Illness in Prisons and Jails*, pp. 14–18.

40. Jennifer Skeem, Sara Manchak, and Jillian K. Peterson, "Correctional Policy for Offenders with Mental Illness: Creating a New Paradigm for Recidivism Reduction," *Law and Human Behavior* 35 (2011): 110–126.

41. James Mayfield, *The Dangerously Mentally Ill Offender Program: Four-Year Felony Recidivism and Cost Effectiveness* (Olympia, WA: Washington State Institute for Public Policy, 2009).

42. Thanks to Dr. Glenn R. Young, psychologist in the Federal Bureau of Prisons for providing information regarding careers in correctional psychology. He served as the Chief, Psychological Services at FCI Greenville and FCC Victorville before retiring on December 31, 2012.

43. U.S. Census Bureau, Table 1, "Population by Age and Sex: 2012," available at https://www.census.gov/population/age/data/2012.html (accessed November 17, 2014).

44. U.S. Census Bureau, *U.S. Census Bureau Quick Facts*, available at https://www.census.gov/quickfacts/fact/table/US/AGE765210#viewtop (accessed October 2, 2017).

45. Karishma A. Chari, Alan E. Simon, and Carol J. DeFrances, "National Survey of Prison Health Care: Selected Findings," *National Health Statistics Reports* (Washington, D.C.: U.S. Department of Health and Human Services, 2016).

46. A good overview of this issue can be found in Inimal M. Chettiar, W.C. Bunting, and Georffrey Schotter, *At American's Expense: The Mass Incarceration of the Elderly* (New York, NY: American Civil Liberties Union, 2012).

47. Kenneth Moritsugu, "Inmate Chronological Age versus Physical Age," *Long-Term Confinement and the Aging Inmate Population* (Washington, D.C.: U.S. Department of Justice, Federal Bureau of Prisons, 1990).

48. Carson, "Prisoners in 2016," p. 15.

49. E. Ann Carson and William J. Sabol, "Aging of the State Prison Population, 1993–2013," *BJS Special Reports* (Washington, D.C.: U.S. Department of Justice, 2016).

50. Mike Mitka, "Aging Prisoners Stressing Health Care System," *Journal of the American Medical Association* 292, no. 4 (2004): 423–424.

51. McArthur Foundation, *Managing Prison Health Care Spending* (Philadelphia, PA: Pew Charitable Trusts, 2013).

52. A 2004 report by the National Institute of Corrections noted health care costs in that year of $70,000 for older offenders. Since that time, prison health care costs have risen at between 10 percent and 15 percent per year.
B. Jaye Anno et al., *Correctional Health Care: Addressing the Needs of Elderly, Chronically Ill, and Terminally Ill Inmates* (Washington, D.C.: U.S. Department of Justice, National Institute of Corrections, 2004).

53. Christine Vestal, *Aging Inmates: Care Outside Prison Walls* (Washington, D.C.: Pew Charitable Trust, 2014).

54. Association of State Correctional Administrators, "Prison Dilemma: Surging Numbers of Older Inmates," *Corrections Directions* 24, no. 1 (February–March 2012): 11.

55. Vestal, op. cit.

56. CorrectionsOne Staff, *How Should Correctional Facilities Manage Transgender Offenders?*, available at https://www.correctionsone.com/correctional-healthcare/articles/2082675-How-should-correctional-facilitiesmanage-transgender-offenders (accessed December 11, 2017).

57. Douglas Routh, Gassan Abess, and David Makin, "Transgender Inmates in Prisons: A Review of Applicable Statutes and Policies," *International Journal of Offender Therapy and Comparative Criminology* 61, no. 6 (2017): 645–666.

58. The Editorial Board, "Prisons and Jails Put Transgender Inmates at Risk," *The New York Times*, November 9, 2015, available at https://www.nytimes.com/2015/11/09/opinion/prisons-and-jails-put-transgender-inmates-at-risk.html?_r=0 (accessed December 11, 2017).

59. Federal Bureau of Prisons, *Transgender Offender Manual* (Washington, D.C.: U.S. Department of Justice, January 18, 2017).

60. Ibid., p. 5.

61. Association of State Correctional Administrators, meeting discussion regarding transgender inmates, August 19, 2017, St. Louis, Missouri.

62. National Commission on Correctional Health Care, "Transgender, Transsexual, and Gender Nonconforming Health Care in Correctional Settings," *NCCHC Position Statements*, adopted October 18, 2009 and reaffirmed with revision April 2015, available at https://www.ncchc.org/transgender-transsexual-and-gender-nonconforming-health-care (accessed December 11, 2017).

63. Most of this information was provided in an interview with Heidi R. Steward, assistant director, Office of Management and Rehabilitation, the Oregon Department of Corrections. As well, the Basic Rights Oregon reviewed the case study prior to it being finalized.

64. Carson, "Prisoners in 2016," pp. 19–20.

65. Robert Perkinson, "Shackled Justice: Florence Federal Penitentiary and the New Politics of Punishment," *Social Justice* 21, no. 3 (1994): 119.

66. *Bruscino v. Carlson*, 854 F.2d 162 (7th Cir. 1988).

67. Interview With Jerry T. Williford. Reprinted with Permission.

68. Chase Riveland, *Supermax Prisons: Overview and General Considerations* (Washington, D.C.: U.S. Department of Justice, National Institute of Corrections, January 1999), p. 3.

69. John wooldredge and Benjamin Steiner, "A Macro-Level Perspective on Prison Inmate Deviance, *Punishment & Society* 17, no. 2 (2015): 230–257.

70. Robert G. Morris, "Exploring the Effect of Exposure to Short-Term Solitary Confinement Among Violent Prison Inmates," *Journal of Quantitative Criminology* 32, no. 1 (2015): 1–22, and Ryan M. Labrecqaue, *The Effect of Solitary Confinement on Institutional Misconduct: A Longitudinal Evaluation*, Doctoral Dissertation, University of Cincinnati, available at https://www.ncjrs.gov/pdffiles1/nij/grants/249013.pdf (accessed October 17, 2017).

71. A good overview of a variety of inmate experiences in solitary confinement can be found in Nathaniel Penn, "Buried Alive: Stories From Inside Solitary Confinement," *CQ Magazine*, March 2, 2017, available at https://www.gq.com/story/buried-alive-solitary-confinement (accessed October 2, 2017).

72. For a good overview of this issue, see Craig Haney, "Mental Health Issues in Long-Term Solitary and "Supermax" Confinement," *Crime and Delinquency* 49, no. 1 (2003): 124–156.

73. Maureen L. O'Keefe and Kelli J. Klebe, "One Year Longitudinal Study of the Psychological Effects of Administrative Segregation" (Colorado Springs, CO: Colorado Department of Corrections and University of Colorado 2010), available at www.ncjrs.gov/pdffiles1/nij/grants/232973.pdf (accessed June 20, 2013).

74. Grant Duwe, *The Use and Impact of Correctional Programming for Inmates on Pre- and Post-Release Outcomes* (Arlington, VA: CSR Incorporated, 2017), pp. 13–15.

75. Carson, "Prisoners in 2016," p. 18.

76. Federal Bureau of Investigation, Table 1, Offenses Known to Law Enforcement, *Crime in the United States 2016*, available at https://ucr.fbi.gov/crime-in-the-u.s/2016/crime-in-the-u.s.-2016/topic-pages/tables/table-1(accessed October 2, 2017). Note: this figure uses the UCR revised definition of rape, used since 2013.

77. "Estimated Number and Rate of Personal Victimizations," Table 3.10.2008, *Sourcebook of Criminal Justice Statistics*, available at http://www.albany.edu/sourcebook/pdf/t3102008.pdf (accessed November 18, 2014).

78. Lawrence A. Greenfeld, *Sex Offenses and Offenders: An Analysis of Data on Rape and Sexual Assault* (Washington, D.C.: U.S. Department of Justice, Bureau of Justice Statistics, February 1997), p. 24.

79. Op. cit., p. 21.

80. As reported from a survey by the National Center for Missing & Exploited Children, available at http://www.missingkids.com/en_US/documents/Sex_Offenders_Map.pdf, updated on May 24, 2017 (accessed October 2, 2017).

81. Greenfeld, *Sex Offenses and Offenders*, p. 17.

82. Carson, "Prisoners in 2016," p. 19.

83. *Sourcebook of Criminal Justice Statistics, 2006*, Table 5.48 (Washington, D.C.: U.S. Department of Justice, 2009), available at http://www.albany.edu/sourcebook/pdf/t5482006.pdf (accessed October 2, 2017).

84. Kim English, Suzanne Pullen, and Linda Jones, *Managing Sex Offenders in the Community—A Containment Approach* (Washington, D.C.: U.S. Department of Justice, 1997), p. 3.

85. Op. cit., p. 2.

86. K.E. Aytes, S.S. Olsen, T. Zakrajsek, P. Murray, and R. Ireson, "Cognitive/behavioral Treatment for Sexual Offenders: An Examination of Recidivism," *Sexual Abuse: A Journal of Research and Treatment* 13, no. 4 (2001): 223–231.

87. For examples, see Chris Lobanov-Rostovsky and Jesse Hansen, *Evidence-Based Practices for the Treatment and Management of Adults and Juveniles Who Have Committed Sexual Offenses* (Denver, CO: Colorado Department of Public Safety, 2014).

88. Center for Sex Offender Management, *Adult Sex Offender Management* (Washington, D.C.: U.S. Department of Justice, 2015).

89. Greenfeld, *Sex Offenses and Offenders*, p. 25.

90. Op. cit., pp. 25–26.

91. Steven Patrick and Robert Marsh, "Recidivism among Child Sexual Abusers: Initial Results of a 13-Year Longitudinal Random Sample," *Journal of Child Sexual Abuse* 18, no. 2 (2009): 123–136.

92. R.K. Hanson, G. Bourgon, L. Helmus, and S. Hodgson, *A Meta-Analysis of the Effectiveness of Treatment for Sex Offenders: Risk, Need, and Responsivity* (Ottawa: ON: Public Safety Canada, 2009). R.K. Hanson et al., "First Report of the Collaborative Outcome Data Project on the Effectiveness of Psychological Treatment for Sex Offenders," *Sexual Abuse: A Journal of Research and Treatment* 14 (2002): 169–194. F. Losel and M. Schmucker, "The Effectiveness of Treatment for Sex Offenders: A Comprehensive Meta-Analysis," *Journal of Experimental Criminology* 1 (2005): 117–146.

93. Duwe, op. cit., p. 14.

94. Rebecca L. Jackson and Derek T. Hess, "Evaluation of Civil Commitment for Sex Offenders: A Survey of Experts," *Sexual Abuse: A Journal of Research and Treatment* 19, no. 4 (December 2007): 425–448.

95. *Kansas v. Hendricks*, 117 U.S. 2072 (1997); *Seling v. Young*, 531 U.S. 215 (2001); *Kansas v. Crane*, 534 U.S. 407 (2002).

96. Christopher Lobanov-Rostovsky, chapter 8, "Sex Offender Management Strategies," *Sex Offender Management Assessment and Planning Initiative* (Washington, D.C.: U.S. Department of Justice, 2014).

97. Interview with Adam H Deming, Psy.D. Reprinted with Permission.

98. Theodore M. Hammett, Cheryl Roberts, and Sofia Kennedy, "Health Related Issues in Prisoner Reentry," *Crime & Delinquency* 47, no. 3 (July 2001): 390–409.

99. Center for Disease Control and Prevention, *HIV/AIDS*, available at https://www.cdc.gov/hiv/basics/statistics.html (accessed October 2, 2017).

100. Center for Disease Control and Prevention, *HIV Among Incarcerated Populations*, available at http://www.cdc.gov/hiv/risk/other/correctional.html (accessed October 2, 2017).

101. Laura M. Maruschak and Jennifer Bronson, "HIV in Prisons, 2015 – Statistical Tables," *BJS Statistical Tables* (Washington, D.C.: U.S. Department of Justice, 2017), pp. 1 and 3.

102. Calculated from data on Appendix Table 1, Op. cit., p. 9.

103. Op. cit., p. 4.

104. Ibid.

105. Theodore M. Hammett, Sofia Kennedy, and Sarah Kuck, *National Survey of Infectious Diseases in Correctional Facilities: HIV and Sexually Transmitted Diseases* (Washington, D.C.: National Institute of Justice, March 2007), p. 8.

106. Curt Beckwith, et al., *CDC HIV Testing Implementation Guidance for Correctional Settings* (Atlanta, GA: Center for Disease Control and Prevention, 2009).

107. Hammett, et al., op. cit., p. 16.

108. Centers for Disease Control and Prevention, *HIV Among Incarcerated Populations* (2017), available at https://www.cdc.gov/hiv/pdf/group/cdc-hiv-incarcerated-populations.pdf (accessed October 3, 2017).

109. Christopher P. Krebs, "Inmate Factors Associated with HIV Transmission in Prison," *Criminology and Public Policy* 5, no. 1 (February 2006): 113–136.

110. Theodore M. Hammett, M. P. Harmon, and W. Rhodes, "The Burden of Infectious Disease among Inmates and Releasees from U.S. Correctional Facilities," *American Journal of Public Health* 92 (1997): 189–194.

111. Theodore Hammett, "Editorial Introduction: HIV in Prisons," *Criminology and Public Policy* 5, no. 1 (February 2006): 108.

112. CDC, *HIV Among Incarcerated Populations*, 2017, op. cit.

113. M. Dara, M. Grzemska, M. Kimerling, H. Reyes, and A. Zargorskiy, *Guidelines for Control of Tuberculosis in Prisons* (Washington, D.C.: Tuberculosis Coalition for Technical Assistance and the International Committee of the Red Cross, 2009), p. 9.

114. Ibid.

115. Center for Disease Control and Prevention, *TB in Correctional Facilities in the United States*, available at http://www.cdc.gov/tb/topic/populations/correctional/default.htm (accessed November 18, 2014).

116. Karen Wilcock, Theodore M. Hammett, Rebecca Widom, and Joel Epstein, *Tuberculosis in Correctional Facilities 1994–95* (Washington, D.C.: U.S. Department of Justice, 1996), p. 5.

117. Karishma Chari, Alan E. Simon, and Carol J. DeFrances, *National Survey of Prison Health Care: Selected Findings* (Washington, D.C.: U.S. Department of Health and Human Services, 2016), p. 3.

118. Jessica R. McNeil, Mark N. Lobato, and Marisa Moore, "An Unanswered Health Disparity: Tuberculosis among Correctional Inmates, 1993 through 2003," *American Journal of Public Health* 95, no. 10 (2005): 1800–1805.

119. CDC, *TB in Correctional Facilities*, op. cit.

120. Allen J. Beck and Laura Maruschak, "Hepatitis Testing and Treatment in State Prisons," *Bureau of Justice Statistics Special Report* (Washington, D.C.: U.S. Department of Justice, 2004).

121. Alden K. Varan et al., "Hepatitis C Seroprevalence among Prison Inmates Since 2001: Still High but Declining," *Public Health Reports* 129, no. 2 (2014): 187–195.

122. Centers for Disease Control and Prevention, *Viral Hepatitis Specific Settings, Correctional Facilities and Viral Hepatitis,* May 2011, available at http://www.cdc.gov/hepatitis/Settings/corrections.htm (accessed November 18, 2014).

123. Chari, Simon, and DeFrances, op. cit., p. 3.

124. Centers for Disease Control and Prevention, *Hepatitis C and Incarceration* (Washington, D.C.: U.S. Department of Health and Human Services, 2014).

125. Beck and Maruschak, op. cit.

Chapter 10

1. Federal Bureau of Prisons, data from website, available at http://www.bop.gov/about/statistics/population_statistics.jsp (accessed November 20, 2017).

2. E. Ann Carson, "Prisoners in 2016," *BJS Bulletin* (Washington, D.C.: U.S. Department of Justice, 2018), p. 4.

3. Ohio Department of Rehabilitation and Correction, *Fact Sheet*, September 2017, available at http://www.drc.ohio.gov/Portals/0/Reentry/Reports/Monthly/2017/Sept%202017%20Fact%20Sheet.pdf?ver=2017-09-12-112010-787 (accessed October 4, 2017).

4. United States Courts, "Civil Cases Filed, by Nature of Suit," *U.S. District Courts – Judicial Business 2016*, available at http://www.uscourts.gov/statistics-reports/us-district-courts-judicial-business-2016 (accessed October 3, 2017).

5. Carson, "Prisoners in 2016," p. 1.

6. Tracey Kyckelhahn, "State Corrections Expenditures, FY 1982-2010," *BJS Bulletin* (Washington, D.C.: U.S. Department of Justice, 2012), p. 1.

7. Camille Graham Camp and George M. Camp, *The 2002 Corrections Yearbook, Adult Systems* (Middletown, Conn.: Criminal Justice Institute, 2002), pp. 7, 92, 154, and 187.

8. Camille Graham Camp and George M. Camp, *The 2002 Corrections Yearbook* (Middletown, Conn.: Criminal Justice Institute, 2003), pp. 82–83, 84, 97 and 98.

9. James J. Stephan, "Census of State and Federal Correctional Facilities, 2005," *National Prisoner Statistics Program* (Washington, D.C.: U.S. Department of Justice, October 2008), pp. 1 and 2.

10. Using capacities taken from William J. Sabol, Heather C. West, and Matthew Cooper, "Prisoners in 2008," *Bureau of Justice Statistics Bulletin* (Washington, D.C.: U.S. Department of Justice, 2009), p. 9, and from Carson (2014), p. 22.

11. This was determined by comparing capacities from 2008 until 2016, "Prisoners in 2008" and "Prisoners in 2016."

12. For a discussion of the history of unit management in the Bureau of Prisons, see Robert Levinson and Roy Gerard, "Functional Units: A Different Correctional Approach," *Federal Probation* 37, no. 4 (1973): 8–16.

13. Federal Bureau of Prisons, *Unit Management Manual* (Washington, D.C.: U.S. Department of Justice, Bureau of Prisons, August 10, 2017).

14. Op. cit., pp. 2–3.

15. Everett C. Hughes, "Professions," in *The Professions in America*, edited by Kenneth S. Lynn (Boston: Houghton-Mifflin, 1965), p. 4.

16. American Correctional Association, *Manual of Accreditation: Policy and Procedure* (Alexandria: VA: American Correctional Association, 2017), p. 9.

17. Mary Dallao, "Keeping Classification Current," *Corrections Today* 59, no. 4 (July 1997): 87.

18. Tim Brennan, "Classification for Control in Jail and Prisons," in *Prediction and Classification: Criminal Justice Decision Making*, edited by Don M. Gottfredson and Michael Tonry (Chicago: University of Chicago Press, 1987), p. 343.

19. Stephan, "Census of State and Federal Correctional Facilities, 2005," p. 2.

20. Joan Mullen, *American Prisons and Jails, Volume I: Summary and Policy Implications of a National Survey* (Washington, D.C.: U.S. Department of Justice, 1980), p. 57.

21. Federal Bureau of Prisons, *Inmate Discipline Program*, Program Statement #5270.09 (Washington, D.C.: U.S. Department of Justice, August 1, 2011), p. 3.

22. Op. cit., pp. 9–10.

23. Clair A. Cripe, "Inmate Disciplinary Procedures," in *Prison and Jail Administration: Practice and Theory*, 3rd ed., edited by Peter M. Carlson (Burlington, Mass.: Jones and Bartlett, 2015), p. 349.

24. Tracey Kyckelhahn, *Justice Expenditure and Employment Extracts, 2012 – Preliminary*, Table 2 (Washington, D.C.: U.S. Department of Justice, December 2015), Table 2, jeeus1202.cvs.

25. Donald Cressey, "Prison Organizations," in *Handbook of Organizations*, edited by J. March (New York: Rand McNally, 1965), p. 1024.

26. American Correctional Association, "Resolution on the Term 'Correctional Officer,'" *Corrections Today* 55, no. 2 (April 1993): 60.

27. Kelsey Kauffman, *Prison Officers and Their World* (Cambridge, Mass.: Harvard University Press, 1988), p. 167.

28. John J. DiIulio, *Governing Prisons: A Comparative Study of Correctional Management* (New York, NY: Free Press, 1987), p. 95.

29. Gregg W. Etter, "Recruiting the Best!" *American Jails* 22, no. 2 (May/June 2008): 22.

30. Roderick S. Osborne, "Recruiting for Corrections in Today's World," *American Jails* 22, no. 3 (July/August 2008): 22.

31. Nicole Baker and Max Carrera, "Unlocking the Door to Relationship-Based Corrections Recruiting," *Corrections Today* 69, no. 1 (February 2007): 36.

32. Jeanne B. Stinchcomb and Susan W. McCambell, "The 21st Century Jail Workforce," *American Jails* 23, no. 2 (May/June 2009): 15–20.

33. V. Wolfe Mahfood, Wendi Pollock, and Dennis Longmire, "Leave It at the Gate: Job Stress and Satisfaction in Correctional Staff," *Criminal Justice Studies* 26, no. 3 (September 2013): 308–325.

34. Jane Lommel, "Turning Around Turnover," *Corrections Today* 66, no. 5 (August 2004): 54–57.

35. Leslie A. Leip and Jeanne B. Stinchcomb, "Should I Stay or Go?: Job Satisfaction and Turnover Intent of Jail Staff throughout the United States," *Criminal Justice Review* 38, no. 2 (June 2013): 226–241.

36. Association of State Correctional Administrators, "Critical Issue Surveys" (June 2013), available at http://www.asca.net/system/assets/attachments/6468/ASCA%20June%202103%20Current%20Issues%20 in%20Corrections%20Surveyfin.pdf (accessed November 20, 2014).

37. Brian E. Cronin, Ralph Klessig, and William D. Sprenkle, "Recruiting and Retaining Staff through Culture Change," *Corrections Today* 70, no. 4 (August 2008): 48–51.

38. Gary C. Mohr, "Samberg Program Improves Leadership and Addresses Turnover," *Corrections Today* 71, no. 2 (April 2009): 56–58.

39. David W. Reeves, Benjamin M. Walsh, Michael D. Tuller, and Vicki J. Magley, "Positive Effects of Participative Decision Making for Midlevel Correctional Management," *Criminal Justice and Behavior* 39, no. 10 (October 2012): 1361–1372.

40. A good discussion of this can be found in Kevin P. Coyne and Shawn T. Coyne, "The Baby Boom Retirement Fallacy and What It Means to You," *Harvard Business Review Blog*, May 16, 2008, http://blogs. harvardbusiness.org/cs/2008/05/the_baby_boomer_retirement_fal. html (accessed December 23, 2009).

41. John Irwin, "The Changing Social Structure of the Men's Correctional Prison," in *Corrections and Punishment*, edited by D. Greenberg (Beverly Hills, Calif.: Sage, 1977), pp. 21–40.

42. Susan Philliber, "Thy Brother's Keeper: A Review of Literature on Correctional Officers," *Justice Quarterly* 4, no. 1 (1987): 9–33.

43. M. Robert Montilla, *Prison Employee Unionism: Management Guide for Correctional Administrators* (Washington, D.C.: U.S. Department of Justice, National Institute of Law Enforcement and Criminal Justice, 1978), p. 2.

44. Bureau of Labor Statistics, *Press Release: Union Members—2015* (Washington, D.C.: U.S. Department of Labor, 2016).

45. Andrew A. Peterson, "Deterring Strikes by Public Employees: New York's Two-for-One Salary Penalty and the 1979 Prison Guard Strike," *Industrial and Labor Relations Review* 34, no. 4 (July 1981): 545–562.

46. Lynn Zimmer and James B. Jacobs, "Challenging the Taylor Law: Prison Guards on Strike," *Industrial and Labor Relations Review* 34, no. 4 (July 1981): 531–544.

47. Michael Schwirtz and Michael Winerip, "At Rikers Island, Union Chief's Clout Is a Roadblock to Reform," *New York Times*, December 14, 2014, available at http://www.nytimes.com/2014/12/15/nyregion/ at-rikers-a-roadblock-to-reform.html?emc=edit_th_20141215&nl=tod aysheadlines&nlid=66581080&_r=1 (accessed December 16, 2014).

Chapter 11

1. Erving Goffman, *Asylums: Essays on the Social Situation of Mental Patients and Other Inmates* (New York: Doubleday, 1961).

2. Phillip G. Zimbardo, "Pathology of Imprisonment," *Society* 9 (April 1972): 4–8.

3. Op. cit., p. 4.

4. Donald Clemmer, *The Prison Community* (New York: Rinehart, 1940), p. 8.

5. Gresham Sykes, *The Society of Captives: A Study of a Maximum Security Prison* (Princeton, N.J.: Princeton University Press, 1958).

6. John Irwin and Donald Cressey, "Thieves, Convicts, and the Inmate Culture," *Social Problems* 10 (1962): 145–157.

7. Ann Coppola, "In the Year 2028," *The Corrections Connection*, March 10, 2008, available at http://www.corrections.com/news/article/17986 (accessed November 12, 2017).

8. These prison terms are a part of a longer list collected by Kate King, professor of sociology at Western Kentucky University. Reprinted with Permission.

9. E. Ann Carson, "Prisoners in 2016," *BJS Bulletin* (Washington, D.C.: U.S. Department of Justice, 2018), p. 18.

10. Karen F. Lahm, "Inmate-on-Inmate Assault: A Multilevel Examination of Prison Violence," *Criminal Justice and Behavior* 35, no. 1 (January 2008): 120–137.

11. Stephan, J. J., and Karberg, J. C., *Census of State and Federal Correctional Facilities, 2000* (No. NCJ 198272). (Washington, D.C.: Bureau of Justice Statistics, U.S. Department of Justice, 2003). Also see Wolff, N., Blitz, C., Shi, J., Siegel, J., and Bachman, R., "Physical Violence Inside Prison: Rates of Victimization." *Criminal Justice and Behavior* 34 (2007): 588–599.

12. S. Ekland-Olson, "Crowding, Social Control, and Prison Violence: Evidence from the Post-*Ruiz* Years in Texas," *Law and Society Review* 20, no. 3 (1986): 289–421. Also see Gerald G. Gaes and W. J. McGuire, "Prison Violence: The Contribution of Crowding Versus Other Determinants of Prison Assault Rates," *Journal of Research in Crime and Delinquency* 22, no. 1 (1985): 41–65; and Maryland Department of Public Safety and Correctional Services, *Report of the Task Force to Study Prison Violence in Maryland* (Towson, Md.: State of Maryland, 2009).

13. For an early work, see John Irwin, *Prisons in Turmoil* (Boston: Little, Brown, 1980). A good and more recent study is Rebecca Trammell, *Enforcing the Convict Code: Violence and Prison Culture* (Boulder, Colo.: Lynne Rienner Publishers, 2012).

14. James B. Jacobs, *Statesville, a Penitentiary in Mass Society* (Chicago: University of Chicago Press, 1977); and Rebecca Trammell, "Symbolic Violence and Prison Wives: Gender Roles and Protective Pairings in Men's Prisons," *Prison Journal* 91, no. 3 (September 2011): 305–324.

15. Mark S. Fleisher, *Warehousing Violence* (Newbury Park, Calif.: Sage, 1989), p. 198. See also Kristie R. Blevins, Shelley Johnson Listwan, Francis T. Cullen, and Ceryl Lero Jonson, "General Strain Theory of Prison Violence and Misconduct: An Integrated Model of Behavior," *Journal of Contemporary Criminal Justice* 26, no. 2 (May 2010): 148–166.

16. Victor Hassine, *Life without Parole: Living in Prison Today*, 2nd ed. (Los Angeles: Roxbury, 1999), p. 39.

17. Michael C. Braswell, Reid H. Montgomery, and Lucien X. Lombardo, *Prison Violence in America*, 2nd ed. (Cincinnati, Ohio: Anderson, 1994).

18. Robert Johnson, *Hard Time: Understanding and Reforming the Prison*, 3rd ed. (Belmont, Calif.: Wadsworth, 2002), p. 149.

19. Charles M. Terry, *The Fellas: Overcoming Prison and Addiction* (Belmont, Calif.: Wadsworth, 2003), p. 72.

20. Christopher A. Innes and Vicki D. Verdeyen, "Conceptualizing the Management of Violent Inmates," *Corrections Management Quarterly* 1, no. 4 (1997): 1–9.

21. Margaret E. Noonan and Scott Ginder, "Mortality in Jails and State Prisons, 2000–2012," *BJS Statistical Tables* (Washington, D.C.: U.S. Department of Justice, 2014), pp. 18–19.

22. Ryan M. Labrecque, Paula Smith, and John D. Wooldredge, "Creation and Validation of an Inmate Risk Assessment for Violent, Nonsexual Victimization, Victims and Offenders: An International Journal of Evidence-Based Research," *Policy, and Practice* 9, no. 3 (2014): 317–333.

23. Margaret Noonan, Harley Rohloff, and Scott Ginder, "Mortality in Local Jails and State Prisons, 2000–2013 – Statistical Tables," *BJS Statistical Tables* (Washington, D.C.: U.S. Department of Justice, 2015), p. 20.

24. Ibid.

25. Erika Harrell, "Violence by Gang Members, 1993–2002," *Bureau of Justice Statistics Crime Data Brief* (Washington, D.C.: U.S. Department of Justice, June 2005), p. 1.

26. National Gang Intelligence Center, *National Gang Report, 2015* (Tallahassee, FL: National Gang Center, 2016).

27. National Gang Intelligence Center and the National Drug Intelligence Center, *2011 National Gang Threat Assessment: Emerging Trends* (Washington, D.C.: National Gang Intelligence Center, 2012).

28. Gerald G. Gaes, Susan Wallace, Evan Gilman, Jody Klein-Saffran, and Sharon Suppa, "Influence of Prison Gang Affiliation on Violence and Other Prison Misconduct," *Prison Journal* 82, no. 3 (2002): 359–385.

29. National Institute of Corrections, *Management Strategies in Disturbances and with Gangs/Disruptive Groups* (Washington, D.C.: U.S. Department of Justice, 1991), p. 2.

30. George M. Camp and Camille Graham Camp, *Prison Gangs: Their Extent, Nature, and Impact on Prisons* (Washington, D.C.: U.S. Government Printing Office, 1985).

31. American Correctional Association, *Gangs in Correctional Facilities: A National Assessment* (Laurel, Md.: American Correctional Association, 1993).

32. George W. Knox, "The Problems of Gangs and Security Threat Groups (STG's) in American Prisons Today: Recent Research Findings from the 2004 Prison Gang Survey," *Journal of Gang Research* 12, no. 1 (Fall 2006): 1–50.

33. George W. Knox, "Problems of Gangs and Security Threat Groups in American Prisons and Jails Today: Recent Findings from the 2012 NGCRC National Gang/STG Survey," *Journal of Gang Research* 20, no. 1 (Fall 2012): 51–76.

34. National Gang Intelligence Center, op. cit., p. 30.

35. Gregory Scott, "Broken Windows behind Bars: Eradicating Prison Gangs through Ecological Hardening and Symbol Cleansing," *Corrections Management Quarterly* 5, no. 1 (2001): 23–36.

36. John L. Worral and Robert G. Morris, "Prison Gang Integration and Inmate Violence," *Journal of Criminal Justice* 40, no. 5 (2012): 425–432.

37. Op. cit., p. 24.

38. Sykes, op. cit.

39. Mark S. Fleisher and Scott H. Decker, "An Overview of the Challenge of Prison Gangs," *Corrections Management Quarterly* 5, no. 1 (2001): 5.

40. Stephen Gies, "GPS Supervision in California: One Technology, Two Contrasting Goals," *NIJ Journal* 275 (2015): 1–3.

41. Richard P. Seiter, "Winning a Battle of Wills: Correctional Administrators and Prison Gangs," *Corrections Management Quarterly* 5, no. 1 (2001): iv.

42. Tony Lesce, "How to Cope with Prison Gangs," *Corrections Technology and Management* 4, no. 2 (March/April 2000): 22–25.

43. James Byrne and Don Hummer, "In Search of the 'Tossed Salad Man' (and Others Involved in Prison Violence): New Strategies for Predicting and Controlling Violence in Prison," *Aggression and Violent Behavior* 12, no. 5 (September–October 2007): 531–541.

44. Intelligence Section, Federal Bureau of Prisons, *Gang Interdiction Strategies Briefing Guide* (Washington, D.C.: U.S. Department of Justice, April 29, 1996), p. 17.

45. *Johnson v. California*, 321 F.3d 791 (2005).

46. Peter L. Nacci and Thomas R. Kane, "The Incidence of Sex and Sexual Aggression in Federal Prisons," *Federal Probation* 47, no. 4 (December 1983): 31–36.

47. Victor Hassine, *Life without Parole: Living in Prison Today* (Los Angeles: Roxbury, 1997), p. 138.

48. T. J. Fagan, D. Wennerstrom, and J. Miller, "Sexual Assault of Male Inmates: Prevention, Identification, and Intervention," *Journal of Correctional Health Care* 3, no. 1 (1996): 49–63.

49. Allen J. Beck and Ramona R. Rantala, "Victimization Reported by Adult Correctional Authorities, 2005–11," *BJS Special Report* (Washington, D.C.: U.S. Department of Justice, 2014), p. 1.

50. Review Panel on Prison Rape, *Report on Sexual Victimization in Prisons, Jails, and Juvenile Correctional Facilities* (Washington, D.C.: U.S. Department of Justice, 2016), p. 2.

51. Allen J. Beck and Marcus Berzofsky, *Sexual Victimization in Prisons and Jails Reported by Inmates, 2001–2012* (Washington, D.C.: U.S. Department of Justice, 2014), pp. 2–3.

52. Op. cit., p. 8.

53. Op. cit. p. 23.

54. John Blackmore and Janine Zweig, "Developing State Prison Policies to Respond to Sexual Violence," *Corrections Today* 70, no. 4 (August 2008): 78–81.

55. R. Alan Thompson, Lisa S. Nored, and Kelly Cheeseman Dial, "Prison Rape Elimination Act: An Evaluation of Policy Compliance with Illustrative Excerpts," *Criminal Justice Policy Review* 19, no. 4 (December 2008): 414–437.

56. Aviva N. Moster and Elizabeth L. Jeglic, "Prison Warden Attitudes toward Prison Rape and Sexual Assault," *The Prison Journal* 89 (April 2009): 65–78.

57. The Urban Institute, "Strategies to Prevent Prison Rape by Changing the Correctional Culture," *NIJ Research in Practice* (Washington, D.C.: U.S. Department of Justice, October 2008).

58. Camille Graham Camp and George M. Camp, *2002 Corrections Yearbook* (Middletown, Conn: Criminal Justice Institute, 2003), p. 149.

59. Carson, "Prisoners in 2016," pp. 18–20.

60. Christopher J. Mumola and Jennifer C. Karberg, *Drug Use and Dependence, State and Federal Prisoners, 2004* (Washington, D.C.: U. S. Department of Justice, Bureau of Justice Statistics, October 2006), p. 1.

61. Camp and Camp, *2002 Corrections Yearbook*, 2003, pp. 138–139.

62. Faye S. Taxman, Matthew L. Perdoni, and Michael Caudy, "Plight of Providing Appropriate Substance Abuse Treatment Services to Offenders: Modeling the Gaps in Service Delivery," *Victims and Offenders* 8, no. 1 (2013): 70–93.

63. Steven Belenko and Kimberly A. Houser, "Gender Differences in Prison-Based Drug Treatment Participation," *International Journal of Offender Therapy and Comparative Criminology* 56, no. 5 (2012): 790–810.

64. Charles M. Terry, "The Function of Humor for Prison Inmates," *Journal of Contemporary Criminal Justice* 13, no. 1 (February 1997): 23–40.

65. Goffman, op. cit.

66. S. Ungar, "Self-Mockery: An Alternative Form of Self-Presentation," *Symbolic Interaction* 71, no. 1 (1984): 121–133.

67. Terry, op. cit., p. 24.

68. Interview with Clark E. Porter. Reprinted with Permission.

69. Henry Elmer Barnes, *The Evolution of Penology in Pennsylvania: A Study in American Social History* (Montclair, N.J.: Patterson Smith, 1968).

70. Russell P. Dobash, R. Emerson Dobash, and Sue Gutteridge, *The Imprisonment of Women* (Oxford, England: Basil Blackwell, 1986), p. 52.

71. Allison Morris, *Women, Crime and Criminal Justice* (Oxford, England: Basil Blackwell, 1987).

72. Nicole H. Rafter, *Partial Justice: Women, Prison, and Social Control*, 2nd ed. (New Brunswick, N.J.: Transaction, 1990).

73. Nicole H. Rafter, "Gender and Justice: The Equal Protection Issues," in *The American Prison*, edited by Lynne Goodstein and Doris MacKenzie (New York: Plenum Press, 1989), pp. 89–109.

74. Clarice Feinman, "A Historical Overview of the Treatment of Incarcerated Women: Myths and Realities of Rehabilitation," *Prison Journal* 63 (1983): 12–26.

75. Clarice Feinman, "Sex-Role Stereotypes and Justice for Women," in *Women and Crime in America*, edited by L. H. Bowker (New York: Macmillan, 1981), pp. 383–391.

76. See Mark S. Fleisher, Richard H. Rison, and David W. Helman, "Federal Inmates: A Growing Constituency in the Federal Bureau of Prisons," *Corrections Management Quarterly* 1, no. 4 (1997): 28–35.

77. Ann Booker Loper, L. Wrenn Carlson, Lacey Levitt, and Kathryn Scheffel, "Parenting Stress, Alliance, Child Contact, and Adjustment of Imprisoned Mothers and Fathers," *Journal of Offender Rehabilitation* 48, no. 6 (August–September 2009): 483–503.

78. Barbara Owens, *In the Mix: Struggle and Survival in a Women's Prison* (Albany, N.Y.: State University of New York Press, 1998), p. 120.

79. Alice M. Propper, "Make Believe Families and Homosexuality among Imprisoned Girls," *Criminology* 20, no. 1 (1982): 120.

80. Joycelyn M. Pollock-Byrne, *Women, Prison, and Crime* (Belmont, Calif.: Wadsworth, 1990).

81. Denise W. Huggins, Loretta Capeheart, and Elizabeth Newman, "Deviants or Scapegoats: An Examination of Pseudofamily Groups and Dyads in Two Texas Prisons," *Prison Journal* 86, no. 1 (March 2006): 114–139.

82. Cynthia B. Hart, "Gender Differences in Social Support among Inmates," *Women and Criminal Justice* 6, no. 2 (1995): 67–68.

83. Ira J. Silverman, *Corrections: A Comprehensive View*, 2nd ed. (Belmont, Calif.: Wadsworth, 2001), p. 200.

84. J. Diaz-Cotto, *Gender, Ethnicity, and the State: Latina and Latino Prison Politics* (Albany, N.Y.: New York State University Press, 1996).

85. Katherine S. Van Wormer and Clemens Bartolas, *Women and the Criminal Justice System* (Boston: Allyn and Bacon, 2000), p. 66.

86. Imogene L. Moyer, "Differential Social Structures and Homosexuality among Women in Prison," *Virginia Social Science Journal* 13 (1978): 13–19.

87. Owens, *In the Mix*, p. 198.

88. Allen J. Beck and Paige M. Harrison, *Sexual Victimization in Prisons and Jails Reported by Inmates, 2008–09* (Washington, D.C.: U.S. Department of Justice, August 2010), Table 6, p. 12. Also Allen J. Beck and Marcus Berzofsky, *Sexual Victimization in Prisons and Jails Reported by Inmates, 2001–12* (Washington, D.C.: U.S. Department of Justice, 2014), p. 4.

89. Barbara Owen, James Wells, Joycelyn Pollock, Bernadette Muscat, and Stephanie Torres, *Gendered Violence and Safety: A Contextual Approach to Improving Security in Women's Facilities* (Washington, D.C.: U.S. Department of Justice, November 2008), p. vi.

90. Fleisher, Rison, and Helman, "Female Inmates," p. 34.
91. Michael Winsett, "Take a Look Inside Prison's Underground Economy," *Prison Writers* (2017), available at http://prisonwriters.com/the-underground-economy-in-prison (accessed October 15, 2017).
92. Ibid.
93. Ben Paynter, "Prison Economics: How Fish And Coffee Become Cash," *Wired Magazine*, January 3, 2011, available at https://www.wired.com/2011/01/st_prisoncurrencies (accessed October 15, 2017).

Chapter 12

1. James B. Jacobs, *Stateville: The Penitentiary in Mass Society* (Chicago: University of Chicago Press, 1977).
2. "At Stateville: The Calm Is Tense," *Corrections Magazine* 61, no. 3 (June 1980): 6–10, 15–19.
3. Nathan Kantrowitz, *Close Control: Managing a Maximum Security Prison: The Story of Ragen's Stateville Penitentiary* (Albany, N.Y.: Harrow and Heston, 1996).
4. Robert Freeman, "Management and Administrative Issues," in *Prisons: Today and Tomorrow*, edited by Jocelyn M. Pollock (Gaithersburg, Md.: Aspen, 1997), p. 279.
5. James MacGregor Burns, *Leadership* (New York: Harper & Row, 1978).
6. M. Kay Harris, "A Call for Transformational Leadership for Corrections," *Corrections Management Quarterly* 3, no. 1 (1997): 22–25.
7. John P. Kotter, *Leading Change* (Boston: Harvard Business Review Press, 2012).
8. Thomas Baker, Jill A. Gordon, and Faye S. Taxman, "A Hierarchical Analysis of Correctional Officers' Procedural Justice Judgments of Correctional Institutions: Examining the Influence of Transformational Leadership," *Justice Quarterly*, 2014, available at http://dx.doi.org/10.1080/07418825.2013.877517 (accessed March 25, 2014).
9. John J. DiIulio, Jr., *Governing Prisons: A Comparative Study of Correctional Management* (New York: Free Press, 1987), pp. 188–189.
10. James J. Stephan, "Census of State and Federal Correctional Facilities, 2005," *National Prisoner Statistics Program* (Washington, D.C.: U.S. Department of Justice, October 2008), p. 4.
11. Tracey Kyckelhahn and Tara Martin, "Justice Expenditure and Employment Extracts, 2010—Preliminary," *Justice Expenditure and Employment Series* (Washington, D.C.: U.S. Department of Justice, Table 2, available at http://www.bjs.gov/index.cfm?ty=pbdetail&iid=4679 (accessed January 7, 2018).
12. Ibid.
13. Op. cit., p. 5.
14. Bureau of Labor Statistics, "Occupational Employment and Wages, May 2016: Correctional Officers and Jailers," *Occupational Employment Statistics* (Washington, D.C.: U.S. Department of Labor, 2017). Stephan, op. cit.
15. Bureau of Labor Statistics, "Women in the Labor Force: A Databook," *BLS Reports* (Washington, D.C.: U.S. Department of Labor, 2014), p. 38.
16. Curtis Prout and Robert N. Ross, *Care and Punishment: The Dilemmas of Prison Medicine* (Pittsburgh, Pa.: University of Pittsburgh Press, 1988), p. 152.
17. Lucien X. Lombardo, *Guards Imprisoned*, 2nd ed. (Cincinnati, Ohio: Anderson, 1989).
18. Andrew Metz, "Life on the Inside: The Jailers," in *Exploring Corrections: A Book of Readings* (Boston: Allyn and Bacon, 2002), p. 65.
19. Op. cit., p. 64.
20. M. A. Farkas and P. K. Manning, "The Occupational Cultures of Corrections and Police Officers," *Journal of Crime and Justice* 20, no. 2 (1997): 51–68.
21. Lee Dickenson, *The Keepers of the Keys* (Fort Bragg, Calif.: Lost Coast, 1999), pp. 142–143.
22. National Institute of Justice, *Correctional Officer Safety and Wellness – What We Learned from the Research Literature* (Washington, D.C.: U.S. Department of Justice, 2017).
23. Peter Finn, *Addressing Correctional Officer Stress: Programs and Strategies* (Washington, D.C.: U.S. Department of Justice, National Institute of Justice, December 2000).
24. Op. cit., p. 13.
25. Kelly Ann Cheeseman and Wendi Goodin-Fahncke, "The Impact of Gender on Correctional Employee Perceptions of Work Stress," *Corrections Compendium* 36, no. 2 (2011): 1–2.
26. Jon R. Sorenson, Mark D. Cunningham, Mark P. Vigen, and S.O. Woods, "Serious Assaults on Prison Staff: A Descriptive Analysis," *Journal of Criminal Justice* 39, no. 2 (March/April 2011): 143–150.
27. From the Correctional Peace Officer Foundation, http://cpof.org/fallen-officers/by-year/ (accessed October 15, 2017).
28. United States Government Accountability Office, *Bureau of Prisons: Evaluating the Impact of Protective Equipment Could Help Enhance Officer Safety* (Washington, D.C.: U.S. Government Accountability Office, 2011).
29. V. Wolfe Mahfoed, Wendi Pollock, and Dennis Longmire, "Leave it at the Gate: Job Stress and Satisfaction in Correctional Staff," *Criminal Justice Studies* 26, no. 3 (2013): 308–325.
30. Frank V. Ferdik and Hayden P. Smith, *Correctional Officer Safety and Wellness Literature Synthesis* (Washington, D.C.: U.S. Department of Justice, 2017).
31. Michael Pittaro, "Stress, Burnout, and Suicide Among Correctional Workers: The Silent Killers," *Medium*, February 11, 2016, available at https://medium.com/@michaelpittaro/correctional-officers-are-killing-themselves-22222af7912 (accessed October 21, 2017).
32. Colette S. Peters, "Helping Ourselves: Working Together to Promote Staff Well-Being," *Corrections Today* (November/December 2017): 7–8.
33. American Correctional Association, "Resolution on the Term 'Correctional Officer,'" *Corrections Today* (April 1993): 60.
34. Bureau of Labor Statistics, "Occupational Employment and Wages, May 2016: Correctional Officers and Jailers," *Occupational Employment Statistics* (Washington, D.C.: U.S. Department of Labor, 2017).
35. Bureau of Labor Statistics, "Women in the Labor Force: A Databook," *BLS Reports* (Washington, D.C.: U.S. Department of Labor, 2014), p. 38.
36. Texas Department of Criminal Justice (Corrections), salaries effective 9-1-17, available at https://www.tdcj.state.tx.us/divisions/hr/coinfo/cosalary.html (accessed October 15, 2017); and California Department of Corrections and Rehabilitation, available at http://cdcr.ca.gov/Career_Opportunities/POR/pay.html (accessed October 15, 2017).
37. Frank E. Riley and Beverly A. Wilder, "Hiring Correctional Staff with the Right Stuff," *Corrections Today* (June 2000): 91.
38. Interview with Gary D. Zavislak. Reprinted with Permission.
39. Gary F. Cornelius and Kevin Courtright, "Colleges and Corrections: The Value of Partnerships," *Corrections Today* (November/December 2017): 15–17.
40. Quoting correctional officer Donna Verrastro in an AP National article by David Crary, "High Stress, Low Glamor: Correctional Officers Struggle with Workplace Strains," PoliceOne.com *News*, May 8, 2005, available at https://www.policeone.com/health-fitness/articles/100392-High-Stress-Low-Glamor-Correctional-Officers-Struggle-with-Workplace-Strains/ (accessed November 1, 2017).
41. Jeanne B. Stinchcomb, Susan W. McCampbell, and Leslie Leip, *The Future is Now: Recruiting, Retaining, and Developing the 21st Century Jail Workforce* (Naples, Fla.: Center for Public Policies, 2009), p. 18.
42. Ibid.
43. Glen Castlebury, "Correctional Officer Recruitment and Retention in Texas," *Corrections Today* 64, no. 3 (June 2001): 80–83.
44. Jane Lommel, "Turning Around Turnover," *Corrections Today* 66, no. 5 (August 2004): 54–57.
45. Cece Hill, "Staff Recruitment and Workforce Issues," *Corrections Compendium* 31, no. 3 (May/June 2006): 15–32.
46. Lacey, T. A. & Wright, B. (2009). Employment outlook: 2008–18: Occupational employment projections to 2018. Bureau of Labor Statistics, available at http://www.bls.gov/opub/mlr/2009/11/art5full.pdf (accessed October 30, 2017).
47. Pew Center on the States, *Ten Steps Corrections Directors Can Take to Strengthen Performance* (Washington, D.C.: The Pew Charitable Trusts, May 2008).
48. Brian E. Cronin, Ralph Klessig, and William D. Sprenkle, "Recruiting and Retaining Staff through Culture Change," *Corrections Today* 70, no. 4 (August 2008): 48–51.

49. Gary C. Mohr, "Samberg Program Improves Leadership and Addresses Turnover," *Corrections Today* 71, no. 2 (April 2009): 56–58.

50. Craig Runde and William K. Rusak, "Want to Improve Safety and Security? Manage Conflict Effectively!" unpublished white paper, 2015.

51. Stan Stojkovic and Mary Ann Farkas, *Correctional Leadership: A Cultural Perspective* (Belmont, Calif.: Wadsworth/Thompson, 2003), p. 5.

52. For a good discussion of the various models of prison organizational culture, see Stojkovic and Farkas, *Correctional Leadership*, pp. 37–47.

53. M. A. Farkas and P. K. Manning, "The Occupational Cultures of Policing and Correctional Work," *Journal of Crime and Justice* 22, no. 2 (1997): 51–68.

54. These two culture types were created by Richard P. Seiter, based on his thirty-five year career of working in or overseeing prisons.

55. Richard P. Seiter, *Correctional Administration: Integrating Theory and Practice*, 3rd ed. (Boston, Mass.: Pearson, 2017), p. 195.

56. Norman A. Carlson, Karen M. Hess, and Christine M. H. Orthmann, *Corrections in the Twenty-First Century: A Practical Approach* (Belmont, Calif.: Wadsworth, 1999), p. 441.

57. 42 U.S.C. 2000e-2 (1976), p. 703(e).

58. *Dothard v. Rawlinson*, 433 U.S. 321 (1977).

59. *Gunther v. Iowa*, 462 F., Suppl. 952 (N.D. Iowa 1979).

60. Camp and Camp, *2002 Corrections Yearbook*, 2003, pp. 159, 164, 165.

61. Bureau of Labor Statistics, "Women in the Labor Force: A Databook," *BLS Reports* (Washington, D.C.: U.S. Department of Labor, 2014), p. 38. In addition, this report shows 45.7 percent of the 105,000 probation officers and prison correctional treatment specialists are women (p. 36).

62. Lynn E. Zimmer, *Women Guarding Men* (Chicago: University of Chicago Press, 1986), pp. 53–54.

63. See Nancy C. Jurik and Gregory J. Halembia, "Gender, Working Conditions and the Job Satisfaction of Women in a Non-Traditional Occupation: Female Correctional Officers in Men's Prisons," *Sociological Quarterly* 25 (1984): 551–566. Also see Lincoln J. Fry and Daniel Glaser, "Gender Differences in Work Adjustment of Prison Employees," *Journal of Offender Counseling, Services and Rehabilitation* 12 (1987): 39–52.

64. Herbert Holeman and Barbara Krepps-Hess, *Women Correctional Officers in the California Department of Corrections* (Sacramento, Calif.: California Department of Corrections, Research Unit, 1983).

65. See Kevin Wright and William Saylor, "Male and Female Employees' Perceptions of Prison Work: Is There a Difference?" *Justice Quarterly* 8 (1991): 505–524.

66. Kelly A. Cheeseman, Janet L. Mullings, and James W. Marquart, "Inmate Perceptions of Security Staff across Various Custody Levels," *Corrections Management Quarterly* 5, no. 2 (2001): 44.

67. Mark R. Pogrebin and Eric D. Poole, "Sex, Gender, and Work: The Case of Women Jail Officers," *Sociology of Crime, Law, and Deviance* 1 (1998): 105–124.

68. Joycelyn M. Pollock, "Women in Corrections: Custody and the 'Caring Ethic,'" in *Women, Law, and Social Control*, edited by Alida V. Merlo and Joycelyn M. Pollock (Boston: Allyn and Bacon, 1995), p. 111.

69. Interview with Pamela McBride. Reprinted with Permission.

Chapter 13

1. Richard P. Seiter, *Correctional Administration: Integrating Theory and Practice*, 3rd ed. (Boston, MA: Pearson, 2017), pp. 291–292.

2. *The Security Audit Program: A "How To" Guide and Model Instrument for Adaptation to Local Standards, Policies, and Procedures* (Washington, D.C.: U.S. Department of Justice, National Institute of Corrections, 1999), p. 1.

3. James D. Henderson, W. Hardy Rauch, and Richard L. Phillips, *Guidelines for the Development of a Security Program*, 3rd ed. (Alexandria, Va.: American Correctional Association, 2013), p. 21.

4. Interview by A Director of Corrections - George A. Lombardi. Reprinted with Permission.

5. Henderson, Rauch, and Phillips, op. cit., pp. 143–144.

6. "Use of Smuggled Cell Phones on the Rise in Florida Prisons," *CBS/Miami/AP* (February 16, 2014), available at http://miami.cbslocal.com/2014/02/16/use-of-smuggled-cell-phones-on-the-rise-in-floridas-prisons (accessed October 23, 2017).

7. Michele Coppola, "Corrections Department Allowing Use of Cordless Phones for Inmates," *TECHBeat* (July/August 2014): 11–13.

8. Becky Lewis, "Minnesota Reduces Phone Rates to Combat Contraband Cellphones," *TECHBeat* (March/April 2014): 14–15.

9. Letter from four U.S. Senators and 48 Members of Congress to Chairman Ajit Pai and Commissioner Mignon Clyburn, October 4, 2017.

10. William Falcon, "Special Technologies for Law Enforcement and Corrections," *NIJ Journal* 252 (July 2005): 22–27.

11. National Law Enforcement and Corrections Technology Center, *Introduction to Portal Contraband Detection Technology* (Gaithersburg, Md.: National Institute of Justice, 2013).

12. Timothy L. Smith, *Technology Advantage: Using Shoulder Mounted Cameras within a Detention Facility* (Washington, D.C.: U.S. Department of Justice, 2013).

13. Henderson, Rauch, and Phillips, op. cit., p. 129.

14. Federal Bureau of Prisons, "Inmate Discipline," *Policy Statement Number 5270.09* (Washington, D.C.: U.S. Department of Justice, Bureau of Prisons, August 1, 2011), chapter 5, pp. 4–6.

15. For a good historical overview, see Reid H. Montgomery, Jr., and Gordon A. Crews, *A History of Correctional Violence: An Examination of Reported Causes of Riots and Disturbances* (Lanham, Md.: American Correctional Association, 1998); and Randy James, "Prison Riots," *Time Magazine*, August 11, 2009, available at http://content.time.com/time/magazine/article/0,9171,1916301,00.html (accessed December 1, 2017).

16. Alene Tchekmedyian, "One Inmate Is Killed and Several Injured in Prison Riot Near San Luis Obispo," *Los Angeles Times*, September 24, 2017, available at http://www.latimes.com/local/lanow/la-me-ln-prison-riot-20170924-story.html (accessed October 18, 2017).

17. There are several official and government reports on this riot. However, a source of interesting reading is Tom Wicker, *A Time to Die* (New York: Quadrangle/New York Times Book Company, 1975).

18. Attorney General's Office, *Report of the Attorney General on the February 2 and 3, 1980 Riot at the Penitentiary of New Mexico* (Santa Fe, N.Mex.: State of New Mexico, Office of the Attorney General, 1980).

19. A BBC documentary describes the New Mexico Penitentiary riot and the savagery that resulted. It can be seen at https://youtu.be/3M-hPpuAqwQ.

20. Reginald A. Wilkinson and Thomas J. Stickrath, "After the Storm: Anatomy of a Riot's Aftermath," *Corrections Management Quarterly* 1, no. 1 (1996): 16.

21. Henderson, Rauch, and Phillips, pp. 180–181.

22. R. Arjen Boin and Menno J. Van Duin, "Prison Riots as Organized Failures: A Managerial Perspective," *Prison Journal* 75, no. 3 (1995): 365.

23. Russ Savage, Meg Savage, and Eugene Atherton, *Preventing and Managing Riots and Disturbances: Using the Incident Command System for Corrections* (Alexandria, Va.: American Correctional Association, 2014).

24. Earnest A. Step, "Emergency Management," in *Prison and Jail Administration: Practice and Theory*, edited by Peter M. Carlson, 3e (Sudbury, Mass.: Jones and Bartlett, 2015), p. 463.

25. A good description of the negotiation process is presented in Thomas J. Fagan and Dyone Augustin, "Crisis Negotiation in Correctional Settings," in *Prison and Jail Administration: Practice and Theory*, edited by Peter M. Carlson, 3e (Sudbury, Mass.: Jones and Bartlett, 2015), pp. 471–484.

Chapter 14

1. President's Commission on Law Enforcement and the Administration of Justice, *The Challenge of Crime in a Free Society* (Washington, D.C.: U.S. Government Printing Office, 1967), p. 183.

2. Douglas Lipton, Robert Martinson, and Judith Wilks, *The Effectiveness of Correctional Treatment* (New York: Praeger, 1975).

3. Robert Martinson, "What Works? Questions and Answers about Prison Reform," *The Public Interest* 35 (1974): 25.

4. Barry Krisberg and Susan Marchionna, "Attitudes of US Voters toward Prisoners Rehabilitation and Reentry Policies," *Focus: Views from the National Council on Crime and Delinquency* (Washington, D.C.: National Council on Crime and Delinquency, April 2006).

5. The Opportunity Agenda, *An Overview of Public Opinion and Discourse on Criminal Justice Issues* (New York, NY: The Opportunity Agenda, 2014).

6. Francis T. Cullen and Brandon K. Applegate, eds., *Offender Rehabilitation: Effective Correctional Intervention* (Aldershot, England: Ashgate, Dartmouth, 1998), p. xiv.

7. Tolbert, M., *A Reentry Education Model: Supporting Education and Career Advancement for Low-Skill Individuals in Corrections*, MPR Associates, Inc., Prepared for the U.S. Department of Education Office of Vocational and Adult Education (OVAE), 2012.

8. Jennifer Bronson and Marcus Berzofsky, "Indicators of Mental Health Problems Reported by Prisoners and Jail Inmates, 2011–12," *BJS Special Report* (Washington, D.C.: U.S. Department of Justice, 2017), p. 13.

9. National Center for Education Statistics, *Literacy behind Bars* (Washington, D.C.: U.S. Department of Education, 2007). Similar findings were reported in Grant Duwe and Valerie Clark, "The Effects of Prison-Based Programming on Recidivism and Employment," *The Prison Journal* 94 (2014): 454–478.

10. James J. Stephan, "Census of State and Federal Correctional Facilities, 2005," *BJS National Prisoner Statistics Program* (Washington, D.C.: U.S. Department of Justice, 2008), p. 5.

11. Caroline Wolf Harlow, *Education and Correctional Populations* (Washington, D.C.: U.S. Department of Justice, Bureau of Justice Statistics, January 2003), p. 5.

12. Stephan, op. cit.

13. Stephen J. Steurer, John Linton, John Nally, and Susan Lockwood, "The Top Nine Reasons to Increase Correctional Education Programs," *Corrections Today* 72, no. 4 (August 2010): 40–43.

14. Commission on Accreditation for Corrections, "Comprehensive Education Program, Standard 4-44070," *Standards for Adult Correctional Institutions* (College Park, Md.: American Correctional Association, 2003), p. 149.

15. Two studies that did not link education achievement in prison with reduced recidivism are Gennaro F. Vito and Richard Tewksbury, "Improving the Educational Skills of Inmates: The Results of an Impact Evaluation," *Corrections Compendium* 24, no. 10 (1999): 1–17. Also see Stephen J. Bahr, Lish Harris, James K. Fisher, and Anita Harker Armstrong, "Successful Reentry: What Differentiates Successful and Unsuccessful Parolees?" *International Journal of Offender Therapy and Comparative Criminology* 54, no. 5 (October 2010): 667–692.

16. See J. Gerber and E. J. Fritsch, "Adult Academic and Vocational Correctional Education Programs: A Review of Recent Research," *Journal of Offender Rehabilitation* 22 (1995): 199–242; M. D. Harer, "Recidivism among Federal Prisoners Released in 1987," *Journal of Correctional Education* 46, no. 3 (1995): 98–128; Mitchell Jancic, "Does Correctional Education Have an Effect on Recidivism?" *Journal of Correctional Education* 49, no. 4 (1998): 152–161; and K. Adams, K. J. Bennett, T. J. Flanagan, J. W. Marquart, S. J. Cuvelier, E. Fritsch, J. Gerber, D. R. Longmire, and V. S. Burton, Jr., "Large-Scale Multidimensional Test of the Effect of Prison Education Programs on Offenders' Behavior," *Prison Journal* 74, no. 4 (December 1994): 433–449. Also for a good summary of other studies, see James S. Vacca, "Educated Prisoners are Less Likely to Return to Prison," *Journal of Correctional Education* 55, no. 4 (December 2004): 297–305.

17. Lois M. Davis, Robert Bozick, Jennifer L. Steele, Jessica Saunders, and Jeremy N.V. Miles, *Evaluating the Effectiveness of Correctional Education* (Santa Monica, Calif.: The Rand Corporation, 2013), p. 29.

18. William G. Saylor and Gerald G. Gaes, "Training Inmates through Industrial Work Participation and Vocational and Apprenticeship Instruction," *Corrections Management Quarterly* 1, no. 2 (1997): 40.

19. Shakoor A. Ward, "Career and Technical Education in United States Prisons: What Have We Learned," *Journal of Correctional Education* 60, no. 3 (September 2009): 191–200.

20. John Linton, "Inmate Education Makes Sense," *Corrections Today* 60, no. 3 (1998): 18.

21. Steve Peacock, "BOP Proposes Inmates Pay All Tuition Costs for College," *Corrections Journal* 4, no. 10 (2000): 7.

22. Cathryn A. Chappell, "Post-Secondary Correctional Education and Recidivism: A Meta-Analysis of Research Conducted 1990–1999," *Journal of Correctional Education* 55, no. 2 (June 2004): 148–169.

23. Duwe and Clark, 2014, op. cit. Also, Ryang Hui Kim and David Clark, "Effect of Prison-Based College Education Programs on Recidivism: Propensity Score Matching Approach," *Journal of Criminal Justice* 41, no. 3 (2013): 196–204.

24. Jennifer C. Kerr, "Obama to Extend College Aid Grants to Some Prisoners," *PBS News Hour*, July 31, 2015, available at https://www.pbs.org/newshour/nation/obama-extend-college-aid-grants-prison-inmates (accessed November 1, 2017).

25. Michigan Department of Corrections, *Post Secondary Expansion – Correctional Education* (Lansing, MI: Department of Corrections, 2017).

26. Information on recent issues regarding corrections education was provided by Stephen J. Steurer, Executive Director of the Correctional Education Association in a January 6, 2014, telephone interview.

27. Daniel McGraw, "The Giant GED Gap," *CityBeat*, January 7, 2015, available at http://citybeat.com/cincinnati/article-31883-the_giant_ged_gap.html (accessed October 22, 2017).

28. Interview by A Correctional Educator Catherine L. Linaweave. Reprinted with Permission.

29. Doris J. James and Lauren E. Glaze, "Mental Health Problems of Prison and Jail Inmates," *Bureau of Justice Statistics Special Report* (Washington, D.C.: U.S. Department of Justice, September 2006), p. 1.

30. Paula M. Ditton, *Mental Health and Treatment of Inmates and Probationers* (Washington, D.C.: U.S. Department of Justice, Bureau of Justice Statistics, 1999).

31. E. Fuller Torrey et al., *The Treatment of Persons with Mental Illness in Prisons and Jails: A State Survey* (Washington, D.C.: Treatment Advocacy Center, 2014), p. 6.

32. Jennifer Bronson and Marcus Berzofsky, "Indicators of Mental Health Problems Reported by Prisoners and Jail Inmates, 2011–12," *BJS Special Report* (Washington, D.C.: U.S. Department of Justice, 2017).

33. Seth Jacob Prins and Laura Draper, *Improving Outcomes for People with Mental Illnesses Under Community Corrections Supervision* (New York: Council of State Government Justice Center, 2009).

34. Allen J. Beck and Laura J. Maruschak, *Mental Health Treatment in State Prisons, 2000* (Washington, D.C.: U.S. Department of Justice, Bureau of Justice Statistics, July 2001).

35. James and Glaze, "Mental Health Problems of Prison and Jail Inmates," p. 9.

36. Ibid.

37. Beck and Maruschak, 2000, op. cit., p. 3.

38. Department of Rehabilitation and Correction, *Mental Health Care in Ohio Corrections* (Columbus: Ohio Department of Rehabilitation and Correction, 1997), p. 4.

39. Grant Duwe, *The Use and Impact of Correctional Programming for Inmates on Pre- and Post-Release Outcomes* (Washington, D.C.: U.S. Department of Justice, 2017).

40. Michael S. Caudy, Joseph M. Durso, and Faye S. Taxman, "How Well do Dynamic Needs Predict Recidivism? Implications for Risk Assessment and Risk Reduction," *Journal of Criminal Justice* 41 (2013): 458–466.

41. Christopher J. Mumola and Jennifer C. Karberg, "Drug Use and Dependence, State and Federal Prisoners, 2004," *Bureau of Justice Statistics Special Report* (Washington, D.C.: U.S. Department of Justice, Bureau of Justice Statistics, October 2006), p. 1.

42. Ibid., p. 9.

43. Office of National Drug Control Policy, *The National Drug Control Strategy: 1998* (Washington, D.C.: The White House, February 1998).

44. Ojmarrh Mitchell, David B. Wilson, and Doris L. MacKenzie, "Dores Incarceration-Based Drug Treatment Reduce Recidivism? A Metal-Analytic Synthesis of the Literature," *Journal of Experimental Criminology* 3 (2007): 353–375.

45. Federal Bureau of Prisons, "Drug Treatment Programs in Federal Prisons," in *Best Practices: Excellence in Corrections*, edited by Edward E. Rhine (Lanham, Md.: American Correctional Association, 1998), pp. 427–430.

46. Federal Bureau of Prisons, *TRIAD Drug Treatment Evaluation Six-Month Report: Executive Summary* (Washington, D.C.: U.S. Department of Justice, 1998).

47. For an overview of several studies, see Duwe, 2017, op. cit.

48. Stephen J. Bahr, Amber L. Masters, and Bryan M. Taylor, "What Works in Substance Abuse Treatment Programs for Offenders?" *The Prison Journal* 92, no. 2 (June 2012): 155–174.

49. Texas Department of Criminal Justice, *Community and Public Work Project*, Press Release on August 17, 2015, available at http://www.tdcj.texas.gov/TDCJ_community_work.html (accessed October 31, 2017)

50. Richard P. Seiter, *Correctional Administration* (Boston, MA: Pearson Education, 2017), p. 340.

51. Camille Graham Camp and George M. Camp, *The 2001 Corrections Yearbook* (Middletown, Conn.: The Criminal Justice Institute, 2002), pp. 118 and 124.

52. Camp and Camp, op. cit., p. 120.

53. National Institute of Justice, *Developing Private Sector Prison Industries: From Concept to Start Up* (Washington, D.C.: U.S. Government Printing Office, 1990), p. 22.

54. Marilyn C. Moses and Cindy J. Smith, "Factories behind Fences: Do Prison 'Real Work' Programs Work?" *NIJ Journal*, Issue 257 (2007): pp. 36–39.

55. Bureau of Justice Assistance, "Prison Industry Enhancement Certification Program," *Bureau of Justice Assistance: Program Brief* (Washington, D.C.: U.S. Department of Justice, March 2004).

56. Ibid.

57. Cindy J. Smith et al., *Correctional Industries Preparing Inmates for Re-Entry: Recidivism & Post-release Employment* (Washington, D.C.: U. S. Department of Justice, 2006).

58. William G. Saylor and Gerald G. Gaes, "The Post-Release Employment Project: Prison Work Has Measurable Effects on Post-Release Success," *Federal Prisons Journal* 2, no. 4 (1992): 33–36.

59. See Mark W. Lipsey, Gabrielle L. Chapman, and Nana A. Landenberger, "Cognitive-Behavior Programs for Offenders," *The Annuals of the American Academy of Political and Social Science* 578 (2001): 144–157. Also Mark W. Lipsey, Nana A. Landenberger, and Sandra J. Wilson, "Effects of Cognitive-Behavioral Programs for Criminal Offenders: A Systematic Review," *Campbell Systematic Reviews* 6 (2007), available at https://www.campbellcollaboration.org/media/k2/attachments/1028_R.pdf (accessed November 1, 2017).

60. Christopher T. Lowenkamp, Dana Hubbard, Matthew D. Makarios, and Edward J. Latessa, "A Quasi-Experimental Evaluation of Thinking for Change: A 'Real World' Application," *Criminal Justice and Behavior* 36 (2009): 137–146.

61. Stephanie C. Boddie and Cary Funk, *Religion in Prisons: A 50-State Survey of Prison Chaplains* (Baltimore, MD: Annie E. Casey Foundation, 2012).

62. Grant Duwe and Michele King, "Can Faith-Based Correctional Programs Work? An Outcome Evaluation of the InnerChange Freedom Initiative in Minnesota," *International Journal of Offender Therapy and Comparative Criminology* 57 (2013): 813–841.

63. Scott D. Camp, Dawn M. Daggett, Okyun Kwon, and Jody Klein-Saffan, "The Effect of Faith Program Participation on Prison Misconduct: The Life Connections Program," *Journal of Criminal Justice* 36 (2008): 389–395.

64. The weightlifting issue is discussed in Reginald A. Wilkinson and Thomas J. Stickrath, "Public Opinion: Sometimes You're the Windshield, Sometimes You're the Bug," *Corrections Management Quarterly* 1, no. 3 (1997): 10–14.

65. Richard P. Seiter. "Managing Within Political Comfort Zones: An Interview with Allen Ault," *Corrections Management Quarterly* 1, no. 1 (1997): 74–75.

66. Douglas Lipton, Robert Martinson, and Judith Wilks, *The Effectiveness of Correctional Treatment and What Works: A Survey of Treatment Evaluation Studies* (New York, NY: Praeger, 1975).

67. Francis T. Cullen and Paul Gendreau, "Assessing Correctional Rehabilitation: Policy, Practice, and Prospects," in *Policies, Processes, and Decisions of the Criminal Justice System*, edited by Julie Horney (Washington, D.C.: U.S. Department of Justice, National Institute of Justice, 2000), pp. 109–175.

68. Cullen and Gendreau, op. cit., p. 127.

69. See D. A. Andrews, Ivan Zinger, Robert D. Hoge, James Bonta, Paul Gendreau, and Francis D. Cullen, "Does Correctional Treatment Work? A Clinically Relevant and Psychologically Informed Meta-Analysis," *Criminology* 28 (August 1990): 369–404; and D. A. Andrews and James Bonta, *The Psychology of Criminal Conduct*, 2nd ed. (Cincinnati, Ohio: Anderson, 1998).

70. Andrews et al., "Does Correctional Treatment Work?" p. 374.

71. Mark W. Lipsey and David B. Wilson, "The Efficacy of Psychological, Educational, and Behavioral Treatment," *American Psychologist* 48, no. 12 (1993): 1181–1209.

72. Friedrich Losel, "The Efficacy of Correctional Treatment: A Review and Synthesis of Meta-Evaluations," in *What Works: Reducing Reoffending*, edited by James McGuire (West Sussex, England: Wiley, 1995): 79–111.

73. A good overview of these approaches is available in Edward J. Latessa, "Evaluating Correctional Programs," *151st International Training Course: Visiting Experts' Papers* (New York, NY: United Nations Institute for the Prevention of Crime and Treatment of Offenders, 2013): 64–76.

74. Matthew Makarios, Lori Lovins, Edward Latessa, and Paula Smith, "Staff Quality and Treatment Effectiveness: An Examination of the Relationship between Staff Factors and the Effectiveness of Correctional Program," *Justice Quarterly* Online (June 2014), available at http://www.tandfonline.com/doi/abs/10.1080/07418825.2014.924546?queryID=%24%7BresultBean.queryID%7D#.VJB-t8aRWyS (accessed December 15, 2017).

75. For a good overview of the results of correctional treatment in reducing recidivism, see Gerald G. Gaes, Timothy F. Flanagan, Laurence L. Motiuk, and Lynn Stewart, "Adult Correctional Treatment," in *Prisons*, edited by Michael Tonry and Joan Petersilia (Chicago, Ill.: The University of Chicago Press, 1999), pp. 361–426. Another useful report is Edward J. Latessa, *Evaluating Correctional Programs* (New York, NY: United Nations Publications, 2013).

76. Matthew Durose, Alexia D. Cooper, and Howard N. Snyder, "Recidivism of Prisoners Released in 30 States in 2005: Patterns from 2005 to 2010," *BJS Special Report* (Washington, D.C.: U.S. Department of Justice, 2014).

77. Steve Aos, Marna Miller, and Elizabeth Drake, *Evidence-Based Public Policy Options to Reduce Future Prison Construction, Criminal Justice Costs, and Crime Rates* (Olympia, Wash.: Washington State Institute for Public Policy, 2006).

78. Michael Antonio and Frederick R. Klunk, "Examining Offender Programming in Pennsylvania's Board of Probation and Parole," *Corrections Today* 76, no. 6 (November/December 2014): 42–44.

79. As noted on the ODRC website. See John Jarvis, "Prison Director Details Reform Plan," *The Marion Star,* March 6, 2012, available at http://pqasb.pqarchiver.com/marionstar/access/2602716871.html?FMT=ABS&date=Mar+06%2C+2012 (accessed December 12, 2014).

80. Department of Rehabilitation and Correction, *DRC Recidivism Rates*, available at http://www.drc.ohio.gov/Portals/0/Reentry/Reports/Key%20Recidivism%20Info/Recidivism%20Report%202016%20Final.pdf?ver=2017-05-30-131308-220 (accessed October 22, 2017).

Chapter 15

1. "Prisoner Petitions Filed in U.S. District Courts," Table C-2, *United States Courts: Statistics & Reports*, available at http://www.uscourts.gov/statistics-reports/caseload-statistics-data-tables?tn=&pn=78&t=68&m%5Bvalue%5D%5Bmonth%5D=12&y%5Bvalue%5D%5Byear%5D=2015 (accessed November 20, 2017).

2. *Ruffin v. Commonwealth of Virginia*, 62 Va. (21 Gratt.) 790, 796 (1871).

3. *Price v. Johnston*, 334 U.S. 266 (1948).

4. *Cooper v. Pate*, 378 U.S. 546 (1964).

5. Roger A. Hanson and Henry W. K. Daley, *Challenging the Conditions of Prisons and Jails: A Report on Section 1983 Litigation* (Washington, D.C.: U.S. Department of Justice, Bureau of Justice Statistics, 1994), pp. 1–2.

6. *Holt v. Sarver*, 309 F. Supp. 362 [E.D. Ark. 1970], aff'd 442 F.2d 304 9th Cir. (1971).

7. *Bell v. Wolfish*, 441 U.S. 520 (1979).

8. *Solem v. Helm*, 463 U.S. 277 (1983).

9. *Pell v. Procunier*, 417 U.S. 817 (1974).

10. *United States v. Georgia*, 546 U.S. 151 (2006).

11. *Pugh v. Locke*, 406 F. 2d 318 (1976).

12. *Bell v. Wolfish*, 441 U.S. 520 (1979).

13. *Rhodes v. Chapman*, 452 U.S. 337 (1981).

14. *Wilson v. Seiter*, 111 S. Ct. 2321 (1991).

15. *Brown v. Plata*, 131 S. Ct. 1910, 179 L. Ed. 2d 969 (2011).

16. *Brown v. Plata*, 134 S.Ct. 436 (U.S. 2013)

17. *Cooper v. Pate*, 378 U.S. 546 (1964).

18. *Cruz v. Beto*, 405 U.S. 319 (1972).

19. *Theriault v. Silber*, 391 F. Supp. 579 (1977).

20. *Kahane v. Carlson*, 527 F.2d 492 (2d Cir. 1975).

21. *O'Lone v. Estate of Shabazz*, 482 U.S. 342 (1987).
22. *Hamilton v. Schriro*, 74 F.3d 1545 (8th Cir. 1996).
23. *Fowler v. Crawford*, U.S. App. LEXIS 15841 (8th Cir. 2008).
24. *Turner v. Safley*, 482 U.S. 78 (1987).
25. *Gittlemacker v. Prasse*, 428 F.2d 1 (3d Cir. 1970).
26. *Walker v. Blackwell*, 411 F.2d 23 (1969).
27. 42 U.S.C. 2000cc-1(a)(1)-(2), passed in 2000.
28. *Cutter v. Wilkinson*, 544 U.S. 709 (2005).
29. *Americans United for Separation of Church and State v. Prison Fellowship Ministries*, 432 F. Supp. 2d 862 (2006).
30. *Americans United for Separation of Church and State v. Prison Fellowship Ministries*, 509 F.3d 406 (2007).
31. *Hazel v. Crofoot*, 727 F.3d 983 (9th Cir Cal. 2013).
32. *Holt v. Sarver*, 309 F. Supp. 362 [E.D. Ark. 1970], *aff'd* 442 F.2d 304 9th Cir. (1971).
33. *Estelle v. Gamble*, 429 U.S. 97 (1976).
34. *Ramos v. Lamm*, 639 F.2d 559, 576 (1980).
35. *Fernandez v. United States*, 941 F.2d 1488 (1991).
36. *Portalatin v. Department of Corrections*, 979 A. 2d 944 (2009).
37. *Procunier v. Martinez*, 416 U.S. 396 (1974).
38. *McNamara v. Moody*, 606 F. Supp. 2d 621 (5th Cir. 1979).
39. *Turner v. Safley*, 482 U.S. 78 (1987).
40. *Jones v. North Carolina Prisoners' Labor Union, Inc.*, 433 U.S. 119 (1977).
41. *Sostre v. Otis*, 330 F. Supp. 941 (1971).
42. *Thornburgh v. Abbott*, 109 S. Ct. 1874 (1989).
43. *Guajardo v. Estelle*, 580 F.2d 748 (1978).
44. *Johnson v. Avery*, 393 U.S. 483 (1969).
45. *Younger v. Gilmore*, 404 U.S. 15 (1971).
46. *Bounds v. Smith*, 430 U.S. 817 (1977).
47. *Hudson v. Palmer*, 468 U.S. 517 (1984).
48. *Bell v. Wolfish*, 441 U.S. 520 (1979).
49. *Tribble v. Gardner*, 860 F.2d 321 (9th Cir. 1988).
50. *Grummett v. Rushen*, 587 F. Supp. 913 (9th Cir. 1984).
51. *Johnson v. Phelan*, 69 F.3d 144 (7th Cir. 1995).
52. *Boone v. City of Philadelphia*, 668 F. Supp. 2d 693 (2009).
53. *McBean v. City of New York*, Case No. 02 Civ 05426 (SDNY) (2010).
54. *Bull v. City and County of San Francisco*, 595 F. 3d 964 (2010).
55. *Florence v. Board of Chosen Freeholders for the County of Burlington*, 621 F. 3d 296 (2012).
56. *Wolff v. McDonnell*, 418 U.S. 539 (1974).
57. *Sandin v. Conner*, 515 U.S. 472 (1995).
58. *Turner v. Safley*, 482 U.S. 78 (1987).
59. *Wilson v. Seiter*, 111 S. Ct. 2321 (1991).
60. *Sandin v. Conner*, 515 U.S. 472 (1995).
61. As suggested in David Crary, "Law Curbing Inmates' Lawsuits Questioned," *USA Today*, February 13, 2008, available at http://usatoday30.usatoday.com/news/nation/2008-02-13-3685431048_x.htm (accessed December 8, 2014). And data from "Petitions Filed in U.S. District Courts by Federal and State Prisoners," Table 5.65.2012, *Sourcebook of Criminal Justice Statistics*, http://www.albany.edu/sourcebook/pdf/t5652012.pdf (accessed December 8, 2014).
62. James J. Stephan, "Census of State and Federal Correctional Facilities, 2005," *National Prisoner Statistics Program* (Washington, D.C.: U.S. Department of Justice, October 2008), p. 3.
63. Tracy L. Snell, "Capital Punishment 1999," *BJS Bulletin* (Washington, D.C.: U.S. Department of Justice, 2000).
64. Tracey Snell, "Capital Punishment, 2014–2015," *BJS Statistical Brief* (Washington, D.C.: U.S. Department of Justice, 2017).
65. From Snell, advanced count of executions, 2016, Ibid.
66. *Furman v. Georgia*, 408 U.S. 238 (1972).
67. *Robert v. Louisiana*, 428 U.S. 325 (1976); *Woodson v. North Carolina*, 428 U.S. 280 (1976).
68. *Gregg v. Georgia*, 428 U.S. 153 (1976).
69. *Coker v. Georgia*, 433 U.S. 584 (1977).
70. *Godfrey v. Georgia*, 446 U.S. 420 (1980).
71. *Tison v. Arizona*, 107 S. Ct. 1676 (1987).
72. *Ford v. Wainwright*, 477 U.S. 399 (1986).
73. *Penry v. Lynaugh*, 45 Cr. L. Rptr. 3188 (1989).
74. *Atkins v. Virginia*, 536 U.S. 304 (2002).

75. *Eddings v. Oklahoma*, 455 U.S. 104 (1982).
76. *Stanford v. Kentucky*, 492 U.S. 361 (1989).
77. *In re Stanford*, 123 S. Ct. 472 (2002).
78. As quoted in a story by the Associated Press, "Supreme Court Appears One Vote Shy of Rejecting Death Penalty for Young Killers," *St. Louis Post-Dispatch*, January 28, 2003, p. 2.
79. Thomas P. Bonczar and Tracy L. Snell, "Capital Punishment, 2004," *Bureau of Justice Statistics Bulletin* (Washington, D.C.: U.S. Department of Justice, 2005), p. 4.
80. *Roper v. Simmons*, 543 U.S. 551 (2005).
81. Bonczar and Snell, op. cit., p. 1.
82. *Kennedy v. Louisiana*, 554 U.S. 407 (2008).
83. Ibid.
84. Note that while only thirty-one states have a death penalty statute, some states that recently abolished it still have inmates on death row under a sentence of execution.
85. Tracy L. Snell, "Capital Punishment, 2014–2015, op. cit.
86. Tracy L. Snell, "Capital Punishment 2013—Statistical Tables, *BJS Statistics* (Washington, D.C.: U.S. Department of Justice, 2014), pp. 8–9.
87. *McCleskey v. Kemp*, 481 U.S. 279 (1989).
88. David C. Baldus, George F. Woodworth, and Charles A. Pulaski, Jr., *Equal Justice and the Death Penalty: A Legal and Empirical Analysis* (Boston: Northeastern University Press, 1990).
89. Snell, "Capital Punishment 2013," op. cit., p. 14.
90. Ibid.
91. Ibid., p. 16, updated with Snell, 2017.
92. *Baze et al. v. Rees*, 553 U.S. 35 (2008).
93. Greg Zoroya, "States Engage in Shadowy Deals as Death Penalty Drugs Dwindle," *USA Today* (March 18, 2014): pp. 1–2.
94. Greg Zoroya, "Oklahoma Delays 2 Executions because of Drug Shortage," *USA Today*, March 18, 2014, available at http://www.usatoday.com/story/news/nation/2014/03/18/oklahoma-execution-drugs-lethal-injection/6569749/ (accessed December 9, 2017).
95. Michael Graczyk, "Federal Appeals Court Overrules Judge Who Ordered Texas to Name Supplier of Lethal Drug," *Washington Post*, April 2, 2014, available at http://www.washingtonpost.com/politics/federal-judge-stops-two-texas-executions-demanding-state-name-supplier-of-lethal-drug/2014/04/02/5e0bf49e-bab3-11e3-96ae-f2c36d2b1245_story.html (accessed December 9, 2017).
96. Erik Eckholm, "One Execution Botched, Oklahoma Delays the Next," *New York Times*, April 29, 2014, available at http://www.nytimes.com/2014/04/30/us/oklahoma-executions.html?_r=0 (accessed December 9, 2017).
97. Debbie Elliott, "States Find Other Execution Methods After Difficulties with Lethal Injection," NPR, April 6, 2017.
98. Faith Karimi, Dakin And one, and Jason Hanna, "Arkansas Executes Kenneth Williams, 4th Inmate in 8 Days," CNN, April 28, 2017.
99. Elliott, op. cit.
100. As an example, see Isaac Ehrlich, "The Deterrent Effect of Capital Punishment: A Question of Life and Death," *American Economic Review* 65 (1975): 397–417.
101. Naci H. Mocan and R. Kaj Gittings, "Getting Off Death Row: Commuted Sentences and the Deterrent Effect of Capital Punishment," *Journal of Law and Economics* 21, no. 11 (2003): 453–478.
102. Scott H. Decker and Carol W. Kohfeld, "A Deterrence Study of the Death Penalty in Illinois," *Journal of Criminal Justice* 12 (1984): 367–377.
103. Ethan Cohen-Cole et al., *Reevaluating the Deterrent Effect of Capital Punishment: Model and Data Uncertainty* (Washington, D.C.: U.S. Department of Justice, December 2006).
104. John J. Donaohue and Justin Wolfers, "The Death Penalty: No Evidence for Deterrence," *The Economists' Voice*, April 2006, available at http://users.nber.org/~jwolfers/policy/DeathPenalty(BEPress).pdf (accessed December 9, 2017).
105. See Scott H. Decker and Carol W. Kohfeld, "The Deterrent Effect of Capital Punishment in the Five Most Active Execution States: A Time Series Analysis," *Criminal Justice Review* 15 (1990): 173–191; and W. C. Bailey, "Desegregation in Deterrence and Death Penalty Research: The Case of Murder in Chicago," *Journal of Criminal Law and Criminology* 74 (1983): 827–859.

106. National Research Council, "Committee on Deterrence and the Death Penalty," *Deterrence and the Death Penalty*, edited by Daniel S. Nagin and John V. Pepper (Washington, D.C.: The National Academies Press, 2012), p. 2.

107. "Respondents Belief as to the Deterrence of the Death Penalty," Table 2.57.2011, *Sourcebook of Criminal Justice Statistics Online*, available at http://www.albany.edu/sourcebook/pdf/t2572011.pdf (accessed December 9, 2017).

108. Interview with Stephen Huffman, A Warden Who Oversees Executions. Reprinted with Permission.

109. The most recent survey as to why people support the death penalty (2003) indicated that for those who support the death penalty for the crime of murder, 37 percent stated their reason was for "an eye for an eye/they took a life/it fits the crime." Table 2.55, available at http://www.albany.edu/sourcebook/pdf/t255.pdf (accessed December 9, 2017).

110. Robert M. Bohm, "Retribution and Capital Punishment: Toward a Better Understanding of Death Penalty Opinion," *Journal of Criminal Justice* 20 (1992): 227–236.

111. T. J. Keil and G. F. Vito, "Race and the Death Penalty in Kentucky Murder Trials," *American Journal of Criminal Justice* 20, no. 1 (Fall 1995): 17–36; Rebecca A. Rofferty, "In the Shadow of *McClesky v. Kemp*: Discriminatory Impact of the Death Sentencing Process," *New England Journal on Criminal and Civil Confinement* 21, no. 1 (Winter 1995): 271–312; R. N. Stone, "Killing of Charles Walker: Racial Bias and the Death Sentence," *Criminal Justice* 7, no. 2 (Summer 1992): 22–27, 54–55; and Jonathan R. Sorensen and Donald H. Wallace, "Capital Punishment in Missouri: Examining the Issue of Racial Disparity," *Behavioral Sciences and the Law* 13, no. 1 (Winter 1995): 61–80.

112. Jon Sorensen, Robert Wrinkle, Victoria Brewer, and James Mauquaut, "Capital Punishment and Deterrence: Examining the Effect of Executions on Murder in Texas," *Crime and Delinquency* 45, no. 4 (October 1999): 481–493; and Gennaro F. Vito and Deborah G. Wilson, "Back from the Dead: Tracking the Progress of Kentucky's *Furman*-Commuted Death Row Population," *Justice Quarterly* 5, no. 1 (1988): 101–111.

113. "Attitudes Toward the Better Penalty for Murder," Table 2.49.2010, *Sourcebook of Criminal Justice Statistics Online*, available at http://www.albany.edu/sourcebook/pdf/t2492010.pdf (accessed December 9, 2017).

114. Snell, "Capital Punishment 2013," op. cit., p. 12.

115. Hugo A. Bedau, *The Case Against the Death Penalty* (Washington, D.C.: American Civil Liberties Union, Capital Punishment Project, 1992).

116. Bohm, "Retribution and Capital Punishment."

117. Philip J. Cook and Donna B. Slawson, *The Costs of Processing Murder Cases in North Carolina* (Durham, N.C.: Duke University, Jerry Sanford Institute of Public Policy, 1993).

118. Robert S. Spangenberg and Elizabeth R. Walsh, "Capital Punishment or Life Imprisonment? Some Cost Considerations," *Loyola University of Los Angeles Law Review* 23, no. 1 (November 1989): 45–58.

119. John Roman et al., *The Cost of the Death Penalty in Maryland* (Washington, D.C.: The Urban Institute, March 2008).

120. Globe Editorial Writers, "The Cost of Capital Punishment," *Boston Globe.com*, April 15, 2009, available at http://www.boston.com/bostonglobe/editorial_opinion/editorials/articles/2009/04/15/the_cost_of_capital_punishment/ (accessed December 9, 2017).

121. Ed Barnes, "Just or Not, Cost of Death Penalty is a Killer for State Budgets," Fox *News.com*, March 27, 2010, available at http://www.foxnews.com/us/2010/03/27/just-cost-death-penalty-killer-state-budgets/ (accessed December 9, 2017).

122. R. Dieter, *Innocence and the Death Penalty: The Increasing Danger of Executing the Innocent* (Washington, D.C.: Death Penalty Information Center, 1997).

123. "Innocence: List of Those Freed from Death Row," *Death Penalty Information Center*, available at https://deathpenaltyinfo.org/innocence-list-those-freed-death-row (accessed December 9, 2017).

124. Bryan Stevenson, *Just Mercy: A Story of Justice and Redemption* (New York: NY: Spiegel & Grau, 2015).

125. Renee Cardwell Hughes, "The Death Penalty: A Failed System," in *The State of Corrections: 2001 Proceedings of the ACA Annual Conference* (Lanham, Md.: American Correctional Association, 2002), p. 123.

126. *The Harris Poll*, 2001, available at http://www.prodeathpenalty.com/news.htm (accessed December 9, 2014).

127. "Are you in Favor of the Death Penalty for Murder?" *Sourcebook of Criminal Justice Statistics*, available at http://www.albany.edu/sourcebook/pdf/t2512013.pdf (accessed December 9, 2017).

128. Ibid.

129. Michael Lipka, "Support for Death Penalty Drops among Americans," *Pew Research Center FactTank*, available at http://www.pewresearch.org/fact-tank/2014/02/12/support-for-death-penalty-drops-among-americans/ (accessed December 9, 2017).

130. Sourcebook, op. cit.

Chapter 16

1. An Interview With Reginald A. Wilkinson. Reprinted with Permission.

2. Danielle Kaeble and Lauren E. Glaze, "Correctional Populations in the United States, 2015," *BJS Bulletin* (Washington, D.C.: U.S. Department of Justice, December 2016), p. 2.

3. See "Prisoners in 2000," *Bureau of Justice Statistics Bulletin* (Washington, D.C.: U.S. Department of Justice, 2001).

4. Kaeble and Glaze, op. cit.

5. E. Ann Carson, "Prisoners in 2013," *BJS Bulletin* (Washington, D.C.: U.S. Department of Justice, 2014), p. 6.

6. E. Ann Carson, "Prisoners in 2016," *BJS Bulletin* (Washington, D.C.: U.S. Department of Justice, 2018), p. 8.

7. James Austin and Garry Coventry, *Emerging Issues on Privatized Prisons* (Washington, D.C.: U.S. Department of Justice, Bureau of Justice Assistance, February 2001), p. xi.

8. Richard F. Culp, "The Rise and Stall of Prison Privatization" (paper presented at the Academy of Criminal Justice Sciences, Boston, March 2003).

9. Peter Greenwood et al., "Estimated Benefits and Costs of California's New Mandatory Sentencing Law," in *Three Strikes and You're Out*, edited by David Shichor and Dale K. Sechrest (Thousand Oaks, Calif.: Sage, 1996), pp. 53–89.

10. For a good review of this issue, see Joseph W. Rogers, "The Greatest Correctional Myth: Winning the War on Crime through Incarceration," in *Public Policy, Crime, and Criminal Justice*, 2nd ed., edited by Barry W. Hancock and Paul M. Sharp (Upper Saddle River, N.J.: Prentice Hall, 2000), pp. 308–321.

11. Pretrial Services Resource Center, *A Second Look at Alleviating Jail Overcrowding: A Systems Perspective* (Washington, D.C.: U.S. Department of Justice, Bureau of Justice Assistance, October 2000), p. 2.

12. Pretrial Services Resource Center, op. cit., p. 66.

13. Danielle Kaeble and Lauren E. Glaze, "Correctional Populations in the United States, 2015," *BJS Bulletin* (Washington, D.C.: U.S. Department of Justice, 2016), p. 1.

14. Data from Bureau of Justice Statistics, U.S. Department of Justice, Corrections Facts at a Glance, Selected Years, available at http://www.bjs.gov/index.cfm?ty=pbse&sid=5 (accessed December 8, 2017) and from Danielle Kaeble and Lauren E. Glaze, "Correctional Populations in the United States, 2015, *BJS Bulletin* (Washington, DC: U.S. Department of Justice, 2016, p. 2).

15. Tracey Kyckelhahn, "State Correctional Expenditures, FY 1982–2010," *BJS Bulletin* (Washington, D.C.: U.S. Department of Justice, 2012. Expanded to 2016 by National Association of State Budget Officers (NASBO), *State Expenditures Report*, each year, 2011 to 2016 (Washington, D.C.: NASBO, 2017).

16. Christian Henrichson and Ruth Delany, *The Price of Prisons: What Incarceration Cost Taxpayers* (New York: Vera Institute of Justice, January 2012).

17. Elizabeth McNichol, Phil Oliff, and Nicholas Johnson, *States Continue to Feel Recession Impact* (Washington, D.C.: Center on Budget and Policy Priorities, March 2012).

18. The Pew Charitable Trusts, "Real Tax Revenue in 28 States has Recovered from Recession," *Fiscal 50: State Trends and Analysis*, November 7, 2017, available at http://www.pewtrusts.org/~/media/assets/2017/10/real_taxrevenue_map_v1_1012.pdf (accessed December 6, 2017).

19. Pew Center of the States, *One in 31: The Long Reach of American Corrections* (Washington, D.C.: Pew Charitable Trusts, March 2009), p. 11.

20. Pew Center of the States, op. cit., p. 15.

21. Christine S. Scott-Hayward, *The Fiscal Crisis in Corrections: Rethinking Policies and Practices* (New York: Vera Institute of Justice, 2009).

22. Scott-Hayward, op. cit., p. 3.

23. Vera Institute of Justice, *Managing State Prison Growth: Key Trends in Sentencing Policy* (New York: Vera Institute of Justice, January 2008).

24. E. Ann Carson and William J. Sabol, "Prisoners in 2011," *BJS Bulletin* (Washington, D.C.: U.S. Department of Justice 2012), p. 11.

25. Jeremy W. Peters, "Albany Reaches Deal to Repeal '70s Drug Laws," *The New York Times*, March 26, 2009, p. A21.

26. John Gramlich, "States Seek Alternatives to More Prisons," *Stateline.org*, June 18, 2007, http://www.stateline.org/live/details/story?contentId=217204 (accessed August 16, 2009).

27. "$30 million in Stimulus for Public Safety," A Report WKOW Television in Madison, Wisconsin, April 9, 2009, www.wkowtv.com/Gloval/story.asp?S=10157862 (accessed August 16, 2009).

28. William J. Sabor et al., *Prison and Jail Inmates at Midyear 2006* (Washington, D.C.: U.S Department of Justice, Bureau of Justice Statistics, June 2007).

29. Danielle Kaeble and Thomas P. Bonczar, *Probation and Parole in the United States, 2015* (Washington, D.C.: U.S. Department of Justice, Bureau of Justice Statistics, December 2016), p. 6.

30. E. Ann Carson and Elizabeth Anderson, "Prisoners in 2015," *BJS Bulletin* (Washington, D.C.: U.S. Department of Justice 2016), p. 11.

31. As cited in Janet Mandelstam, "California Study Looks at Factors Leading to Parole Revocation," *Corrections Today* 71, no. 5 (October 2009): 122–123.

32. Steve Aos, Marna Miller, and Elizabeth Drake, *Evidence-Based Public Policy Options to Reduce Future Prison Construction, Criminal Justice Costs, and Crime Rates* (Olympia, WA: Washington State Institute for Public Policy, 2006).

33. All of these examples were taken from Keith B. Richburg and Ashley Surdin, "Fiscal Pressures Lead Some States to Free Inmates Early," *Washington Post*, May 5, 2008, p. A01.

34. Gary C. Mohr in "Reforming the System: An Inside Perspective of how Ohio Achieved a Record-Low Recidivism Rate," *Council of State Governments Justice Center Newsletter* (March 2012), available at http://www.nationalreentryresourcecenter.org/announcements/3-12-12 (accessed March 20, 2012).

35. States participating in Justice Reinvestment Act approaches include Alabama, Arizona, Arkansas, Connecticut, Delaware, Georgia, Hawaii, Idaho, Indiana, Kansas, Kentucky, Louisiana, Massachusetts, Michigan, Missouri, Montana, Nebraska, Nevada, New Hampshire, North Carolina, Ohio, Oklahoma, Oregon, Pennsylvania, Rhode Island, South Carolina, South Dakota, Texas, Vermont, Washington, West Virginia, and Wisconsin.

36. Justice Center, *Reducing Recidivism: States Delivering Results* (New York, NY: Council of State Governments, 2017).

37. The Urban Institute, *Justice Reinvestment Initiative: Experiences from the States* (Washington, D.C.: U.S. Department of Justice, 2013).

38. Justice Center, *Justice Reinvestment in North Carolina: Three Years Later* (New York, NY: The Council of State Governments, 2014).

39. Presentation by Justice Michael Boggs of the Georgia Supreme Court, who was co-chair of the Georgia Justice Reinvestment Initiative. Association of State Correctional Administrators meetings, St. Louis, MO, August 19, 2017.

40. Justice Center, *Georgia's Justice Reinvestment Approach: Strengthening Probation and Increasing Public Safety* (New York: Council of State Governments, 2017).

41. Washington State Institute for Public Policy, *Benefit-Cost Ratio: Adult Criminal Justice*, updated May 2017, available at http://www.wsipp.wa.gov/BenefitCost?topicId=2 (accessed December 8, 2017).

42. Carl Hulse and Jennifer Steinhauer, "Sentencing Overhaul Proposed in Senate with Bipartisan Backing," *New York Times*, October 1, 2015, available at http://www.nytimes.com/2015/10/02/us/politics/senate-plan-to-ease-sentencing-laws.html?smid=nytcore-iphone-share&smprod=nytcore-iphone&_r=0 (accessed October 1, 2015).

43. Maya Rhodan, "Department of Justice to Release 6,000 Prisoners," *Time*, October 6, 2015, available at http://time.com/4063277/justice-department-6000-prisoners/ (accessed October 12, 2015).

44. Rebecca R. Ruiz, "Attorney General Orders Tougher Sentences, Rolling Back Obama Policy," *The New York Times*, May 12, 2017, available at https://www.nytimes.com/2017/05/12/us/politics/attorney-general-jeff-sessions-drug-offenses-penalties.html?_r=0 (accessed December 6, 2017).

45. BBC News, *Special Report: World Prison Populations*, available at http://news.bbc.co.uk/2/shared/spl/hi/uk/06/prisons/html/nn2page1.stm (accessed November 12, 2017).

46. The Prison Policy Initiative, *States of Incarceration: The Global Context*, available at https://www.prisonpolicy.org/global (accessed November 12, 2017).

47. The Mellman Group and Public Opinion Strategies, *National Survey Key Findings – Federal Sentencing and Prisons* (New York, NY: Pew Charitable Trusts, 2016).

48. Ibid.

49. Jeremy Travis, Bruce Western, and Steve Redburn, Editors, *The Growth of Incarceration in the United States: Exploring Causes and Consequences* (Washington, D.C.: The National Academies Press, 2014).

50. Ibid.

51. Op. cit., p. 315.

52. US Inflation Calculator, available online at http://www.usinflationcalculator.com (accessed November 12, 2017.

53. Danielle Kaeble and Thomas P. Bonczar, "Probation and Parole in the United States, 2015," *BJS Bulletin* (Washington, D.C.: U.S. Department of Justice, 2016).

54. Harry Allen, Evelyn Parks, Eric Carlson, and Richard Seiter, *Program Models, Halfway Houses* (Washington, D.C.: U.S. Department of Justice, 1978).

55. Edmund R. McGarrell and Timothy Flanagan, *Sourcebook of Criminal Justice Statistics, 1984* (Washington, D.C.: U.S. Department of Justice, 1985).

56. Camp and Camp, *2002 Corrections Yearbook*, pp. 100 and 101.

57. Ibid., pp. 103 and 104.

58. Andrew Cohen, "The Private Probation Problem is Worse than Anyone Thought," *The Atlantic Magazine*, February 5, 2014, available at https://www.theatlantic.com/national/archive/2014/02/the-private-probation-problem-is-worse-than-anyone-thought/283589/ (accessed August 23, 2017). Also see Malik Yoba, "How Private Probation Perpetuates Debtors Prisons," *Huffington Post*, September 29, 2016, available at http://www.huffingtonpost.com/malik-yoba/how-private-probation-per_b_12257216.html (accessed August 23, 2017).

59. Michael Welch, *Corrections: A Critical Approach* (New York: McGraw-Hill, 1996), p. 416.

60. Charles Logan, *Private Prisons: Cons and Pros* (New York: Oxford University Press, 1990), p. 20.

61. Carson, "Prisoners in 2016," p. 22.

62. Hawaii, for example, contracts for the housing of approximately 800 inmates with the Correctional Corporation of America in a prison located in Minnesota. Although this is inconvenient for administrators and inmate families, inmates do not have a right to be imprisoned close to their home state.

63. Dale K. Sechrest and David Shichor, "Comparing Public and Private Correctional Facilities in California: An Exploratory Study," in *Privatization and the Provision of Correctional Services: Context and Consequences*, edited by G. Larry Mays and Tara Gray (Cincinnati, Ohio: Anderson Publishing, Co., 1996), p. 135.

64. Logan, *Private Prisons*.

65. Ira P. Robbins, "Privatization of Corrections: Defining the Issues," in *The Dilemmas of Corrections: Contemporary Readings*, 3rd ed., edited by Kenneth C. Haas and Geoffrey P. Alpert (Prospect Heights, Ill.: Waveland Press, 1995), pp. 592–594.

66. Logan, *Private Prisons*, pp. 52–54.

67. Ira P. Robbins, "Privatization of Corrections: Defining the Issues," *Judicature* 69, no. 6 (April–May 1986): 325–331.

68. *Lugar v. Edmonson Oil Co.*, 457 US 922 (1982).

69. *Medina v. O'Neill*, 589, F. Supp. 1028 (1984).

70. Charles Logan, *Looking at Hidden Costs: Public and Private Corrections* (Washington, D.C., U.S. Department of Justice, 1989), pp. 52–54.

71. Sechrest and Shichor, "Comparing Public and Private Correctional Facilities in California."

72. James F. Blumstein, Mark A. Cohen, and Suman Seth, "Do Government Agencies Respond to Market Pressures? Evidence from Private Prisons," *Virginia Journal of Social Policy & the Law* 15, no. 3 (Spring 2008): 466.

73. James F. Blumstein and Mark A. Cohen, "Developments in the Law of Prisons: A Tale of Two Systems: Cost, Quality, and Accountability in Private Prisons," *Harvard Law Review* 115, no. 7 (May 2002): 1891.

74. Geoffrey F. Segal, *Comparing Public and Private Prisons on Quality* (Los Angeles: The Reason Foundation, 2005), http://www.reason.org/ps290.pdf (accessed August 16, 2009).

75. Arizona Department of Corrections, *FY 2010 Operating Cost Report: Cost Identification and Comparison of State and Private Contract Beds* (Phoenix: State of Arizona, 2011).

76. Geoffrey F. Segal and Adrian T. Moore, *Weighing the Watchmen: Evaluating the Costs and Benefits of Outsourcing Correctional Services* (Los Angeles: Reason Public Policy Institute, January 2002), p. 17.

77. Cody Mason, *Too Good to be True: Private Prisons in America* (Washington, D.C.: The Sentencing Project, 2012).

78. Simon Hakim and Erwin A. Blackstone, *Prison Break: A New Approach to Public Cost and Safety* (Oakland, CA: The Independent Institute, 2014).

79. J. Austin and G. Coventry, *Emerging Issues on Privatized Prisons* (San Francisco: National Council of Crime and Delinquency, March 1999).

80. Culp, op. cit.

81. Douglas McDonald and Carl Patten, *Governments' Management of Private Prisons* (Washington, D.C.: U.S. Department of Justice, January 2004), p. 102.

82. J. Hackett and H. Hatry, *Issues in Contracting for the Private Operation of Prisons and Jails* (Washington, D.C.: U.S. Department of Justice, 1987).

83. Lonn Lanza-Kaduce, Karen F. Parker, and Charles W. Thomas, "A Comparative Recidivism Analysis of Releasees from Private and Public Prisons," *Crime and Delinquency* 45, no. 1 (1999): 28–47.

84. U.S. General Accounting Office, *Private and Public Prisons: Studies Comparing Operational Costs and/or Quality of Service* (Washington, D.C.: GAO, 1996).

85. Studies showing little evidence of cost savings include A. Cheung, *Prison Privatization and the Use of Incarceration* (Washington, D.C.: Sentencing Project, January 2002); P. Mattera and M. Khan, *Jail Breaks: Economic Development Subsidies Given to Private Prisons* (Washington, D.C.: Institute on Taxation and Economic Policy, October 2001).

86. Scott D. Camp and Gerald G. Gaes, "Growth and Quality of U.S. Private Prisons: Evidence from a National Survey," *Criminology and Public Policy* 1, no. 3 (July 2002): 427–449.

87. Douglas C. McDonald and Kenneth Carlson, *Contracting for Imprisonment in the Federal Prison System: Cost and Performance of the Privately Operated Taft Correctional Institution* (Washington, D.C.: U.S. Department of Justice, November 2005).

88. Robert J. Lilly and Paul Knepper, "The Corrections-Commercial Complex," *Crime and Delinquency* 39, no. 2 (April 1993): 150–166.

89. See Karyl Dicenski, *Cashing in on Crime: The Drive to Privatize California State Prisons* (Boulder, C.O.: First Forum Press, 2014).

90. Carson, op. cit., Table 17, p. 22.

91. An Interview With Damon Hininger. Reprinted with Permission.

92. Voncile B. Gowdy, "Should We Privatize Our Prisons? The Pros and Cons," *Corrections Management Quarterly* 1, no. 2 (1997): 61.

93. James Austin and Garry Coventry, *Emerging Issues on Privatized Prisons* (Washington, D.C.: U.S. Department of Justice, Bureau of Justice Assistance, February 2001), p. xi.

94. Culp, "The Rise and Stall of Prison Privatization."

95. Sharon Dolovich, "State Punishment and Private Prisons," *Duke Law Journal* 55, no. 3 (2005): 439–546.

96. Allen J. Beck, "Use of Restrictive Housing in U.S. Prisons and Jails, 2011–12," *BJS Special Report* (Washington, D.C.: U.S. Department of Justice, 2015).

97. United Nations, United Nations Standard Minimum Rules *for the Treatment of Prisoners (the Mandela Rules)* (New York, NY: The United Nations, Revised 2015).

98. For a good discussion of this, see Jacob McCleland, "The High Cost of High Security at Supermax Prisons," *NPR News*, June 19, 2012, available at http://www.npr.org/2012/06/19/155359553/the-high-costs-of-high-security-at-supermax-prisons (accessed December 18, 2014).

99. Erica Godde, "Rethinking Solitary Confinement," The New *York Times*, March 11, 2012, pp. 1 and 18.

100. Pat Gauen, "Budget Woes End Illinois' 14-Year Experiment with Super-Max Prison," *The St. Louis Post Dispatch*, February 24, 2012, available at www.stltoday.com/news/local/columns/pat-gauen/budget woes-end-illinois-year-experiment-with-super-max/article (accessed February 24, 2012).

101. ASCA is an organization of individuals that oversee the correctional systems of all the fifty states as well as the U.S. Bureau of prisons and the largest city correctional agencies.

102. See Hope Metcalf, Jamilia Morgan, Samuel Oliker-Friedland, Judith Resnik, Julia Spiegel, Haran Tae, Alyssa Work, and Brian Holbrook, *Administrative Segregation, Degrees of Isolation, and Incarceration: A National Overview of State and Federal Policies* (New Haven, Conn: Linman Public Interest Program at Yale Law School, 2013).

103. ASCA Resolution regarding Restrictive Status Housing, September 4, 2013, available at http://www.asca.net/system/assets/attachments/6386/ASCA%20Resolution%20%23%2024%20Final.pdf?1381938344 (accessed November 17, 2014).

104. Ibid.

105. For a good description of some of these changes, see Greg Markway and Scott O'Kelly, "Addressing Rehabilitation in Restrictive Housing: The Potosi Experience," *Corrections Today* 76, no. 5 (September/October 2014): 70–74, 78.

106. Ian Lovett, "California Agrees to Overhaul Use of Solitary Confinement," *New York Times*, September 1, 2015, available athttps://www.nytimes.com/2015/09/02/us/solitary-confinement-california-prisons.html?_r=0 (accessed October 23, 2017).

107. *Davis v. Ayala*, 576 U.S. (2015).

108. Robert D. Morgan, Ryan M. Labrecque, Paul Gendreau, Taylor R. Ramler, and Brieann Olafsson, "Questioning Solitary Confinement: Is Administrative Segregation as Bad as Alleged?" *Corrections Today* (September/October 2017): 18–24, 78.

109. Ibid., pp. 19–20.

110. Ibid., p. 20.

111. Kevin N. Wright, *Effective Prison Leadership* (Binghamton, N.Y.: William Neil, 1994), p. 14.

112. Kristin Hughes, *Criminal Justice Expenditure Extracts, 2010, Sourcebook of Criminal Justice Statistics* (Washington, D.C.: U.S. Department of Justice, Bureau of Justice Statistics, 2014), Table 2.

113. Bureau of Justice Statistics, *Sourcebook of Criminal Justice Statistics, 1994* (Washington, D.C.: U.S. Department of Justice, updated March 2003), p. 26.

GLOSSARY

A

ACA accreditation: a process to promote and recognize improvement in the management of correctional agencies through the administration of voluntary standards

adjudicate: to find a juvenile guilty of a delinquent act

administrative appeals process: an informal process for inmates to appeal a disciplinary sanction or to seek remedy of any other injustice they feel they have received at the hands of correctional officials

administrative detention: a nonpunitive confinement in SHU used to house inmates whose continued presence in the general population may pose a serious threat to the security or orderly running of the prison

administrative form of sentencing: administrative bodies (correctional officials and parole/release boards) have primary discretion in granting good time and determining the release time of offenders

adultification: a move to make the juvenile justice system look and operate more like an adult correctional system

affirmative action programs: activities to aggressively recruit and provide opportunities for employment to women and minorities

aftercare: supervision of a juvenile in the community after serving time in a juvenile correctional institution; similar to parole for adults

age of original jurisdiction: the upper or oldest age that a juvenile court will have jurisdiction over categories of offenders

Alexander Maconochie: the superintendent of the British penal colony on Norfolk Island from 1841 to 1844, who created a system of marks for good behavior that could lead to a graduated release from prison

American Correctional Association: the largest professional organization for corrections in the United States

Americans with Disabilities Act: a law that prohibits any entity from discriminating against an individual with a disability in regard to employment, public service and transportation, public accommodations, and telecommunications services

antipsychotic drugs: drugs administered to mentally ill individuals to counteract the symptoms of their mental illness, often allowing them to live successfully in the community rather than needing to be institutionalized

arrestee drug abuse monitoring: surveys of arrested individuals by the U.S. Office of Drug Control Policy to determine the extent of drug use related to criminality

asset forfeiture: the authorized seizure by the government of money, negotiable instruments, securities, or other things of value that were obtained through illegal activities

atavism: the existence of features common in the early stages of human evolution; implied the idea that criminals are born, and criminal behavior is *predetermined*

Auburn system: the congregate and silent operation of prisons, in which inmates were allowed to work together during the day, but had to stay separate and silent at other times

B

bail: the pledge of money or property in exchange for a promise to return for further criminal processing

balancing test: established in *Pell v. Procunier*, finding that prison inmates retain those First Amendment rights that are not inconsistent with their status as prisoner or with legitimate penological objectives

Barefield v. Leach: a 1974 federal court decision that a disparity of programs for female inmates could not be justified because the smaller number of female inmates made it more costly to provide program parity

Bell v. Wolfish: a 1979 U.S. Supreme Court case in which the punitive intent standard was adopted for considering violations of the Eighth Amendment regarding jail operations

BFOQ: a bona fide occupational qualification reasonably necessary to the normal operation of that particular business or enterprise that may allow for some discriminatory practices to occur

bifurcated trial: used in capital cases, with guilt first established at a traditional trial, and if found guilty, a second stage of sentencing considers between death or life imprisonment

blended sentencing: a middle ground between juvenile and adult sentences that allows judges to choose from a broad array of both juvenile and adult sanctions

brig: a military term meaning a correctional facility

Bruscino v. Carlson: a 1985 federal court decision that the lockdown of inmates at the U.S. Penitentiary in Marion, Illinois, was not a violation of the Constitution

C

call out: a schedule of all the appointments and required moves for a day, including the name and expected times of the moves

capital punishment: punishment for the most serious crimes (generally first-degree murder); most states and the federal government provide for the death penalty

career in corrections: beginning work for a correctional agency with a possibility of working in corrections from now until retirement

case manager: sometimes called social worker or caseworker; responsible for developing the program of work and rehabilitation for inmates assigned to him or her

casework style of supervision: a style of supervising community offenders that places emphasis on assisting the offender with problems, counseling, and working to make sure the offender successfully completes supervision

census counts: a less formal count conducted at program and work assignments by the staff responsible for supervising inmates

Cesare Beccaria: the Italian theorist who in the eighteenth century first suggested linking crime causation to punishments and became known as the founder of the Classical School of criminology

Cesare Lombroso: the Italian physician who in the nineteenth century founded the Positive School

chain of command: the vertical hierarchy in an organization, identified in terms of authority, and the order through which persons receive directives from the person immediately above them and pass these directives to the person immediately below them

civil commitment statutes: laws to continue incarceration of sexual predators even after they have completed their maximum criminal sentence

Civil Rights Act of 1871: this act of Congress guaranteed the rights of freed slaves and provided access to federal courts for violations of the act

Classical School: the theory linking crime causation to punishment, based on offenders' free will and hedonism

closed systems: prison systems that consist of only the internal environment, under the direct control of the warden, and without much interest or any interference from external groups

collective bargaining: the formal recognition of employee organizations and their right to negotiate with management regarding workplace issues

collective violence: prison violence that is between and initiated by groups of inmates and includes prison riots and disturbances; it can be groups of inmates against staff or against one another, as this violence stems from the fundamental difference in values and positions of the two groups

community classification systems: risk assessments that predict the chance of new crimes being committed; they are used to determine the level of supervision an offender will receive in the community

community corrections: those criminal sanctions that involve community supervision of offenders, make use of correctional and program resources available in the community, and require offenders to abide by specified conditions to remain in the community

community residential centers: houses in which offenders live in the community that provide supervision, room and board, and some treatment as an alternative to prison

community service: an economic sanction used when offenders do not have funds from which to pay a fine or make restitution; referred to as a "fine on their time," so that indigent offenders do not have to serve prison or jail time merely because they lack the fiscal ability to pay a fine

community standards: the test established in *Fernandez v. United States* that medical care for inmates must be reasonably commensurate with medical care they would receive if not imprisoned

concurrent sentences: sentences that run at the same time

conjugal visiting: sometimes referred to as family visiting, these are private visiting opportunities between inmates and their spouses, and it is expected that they will engage in sexual relations

consecutive sentences: sentences that run one after the other

consent decree: an informal handling of a juvenile justice case, in which the delinquent juvenile admits to wrongdoing and agrees to specific conditions of behavior; sometimes called informal probation

containment model: an approach to managing sex offenders that includes treatment to develop internal control over deviant thoughts, supervision and surveillance to control external behaviors, and polygraph examinations to monitor conformance to treatment plans and supervision conditions

continuum of care: provision of mental health programs based on the intensity of needs for each inmate, including as inmates prepare for release to the community

contraband: any item that inmates are not allowed to possess, including items that can assist in an escape, are dangerous, can undermine prison physical security, or are nuisance items

controlled movement: the procedure used by prisons to maintain accountability for inmates as they move throughout the prison

convicts: long-term inmates who become used to the prison society and find a way to live in this environment with a minimal amount of problems and disruptions

correctional counselor: a former correctional officer who works with inmates on prison issues such as creating a visiting or telephone list or getting a prison job assignment

correctional officer: staff person in a prison or jail who accomplishes the institution's mission by maintaining control and order within the prison

CoreCivic: formerly Corrections Corporation of America; the largest of the private prison corporations that opened the first private, for-profit correctional facility in 1984 in Tennessee; currently operates seventy correctional facilities

corrections: the range of community and institutional sanctions, treatment programs, and services for managing criminal offenders

cost of supervision: offenders have to pay for some costs associated with their supervision in the community, such as drug testing or electronic monitoring

cottage-style architecture: a style of prison design used for women's prisons, with several small housing units holding approximately thirty inmates; each cottage included kitchens, living rooms, and sometimes nurseries for inmates with children

custody: the functions within a prison that come under the security activities; includes all "uniformed" employees such as correctional officers and correctional supervisors

D

debrief: gang members tell correctional officials everything they know about the gang operations and membership; once inmates debrief, they become an enemy of the gang

deinstitutionalize: the move to remove juveniles from correctional institutions and place them in community alternatives

deliberate indifference: as established in *Wilson v. Seiter*, the standard that conditions at prison are not unconstitutional unless prison administrators show deliberate indifference toward inmates' basic needs

delinquency petition: a statement of the delinquent acts a juvenile is alleged to have committed; similar to an indictment for adults

delinquent children: children who have committed an act that would be considered criminal if committed by an adult

dependent children: children who, although committing no legal offense, may be without a parent or guardian, possibly because the parent is physically or mentally unable to act in that capacity

determinate sentences: sentences of fixed terms

direct supervision: a style of inmate supervision with staff located in direct contact with inmates; requires staff to continuously supervise and communicate with inmates, reducing tension and avoiding the development of conflicts between inmates or inmates and staff

director: the chief executive officer of a state or federal department of corrections

disciplinary segregation: a punitive assignment in SHU after a finding of guilt for a serious prison rule violation; disciplinary segregation is for a set amount of time established by the authorized hearing official

discretionary parole: release of inmates in which the decision to release is made by a parole board

disturbance control team: an emergency team with the primary mission of controlling inmates during riot situations by using defensive tactics and equipment to move, isolate, and get them to give up and stop the disturbance

Dothard v. Rawlinson: a 1977 U.S. Supreme Court case regarding a woman who was denied a position as a correctional officer in an Alabama male prison; the Court ruled that a BFOQ against women correctional officers was allowable because of the deplorable conditions of the Alabama prisons and the presence of predatory male sex offenders as inmates

drug courts: an alternative to traditional court models to deal with the underlying drug problem as the basis of the offenders' criminality

drug offenders: those convicted of crimes regarding the possession or sale of drugs

E

economic sanction: a requirement that an offender pay a fine or restitution to the victim as a part of his or her sentence

Eighth Amendment: states that no cruel or unusual punishment may be inflicted

electronic monitoring: the use of technology to monitor an offender's location

Elizabeth Fry: a Quaker who formed the Ladies Society for Promoting the Reformation of Female Prisoners in 1816; she tried to convince officials that women prisoners should be separated from male prisoners and that female guards should be hired to supervise them

Elmira Reformatory: the first reformatory in the United States; it opened in 1876 and used the principles of the Irish system, indeterminate sentences, and parole

employee awards program: a program to recognize and reward staff members who perform beyond their expected level

environmental factors: factors that create tension and an underlying unrest among inmates; they can include hot weather, reduction in budgets for recreation equipment, prison crowding, poor food service or medical care, a perceived pattern of unfairness in the management of the prison, or poor security procedures that allow inmates to create an unsafe environment

evidence based: a focus on provision of programs where there is evidence of success, generally defined as reducing recidivism

F

Federal Bureau of Prisons: an agency within the U.S. Department of Justice charged with housing and managing federal law offenders

federalized: the making of a crime a federal rather than a state offense; results when the U.S. Congress decides that it desires federal law enforcement and prosecution of certain offenses

felony: crime that is punishable by a year or more of incarceration

female offenders: women who are convicted and sentenced; just over 7 percent of prison inmates are females

fines: a requirement that offenders pay some dollar amount to the court as punishment for committing the offense

first-generation jails: jails using a linear design for housing inmates, in which cells are aligned in long, straight rows, with walkways in the front of the cells for jail correctional officers to walk intermittently to observe what is going on in the cells

Fourteenth Amendment: no state shall deprive any person of life, liberty, or property without the due process of the law; states may not deny any person the equal protection of the law

furlough: a program in which prison inmates are allowed to leave the prison early to reside in a halfway house and prepare for reentry to the community

G

Gagnon v. Scarpelli: a 1973 U.S. Supreme Court decision that created the due process requirements for revoking probation

gang intelligence officers: prison staff charged with collecting intelligence and advising administrators regarding strategies to manage and contain prison gang activity

gang validation process: an identification of the number of identifiers of gang activity used to confirm individuals' gang involvement level

gaol: an early English term for a jail

general deterrence: the recognition that criminal acts result in punishment, and the effect of that recognition on society that prevents future crimes

general population: inmates in prison who do not have any specific designation as a special type of offender

Girl Scouts Beyond Bars: Girl Scout troops that have their chapter based in a prison so inmates with children can participate as Scout parents

good time: affords inmates the opportunity to reduce their eligibility for release by good behavior in prison

graduated incarceration: a system in which juveniles handled by adult courts are placed in juvenile facilities until they reach the age of eighteen; they are then transferred to an adult prison to complete the sentence

Gunther v. Iowa: a 1979 case in the U.S. District Court of Iowa in which the court determined that inmate privacy was not a valid reason to refuse to hire women as correctional officers; the *Gunther* decision eliminated the major support used for the BFOQ by states in not hiring female correctional officers

H

hands-off doctrine: an avoidance by the U.S. Supreme Court of judicial intervention in the operations of prisons and the judgment of correctional administrators

hearing officers: officials who are not appointed parole board members, yet they hold parole hearings and make recommendations to the parole board regarding inmates' release

hedonistic calculus: the idea that the main objective of an intelligent person is to achieve the most pleasure and the least pain and that individuals are constantly calculating the pluses and minuses of their potential actions

hostage negotiation teams: a team of eight to ten prison employees, with excellent communication skills and ability to perform under stress, with the principal role to open lines of communications between staff and hostage takers

house arrest: offenders live at home and must be at home except for times they are to be at work or participating in other activities approved by their probation officer

human immunodeficiency virus (HIV): a virus that attacks the body's immune system, increasing the chance of infection and other diseases

I

Immigration and Customs Enforcement (ICE): formerly the U.S. Immigration and Naturalization Service (INS), responsible for housing illegal aliens pending a hearing or deportation back to their home country

imprisonment: a sentence in a prison of a year or more

incapacitation: reducing offenders' ability or capacity to commit further crimes

incarceration rates: the number of persons per 100,000 who are in jail or prison

indeterminate sentences: sentences that have a minimum and maximum time to serve; a decision by a release authority determines the actual time served within that range

Industrial Prison Era: prison operations with emphasis on having inmates work and produce products that could help to make the prisons self-sustaining

inmate accountability: the staff's ability to locate and identify inmates at any point in time within a prison

inmate code: the expected rules and behaviors represented by the model prisoner and reflecting the values and norms of prison society

inmate disciplinary system: a policy that clearly prescribes the process required to find that an inmate committed a proscribed act and identifies allowable punishments for each act; a key to controlling inmate behavior

In re Gault: a 1967 U.S. Supreme Court case requiring that in hearings in which a juvenile may be committed to an institution, they must have the right to counsel, to notice of the charges against them, to question witnesses, and to protection against self-incrimination

inspector: a person in a department of corrections who investigates allegations by inmates against staff

intake: determination if a juvenile case should be dismissed, handled informally, or referred to the juvenile court

integrity interview: interviews of candidates for correctional employment used to determine if candidates have issues or conditions that could put them in a compromising situation or make them more likely to accept a bribe to show favored treatment to an inmate

intensive supervised probation: supervision of community offenders with higher than average risk, through smaller caseloads and very close monitoring of activities

intensive-supervision caseload: caseload for offenders with too high a risk or need to be on regular supervision; created as an alternative to sending these offenders to prison

intermediate sanctions: midrange dispositions that fall between probation and imprisonment

internal classification system: instruments used to assign inmates to housing or programs after they are placed in a particular prison

interpersonal violence: prison violence that occurs between two or more individual inmates; the reason for the violence is a personal issue between the individuals

J

jails: locally operated correctional facilities that confine persons before or after adjudication

Jeremy Bentham: creator of the hedonistic calculus suggesting that punishments outweigh the pleasure criminals get from committing their crime

John Augustus: the Boston shoemaker who became the "father" of probation

John Howard: the sheriff of Bedfordshire, England, who encouraged reform of English jails in the late 1700s

judicial form of sentencing: judges have primary discretion in creating the sentence

just deserts model: a model for sentencing proposed by von Hirsch that had fixed sentences for each crime so that the punishment fit the crime

justice model: the model for sentencing proposed by Fogel that would use flat, determinate sentences, eliminate parole boards, and make all treatment voluntary

juvenile detention: the temporary care of children in physically restricted facilities pending court disposition or transfer to another jurisdiction or agency

juvenile gangs: groups of adolescents or young adults who see themselves as a group and have been involved in enough crime to be of considerable concern to law enforcement and the community

juvenile justice system: a system to handle juveniles separate from adult offenders, based on the concept of *parens patriae*, which was used as the basis for giving the court the authority to take over supervision of children when their parents failed to provide proper care and guidance

L

lease system: state prisons accepted bids and leased out prisoners to the private sector, which would work the inmates in their industrial operations

legislative form of sentencing: legislative bodies create very structured sentencing codes, and therefore have primary discretion in the length of time served by offenders

length of stay: the time served in a jail or prison by any inmate

lethal injection: a method of execution in which drugs are injected into a person's body, making the heart stop and causing death

lockup: refers to a small jail with only a few cells and no accommodations for food services, medical care, or recreation

M

male offenders: men who are convicted and sentenced; they constitute over 93 percent of all prison inmates

management culture: a culture based on the way prison leadership deals and communicates with subordinate staff; it falls into a continuum between autocratic and empowered

Management Training Corporation: a private correctional company headquartered in Utah that operates nineteen correctional facilities in the United States

mandatory minimum sentences: a requirement that for certain crimes or for certain types of offenders, there must be a sentence to prison for at least a minimum term

mandatory prison education: many states and the Federal Bureau of Prisons require inmates without a high school diploma or GED to attend school

Manhattan Bail Project: a program started in the 1960s to assist judges in identifying individuals who were good candidates to be released on their own recognizance without commercial or monetary bond

mark system: credits against a sentence that allowed for inmates to be released once they earned the required level of marks through work and good behavior

medical model: a theory of corrections that offenders were sick, inflicted with problems that caused their criminality, and needed to be diagnosed and treated, and that rehabilitative programs would resolve offenders' problems and prepare them for release into the community able to be productive and crime-free

medical parole: placement of aging or disabled inmates in a nursing home or hospital to receive care while still serving their sentence and costs being covered by Medicaid

meta-analysis: a statistical measure of the average effect an intervention has on recidivism across all studies while identifying and controlling for various study conditions

misdemeanors: crimes that are punishable by less than a year of incarceration

mission: a statement of an organization's major function and what it is to accomplish, or its basic purposes, to include general outcomes that it is committed to achieving

Morrissey v. Brewer: a 1972 U.S. Supreme Court decision that once parole is granted, a liberty interest is created and offenders must have certain due process rights to revoke that liberty

N

neglected children: children who have a family or guardian, but are not receiving proper care or the situation in the home is harmful to them and their upbringing

Neoclassical School: a compromise between Classical and Positive Schools, while holding offenders accountable for their crimes, allowing for some consideration of mitigating and aggravating circumstances

net widening: the overlapping of criminal sanctions and added supervision for community-placed offenders, rather than diversion of offenders from prison

new penology: an emphasis on the rational and efficient deployment of control strategies for managing and confining high-risk criminal populations

new-crime violations: violation of the condition of probation prohibiting the commission of any additional crimes

"nothing works": a conclusion by Robert Martinson that no correctional treatment program reduces recidivism; it effectively spelled the end to the medical model

O

objective classification systems: statistical approaches to consider the risk of escape and violence by inmates

offender restitution: a requirement that offenders repay society for the harm created by the offense

open systems: prison systems that have frequent interactions between the organization and other groups, in order to obtain resources, gain support, and accomplish goals

order: the sanction for a juvenile found delinquent by juvenile court; similar to the sentence for an adult

organizational culture: the values, beliefs, and behaviors that form the way of life within that organization

overclassification: the placement of offenders in prisons more secure than needed for their level of risk

P

parens patriae: means "parents of the nation," established in 1601 to allow officials to take charge of delinquent children and place them in poorhouses or orphanages to gain control of them; in more modern times, this doctrine was expanded as the basis for juvenile court and correctional systems to take responsibility for educating and nurturing delinquents, with an emphasis on reform and rehabilitation

parenting programs: prison programs to assist inmates to improve their parenting skills, even while in prison

Pargo v. Elliott: the 1995 Eighth Circuit Court case that allowed that differences in programs between male and female prisons does not necessarily violate the equal protection clause of the Constitution

parole guidelines: similar to sentencing guidelines, these use predictive factors to determine the offenders' risk to the community and chance for success; guidelines prescribe a presumptive time to be served based on the seriousness of the crime and the factors predictive of success for each inmate

parole: the conditional release of inmates by a parole board prior to the expiration of their sentence

pass system: a form of inmate movement in which an inmate is issued a pass by the work or program supervisor to go to a scheduled appointment

pedophile: someone who is sexually attracted to and molests children

Pell grants: grants for disadvantaged individuals used to cover tuition costs for college courses

penal code: a legislative authorization to provide a specific range of punishment for a specific crime

penitentiary: the term first used to describe secure facilities used to hold offenders serving a criminal sentence; still used today for some older or highly secure prisons

Pennsylvania system: the "separate and silent" system of prison operations emphasizing reformation and avoidance of criminal contamination

penology: the study of the use of punishment for criminal acts

Period of Transition: an era of prison operations in which enforced idleness, lack of professional programs, and excessive size and overcrowding of prisons resulted in an increase in prisoner discontent and prison riots

PIE Program: prison industry programs operated by private companies, with prison goods authorized to be sold on the open market if the program is certified as meeting certain conditions

plea bargaining: an agreement in which the defendant enters a plea of guilty in exchange for a reduced sentence in comparison to the sentence allowable for the charged offense

podular designs: a design of prisoner housing that provides common dayroom areas in the center of the unit to allow inmates to watch television or play table games, thereby getting out of their cells and reducing idleness and tension; podular designs make it easier for officers to view inmate activities in the cells and the dayrooms from one central location

policy audit: a review to ascertain whether broad agency policy is in place at the prison

policy implementation audit: a review to identify whether the procedures prescribed by policy are consistently being carried out by staff members in their daily duties

positive contact: face-to-face contact between a parole officer and an offender

Positive School: the belief that criminals do not have complete choice over their criminal actions and may commit acts that are beyond their control

post orders: the detailed description of the activities that are required to be performed throughout the day, often including the time they are to occur

precedents: decisions of the courts that come before and are therefore binding on later decisions of courts within the same jurisdiction

precipitating event: the "spark in the haystack" that sets off an inmate riot; usually must be preceded by the right environmental factors before a precipitating event creates the beginning of a prison riot

presentence investigation: a report used during the sentencing process that details the background of a convicted offender, to include criminal, social, education, employment, mental and physical health, and other significant factors

presumptive parole date: a date the inmate can expect to be released on parole, even if it is five or ten years later than the hearing

presumptive sentencing: a predetermined range of a minimum, average, and maximum term for a specific crime for a "typical" offender, with allowances for mitigating and aggravating circumstances to be considered

pretrial diversion: the suspension of criminal process while the offender is provided the chance to participate in treatment programs and avoid further criminal activity

preventive detention: detaining an accused person in jail to protect the community from crimes they are likely to commit if set free pending trial

prison gangs: groups that form in prison and use the threat of violence to intimidate other inmates, control drug sales and prostitution, and gain power and influence

prisoner reentry: the process of an inmate leaving prison and returning to the community

prisonization: the process whereby inmates take on the folkways, mores, customs, and general culture of the penitentiary

prisons: institutions designed to house convicted, adult felons, serving a sentence of one year or more

private prison: any secure correctional facility, operated by other than a governmental agency and usually in a for-profit manner, which contracts with a governmental entity, to provide security, housing, and programs for adult offenders

probation supervision: the role of a probation or parole officer in monitoring an offender's behavior through office visits; contacts with family, friends, bosses, or treatment providers; and visits to their home or place of work

probation: a prison sentence that is suspended on the condition that the offender follows certain prescribed rules and commits no further crimes

professional staff: prison or jail staff members in a specialty area that requires distinctive training and education and may also require a professional certification to deliver a program

pseudofamilies: family organizations formed by female inmates who have roles of parents and children

punishment: the correctional goal emphasizing the infliction of pain or suffering

R

racial disparity: the fact that minorities make up a greater percentage of those under correctional supervision than their makeup in the U.S. population

random counts: counts done at any time, freezing inmates at whatever location they are in when the random count is called

random drug testing: randomly selecting a percentage of inmates to urine test to see whether they have used any drug recently; a good deterrent to and source of data about prisoner drug use

recidivism: the state of relapse that occurs when offenders complete their criminal punishment and then continue to commit crimes

referral: the formal processing of a juvenile offense through the juvenile court

Reformatory Era: an environment emphasizing reformation that expanded education and vocational programs and focused offenders' attention on their future

Refuge Period: a period from 1824 to 1899 when delinquent or neglected children were placed in a home for training and discipline

regional jail: a jail that serves more than one county and is overseen by a regional jail commission

regular caseload: caseload made up of standard probationers, requiring no special program or supervision

regular counts: the scheduled counting of inmates in their housing units to ensure that they are in the prison and have not escaped

rehabilitation: a programmed effort to alter the attitudes and behaviors of inmates and improve their likelihood of becoming law-abiding citizens

Rehabilitative Era: an era of prison management emphasizing the professionalizing of staff through recruitment and training and implementation of many self-improvement programs of prison management

reintegration: a belief that after offenders complete their treatment in prison they need transitional care, and that the community must be involved in their successful return to society

relationship culture: a culture based on how staff members view and communicate with inmates; it falls into a continuum between authoritarian and reasoned

release on recognizance: release from jail based only on the defendant's promise to appear for further court procedures

restitution: acts by which criminals make right or repay society or their victims for their wrongs

restorative justice: models of sentencing that shift the focus away from punishment of the offender and emphasize involving the victim while holding offenders accountable for the harm they caused and finding opportunities for them to repair the damage

retribution: infliction of punishment on those who deserve to be punished

Retributive Era: an era of corrections that emphasizes holding offenders accountable for their acts and being tough on criminals while keeping them isolated from law-abiding citizens and making them serve "hard" time

Rhodes v. Chapman: a 1981 U.S. Supreme Court decision that overcrowded conditions resulting in two inmates housed in cells designed for one person was not a violation of the Eighth Amendment right of protection from cruel and unusual punishment

S

salient factor score: a point determination for each inmate for use with parole guidelines; the score is based on factors predictive of success on parole

Sanford Bates: the first director of the Federal Bureau of Prisons

second-generation jails: jails using podular housing designs and remote supervision; officers are located in a secure control room overlooking the cells and dayroom, with electronic controls to open and close individual cell doors

Section 1983: a section of the Civil Rights Act that prohibits any person acting under the color of any statute, ordinance, or regulation (color of law) from depriving another person of his or her constitutional rights

security classification: to match offenders to institutions that have the physical security and staff resources to prevent escapes and control their behavior

security levels: levels such as minimum, low, medium, high, or maximum are distinct by such features as the presence of towers and other perimeter security barriers (fences or walls) with detection devices, the type of housing for prisoners (cells or dormitory), and the staff-to-inmate ratio

segregated incarceration: a form of incarceration in which juveniles handled by adult courts are assigned to an adult prison, yet they are housed separately and placed in specialized educational, vocational, life skills training, and substance abuse programs that meet their age and needs

selective incapacitation: incarceration of high-risk offenders for preventative reasons based on what they are expected to do, not what they have already done

seniority: the use of the length of employment to determine an employee's assignment, days off, or other job-related functions

sentencing guidelines: structured sentences, based on measures of offense severity and criminal history, to determine the length of the term of imprisonment

Sentencing Reform Act of 1984: the act of Congress that abolished parole, established determinate sentencing, and reduced the amount of good time available to federal offenders

sentencing: the imposition of a criminal sanction by a judicial authority

services: the functions required to operate a prison such as budget and financial, maintenance, human resource management, food and health services, work programs, commissary function, and laundry operations

sex offenders: offenders who have committed a legally prohibited sexual act or in some states any offender who commits any crime that was statutorily defined as sexually motivated

sexual triangles: two inmates become jealous and fight over another one

shadow board: a light-colored background with the outline of the tool painted on it, allowing for a missing tool or knife to be quickly noticed

sheriff: the elected official who oversees both policing activities within the county and the operation of the jail

shock incarceration/boot camp: alternatives to traditional incarceration that are operated similar to a military boot camp; offenders are required to have short hair, shine their shoes, wear uniforms, do extensive physical exercise, and perform hard physical labor; at times, these are complemented with education or drug programming, but the major components of boot camps are military regimentation, discipline, exercise, and hard work

shock probation: a short period of imprisonment to "shock" the offender, with a return to the community within a few weeks to continue supervision on probation

short-term confinement: a sentence in a jail for one year or less

Sir Walter Crofton: the director of Irish prison system in 1854, who began to implement many of the ideas of Maconochie's work

slave-of-the-state doctrine: as decided in the 1871 decision of *Ruffin v. the Commonwealth of Virginia*, which held inmates were slaves of the state and had no rights that were not granted them by the state

special caseload: caseload is made up of offenders with a particular type of problem, such as substance abuse, mental illness, or a history of sex offenses

special conditions of probation: conditions of probation tailored to meet the needs for a particular offender; they can be imposed to meet the specific risks or needs of an individual offender

special emergency response team: an emergency team trained in the use of lethal force when all else fails to resolve an emergency situation

special housing unit: a temporary housing assignment for inmates who present a danger to the security of the prison, need protection from other inmates, or are being punished for violating prison rules

special offenders: offenders whose circumstances, conditions, or behaviors require management or treatment outside of the normal approach to supervision

specific deterrence: the effect of punishment on an individual offender that prevents that person from committing future crimes

split sentence: a combination of a short jail sentence and then return to the community on probation

square johns: inmates who are usually first-time offenders and have more identification with "straight" society and norms of the noncriminals

staff diversity: the representation of a wide variety (in gender, race, and ethnicity) of people working for a correctional agency

standard conditions of probation: conditions that must be followed by every probationer

stand-up count: the most formal count of the day, at which inmates must stand at their cell door or by their dormitory bed to be counted and matched to the number of inmates assigned to each housing area

state-use system: only allowing prison-made goods to be sold to and used by the state and federal government agencies

status offense: an activity that is considered a crime only because the offender is under the age of eighteen and would not be a crime if committed by an adult; includes acts such as running away from home, ungovernability, truancy, or underage drinking

straight adult incarceration: a form of incarceration in which juveniles handled by adult courts are placed in adult prisons with no separate housing or differentiation in programming or job assignments

street crimes: traditional reference to crimes with little sophistication required, such as murder, robbery, burglary, assault, and theft

substance abuse programs: programs for offenders to reduce their likelihood of further abuse of alcohol or drugs

suicide prevention programs: jail and prison programs that include early detection of suicide risks, staff education to recognize signs of potential suicide, and procedures for managing inmates who are now suicidal

suicide watch: management of suicidal inmates who are placed in a specially designed cell and have constant supervision

supermax prisons: either freestanding or distinct units within other prisons that provide for the management and secure control of inmates designated as violent or seriously disruptive in other prisons

superpredator: a term created by DiIulio to describe a generation of violent youths who practiced almost indiscriminant violence on the streets

supervised mandatory release: a type of release in which inmates serve a determinate sentence and are then released, but with a period of supervision to follow

supervised pretrial release programs: supervision of offenders released on their own recognizance, similar to supervision while on probation

Sureños: formed from the Mexican Mafia; *Sureños* means "Southerner" in Spanish and is one of the largest and most violent prison gangs in America

surety: a person who is legally liable for the conduct of another; someone who guarantees the accused person's appearance in court

surveillance style of supervision: a style of supervising community offenders that places emphasis on monitoring and enforcing compliance with the rules or supervision and the detection of violations leading to revocation and return to custody

T

technical violations: violations of conditions of community supervision, without commission of a new crime

test of proportionality: the result of the 1983 case of *Solem v. Helm*; a test used to guide sentencing based on the gravity of the offense and consistency of the severity of punishment

The GEO Group, Inc.: a private correctional company headquartered in Florida that operates 110 correctional facilities in the United States

thieves: inmates who have adopted a career of crime and are doing their prison time until they can get out and hit the "big score"

third-generation jails: jail designs without remote control centers, in which correctional officers are located in the housing unit in direct contact with inmates

Three Penitentiary Act: the 1891 act of Congress that authorized the construction of the first three federal prisons

three-strikes laws: a legislative mandate that judges sentence third-time felons to extremely long or life prison sentences

ticket of leave: a form of release used by Maconochie; on earning the required level of marks, prisoners received a conditional pardon and were released to the community

total institution: Goffman's concept of a setting isolating people from the rest of society and unnecessarily manipulating them through the actions of the administrative staff

totality-of-conditions test: a test created in *Pugh v. Locke* that examines the aggregate of circumstances in a prison to determine whether cruel and unusual conditions exist

"tough on crime": an attitude that criminals should be severely punished for their wrongdoings, and long prison sentences are the most effective criminal sanction

transactional leaders: traditional authorities within an organization who were involved in exchange relationships between leaders and followers; they provided answers and direction for any issue the agency confronted

transformational leaders: organizational leadership based on principles, while motivating staff to jointly address challenges and find solutions to new problems

transportation: used in England during the seventeenth and eighteenth centuries to remove criminals from society by sending them to British colonies such as America

treatment: the creation of an environment and provision of rehabilitative programs that encourage inmates to accept responsibility and to address personal disorders that make success in the community more difficult

truth in sentencing: requires completion of 85 percent of the sentence before prisoners are eligible for release

U

unconditional mandatory release: a type of release in which inmates serve the full portion of their sentence and have no supervision after release from prison

uniformed staff: those prison or jail staff members who work in the security or custody department and are responsible for the implementation of security policies and procedures

unit management: organizing a prison into smaller components by decentralizing the authority to manage the inmate population while making staff more accessible to inmates

unit manager: the staff person who is in charge of the unit, including housing, security, and treatment issues

V

victim compensation: offenders repay their victims directly for their losses and harm caused by the offense

victims' movement: the criminal justice system's recognition that victims should be involved in the process of sentencing criminals

violation: failure to follow conditions of parole supervision

vocational training: specific training in a trade area to prepare students to work in that trade

W

waiver to adult courts: because of the serious nature of a juvenile offender's crime, statutory exceptions were granted to allow the movement from juvenile to adult courts for criminal processing

Walnut Street Jail: the first penitentiary in the United States

war on drugs: a Reagan initiative to reduce the availability and dependence on illicit drugs through interdiction, criminal sanctions, and treatment

warden: the chief executive officer of a prison, responsible for the day-to-day operations

work call: the time when inmates move to their assigned jobs or programs assignments

Z

Zebulon R. Brockway: a leading U.S. penologist in the mid-1800s who was a proponent of adopting the Irish system in the United States and who became the first superintendent of the Elmira Reformatory

INDEX

Note: Page numbers followed by f or t indicate Figures or Tables.